The Ultimate

Trivial Pursuit

Question &
Answer Book

**PUZZLE
WRIGHT
PRESS**

An imprint of Sterling
Publishing Co., Inc.

www.puzzlewright.com

Puzzlewright Press and the distinctive Puzzlewright Press logo are registered trademarks of Sterling Publishing Co., Inc.

2 4 6 8 10 9 7 5 3

Published by Sterling Publishing Co., Inc.
387 Park Avenue South, New York, NY 10016
© 2010 by Hasbro.
All rights reserved.
Distributed in Canada by Sterling Publishing
c/o Canadian Manda Group, 165 Dufferin Street
Toronto, Ontario, Canada M6K 3H6
Distributed in the United Kingdom by GMC Distribution Services
Castle Place, 166 High Street, Lewes, East Sussex, England BN7 1XU
Distributed in Australia by Capricorn Link (Australia) Pty. Ltd.
P.O. Box 704, Windsor, NSW 2756, Australia

HASBRO and its logo, TRIVIAL PURSUIT, the associated logo, the distinctive design of the game board, trivia cards, game tokens, and scoring wedges are trademarks of Hasbro and are used with permission. © 2010 Hasbro. All Rights Reserved.

Printed in China
All rights reserved

Sterling ISBN 978-1-4027-7065-4

For information about custom editions, special sales, premium and corporate purchases, please contact Sterling Special Sales Department at 800-805-5489 or specialsales@sterlingpublishing.com.

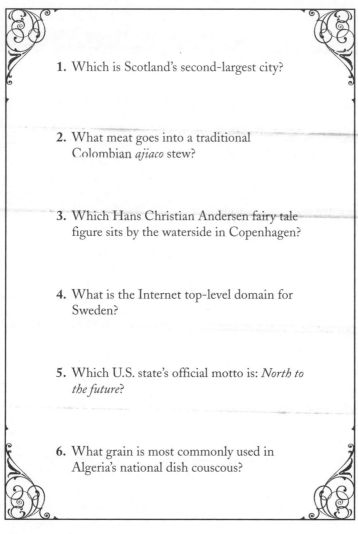

1. Which is Scotland's second-largest city?

2. What meat goes into a traditional Colombian *ajiaco* stew?

3. Which Hans Christian Andersen fairy tale figure sits by the waterside in Copenhagen?

4. What is the Internet top-level domain for Sweden?

5. Which U.S. state's official motto is: *North to the future*?

6. What grain is most commonly used in Algeria's national dish couscous?

1. Edinburgh

2. Chicken

3. The Little Mermaid

4. .se

5. Alaska's

6. Semolina (Durum wheat)

1. What country's name means Land of the Afghans?

2. What is the better-known name for the Hellenic Republic?

3. Which Venetian canal does the Rialto Bridge span?

4. Which city boasts Antoni Gaudi's spectacular, yet unfinished, Sagrada Familia church?

5. What is the closest city to South Africa's Soweto?

6. How many Berlin streets are named after Adolf Hitler?

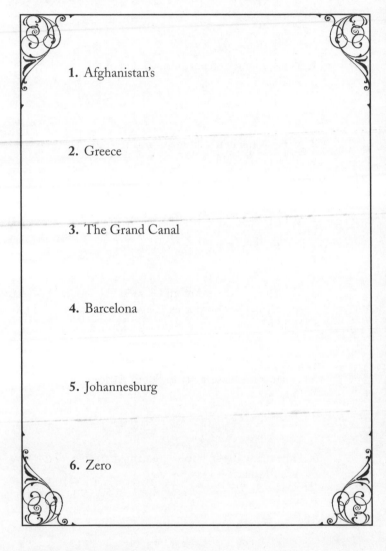

1. What is Latin America's northernmost nation?

2. What nickname is attached to the circle of volcanoes around the Pacific Basin?

3. What country shares Lake Titicaca with Bolivia?

4. What is alternatively known as the Will Rogers Highway?

5. Which country contains Lake Assal, the lowest point on mainland Africa?

6. Which city's annual *Fringe* is the world's largest arts festival?

1. Which Scandinavian country's longest and deepest fjord is the Sognafjorden?

2. Who was king of Spain at the start of the 21st century?

3. How many zeros were dropped when Turkish Lira became New Turkish Lira in 2005?

4. What often splashes down the clothes of unwary visitors when they bite into the Tunisian dish called *brik*?

5. Which island on the Pearl River delta has a name meaning *fragrant harbor*?

6. Which of the Twelve Apostles is said to be buried in North West Spain and is that country's patron saint?

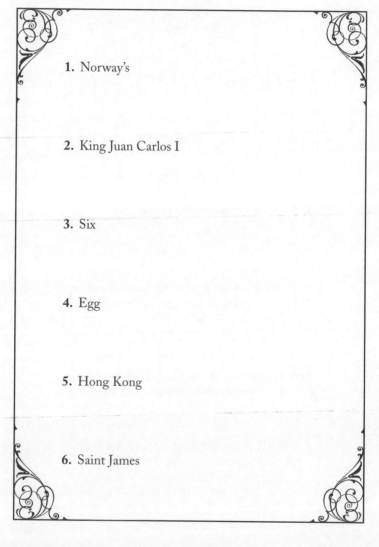

1. Norway's

2. King Juan Carlos I

3. Six

4. Egg

5. Hong Kong

6. Saint James

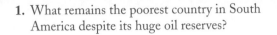

1. What remains the poorest country in South America despite its huge oil reserves?

2. Which is the largest of the Balearic Islands?

3. What decade saw Nigeria become independent?

4. Which river is Nigeria named after?

5. Which is the third-largest Mediterranean island after Sicily and Sardinia?

6. Which of the Seven Wonders of the World was situated approximately 50 miles south of modern Baghdad?

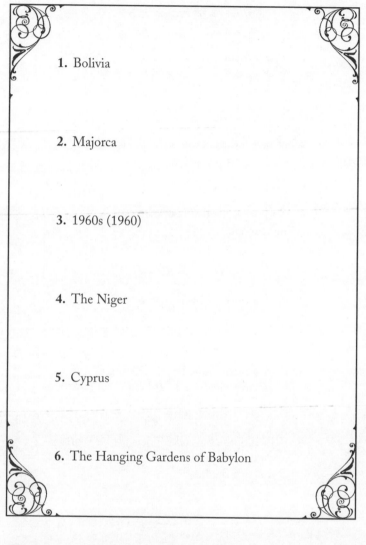

1. Bolivia

2. Majorca

3. 1960s (1960)

4. The Niger

5. Cyprus

6. The Hanging Gardens of Babylon

1. How many fillérs are there in one Hungarian forint?

2. Which popular cocktail was created at the Raffles Hotel, Singapore around 1915?

3. What are stolen in Amsterdam at the rate of 80,000 a year with around 25,000 ending up in the canals?

4. What country is known as the Cradle of Civilization?

5. What was once mined in Salzburg?

6. Which is the world's largest container port?

1. One hundred

2. Singapore Sling

3. Bicycles

4. Iraq

5. Salt

6. Singapore

1. What word describes Danish coastal valleys shaped by glaciers and partially filled by the sea?

2. What is Finland's most northerly province?

3. What strait links the Mediterranean Sea and the Atlantic Ocean?

4. What eastern country's highest mountain is the extinct volcano Mount Damavand?

5. What New York location is popularly called the Crossroads of the World?

6. What island's Argentinean section is the world's most southerly National Park?

1. Fjords

2. Finnish Lapland

3. The Strait of Gibraltar

4. Iran's

5. Times Square

6. Tierra del Fuego

1. What Latin American city hosted the 1992 World Earth Summit?

2. What is the official state sport of Alaska?

3. What would a Bolivian do with his Chica—smoke it, drink it or wear it?

4. Which U.S. city's *Elvis Wedding Chapel* advertises: "The best wedding with best value"?

5. What is the world's largest volcano?

6. What color is the cross on the Swedish flag?

1. Rio de Janeiro

2. Dog mushing

3. Drink it

4. Las Vegas'

5. Mauna Loa

6. Yellow

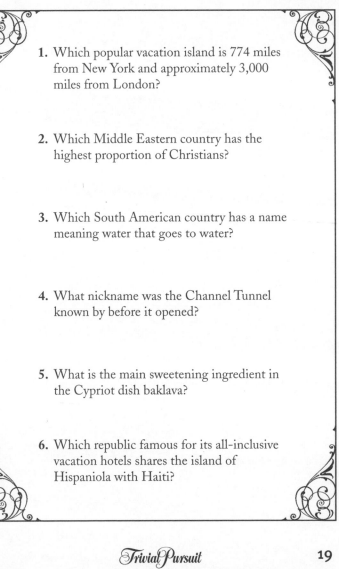

1. Which popular vacation island is 774 miles from New York and approximately 3,000 miles from London?

2. Which Middle Eastern country has the highest proportion of Christians?

3. Which South American country has a name meaning water that goes to water?

4. What nickname was the Channel Tunnel known by before it opened?

5. What is the main sweetening ingredient in the Cypriot dish baklava?

6. Which republic famous for its all-inclusive vacation hotels shares the island of Hispaniola with Haiti?

1. Bermuda

2. Lebanon

3. Paraguay

4. The Chunnel

5. Honey

6. Dominican Republic

1. Which territory's people voted in 1967 and 2002 to remain British citizens?

2. What precious stone is Colombia the world's leading producer of?

3. What gave a boost to Libya's standard of living in the 1960s?

4. What dam regulates the flow of the Nile?

5. What was Iran known as until 1935?

6. Which European capital, known as the Venice of the North, is built on 14 islands?

1. Gibraltar's

2. Emerald

3. The discovery of oil

4. Aswan

5. Persia

6. Stockholm

1. Whose birthday do the people of Bermuda celebrate on the second Monday in June?

2. What nation did Premier Lee Kuan Yew lead for 34 years, turning it into the world's seventh-wealthiest country by 1996?

3. What does Djibouti have on only 26 days of its average year?

4. What defensive item is pictured in front of two spears on the flag of Kenya?

5. Which country, famous through the ages for its mercenary soldiers, still supplies a guard for the Pope?

6. What does John Steinbeck refer to as the "Mother Road" in *The Grapes of Wrath*?

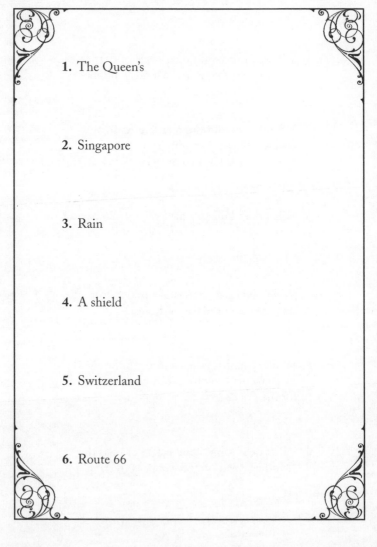

1. The Queen's

2. Singapore

3. Rain

4. A shield

5. Switzerland

6. Route 66

1. What is SoHo short for?

2. What is Europe's longest river?

3. What country did Maoris name *Aotearoa*, Land of the Long White Cloud?

4. What is the official language of Latvia?

5. Which country's Kayan women stretch their necks with brass rings?

6. What city would you be in if you were feeding the pigeons in the Piazza San Marco?

1. South of Houston

2. Volga

3. New Zealand

4. Latvian

5. Burma's (Myanmar's)

6. Venice

1. What vegetable takes its name from the capital of Belgium?

2. Which country's city of Kairouan is said to have given us the word *caravan*, meaning a string of camels?

3. What major river's source is Lake Tana in Ethiopia?

4. What ingredient does the word *sushi* refer to?

5. Which British castle is said to include columns from the Roman city of Leptic Magna in Libya?

6. What name was Argentina's Eva Peron known by?

1. Brussels sprouts

2. Tunisia's

3. The Blue Nile's

4. Rice

5. Windsor Castle

6. Evita

1. What did singer Kyu Sakamoto once have carried to the summit of Mount Fuji for a concert?

2. Where can you enjoy a close encounter with Barbary apes, the only wild monkeys living in Europe?

3. What animal is the symbol of Thailand?

4. What is the capital of Tunisia?

5. What is Uganda's main export?

6. What religion do many Haitians practice alongside Christianity?

1. Grand piano

2. Gibraltar

3. Elephant

4. Tunis

5. Coffee

6. Voodoo

1. What $15 billion tunnel is the largest privately financed engineering project in history?

2. Which ocean covers a greater area of the world's surface than all the dry land?

3. What country produces the world's finest rubies?

4. What U.S. city takes its tourists to the Adler Planetarium and Grant Park?

5. What day traditionally sees the end of Rio's Carnaval?

6. What is the most famous product from Murano, Venice?

1. The Channel Tunnel

2. Pacific

3. Burma (Myanmar)

4. Chicago

5. Shrove Tuesday (Mardi Gras)

6. Glass

1. What country is most associated with Internet 419 scams, also known as advance-fee frauds?

2. What month sees the start of the annual Beaujolais Nouveau celebration?

3. Where's the Isthmus of Corinth?

4. Which island's Mount Teide can be seen from Africa on a clear day?

5. What Scandinavian country's flag flies over Spitsbergen?

6. What city on Route 66 has a name you might expect to see the Stars and Stripes flying from?

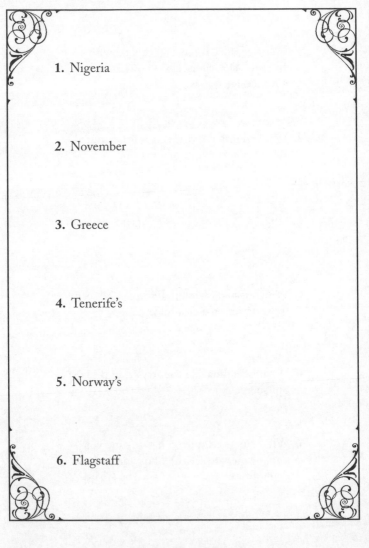

1. Nigeria

2. November

3. Greece

4. Tenerife's

5. Norway's

6. Flagstaff

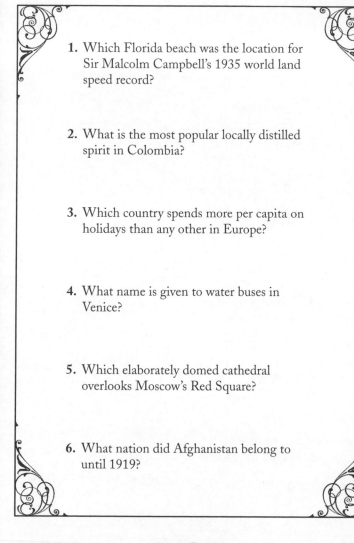

1. Which Florida beach was the location for Sir Malcolm Campbell's 1935 world land speed record?

2. What is the most popular locally distilled spirit in Colombia?

3. Which country spends more per capita on holidays than any other in Europe?

4. What name is given to water buses in Venice?

5. Which elaborately domed cathedral overlooks Moscow's Red Square?

6. What nation did Afghanistan belong to until 1919?

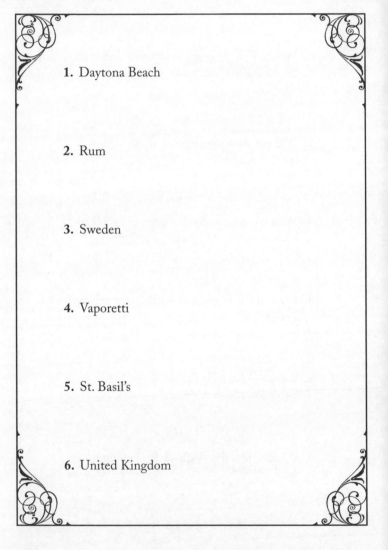

1. Daytona Beach

2. Rum

3. Sweden

4. Vaporetti

5. St. Basil's

6. United Kingdom

1. What desert surrounds Las Vegas?

2. Which U.S. state's highest point is the lowest of all the states?

3. Which is the world's northernmost capital city?

4. What is Norway's Jostedalsbreen Northern Europe's largest example of?

5. What is *nori*, an important ingredient in some forms of sushi?

6. What country sprang from the union of Tanganyika and Zanzibar?

1. The Mojave Desert

2. Florida

3. Reykjavik

4. Glacier

5. Seaweed

6. Tanzania

1. What kind of drum shares its name with the man who became president of the Gabonese Republic in 1967?

2. Which author built a home called *Goldeneye* in Jamaica?

3. What is the American equivalent of the annual celebration known as *Erntedankfest* in Germany?

4. What is Africa's second-largest country after Sudan?

5. What is Burma's main food crop?

6. Which southern country's national anthem boasts: "Our land is girt by the sea"?

1. Bongo

2. Ian Fleming

3. Thanksgiving

4. Algeria

5. Rice

6. Australia's

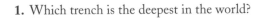

1. Which trench is the deepest in the world?

2. What was known as Seward's Folly when the U.S. purchased it in 1867?

3. What sea gives Iran its northern coastline?

4. What is the most famous drink from Jamaica's Blue Mountains?

5. What is South Africa's national animal?

6. What is the world's most populous Spanish-speaking country?

1. The Marianas Trench

2. Alaska

3. Caspian Sea

4. Coffee

5. Springbok

6. Mexico

1. Which South American country boasts the Cartagena World Heritage site?

2. What large apes are Uganda's *Kigezi Game Reserve* best known for?

3. What is the colorful English name for Amsterdam's De Wallen area?

4. What country's flag was reversed to become the flag of the Red Cross?

5. What is Rio de Janeiro's most popular beach?

6. What Middle Eastern country's cities include Isfahan, Shiraz and Tabriz?

1. Colombia

2. Gorillas

3. Red Light District

4. Switzerland's

5. Copacabana

6. Iran's

1. What sea does the Danube empty into?

2. Which African country's capital, Libreville, was founded in 1849 by freed slaves?

3. Which U.S. mountain has the highest visible base-to-summit elevation of any on Earth?

4. What is mainland Europe's northernmost capital?

5. Which capital city was once known as Byzantium?

6. What city is known as Auld Reekie?

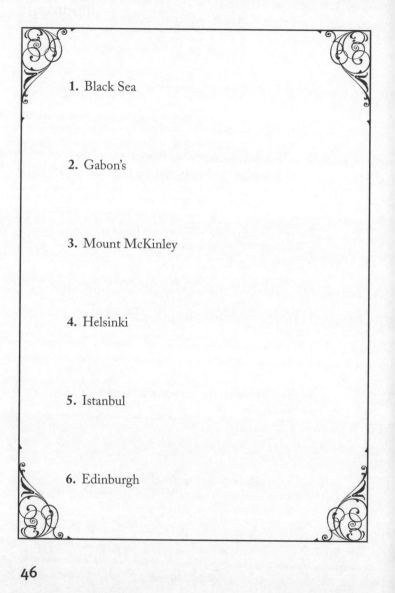

1. Black Sea

2. Gabon's

3. Mount McKinley

4. Helsinki

5. Istanbul

6. Edinburgh

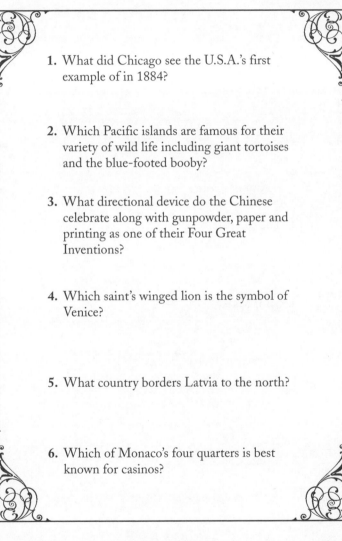

1. What did Chicago see the U.S.A.'s first example of in 1884?

2. Which Pacific islands are famous for their variety of wild life including giant tortoises and the blue-footed booby?

3. What directional device do the Chinese celebrate along with gunpowder, paper and printing as one of their Four Great Inventions?

4. Which saint's winged lion is the symbol of Venice?

5. What country borders Latvia to the north?

6. Which of Monaco's four quarters is best known for casinos?

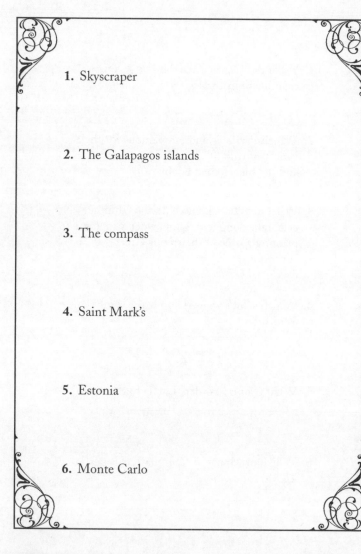

1. Skyscraper

2. The Galapagos islands

3. The compass

4. Saint Mark's

5. Estonia

6. Monte Carlo

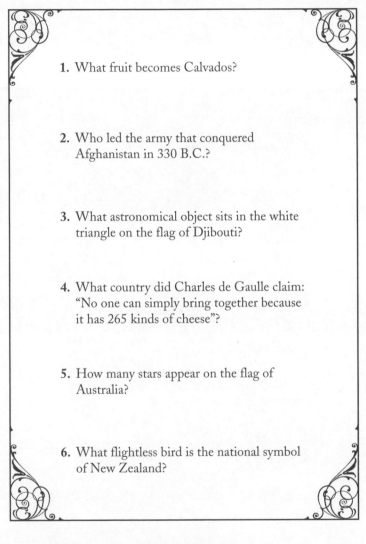

1. What fruit becomes Calvados?

2. Who led the army that conquered Afghanistan in 330 B.C.?

3. What astronomical object sits in the white triangle on the flag of Djibouti?

4. What country did Charles de Gaulle claim: "No one can simply bring together because it has 265 kinds of cheese"?

5. How many stars appear on the flag of Australia?

6. What flightless bird is the national symbol of New Zealand?

1. Apple

2. Alexander the Great

3. Star

4. France

5. Six

6. Kiwi

1. What is Ethiopia's main commercial crop?

2. What country would you be heading to on the Road to Mandalay?

3. What didn't operate in Iceland in July until 1983 or on Thursdays until 1987?

4. What city takes tourists to the Anne Frank House?

5. What is the largest city in Iran?

6. Which explorer's day is celebrated on the second Monday in October?

1. Coffee

2. Burma (Myanmar)

3. Television

4. Amsterdam

5. Tehran

6. Christopher Columbus'

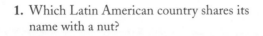

1. Which Latin American country shares its name with a nut?

2. What was Jamaica the world's leading exporter of during its first 200 years of British rule?

3. Which company's *finger lickin' good* slogan became *eat your fingers off* when launched in China?

4. What mountain is known in Nepal as *Sagarmatha* or Forehead of the Sky?

5. Which African country is said to have been named from a Greek term describing its natives' sunburned features?

6. What mountain range runs through Morocco and Algeria into Tunisia?

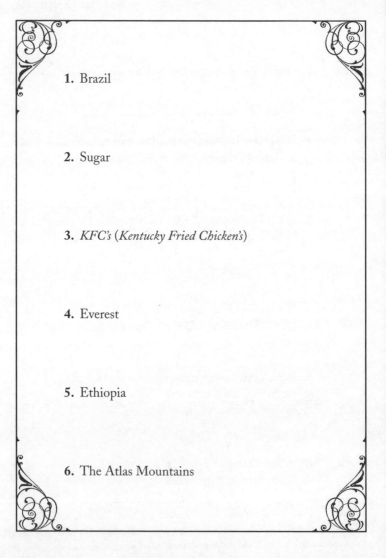

1. Brazil

2. Sugar

3. *KFC's* (*Kentucky Fried Chicken's*)

4. Everest

5. Ethiopia

6. The Atlas Mountains

1. What is the official residence of the Head of State of New Zealand?

2. Which iconic Japanese volcano last erupted in 1707?

3. What was the only country you were allowed to drive into Israel from in 1979?

4. What is the official language of Egypt?

5. Which country boasts the highest and lowest points in South America?

6. Which very small people was the first group to inhabit Gabon?

1. Buckingham Palace

2. Mount Fuji

3. Jordan

4. Arabic

5. Argentina

6. Pygmy

1. How many U.S. states are there?

2. What desert covers approximately 80 percent of Algeria?

3. Which European country's native people are known as Letts?

4. Which is the world's highest capital?

5. Which South African city is overlooked by Table Mountain?

6. Who lives with his wife and helpers on a mountain called Korvatunturi, according to Finnish folklore?

1. Fifty

2. Sahara Desert

3. Latvia's

4. La Paz

5. Cape Town

6. Father Christmas

1. What is the approximate number of languages spoken in Nigeria: 3, 30 or 300?

2. Which city boasts the Supreme Court of Canada?

3. What agricultural crop is Cuba's main export?

4. What is the most popular spirit produced in Jamaica?

5. What title do Germans give to their motorways?

6. What city has been dubbed the Venice of the East?

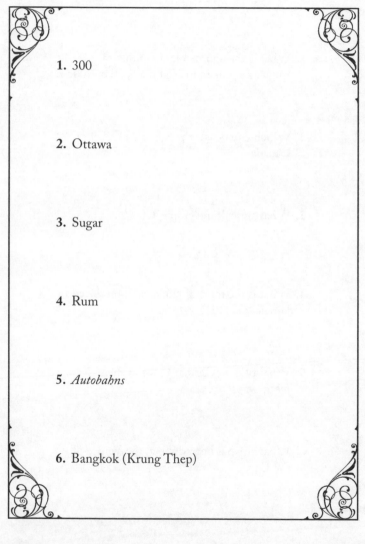

1. 300

2. Ottawa

3. Sugar

4. Rum

5. *Autobahns*

6. Bangkok (Krung Thep)

1. What cotton fabric takes its name from the city of Mosul in Northern Iraq?

2. What company was established in Switzerland in 1866 to market baby milk?

3. What female artist had more number one hits in the 1980s than anyone else?

4. Which hurricane caused Florida an estimated $30 billion of damage in 1992?

5. Which city on the old Route 66 was Gene Pitney 24 hours from?

6. Which colorful sea washes the northernmost beaches of Djibouti?

1. Muslin

2. *Nestlé*

3. Madonna

4. Hurricane Andrew

5. Tulsa

6. Red Sea

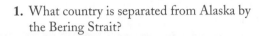

1. What country is separated from Alaska by the Bering Strait?

2. What is the three-word title of the anthem sung by the Wallabies rugby squad?

3. Who was president of Kenya from 1963 to 1978?

4. What item of clothing, adapted from British military trousers, takes its name from an Atlantic island?

5. Which is the most densely populated country in the world?

6. Which city's attractions include Rembrandt's House and the Rijksmuseum?

1. Russia

2. *Advance Australia Fair*

3. Jomo Kenyatta

4. Bermuda shorts

5. Monaco

6. Amsterdam's

1. What was the former name of Bangladesh?

2. What is the Japanese name for Japan?

3. Which country boasts the town of Corinth that gave its name to currants and a canal?

4. What country was known as the Gift of the Nile?

5. What popular Greek dish is mostly smoked fish roe?

6. Which city boasts the State Hermitage art museum and St. Isaac's Cathedral?

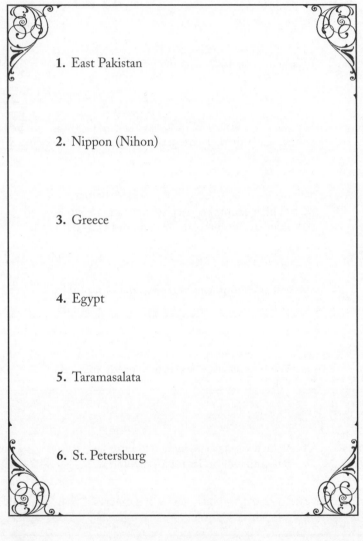

1. East Pakistan

2. Nippon (Nihon)

3. Greece

4. Egypt

5. Taramasalata

6. St. Petersburg

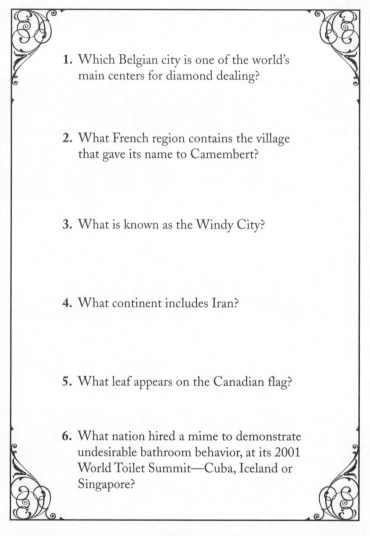

1. Which Belgian city is one of the world's main centers for diamond dealing?

2. What French region contains the village that gave its name to Camembert?

3. What is known as the Windy City?

4. What continent includes Iran?

5. What leaf appears on the Canadian flag?

6. What nation hired a mime to demonstrate undesirable bathroom behavior, at its 2001 World Toilet Summit—Cuba, Iceland or Singapore?

1. Antwerp

2. Normandy

3. Chicago

4. Asia

5. Maple leaf

6. Singapore

1. Which is the largest of the seven Canary Islands?

2. Where were 30,000 British citizens living when it became a Special Administrative Region of China in 1997?

3. What cheese is served with a classic Greek salad?

4. What killed more than 2,000 people in Algeria in May 2003?

5. What sea creature gave its name to the only cards accepted for payment by Hong Kong parking meters?

6. Which river can ocean-going ships travel the entire length of in Brazil?

1. Tenerife

2. Hong Kong

3. Feta

4. Earthquake

5. Octopus

6. Amazon

1. What valley runs the length of Kenya?

2. Which country's president kicked up a fuss when a Spanish version of its national anthem was recorded in 2006?

3. Which sunny spot in the Atlantic is Britain's oldest colony?

4. How many times is Britain mentioned in the anthem *God Save the Queen*?

5. What religion is followed by 90 percent of the population of Thailand?

6. What name is given to local porters who help climbers on Everest?

1. Great Rift Valley

2. U.S.A.'s

3. Bermuda

4. Once

5. Buddhism

6. Sherpas

1. Who ruled Monaco until 2005?

2. What London traffic circle was known as the "Hub of the British Empire"?

3. What Asian country's name means Land of the Bengalis?

4. What traditional belief in natural forces has been taken into consideration in the design and furniture layout of many Hong Kong hotels and offices?

5. Which Latvian city was dubbed the Paris of the Baltic?

6. What became the world's first independent black-led republic?

1. Prince Rainier III

2. Picadilly Circus

3. Bangladesh's

4. Feng Shui

5. Riga

6. Haiti

1. What does a dirty Turk know as a *hamam*?

2. What country is home to Shakespeare's Hamlet?

3. Which city is the home of more than 40 percent of the entire population of the Hawaiian Islands?

4. Which country made history in 1893 by giving its women the vote?

5. What shape is the main part of Las Vegas' *Luxor Hotel*?

6. Which country's prostitutes were given funding to retrain as geriatric nurses?

1. Turkish bath

2. Denmark

3. Honolulu

4. New Zealand

5. Pyramid

6. Germany's

1. What named line of latitude cuts through Gabon?

2. What two symbols of the Islamic religion appear on the flag of Algeria?

3. What heavy wood is Burma's main timber export?

4. What children's construction kit is the subject of a Danish theme park?

5. What M-word describes the old town or market in a Tunisian city?

6. Who founded a hospital at Lambarene, Gabon, in 1913?

1. The Equator

2. Star and crescent

3. Teak

4. *Lego*

5. Medina

6. Albert Schweitzer

1. What river separates Buda from Pest?

2. What is the traditional color of Venetian gondolas?

3. What book did Elspeth Huxley base on her childhood at a Kenyan coffee plantation?

4. What does a citizen of Edinburgh call New Year?

5. What is the name for Argentinean cowboys?

6. What French river shares its name with a type of fishing net?

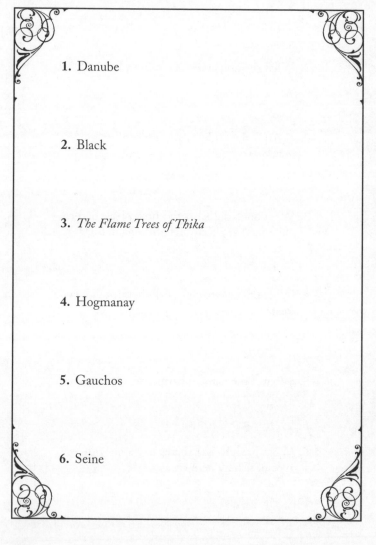

1. Danube

2. Black

3. *The Flame Trees of Thika*

4. Hogmanay

5. Gauchos

6. Seine

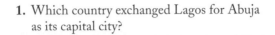

1. Which country exchanged Lagos for Abuja as its capital city?

2. What country is completely enclosed by South Africa?

3. What is New York City's most popular nickname?

4. Which British overseas territory's name is derived from the Arabic for *Mountain of Tariq*?

5. What was abolished in Colombia in 1849?

6. What crazy nickname is given to the Canadian dollar coin due to the bird pictured on it?

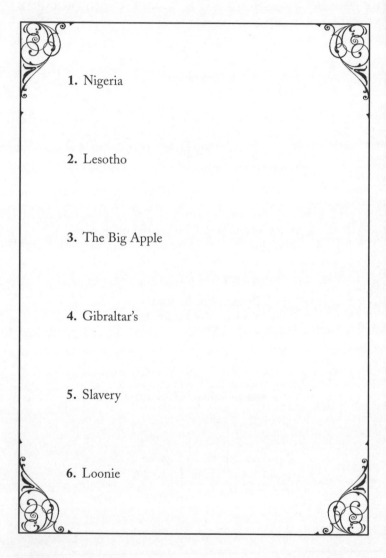

1. Nigeria

2. Lesotho

3. The Big Apple

4. Gibraltar's

5. Slavery

6. Loonie

1. What is Djibouti's main religion?

2. What nationality by birth was Joseph Pulitzer of Pulitzer Prize fame?

3. Which vacation island is named after Spanish seafarer Juan de Bermudez?

4. Which South American country speaks and spends Guarani?

5. What large island is due south of Melbourne, Australia?

6. What is the most populous country on the African continent?

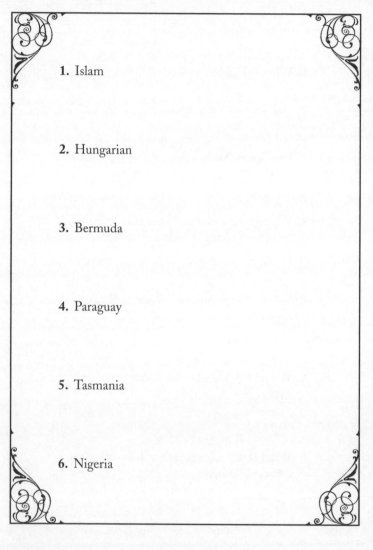

1. Islam

2. Hungarian

3. Bermuda

4. Paraguay

5. Tasmania

6. Nigeria

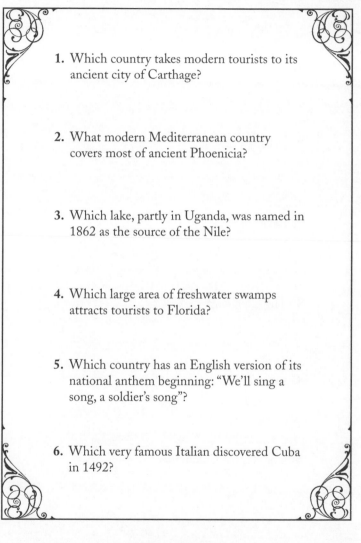

1. Which country takes modern tourists to its ancient city of Carthage?

2. What modern Mediterranean country covers most of ancient Phoenicia?

3. Which lake, partly in Uganda, was named in 1862 as the source of the Nile?

4. Which large area of freshwater swamps attracts tourists to Florida?

5. Which country has an English version of its national anthem beginning: "We'll sing a song, a soldier's song"?

6. Which very famous Italian discovered Cuba in 1492?

1. Tunisia

2. Lebanon

3. Lake Victoria

4. The Everglades

5. Ireland

6. Christopher Columbus

1. What accounts for almost 75 percent of Iceland's exports?

2. What is the largest island in the Atlantic?

3. What beer shares its name with the river that runs through Amsterdam?

4. What is the standard unit of currency in Gibraltar?

5. What's the northernmost Scandinavian country?

6. What country is sometimes called the Land of Fire and Ice?

1. Fish

2. Greenland

3. *Amstel*

4. Gibraltar pound

5. Norway

6. Iceland

1. Which is the largest of the Caribbean islands?

2. What area of the Atlantic is said to be responsible for the disappearance of ships and aircraft?

3. What nationality is the *Muppet Show* chef?

4. Which was the first ocean to be crossed by ship and by plane?

5. Which is the only independent state smaller than Monaco?

6. What name is given to the continuous strong winds between South Africa and South America?

1. Cuba

2. Bermuda Triangle

3. Swedish

4. Atlantic Ocean

5. The Vatican

6. Roaring Forties

1. Which U.S. city takes tourists to Martin Luther King Jr.'s tomb and the *World of Coca-Cola*?

2. What modern country includes the ancient region of Mesopotamia?

3. What color is the cross on the flag of Finland?

4. Who co-opened the Channel Tunnel with the Queen of England?

5. Who became Queen of Denmark in 1972?

6. What is the main export crop of the Canary Islands?

1. Atlanta

2. Iraq

3. Blue

4. French President Mitterrand

5. Queen Margrethe II

6. Bananas

1. What exotic bloom is the national flower of Singapore?

2. What is *lokum* to a sweet-toothed Turk?

3. What limestone rock is dubbed the northern Pillar of Hercules?

4. What were the women of Libya given in 1963?

5. What color joins green, white and black on the flag of Afghanistan?

6. Which is the only Southeast Asian country never ruled by a European power?

1. Orchid

2. Turkish Delight

3. Gibraltar

4. The right to vote

5. Red

6. Thailand

1. What Brussels landmark boasting nine huge spheres was created for the 1958 World Fair?

2. What transport system did British engineers construct in Paraguay between 1858 and 1861?

3. Which waterfalls are between Lake Erie and Lake Ontario?

4. Which is by far the best-known harbor in the Hawaiian Islands?

5. What is the official language of Gabon?

6. What famous dance did Andalusian Gypsies invent?

1. The *Atomium*

2. Railway

3. Niagara Falls

4. Pearl Harbor

5. French

6. Flamenco

1. Which South American country is named after Christopher Columbus?

2. What hot room invented in Finland has become used as a term for almost anywhere with intense heat?

3. Which country's postage stamps are marked *Magyar Posta*?

4. What country was historically known as Cathay?

5. What color pencil was used to draw the Greek/Turkish border on a map of Cyprus and determined its name?

6. What African mountain was formerly known as Kaiser-Wilhelm-Spitze?

1. Colombia

2. Sauna

3. Hungary's

4. China

5. Green (*The Green Line*)

6. Mount Kilimanjaro

1. What country has been called the Cradle of Western Civilization and the Birthplace of Democracy?

2. What is the main ingredient in the traditional Egyptian dish *Ful Mudammas*?

3. Which Middle Eastern country boasts the ancient city of Byblos, which is said to have given the Bible its name?

4. What meat traditionally becomes a Wiener Schnitzel?

5. What is the closest tropic to the Hawaiian Islands?

6. What creature is pictured on the German coat of arms?

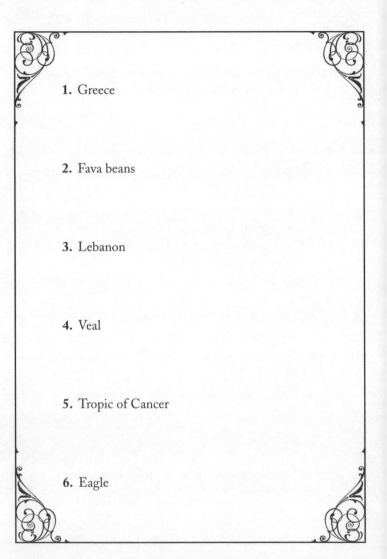

1. Greece

2. Fava beans

3. Lebanon

4. Veal

5. Tropic of Cancer

6. Eagle

1. How many time zones are spanned by Russia?

2. What is Alaska's most populous city but not its capital?

3. Which German city is twinned with Edinburgh?

4. What creatures are said to have given their Latin name to the Canary Islands?

5. Which ocean can be reached from Bolivia along the Paraguay River?

6. What Caribbean republic is the least-developed country in the Western Hemisphere?

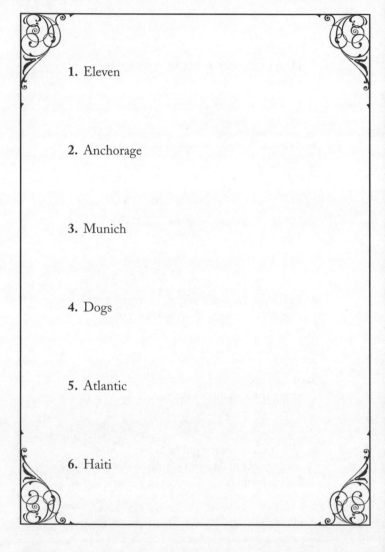

1. Eleven

2. Anchorage

3. Munich

4. Dogs

5. Atlantic

6. Haiti

1. Who was born in the Austrian village of Thal and became the 38th governor of California?

2. What form of drink is Paraguayan *maté*, which is made from the leaves and roots of a holly tree?

3. Which country's national anthem is *La Marseillaise*?

4. Which of the Great Lakes touches Chicago?

5. Which mountain range covers approximately two-thirds of southern Switzerland?

6. What make up more than 90 percent of Algeria's exports?

1. Arnold Schwarzenegger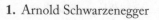

2. Tea

3. France's

4. Lake Michigan

5. Alps

6. Oil and gas

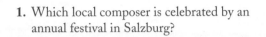

1. Which local composer is celebrated by an annual festival in Salzburg?

2. Which African country was historically known as Abyssinia?

3. What is the only U.S. state with a single-syllable name?

4. What is the highest peak in Turkey and the supposed resting place of Noah's Ark?

5. What collective name is given to the islands at the tip of the Florida peninsula?

6. What location on the Danish island of Sjaelland is the setting for Shakespeare's *Hamlet*?

1. Mozart

2. Ethiopia

3. Maine

4. Mount Ararat

5. The Florida Keys

6. Helsingør (Elsinore)

1. Which country claims to have a Loch Ness–like monster in its Lake Storsjön?

2. What warm Atlantic current keeps many northern European ports free of winter ice?

3. What strait separates Tierra del Fuego from mainland Argentina?

4. Which is America's largest state, by land area?

5. What country is the world's second-largest producer of opium after Myanmar despite its ban by the Taliban in 2001?

6. What did Amsterdam cab drivers have to sell from machines in their cars beginning January 2001?

1. Sweden

2. The Gulf Stream

3. Strait of Magellan

4. Alaska

5. Afghanistan

6. Condoms

1. What nation protects dugong and turtles in a marine park called *Gumoo Woojabuddee*?

2. What is the world's largest country?

3. Which leader's thoughts are set out in *The Green Book*?

4. What might appear on a Chinese menu as *fragrant meat*?

5. Which is the world's largest coral reef?

6. Which is the only remaining example of the Seven Wonders of the Ancient World?

1. Australia

2. Russia

3. Muammar Al Qadhafi's

4. Dog

5. The Great Barrier Reef

6. The Great Pyramid

1. What hotel did Bugsy Siegel open on the Las Vegas Strip in 1946?

2. What is the longest river in the U.S.?

3. What religion that emerged in Jamaica accepts Ethiopian Emperor Haile Selassie I as its God incarnate?

4. Which country has the world's longest coastline?

5. What metal was mined in Cyprus and is said to have given the island its name from the Greek word for that metal, *kypros*?

6. What is New Zealand's highest mountain?

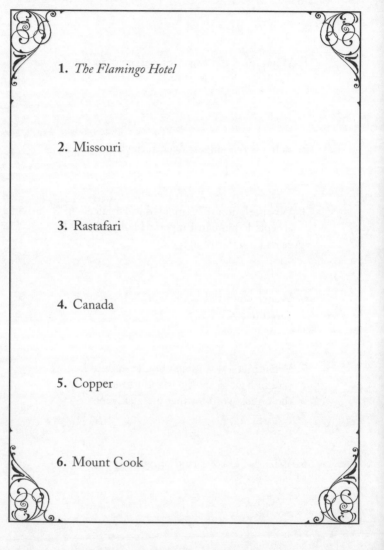

1. *The Flamingo Hotel*

2. Missouri

3. Rastafari

4. Canada

5. Copper

6. Mount Cook

1. What state boasts the easternmost desert in the U.S.?

2. What is the capital of Uganda, known as the city of seven hills even though it now covers more than 20?

3. What valuable commodity was found at Kimberley, South Africa, in 1871?

4. What is the named line of latitude running through Kenya?

5. Which European country produces more hydroelectricity per capita than any other in the world?

6. What cheese joins Gruyere in a traditional Swiss fondue?

1. Maine

2. Kampala

3. Diamonds

4. The Equator

5. Norway

6. Emmental

1. What weren't worn in the Hawaiian Islands until the 1870s?

2. What is the largest city in Libya?

3. Which islands off the coast of Africa introduced bananas to Jamaica in the 16th century?

4. How many years must you wait for each animal to come around again in the Chinese calendar?

5. What river forms in Montana at the junction of the Jefferson, Madison and Gallatin Rivers?

6. What is the most widely spoken European language in Paraguay?

1. Grass skirts

2. Tripoli

3. Canary Islands

4. Twelve

5. The Missouri River

6. Spanish

1. Which European country offers shoppers the opportunity to spend lats?

2. How many times is the United States mentioned in its national anthem?

3. What was the four-letter name of Thailand prior to 1949?

4. Who was the last Governor of Hong Kong?

5. What active Mexican volcano has a name meaning smoking mountain?

6. Which country's government building is a vast wooden structure known as the Beehive?

1. Latvia

2. Zero

3. Siam

4. Chris Patten

5. Popocatepetl

6. New Zealand's

1. What is the name of Spain's famous cold soup made mostly from tomatoes?

2. What Cuban naval base has been leased to the U.S. until 2033?

3. How many of the world's ten highest mountains are in Asia?

4. What river, celebrated as being blue, looks decidedly brown as it flows through Vienna?

5. Which planet boasts the tallest mountain in the solar system?

6. What commodity is collected from the lakes of Cyprus when they dry up in the summer?

1. *Gazpacho*

2. Guantanamo Bay

3. Ten

4. Danube

5. Mars

6. Salt

1. Which European country drinks more coffee per capita than any other in the world?

2. Which Scandinavian country awards the Nobel Peace prize?

3. Which eastern island city-state has a name meaning Lion Town?

4. What river joins the Brahmaputra in Bangladesh to form the world's largest river delta?

5. What is the Grand Place market in Brussels carpeted with once every other year as part of a festival?

6. What dinky dog takes its name from the capital of a Mexican state?

1. Finland

2. Norway

3. Singapore

4. Ganges

5. Flowers

6. Chihuahua

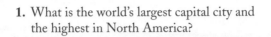

1. What is the world's largest capital city and the highest in North America?

2. What Mexican revolutionary began life as baby Doroteo Arango?

3. What English town does the Channel Tunnel connect directly to Coquelles in France?

4. What became the second independent country in the Americas after the United States?

5. What sung-about route connected Chicago to Los Angeles?

6. What are the two red stripes on the flag of Latvia said to represent?

1. Mexico City

2. Pancho Villa

3. Folkestone

4. Haiti

5. Route 66

6. The blood of a hero

1. What is the French name for the gourmet dish that in English translates as *fat liver*?

2. Which Pacific island is the second largest in the world?

3. What tree appears on the flag of Lebanon?

4. Which of the Canary Islands has the same national flag as Scotland?

5. Which city is *oh so pretty* in the song *Route 66*?

6. What is South America's second-largest country after Brazil?

1. *Foie Gras*

2. New Guinea

3. Cedar of Lebanon

4. Tenerife

5. Oklahoma City

6. Argentina

1. Which is Europe's second-largest island after Great Britain?

2. What does education and medical care cost in Libya?

3. Which tiny European country claims more millionaires per capita than any other in the world?

4. What ancient proclamation is Britain's equivalent of Hungary's *Golden Bull*?

5. Which churchman first called South Africa the Rainbow Nation?

6. What is Cuba's most common mammal?

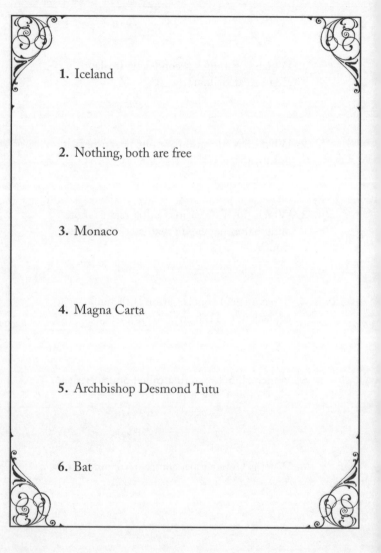

1. Iceland

2. Nothing, both are free

3. Monaco

4. Magna Carta

5. Archbishop Desmond Tutu

6. Bat

1. What name was Haitian dictator François Duvalier better known by?

2. What would a Bangladeshi man do with his *lungi*?

3. Who is by far the most famous, yet least celebrated, person to have been born in Braunau am Inn, Austria?

4. What political party with civilian and military arms was founded in Lebanon in 1985?

5. Which New York City building is nicknamed after something you could press your clothes with?

6. Who gave the Asian community 90 days to leave Uganda in 1972?

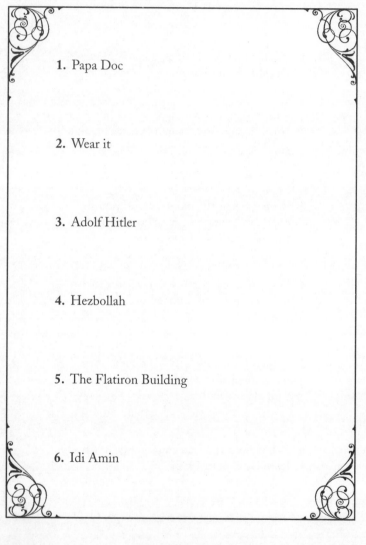

1. Papa Doc

2. Wear it

3. Adolf Hitler

4. Hezbollah

5. The Flatiron Building

6. Idi Amin

1. Which chilly country's native cuisine is called *porramatur*, which includes such mouth-watering delicacies as pickled ram's testicles and putrefied shark?

2. What kind of vehicle would you be in if you took a sampan to a restaurant in Hong Kong?

3. What country borders the entire northern side of Bolivia?

4. What did the name of Burma officially change to in 1989?

5. Which city in Nevada has a name based on *The Meadows* in Spanish?

6. Which capital city touches two continents?

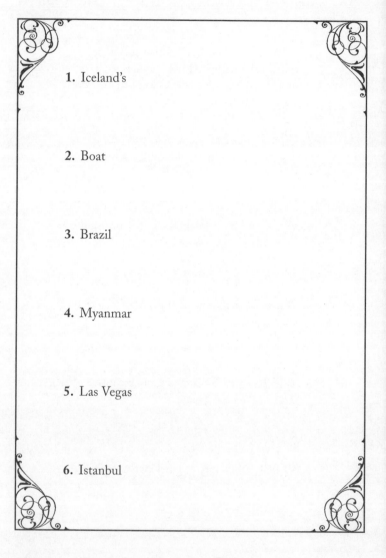

1. Iceland's

2. Boat

3. Brazil

4. Myanmar

5. Las Vegas

6. Istanbul

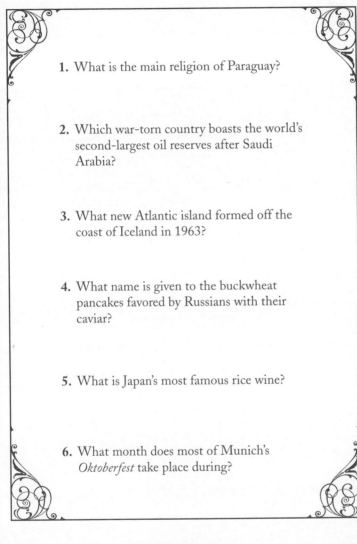

1. What is the main religion of Paraguay?

2. Which war-torn country boasts the world's second-largest oil reserves after Saudi Arabia?

3. What new Atlantic island formed off the coast of Iceland in 1963?

4. What name is given to the buckwheat pancakes favored by Russians with their caviar?

5. What is Japan's most famous rice wine?

6. What month does most of Munich's *Oktoberfest* take place during?

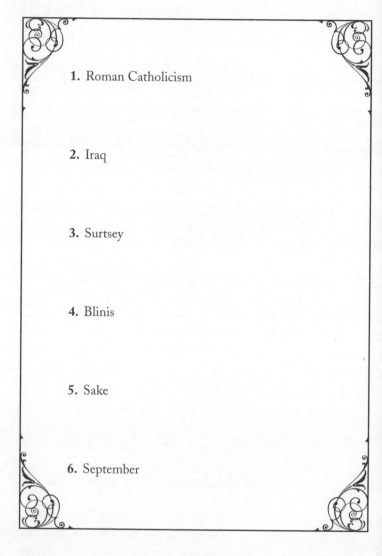

1. Roman Catholicism

2. Iraq

3. Surtsey

4. Blinis

5. Sake

6. September

1. What river forms the border between Thailand and Laos?

2. What is the largest city in the U.S., in terms of population?

3. What Greek goddess of love and beauty is said to have been born in Cyprus?

4. Which river flows past the Eiffel Tower?

5. What is the official name for what was once known as Ayers Rock?

6. Which is the only Portuguese-speaking Latin American country?

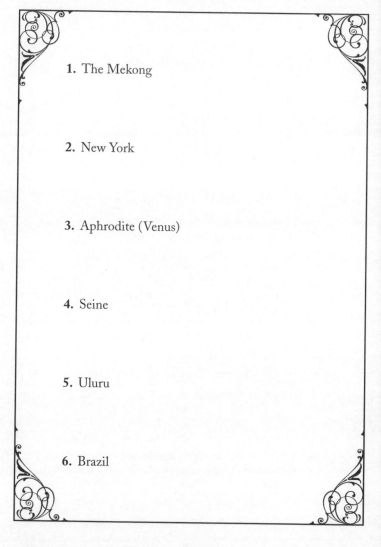

1. The Mekong

2. New York

3. Aphrodite (Venus)

4. Seine

5. Uluru

6. Brazil

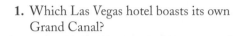

1. Which Las Vegas hotel boasts its own Grand Canal?

2. Which famous Jamaican, who died in 1981, had the middle name Nesta?

3. What is the main flavor in the French drink pastis?

4. What country's famine inspired *Live Aid*?

5. What literary sleuth was based on Edinburgh University lecturer Dr. Joseph Bell?

6. What luxury Cuban products include *Montecristo*, *Cohiba* and *Romeo y Julieta*?

1. *The Venetian*

2. Bob Marley

3. Aniseed (anise)

4. Ethiopia's

5. Sherlock Holmes

6. Cigars

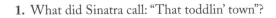

1. What did Sinatra call: "That toddlin' town"?

2. Which Belgian city claims to be the home of Europe's first stock exchange?

3. What was blamed for killing 500,000 people in the region now called Bangladesh in 1970?

4. Which country owns the Canary Islands?

5. What color is the bottom strip on the flag of Egypt?

6. Which city in Tennessee is the country music capital?

1. Chicago

2. Bruges

3. A cyclone

4. Spain

5. Black

6. Nashville

1. What city is the capital of New York State?

2. What is each household in Bermuda only
   permitted one of to protect the
   environment?

3. Which ocean's name means peaceful?

4. What tunnel's 23.55-mile undersea section
   is the longest undersea passenger tunnel in
   the world?

5. What is Africa's second-highest mountain?

6. What sea can you dip your toes in from the
   Western beaches of Lebanon?

1. Albany

2. Car

3. Pacific

4. The Channel Tunnel's

5. Mount Kenya

6. Mediterranean

1. Which European country was the site for the Battle of Waterloo?

2. What is by far the best-known product by *Victorinox*?

3. Which European country's capital has two halves, Buda and Pest, linked by nine bridges across a river?

4. What is Chicago's main international airport?

5. What was the original French name for what is now Djibouti?

6. What's the capital of Monaco?

1. Belgium

2. *Swiss Army Knife*

3. Hungary's

4. O'Hare

5. French Somaliland

6. Monaco

1. What comedy character drives the golden limo in Madonna's *Music* video?

2. What does Elwood only remove three times in *The Blues Brothers*?

3. What movie was hyped: "Five Criminals. One Line Up. No Coincidence"?

4. What Greek city gave its name to the town in Georgia where R.E.M. were formed?

5. What is Beyoncé's surname?

6. Who is the subject of Sting's *An Englishman in New York*?

1. Ali G.

2. His hat

3. *The Usual Suspects*

4. Athens

5. Knowles

6. Quentin Crisp

1. Who wed Cris Judd after paying him to dance in her *Love Don't Cost a Thing* video?

2. What color beret was a huge hit for Prince?

3. What is the subtitle to the second *Pirates of the Caribbean* movie?

4. Which famous comic actor voiced characters Lovelace and Ramón in *Happy Feet*?

5. What is E.T.'s job in the Spielberg movie?

6. What movie caused Nicole Kidman's knee injury that resulted in Jodie Foster having to replace her in *Panic Room*?

1. Jennifer Lopez

2. Raspberry

3. *Dead Man's Chest*

4. Robin Williams

5. Botanist

6. *Moulin Rouge*

1. What Queen hit did Sylvester Stallone nearly use for the *Rocky III* theme song?

2. What foursome is known in Spain as U-Dos?

3. What character in *The Lord of the Rings: The Return of the King* was based on a New Zealand tunnel web spider?

4. What name was shared by the drummers for Duran Duran and Queen?

5. What 1993 dinosaur movie featured Samuel L. Jackson as Ray Arnold?

6. What movie gave Julia Roberts the chance to explain to Hugh Grant: "I'm just a girl standing in front of a boy asking him to love her"?

1. *Another One Bites the Dust*

2. U2

3. Shelob

4. Roger Taylor

5. *Jurassic Park*

6. *Notting Hill*

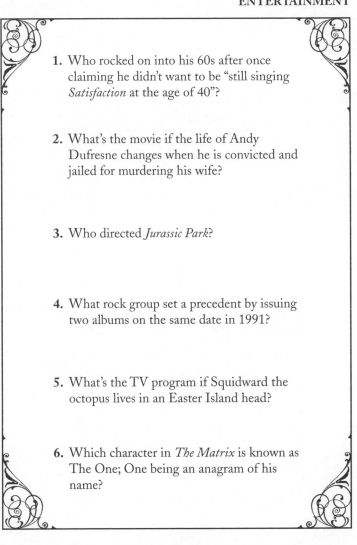

1. Who rocked on into his 60s after once claiming he didn't want to be "still singing *Satisfaction* at the age of 40"?

2. What's the movie if the life of Andy Dufresne changes when he is convicted and jailed for murdering his wife?

3. Who directed *Jurassic Park*?

4. What rock group set a precedent by issuing two albums on the same date in 1991?

5. What's the TV program if Squidward the octopus lives in an Easter Island head?

6. Which character in *The Matrix* is known as The One; One being an anagram of his name?

1. Mick Jagger

2. *The Shawshank Redemption*

3. Steven Spielberg

4. Guns N' Roses

5. *SpongeBob SquarePants*

6. Neo

1. What *South Park* character has been killed the most times?

2. What Scientologist was trapped in the closet in the controversial "Trapped in the Closet" episode of *South Park*?

3. What TV series, based on a novel by Candace Bushnell, ended with an episode called "An American Girl in Paris (Part Deux)"?

4. What Quentin Tarantino movie sees something go very wrong when five total strangers team up for the perfect crime?

5. Who is the voice of Jack in the video game *Pirates of the Caribbean: The Legend of Jack Sparrow*?

6. What 1993 blockbuster was set on Isla Nublar near Costa Rica?

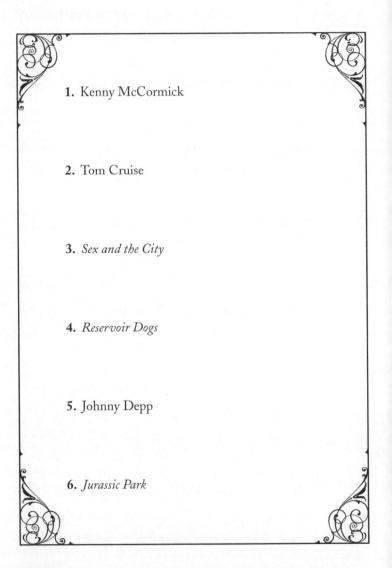

1. Kenny McCormick

2. Tom Cruise

3. *Sex and the City*

4. *Reservoir Dogs*

5. Johnny Depp

6. *Jurassic Park*

1. What fashion company did *Friends* character Rachel become a buyer for after leaving *Bloomingdale's*?

2. What dance DJ was featured on Beyoncé's hit *Baby Boy*?

3. Which of the Rolling Stones was expelled from Dartford Technical College for truancy?

4. What disco spin-off dance gave Van McCoy his biggest hit?

5. Whose memory is the movie *Gladiator* dedicated to?

6. What's the movie if the songs include *You're the One That I Want* and *Look at Me I'm Sandra Dee*?

1. *Ralph Lauren*

2. Sean Paul

3. Keith Richards

4. The Hustle

5. Oliver Reed's

6. *Grease*

1. What initials are formed by Homer Simpson's hair and ear?

2. Who did Kermit the Frog unwittingly marry in *The Muppets Take Manhattan*?

3. Who said at a 2006 London movie premiere he hoped to sell his 11-year-old son's newborn baby to "singing transvestite Madonna"?

4. What comedy movie set in Punxsutawney was actually filmed in Woodstock, Illinois?

5. What movie character was: "Afraid, alone and three million light years from home"?

6. What sitcom most often preceded *The Bob Newhart Show* during its six-year run on CBS?

1. M.G.

2. Miss Piggy

3. Sacha Baron Cohen (Borat)

4. *Groundhog Day*

5. E.T.

6. *The Mary Tyler Moore Show*

1. Who performed a duet with Elton John on the 1991 hit version of *Don't Let the Sun Go Down on Me*?

2. What role in *The Usual Suspects* was taken by Chazz Palminteri after Robert De Niro and Christopher Walken both turned it down?

3. How many movies did Peter Jackson's *The Lord of the Rings* sprawl across?

4. What movie character is told by Donkey: "You're not ugly. All right, you are ugly but you're only ugly at night. Shrek's ugly 24/7"?

5. Which actor, whose first name is Hawaiian for "cool breeze over the mountain," starred as Neo in *The Matrix*?

6. What David Bowie video from the *Let's Dance* album was censored because of nudity?

1. George Michael

2. Dave Kujan

3. Three

4. Princess Fiona

5. Keanu Reeves

6. *China Girl*

1. Who provided the voice for Maggie Simpson's first word, which none of her family heard her say?

2. What Peter Sellers *Inspector Clouseau* movie doesn't have Pink Panther in its title?

3. Who would be most likely to telephone Moe's Tavern asking for Mike Rotch or Seymore Butts?

4. What musical group originally included LaTavia Roberson and LeToya Luckett?

5. Who took the lead role in *King Creole* that had originally been offered to James Dean?

6. What singing, dancing Scientologist played Vincent Vega in *Pulp Fiction*?

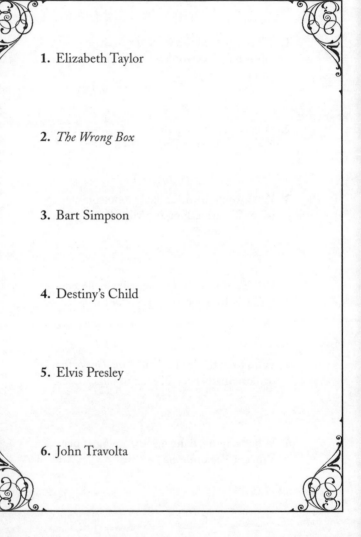

1. Elizabeth Taylor

2. *The Wrong Box*

3. Bart Simpson

4. Destiny's Child

5. Elvis Presley

6. John Travolta

1. Which actor had top billing as Lester Burnham in *American Beauty*?

2. Whose first world tour was called the *Oops! ... I Did It Again* Tour?

3. What was the title of desperate housewife Susan's first children's book?

4. Who was the *Muppet Show* announcer?

5. How many times does the postman always ring, according to the title of a 1981 Jack Nicholson movie?

6. What *Saturday Night Live* star is the voice of Shrek?

1. Kevin Spacey

2. Britney Spears'

3. *Ants in My Picnic Basket*

4. Kermit the Frog

5. Twice

6. Mike Myers

1. What three words appear on the helmet pictured in the poster for *Full Metal Jacket*?

2. What animal is Shrek's best buddy?

3. What band rewrote their *Shiny Happy People* so it became *Furry Happy Monsters* when they appeared on *Sesame Street*?

4. What's the movie if Andy Dufresne says: "Hope is a good thing. Maybe the best of things. And a good thing never dies"?

5. Who originally wrote and performed the song Norma Jean sang to Memphis in *Happy Feet*?

6. Which former member of the Rolling Stones was 47 when he started dating 13-year-old Mandy Smith, his future wife?

1. "Born to kill"

2. Donkey

3. R.E.M.

4. *The Shawshank Redemption*

5. Prince

6. Bill Wyman

1. What playwright's bust disguises Batman's bat phone?

2. What's the three-letter title of the song that U2 stretched to a 13-minute epic at the *Live Aid* concert?

3. What TV series did Kim Cattrall describe as: "A valentine to being single"?

4. Whose $20 million for *King Kong* was the highest fee paid to a director in advance of production?

5. What four words appear in parentheses after the R.E.M. hit title *It's the End of the World as We Know It*?

6. Who became a major star after dropping out from a scheduled world tour as one of Janet Jackson's backup dancers?

1. William Shakespeare's

2. *Bad*

3. *Sex and the City*

4. Peter Jackson's

5. *(And I Feel Fine)*

6. Jennifer Lopez

1. What creatures produce delicious jelly on *SpongeBob SquarePants*?

2. What 1997 movie finally sank *Star Wars* from its position as all-time box office champ?

3. What movie stars Eddie Murphy in four roles including Prince Akeem who visits the U.S. in search of a bride?

4. What fishy movie held the all-time box office record until *Star Wars* came along?

5. What was the first movie from Dreamworks SKG to win a Best Picture Oscar?

6. What Jack Nicholson movie was hyped: "Brace yourself for Melvin"?

1. Jellyfish

2. *Titanic*

3. *Coming to America*

4. *Jaws*

5. *American Beauty*

6. *As Good as It Gets*

1. What movie was hyped: "He's having the worst day of his life… over, and over…"?

2. What U.S. state is the home of Tony, head of the Sopranos household?

3. What member of *NSYNC had a much-publicized relationship with Britney Spears?

4. Who is the oldest of the four main characters in *Sex and the City*?

5. What actually is an *American Beauty* in the movie of that title?

6. What rock star married Trudie Styler in 1992?

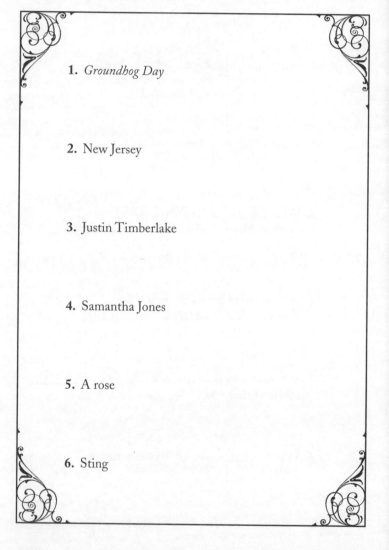

1. *Groundhog Day*

2. New Jersey

3. Justin Timberlake

4. Samantha Jones

5. A rose

6. Sting

1. Whose role in *Jungle Fever* was so acclaimed that the Cannes Film Festival created a Supporting Actor award just for him?

2. What's the movie if Neo works for Metacortex?

3. What movie brought Nicole Kidman an Oscar nomination for her performance as the courtesan Satine?

4. What comedy series' theme tune was *Liberty Bell* by John Philip Sousa?

5. What Queen epic topped the charts in 1976 and again in 1992?

6. What rock star was Johnny Depp's inspiration for Jack Sparrow?

1. Samuel L. Jackson's

2. *The Matrix*

3. *Moulin Rouge*

4. *Monty Python's Flying Circus'*

5. *Bohemian Rhapsody*

6. Keith Richards

1. Who enjoyed her first chart-topper with
   ...*Baby One More Time*?

2. What kind of animals starred in the movie
   Happy Feet?

3. What Eminem chart-topper sampled Dido's
   Thank You?

4. What is the name of the Teletubbies'
   vacuum cleaner friend?

5. What was The Police's biggest selling
   single?

6. What is the name of Julia Roberts' character
   in *Notting Hill*?

1. Britney Spears

2. Penguins

3. *Stan*

4. Noo-Noo

5. *Every Breath You Take*

6. Anna Scott

1. What Richard Rodgers show suggests: "It might as well be spring"?

2. What's the movie if Redfoot flicks his cigarette into the face of McManus?

3. What is the name of the White Stripes' drummer?

4. What band did Jack White of the White Stripes co-form in 2005?

5. What 1999 movie was hyped: "Ever want to be someone else? Now you can"?

6. What movie has Bill Murray as a TV weatherman covering a story about what he calls "a weather-forecasting rat"?

1. *State Fair*

2. *The Usual Suspects*

3. Meg White

4. The Raconteurs

5. *Being John Malkovich*

6. *Groundhog Day*

1. What 1978 movie was hyped: "You'll believe a man can fly"?

2. What star of *Jerry Maguire* and *As Good as It Gets* had his first movie role as a kid in the barber's shop in Eddie Murphy's *Coming to America*?

3. What 2006 thriller starring Samuel L. Jackson caused controversy by being released without any advance screenings for critics?

4. What TV show's tough guys drink scotch at the Bada Bing?

5. What do Brad Pitt and Edward Norton shoot at factories while drunk in *Fight Club*?

6. What charismatic British rock star, once known as the Thin White Duke, fronted a band called the Spiders from Mars?

1. *Superman*

2. Cuba Gooding Jr.

3. *Snakes on a Plane*

4. *The Sopranos'*

5. Golf balls

6. David Bowie

1. What is the name of the ten-year-old boy who finds E.T.?

2. What female British rock star did Prince mysteriously thank in the credits of his *Diamonds and Pearls* album?

3. Who rose to fame as *Billy Elliot* and then had the role of Jimmy, a seaman in *King Kong*, created specially for him?

4. What duo included George Michael before he went solo?

5. What Indiana Jones trademark came from *Herbert Johnson* of Savile Row?

6. What movie star grabbed top billing by playing a movie star in *Notting Hill*?

1. Elliott

2. Kate Bush

3. Jamie Bell

4. Wham!

5. His hat

6. Julia Roberts

1. Who received an estimated $10 million as the voice of Donkey in the movie *Shrek*?

2. What Rolling Stones hit did Guns N' Roses cover for the movie *Interview with the Vampire*?

3. What is Miss Piggy's surname?

4. What TV series' theme song is *Woke Up This Morning* by U.K. band the Alabama 3?

5. What horror movie hears Jack Nicholson announce: "Here's Johnny!"?

6. What soul singer notched top-40 hits in duets with Eurythmics, George Michael and Elton John?

1. Eddie Murphy

2. *Sympathy for the Devil*

3. Lee

4. *The Sopranos*

5. *The Shining*

6. Aretha Franklin

1. What movie's characters include Sick Boy and Renton?

2. What are the only animals ever seen in the land where the Teletubbies live?

3. What movie sees hustler Billy Ray, played by Eddie Murphy, swap identities with Louis Winthorpe III, played by Dan Aykroyd?

4. What male member of the White Stripes took his first wife's surname when they married?

5. What disco dance craze involved using the arms to spell out the four-letter title of a Village People hit?

6. What girlie R&B group topped the charts with *Independent Women Part 1*?

1. *Trainspotting*

2. Rabbits

3. *Trading Places*

4. Jack White

5. The YMCA

6. Destiny's Child

1. What is Prince's surname?

2. What L.A. band's *Fight Like a Brave* is featured on the soundtrack of the video game *Tony Hawk's Pro Skater 3*?

3. What is the name of the coolest guys' gang in the movie *Grease*?

4. What is the name of SpongeBob SquarePants' pet snail that meows like a cat?

5. What Scottish city is the setting for *Trainspotting*, according to the plot?

6. Who did Quentin Tarantino write the *Pulp Fiction* role of Jules Winnfield specifically for?

1. Nelson

2. Red Hot Chili Peppers'

3. The T Birds

4. Gary

5. Edinburgh

6. Samuel L. Jackson

1. What name did Madonna take after her conversion to Kabbalah?

2. Who was the last Beatle to marry and the only one whose first marriage didn't end in divorce?

3. What 2005 movie starred Johnny Depp as Willy Wonka?

4. What are Tinky Winky, Dipsy, Laa-Laa and Po collectively called?

5. What city is King Kong shipped to in the 2005 movie?

6. What was the first TV channel to broadcast *SpongeBob SquarePants*?

1. Esther

2. Paul McCartney

3. *Charlie and the Chocolate Factory*

4. *Teletubbies*

5. New York

6. *Nickelodeon*

1. What pop star posed naked and pregnant on the August 2006 cover of *Harper's Bazaar*?

2. What is the four-letter name of the groundhog in *Groundhog Day*?

3. Who tied the knot with Nicole Kidman on Christmas Eve 1990?

4. What's the four-letter rock 'n' roll stage name of Paul David Hewson?

5. What flamboyant British rock star performed *Wake Up Wendy* for *South Park*'s Chef Aid?

6. What 2002 movie about crop circles didn't include Mel Gibson's face on its posters at the director's request?

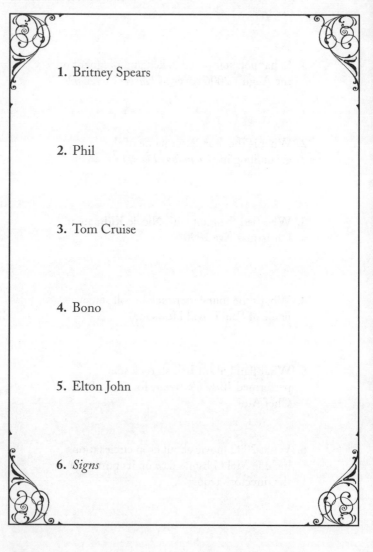

1. Britney Spears

2. Phil

3. Tom Cruise

4. Bono

5. Elton John

6. *Signs*

1. What is the better-known name of the rapper also known as Slim Shady?

2. What track on Coldplay's *A Rush of Blood to the Head* album was recorded a few days after the September 11th attacks?

3. What Bob Dylan classic was a top-ten hit for Guns N' Roses?

4. What short-lived, early 1990s dance craze was launched by the Simpsons?

5. Which song did desperate housewife Susan sing while simultaneously berating her ex-husband Karl for his groping of Edie?

6. What future megastar's first movie role was as Glen Lantz, one of the victims in *A Nightmare on Elm Street*?

1. Eminem

2. *Politik*

3. *Knockin' on Heaven's Door*

4. The Bartman

5. *New York, New York*

6. Johnny Depp's

194

1. What 2004 success had the longest title of any Best Picture Oscar winner?

2. Who directed Robert De Niro and cast in *GoodFellas*?

3. What company bought the *Muppets* in 2004?

4. What fast-food chain sponsored the Destiny's Child 2005 world tour?

5. What's the movie if John Travolta is Danny and Olivia Newton-John is Sandy?

6. What nationality does *Simpsons* Groundskeeper Willie refer to as "cheese-eating surrender monkeys"?

1. *The Lord of the Rings: Return of the King*

2. Martin Scorsese

3. The Walt Disney Company

4. *McDonald's*

5. *Grease*

6. French

1. Who was the only member of the classic Queen lineup never to sing lead on one of the band's album tracks?

2. Which star of the movie *MASH* played Monica and Ross' father on *Friends*?

3. What dance was named for aviator Charles Lindbergh?

4. What colorful rock duo claimed to be brother and sister but were actually a divorced couple?

5. What is the TV show if the local fast-food restaurant is The Chum Bucket?

6. What items of aircraft equipment gave Coldplay the title for their first full-length album?

1. John Deacon

2. Elliott Gould

3. The Lindy Hop

4. The White Stripes

5. *SpongeBob SquarePants*

6. *Parachutes*

1. Which Teletubby comes last alphabetically?

2. What 1999 movie was hyped: "The future will not be user friendly"?

3. What rock diva locked lips with Britney Spears and Christina Aguilera at the 2003 MTV Video Awards?

4. What bathroom product does the character Tyler Durden sell in the movie *Fight Club*?

5. What post-Twist dance was named after an African tribe?

6. Who designed the Rolling Stones' lips and tongue logo?

1. Tinky Winky

2. *The Matrix*

3. Madonna

4. Soap

5. The Watusi

6. Andy Warhol

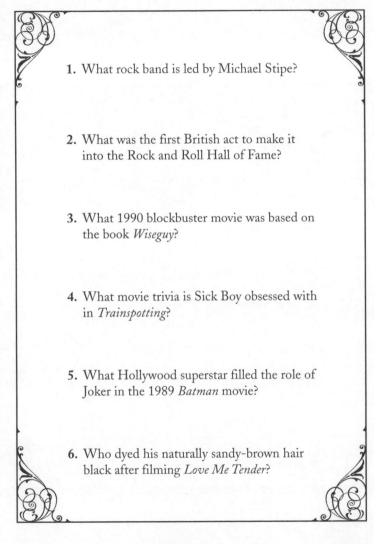

1. What rock band is led by Michael Stipe?

2. What was the first British act to make it into the Rock and Roll Hall of Fame?

3. What 1990 blockbuster movie was based on the book *Wiseguy*?

4. What movie trivia is Sick Boy obsessed with in *Trainspotting*?

5. What Hollywood superstar filled the role of Joker in the 1989 *Batman* movie?

6. Who dyed his naturally sandy-brown hair black after filming *Love Me Tender*?

1. R.E.M.

2. The Beatles

3. *GoodFellas*

4. James Bond

5. Jack Nicholson

6. Elvis Presley

1. What is the name of the president, played by Jack Nicholson, in *Mars Attacks!*?

2. What singer-actress inspired an L.A. producer to warn: "One false move, and she's Charo"?

3. What rock star is credited as a co-writer and backing singer for David Bowie's *Fame*?

4. What color roses appeared on *American Beauty* posters?

5. What color is Shrek?

6. What make of car took Marty McFly *Back to the Future*?

1. James Dale

2. Jennifer Lopez

3. John Lennon

4. Red

5. Green

6. *DeLorean*

1. What 1977 sci-fi movie was hyped: "A long time ago in a galaxy far, far away…"?

2. What is the name of the soap opera that Miranda loves watching in *Sex and the City*?

3. Who was the voice of Rocky in *Chicken Run*?

4. Who was Elvis Presley's manager?

5. Who is U2's bass player?

6. What movie gives Bill Murray time to work on his pickup line for Andie MacDowell by reliving the same day over and over?

1. *Star Wars*

2. *Jules and Mimi*

3. Mel Gibson

4. Colonel Tom Parker

5. Adam Clayton

6. *Groundhog Day*

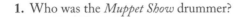

1. Who was the *Muppet Show* drummer?

2. What book that became a huge 1996 movie took its name from the fact that junkies scored their drugs at an abandoned railway station?

3. What is the name of Spider-Man's childhood sweetheart?

4. What fictional Kansas town is the earthly home of the young Superman?

5. What movie required John Cusack to take lessons as a puppeteer?

6. What band had their first major worldwide album success with *Blood Sugar Sex Magik*?

1. Animal

2. *Trainspotting*

3. Mary-Jane Watson

4. Smallville

5. *Being John Malkovich*

6. Red Hot Chili Peppers

1. Which member of Queen's love for "the manic roar of the crowd" is mentioned in Kurt Cobain's suicide note?

2. What is the "Heart of the Ocean" in the movie *Titanic*?

3. What is the city if the TV show is *Sex and the City*?

4. What animal's suspicious death resulted in Tony murdering Ralphie on *The Sopranos*?

5. What hairy character's growl is the last line heard in *Star Wars*?

6. What Stealers Wheel hit is heard in *Reservoir Dogs*?

1. Freddie Mercury's

2. Diamond

3. New York

4. Racehorse's

5. Chewbacca's

6. *Stuck in the Middle with You*

1. Who starred in *Happy Feet* as the voice of Trev, the elephant seal, before his untimely death?

2. Whose is by far the most famous voice provided by Dan Castellaneta?

3. What movie has Michael J. Fox gasping: "Do you mean my mother has the hots for me?"?

4. What Elton John title is followed by *(I Think It's Going to Be a Long Long Time)*?

5. Who co-wrote most of the Beatles' songs with Paul McCartney?

6. What *Simpsons* character endorsed a home pregnancy test kit carrying a warning it could cause birth defects?

1. Steve Irwin

2. Homer Simpson's

3. *Back to the Future*

4. *Rocket Man*

5. John Lennon

6. Krusty the Clown

1. What TV series was narrated by Sarah Jessica Parker in the role of Carrie Bradshaw?

2. What comedy show's theme song is *I'll Be There for You* by the Rembrandts?

3. What song did Prince write for The Family that became a huge hit for Sinead O'Connor?

4. What's the kid's cartoon if the location is Bikini Bottom?

5. What musical comedy was hyped: "They'll never get caught. They're on a mission from God"?

6. Who was the Beatles' bass guitarist?

1. *Sex and the City*

2. *Friends'*

3. *Nothing Compares 2U*

4. *SpongeBob SquarePants*

5. *The Blues Brothers*

6. Paul McCartney

1. What fashion designer daughter of a former Beatle was maid of honor at Madonna's second wedding, after Gwyneth Paltrow reportedly turned down the gig?

2. Who turned down the role of Danny in *Grease* for fear of being typecast, yet will always be known as The Fonz?

3. Who became a major solo star after performing with Andrew Ridgeley?

4. What's the movie if Henry Hill and friends are working their way through the mob hierarchy?

5. What movie star boasts that his surname translates from German as *idiot*?

6. Who was once best known as Magnum P.I. but became Dr. Richard Burke of *Friends* fame to younger viewers?

1. Stella McCartney

2. Henry Winkler

3. George Michael

4. *GoodFellas*

5. Johnny Depp

6. Tom Selleck

1. What female rock star is discussed at the start of *Reservoir Dogs*?

2. What movie, with 14 Oscar nominations, is the most nominated film not to win in any acting categories?

3. What 2005 monster-of-a-title-role did Andy Serkis prepare for by studying wild gorillas in Rwanda?

4. What does Uma Thurman wear on her feet for most of *Pulp Fiction*?

5. What were the names of Mumble's parents in the animated movie *Happy Feet*?

6. What TV show introduced *The Simpsons*?

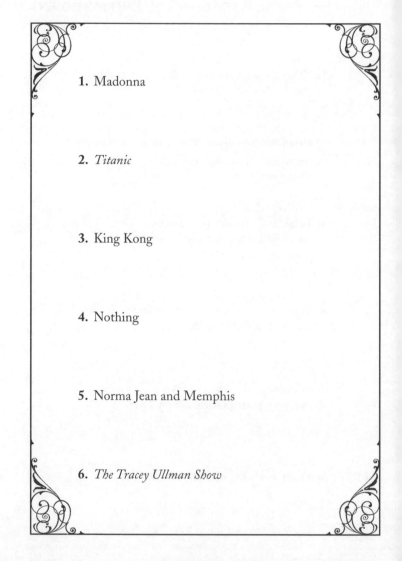

1. Madonna

2. *Titanic*

3. King Kong

4. Nothing

5. Norma Jean and Memphis

6. *The Tracey Ullman Show*

1. What high-ranking character is mentioned in David Bowie's *Space Oddity* and again in *Ashes to Ashes*?

2. Who is the mother of rapper Kevin Federline's sons Sean Preston and Jayden James?

3. What *Monty Python* animator turned down the opportunity to direct *American Beauty*?

4. What *Monty Python* character liked to "put on women's clothing and hang around in bars"?

5. What heavy rock band does Axl Rose lead?

6. Whose first poster called him the Hillbilly Cat?

1. Major Tom

2. Britney Spears

3. Terry Gilliam

4. The lumberjack

5. Guns N' Roses

6. Elvis Presley's

1. What 1999 movie was hyped: "Mischief. Mayhem. Soap."?

2. Who fills the role of Elizabeth Swann in *Pirates of the Caribbean: The Curse of the Black Pearl*?

3. What instrument did Sting play with The Police?

4. Who claimed it was his idea to have his character killed off in the first *Star Wars* movie so he "wouldn't have to go on saying those rubbish lines"?

5. What movie sees five men agreeing to commit a crime together as revenge after being rounded up to stand in a New York police lineup?

6. What Sacha Baron Cohen character welcomed *Boutros Boutros Boutros Boutros-Ghali* when he interviewed the former U.N. Secretary on his TV show?

1. *Fight Club*

2. Keira Knightley

3. Bass guitar

4. Sir Alec Guinness

5. *The Usual Suspects*

6. Ali G.

1. What 1980 movie featured the famed car chase shot inside Dixie Square Mall in Harvey, Illinois?

2. What Vietnam War movie sees marines marching off into the night singing the *Mickey Mouse Club* theme song?

3. Who played Daryl Van Horne, the man who gave the women their powers, in *The Witches of Eastwick*?

4. What quartet live in the Tubbytronic Superdome?

5. What city did U2 form in?

6. What TV show often moved from sketch to sketch with the words: "…And now for something completely different"?

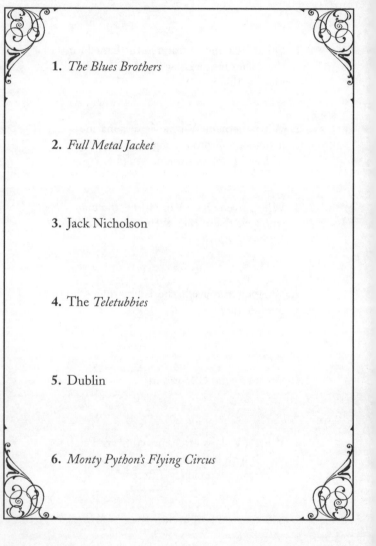

1. *The Blues Brothers*

2. *Full Metal Jacket*

3. Jack Nicholson

4. The *Teletubbies*

5. Dublin

6. *Monty Python's Flying Circus*

1. Who played Batman opposite Burt Ward's Robin?

2. What Eagles song shares its name with a movie starring Mel Gibson as Dale McKussic?

3. What movie starred Hugh Grant as a London bookshop owner who meets the most famous film star in the world?

4. Who is the lead singer of Coldplay?

5. Which blues giant wrote the song that gave the Rolling Stones their name?

6. What is the name of the monkey in *Pirates of the Caribbean: The Curse of the Black Pearl*?

1. Adam West

2. *Tequila Sunrise*

3. *Notting Hill*

4. Chris Martin

5. Muddy Waters

6. Jack

ENTERTAINMENT

1. What British actor was taking a break from filming *Gladiator* when he died after reportedly drinking three bottles of rum in a Maltese bar?

2. What does Samuel L. Jackson's "L" stand for?

3. What Paul McCartney composition is listed as the most-covered song in history?

4. What former rock star's sales took a 21st century boost when *A Little Less Conversation* was heard on a *Nike* TV commercial?

5. What Dolly Parton classic was covered by the White Stripes on the b-side of their *Hello Operator* single?

6. Who appears on the sleeve of his *Aladdin Sane* album with a blue and red lightning bolt painted across his face?

1. Oliver Reed

2. Leroy

3. *Yesterday*

4. Elvis Presley's

5. *Jolene*

6. David Bowie

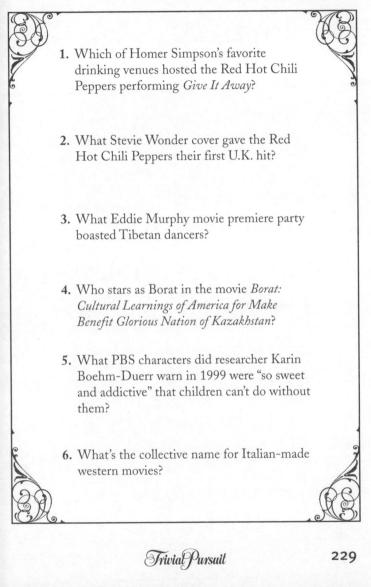

1. Which of Homer Simpson's favorite drinking venues hosted the Red Hot Chili Peppers performing *Give It Away*?

2. What Stevie Wonder cover gave the Red Hot Chili Peppers their first U.K. hit?

3. What Eddie Murphy movie premiere party boasted Tibetan dancers?

4. Who stars as Borat in the movie *Borat: Cultural Learnings of America for Make Benefit Glorious Nation of Kazakhstan*?

5. What PBS characters did researcher Karin Boehm-Duerr warn in 1999 were "so sweet and addictive" that children can't do without them?

6. What's the collective name for Italian-made western movies?

1. Moe's

2. *Higher Ground*

3. *The Golden Child*'s

4. Sacha Baron Cohen

5. *Teletubbies*

6. Spaghetti westerns

1. Who celebrates his 111th birthday during *The Lord of the Rings: The Fellowship of the Ring*?

2. What Céline Dion funeral favorite has *(Love Theme From Titanic)* after its title?

3. Who fills the role of Craig the puppeteer's wife in *Being John Malkovich*?

4. What's the name of Harrison Ford's *Raiders of the Lost Ark* character?

5. What country provided most of the settings for *The Lord of the Rings* movies?

6. What decade did Marty McFly go back to in *Back to the Future*?

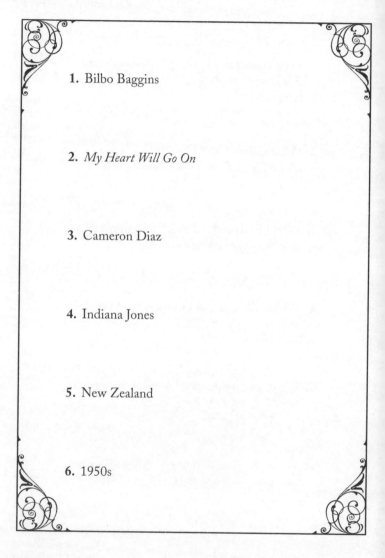

1. Bilbo Baggins

2. *My Heart Will Go On*

3. Cameron Diaz

4. Indiana Jones

5. New Zealand

6. 1950s

1. What is Shawshank in the movie *The Shawshank Redemption*?

2. Who is pictured with her eyes wide open on posters for Kubrick's final movie, *Eyes Wide Shut*?

3. What Welsh songstress has performed the themes for three different Bond movies?

4. What 2002 movie superhero's alter ego is newspaper reporter Peter Parker?

5. What is the general subject of the books sold by Hugh Grant's character in *Notting Hill*?

6. What New York City night spot was the subject of a 1984 Richard Gere movie?

1. A prison

2. Nicole Kidman

3. Shirley Bassey

4. Spider-Man's

5. Travel

6. The Cotton Club

1. What is the name of the technology that enabled the production of *Happy Feet* to use the movements of actual dancers?

2. What movie sees Emperor Marcus Aurelius choose Maximus to be his heir instead of his own son?

3. What was the title of the Carly Simon theme song for *The Spy Who Loved Me*, the first Bond theme since *Dr. No* not to reflect the movie name in its title?

4. Who stars in the semi-autobiographical movie *Purple Rain*?

5. What fruity brand of cigarettes, a Quentin Tarantino trademark, made yet another appearance in *Pulp Fiction*?

6. What was the name of David Bowie's extraterrestrial glam-rock alter ego?

1. Motion capture

2. *Gladiator*

3. *Nobody Does It Better*

4. Prince

5. *Red Apple*

6. Ziggy Stardust

1. Who wrote the famous *Pink Panther* theme music?

2. What movie director played the Cook County Assessor's Office Clerk in *The Blues Brothers*?

3. What band took on Will Champion as its drummer even though he didn't play drums at the time?

4. What movie did Ewan McGregor get in character for by shaving his head and shedding 30 pounds?

5. Who became an international superstar after playing little Gertie in *E.T.: The Extra-Terrestrial*?

6. What movie hears a punk rock girl quip: "Guy with eight hands? Sounds hot!"?

1. Henry Mancini

2. Steven Spielberg

3. Coldplay

4. *Trainspotting*

5. Drew Barrymore

6. *Spider-Man*

1. What is the real first name of rock star Prince?

2. What novel did Universal Studios pay Michael Crichton $2 million for before it was even published?

3. What animated TV show's characters watch the cartoon antics of "Terrance and Phillip"?

4. Who performed *Bitter Sweet Symphony* with Coldplay at the *Live 8* concert?

5. What hit by Los del Rio spawned a flamenco-style dance and was voted the Greatest One Hit Wonder in a 2002 TV show?

6. What superhero sidekick is known as Boy Wonder?

1. Prince

2. *Jurassic Park*

3. *South Park*'s

4. Richard Ashcroft

5. Macarena

6. Robin

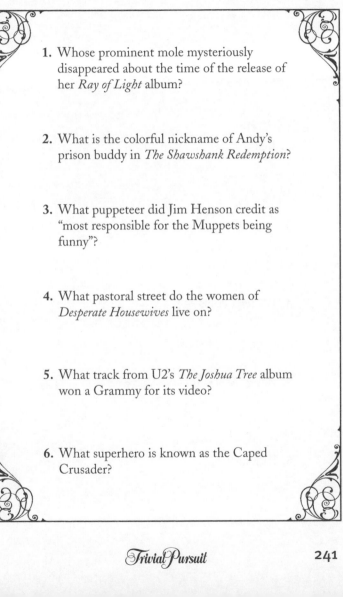

1. Whose prominent mole mysteriously disappeared about the time of the release of her *Ray of Light* album?

2. What is the colorful nickname of Andy's prison buddy in *The Shawshank Redemption*?

3. What puppeteer did Jim Henson credit as "most responsible for the Muppets being funny"?

4. What pastoral street do the women of *Desperate Housewives* live on?

5. What track from U2's *The Joshua Tree* album won a Grammy for its video?

6. What superhero is known as the Caped Crusader?

1. Madonna's

2. Red

3. Frank Oz

4. Wisteria Lane

5. *Where the Streets Have No Name*

6. Batman

1. Who shot Mr. Burns in the "Who Shot Mr. Burns" episode of *The Simpsons*?

2. What 1998 movie with the slogan "The Gang's All Here" starred Mel Gibson as Martin Riggs?

3. What movie star had hit records singing with Ewan McGregor and Robbie Williams?

4. What TV title character is actually lawman John Reid?

5. What George Michael song was banned by the BBC and re-edited three times for MTV?

6. Who are Bart Simpson's favorite cartoon duo?

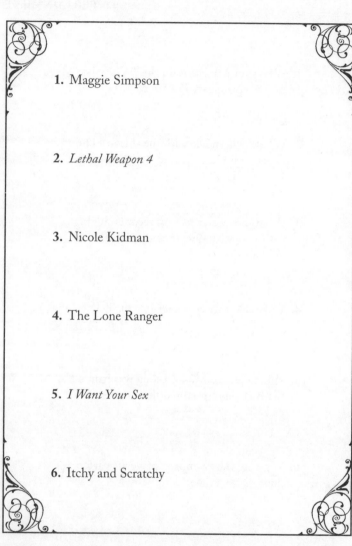

1. Maggie Simpson

2. *Lethal Weapon 4*

3. Nicole Kidman

4. The Lone Ranger

5. *I Want Your Sex*

6. Itchy and Scratchy

1. What movie brought complaints from the American Humane Society that only maggots that had died of natural causes should be fed to a crow?

2. How many main friends are featured on *Friends*?

3. What is the main character's job in *Raiders of the Lost Ark*?

4. What movie was hyped: "Girls like me don't make invitations like this to just anyone"?

5. What TV show's 2003 *It's Christmas in Canada* episode included the capture of Saddam Hussein just three days after the actual event?

6. What is the birth country of *Gladiator* star Russell Crowe?

1. *The Shawshank Redemption*

2. Six

3. Archeologist

4. *Pulp Fiction*

5. *South Park*'s

6. New Zealand

1. What was the first album in history to reach number one in 34 nations?

2. What BBC show did Lorne Michaels screen for NBC executives when he pitched *Saturday Night Live*?

3. What is the five-letter stage name of Gordon Matthew Thomas Sumner?

4. What animated movie takes its name from a Yiddish word meaning monster?

5. What TV show often displays a disclaimer beginning: "All characters and events in this show—even those based on real people—are entirely fictional"?

6. Who was the only fictional character in *Time* magazine's list of the 100 most influential people of the 20th century?

1. *The Beatles 1*

2. *Monty Python's Flying Circus*

3. Sting

4. *Shrek*

5. *South Park*

6. Bart Simpson

1. What 1993 movie saw dinosaurs escaping from their theme park enclosure after the security system was disabled?

2. What time period was the title of Eddie Murphy's first movie, in which he sang a very out of key version of The Police's *Roxanne*?

3. What sitcom character often advised: "Stifle yourself"?

4. What pop diva performed the Bond theme *Die Another Day*?

5. What valuable commodity do the thieves set out to steal in *Reservoir Dogs*?

6. What TV series features the DiMeo crime family?

1. *Jurassic Park*

2. *48 Hrs*

3. Archie Bunker

4. Madonna

5. Diamonds

6. *The Sopranos*

1. What *Monty Python* movie with a religious theme was banned in the Republic of Ireland for eight years?

2. What newspaper does Clark Kent work for?

3. What did Frodo lose just before finally getting rid of the ring in *The Lord of the Rings*?

4. What movie sees puppeteer Craig Schwartz discovering the portal into a film star's mind?

5. What English actor plays Will Turner in the *Pirates of the Caribbean* movies?

6. What rock star with the middle name Louise chose the confirmation name Veronica?

1. *Monty Python's Life of Brian*

2. The Daily Planet

3. A finger

4. *Being John Malkovich*

5. Orlando Bloom

6. Madonna

1. What rapper was born Marshall Bruce Mathers III?

2. What movie's first batch of soap is made out of fat from liposuction clinics?

3. What little guy couldn't take the role of Sallah in *Raiders of the Lost Ark* because he was too busy filming *Taxi*?

4. What Stanley Kubrick movie was hyped: "In Vietnam the wind doesn't blow, it sucks"?

5. What movie title–duo were named Joliet and Elwood after two cities south of Chicago?

6. What band performed the Bond theme *A View to a Kill*?

1. Eminem

2. *Fight Club*'s

3. Danny DeVito

4. *Full Metal Jacket*

5. The Blues Brothers

6. Duran Duran

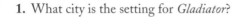

1. What city is the setting for *Gladiator*?

2. What is "Crocodile" Dundee's given name?

3. Who reportedly turned down Meryl Streep's role in *Music of the Heart* and Michelle Pfeiffer's role in *The Fabulous Baker Boys*?

4. What shock rocker's *Rock Is Dead* is heard in *The Matrix*?

5. What band's *A Crazy Little Thing Called Love* was a tribute to Elvis Presley?

6. Who was the first character Johnny Depp portrayed in more than one movie?

1. Rome

2. Michael

3. Madonna

4. Marilyn Manson's

5. Queen's

6. Jack Sparrow

1. Who is the Godfather of Soul who played the Reverend Cleophus James in *The Blues Brothers*?

2. What superhero battles against the evil Green Goblin?

3. What TV animation series takes its name from the fictional Colorado town where it is set?

4. What fruity drink does William spill on Anna the second time they meet in *Notting Hill*?

5. What name is given to the computer-created version of 20th century life in a 1999 movie starring Keanu Reeves?

6. What role did Cesar Romero fill in 19 TV episodes of *Batman*?

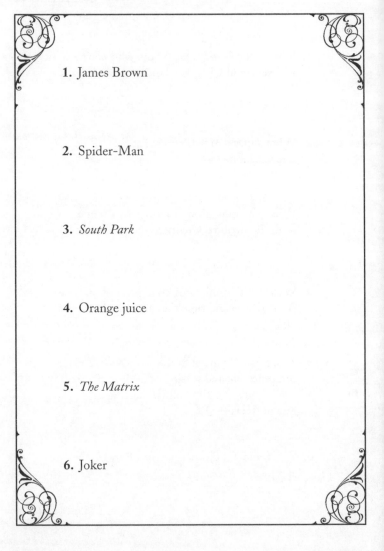

1. James Brown

2. Spider-Man

3. *South Park*

4. Orange juice

5. *The Matrix*

6. Joker

1. What is the name of the mob boss who hires the gang in *Reservoir Dogs*?

2. Whose mother complained about his swearing in the film *GoodFellas*, which features the F-word 246 times?

3. Who performed *The Power of Love* with his band the News in *Back to the Future*?

4. What Elton John album introduced classics including *Candle in the Wind* and *Saturday Night's Alright for Fighting*?

5. Who does Superman take for a flight after falling in love with her?

6. What actor originated the role of Inspector Clouseau?

1. Joe Cabot

2. Joe Pesci's

3. Huey Lewis

4. *Goodbye Yellow Brick Road*

5. Lois Lane

6. Peter Sellers

1. What's the movie if Vincent reads *Modesty Blaise*?

2. What British duo were sampled on Eminem's *My Name Is*?

3. What movie hears John Cusack, as Craig Schwartz, saying: "Nobody's looking for a puppeteer in today's wintry economic climate"?

4. What Spielberg movie had the working title *A Boy's Life*?

5. What Stanley Kubrick war movie takes its name from a bullet with a copper coating covering its lead core?

6. Which town's businesses include the I Can't Believe It's a Law Firm law firm and J.R.R. Toykins toy shop?

1. *Pulp Fiction*

2. Chas and Dave

3. *Being John Malkovich*

4. *E.T.: The Extra-Terrestrial*

5. *Full Metal Jacket*

6. Springfield's

1. What 1960s hit plays on the radio alarm clock in *Groundhog Day*?

2. What is the three-letter name of Jennifer Lopez's clothing line?

3. What bumbling French detective features in the *Pink Panther* movies?

4. What great British soul songstress performed *Son of a Preacher Man* in *Pulp Fiction*?

5. What decade provides the setting for the 2005 movie *King Kong*?

6. What 1981 movie required some 7,000 snakes?

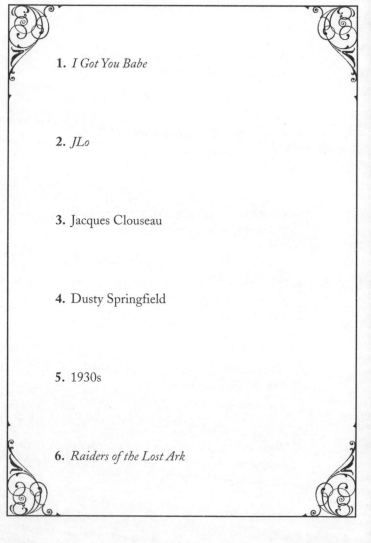

1. *I Got You Babe*

2. *JLo*

3. Jacques Clouseau

4. Dusty Springfield

5. 1930s

6. *Raiders of the Lost Ark*

1. What was the biggest dance craze launched by Chubby Checker?

2. What band's *Paint It Black* is featured in *Full Metal Jacket*?

3. What Icelandic rock diva performs *Amphibian* in *Being John Malkovich*?

4. What 2005 monster movie was the first to be released in the U.K. on DVD and via the Internet at the same time?

5. What movie's Keyser Soze character was inspired by a real-life murderer who went on the run for 17 years?

6. Who was paid $3.7 million plus a percentage of the profits for approximately ten minutes on screen in *Superman*?

1. The Twist

2. The Rolling Stones'

3. Björk

4. *King Kong*

5. *The Usual Suspects'*

6. Marlon Brando

266

1. Who named himself for Long John Baldry and Elton Dean?

2. What Oscar-winning actress, born in Hawaii, holds dual American/Australian citizenship and has parents of Scottish and Irish descent?

3. What's the movie if the *Avon* lady takes a very sharp-fingered Johnny Depp into her home?

4. What country was the movie *Full Metal Jacket* filmed in?

5. What rock star gained his nickname from a black and yellow-striped jersey he wore while playing with the Phoenix Jazzmen?

6. What movie hears Russell Crowe warn: "What we do in life echoes in eternity"?

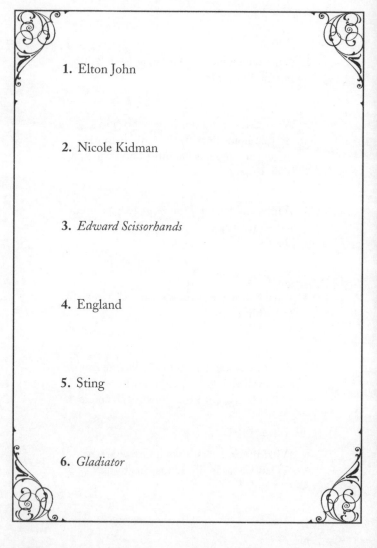

1. Elton John

2. Nicole Kidman

3. *Edward Scissorhands*

4. England

5. Sting

6. *Gladiator*

1. What British band turned down an offer from *Gatorade* to use *Yellow* and from *Gap* to use *Don't Panic*?

2. What is the stage name of Reginald Kenneth Dwight?

3. What star of *Superman Returns* had the fingers of his left hand glued together to make his disability look more real in *The Usual Suspects*?

4. What is the name of Doc Brown's very clever dog in *Back to the Future*?

5. What sport does Samuel L. Jackson reportedly take two days off from each working week to play?

6. What comic led a 2,800-person Carnegie Hall audience to a post-concert snack of milk and cookies at a nearby school cafeteria?

1. Coldplay

2. Elton John

3. Kevin Spacey

4. Einstein

5. Golf

6. Andy Kaufman

1. What was the title of the 2006 *Casino Royale* theme sung by Chris Cornell?

2. Who played Leonardo DiCaprio's love interest in *Titanic*?

3. What creator of Spider-Man made a cameo appearance in the 2002 movie blockbuster?

4. What was the name of the Rolling Stones' 2005 U.S. tour?

5. Who was the first major rock star to perform in the Soviet Union, in 1979?

6. Who played Spider-Man in the 2002 movie?

1. *You Know My Name*

2. Kate Winslet

3. Stan Lee

4. A Bigger Bang

5. Elton John

6. Tobey Maguire

1. What breed was the deceased bird in *Monty Python's* Dead Parrot Sketch?

2. What is the *Pink Panther* in the Peter Sellers movies with that name?

3. What preserved the mosquitoes that provided the DNA to produce the *Jurassic Park* dinosaurs?

4. Who was the last person to join the classic Queen lineup and the first to retire?

5. What three-letter name did the band formerly known as Slut Bank and Twisted Kites finally settle on?

6. What former British politician smoked what was allegedly marijuana offered to him by Ali G.?

1. Norwegian Blue

2. A diamond

3. Amber

4. John Deacon

5. R.E.M.

6. Neil Hamilton

1. Which duo's *7 Nation Army* won the 2004 Grammy for Best Rock Song?

2. What colorful nickname was given to Larry Dimmick, the professional criminal, in *Reservoir Dogs*?

3. What was Paul McCartney's Bond theme?

4. What is baby Superman called on the planet Krypton?

5. What movie starred Mel Gibson as William Wallace?

6. What did Susan "accidentally" do to Edie's house during the first season of *Desperate Housewives*?

1. The White Stripes'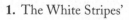

2. Mr. White

3. *Live and Let Die*

4. Kal-El

5. *Braveheart*

6. Set it on fire

1. What is the name of the coolest girls' gang in the movie *Grease*?

2. What TV character's price is $847.63 when she is scanned through a supermarket checkout machine?

3. What circus star tipped the scales at six-and-a-half tons?

4. What 1996 British movie did Senator Bob Dole charge with glorifying drug use before later admitting he hadn't seen it?

5. What, in 1998, became the first movie since *The Sound of Music* to win Best Picture Oscar without being nominated for its screenplay?

6. What was Beyoncé's band before she went solo?

1. The Pink Ladies

2. Maggie Simpson's

3. Jumbo the Elephant

4. *Trainspotting*

5. *Titanic*

6. Destiny's Child

1. What was the name of the Tennessee sheriff portrayed by Joe Don Baker in *Walking Tall*?

2. What heavyweight rock star reportedly didn't bat an eyelid when requested to don a fat suit for his role in *Fight Club*?

3. What movie did Michael J. Fox learn to skateboard for?

4. What Elvis Costello song does Elliott's brother Michael sing while looking in the fridge in *E.T.: The Extra-Terrestrial*?

5. Whose relationship with Jennifer Lopez was mocked in the *South Park* episode Fat Butt and Pancake Head?

6. What movie's *Hopelessly Devoted to You* was added as an afterthought so Olivia Newton-John could sing a ballad?

1. Buford Pusser

2. Meat Loaf

3. *Back to the Future*

4. *Accidents Will Happen*

5. Ben Affleck's

6. *Grease*'s

1. Who was too busy with *Magnum P.I.* to take the role of Indiana Jones?

2. Which former Beatle is heard singing *What Is Life* in the movie *GoodFellas*?

3. What Leonardo DiCaprio movie was hyped: "A woman's heart is a deep ocean of secrets"?

4. What 1993 blockbuster gave Richard Attenborough his first acting role in 15 years?

5. What Eddie Murphy movie was subtitled *The Klumps*?

6. What song by the Buggles was the first ever played on MTV?

1. Tom Selleck

2. George Harrison

3. *Titanic*

4. *Jurassic Park*

5. *Nutty Professor II*

6. *Video Killed the Radio Star*

1. What charity benefited from George Michael's *Last Christmas*?

2. Which *Friends* character jilted her fiancé at the altar at the start of the series?

3. What R.E.M. single repeats the line "Call me when you awake her" 32 times?

4. What cable TV network didn't have to send its 300 staffers far to cover the 1988 Democratic National Convention?

5. What TV series began with head of the family, Tony, being treated by Dr. Jennifer Melfi after suffering an anxiety attack?

6. Whose punk version of *My Way* is heard in the movie *GoodFellas*?

1. *Band Aid*

2. Rachel Green

3. *The Sidewinder Sleeps Tonite*

4. CNN

5. *The Sopranos*

6. Sid Vicious'

1. Who played Mad Max Rockatansky?

2. What band's greatest hits include *Sweet Child o' Mine* and *November Rain*?

3. What London open space was the 2004 venue for the Red Hot Chili Peppers' first full-length live album?

4. What country complained about Sacha Baron Cohen's Borat character then admitted its national bank had misspelled *bank* on its banknotes?

5. What Jimmy Buffett song opens: "Living on spongecake ..."?

6. What movie follows the ins and outs of Lester Burnham's mid-life crisis?

1. Mel Gibson

2. Guns N' Roses'

3. Hyde Park

4. Kazakhstan

5. *Margaritaville*

6. *American Beauty*

1. Who fills the role of serial divorcee Edie Britt on *Desperate Housewives*?

2. What singer was the first Latin-American actress to be paid $1 million for a movie role?

3. Who were dubbed the World's Most Dangerous Band after fans were trampled to death during their *Appetite for Destruction* Tour?

4. Which desperate housewife's husband is very allergic to cats?

5. What episode of *Dallas* filmed five different endings so no one could leak the answer?

6. What actor rode a bomb from a B-52 in *Dr. Strangelove*?

1. Nicolette Sheridan

2. Jennifer Lopez

3. Guns N' Roses

4. Lynette's

5. "Who Shot J.R.?"

6. Slim Pickens

1. What country's space travellers have been called *taikonauts* since 1998?

2. What year saw the end of World War II?

3. Who became prime minister of Cuba in 1959?

4. Which country's Antonine Wall was the northernmost frontier of the Roman Empire?

5. Which state flag has the British Union Jack as part of its design?

6. What name was attached to Germany's World War II submarines?

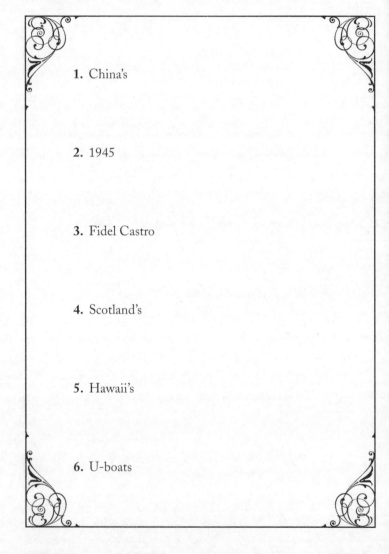

1. China's

2. 1945

3. Fidel Castro

4. Scotland's

5. Hawaii's

6. U-boats

1. Who was president when the agency that would become the FBI was created?

2. What city had recently grown to be the fourth largest in America when a devastating fire broke out in October of 1871?

3. Who did Richard Nixon pass on to Gerald Ford as U.S. Secretary of State?

4. How many dogs survived the sinking of the *Titanic*?

5. What national bulletin did J. Edgar Hoover initiate that is still in use today?

6. What was Paul Revere's occupation, besides midnight riding?

1. Theodore Roosevelt

2. Chicago

3. Henry Kissinger

4. Two

5. The "Ten Most Wanted Fugitives" list

6. Silversmith

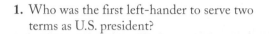

1. Who was the first left-hander to serve two terms as U.S. president?

2. Who were the first Japanese warriors to be officially permitted to carry two swords, one long and one short?

3. Which saint is said to have landed in Ireland in 432 A.D.?

4. What year did the red maple leaf design officially become Canada's flag?

5. What is the largest humanitarian network in the world?

6. What country left the European Union following a 1985 referendum?

1. Bill Clinton

2. Samurai

3. St. Patrick

4. 1965

5. The International Red Cross (and Red Crescent)

6. Greenland

1. How many stars are on Alaska's state flag?

2. Who was "that woman" Bill Clinton claimed he didn't have sexual relations with?

3. Who founded the city of Philadelphia?

4. Who did Mehmet Ali Agca attempt to assassinate in 1981?

5. What did the residence of the U.S. president become formally known as in 1901?

6. Which Indian prime minister was assassinated by two of her Sikh bodyguards?

1. Eight

2. Monica Lewinsky

3. William Penn

4. Pope John Paul II

5. The White House

6. Indira Gandhi

1. Whose tomb did Howard Carter discover in 1922?

2. Which former U.S. Secretary of State's glasses did Homer Simpson find in a toilet?

3. What Chicago attraction required one million gallons of seawater shipped to it in 1930?

4. What joins Chinese, English, Russian, French and Spanish to complete the six official languages of the U.N.?

5. What is the name of the Red Cross organization in Muslim countries?

6. Which state's coastline is over 6,600 miles long?

1. Tutankhamun's

2. Henry Kissinger's

3. The Shedd Aquarium

4. Arabic

5. The Red Crescent

6. Alaska's

1. What four words did boxer Jack Dempsey use when he lost the championship to Gene Tuney that Ronald Reagan echoed to Nancy when he was shot?

2. What was suspended in Northern Ireland in 1972?

3. Which island was Napoleon on at the time of his death?

4. Where was the first basketball game played?

5. Which King allegedly wrote *Greensleeves*?

6. What is the capital of Canada?

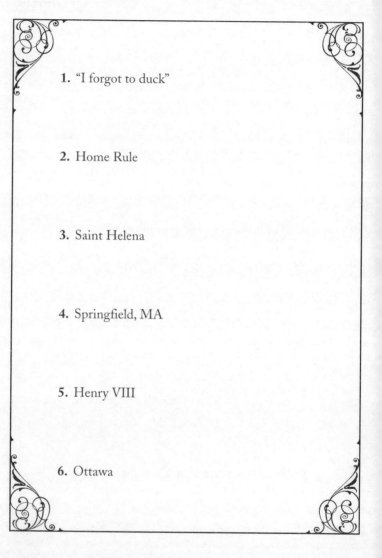

1. "I forgot to duck"

2. Home Rule

3. Saint Helena

4. Springfield, MA

5. Henry VIII

6. Ottawa

1. What river near Sutter's Mill did prospectors find gold in?

2. What was banned in Mississippi in 1907 that didn't become legal there again until 1966?

3. Who is the only president to be buried in Washington, D.C.?

4. Which iconic children's author was born in Chittenango, NY?

5. Whose essay *Civil Disobedience* did Gandhi carry with him during his prison stays?

6. What language was Elizabeth I's coronation conducted in?

1. American River

2. Alcohol

3. Woodrow Wilson

4. L. Frank Baum

5. Henry David Thoreau's

6. Latin

1. What 28-mile structure was started in 1961 and came down in 1989?

2. What country gave the Statue of Liberty to the U.S.?

3. Who was the first woman elected to lead a modern Muslim state?

4. Which structure in Rome is the best preserved Roman building and the oldest important building in the world with its roof intact?

5. Which battle saw the final defeat of Napoleon?

6. How were Theodore and Franklin Roosevelt related?

1. The Berlin Wall

2. France

3. Benazir Bhutto

4. The Pantheon

5. Waterloo

6. They were fifth cousins

1. Who "sailed the ocean blue in 1492," according to the old rhyme?

2. What was the name of the security guard wrongly accused of setting off a bomb at the 1996 Olympics?

3. What Detroit record company, founded in 1959, went on to be one of the most successful of the 20th century?

4. What city was the first American college located in?

5. What city did Yasir Arafat die in?

6. What famous retailer now stands where Field & Leiter's store was at the time of the great Chicago fire?

1. Christopher Columbus

2. Richard Jewell

3. Motown

4. Cambridge, MA

5. Paris

6. Marshall Field's

1. Where did Ray Kroc open the first McDonald's restaurant in 1955?

2. What Scottish garment has a name based on the Middle English term for "fold" or "pleat"?

3. What was Rajiv Gandhi's high-flying job before he turned to politics?

4. What famous construction did newspaper editor Joseph Pulitzer shame citizens into financing?

5. What Revolutionary War spy from Connecticut got caught by the enemy after only a few days on the job?

6. What did you require to obtain legal whiskey during prohibition?

1. Des Plaines, IL

2. Kilt

3. Airline pilot

4. The pedestal for the Statue of Liberty

5. Nathan Hale

6. A doctor's prescription

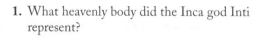

1. What heavenly body did the Inca god Inti represent?

2. Who designed the famous collection of buildings in Oak Park, Illinois?

3. How many presidents have been born in Illinois?

4. What country did the Romans call Hibernia?

5. Who was the subject of a $25 million reward offered by the U.S. State Department in 2001?

6. What did Benjamin Franklin do on April 17, 1790?

1. The Sun

2. Frank Lloyd Wright

3. One (Ronald Reagan)

4. Ireland

5. Osama bin Laden

6. He died

1. Which historic area of Paris must be visited to enter the *Sacré Coeur*?

2. What was the practical purpose of the Pharos of Alexandria, one of the Seven Wonders of the Ancient World?

3. Which U.S. president's disability resulted in the White House being made wheelchair-accessible?

4. Whose 2005 funeral did five kings, four queens plus 70 presidents and prime ministers attend?

5. Who was the first U.S. president to hold a televised news conference?

6. What organization replaced the League of Nations?

1. Montmartre

2. Lighthouse

3. Franklin D. Roosevelt's

4. Pope John Paul II's

5. John F. Kennedy

6. The United Nations

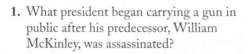

1. What president began carrying a gun in public after his predecessor, William McKinley, was assassinated?

2. What is the Quaker Square Hotel in Akron, Ohio built inside?

3. What U.S. president came up with the title United Nations after spotting it in Byron's "Childe Harold's Pilgrimage"?

4. What was Cape Canaveral's name changed to from 1963 to 1973?

5. What hip museum has drawn thousands of visitors to Cleveland, Ohio, since it opened in 1995?

6. What did the U.S. government tax at one dollar per barrel to help finance the Civil War?

1. Theodore Roosevelt

2. Old grain silos

3. Franklin D. Roosevelt

4. Cape Kennedy

5. The Rock and Roll Hall of Fame

6. Beer

1. What country were Stonehenge's bluestones quarried in?

2. Where, in a 1961 speech, did John F. Kennedy say the U.S. should commit to landing a man before the decade was out?

3. Which U.S. robbers had the surnames Parker and Barrow?

4. Which Egyptian queen is said to have died following a bite from an asp?

5. Where in Beijing did Chinese students build a Goddess of Democracy in May, 1989?

6. How many terms of office did former Prime Minister Benazir Bhutto serve?

1. Wales

2. On the Moon

3. Bonnie and Clyde

4. Cleopatra

5. Tiananmen Square

6. Two

1. Where is the world's largest landlocked harbor?

2. Which gulf gave its name to the 1991 Gulf War?

3. Which English county boasts the final resting place of T.E. Lawrence (of Arabia)?

4. Which civil rights campaigner was awarded the 1964 Nobel Peace Prize?

5. What is the best-known invention of Peace Prize founder Alfred Nobel?

6. Where is the National Ski and Snowboarding Hall of Fame located?

1. San Francisco Bay

2. The Persian Gulf

3. Dorset

4. Martin Luther King Jr.

5. Dynamite

6. Ishpeming, Michigan

1. Who was the only U.S. president to appoint his own brother to a senior cabinet post?

2. Which Soviet leader approved the building of the Berlin Wall?

3. What day was Charlemagne crowned Holy Roman Emperor on?

4. Which part of Alaska was named as the result of a clerical error made by mapmakers?

5. What was the nickname of Arthur Harris who was in charge of the World War II Allied air campaign against Germany?

6. What is the name of the legendary graveyard in Tombstone, Arizona?

1. John F. Kennedy

2. Nikita Khrushchev

3. Christmas Day

4. Cape Nome

5. Bomber

6. Boot Hill

1. Where does Pennsylvania's most famous groundhog reside?

2. What was the popular name for the European Economic Community?

3. Where is the Cereal Capital of the World?

4. What triumphal arch became an East/West German border crossing in December 1989?

5. How did the founder of Vassar College accumulate his wealth?

6. Who was Elizabeth I's father?

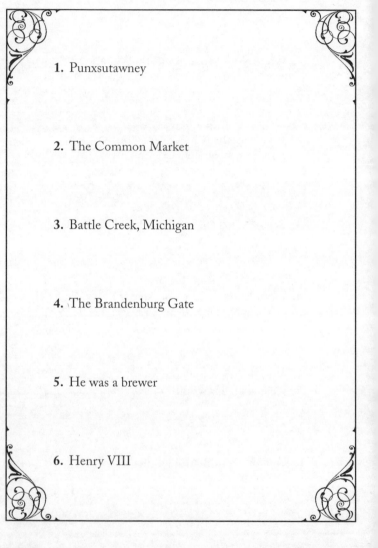

1. Punxsutawney

2. The Common Market

3. Battle Creek, Michigan

4. The Brandenburg Gate

5. He was a brewer

6. Henry VIII

1. How many members of the *Titanic*'s orchestra survived to tell the tale?

2. Who was Charlemagne's brother?

3. Who was known as the Virgin Queen?

4. What name was given to the hanging bits of paper that confused vote counters in 2000?

5. Who was the first Roman Catholic president of the U.S.?

6. What Broadway musical celebrates the life of King Charlemagne's son?

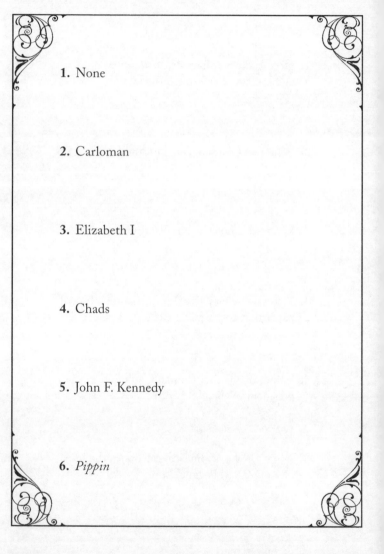

1. None

2. Carloman

3. Elizabeth I

4. Chads

5. John F. Kennedy

6. *Pippin*

1. Which city's Leinster House was the U.S.A.'s White House modeled after?

2. Which Italian city did Christopher Columbus claim he was born in?

3. Which country had the most seats in the European Parliament at the start of 2007?

4. How many times has Nelson Mandela been married?

5. Whose state flower is the bluebonnet?

6. Who was the first U.S. president born in the 20th century?

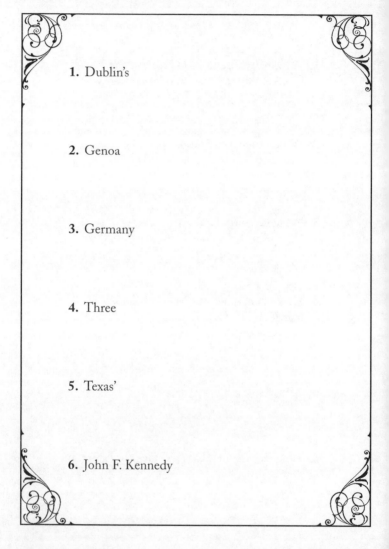

1. Dublin's

2. Genoa

3. Germany

4. Three

5. Texas'

6. John F. Kennedy

1. What illness incapacitated Woodrow Wilson during his second term?

2. Which mountain witnessed the deaths of George Mallory and Andrew Irvine?

3. What is the FBI's motto?

4. Who was prime minister of the United Kingdom from 1997 to 2007?

5. Which future president founded the Free French movement during the Second World War?

6. Who shared the 1998 Nobel Peace Prize with David Trimble?

1. A cerebral hemorrhage (stroke)

2. Mount Everest

3. "Fidelity, Bravery, and Integrity."

4. Tony Blair

5. Charles de Gaulle

6. John Hume

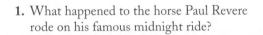

1. What happened to the horse Paul Revere rode on his famous midnight ride?

2. Which country was at war with Iran from 1980 to 1988?

3. What was the country of birth of Henry Kissinger?

4. What fun-loving state boasts town names of Christmas, Holiday and Panacea?

5. How many of Henry VIII's wives were executed?

6. Which ancient Roman building's nighttime lighting is changed from white to gold when someone anywhere in the world has the death penalty commuted?

1. The British took it away from him

2. Iraq

3. Germany

4. Florida

5. Two

6. The Colosseum's

1. What did Al Capone largely fund his criminal empire on?

2. Which mountain was given its English name in 1865 by the British Surveyor-General in India, Andrew Waugh?

3. Which nation's Conquistadors took over from the Incas?

4. What European capital was first dubbed the City of Light in the 19th century?

5. Which Scottish island boasts the historic site of Skara Brae?

6. What secret transportation service involved at least 21 states and moved more than 100,000 people during most of the 19th century?

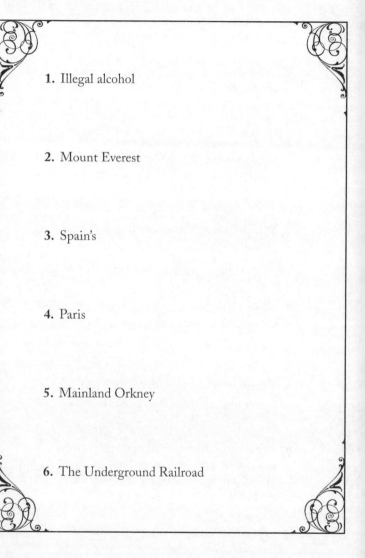

1. Illegal alcohol

2. Mount Everest

3. Spain's

4. Paris

5. Mainland Orkney

6. The Underground Railroad

1. Where was the world's first nuclear-powered submarine built?

2. What famous explorer was married to Felipa Perestrello e Moniz and had a son named Diego?

3. Who negotiated with Colonel Qadhafi to bring the Lockerbie suspects to trial?

4. What organization owns Stonehenge?

5. What was completed in 1825 to connect the Hudson River with Lake Erie?

6. Who was Charlemagne's father?

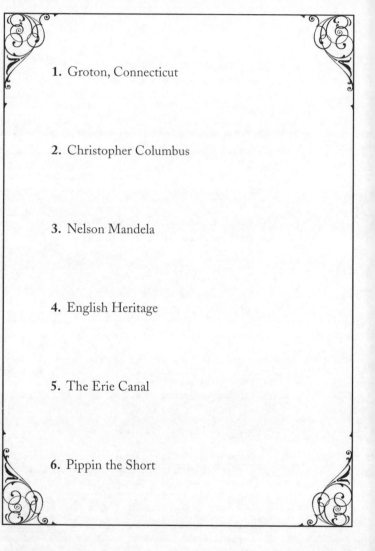

1. Groton, Connecticut

2. Christopher Columbus

3. Nelson Mandela

4. English Heritage

5. The Erie Canal

6. Pippin the Short

1. What name was given to people who made illegal booze during prohibition?

2. Which American inventor held an astonishing 1,093 patents?

3. What city was R.M.S. *Titanic* built in?

4. What woman's name was the last word spoken by Napoleon?

5. What was the only state George McGovern carried in the 1972 presidential election?

6. Which is the 28th U.S. state?

1. Bootleggers

2. Thomas Edison

3. Belfast

4. Josephine

5. Massachusetts

6. Texas

1. What was the real identity of 18th century American essay writer Silence Dogood?

2. Which U.S. president once wore a Nazi uniform in a movie?

3. What priceless object is Cleopatra said to have dissolved in a cup of vinegar before drinking it?

4. Which country did the first European settlers of New York come from?

5. What country's liberation was the purpose of the 1991 Gulf War?

6. What state opened America's first free public schools?

1. Benjamin Franklin

2. Ronald Reagan

3. A pearl

4. The Netherlands

5. Kuwait's

6. Massachusetts

1. Which ruler brought the whole of Greece together following the internal struggles between Athenians and Spartans?

2. What was the administrative and political center of the Incas?

3. Who replied: "Because it's there," when asked why he intended climbing Mount Everest?

4. Which of Henry VIII's ships was rescued from the Solent and can be seen in the *Portsmouth Naval Museum*?

5. Which exiled Middle Eastern leader returned home in 2007, only to be assassinated two months later?

6. What is Ohio's official state rock song?

1. Alexander the Great

2. Cuzco

3. George Mallory

4. *Mary Rose*

5. Benazir Bhutto

6. *Hang On Sloopy*

1. Who played the role of Lawrence in the movie *Lawrence of Arabia*?

2. What month in 1912 saw the *Titanic* go down?

3. What is the tallest building in the U.S.?

4. Who gave the state of Florida its name?

5. How many years are there in a French president's term?

6. What stands today on the site of the O'Leary barn, where the Chicago fire began?

1. Peter O'Toole

2. April

3. The Sears Tower

4. Juan Ponce de León

5. Seven

6. The Chicago Fire Academy

1. Who was made director of the FBI as of September 4, 2001?

2. What had 1,919 people reached the top of by the end of 2003?

3. What kind of gun was used to kill Abraham Lincoln?

4. What other man, besides Paul Revere, was originally sent out to warn patriots that the British were coming on April 18, 1775?

5. What was Al Capone's nickname?

6. Which king was crowned in Scotland in 1651?

1. Robert S. Mueller III

2. Mount Everest

3. A Derringer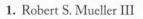

4. William Dawes

5. Scarface

6. Charles II

1. What school's original name was the Catholepistimiad?

2. What is the meaning of *Imam*, the title by which Ayatollah Khomeini was known in Iran?

3. What was Al Capone's alibi for the St. Valentine's Day Massacre?

4. Who was the first British astronaut?

5. What is the second-largest country in the world?

6. What critter was the subject of a famous speech by Richard Nixon, defending himself against charges of accepting illegal campaign contributions?

1. The University of Michigan

2. Leader

3. Vacationing in Florida

4. Helen Sharman

5. Canada

6. Checkers, his cocker spaniel

1. What popular soft drink had its birthplace in Waco, Texas?

2. How many years was Tony Blair the prime minister of the United Kingdom?

3. How many times did Henry VIII marry in 1540?

4. Who succeeded Tony Blair as prime minister of the U.K.?

5. Who topped the FBI's list of most wanted terrorists in October 2001?

6. What British royal was depicted on the first adhesive postage stamps, in 1840?

1. Dr Pepper

2. Ten

3. Twice

4. Gordon Brown

5. Osama bin Laden

6. Queen Victoria

1. What did the Incas believe happened to them after death?

2. Which islands did Columbus visit to stock up before setting sail for the Americas?

3. How many people showed up to take a ride on New York's subway on its opening day?

4. What was played in Holyoke, MA, in 1895?

5. Which two famous late-19th-century authors lived next door to one another in Hartford, CT?

6. Which French president personally authorized the sinking of the *Greenpeace* ship *Rainbow Warrior*?

1. Reincarnation

2. Canary Islands

3. 150,000

4. The first volleyball game

5. Harriet Beecher Stowe and Mark Twain

6. François Mitterrand

1. Which British queen presented a desk to America that remained unused until John F. Kennedy's presidency?

2. What shortage killed one million Irish people in the 1840s?

3. What name did Joseph Alois Ratzinger adopt in 2005 when he became the first German Pope since Adrian VI in 1523?

4. Which Middle Eastern country was Benazir Bhutto prime minister of?

5. What island was connected to mainland Scotland by a bridge opened in 1995?

6. Which Egyptian queen's name is Greek for *father's glory*?

1. Queen Victoria

2. Potatoes

3. Pope Benedict XVI

4. Pakistan

5. Skye

6. Cleopatra's

HISTORY

1. Who owned the sawmill where the Gold
   Rush began in 1848?

2. What name is given to the ancient Christian
   and Jewish underground burial chambers in
   and around Rome?

3. Which veteran American astronaut made a
   trip into space at the age of 77?

4. How long did William Penn live in
   Pennsylvania?

5. Whose state animal is the sperm whale?

6. What date in 1929 saw the shooting of
   seven members of Bugs Moran's gang in
   Chicago?

1. John Sutter

2. Catacombs

3. John Glenn

4. Three and a half years

5. Connecticut's

6. February 14 (Valentine's Day)

1. What did President Lyndon Johnson do to his beagle dog that caused a flap?

2. What garments gave Bill Clinton's cat its name?

3. Who became King of Italy in 1804?

4. Who is said to have been presented to Julius Caesar in a carpet?

5. Who was director of the FBI from 1924 to 1972?

6. Which organization did the U.S. refuse to join, despite being enthusiastically supported by Woodrow Wilson?

1. Lifted him up by the ears

2. Socks

3. Napoleon I

4. Cleopatra

5. J. Edgar Hoover

6. The League of Nations

1. Who was the father of Cleopatra's twins?

2. What disease killed 20,000 Parisians in 1832?

3. Which U.S. gangster described himself as a used furniture dealer on his business card?

4. Who became the first Englishman to circumnavigate the globe?

5. Who made a contract with King Ferdinand and Queen Isabella entitling him to be appointed Viceroy and Governor of any new lands he discovered?

6. Which carved stone was the key to the understanding of Egyptian hieroglyphics?

1. Mark Antony

2. Cholera

3. Al Capone

4. Sir Francis Drake

5. Christopher Columbus

6. The Rosetta Stone

1. What was 16-year-old Thomas Edison's job?

2. Who was the 32nd president of the U.S.?

3. How many days were there in an ancient Egyptian year?

4. Who is the only person to have become vice president and president of the U.S. without being elected to either position?

5. Where in the United States is coffee grown?

6. Which French president adopted a boat person refugee who he'd found crying at Charles de Gaulle Airport?

1. Telegrapher

2. Franklin D. Roosevelt

3. 365

4. Gerald Ford

5. Hawaii

6. Jacques Chirac

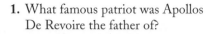

1. What famous patriot was Apollos De Revoire the father of?

2. Which organization shared the 2001 Nobel Peace Prize with Kofi Annan?

3. What did the building originally known as the Mission San Antonio de Valero become known as?

4. What creature appears rampant on Scotland's coat of arms?

5. Which Greek island was the center of the Minoan civilization?

6. How many main islands make up the state of Hawaii?

1. Paul Revere

2. United Nations

3. The Alamo

4. Lion

5. Crete

6. Eight

1. What nationality was Pope John Paul II?

2. Who was George W. Bush's main competitor in the 2004 presidential election?

3. What ranch hands from the days of American cowboys gave their name to a brand of jeans?

4. What religion was introduced to Japan in the mid-6th century?

5. Who was South Africa's first leader to be elected in fully representative democratic elections?

6. Who did the U.S. purchase Alaska from?

1. Polish

2. John F. Kerry

3. Wranglers

4. Buddhism

5. Nelson Mandela

6. Russia

1. What empire arose in the Peruvian highlands around 1200 A.D.?

2. What portable ice cream treat did a candy maker from Youngstown, Ohio invent?

3. What F-word did Tony Blair fight to have removed from the European Constitution?

4. What country did the Battle of the Bulge take place in?

5. Who announced at the Berlin Wall: "Ich bin ein Berliner"?

6. Who reached the summit of Mount Everest in 1953 with Tenzing Norgay?

1. The Inca Empire

2. The *Good Humor* bar

3. Federal

4. Belgium

5. John F. Kennedy

6. Edmund Hillary

1. What Florida governor was in office at the same time his big brother was president of the U.S.?

2. What Caribbean island did Columbus originally name Juana?

3. What animal is on the California state flag?

4. What famed English site is found on Salisbury Plain?

5. Who was Bill Clinton's main competitor in the 1996 presidential election?

6. What was the name of the secret system for runaway slaves to escape to the North?

1. Jeb Bush

2. Cuba

3. A grizzly bear

4. Stonehenge

5. Bob Dole

6. The Underground Railroad

1. Which fashionable street in Paris boasts the site where the guillotine stood?

2. What was the original Dutch name of New York City?

3. What was George Bush's famous book-writing dog's name?

4. What city saw work start on the United Nations headquarters in 1950?

5. What are the "three Ps" that Georgia produces?

6. What more pronounceable first name was given to little Rolihlahla Mandela when he went to school?

1. *Place de la Concorde*

2. New Amsterdam

3. Millie

4. New York

5. Peaches, pecans and peanuts

6. Nelson

1. What hatchet-wielding activist stormed many a Kansas saloon to break up the party?

2. What political party did Nelson Mandela represent as president of South Africa?

3. Whose 1939 nomination for the Nobel Peace Prize was retracted in February of that same year?

4. What addiction-inducing crop did Christopher Columbus discover in Cuba in 1492?

5. What was the southernmost of the thirteen original American colonies?

6. Which city's Bastille was stormed in 1789?

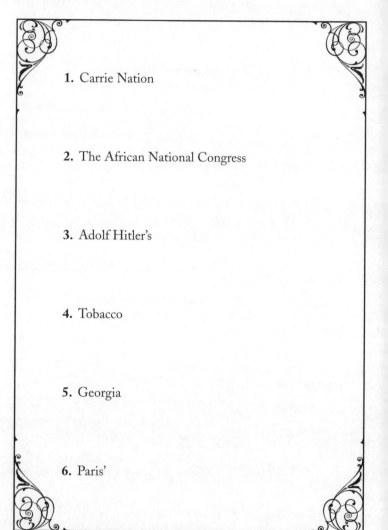

1. Carrie Nation

2. The African National Congress

3. Adolf Hitler's

4. Tobacco

5. Georgia

6. Paris'

1. Which state is bordered by Vermont, Massachusetts and Connecticut?

2. Where is the Land of Steady Habits?

3. Who was Henry VIII's widow?

4. How many cameras was *I Love Lucy* the first TV show to use?

5. Which U.S. naval base did Japan attack in 1941 to declare war on the Allies?

6. What language did King Robert the Bruce hold his parliaments in?

1. New York

2. Connecticut

3. Catherine Parr

4. Three

5. Pearl Harbor

6. Gaelic

1. What TV series starred Efrem Zimbalist Jr. as Inspector Lewis Erskine?

2. What state saw the start of the American Revolution?

3. How many shillings more than 20 were there in a guinea?

4. What prime minister oversaw the move to independence of 11 former British colonies?

5. Which European country was Ayatollah Khomeini's home for the final years of his exile?

6. What surname did T.E. Lawrence use for anonymity when he joined the Royal Tank Corps?

1. *The F.B.I.*

2. Massachusetts

3. One

4. Harold Macmillan

5. France

6. Shaw

1. What name was given to the leather protection cowboys wore over the front of their pants?

2. How old was Clara Barton when she founded the American Red Cross?

3. Where can you find the Great Serpent Mound?

4. What happened to the firefighters who responded to the first alarm of the great Chicago fire?

5. How many funnels did the *Titanic* have?

6. What was James I of England's Scottish title?

1. Chaps

2. Sixty

3. Ohio

4. They were sent to the wrong address

5. Three (and a false one)

6. James VI

1. What is the "Big Mac" that was built in Michigan in 1957?

2. What is the name of the sonnet by Emma Lazarus that is inside the pedestal of the Statue of Liberty?

3. What shape is the White House office constructed in 1909 for U.S. presidents?

4. What name was given to bars selling illegal alcohol during prohibition?

5. What goopy attraction has been a part of the Los Angeles area for more than 40,000 years?

6. Whose 2004 U.S. election campaign slogans included: "Stronger at home, respected in the World"?

1. The Mackinac Bridge

2. "The New Colossus"

3. Oval

4. Speakeasies

5. The La Brea Tar Pits

6. George W. Bush's

1. How much did it cost to take the New York City subway when it began in 1904?

2. Where in the Americas did Europeans first settle?

3. Who was the first American in space?

4. What did the Romans consider to be their most important road?

5. Which prime minister's Munich Agreement wasn't worth the paper it was written on?

6. How long did New York City's first subway system take to build?

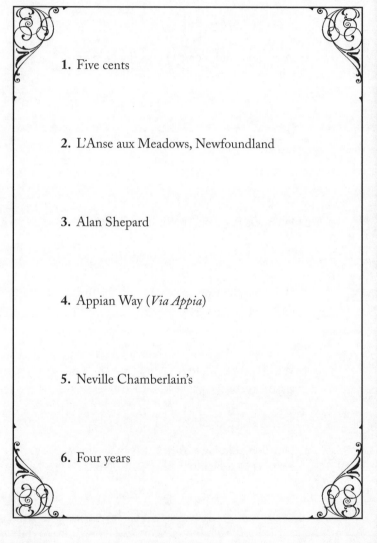

1. Five cents

2. L'Anse aux Meadows, Newfoundland

3. Alan Shepard

4. Appian Way (*Via Appia*)

5. Neville Chamberlain's

6. Four years

1. What battle of the War of American Independence was fought on Breed's Hill?

2. Which 2006 Nobel Peace Prize nominee has sold the most records?

3. What group of people was banned from gaining jobs with the U.N.'s World Health Organization after December 1, 2005?

4. What year was the famous Chicago fire?

5. What organization did Henri Dunant found in 1863 with the title International Committee for the Relief of the Wounded?

6. Which anti-trade union U.S. president was a former head of the Screen Actors Guild?

1. The Battle of Bunker Hill

2. Bono

3. Smokers

4. 1871

5. The Red Cross

6. Ronald Reagan

1. What controversial Middle Eastern leader was assassinated on December 27, 2007?

2. Who crowned Charlemagne in the year 800?

3. What did a dispute with Mexico over where Texas land ended and where Mexican land began lead to?

4. What was the ultimate destination for most travelers of the Underground Railroad?

5. What sea did Plato describe the ancient Greeks living by: "Like frogs around a pond"?

6. Which modern country included ancient Caledonia and its population of Picts?

1. Benazir Bhutto

2. Pope Leo III

3. The Mexican War

4. Canada

5. Aegean

6. Scotland

1. What island country announced its neutrality the day after the 1939 German invasion of Poland?

2. Which U.S. state was an independent nation for ten years during the 19th century?

3. What barrier did one man get through by driving a very low sports car underneath Checkpoint Charlie?

4. Who was India's first prime minister and the father of Indira Gandhi?

5. What year did Alfred Beach open his pneumatic underground railroad in New York City?

6. What Japanese term meaning "divine wind" was adopted into the English language to describe World War II suicide pilots?

1. Ireland

2. Texas

3. The Berlin Wall

4. Jawaharlal Nehru

5. 1870

6. *Kamikaze*

1. What was John F. Kennedy called by his friends?

2. Which country celebrated the 500th anniversary of its whisky production in 1994?

3. Whose body was exposed to the world in 1989 as fanatical mourners ripped shreds from his shroud?

4. Who was Scotland's first First Minister?

5. What is the Flavian Amphitheatre now called by tourists in Rome?

6. What do Keanu Reeves, Pamela Anderson, Shania Twain and Romeo Dallaire have in common?

1. Jack

2. Scotland

3. Ayatollah Khomeini's

4. Donald Dewar

5. The Colosseum

6. They are all Canadians

1. Which U.S. president saw the last cow living at the White House?

2. Which future president's campaign advisors formed the first so-called "Brain Trust"?

3. What island off Georgia's coast was named for a famous pirate who frequented the area?

4. What city became capital of Cuba in 1519?

5. What Hawaiian island was used for bombing target practice during World War II and is now closed to visitors because it's considered unsafe?

6. What record-breaking building stands on an island in Oneida, NY?

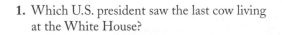

1. William Taft

2. Franklin D. Roosevelt's

3. Blackbeard Island

4. Havana

5. Kaho'olawe

6. The world's smallest church

1. What color suits are associated with Japanese Ninja?

2. Which of America's original 13 states took its name from Elizabeth I?

3. What president had a dog named Fala?

4. What is Canada's official name?

5. Which British king was born at Greenwich on June 28, 1491?

6. Who was known as "Moses" of the Underground Railroad?

1. Black

2. Virginia

3. Franklin D. Roosevelt

4. Canada

5. Henry VIII

6. Harriet Tubman

1. What name was given to the defensive mission launched to prevent Iraq from invading Saudi Arabia prior to the 1991 Gulf War?

2. Who performed *The Wall* by the Berlin Wall?

3. Where is the only royal palace in the United States?

4. What weekend retreat saw Menachim Begin and Anwar Sadat hammer out an Israeli-Egyptian peace accord in 1978?

5. Who was the mysterious author of *Poor Richard's Almanack*?

6. Which U.S. president walked down the aisle with a three-months pregnant Nancy?

1. Operation Desert Shield

2. Pink Floyd

3. In Hawaii

4. Camp David

5. Benjamin Franklin

6. Ronald Reagan

1. What was the name of Franklin Roosevelt's longtime supposed mistress?

2. Who were the first people to separate copper from its ore?

3. What was the official U.S. name for the 1991 Gulf War?

4. Who was Ronald Reagan's first wife?

5. Who was "The Wizard of Menlo Park"?

6. Which British author did Ayatollah Khomeini sentence to death?

1. Lucy Mercer

2. Ancient Egyptians

3. Operation Desert Storm

4. Jane Wyman

5. Thomas Edison

6. Salman Rushdie

1. What does legend say started the great Chicago fire of 1871?

2. Which U.S. vice president shot a Texas attorney while out hunting quail in 2006?

3. Who first became president of France in 1995?

4. Which battle's horrors inspired Henri Dunant to create the relief agency that became the Red Cross?

5. Who was the leader of the successful 1953 ascent of Everest?

6. Which president had a swimming pool installed in the White House?

1. A cow

2. Dick Cheney

3. Jacques Chirac

4. The Battle of Solferino

5. John Hunt

6. Franklin Roosevelt

1. What speech did FDR deliver and proclaim, "The only thing we have to fear is fear itself"?

2. What is the first name of Fidel Castro's younger brother, who became president of Cuba's Council of State during Castro's 2006 illness?

3. Which former American president was also a Nobel laureate and a Princeton professor?

4. Who is Cleveland, Ohio, named after?

5. What ancient city's capture resulted in T.E. Lawrence's promotion to lieutenant colonel in 1918?

6. Where do "Nutmeggers" come from?

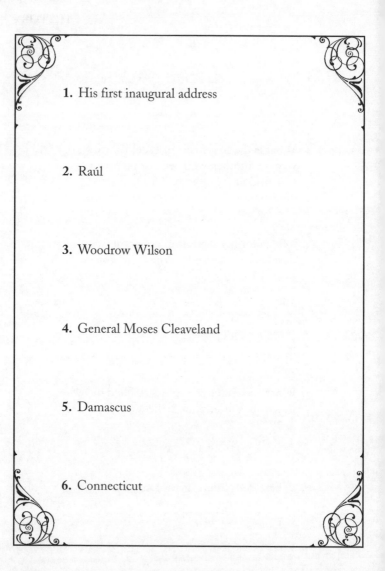

1. His first inaugural address

2. Raúl

3. Woodrow Wilson

4. General Moses Cleaveland

5. Damascus

6. Connecticut

1. What were Pablo, Famo, Vivo, Lux-O and Bevo?

2. What animal is said to have nurtured the founders of Rome, Romulus and Remus?

3. Who served as vice president to Bill Clinton and gained over half a million votes more than George W. Bush when Bush was elected president in 2000?

4. What connection did Thomas Edison have with the construction of Yankee Stadium?

5. What very large and famous piece of artwork has a sonnet by Emma Lazarus on it?

6. What defensive line was supposed to keep the Germans out of France in World War II?

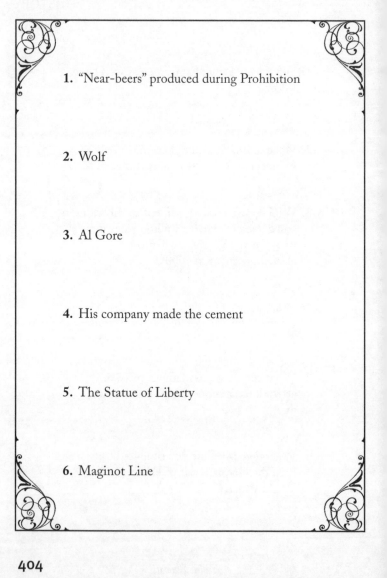

1. "Near-beers" produced during Prohibition

2. Wolf

3. Al Gore

4. His company made the cement

5. The Statue of Liberty

6. Maginot Line

1. What were the first words Edison spoke into the phonograph he had just invented?

2. What was writer and war hero T.E. Lawrence popularly known as?

3. What did cowboys refer to as "tonsil paint"?

4. What was New York's Liberty Island called before its name was changed in 1956?

5. Which South African State president ordered the release of Nelson Mandela?

6. Who played Benjamin Franklin in the movie musical "1776"?

1. "Mary had a little lamb ..."

2. Lawrence of Arabia

3. Whiskey

4. Bedloe's Island

5. F.W. de Klerk

6. Howard da Silva

1. Who was already the husband of Octavia Minor when he married Cleopatra?

2. How many stones make up each of Stonehenge's trilithons?

3. Which Greek goddess gave her name to the city of Athens?

4. Which country was former Prime Minister Tony Blair born in?

5. Whose more articulate quotes include: "I tell people, let's don't fear the future, let's shape it"?

6. What country saw the 1979-80 hostage crisis that ended as Ronald Reagan took his oath of office?

1. Mark Antony

2. Three

3. Athena

4. Scotland

5. George W. Bush's

6. Iran

1. Which ancient monument, close to the Pyramids of Giza, is said to have been partly formed by natural erosion?

2. What Harvard dropout held 535 U.S. patents upon his death in 1991, second only to Thomas Edison?

3. Which pass connects Afghanistan to Pakistan?

4. Which country helped Italian investors support Columbus' expedition to the Americas after Portugal had turned him down?

5. What Miss America Pageant winner turned in her tiara on July 23, 1984?

6. Which president's wife helped fund the war effort by auctioning wool from sheep grazing on the White House lawn?

1. The Sphinx

2. Edwin Land

3. The Khyber Pass

4. Spain

5. Vanessa Williams

6. Woodrow Wilson's

1. Which island boasts of being Napoleon's birthplace?

2. Who was the first Holy Roman Emperor?

3. Who did Sudanese-American author Kola Boof claim kept her against her will as his mistress?

4. How many letters are in the Hawaiian alphabet?

5. Which country joined the European Economic Community along with Ireland and the United Kingdom in 1973?

6. Where is the oldest continuously settled city in the U.S.?

1. Corsica

2. Charlemagne

3. Osama bin Laden

4. Twelve

5. Denmark

6. Saint Augustine, FL

1. What Canadian city boasts the world's richest rodeo that was first staged in 1912?

2. Who was Jimmy Carter's vice president?

3. Which Argentinean Marxist, who became a bedroom poster icon of the 1960s, was once one of Fidel Castro's closest advisors?

4. What was U.S. President Wilson's first name?

5. Who wrote the not-quite-accurate poem "Paul Revere's Ride"?

6. Who was the first Pope with two names and the first to use *The First* as part of his title?

1. Calgary

2. Walter (Fritz) Mondale

3. Ernesto (Che) Guevara

4. Thomas (Woodrow was his middle name)

5. Henry Wadsworth Longfellow

6. Pope John Paul I

1. What hill in Athens does the Parthenon stand on?

2. Which U.N. Secretary-General was sandwiched between Javier Pérez de Cuéllar and Kofi Annan?

3. What was the official name for the World War II evacuation of Dunkirk?

4. What Christian sect did a Huguenot belong to?

5. Who first saw Benjamin Franklin walking down the street with a Puffy Bun in his mouth and thought he looked ridiculous?

6. Who was one of the founding members of the little-known British rock band Ugly Rumours?

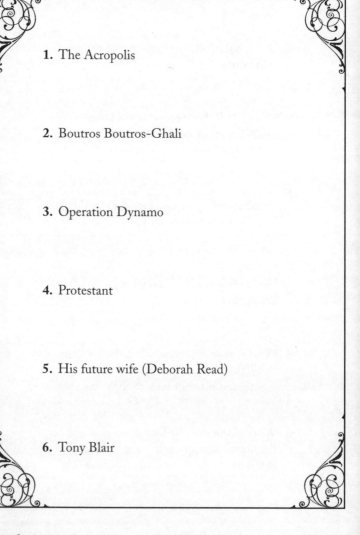

1. The Acropolis

2. Boutros Boutros-Ghali

3. Operation Dynamo

4. Protestant

5. His future wife (Deborah Read)

6. Tony Blair

1. What was Norman Schwarzkopf Jr.'s Gulf War nickname?

2. Which U.S. president said he didn't inhale, when asked if he'd smoked marijuana?

3. What national landmark has railroad enthusiasts steaming to just west of Altoona, PA?

4. What's the name of the building that stands at 1600 Pennsylvania Avenue, Washington, D.C.?

5. Which state was the first to ratify the 13th Amendment to abolish slavery?

6. Which beverage was promoted during the 1990s by three frogs croaking out its name?

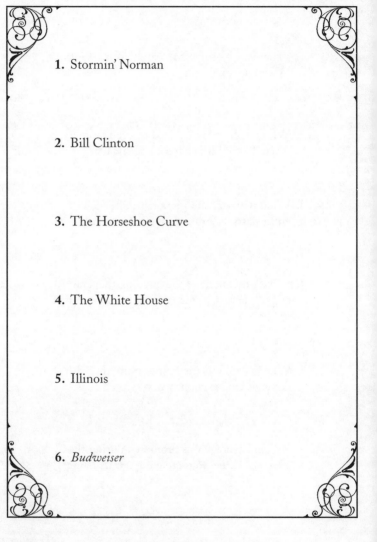

1. Stormin' Norman

2. Bill Clinton

3. The Horseshoe Curve

4. The White House

5. Illinois

6. *Budweiser*

1. Who was head of New York City's Interborough Transit System in 1904?

2. Which was the first city to be devastated by the dropping of an atomic bomb?

3. What was the *agora* in an ancient Greek city?

4. Who was the sculptor who designed the Statue of Liberty?

5. Which political party was former Prime Minister Tony Blair the leader of?

6. What is Henry Kissinger's actual first name?

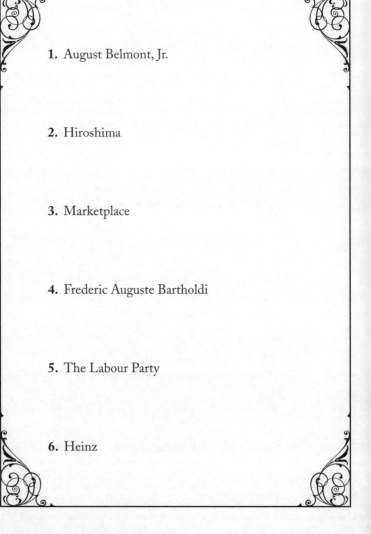

1. August Belmont, Jr.

2. Hiroshima

3. Marketplace

4. Frederic Auguste Bartholdi

5. The Labour Party

6. Heinz

1. What was T.E. Lawrence (of Arabia) riding when he had the accident that killed him?

2. What disability did talented Thomas Edison have?

3. Which famous family owned a cat named Socks?

4. What replaced the Royal Ulster Constabulary in 2001?

5. What wiped out Napoleon's Caribbean troops, leading him to scrap plans to conquer the New World?

6. Which country's parliament passed the Act of Union in 1801?

1. A motorcycle

2. He was hearing impaired

3. The Clintons

4. The Police Service of Northern Ireland

5. Yellow fever

6. Ireland's

1. What U.S. Secretary of State said: "There can't be a crisis next week. My schedule is already full"?

2. Which U.S. president used his wife's astrologer for advice on "virtually every move and decision"?

3. What is widely considered to be man's first celestial observatory?

4. Which U.S. vice president became president when John F. Kennedy was assassinated?

5. What was the name of Clyde Barrow's brother who joined Bonnie and Clyde in some of their heists?

6. Where is the Fakahatchee Strand?

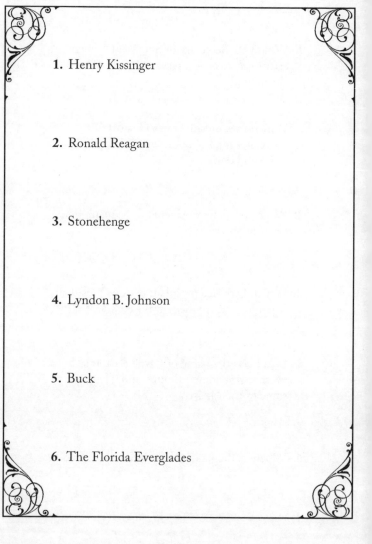

1. Henry Kissinger

2. Ronald Reagan

3. Stonehenge

4. Lyndon B. Johnson

5. Buck

6. The Florida Everglades

1. Who was chairman of the Joint Chiefs of Staff during the 1991 Gulf War?

2. What Frenchman was first president of the Fifth Empire?

3. What exciting new form of transportation opened on October 27, 1904, in New York City?

4. Which country did Osama bin Laden head for when expelled from Sudan?

5. What subject of hundreds of Wild West movies do the Spaniards, who called them *vaquero*, lay claim to originating?

6. What nation's land did Vicente Yanez discover in 1500 and claim for Portugal?

1. Colin Powell

2. Charles De Gaulle

3. The subway

4. Afghanistan

5. Cowboys

6. Brazil's

1. What building first appeared on the back of a $20 bill in 1928?

2. Who was Pakistan's leader at the time Benazir Bhutto was assassinated?

3. What did Quaker Levi Coffin assist more than 3,000 of?

4. Who did the U.S. Senate condemn on January 2, 1954?

5. Whose death resulted in Elizabeth I becoming Queen?

6. Which ship was the subject of an inquiry that heard U.S. Senator W.A. Smith ask: "What is an iceberg composed of"?

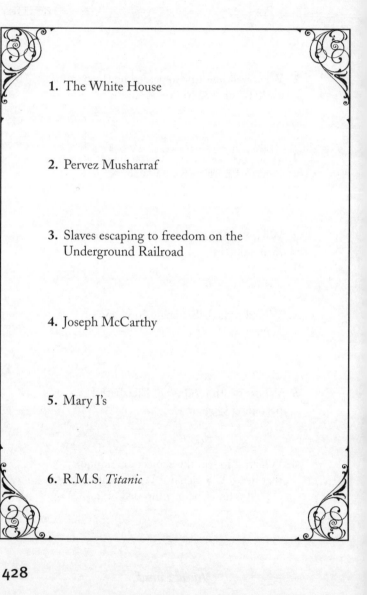

1. The White House

2. Pervez Musharraf

3. Slaves escaping to freedom on the Underground Railroad

4. Joseph McCarthy

5. Mary I's

6. R.M.S. *Titanic*

1. Which state's ballot counting, said by some to be ballot rigging, held up the 2000 U.S. presidential election result for more than a month?

2. Which Indian prime minister was awarded the 1983-84 Lenin Peace Prize?

3. What company did Henry Ford found in 1899?

4. Who was Crispus Attucks?

5. Where do the Allegheny, Monongahela and Ohio Rivers meet?

6. What archaeological site is known as the Lost City of the Incas?

1. Florida's

2. Indira Gandhi

3. The Detroit Automobile Company

4. First person to die in the Boston Massacre

5. Pittsburgh, PA

6. Machu Picchu

1. What is the four-letter Gaelic name for Scotland?

2. Where were the 1996 Summer Olympics held?

3. What animal was Bill Clinton mauled by when he was eight, which he described as: "the awfullest beating I ever took"?

4. Who became India's youngest prime minister shortly after his mother's assassination?

5. What was banned in the U.S. under the terms of the 21st Amendment?

6. What year was the first beer brewed?

1. Alba

2. Atlanta, Georgia

3. Sheep

4. Rajiv Gandhi

5. Alcohol

6. 6000 B.C.

1. What museum inspired a setting in the Lara Croft video game *Tomb Raider, The Angel of Darkness*?

2. What is Patricia Reichardt better known as in the *Peanuts* cartoon strips?

3. What H-word means designing, displaying and describing coats of arms and badges?

4. What Agatha Christie novel was made up of two parts, England and Egypt?

5. What is the first name of Professor Dumbledore in the *Harry Potter* books?

6. Which cartoon character made his debut with his girlfriend Minnie in the 1928 movie *Steamboat Willie*?

1. The Louvre

2. Peppermint Patty

3. Heraldry

4. *Death on the Nile*

5. Albus

6. Mickey Mouse

1. What note is the highest string of a violin usually tuned to?

2. What three words follow *The Most Excellent and Lamentable Tragedy of*, to complete the full original title of a Shakespeare play?

3. What did Disney drop from the name of *Winnie-the-Pooh*?

4. What is Tchaikovsky's ballet *Le Lac des Cygnes* commonly called?

5. Which monarch is said to have given Sherlock Holmes his emerald tiepin?

6. What book about little creatures was Roald Dahl's first work for children?

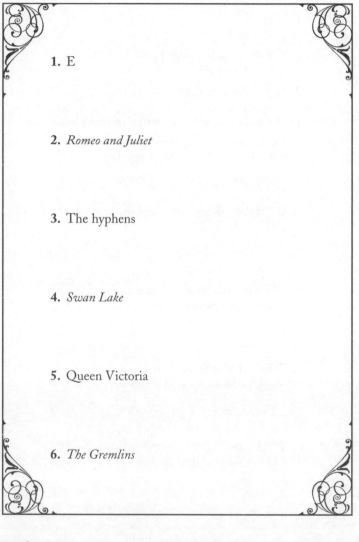

1. E

2. *Romeo and Juliet*

3. The hyphens

4. *Swan Lake*

5. Queen Victoria

6. *The Gremlins*

1. When does Mary Poppins say she will leave?

2. What Andrew Lloyd Webber musical sees naïve singer Christine Daaé seduced by a disfigured musical genius?

3. What nationality was Rembrandt?

4. Who was famous for saying: "All you need to fly are lovely things and fairy dust"?

5. What *Wind in the Willows* character "simply hates society"?

6. What war is the Tribe fighting against conscription into in the musical *Hair*?

1. When the wind changes

2. *The Phantom of the Opera*

3. Dutch

4. Peter Pan

5. Badger

6. Vietnam

1. Whose treasure is said to be the subject of the *Treasure Island* map?

2. Whose novel is the basis for the Lloyd Webber musical *The Phantom of the Opera*?

3. What artist stopped talking to van Gogh after the ear cutting incident?

4. What did J.R.R. Tolkien start to write as a sequel to *The Hobbit*?

5. Who wrote *The Young Lions* and *Rich Man, Poor Man*?

6. What musical is based on a series of children's books by P.L. Travers?

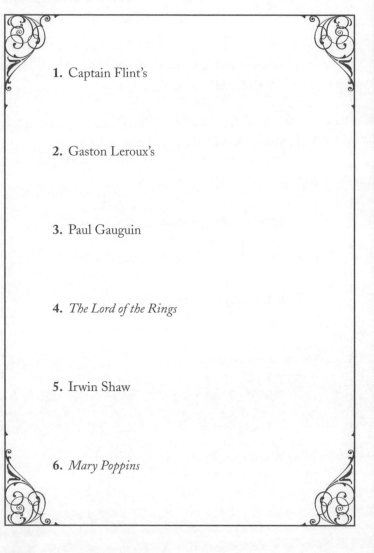

1. Captain Flint's

2. Gaston Leroux's

3. Paul Gauguin

4. *The Lord of the Rings*

5. Irwin Shaw

6. *Mary Poppins*

1. What format was *The Hitchhiker's Guide to the Galaxy* first produced in?

2. Which musical's title character is adopted by billionaire Oliver (Daddy) Warbucks?

3. Who created Hercule Poirot and Miss Marple?

4. What Anglo-Irish writer had the middle names Fingal O'Flahertie Wills?

5. What is the title of Constance, the D.H. Lawrence character who has an affair with her gamekeeper Oliver Mellors?

6. What is the stolen *Heart of Gold* in *The Hitchhiker's Guide to the Galaxy*?

1. Radio play

2. *Annie*'s

3. Agatha Christie

4. Oscar Wilde

5. Lady Chatterley

6. Space ship

1. Who starred as Amos Hart in the Broadway production of *Chicago* after serving as a writer and performer on the Imus in the Morning show?

2. What fictional Harvard professor appears in Dan Brown novels including *The Da Vinci Code*?

3. Which Shakespeare play tells the story of Miss Capulet who loves Mr. Montague?

4. What orchestral drums consist of skin stretched over a large bowl commonly made of copper?

5. What musical features *Edelweiss*, the last song Oscar Hammerstein II wrote before his death?

6. What kind of creature is the ballet dancing Hyacinth in *Fantasia*?

1. Rob Bartlett

2. Robert Langdon

3. *Romeo and Juliet*

4. Timpani

5. *The Sound of Music*

6. Hippopotamus

1. What role did multi-platinum singer Brian McKnight fill in the Broadway production of *Chicago*?

2. What nursery rhyme character was warned that the cow was in the corn?

3. What town in northern Italy is the home of Valentine and Proteus, Shakespeare's *Two Gentlemen*?

4. What song in *The Sound of Music* do Julie Andrews and the von Trapps reprise at the folk festival?

5. What musical is set in the fictional English town of Everington?

6. Whose operatic marriage was a sequel to *The Barber of Seville*?

1. Billy Flynn

2. Little Boy Blue

3. Verona

4. *Do-Re-Mi*

5. *Billy Elliot*

6. Figaro's

1. Who painted the *Mona Lisa*?

2. What metal is the *The Statue of Liberty*'s visible surface constructed from?

3. What did Mickey Mouse first wear on his hands in the 1929 movie *The Opry House*?

4. Whose painting *London, the Parliament, Effects of Sun in the Fog* sold for over $20 million in 2004?

5. Whose assassination was announced to the cast of *My Fair Lady* by Audrey Hepburn after filming *Wouldn't It Be Loverly* in November 1963?

6. What is the name of the paranoid android in *The Hitchhiker's Guide to the Galaxy*?

1. Leonardo da Vinci

2. Copper

3. Gloves

4. Claude Monet's

5. John F. Kennedy's

6. Marvin

1. Who made the One Ring in *The Lord of the Rings*?

2. What is the singular of timpani?

3. Which of the Three Tenors would be first in the telephone directory if they all lived in the same town?

4. How many eyes does a Cyclops have?

5. What nationality is the girl who is rescued by Phileas Fogg in *Around the World in Eighty Days*?

6. What Ian Fleming novel's title is the nickname of the character Francisco Scaramanga?

1. Dark Lord Sauron

2. Timpano

3. José Carreras

4. One

5. Indian

6. *The Man with the Golden Gun*

1. What musical did the Simpsons parody in the episode *Simpsoncalifragilisticexpiala(Annoyed Grunt)cious*?

2. What form of theater was the subject of many of Degas' paintings?

3. What was the first *James Bond* novel?

4. What rock star wrote the music for the stage version of *Billy Elliot*?

5. What three-letter word does Marcie always use to address Peppermint Patty in the *Peanuts* cartoon strip?

6. What sport did Billy Elliot's father encourage his son to take up?

1. *Mary Poppins*

2. Ballet

3. *Casino Royale*

4. Elton John

5. Sir

6. Boxing

1. Who filled the role of the Sorcerer's Apprentice in *Fantasia*?

2. What author signed into Harrogate's Old Swan Hotel using the name of her hubby's mistress, during her notorious 1926 disappearance?

3. Who is the second bag of wool for in *Baa, Baa, Black Sheep*?

4. What musical's most memorable songs include *Tomorrow* and *It's the Hard-Knock Life*?

5. Which famous artist made all his scientific notes in mirror writing?

6. What creature is the back end of a Centaur?

1. Mickey Mouse

2. Agatha Christie

3. The Dame

4. *Annie*'s

5. Leonardo da Vinci

6. Horse

1. What Canadian Island was the setting for *Anne of Green Gables*?

2. Who joined José Carreras and Placido Domingo for the bestselling *Three Tenors* concert album?

3. What novel is said to have boosted the number of visitors to the Louvre by 22 percent in 2005?

4. How many spikes are on the *The Statue of Liberty*'s crown?

5. What prolific Frenchman wrote *Notre-Dame de Paris*, better known as *The Hunchback of Notre Dame*?

6. Which Italian fashion house owns the *Yves Saint Laurent* brand for clothes, watches and perfume?

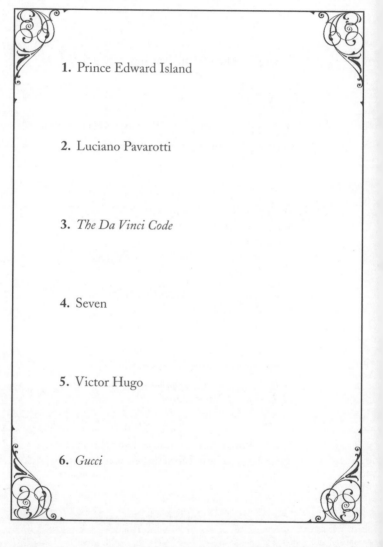

1. Prince Edward Island

2. Luciano Pavarotti

3. *The Da Vinci Code*

4. Seven

5. Victor Hugo

6. *Gucci*

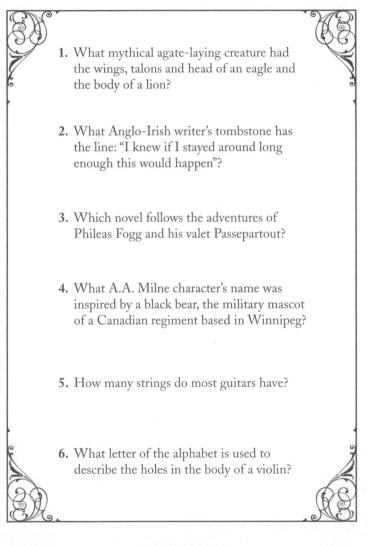

1. What mythical agate-laying creature had the wings, talons and head of an eagle and the body of a lion?

2. What Anglo-Irish writer's tombstone has the line: "I knew if I stayed around long enough this would happen"?

3. Which novel follows the adventures of Phileas Fogg and his valet Passepartout?

4. What A.A. Milne character's name was inspired by a black bear, the military mascot of a Canadian regiment based in Winnipeg?

5. How many strings do most guitars have?

6. What letter of the alphabet is used to describe the holes in the body of a violin?

1. Griffin

2. George Bernard Shaw's

3. *Around the World in Eighty Days*

4. Winnie-the-Pooh's

5. Six

6. F

1. What are the ladies doing in the song *The Twelve Days of Christmas*?

2. What ballet term translates literally as "in Arabic fashion"?

3. What does Honeychile Rider collect from the beach in *Dr. No*?

4. Which musical's lead male character ends many sentences with "et cetera, et cetera, et cetera"?

5. What French museum's curator is murdered in *The Da Vinci Code*?

6. What name is given to the carved piece of wood that lifts the strings of a violin from the body?

1. Dancing

2. Arabesque

3. Shells

4. *The King and I*'s

5. The Louvre's

6. Bridge

1. What Saint's Day is said to have seen the birth and the death of William Shakespeare?

2. Who was cast as Mrs. Molly Weasley in *Harry Potter and the Sorcerer's Stone* before becoming Billy's dance instructor in the movie *Billy Elliot*?

3. What was the sequel to *Little Women*?

4. What does Lucy charge for psychiatric help in the *Peanuts* cartoon strip?

5. What P-word means an electric guitar's transducers?

6. What does Jo sell, in *Little Women*, to raise money for her mother to visit her father?

1. St. George's Day

2. Julie Walters

3. *Good Wives*

4. Five cents

5. Pickups

6. Her hair

1. What university do Charles and Sebastian meet at, in *Brideshead Revisited*?

2. What saint's keys appear on the Pope's personal coat of arms?

3. Who founded the cubism movement with George Braque?

4. What was the only musical running on Broadway at the start of 2006 that shared its title with the name of a U.S. city?

5. What school of witchcraft and wizardry does Harry Potter attend?

6. What city must you visit to see Leonardo's famous *The Last Supper*?

1. Oxford

2. St. Peter's

3. Pablo Picasso

4. *Chicago*

5. Hogwarts

6. Milan

1. How many von Trapp children are involved in *The Sound of Music*?

2. What actress are we advised to think of in the title of a song from the musical *Fame*?

3. Who wrote *Treasure Island*?

4. What museum was first opened to the public during the French Revolution?

5. What model was the inspiration for the helpmate character in Roald Dahl's *The Big Friendly Giant*?

6. Which nursery rhyme character "kissed the girls and made them cry"?

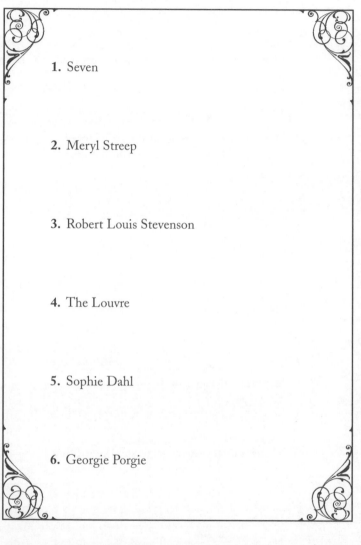

1. Seven

2. Meryl Streep

3. Robert Louis Stevenson

4. The Louvre

5. Sophie Dahl

6. Georgie Porgie

1. Which author's *A Widow for One Year* was adapted into the movie *The Door in the Floor*?

2. What musical movie's researchers had problems finding corn "as high as an elephant's eye"?

3. What country is the setting of John Fowles' *The French Lieutenant's Woman*?

4. What statue in St. Peter's Basilica, Rome, is considered to be Michelangelo's second most famous?

5. What collective name was given to the trio of opera singers who first performed together in Rome on the eve of the 1990 World Cup Final?

6. Which French designer whose perfume range includes *J'adore* was the heir to a fertilizer fortune?

1. John Irving's

2. *Oklahoma!*'s

3. England

4. *Pietà*

5. The Three Tenors

6. Christian Dior

1. What children's writer's name was given to newly discovered asteroid 43844 in 2006?

2. What Irish city was the birthplace of George Bernard Shaw?

3. Who is the mistress of Satis House in *Great Expectations*?

4. What was the title of the first *Harry Potter* book?

5. What was the name of the devilish cat in Walt Disney's *Cinderella*?

6. What flowers did van Gogh paint most regularly?

1. J.K. Rowling's

2. Dublin

3. Miss Havisham

4. *Harry Potter and the Sorcerer's Stone*

5. Lucifer

6. Sunflowers

1. What artist's 400th birthday anniversary saw 2006 celebrated as a special year in the Netherlands?

2. What German composer's musical works include a Freemasonry-influenced opera called *The Magic Flute*?

3. What must be held by anyone wishing to speak during meetings in *Lord of the Flies*?

4. What term is used to describe a pair of cymbals clashed together by operating a foot pedal?

5. What nationality was Pablo Picasso?

6. Who left Ireland after falling in love with Florence Balcome and then hearing she'd become engaged to Bram Stoker?

1. Rembrandt's

2. Wolfgang Amadeus Mozart's

3. Conch shell

4. Hi-hat

5. Spanish

6. Oscar Wilde

1. How many mechanical birds are there in Paul Klee's playful watercolor *Twittering Birds*?

2. What returned to Johann Sebastian Bach in 1750, helping him dictate his last choral prelude?

3. What city boasts the Rembrandt House Museum?

4. How many strings does a standard violin have?

5. What breed of dog was John Steinbeck's canine companion in *Travels with Charley*?

6. What was Leonardo da Vinci's hometown?

1. Four

2. His sight

3. Amsterdam

4. Four

5. French Poodle

6. Vinci

1. Who killed the Minotaur?

2. Who wrote *Great Expectations*?

3. What great composer's only opera was *Fidelio*?

4. What fairy tale character has two ugly stepsisters?

5. What Douglas Adams bestseller became a computer game in 1984?

6. What musical's songs include *I Want to Make Magic* and *Tyrone's Rap*?

1. Theseus

2. Charles Dickens

3. Ludwig van Beethoven's

4. Cinderella

5. *The Hitchhiker's Guide to the Galaxy*

6. *Fame*'s

1. What kind of house do Hunca Munca and Tom Thumb vandalize in the Beatrix Potter story *The Tale of Two Bad Mice*?

2. What fashion designer was 18 when he became an apprentice to Christian Dior?

3. What author had a house in Jamaica called Goldeneye?

4. What hugely successful movie was based on a book by Margaret Mitchell?

5. Who, in 2004, became the first person to become a billionaire by writing books?

6. Who runs the orphanage in the musical *Annie*?

1. A doll's house

2. Yves Saint Laurent

3. Ian Fleming

4. *Gone with the Wind*

5. J.K. Rowling

6. Miss Hannigan

1. What Italian city was Michelangelo raised in?

2. Which artist is played by John Leguizamo in the 2001 Oscar-winning musical *Moulin Rouge!*?

3. What country is the setting for Edgar Allan Poe's *The Pit and the Pendulum*?

4. What Rodgers and Hammerstein musical is based on Lynn Riggs' play *Green Grow the Lilacs*?

5. How many lords are leaping in the song *The Twelve Days of Christmas*?

6. What age is dawning in the musical *Hair*?

1. Florence

2. Henri de Toulouse-Lautrec

3. Spain

4. *Oklahoma!*

5. Ten

6. Aquarius

1. Who's the hero of Kenneth Grahame's children's classic *The Wind in the Willows*?

2. Which daughter of a famous singer resigned from *Chloé* in 2001 to enter into a venture with *Gucci*?

3. Who had the Ring immediately before Bilbo took it in *The Hobbit*?

4. Whose best-selling diary was written by Helen Fielding?

5. What does the fairy godmother transform into a coach for Cinderella?

6. What did *Fender* name the follow up to their *Telecaster* guitar with the intention of evoking the new age of jet aircraft?

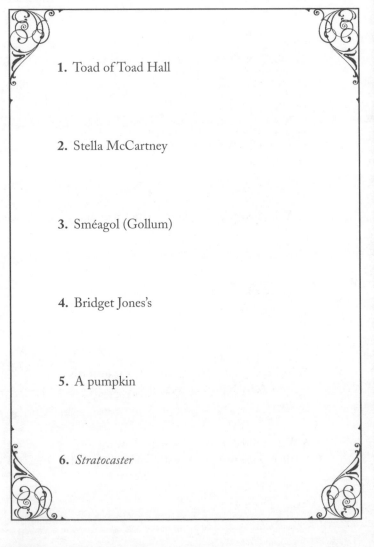

1. Toad of Toad Hall

2. Stella McCartney

3. Sméagol (Gollum)

4. Bridget Jones's

5. A pumpkin

6. *Stratocaster*

1. What Lionel Bart musical is based on a Dickens novel about an orphan?

2. Which champagne company took over the perfume wing of the *Givenchy* fashion house in 1981?

3. What nationality was Paul Cézanne?

4. What annual celebration is taking place at the start of *Great Expectations*?

5. What musical famously saw Yul Brynner enjoying its *Shall We Dance* routine?

6. Who painted the Sistine Chapel ceiling?

1. *Oliver!*

2. *Veuve Clicquot*

3. French

4. Christmas Eve

5. *The King and I*

6. Michelangelo

1. What city were people generally heading for if they stayed at the Admiral Benbow Inn in *Treasure Island*?

2. What book mentions Colin Firth and Hugh Grant who both went on to star in the movie?

3. What mythical creature was born from the blood when Perseus chopped off Medusa's head?

4. What was the name of Vincent van Gogh's art dealer brother?

5. What armless statue in the Louvre is described as "the most famous work of art of the ancient Greek era"?

6. What are the surnames of Italian fashion designers Domenico and Stefano whose celebrity clients have included Madonna and Demi Moore?

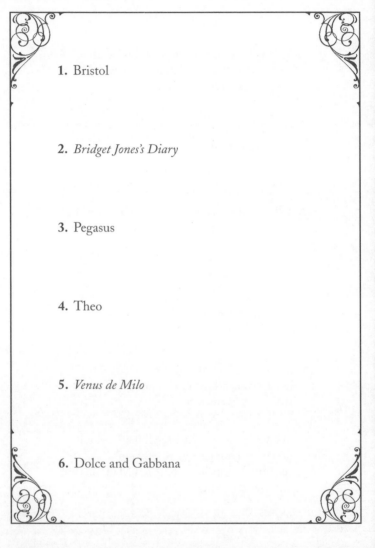

1. Bristol

2. *Bridget Jones's Diary*

3. Pegasus

4. Theo

5. *Venus de Milo*

6. Dolce and Gabbana

1. What writer invented a middle initial to go with her real first one, as her publisher feared boys wouldn't buy books by a woman?

2. What 1955 musical movie was filmed in Arizona because its title state was so heavily developed?

3. Which of the Three Tenors set up his own international competition for young singers in 1982?

4. What color is known as "vert" on a coat of arms?

5. What do the boys use to start a signal fire in *Lord of the Flies*?

6. What fashion designer owns Maxim's restaurant in Paris?

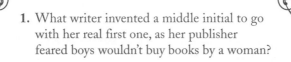

1. Joanne Rowling

2. *Oklahoma!*

3. Luciano Pavarotti

4. Green

5. Piggy's glasses

6. Pierre Cardin

1. What novel-inspired cannibalistic role did Anthony Hopkins say he based partly on *HAL 9000*, the *Space Odyssey* computer?

2. How many times does Conan Doyle refer to Sherlock Holmes wearing a deerstalker hat in his four novels and 56 short stories?

3. What creatures in *The Lord of the Rings* are referred to as goblins in *The Hobbit*?

4. Which famous guitarist pioneered the solid-body electric guitar with the *Gibson* guitar company?

5. Which French museum's entrance is beneath a giant glass pyramid?

6. What feisty film duo ends a road trip by driving a *Thunderbird* off a cliff?

1. Hannibal Lecter

2. Zero

3. Orcs

4. Les Paul

5. The Louvre's

6. Thelma & Louise

1. What kind of flowers did Mary Poppins wear in her hair?

2. What is the name of cartoon character Charlie Brown's dog?

3. What type of drum has vibrating wires across its bottom?

4. What diet did George Bernard Shaw stick to throughout his adult life?

5. Who provided the voice of Mickey Mouse from 1928 to 1946?

6. What D-word is most commonly given to the percussionist in a rock band?

1. Daisies

2. Snoopy

3. Snare drum

4. Vegetarianism

5. Walt Disney

6. Drummer

1. What William Golding novel tells the story of a group of boys cast away on a desert island?

2. What children's author wrote screenplays for the movies *You Only Live Twice* and *Chitty Chitty Bang Bang*?

3. Which French fashion designer created the conical bra for Madonna's Blond Ambition tour?

4. What novel by D.H. Lawrence finds Gudrun and Ursula Brangwen from *The Rainbow* all grown up?

5. Which ballet star, who was born on a train traveling across Siberia, defected to the West in 1961?

6. What Paris cathedral's bells were rung by Quasimodo?

1. *Lord of the Flies*

2. Roald Dahl

3. Jean-Paul Gaultier

4. *Women in Love*

5. Rudolf Nureyev

6. Notre Dame's

1. Who remarked when Gertrude Stein complained she didn't look like a portrait he'd painted: "You will Gertrude, you will"?

2. Who illustrated the original *Winnie-the-Pooh* books?

3. What movie starring Tobey Maguire and Michael Caine won a Best Adapted Screenplay Oscar for John Irving?

4. Which of the Bennet sisters is 15 years old at the start of *Pride and Prejudice*?

5. What Dublin-born author won both a Nobel Prize and an Academy Award during his lifetime?

6. What name was given to the O'Hara plantation in *Gone with the Wind*, which author Margaret Mitchell originally called Fountenoy Hall?

1. Pablo Picasso

2. E.H. Shepard

3. *The Cider House Rules*

4. Lydia

5. George Bernard Shaw

6. Tara

1. What kinds of animals temporarily take over Toad Hall, in *The Wind in the Willows*?

2. What Mozart opera focuses on fiancée swapping as its theme?

3. What job does Joe teach to Pip in *Great Expectations*?

4. What kind of creatures are Nag and Nagaina who plan to kill Rikki-Tikki-Tavi in *The Jungle Book*?

5. What four-letter girl's name gave Jane Austen the title for a comic novel?

6. Who is overawed by the hustle and bustle of riverside life when he is the first character introduced to readers of *The Wind in the Willows*?

1. Weasels

2. *Così fan tutte*

3. Blacksmith

4. Cobras

5. Emma

6. Mole

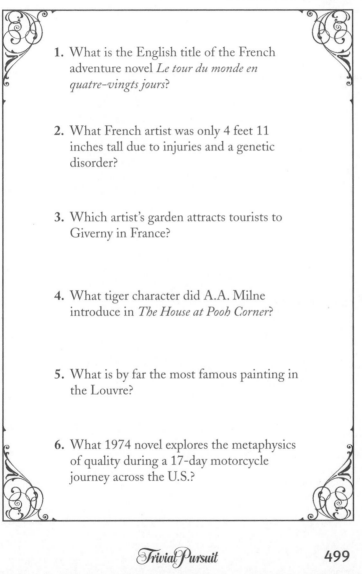

1. What is the English title of the French adventure novel *Le tour du monde en quatre-vingts jours*?

2. What French artist was only 4 feet 11 inches tall due to injuries and a genetic disorder?

3. Which artist's garden attracts tourists to Giverny in France?

4. What tiger character did A.A. Milne introduce in *The House at Pooh Corner*?

5. What is by far the most famous painting in the Louvre?

6. What 1974 novel explores the metaphysics of quality during a 17-day motorcycle journey across the U.S.?

1. *Around the World in Eighty Days*

2. Henri de Toulouse-Lautrec

3. Claude Monet's

4. Tigger

5. The *Mona Lisa*

6. *Zen and the Art of Motorcycle Maintenance*

1. What eye complaint is blamed for the reddish tone of some of Monet's paintings?

2. What musical is based on the book *Anna and the King of Siam*?

3. What war is taking place in the novel *Lord of the Flies*?

4. Who, according to *The Da Vinci Code*, sits next to Jesus' right hand in Leonardo's *The Last Supper*, rather than St. John as always thought?

5. Which artist did Matisse and Picasso call "the father of us all"?

6. What musical instrument does Goody King play in the musical *Fame*?

1. Cataracts

2. *The King and I*

3. World War II

4. Mary Magdalene

5. Paul Cézanne

6. Saxophone

1. What was Tchaikovsky's first ballet?

2. What did a Seoul cinema owner cut out of the *The Sound of Music* when it was released in South Korea so he could fit in more screenings each day?

3. Which painting's eyes gaze out from the cover of *The Da Vinci Code*?

4. What was Cinderella's real name?

5. Who murders Nancy in *Oliver Twist*?

6. What British city's name is attached to Michelangelo's *The Virgin and Child with Saint John and Angels* now displayed in London's National Gallery?

1. *Swan Lake*

2. The songs

3. The *Mona Lisa*'s

4. Ella

5. Bill Sikes

6. Manchester's (Manchester Madonna)

1. What colorful book introduced readers to 11-year-old Anne Shirley?

2. Which city's Merrion Square boasts a statue of Oscar Wilde?

3. What musical instrument is Antonio Stradivari most famous for making?

4. What is the first name of Agatha Christie's tweedy sleuth Miss Marple?

5. What town was the home of Mistress Ford and Mistress Page, Shakespeare's *Merry Wives*?

6. What musical's movie premiere was preceded by a parade of horse drawn surreys with fringes on top?

1. *Anne of Green Gables*

2. Dublin's

3. Violin

4. Jane

5. Windsor

6. *Oklahoma!*'s

1. Whose mother helped fund a museum to his memory at Albi, his birthplace, after he died of alcoholism and syphilis?

2. What is the English title of the Manet painting depicting a nude woman enjoying a picnic with two clothed men?

3. Who spent months rehearsing for *My Fair Lady* then had most of her singing dubbed by Marni Nixon?

4. What nursery rhyme character was arachnophobic?

5. Which 18-year-old married 26-year-old Anne Hathaway in November 1582?

6. Which *James Bond* novel is told in the first person by a fictional character called Vivienne Michel who Ian Fleming also gives co-author credit?

1. Henri de Toulouse-Lautrec's

2. *The Luncheon on the Grass*

3. Audrey Hepburn

4. Little Miss Muffet

5. William Shakespeare

6. *The Spy Who Loved Me*

1. What is the better-known name of crime fiction writer Lady Mallowan D.B.E.?

2. Who replaced Severus Snape as Potions Master at Hogwarts School?

3. What Jane Austen novel has a main character named Fanny Price?

4. What was the first Mickey Mouse movie with synchronized sound?

5. Which planet's satellites are mostly named after Shakespeare characters?

6. Which artist is known as the Father of Impressionism?

1. Agatha Christie

2. Horace Slughorn

3. *Mansfield Park*

4. *Steamboat Willie*

5. Uranus'

6. Camille Pissarro

1. What horse-like animal with a single horn often appears as a supporter on coats of arms?

2. What zoo animals were set free in the title of John Irving's first novel?

3. What century did Rembrandt live in?

4. What sport was most frequently featured in Degas' paintings?

5. Where does Harry Potter have a lightning-shaped scar?

6. What century saw the death of Paul Cézanne?

1. Unicorn

2. Bears

3. 17th

4. Horseracing

5. On his forehead

6. 20th (1906)

1. What major musical of the 1960s was written by James Rado, Gerome Ragni and Galt MacDermot?

2. What sport is most frequently featured in John Irving novels?

3. What is replaced in the hand of William Shakespeare's graveside memorial bust each year on the anniversary of his claimed birthday?

4. Who is the last remaining survivor from Earth when it is destroyed in *The Hitchhiker's Guide to the Galaxy*?

5. What rock band's album *The Piper at the Gates of Dawn* was named after a chapter title from *The Wind in the Willows*?

6. What card game is featured in the novel *Casino Royale*?

1. *Hair*

2. Wrestling

3. Pen (Quill)

4. Arthur Dent

5. Pink Floyd's

6. Baccarat

1. What disability do both Quasimodo and the judge who sentenced him to the pillory suffer from in *The Hunchback of Notre Dame*?

2. What kind of creature is Rikki-Tikki-Tavi?

3. What Verdi opera includes the popular La donna è mobile?

4. Which Roald Dhal duo is cruel to animals until the Roly-Poly Bird arrives from Africa to help the monkeys get revenge?

5. Who is the tomboy main character in *Little Women*?

6. What island does the *The Statue of Liberty* stand on?

1. Deafness

2. Mongoose

3. *Rigoletto*

4. The Twits

5. Josephine (Jo) March

6. Liberty Island

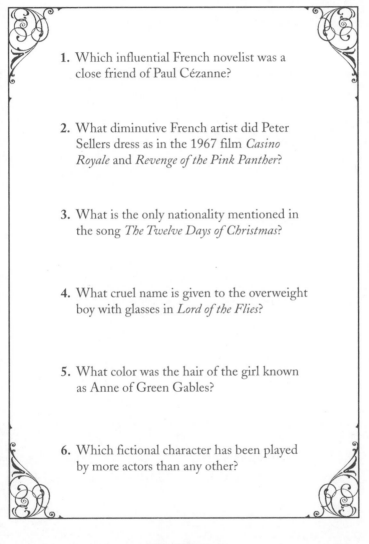

1. Which influential French novelist was a close friend of Paul Cézanne?

2. What diminutive French artist did Peter Sellers dress as in the 1967 film *Casino Royale* and *Revenge of the Pink Panther*?

3. What is the only nationality mentioned in the song *The Twelve Days of Christmas*?

4. What cruel name is given to the overweight boy with glasses in *Lord of the Flies*?

5. What color was the hair of the girl known as Anne of Green Gables?

6. Which fictional character has been played by more actors than any other?

1. Émile Zola

2. Henri de Toulouse-Lautrec

3. French

4. Piggy

5. Red

6. Sherlock Holmes

1. What subject does Miss Sherman teach in the musical *Fame*?

2. Who conducted the Philadelphia Orchestra and shook hands with Mickey Mouse in *Fantasia*?

3. Which Dickens character asked for more?

4. What Christmas treat does Pip give to the hungry convict in *Great Expectations*?

5. What barbecue snack gave Mickey Mouse his first spoken words?

6. What name did the meaner of Cinderella's stepsisters call her in the story by Charles Perrault?

1. English

2. Leopold Stokowski

3. Oliver Twist

4. Pork pie

5. Hot dogs

6. Cinderwench

1. What was the follow-up book to *Bridget Jones's Diary*?

2. What war provides the background for *Gone with the Wind*?

3. What Beatrix Potter character has roasted grasshopper for supper after failing to catch minnows?

4. What eight words from *Gone with the Wind* were voted the number one movie quote by the American Film Institute?

5. What gift is first presented on the fifth day in the song *The Twelve Days of Christmas*?

6. Who is the well-known wife of anesthetist Dr. Neil Murray?

1. *Bridget Jones: The Edge of Reason*

2. The Civil War

3. Mr. Jeremy Fisher

4. "Frankly, my dear, I don't give a damn"

5. Five golden rings

6. J.K. Rowling

1. What classic movie's lead role did Gary Cooper turn down with the words: "[It] will be the biggest flop in Hollywood history"?

2. What road film highlights two buddies' search for freedom on their way to Mardi Gras?

3. How old is the teenage lead character at the end of *Anne of Green Gables*?

4. Who composed the *Brandenburg Concertos*?

5. How many of the gifts in the song *The Twelve Days of Christmas* include humans?

6. Who was married to Andrew Lloyd Weber when he composed *The Phantom of the Opera* for her voice?

1. *Gone with the Wind*

2. *Easy Rider*

3. 16

4. Johann Sebastian Bach

5. Five

6. Sarah Brightman

1. What screenplay won George Bernard Shaw a 1938 Oscar and was the first British film to include the word *bloody*?

2. Which literary animal lost his jacket and shoes while raiding Mr. McGregor's garden?

3. What is the alternative name for the *Mona Lisa*?

4. Which artist's *Impression Sunrise* gave its name to the whole impressionist movement?

5. What musical's show-stopping songs include *Mr. Cellophane* and *Razzle Dazzle*?

6. Who considered founding a utopian art colony at Arles in France prior to his suicide?

1. *Pygmalion*

2. Peter Rabbit

3. *La Gioconda*

4. Claude Monet's

5. *Chicago*'s

6. Vincent van Gogh

1. What novel by Louisa May Alcott tells about the lives and loves of four sisters?

2. What was the four-letter nickname of French fashion designer Gabrielle Bonheur Chanel?

3. What children's book hero did the cruel Dursleys bring up after an evil wizard killed his parents?

4. What Disney musical movie was the first to be shown to large public audiences with stereophonic sound?

5. What painter's mental state is revealed in 750 letters he wrote to his brother, Theo?

6. Whose wife was turned into a pillar of salt?

1. *Little Women*

2. Coco

3. Harry Potter

4. *Fantasia*

5. Vincent van Gogh's

6. Lot's

1. What John Irving novel with an armadillo on its cover tells the story of an extremely short boy with a very high-pitched voice?

2. What Shakespeare play asks: "To be or not to be"?

3. Which city staged the premiere of *Gone with the Wind* that actress Hattie McDaniel couldn't attend due to Georgia's segregation laws?

4. What Welsh actress filled the role of Velma Kelly in the movie version of *Chicago*?

5. What movie features singing siblings named Liesl, Friedrich, Brigitta, Louisa, Kurt, Marta and Gretl?

6. What's the Shakespeare play if "All the world's a stage"?

1. *A Prayer for Owen Meany*

2. *Hamlet*

3. Atlanta

4. Catherine Zeta-Jones

5. *The Sound of Music*

6. *As You Like It*

1. Which French writer wrote the novel
   Around the World in Eighty Days?

2. Whose still-life painting, *Rideau, Cruchon et
   Compotier*, sold for $60.5 million in 1999?

3. What writer is known as the Bard?

4. What musical instrument does Sherlock
   Holmes play for relaxation?

5. Who took the role of Lysander in the
   Disney version of *A Midsummer Night's
   Dream*?

6. Which of the Three Tenors lived in Mexico
   from the age of eight?

1. Jules Verne

2. Paul Cézanne's

3. William Shakespeare

4. Violin

5. Mickey Mouse

6. Plácido Domingo

1. What flowers was Monet most famous for painting?

2. What nationality was Roald Dahl?

3. What name is given to the metal bars running across the neck of a guitar?

4. What country provides the setting for *The King and I*?

5. What did Hannibal Lecter say French people taste like?

6. What is the name of Frodo's faithful gardener in *The Lord of the Rings*?

1. Water lilies

2. Welsh

3. Frets

4. Siam (Thailand)

5. Chicken

6. Sam Gamgee

1. What is the name of Squire Trelawney's ship in *Treasure Island*?

2. What Broadway musical was based on the comic strip Little Orphan Annie?

3. What kinds of creatures were Flopsy and Mopsy in the first book by Beatrix Potter?

4. What is Mr. Sowerberry's job in *Oliver Twist*?

5. Who produced two booklets for *Comic Relief* under the names of Newt Scamander and Kennilworthy Whisp?

6. What 1928 novel by D.H. Lawrence was banned in the U.S. until 1959?

1. *Hispaniola*

2. *Annie*

3. Rabbits

4. Undertaker

5. J.K. Rowling

6. *Lady Chatterley's Lover*

1. What musical character came from the easterly wind with an umbrella and a carpet bag?

2. What musical is based on the play *Pygmalion*?

3. What New York landmark stands in size 879 sandals?

4. What decade was Agatha Christie's *Murder on the Orient Express* set in?

5. What are the six characters in the title of Luigi Pirandello's play in search of?

6. What animal's head is placed on a stick in *Lord of the Flies*?

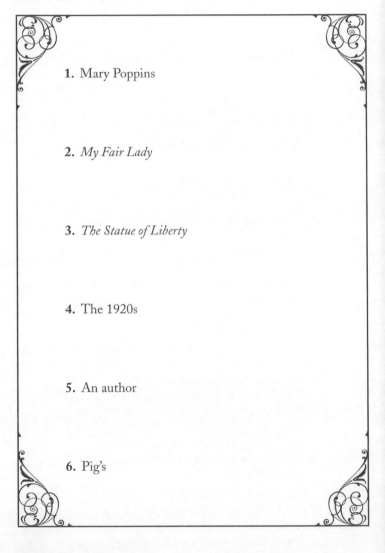

1. Mary Poppins

2. *My Fair Lady*

3. *The Statue of Liberty*

4. The 1920s

5. An author

6. Pig's

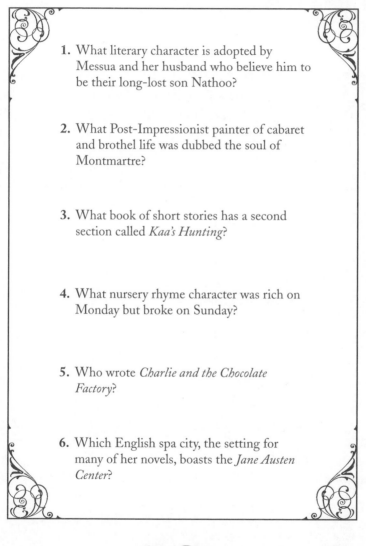

1. What literary character is adopted by Messua and her husband who believe him to be their long-lost son Nathoo?

2. What Post-Impressionist painter of cabaret and brothel life was dubbed the soul of Montmartre?

3. What book of short stories has a second section called *Kaa's Hunting*?

4. What nursery rhyme character was rich on Monday but broke on Sunday?

5. Who wrote *Charlie and the Chocolate Factory*?

6. Which English spa city, the setting for many of her novels, boasts the *Jane Austen Center*?

1. Mowgli

2. Henri de Toulouse-Lautrec

3. *The Jungle Book*

4. Solomon Grundy

5. Roald Dahl

6. Bath

1. Which character narrates all but four of the Sherlock Holmes stories?

2. Who spent a month in jail for insubordinate behavior—Johann Sebastian Bach or Jerry Lee Lewis?

3. How old is Annie, according to the musical's script?

4. Who described his *Lady Windermere's Fan* as: "One of those modern drawing-room plays with pink lampshades"?

5. Who had to face the multi-headed Hydra in the second of his labors?

6. What artist's largest work is called *The Night Watch*?

1. Dr. Watson

2. Johann Sebastian Bach

3. 11

4. Oscar Wilde

5. Hercules

6. Rembrandt's

1. What Jane Austen book has many parallels with *Bridget Jones's Diary* including the main male character's surname?

2. What book does each girl receive as a Christmas present at the start of *Little Women*?

3. What war saw the bombing of Guernica that inspired one of Picasso's most moving paintings?

4. Who was the subject of almost 100 Rembrandt paintings, drawings and etchings?

5. What style of painting are Cézanne, Degas, Manet and Monet all linked with?

6. What English writer died on the same date as Spanish author and poet Miguel de Cervantes?

1. *Pride and Prejudice*

2. A Bible

3. Spanish Civil War

4. Rembrandt

5. Impressionism

6. William Shakespeare

1. How many people dance a *pas de deux*?

2. Which city sees Pip striving to become a gentleman in *Great Expectations*?

3. Who took Oliver Twist into his home even though he had been accused of picking his pockets?

4. Who devised the towering framework that supports the *The Statue of Liberty*?

5. What birthday does Bridget celebrate in the course of the book *Bridget Jones's Diary*?

6. What was the middle name of composer Bach?

1. Two

2. London

3. Mr. Brownlow

4. Alexandre-Gustave Eiffel

5. 33rd

6. Sebastian

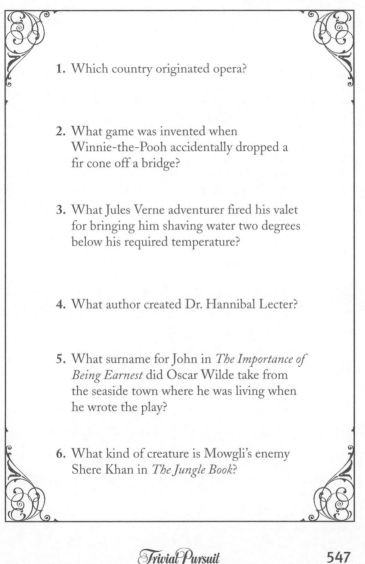

1. Which country originated opera?

2. What game was invented when Winnie-the-Pooh accidentally dropped a fir cone off a bridge?

3. What Jules Verne adventurer fired his valet for bringing him shaving water two degrees below his required temperature?

4. What author created Dr. Hannibal Lecter?

5. What surname for John in *The Importance of Being Earnest* did Oscar Wilde take from the seaside town where he was living when he wrote the play?

6. What kind of creature is Mowgli's enemy Shere Khan in *The Jungle Book*?

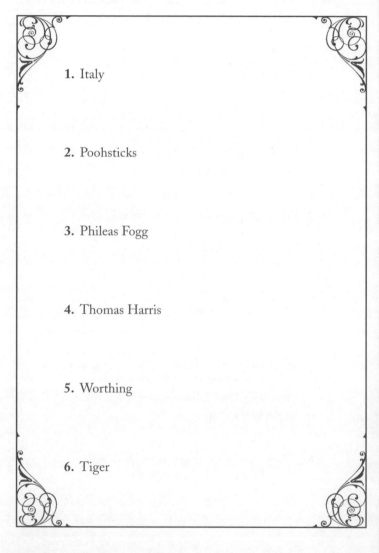

1. Italy

2. Poohsticks

3. Phileas Fogg

4. Thomas Harris

5. Worthing

6. Tiger

1. What is by far the most famous New York–based piece of work by French sculptor Auguste Bartholdi?

2. What major comedy star played Garp in the movie adaptation of John Irving's *The World According to Garp*?

3. What D.H. Lawrence novel with a colorful title was banned in the U.K. following a 1915 obscenity trial?

4. Who reputedly told a customs officer: "I have nothing to declare except my genius"?

5. What city provides the setting for *The Phantom of the Opera*?

6. What is the first name of Gianni Versace's sister who took control of the business after his death in 1997?

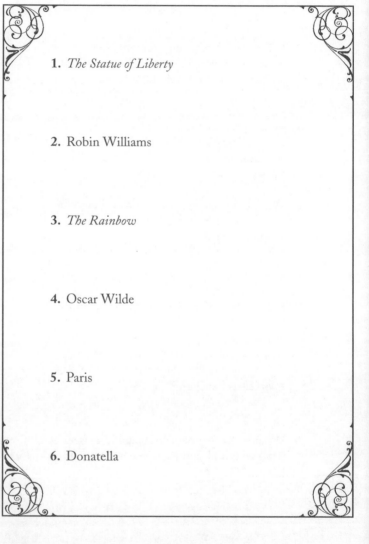

1. *The Statue of Liberty*

2. Robin Williams

3. *The Rainbow*

4. Oscar Wilde

5. Paris

6. Donatella

1. Which Wings album includes *Picasso's Last Words (Drink to Me)*?

2. Who put Humpty Dumpty together again in the traditional nursery rhyme?

3. What form of transportation did George Bernard Shaw give to T.E. Lawrence?

4. What song about her age did 22-year-old Charmain Carr sing in the movie version of *The Sound of Music*?

5. What's the Shakespeare play if Antonio owes Shylock a pound of flesh?

6. What is Jack Dawkins' nickname in *Oliver Twist*?

1. *Band on the Run*

2. No one

3. Motorcycle

4. *Sixteen Going on Seventeen*

5. *The Merchant of Venice*

6. The Artful Dodger

1. Whose paintings include the sensitively titled *Two Half-Naked Women Seen from Behind in the Rue des Moulins Brothel*?

2. What title role was filled by Lon Chaney in 1923, Charles Laughton in 1939 and Anthony Hopkins in 1982?

3. Who's Kanga's son, in the Winnie-the-Pooh stories?

4. Whose *Luncheon of the Boating Party* prints and posters hung in millions of homes in the 1980s?

5. What is the name of the Hobbit in the book with that title?

6. What creepy movie character was briefly known as the Chesapeake Ripper?

1. Henri de Toulouse-Lautrec's

2. The Hunchback of Notre Dame

3. Roo

4. Pierre-Auguste Renoir's

5. Bilbo Baggins

6. Hannibal Lecter

1. How many of the gifts in the song *The Twelve Days of Christmas* do not involve birds?

2. When is Cinderella required to leave the ball?

3. What Shakespeare play is set on January 5?

4. What did Coco Chanel call her bestselling perfume because it was her lucky number?

5. What war do the girls in *Little Women* grow up during?

6. Which impressionist featured his wife, Camille, in *The Woman in the Green Dress*?

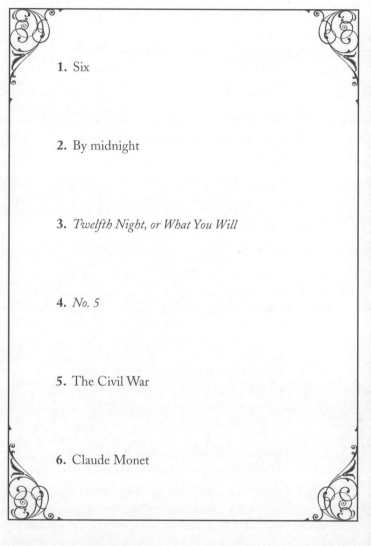

1. Six

2. By midnight

3. *Twelfth Night, or What You Will*

4. *No. 5*

5. The Civil War

6. Claude Monet

1. Who wrote *The Da Vinci Code*?

2. Whose *Coffee Cantata* concerns a girl whose father demands she loses her addiction to coffee before she can marry?

3. What was the first movie adaptation of a Hannibal Lecter novel to feature Anthony Hopkins?

4. What D.H. Lawrence novel was originally titled *Tenderness*?

5. Which Shakespeare play sees the brother of a novice nun sentenced to death for fornication?

6. What snack shares its name with the famous cartoon strip by Charles M. Schulz?

1. Dan Brown

2. Johann Sebastian Bach's

3. *The Silence of the Lambs*

4. *Lady Chatterley's Lover*

5. *Measure for Measure*

6. *Peanuts*

1. Which artist had his wish for 60 beggars to follow his coffin to the grave?

2. What are bongo drums traditionally held between for playing?

3. What musical is based on the trials of murderesses Beulah Annan and Belva Gaertner?

4. What is the name of the gypsy girl who Quasimodo, the Hunchback of Notre Dame, fell in love with?

5. Who was Anne of Green Gables' best friend?

6. What is the only American state with its official song taken from a Rodgers and Hammerstein musical?

1. Leonardo da Vinci

2. The knees

3. *Chicago*

4. Esmeralda

5. Diana Barry

6. Oklahoma

1. Who is the richest character in *The Wind in the Willows*?

2. What does the sailor hold in his right hand on Margaret Thatcher's coat of arms?

3. What crashes from the ceiling to provide one of the highlights of Lloyd Weber's *The Phantom of the Opera*?

4. What was the name of the man cub in *The Jungle Book*?

5. What is the name of the dog in the musical *Annie*?

6. What's the musical if *I Whistle a Happy Tune*?

1. Mr. Toad

2. Binoculars

3. Chandelier

4. Mowgli

5. Sandy

6. *The King and I*

1. Where does Spanish rain fall, according to *My Fair Lady*?

2. What Tchaikovsky ballet includes *Dance of the Sugar-Plum Fairy* and *Waltz of the Flowers*?

3. What is Bridget Jones's home city?

4. Which composer of the *Rite of Spring* was still alive to see his music used in Disney's *Fantasia*?

5. What Italian town takes tourists to the workshop of renowned stringed-instrument maker Antonio Stradivari?

6. What nationality was Vincent van Gogh?

1. On the plain

2. *The Nutcracker*

3. London

4. Igor Stravinsky

5. Cremona

6. Dutch

1. What kind of creature is Mrs. Tiggy-Winkle in a book by Beatrix Potter?

2. Which Shakespeare play opens with the King of Navarre and three companions taking an oath to devote three years to studying?

3. What English actress did Rex Harrison want as his movie Eliza Doolittle because she'd played the role opposite him on Broadway?

4. What fictional detective is often depicted smoking a pipe while wearing a deerstalker hat?

5. What famous fictional cannibal made his first appearance in the 1981 novel *Red Dragon*?

6. What M-word means the words at the bottom of a coat of arms?

1. Hedgehog

2. *Love's Labor's Lost*

3. Julie Andrews

4. Sherlock Holmes

5. Hannibal Lecter

6. Motto

1. What period preceded Picasso's *Rose Period*?

2. What British musical made 13-year-old Liam Mower the youngest Laurence Olivier Award-winner in 2006?

3. What was subtitled *The American Tribal Love/Rock Musical*?

4. What color spot led to the death of Billy Bones in *Treasure Island*?

5. What Beatrix Potter character was rescued by a collie and two foxhounds?

6. What name is usually given to hideously deformed Quasimodo who features in a French novel first published in 1831?

1. *Blue Period*

2. *Billy Elliot*

3. *Hair*

4. Black

5. Jemima Puddleduck

6. The Hunchback of Notre Dame

1. Who aimed his *Emporio* clothing line at younger buyers?

2. Whose chest contained the *Treasure Island* map?

3. Whose *Small House* is the subject of the play acted out during *The King and I*?

4. Which British writer was condemned as a pornographer yet called: "The greatest imaginative novelist of our generation," in an obituary by E.M. Forster?

5. Which great Renaissance artist designed the dome of St. Peter's Basilica in Rome?

6. What car model gave its name to an alien in *The Hitchhiker's Guide to the Galaxy*?

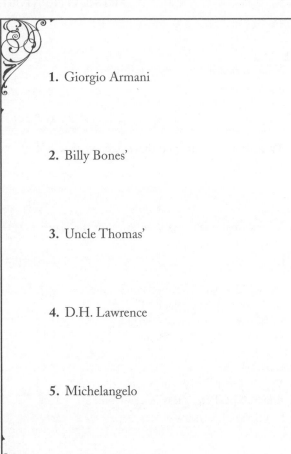

1. Giorgio Armani

2. Billy Bones'

3. Uncle Thomas'

4. D.H. Lawrence

5. Michelangelo

6. *Ford Prefect*

1. What American writer went *On the Road* to find life's answers?

2. What lung disease killed Paul Cézanne a week after he caught a chill and collapsed while painting in a thunderstorm?

3. Who became an animated Disney megastar after replacing Oswald the Lucky Rabbit?

4. What novel by Lucy Maud Montgomery became Canada's longest-running main stage musical?

5. What does Peppermint Patty always call Charlie Brown in the *Peanuts* cartoon strip?

6. What Chaucer collection of stories was told by a group of pilgrims on their way to a shrine?

1. Jack Keroauc

2. Pneumonia

3. Mickey Mouse

4. *Anne of Green Gables*

5. Chuck

6. *Canterbury Tales*

1. What country was the birthplace of two of the Three Tenors?

2. What form of transportation did the *Around the World in Eighty Days* travelers use to cover the gap between stations on the unfinished Indian railroad?

3. Which Biblical figure by Michelangelo has been called "the most recognizable statue in the history of art"?

4. What future Broadway hit closed in Boston rather than obey a court order to cut the nudity in 1970?

5. What is the alternative name for a guitar pick?

6. What do sisters Elinor and Marianne Dashwood represent in the title of a Jane Austen novel?

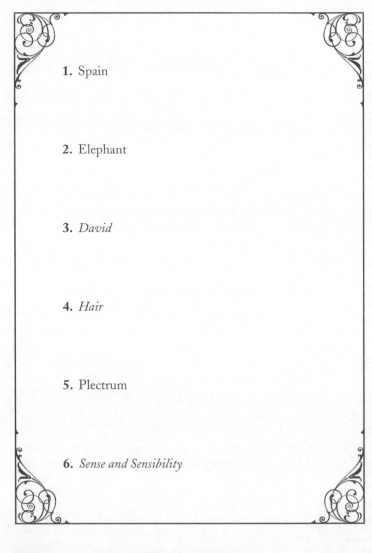

1. Spain

2. Elephant

3. *David*

4. *Hair*

5. Plectrum

6. *Sense and Sensibility*

1. What is the name of the chubby diva in the musical *Fame*?

2. What was William Shakespeare's hometown?

3. What evolutionist penned *The Descent of Man* in 1871?

4. What church must be visited to see the tomb of Sir Isaac Newton, which is instrumental to the plot of *The Da Vinci Code*?

5. What nationality was composer Johann Sebastian Bach?

6. What popular musical was shut down by the government and its cast forced to leave the country when it opened in Mexico in 1968?

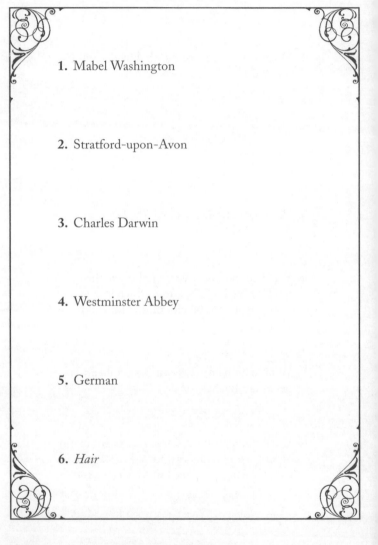

1. Mabel Washington

2. Stratford-upon-Avon

3. Charles Darwin

4. Westminster Abbey

5. German

6. *Hair*

1. What part of the body does an orthopedic doctor treat?

2. What astrological chart takes its name from a Greek word meaning "circle of little animals"?

3. What fruit did Algerian priest Pierre Clément create in 1902?

4. What shape is the piston in a *Wankel* engine?

5. What element did Pierre and Marie Curie discover in 1898?

6. What acid gives citrus fruits their distinctive sharp flavor?

1. Bones

2. Zodiac

3. Clementine

4. Triangular

5. Radium

6. Citric acid

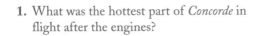

1. What was the hottest part of *Concorde* in flight after the engines?

2. What does the computer term WORM stand for?

3. What was the main method of food preservation used by the Incas to store their potatoes?

4. What sign of the zodiac is the first air sign of the calendar year?

5. What valuable product is obtained from the sturgeon?

6. What is at an average distance of 238,857 miles from the Earth?

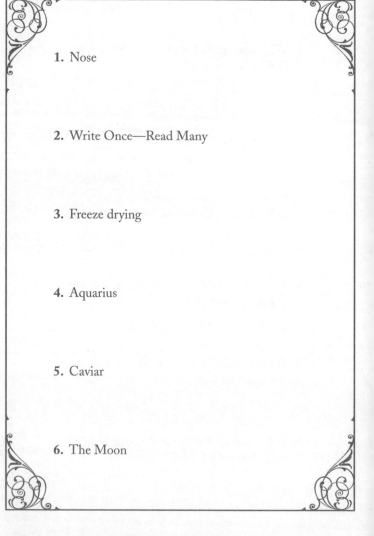

1. Nose

2. Write Once—Read Many

3. Freeze drying

4. Aquarius

5. Caviar

6. The Moon

1. What is the popular name for what *NASA* refers to as its Space Transportation System?

2. What do the British call gasoline?

3. What layer of the Earth's atmosphere sits between the troposphere and mesosphere?

4. What is the common name for the main vent at the top of a volcano?

5. How many carats is pure gold?

6. What disease takes its name from medieval Italian words for "bad air"?

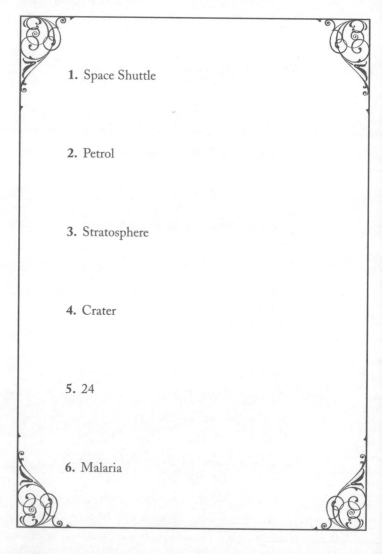

1. Space Shuttle

2. Petrol

3. Stratosphere

4. Crater

5. 24

6. Malaria

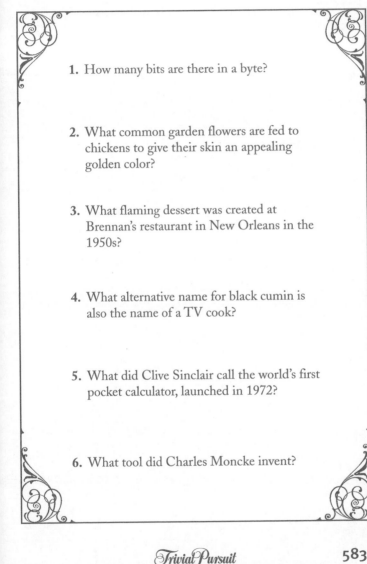

1. How many bits are there in a byte?

2. What common garden flowers are fed to chickens to give their skin an appealing golden color?

3. What flaming dessert was created at Brennan's restaurant in New Orleans in the 1950s?

4. What alternative name for black cumin is also the name of a TV cook?

5. What did Clive Sinclair call the world's first pocket calculator, launched in 1972?

6. What tool did Charles Moncke invent?

1. Eight

2. Marigolds

3. Bananas Foster

4. Nigella

5. *Sinclair Executive*

6. The monkey wrench

1. What name is given to male rhinoceroses?

2. What British breed of cat is tailless?

3. What is the five-letter name for a young dog?

4. What name, originally describing a person who performed calculations, has now come to mean an electronic machine that performs multiple tasks?

5. Which English sci-fi writer first conceived the idea of artificial communication satellites in 1945?

6. Who developed the classifications we use for clouds?

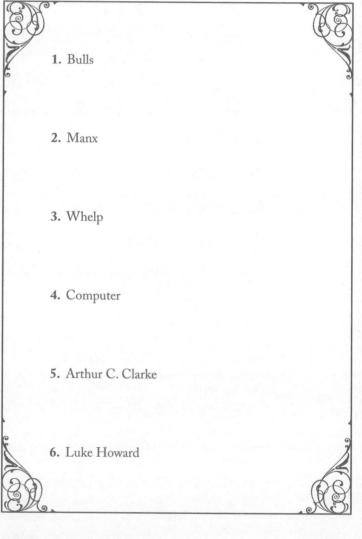

1. Bulls

2. Manx

3. Whelp

4. Computer

5. Arthur C. Clarke

6. Luke Howard

1. What garden visitors are classified in two main families, *hesperioidea* and *papilionoidea*?

2. What berry has the highest antioxidant content?

3. What is the largest dinosaur so far discovered?

4. What is the only dog rated above the Basset Hound for its sense of smell?

5. What is defined as a "ferrous alloy with a minimum of 10 percent chromium content"?

6. Which was the first *iPod* without a screen or scroll wheel?

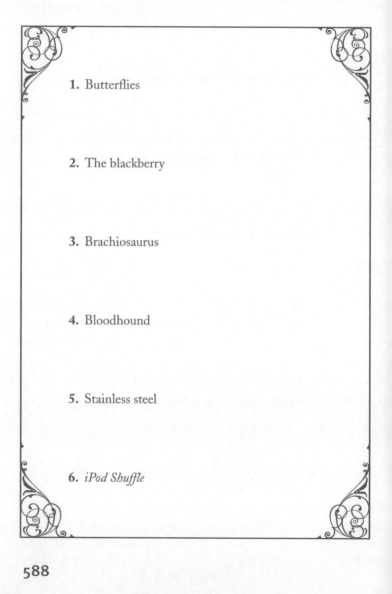

1. Butterflies

2. The blackberry

3. Brachiosaurus

4. Bloodhound

5. Stainless steel

6. *iPod Shuffle*

1. What is the clever-sounding name for a human third molar?

2. What metal is the essential ingredient in a dental amalgam filling?

3. What kind of tree is the General Sherman, which is generally accepted as the world's largest living organism?

4. Who became a household name after inventing fast frozen foods?

5. What is gymnophobia the fear of?

6. What did Thomas Sullivan accidentally invent in 1908 by sending his customers samples in small silk packets?

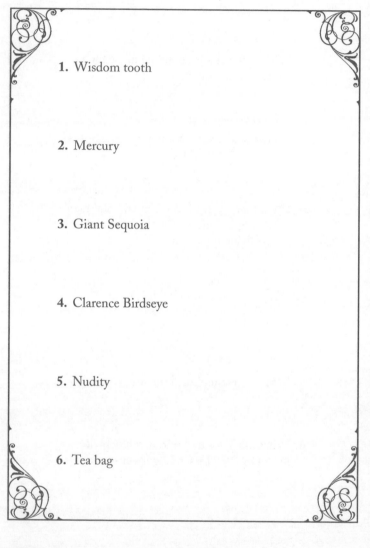

1. Wisdom tooth

2. Mercury

3. Giant Sequoia

4. Clarence Birdseye

5. Nudity

6. Tea bag

1. What registered brand name is now used for the cotton swabs invented in 1923 by Leo Gerstenzang?

2. What did Waldo Hanchett patent in 1848 to make things more comfortable for dental patients?

3. What do whales feed their young?

4. What bird lays the largest eggs?

5. What did James Murray Spangler add to the vacuum cleaner to loosen dust before it was sucked up?

6. What did dentist Levi Spear Parmly first recommend a piece of silk thread for in 1815?

1. *Q-tips*

2. Dentist's chair

3. Milk

4. Ostrich

5. Rotating brushes

6. Dental floss

1. What 1941 invention by *Heinz* and *ICI* kept the troops warm during the D-Day landings?

2. What modern treat takes its name from a stimulating Aztec drink called *Xocoatl*?

3. What simple telescope magnifies the view of distant objects through lenses mounted in a tube and viewed directly through the eyepiece?

4. What is *Canis lupus familiaris*?

5. What method of food preservation was invented for the British Navy in 1813?

6. What tube connects the larynx to the lungs?

1. Self-heating can

2. Chocolate

3. Refracting telescope

4. Pet dog

5. Canning

6. The trachea

1. What is crossed with a blackberry and loganberry to produce a boysenberry?

2. What company did Edwin Land, who developed the world's best-selling instant print camera, found?

3. What name is given to the process of creating fabric from a woolen yarn using a single hook?

4. What prevents the Earth's atmosphere from drifting into space?

5. What four-letter name is given to the killer whale?

6. What does MRI stand for?

1. Raspberry

2. *Polaroid*

3. Crochet

4. Gravity

5. Orca

6. Magnetic resonance imaging

1. Who designed the *Cambridge Z88* mini computer?

2. What does MW stand for on a radio?

3. Which planet was once thought to have canals?

4. How many gigabytes capacity did the first commercially available *iPod* have?

5. What sign of the zodiac is represented by a bull?

6. What has Bill Mogridge's *GRiD Compass 1101* been described as the first true example of?

1. Clive Sinclair

2. Medium wave

3. Mars

4. Five

5. Taurus

6. Laptop computer

1. What symbol shares a key with the number 4 on a standard computer keyboard?

2. Why did celluloid dentures fail to catch on with tea drinkers?

3. What breakfast dish is mostly made from Seville oranges?

4. What name is given to a hybrid formed by a cross between a false killer whale and a bottlenose dolphin?

5. What fishing industry results in the deaths of thousands of dolphins?

6. What bird has the scientific name *struthio camelus*, meaning *sparrow camel*?

1. $ (Dollar sign)

2. Hot liquid softened them

3. Marmalade

4. Wolphin

5. Tuna fishing

6. Ostrich

1. What is the second most common element in the Sun after hydrogen?

2. What birds were traditionally used as gas detectors in coal mines?

3. What is an EKG?

4. What method was first used to send a message across the U.S.A. in March 1955?

5. What three-letter word means the smallest piece of information used by a computer?

6. What is the lowest layer of the Earth's atmosphere called?

1. Helium

2. Canaries

3. An electrocardiogram

4. Fax (Facsimile)

5. Bit

6. Troposphere

1. What has four true varieties: black, white, green and oolong?

2. What item of office equipment, patented in 1883 by William Purvis, enabled secretaries to "sign" letters for their boss?

3. What does an ichthyologist study?

4. What land animal has the longest gestation period?

5. How many fingerlike projections does an African elephant have at the end of its trunk?

6. What did H. Cecil Booth invent the first powered example of after watching a device used for blowing dust off train seats?

1. Tea

2. Rubber stamp

3. Fish

4. Elephant

5. Two

6. Vacuum cleaner

1. What is the common name for the fluid expelled from the body by the process of lacrimation?

2. What element with the symbol I is found in seawater and has a name based on the Greek for *violet*?

3. What company produces the *iPod*?

4. What was the name of the Earth's first artificial satellite?

5. What does an entomologist study?

6. What parts of a Space Shuttle's power system are referred to as S.R.B.s?

1. Tears

2. Iodine

3. Apple Inc.

4. *Sputnik I*

5. Insects

6. Solid rocket boosters

1. What arrived in Britain in 1967 and wiped out most of the country's elm trees?

2. What 1947 invention by Bell Telephone Laboratories spawned pocket-sized radios?

3. Which Space Shuttle comes first alphabetically?

4. What breed of dog is guilty of the most appearances at sheepdog trials?

5. How many wings does a butterfly have?

6. What was the 1914 *Eagle* the first example of from the *Rolls-Royce* factory?

1. Dutch elm disease

2. The transistor

3. *Atlantis*

4. Border Collie

5. Four

6. Aircraft engine

1. What is the national tree of England, Germany, France and the U.S.?

2. What name is given to rain with a particularly low pH?

3. What dog breed spiked in popularity when one starred in the "Yo quiero Taco Bell" TV ads?

4. Which British designer invented the *Dual Cyclone* bagless vacuum cleaner?

5. What did *Nestlé* freeze dry in 1938 that led to the development of powdered food products?

6. What liquid did Swiss candle maker Daniel Peter first add to chocolate in 1867?

1. Oak

2. Acid rain

3. The Chihuahua

4. James Dyson

5. Coffee

6. Milk

1. What name is given to the study of volcanoes?

2. What rank fourth after rice, wheat and maize in terms of human food production?

3. What A-word describes the amount of light allowed to pass through a camera lens?

4. What is the heaviest breed of bear?

5. What occurs when the Sun and the Moon are in conjunction as viewed from Earth?

6. What is the common name for any member of the delphinidae family of swimming mammals?

1. Volcanology or vulcanology

2. Bananas

3. Aperture

4. Polar bear

5. A solar eclipse

6. Dolphin

1. What did the ancient Mayans drink some 2,600 years ago that was turned into a solid treat during the 18th century?

2. What kind of tails do New World monkeys have that Old World monkeys don't?

3. What word describes the habit of some bears for sleeping through the winter?

4. What might you now use to fix the handle of a coffee mug that Dr. Harry Coover discovered in 1952 and rejected because it was too sticky?

5. What South American monkey takes its name due to its similarity in appearance to a nocturnal bird?

6. Which was the first Space Shuttle to be launched?

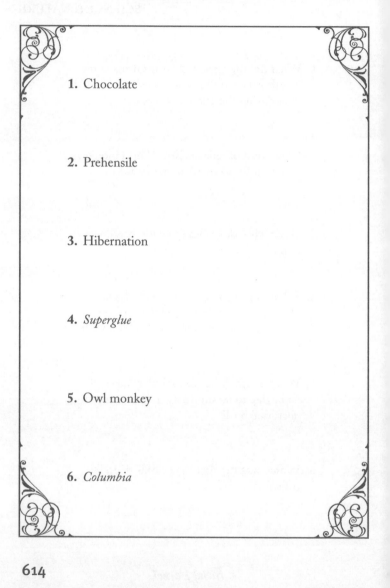

1. Chocolate

2. Prehensile

3. Hibernation

4. *Superglue*

5. Owl monkey

6. *Columbia*

1. What are categorized as the biological class *aves*?

2. What potentially fatal disease is also known as "rabbit fever"—ebola, influenza or tularemia?

3. What do most lobsters and crayfish do with their shell after it has molted?

4. Which is the fourth planet from the Sun?

5. What two metals form the alloy white gold?

6. Where in the U.S. has the maximum wind speed been recorded?

1. Birds

2. Tularemia

3. Eat it

4. Mars

5. Gold and silver

6. Mount Washington, NH

1. What name is given to the sieve-like structure in the upper jaw of plankton-eating whales?

2. What is the common name for butterfly larvae?

3. What is the common name for the *Boeing 747*?

4. What was Alexander Parkes' invention *Parkesine* the first man-made example of?

5. What bird lays the smallest egg in relation to its size?

6. What tree's fruit is candied to produce *marrons glacés*?

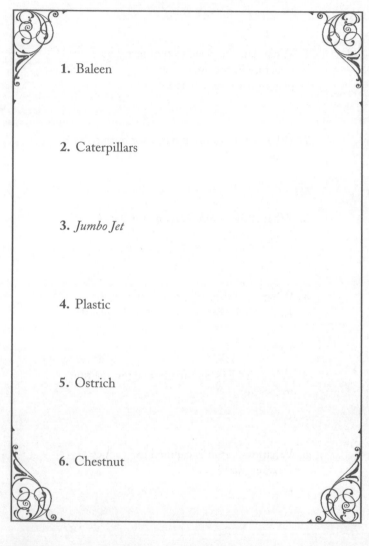

1. Baleen

2. Caterpillars

3. *Jumbo Jet*

4. Plastic

5. Ostrich

6. Chestnut

1. What U-word describes a vacuum cleaner with a bag attached to its vertical handle?

2. What *Volkswagen* car model appears in the International Radio Alphabet?

3. What is the most abundant metal on Earth?

4. What spice comes from the herb called cilantro or Chinese parsley?

5. Which is the largest planet in the solar system?

6. What comes out of a hawsehole?

1. Upright

2. *Golf*

3. Iron

4. Coriander

5. Jupiter

6. Ship's cable

1. What can be found under the hood of a car to visually measure the oil level?

2. What animal produces cashmere wool?

3. What gas makes up approximately 74 percent of the Sun's mass?

4. What does a coleopterist study?

5. What type of dinosaur snatched the man off the toilet in the movie *Jurassic Park*?

6. What is your shirt made from if the fiber was produced by the gossypium shrub?

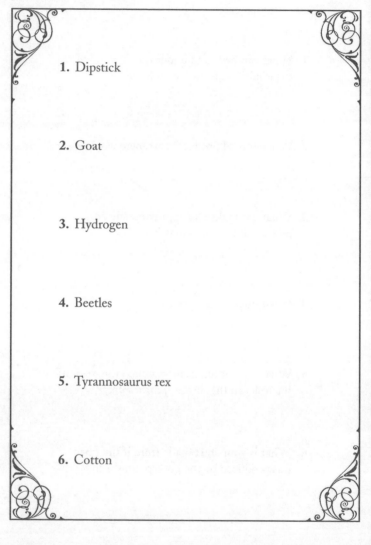

1. Dipstick

2. Goat

3. Hydrogen

4. Beetles

5. Tyrannosaurus rex

6. Cotton

1. How many horns does the average African black rhino have?

2. What is the name for a baby alligator?

3. What essential tool did Ezra Warner patent 45 years after the invention of canned food?

4. How many seats were there across a *Concorde* cabin?

5. Which American airline was the first to order *Boeing 747*s?

6. What is the name for a baby turkey?

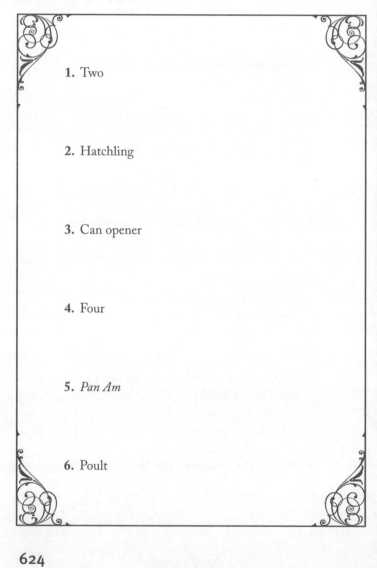

1. Two

2. Hatchling

3. Can opener

4. Four

5. *Pan Am*

6. Poult

1. What type of tea is flavored with oil from the bergamot orange?

2. What are most regularly turned into dagger handles, not an aphrodisiac as commonly thought?

3. What valuable metal has the chemical symbol Au?

4. What is the only phase of the Moon that can produce a solar eclipse?

5. What was the name of the first manned mission to land on the Moon?

6. What are the only vertebrate animals over the weight of 11 pounds that regularly move around by hopping?

1. Earl Grey

2. Rhino horns

3. Gold

4. New Moon

5. *Apollo 11*

6. Kangaroos

1. How many toes on each foot does an ostrich stand on?

2. What was the first vitamin to be discovered and named?

3. Who was the second man to set foot on the Moon?

4. What does a botanist study?

5. What creature boasts the world's largest eyes?

6. What plastic did John Wesley Hyatt invent by combining cellulose and alcoholized camphor?

1. Two

2. Vitamin A

3. Edwin (Buzz) Aldrin

4. Plants

5. Giant squid

6. *Celluloid*

1. What is the name for a young deer?

2. What is the main use for the legume
   phaseolus vulgaris in the canned food
   industry?

3. What P-word is given to birds reared for
   human consumption?

4. What is kept in a ship's binnacle?

5. How many degrees of the sky does each sign
   of the zodiac represent?

6. What type of wool can come from a rabbit?

1. Fawn

2. Baked beans

3. Poultry

4. Compass

5. 30

6. Angora

1. What name is given to domesticated cats that have escaped to live in the wild?

2. What is the three-letter name for a young cheetah?

3. What was the first man-made object to land on the Moon?

4. What was first patented in Britain in 1750 with a recipe consisting mostly of fish and fish bones?

5. What was the first *NASA* program to land an object on Mars that actually sent back information when it got there?

6. What tree measurement do foresters usually make at 4 feet above ground level?

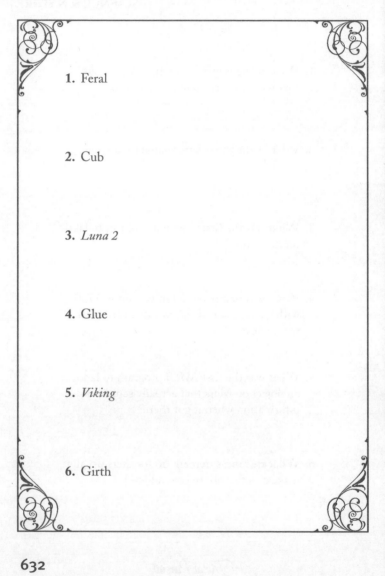

1. Feral

2. Cub

3. *Luna 2*

4. Glue

5. *Viking*

6. Girth

1. What's the common term for precipitation infused by sulfuric and nitric acids?

2. What old type of radio had a cat's whisker?

3. What did the U.S. Postal Service assure weight-conscious customers contains only one-tenth of a calorie?

4. What is the common name for a fruit in which the entire ovary wall ripens to form an edible pericarp?

5. What D-word is the fin on the back of a whale called?

6. What creature was described by the Romans as having the characteristics of a camel and a leopard?

1. Acid rain

2. Crystal set

3. The glue on a stamp

4. Berry

5. Dorsal

6. Giraffe

1. Which rock diva was the first woman to have her signature engraved on a special edition *iPod*?

2. What present-day continent has yielded evidence of the earliest dinosaurs?

3. What name did Neil Armstrong give to the spot where man first touched down on the Moon?

4. What does AM mean to a radio enthusiast?

5. What do astrologers call their chart of predictions based on the position of planets and the signs of the zodiac?

6. What is the only breed of cat that does not have retractable claws?

1. Madonna

2. South America

3. Tranquility Base

4. Amplitude modulation

5. Horoscope

6. Cheetah

1. What does an electroencephalogram show?

2. What name is given to a solar eclipse when the Sun and the Moon are exactly in line but the apparent size of the Moon is smaller than that of the Sun?

3. What metal was Danish astronomer Tycho Brahe's nose made of?

4. What drink is made from the leaves of the *camellia sinensis* bush?

5. Who developed vulcanized rubber and still has his name embossed on the side of tires?

6. What is the only continent without any bees?

1. Electrical activity in the brain

2. Annular eclipse

3. Gold

4. Tea

5. Charles Goodyear

6. Antarctica

1. What collective term describes 2-methylphenol and 4-methylphenol, smelly chemicals found in sweat?

2. What is a dromophobiac afraid to cross?

3. What is a computer's CPU?

4. Where on a fish's body are the growth rings scientists use to determine age?

5. What bird gave its name to the lunar module that took Neil Armstrong to the surface of the Moon?

6. What never works at night and requires a gnomon to tell the time?

1. Odorants

2. A street

3. Central processing unit

4. The ears

5. *Eagle*

6. Sundial

1. What spice takes its name because it is said to taste like a mixture of cloves, pepper, cinnamon and nutmeg?

2. What vitamin is milk fortified with in the U.S. to combat rickets?

3. Which was the only airline other than *British Airways* to buy *Concorde*?

4. What word describes bear-like if feline is cat-like?

5. How many of the engines can a *747* pilot see from his cockpit window?

6. How many neck vertebrae does a giraffe have compared with a human's seven?

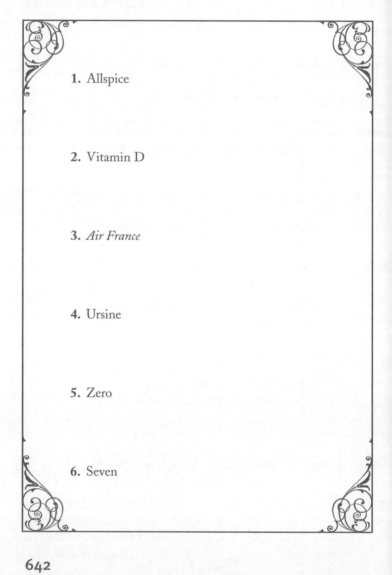

1. Allspice

2. Vitamin D

3. *Air France*

4. Ursine

5. Zero

6. Seven

1. What is the most noticeable physical difference between African and Asian elephants apart from their size?

2. What do postmen and nurses wear that appears in the International Radio Alphabet?

3. What native of Africa ends the International Radio Alphabet?

4. What F-word describes the surface area of a desk occupied by a computer?

5. How many pairs of wings does a bee have?

6. What M-word describes the change from a chrysalis to a butterfly?

1. Ears

2. Uniform

3. Zulu

4. Footprint

5. Two

6. Metamorphosis

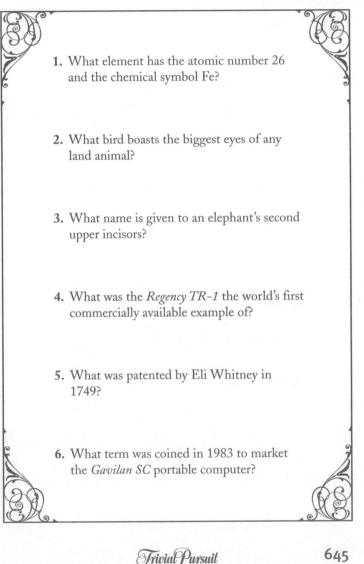

1. What element has the atomic number 26 and the chemical symbol Fe?

2. What bird boasts the biggest eyes of any land animal?

3. What name is given to an elephant's second upper incisors?

4. What was the *Regency TR-1* the world's first commercially available example of?

5. What was patented by Eli Whitney in 1749?

6. What term was coined in 1983 to market the *Gavilan SC* portable computer?

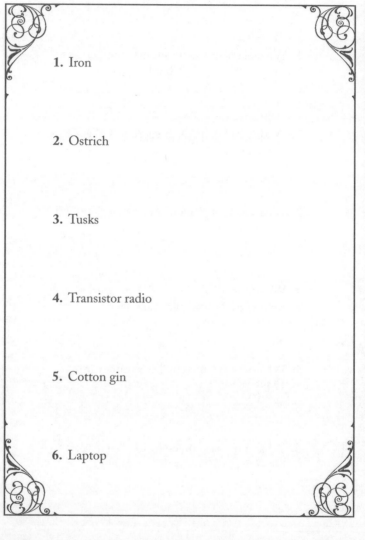

1. Iron

2. Ostrich

3. Tusks

4. Transistor radio

5. Cotton gin

6. Laptop

1. What animal produces most of the world's wool?

2. What is the very common trypanophobia a fear of?

3. What breed is often called the Apollo of Dogs?

4. What was Ceres always classed as until it was touted as a minor planet in 2006?

5. What element with the symbol C occurs in all organic life?

6. How many horns did a triceratops have?

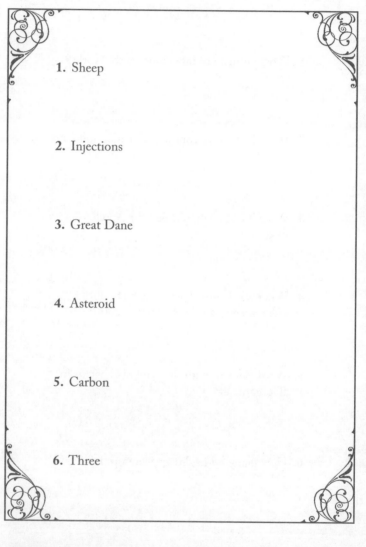

1. Sheep

2. Injections

3. Great Dane

4. Asteroid

5. Carbon

6. Three

648

1. What does a dirty ablutophobiac fear?

2. What name is given to the closest star to the Earth?

3. What is a rhino horn made of?

4. What ancient creature took its name from the Greek words for "terrible lizard"?

5. What was Christian Huygens' swinging invention that made clocks more accurate?

6. What were 5th generation *iPods* the first to offer?

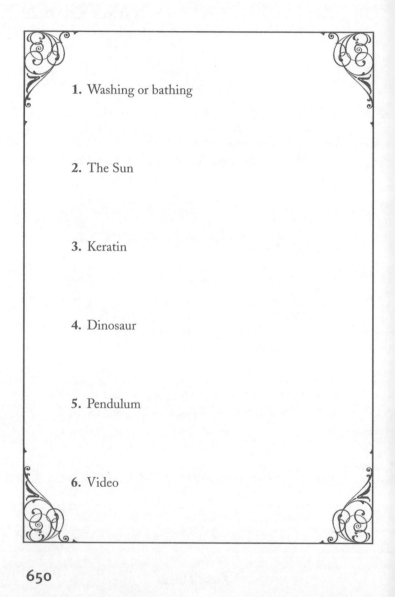

1. Washing or bathing

2. The Sun

3. Keratin

4. Dinosaur

5. Pendulum

6. Video

1. What name is given to the dark areas on the surface of the Sun?

2. What is the name for a baby koala?

3. What is the common name for the seasoning *piper nigrum*?

4. What wild animal kills more people in India each year than tigers and leopards?

5. How many eyelids does a cat have on each eye?

6. What was the name of the U.S.A.'s first Earth-orbiting satellite?

1. Sunspots

2. Joey

3. Black pepper

4. Rhinoceros

5. Three

6. *Explorer I*

1. How many moons does Mars have?

2. What is the more colorful alternative name for the square-lipped rhinoceros?

3. What natural phenomena can be spherical, doughnut-shaped or like parachutes, according to their size?

4. What movie award appears in the International Radio Alphabet?

5. What birds do Chinese and Japanese fishermen commonly use?

6. What's the common name for the fruit *Citrus grandis*?

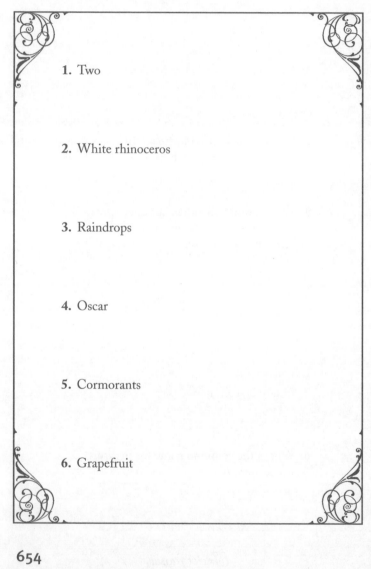

1. Two

2. White rhinoceros

3. Raindrops

4. Oscar

5. Cormorants

6. Grapefruit

1. What animal has the highest blood pressure?

2. What kind of eclipse occurs when the Sun and the Moon aren't exactly in line?

3. What word used in connection with radio and television originally came from an agricultural term referring to the scattering of seeds?

4. What name is usually given to bananas cultivated for cooking?

5. What element joins iron to become steel?

6. What disorder's name is derived from the Greek for "without appetite"?

1. Giraffe

2. Partial eclipse

3. Broadcasting (Broadcast)

4. Plantains

5. Carbon

6. Anorexia's

1. Where in the body will you find your aqueous humor?

2. What three-letter word means the combination of gases surrounding the Earth?

3. What is the large, rotating system of currents in the Atlantic Ocean that takes warm water north?

4. Which American astronomer gave his name to a telescope launched into space in 1990?

5. What orbit the Sun and have a name based on an ancient Greek word meaning *wanderer*?

6. What airport did the first commercial *Boeing 747* flight from JFK land at?

1. Eye

2. Air

3. The Gulf Stream

4. Edwin Hubble

5. Planets

6. London, Heathrow

1. Which is known as the Red Planet?

2. Which of Jupiter's moons is the most volcanically active body in the solar system?

3. What vitamin's principal form is ascorbic acid?

4. What name is attached to volcanoes that haven't erupted since historical times but aren't considered extinct?

5. How many calves does the average giraffe mother give birth to each time?

6. What mixes with the fuel to aid combustion in most car engines?

1. Mars

2. Io

3. Vitamin C's

4. Dormant

5. One

6. Air

1. What venerable fast food chain was the first to sell its precooked frozen burgers in grocery stores?

2. Which country is the world's largest supplier of wool?

3. What was William Fox Talbot a pioneer of?

4. What does S.S.T. stand for when referring to *Concorde*?

5. What period saw the first dinosaurs?

6. What is the longest and heaviest bone in the human body?

1. *White Castle*

2. Australia

3. Photography

4. Supersonic transport

5. Cretaceous

6. Femur (Thighbone)

1. What natural fabric becomes denim?

2. What does the "CAT" in "CAT scan" stand for?

3. What was the surname of William, who bought the patent for James Murray Spangler's newly invented vacuum cleaners?

4. What radioactive element was used in the *Fat Boy* bomb dropped on Nagasaki but not in the *Little Boy* dropped on Hiroshima?

5. What three-letter name can mean a group of dolphins?

6. How many pairs of ribs are there in the average human skeleton?

1. Cotton

2. Computerized axial tomography

3. Hoover

4. Plutonium

5. Pod

6. Twelve

1. What number of varieties is associated with *Heinz*'s products?

2. What is the fruit of the rose?

3. Which was the first *iPod* with a color screen and flash memory?

4. Which British city did *Concorde* make its final flight from Heathrow to?

5. What does B stand for when referring to a camera's shutter speed?

6. What three-letter word describes the material from which iron is extracted?

1. 57

2. Rose hip

3. *iPod Nano*

4. Bristol

5. Bulb

6. Ore

1. What is a male cat if a female is a queen?

2. What flowed through an ancient Egyptian *clepsydra* to tell the time?

3. What is the only bone in the human body that doesn't connect with any other?

4. What is the only supersonic airliner, other than *Concorde*, to have seen commercial service?

5. What's the common name for the disease rubella?

6. What are the primary predecessors that are replaced in later life by succedaneous?

1. Tom

2. Water

3. Hyoid

4. *Tupolev Tu-144*

5. German measles

6. Teeth

1. What group of fruits, in true botanical terms, includes the grape, tomato and eggplant but not the strawberry?

2. What does an agoraphobiac fear?

3. What color is a polar bear's skin?

4. What wild creature does a Shiba Inus dog most look like?

5. What is the only non-human member of the ape family that isn't an agile climber?

6. What is the name for the soft white layer that forms on teeth?

1. Berries

2. Open spaces

3. Black

4. Fox

5. Gorilla

6. Plaque

1. What happened to polar bears in Chicago's Brookfield Zoo when algae appeared in their drinking water during the hot summer of 2005?

2. What area of a giraffe's anatomy is not covered with the characteristic spots?

3. What plastic often has its name shortened to PS?

4. What did Leo Hendrik Baekeland call the plastic he invented in 1907?

5. What name is given to someone who keeps *apis mellifera*?

6. What is the common name for pertussis that causes its usually young victims to make strange noises?

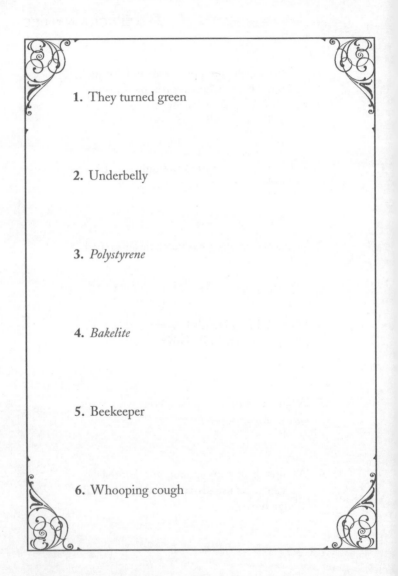

1. They turned green

2. Underbelly

3. *Polystyrene*

4. *Bakelite*

5. Beekeeper

6. Whooping cough

1. What was the next country to launch a satellite after the Soviet Union and U.S.A.?

2. What is *Lipton* the world's biggest-selling brand of?

3. How many engines does a *747* passenger jet have?

4. What fish come in giant 60-pound varieties known to Washingtonians as "June hogs"?

5. What mammal's most common species is the bottlenose?

6. How many bends does a standard paperclip have?

1. France

2. Tea

3. Four

4. Salmon

5. Dolphin's

6. Three

674

1. What ape has a name derived from Malay for *man of the forest*?

2. What is the molten rock magma called once it flows from a volcano?

3. What four-letter name was given to *Hormel Spiced Ham* in the 1930s?

4. What company with a name beginning with X produced the first one-piece, plain paper photocopier?

5. What is the main gas in the Earth's atmosphere?

6. What clock-adjusting scheme was first put into effect in the U.S. in 1918?

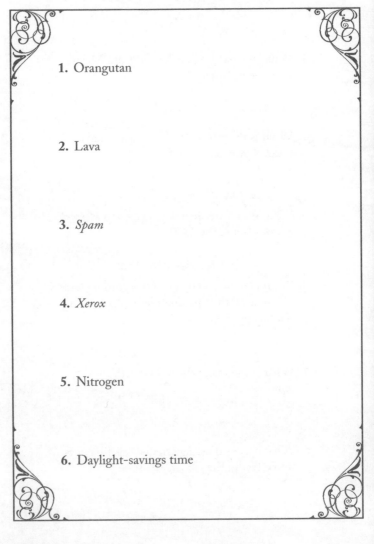

1. Orangutan

2. Lava

3. *Spam*

4. *Xerox*

5. Nitrogen

6. Daylight-savings time

676

1. What name is given to a clock with a face and hands, as opposed to a digital clock that displays the time as numbers?

2. What flowers do florists often refer to as "mums"?

3. Who is fed royal jelly by her workers?

4. How long does a full solar eclipse last?

5. What name is given to an ornamental carving attached to the front of a ship?

6. What direction do growing bananas point?

1. Analog

2. Chrysanthemums

3. A queen bee

4. 450 seconds

5. Figurehead

6. Upwards

1. What does the medical acronym EEG stand for?

2. What common tool might have a claw or a peen?

3. What animal family ranges from the tiny pygmy marmoset up to the mandrill?

4. Which Italian scientist with the initials G.G. made improvements to the telescope and is known as the father of modern astronomy?

5. How many blowholes does a toothed whale have?

6. What causes pollen to stick to bees?

1. Electroencephalogram

2. Hammer

3. Monkey

4. Galileo Galilei

5. One

6. An electrostatic charge

1. What fluid with a four-letter name is stored in the gallbladder?

2. What does a butterfly have 380 of, a chicken 78, a donkey 62 and humans a mere 46?

3. What do dolphins have to think about that humans don't, resulting in dolphins having to only close down half of their brain when sleeping?

4. What is a computer's UPS?

5. What rare natural phenomenon does Yellowstone National Park boast approximately 50 percent of the world's examples of?

6. What month, towards the end of the year, appears in the International Radio Alphabet?

1. Bile

2. Chromosomes

3. Breathing

4. Uninterruptible Power Source

5. Geysers

6. November

1. What name is given to the layer of gases surrounding the Earth?

2. What's the world's oldest science—astronomy, chemistry or physics?

3. What form of food preservation involves removal of the water content from frozen food?

4. What did Jost Burgi first add to a clock in 1577 for those requiring a more accurate timepiece?

5. What country is the world's leading producer of orange juice?

6. What is the most commonly served condiment made from a member of the rapeseed family?

1. Atmosphere

2. Astronomy

3. Freeze drying

4. Minute hand

5. Brazil

6. Mustard

1. What Aussie animal can be Common, Northern Hairy-Nosed or Southern Hairy-Nosed?

2. What vitamin do sufferers from scurvy lack?

3. What is the only weight in the International Radio Alphabet?

4. What U.S. state sees the launch of Space Shuttles?

5. What are scientists hoping to cause when they seed a cloud?

6. What is the common name for the disease tetanus, which can cause facial muscle spasms?

1. Wombat

2. Vitamin C

3. Kilo

4. Florida

5. Rain

6. Lockjaw

1. Where is a ship's bow?

2. Which company took over production of
   Rolls-Royce cars in 2003?

3. What is the main constituent of an
   eggshell?

4. What fiber-producing plant is attacked by
   the boll weevil?

5. What brand name has become a generic
   term in the British dictionary meaning "to
   clean with a vacuum cleaner"?

6. What is dentophobia a common fear of?

1. The front

2. *BMW*

3. Calcium carbonate

4. Cotton

5. *Hoover*

6. Dentists

1. What was the name of the first completed U.S. Space Shuttle, *Constitution*, changed to following pressure from *Star Trek* fans?

2. What tools' variations include mill, geared head and radial arm?

3. What came about when Spencer Silver developed a very weak adhesive that he thought might be used on bookmarks in his Bible?

4. What element has the chemical symbol K?

5. What insulates the ice cream to prevent it from melting in the hot dish *Baked Alaska*?

6. What common fruit's skin did hippie bible *The Anarchist Cookbook* claim could be dried then smoked as a hallucinogenic?

1. *Enterprise*

2. Drills'

3. *Post-it notes*

4. Potassium

5. Meringue

6. Banana

1. What are there 270 of in the average human baby but only 206 in an adult?

2. What part of the cinnamon tree becomes the spice?

3. What bright star in Canis Major has a dim companion, the first white dwarf ever seen?

4. What type of internal combustion engine has one upward stroke and one downward stroke to every power stroke?

5. Which computer company launched its *PowerBook* series in 1991?

6. What does *PDA* stand for in computer terminology?

1. Bones

2. Bark

3. Sirius

4. Two stroke

5. Apple Inc.

6. Personal Digital Assistant

1. What is the name for a baby crocodile?

2. What creature takes its name from Aboriginal words for "no drink"?

3. Which bees in a hive are there to fertilize the queen?

4. Whose *Difference Engine* is often described as the first computer?

5. What vitamin was isolated from fish liver oil in 1917?

6. What became the furthest major planet from the Sun when Pluto was downgraded to minor planet status in 2006?

1. Crocklet

2. Koala

3. Drone bees

4. Charles Babbage's

5. Vitamin D

6. Neptune

1. What organ is inflamed by hepatitis?

2. What does ROM stand for in CD-ROM?

3. What's the chemical symbol for gold?

4. What Indian plant did medieval explorers report bore "tiny lambs on the ends of its branches"?

5. What tool does the Department of Defense refer to as a "manually powered fastener-driving impact device"?

6. Which company's *Silver Ghost* was hailed the best car in the world in 1907?

1. Liver

2. Read-Only Memory

3. Au

4. The cotton plant

5. A hammer

6. *Rolls-Royce's*

1. What sweet treat's main appeal, according to scientists, is that it melts in the mouth at almost human body temperature?

2. What does an agaricologist study?

3. What does a pluviometer measure?

4. Which bodily organ produces urine?

5. What does a little baby elver hope to grow up to become?

6. What term was coined in 1989 to describe computers smaller than regular laptops?

1. Chocolate's

2. Mushrooms

3. Rainfall

4. Kidney

5. An eel

6. Notebook

1. What might a paramedic describe as either simple or compound?

2. What was Hyman Lipman the first person to attach to the end of a pencil?

3. Which island off the coast of India boasts the largest subspecies of Asian elephant?

4. What space orbiter came within 1000 yards of a high-speed collision with a U.S. military satellite?

5. What product that takes its name from a farm animal is a step along the way from iron ore to cast iron?

6. What natural product's main producers are India, China, Sri Lanka and Kenya, in that order?

1. A fracture

2. Eraser

3. Sri Lanka

4. *Mir*

5. Pig iron

6. Tea's

1. What did Henry F. Phillips introduce for carpenters?

2. What did George Green patent in 1875 that was voted the second most terrifying thing known to mankind, after nuclear warfare, in a 2003 poll?

3. What perfume ingredient comes from the intestine of the sperm whale?

4. What does the medical acronym PET stand for?

5. What does it mean if you are surrounded by stellar dendrites?

6. What sign of the zodiac is represented by an archer?

1. Phillips crosshead screw

2. Dentist's electric drill

3. Ambergris

4. Positron emission tomography

5. It's snowing

6. Sagittarius

1. What bird with a unique call lays its eggs in other birds' nests?

2. What color is a huckleberry?

3. What does the average human lose between 40 and 100 of each day?

4. What odd-looking Aussie animal has no nipples but feeds its young on milk that oozes from its body?

5. What name was given to the magnetic radiation belts around the Earth discovered by the first U.S. satellite?

6. What pachyderm comes in three living species: Asian, African Savannah and African Forest?

1. Cuckoo

2. Blue

3. Head hairs

4. Duck-billed platypus

5. Van Allen Belts

6. Elephant

1. What is secured in a ship's cathead?

2. What was the first passenger jet larger than a *747*?

3. What is the world's fastest two-legged creature?

4. What's the common name for what an Olympic sprinter would have if his doctor said he was suffering from *tinea pedis*?

5. Where is your tragus?

6. What is the second-lightest element, often used for inflating balloons?

1. Anchor

2. *Airbus A380*

3. Ostrich

4. Athlete's foot

5. Near your ear

6. Helium

1. What P-word means the visible surface of the Sun?

2. What is the main food of adult echidnas?

3. What did Ralph Wedgwood patent an early version of that was once essential for making instant copies of the written word?

4. What fresh fruit should be squeezed into a margarita?

5. What is actually eclipsed in what is generally known as a solar eclipse?

6. What color are cranberries before they turn red?

1. Photosphere

2. Ants or termites

3. Carbon paper

4. Lime

5. Earth

6. White

1. What N-word describes a lump of natural gold?

2. What is the hardest bone in the human body?

3. What is the alternative name for a laptop's trackpad?

4. What is the name for a tropical cyclone that has wind speeds of 40-73 mph?

5. What common photo flaw is minimized by cameras that use a pre-flash to shrink the subjects' pupil size?

6. What company produced the *Brownie* camera?

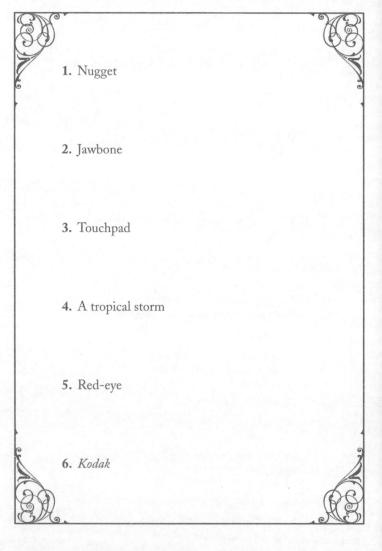

1. Nugget

2. Jawbone

3. Touchpad

4. A tropical storm

5. Red-eye

6. *Kodak*

1. What direction will a field full of sunflowers face at the start of each day?

2. What was Rowland Hill the first to put on the back of a postage stamp?

3. What are the four basic types of clouds?

4. What simple telescope magnifies the view of distant objects by gathering light on curved mirrors?

5. What smelly garden flower has a name that literally means "nose twister"?

6. What single object accounts for more than 99 percent of the solar system's mass?

1. East

2. Adhesive

3. Cumulus, cirrus, stratus and nimbus

4. Reflecting telescope

5. Nasturtium

6. The Sun

1. What C-word is an alternative name for a butterfly's pupa?

2. How many non-retractable claws does a bear have on each paw?

3. What does an ornithologist study?

4. What is the only company to have produced engines that held the world air, land and water speed records simultaneously?

5. What island was the site of Marconi's first radio station?

6. What bodily fluid surrounds a fetus?

1. Chrysalis

2. Five

3. Birds

4. *Rolls-Royce*

5. Isle of Wight

6. Amniotic fluid

1. What is the more common name for a car engine using the *Otto* cycle?

2. How many true legs does a caterpillar have?

3. What is the most malleable and ductile metal known to man?

4. What is the collective name for a group of pet cats?

5. Which of the accepted nine planets at the start of the 21st century was named after a Greek God?

6. What are brails and buntlines on a ship?

1. Four stroke

2. Six

3. Gold

4. A clowder

5. Uranus

6. Ropes

1. What dog gave its name to the 2003 British Mars probe that failed to work?

2. What astronomical aid takes its name from Greek words meaning "far seeing"?

3. What continent produces most of the world's cocoa beans?

4. What part of a *Rolls-Royce* takes one man a whole day to make and five hours to polish?

5. What holds the bit in a drill?

6. What fruit crop is grown in more countries than any other?

1. *Beagle*

2. Telescope

3. Africa

4. Radiator grille

5. Chuck

6. Banana

1. What is the ginko the world's oldest living example of?

2. What animal has been dubbed nature's skyscraper?

3. What is the common name for a flower's colorful corolla?

4. What vitamin is mostly required for blood coagulation?

5. What name does the cosmetics industry use for the greasy yellow substance found in wool?

6. Which was the only one of the accepted nine planets at the start of the 21st century not to be named after a Roman or Greek god?

1. Tree

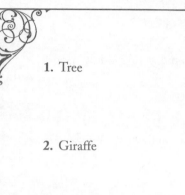

2. Giraffe

3. Petals

4. Vitamin K

5. Lanolin

6. Earth

1. What British boxer trained with people like rock star Sting before being knocked out by Mike Tyson?

2. Who swatted 54 homers the first year the spitball was banned?

3. What type of hobbyist is familiar with the Barber, Saint Gaudens and walking Liberty?

4. What gymnastic event often sees men performing the Iron Cross or Crucifix?

5. What city and its surroundings is the basis for a standard U.S. *Monopoly* board?

6. What item of sports equipment can have a *coquille* or bellguard to protect the fingers?

1. Frank Bruno

2. Babe Ruth

3. Coin collectors

4. Rings

5. Atlantic City

6. Sword

1. What 14th seed became Wimbledon's lowest-ranked female title winner in 2005?

2. What decade sticks out as the one in which the first self-adhesive U.S. postage stamp appeared?

3. What does it mean to "reef" a dinghy's mainsail?

4. What's the women's equivalent to tennis' Davis Cup?

5. What game awards the Stanley Cup?

6. What's the sport if the equipment includes an arm guard and a tab to protect the fingers of the drawing hand?

1. Venus Williams

2. 1960s

3. Reduce its size

4. The Federation Cup

5. Ice hockey

6. Archery

1. What sport, invented in sunny Santa Monica in the 1920s, made its Olympic debut in 1996?

2. What do weather watchers use to measure relative humidity?

3. What reason has been given for retiring the current World Cup in 2038?

4. What items of sports equipment are made by a fletcher?

5. What do you get by mixing ginger ale with grenadine and a cherry?

6. What game have computer programs *Deep Fritz*, *Deep Junior* and *Deep Blue* played against champions?

1. Beach volleyball

2. Psychrometer or Hygrometer

3. The name plaque will be full

4. Arrows

5. A Shirley Temple

6. Chess

1. Which was 1910s baseball player "Shoeless Joe" Jackson's southern home state?

2. What Australian city staged the 2000 games where Sir Steven Redgrave became the first rower to win five consecutive Olympic gold medals?

3. What decade saw the launch of the *PlayStation*?

4. What type of tests were National League umpires ordered to undergo in 1911?

5. What is the actual shape of a C-clamp, found in home workshops?

6. What is the oldest major trophy for which North American athletes have competed since 1893?

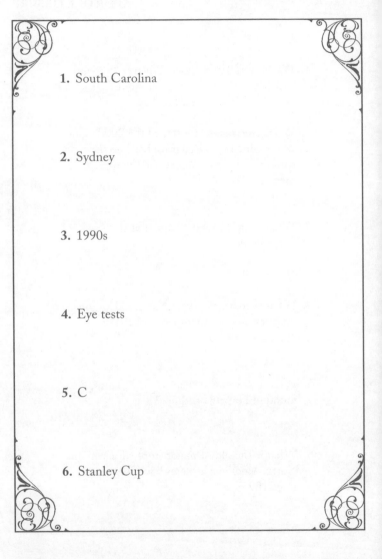

1. South Carolina

2. Sydney

3. 1990s

4. Eye tests

5. C

6. Stanley Cup

1. What would an American cyclist call what his British counterpart would know as mudguards?

2. What domestic art has prairie points, wave panels and cathedral windows?

3. What indoor sport did Marion Van Oosten Ladewig, inductee in the Women's Sports Hall of Fame in 1984, excel in?

4. What conveyance did the Northwest Mounted Police use to reach remote outposts during winter?

5. Which famous Scottish golf club boasts the Ladies Putting Club, the world's oldest miniature golf course?

6. What do common backyard flower garden species ivy, clematis, Virginia creeper and trumpet vine have in common?

1. Fenders

2. Quilting

3. Bowling

4. Dog sled

5. St. Andrews

6. They're climbers

1. Who declared he would "float like a butterfly, sting like a bee" before taking his first world boxing title against Sonny Liston?

2. What three-letter word means the employees' side of a casino table?

3. What modeling material is most commonly used to show a mark if a long jumper takes off from in front of the board?

4. What decade were golf carts introduced in the U.S.?

5. What California-born figure skater overcame a clubfoot to win Olympic women's figure skating gold?

6. What event in a decathlon takes the athletes to the greatest height?

1. Cassius Clay

2. Pit

3. *Plasticine*

4. 1940s

5. Kristi Yamaguchi

6. Pole vault

1. What *Beverly Hills 90210* actor crashed his racecar on the Kentucky Speedway in 2002?

2. What decade saw the first U.S. postage stamp issued?

3. What Italian alpine skier was the first to win medals in three different Olympics, 1988-1994, and grabbed 50 World Cup victories?

4. Who was Triple Crown winner War Admiral's equally famous sire?

5. Where is the stop positioned on traditional roller skates?

6. What store sponsors the annual Thanksgiving Day parade held in New York City?

Trivial Pursuit

1. Jason Priestley

2. 1840s

3. Alberto Tomba

4. Man O'War

5. The toe

6. *Macy's*

1. What is the highest possible snooker break in normal play without the advantage of a foul?

2. How many balls are normally racked in the triangle in pocket billiards?

3. Who lost to Muhammad Ali in a 1975 fight, despite connecting on 440 punches?

4. What is Canada's popular winter ice sport that is not hockey?

5. How many species of birds have been identified by the American Ornithologists' Union as "known species" in North and Central America—246, 2,046 or 20,460?

6. What is the end opposite the nose called on a snowboard?

1. 147

2. Fifteen

3. Joe Frazier

4. Curling

5. 2,046

6. Tail

1. What was the first cat character balloon in the *Macy's* Thanksgiving Day Parade?

2. What basketball powerhouse nicknamed "The Stilt" scored 31,419 points in his career with the Warriors, 76ers and Lakers?

3. What pro sport did Althea Gibson play when her tennis career ended?

4. What sport is featured in the classic movie *Endless Summer*?

5. What lines up alongside lacrosse as one of Canada's two national sports?

6. What was the southern golf course where Gene Sarazen scored a remarkable double eagle on the par 5, 15th hole during the 1935 Masters Golf Tournament?

1. Felix

2. Wilt Chamberlain

3. Golf

4. Surfing

5. Ice hockey

6. Augusta National Golf Club

1. What name is given to the line running across a snooker table?

2. What did Levant M. Richardson add to roller skate wheels in 1884 to increase speed by reducing friction?

3. What French word for sled is given to a Winter Olympic event?

4. What color jackets are winners of the Masters Golf Tournament awarded?

5. What tycoon landed his *Sikorsky Amphibian* on the 8th fairway at Bel-Air Country Club, L.A., to get Katharine Hepburn's attention?

6. What does an amateur weather station anemometer measure?

1. Balk line

2. Ball bearings

3. Luge

4. Green

5. Howard Hughes

6. Wind speed

1. What service organization abides by the motto "Service above self"?

2. What rare bird species was sighted in Arkansas in 2005, launching an enormous search for confirmation?

3. What is the sport of Hilary Swank's character in *Million Dollar Baby*?

4. What name is given to a ball on a wire that is thrown in an Olympic event?

5. Which one of the following baseball players received a phone call from Beaver Cleaver on an episode of *Leave It to Beaver*—Don Drysdale, Babe Ruth or Hank Aaron?

6. What do members of Citizen Weather Observer Program (CWOP) learn from an aneroid barometer?

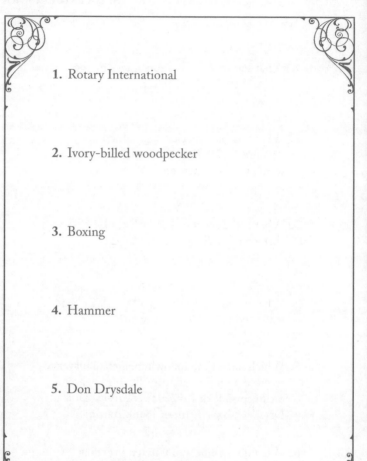

1. Rotary International

2. Ivory-billed woodpecker

3. Boxing

4. Hammer

5. Don Drysdale

6. Air or atmospheric pressure

1. What color hats do lady members of a certain "heady" social organization wear to gatherings?

2. What horse was the first to win the Triple Crown of the Kentucky Derby, Preakness and Belmont Stakes in 1919?

3. What is the "churn dash," popular with sewing Pennsylvania Dutch?

4. What Olympic distance is usually run on the home straight of a 400-meter track with an extension to allow a straight-line race?

5. What do sumo wrestlers call their hair topknots?

6. What travelers relied years ago on octants to find their way?

1. Red

2. Sir Barton

3. Quilt pattern

4. 100 meters

5. Chonmage

6. Sailors

1. What modern event is equivalent to a sport in the ancient Olympics requiring participants to carry hand weights that they swung to increase momentum?

2. What very final sounding name is given to a chess game which white must win to take the match but which black only has to draw?

3. What is the target area in Olympic fencing?

4. Who had a women's tennis record-breaking winning streak of 74 games in 1984?

5. What Winter Olympic sport requires players to slide stones at houses?

6. What flavor is Grand Marnier?

1. Long jump

2. *Armageddon*

3. The torso

4. Martina Navratilova

5. Curling

6. Orange

1. What decade did the Mexico-to-Canada Pacific Coast National Scenic Trail open in?

2. What decade witnessed Gottfried Schmidt invent the automatic bowling pinsetter?

3. What is a judo practitioner's *Judogi*?

4. What continent was the original home to the red tomato?

5. Who beat Bobby Riggs in tennis' famous *Battle of the Sexes*?

6. Which two classic *Monopoly* game tokens are articles that can be worn?

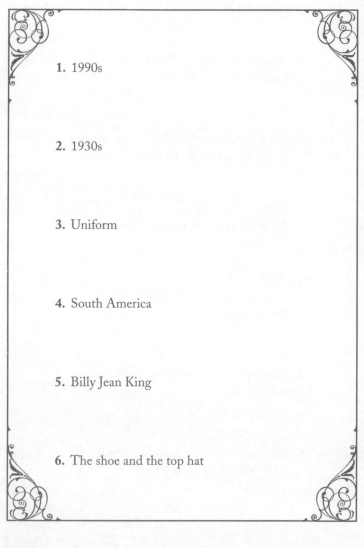

1. 1990s

2. 1930s

3. Uniform

4. South America

5. Billy Jean King

6. The shoe and the top hat

1. What sport is Willard talking about in *Apocalypse Now* when he says: "Don't you think it's a little risky for some R&R"?

2. How many weight classes are there for women sumo wrestlers?

3. How many throwing events are there in a decathlon?

4. What American banged his head on the diving board en route to a 1988 Olympic gold medal?

5. What propelled the "Spirit of America-Sonic I" in which Craig Breedlove set a world land speed record of 600 mph in 1965?

6. What is the first and the shortest running event in a decathlon?

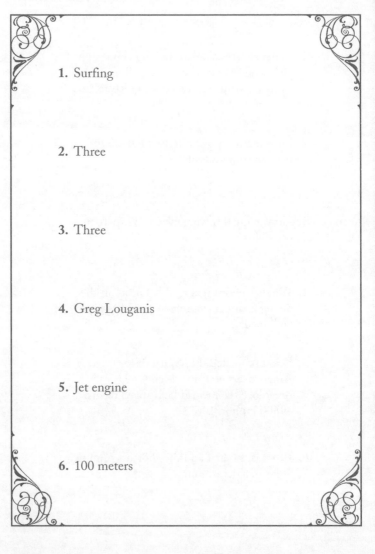

1. Surfing

2. Three

3. Three

4. Greg Louganis

5. Jet engine

6. 100 meters

1. What famous young actress appeared in a revisionist bio film of a famed racehorse, *The Story of Seabiscuit*?

2. What is the figure skating jump launched from the back edge of one skate, followed by a full rotation, and landed on the back edge of the other skate?

3. What was the four-letter name of *Atari*'s 1972 ball and paddle arcade game?

4. What Japanese sport, not for the lean, dates back to the 17th century?

5. Where do members of the mobile organization named for inventor Wally Byam spend many nights?

6. What world record did Jesse Owens hold for 25 years and Bob Beamon for 23?

1. Shirley Temple

2. Lutz

3. *Pong*

4. Sumo wrestling

5. Airstream trailers

6. Long jump

1. Who were the first two daughters of a U.S. president to belong to Girls Scouts of America?

2. What is traditionally the color of a top grade karate belt?

3. Who was the first person to play in both a World Series and Super Bowl?

4. What must a discus competitor wait for before stepping out of the throwing circle if his attempt is to count?

5. What kind of knot do sailboaters commonly use for short-term mooring to a ring or post?

6. What is the shape of a carpenter's square, found in home workshops?

1. Luci and Lynda Johnson

2. Black

3. Deion Sanders

4. The discus to land

5. Clove hitch

6. L

1. What game was born in 1875 when British officers in India got bored with billiards?

2. What is the basketball term for a shot involving a player jumping very high to throw the ball downwards straight through the hoop?

3. What *Scrabble* letter is worth eight points in English, four in Danish and isn't available in an Italian edition?

4. What legendary boxer lit the flame at the 1996 Atlanta Olympics?

5. What sport was featured in the 1940 motion picture *Knute Rockne All American* starring Pat O'Brien?

6. What profession does former *Malcolm in the Middle* star Frankie Muniz now enjoy?

1. Snooker

2. Slam-dunk

3. *J*

4. Muhammad Ali

5. Football

6. Car racing

1. What is the best-known winter sled made by S.L. Allen Co., a firm that also made the *Fire Fly* and the *Yankee Clipper*?

2. What sport has its name abbreviated to *BMX*?

3. Who beat France 5-3 after a penalty shoot out to win the 2006 World Cup?

4. What happened to *Crayola* crayon colors Green Blue, Orange Red, Orange Yellow, Violet Blue, Maize, Lemon Yellow, Blue Gray and Raw Umber in 1990?

5. What was the title of the 1942 motion picture in which Gary Cooper played the legendary baseball player Lou "Iron Horse" Gehrig?

6. What tightwad owner's low salaries do some historians cite as a major reason players agreed to fix the 1919 World Series?

1. *Flexible Flyer* sled

2. Bicycle Moto-cross

3. Italy

4. They were retired

5. *Pride of the Yankees*

6. Charles Comiskey's

1. What decade was the *Macy's* Thanksgiving Day parade first broadcast on television?

2. What decade witnessed Peggy Fleming win Olympic and world champion figure skating medals?

3. Who won the light heavyweight boxing medal at the 1960 Rome Olympics?

4. Who correctly forecast: "When I hit Mike Tyson he's going to think the whole of Ireland hit him"?

5. What is listed as the least-watched major sport in the U.S. and the most-watched in Canada?

6. Where has National Basketball Association star Shaquille O'Neal served in auxiliary police uniform in the off-season?

1. 1940s

2. 1960s

3. Cassius Clay

4. Kevin McBride

5. Ice hockey

6. Miami (or Florida)

1. What position did Hall of Famer Hank Aaron play in his 23 years in *Major League Baseball*?

2. What is the maximum ball weight allowed in a candlepin bowling game—6 pounds, 13 pounds or 16 pounds?

3. Which one of these is not a type of pitch thrown by *Major League Baseball* pitchers—cutter, slider, wobbler or knuckleball?

4. What East Asian state's women won gold, silver and bronze in the Sydney Olympic archery tournament?

5. How many *Major League Baseball* teams today are named for four-footed animals?

6. Who was the catcher when Don Larsen pitched the only perfect game in World Series history, in 1956?

1. Outfield

2. 16 pounds

3. Wobbler

4. South Korea's

5. 2 (Cubs and Tigers)

6. Yogi Berra

1. What is a spinnaker on a boat?

2. What descriptive expression in downhill skiing means to aim straight for the bottom?

3. What other player is on a curling team besides the lead, the second and the third (or vice)?

4. What common household pet's arched back is imitated in a yoga pose?

5. What sport is featured in the 1992 movie *The Cutting Edge*?

6. What decade boasts Jim Thorpe, a football and track star at Carlisle Indian School in Pennsylvania, winning double gold in the Olympics?

1. Type of sail

2. Schuss

3. The skip

4. Cat

5. Figure skating

6. 1910s

1. Which island's *Sandy Lane Hotel* hosted Tiger Woods' wedding at its Green Monkey Golf Course?

2. What martial art has a name beginning with K that means *empty hand*?

3. What is the most common color for basketballs?

4. Who owned the Chicago White Sox baseball team at the time of the 1919 "Black Sox" scandal?

5. What decade saw the *National Hockey League* form, with five teams?

6. What was the only tennis Grand Slam event played on grass at the start of the 21st century?

1. Barbados'

2. Karate

3. Orange

4. Charles Comiskey

5. 1910s

6. Wimbledon

1. What animal was vaulted over in early sporting events to give a modern piece of gymnastics equipment its name?

2. What decade boasts Henry Phillips' invention of the Phillips head screw and screwdriver?

3. What city's 1972 Olympics were staged to celebrate peace but were marred by a terrorist attack?

4. What does a player generally use for a long fairway shot in golf—a wood or an iron?

5. What shaky-sounding case does an archer keep his arrows in?

6. What computer company made its first big break into the arcade game market with *Donkey Kong*?

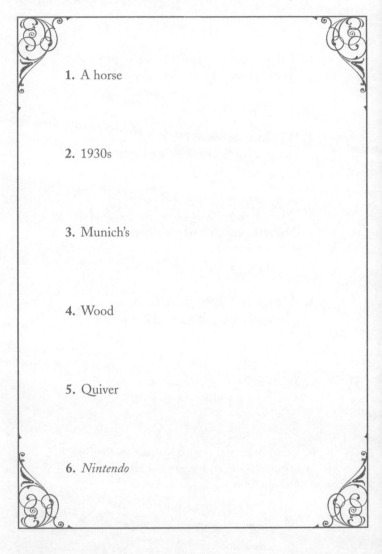

1. A horse

2. 1930s

3. Munich's

4. Wood

5. Quiver

6. *Nintendo*

1. What musical instrument appears on a *Guinness* label?

2. What's the maximum number of players who should be on a basketball court at any one time?

3. What National Basketball Association player, the son of an NBA athlete, was named for a type of steak his parents saw on a menu just before he was born?

4. What Olympic athletics competition includes ten different events?

5. Which state is home to the Attwater Prairie Chicken National Wildlife Refuge, habitat for an endangered bird species of that name?

6. How many points is a jack worth in a game of blackjack?

1. Harp

2. Ten

3. Kobe Bryant

4. Decathlon

5. Texas

6. Ten

1. What does "green lumber" mean to the do-it-yourself carpenter?

2. How many squares are there on a *Scrabble* board?

3. What nationality invented the North American toboggan?

4. What name was adopted by boxing champion Cassius Marcellus Clay Jr.?

5. What R-word is the common name for inline skates?

6. What is the reward for rolling three consecutive doubles in a game of *Monopoly*?

1. Lumber that has not been dried

2. 225

3. Native Americans

4. Muhammad Ali

5. Rollerblades

6. Sent to jail

1. What actor played "Shoeless Joe" Jackson in *Field of Dreams*?

2. How many pieces does each player start a game of chess with?

3. What heavyweight champ lasted all of 91 seconds against Mike Tyson in 1988?

4. What New York Yankee, known for swinging at bad balls, nevertheless had the most career World Series at bats (259) and hits (71)?

5. What stadium saw Roger Maris belt his historic 61st home run, in 1961?

6. Which Georgia golf club is the home of the U.S. Masters?

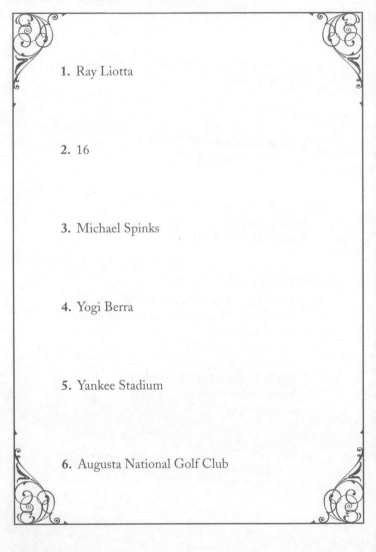

1. Ray Liotta

2. 16

3. Michael Spinks

4. Yogi Berra

5. Yankee Stadium

6. Augusta National Golf Club

1. What popular winter recreation vehicle evolved from logging equipment?

2. What does an athlete from the home country traditionally hold in his/her left hand while taking the Olympic oath?

3. What type of card game did Frank Bank, who played Lumpy Rutherford on TV's *Leave It to Beaver*, later play at a professional level?

4. What sport has players executing snap, slap, wrist and backhand shots?

5. What sport was once contested with a spadroon?

6. What chess piece has a horse's head?

1. Snowmobile

2. A corner of the Olympic flag

3. Poker

4. Ice hockey

5. Fencing

6. Knight

1. What circumference baseball did All-American Girls Professional Baseball League pitchers throw in 1943—8, 12 or 16 inches?

2. What rich term in downhill skiing means a mound of snow on the course?

3. What arcade game's ghosts included Blinky, Pinky and Inky?

4. What Phillies pitcher posted 23 wins in 1955, and batted .253 as a switch-hitter?

5. What century did curling originate in Scotland?

6. What groundbreaking 1978 arcade game involved shooting down advancing armies of aliens with a laser cannon?

1. 12 inches

2. Mogul

3. *Pac-Man*'s

4. Robin Roberts

5. 16th century

6. *Space Invaders*

1. What maritime folk song sailed onto the charts when the Beach Boys released it in 1966?

2. What is the diameter of an official *National Hockey League* puck—3, 3.5 or 4 inches?

3. What Pittsburgh team hired Baseball Hall of Fame and Negro Baseball Leagues athlete Satchel Paige to pitch in the early 1930s?

4. What future decathlon great's foot was once mangled by the rollers of a conveyor belt?

5. What garden vegetable was known for years as green Italian squash?

6. What was the first name of Mr. Guinness who gave his name to the drink?

1. *Sloop John B*

2. 3 inches

3. Crawfords

4. Rafer Johnson's

5. Zucchini

6. Arthur

1. Which species of pigeon is now extinct—passenger, carrier, Bruce's green or royal snow tumbler?

2. What blushing, often prickly flower garden bush species should be pruned each spring for optimum blossoms?

3. What is the longest running event in a decathlon?

4. Who became the highest scorer ever in international women's soccer in 1999?

5. How many times was California-born Nancy Lopez the Ladies Professional Golf Association Player of the Year?

6. What brand name did pigment makers Edwin Binney and C. Harold Smith use to market their waxy 1903 creations?

1. Passenger

2. Rose

3. 1500 meters

4. Mia Hamm

5. Four

6. *Crayola*

1. What decade saw the Providence Steam Rollers become the first National Football League franchise to host a night game under the lights?

2. What low-hit baseball era ended with the advent of a tighter-wound, livelier ball and the banning of the spitball and emery ball?

3. What Olympic field event's two main styles are the glide and the spin?

4. What martial art's name means *way of the sword*?

5. What name is given to the object that is knocked around in a game of ice hockey?

6. What movie actress did tennis star Andre Agassi marry in 1997?

1. 1920s

2. Dead ball era

3. Shot put's

4. Kendo

5. Puck

6. Brooke Shields

1. What winter Olympic event combines cross-country skiing with rifle shooting?

2. What Olympic event is abbreviated to WAG?

3. What's the sport of Sean Penn's character in *Fast Times at Ridgemont High*?

4. What country has won the most Olympic basketball titles?

5. What Dodger teammate and fellow pitcher beat out Sal Maglie for the 1956 MVP award?

6. What did *Crayola* crayon maker Binney & Smith change the name of its Prussian Blue crayon to in 1958 after a late night?

1. Biathlon

2. Women's artistic gymnastics

3. Surfing

4. U.S.A.

5. Don Newcombe

6. Midnight Blue

1. What auto racing actor provided Doc Hudson's voice for the Pixar animated movie *Cars*?

2. How many weeks do the annual Wimbledon Championships last, so long as it doesn't rain?

3. What garden pest has eaten your dahlias if you find a slime trail?

4. Which of your opponent's pieces has to be in checkmate for you to win a game of chess?

5. What two-letter word for "cindery lava" would be the first acceptable *Scrabble* word on an alphabetical list?

6. How many wheels does a pair of roller skates have?

1. Paul Newman

2. Two weeks

3. Snail

4. King

5. Aa

6. Eight

1. What was the better-known name of the old 91 meters sprint race?

2. What part of the body gave its name to the pointed front end of a surfboard?

3. What sport saw America take their dream team, including Magic Johnson, Michael Jordan and Larry Bird, to the Barcelona Olympics in 1992?

4. What was the first year a golfer scored a hole-in-one at the Masters Golf Tournament—1934 or 1944?

5. What decade was Girl Scouts of America formed in?

6. What decade found the Dumont Network carrying the first-ever television broadcast of a National Football League championship game, in which the Rams beat the Browns?

1. 100 yards

2. Nose

3. Basketball

4. 1934

5. 1910s

6. 1950s

1. What career did actress Dolores Hart pursue after starring in two films opposite Elvis Presley?

2. What was *NASCAR* racecar driver Dale Earnhardt Sr.'s nickname?

3. What's the sport in *Field of Dreams*?

4. What is the four-letter name of the computer game credited with sparking the whole genre of first-person adventure-puzzle games?

5. What legendary superhero was featured on the largest balloon ever to appear in a *Macy's* Thanksgiving Day parade?

6. How many states does the Pacific Crest National Scenic Trail traverse?

1. Nun

2. The Intimidator

3. Baseball

4. *MYST*

5. Superman

6. 3

1. What Winter Olympic sport gives tidy-minded women the opportunity to sweep the ice in front of fellow players?

2. How many times is the sumo wrestling woven loincloth, the "mawashi," wound around the waist by male wrestlers?

3. What exercise routine uses the position "downward facing dog"?

4. How many *Major League Baseball* teams today are named for birds?

5. What country gets to go first in the Olympic opening parade because they founded the games?

6. What state after Idaho grows the most potatoes each year?

1. Curling

2. 5

3. Yoga

4. 3 (Blue Jays, Orioles and Cardinals)

5. Greece

6. Washington

1. What NBA team scored 54 points in a 1998 game, the fewest since the advent of the shot clock?

2. What Olympic sport did *Flash Gordon* and *Tarzan* portrayer Buster Crabbe engage in before he took up acting?

3. How many weeks encompass the three races of The Triple Crown of horse racing?

4. Who is the star of the *Tomb Raider* video game?

5. What Olympic field sport was almost banished to the outside of arenas on safety grounds until the projectile was redesigned in 1986 so it couldn't be thrown so far?

6. What is it called in snowboarding to strike an object (other than snow) as part of a routine?

1. The Utah Jazz

2. Swimming

3. Five

4. Lara Croft

5. Javelin

6. Bonk

1. How many states does the Appalachian Trail traverse?

2. What is the name of the first kick (also called the front kick) learned in karate class?

3. What began in Russia in the 1940s with the intention of combining the spirit of sports with the art of classical ballet?

4. What domestic art uses terms such as "hern," "pilling" and "basting"?

5. What Oscar-winning Steven Spielberg movie was partly filmed on the Omaha Beach Golf Club overlooking the D-Day beaches?

6. What brewery convinced Irish bartenders to wear green contact lenses advertising pints of stout, on St. Patrick's Day in 2002?

1. 14

2. Snap kick

3. Rhythmic gymnastics

4. Quilting

5. *Saving Private Ryan*

6. *Guinness*

1. What ballpark provided the backdrop to the 1942 Lou Gehrig film biography *The Pride of the Yankees*?

2. What limbs are extended and elevated in the advanced yoga cobra pose?

3. What famed sprinter won long jump gold at the 1984 and 1988 Olympics?

4. What's the sport in *The Hustler*?

5. What decade was the first Indianapolis 500 race held in?

6. What Baseball Hall of Fame and Negro Baseball Leagues player hit 962 home runs in his 17-year career?

1. Wrigley Field in Los Angeles

2. Arms

3. Carl Lewis

4. Pool

5. 1910s

6. Josh Gibson

1. What sport is most likely to cause pudendal nerve entrapment?

2. What state was the 1989 baseball movie *Field of Dreams* filmed in?

3. What *National Hockey League* player scored the most career points?

4. What video game hero do some of his fans call Chomper?

5. What Olympic throwing object weighs 16 pounds for men and 8.8 pounds for women?

6. What common household cleaning tool is used in the sport of curling?

1. Cycling

2. Iowa

3. Wayne Gretzky

4. *Pac-Man*

5. Shot

6. Broom

1. What was the fourth golf title Tiger Woods picked up in 2001 to give him titles in four consecutive majors?

2. What racehorse established a world speed record of 43.2 mph in 1945?

3. How many current *Major League Baseball* teams have never won a World Series?

4. What sense did Graham Salmon lack, although he ran 100 meters in 11.4 seconds in 1978?

5. What decade was the *National Association of Storm Chasers and Spotters* organized in?

6. What is the only figure skating triple jump that takes off from a forward outside edge?

1. Masters

2. Big Racket

3. 8 (Rays, Mariners, Rangers, Nationals, Astros, Brewers, Padres, Rockies)

4. Sight

5. 1990s

6. Triple Axel

1. How many depth of field settings are there between f2.8 and f32 on a typical adjustable camera lens?

2. What World War II B-24 tail gunner was the first *NASCAR* auto racing points champion in 1948?

3. What tennis legend boycotted Wimbledon in the early 1990s mainly because of the strict "mostly white" dress code?

4. What Hollywood actress who appeared in Danny Thomas specials and toured Vietnam with the USO drove racecars as a sideline?

5. What name is given to the person rolling the dice in a game of craps?

6. What is an albatross in golf scoring?

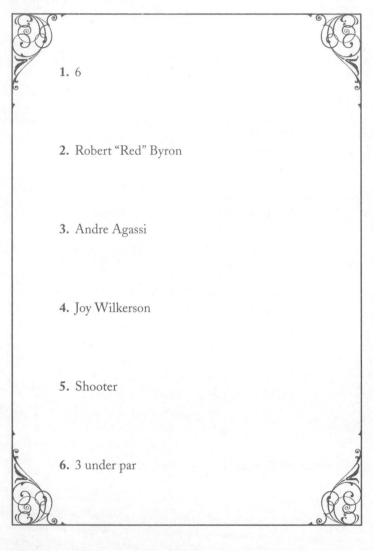

1. 6

2. Robert "Red" Byron

3. Andre Agassi

4. Joy Wilkerson

5. Shooter

6. 3 under par

1. What country invented the Winter Olympic sport of bobsleigh?

2. What event caused *Macy's* to skip its annual Thanksgiving Day parade from 1942 to 1944?

3. What was the first home games console to sell more than 100 million units?

4. What 1996 Olympic event had two U.S. squads playing each other for the gold medal?

5. What year did Hank Aaron best Babe Ruth's career home run record in *Major League Baseball*?

6. What sport is controlled by the *NHL* in North America?

1. Switzerland

2. World War II

3. *PlayStation* (*One* and *Two*)

4. Beach volleyball

5. 1974

6. Ice hockey

1. What *Major League Baseball* team sent three foot, seven inch Eddie Gaedel, the shortest batter ever to appear in a game, to bat as a stunt in 1951?

2. What billiards game shares its name with British military slang for a lowly first-year cadet?

3. What male-dominated sport has Shawna Robinson steered into?

4. What sport boasts such legendary players as Bobby Orr and Gordie Howe?

5. What legendary golf pro, an Augusta National Golf Club founder, had a private cabin built near the 10th tee in the 1940s?

6. What "barely-above-freezing" degree is the ultimate for the Masonic fraternity?

1. St. Louis Browns

2. Snooker

3. *NASCAR* racing

4. Ice hockey

5. Bobby Jones

6. 33

1. What decade was the first *Macy's* Thanksgiving Day parade held in New York City?

2. What kind of patterns are Dutchman's puzzle, log cabin and Irish chain?

3. What sport was featured in the 1992 motion picture *The Mighty Ducks*?

4. What A-word means the same as toxophilite?

5. How many pawns are on the board at the start of a game of chess?

6. What actress and *Playboy* model was once Mrs. Mike Tyson?

1. 1920s

2. Quilts

3. Hockey

4. Archer

5. 16

6. Robin Givens

1. What decade first saw Roger Tory Peterson issue his landmark field guide to birds?

2. What decade heard Red Barber host the first network radio broadcast of a National Football League championship game, over the Mutual Broadcasting System?

3. What was the first home video game to let players take a bead on wildlife with Nintendo's patented "light gun" controller?

4. What nationwide youth organization at different times claimed as members Hank Aaron, Richard Dean Anderson, Neil Armstrong, Michael Moore and John Tesh?

5. What Australian was Wimbledon Men's Singles Champion immediately prior to Roger Federer beginning his winning streak in 2003?

6. What decade witnessed the first *NASCAR* Strictly Stock Series (later renamed Winston Cup Series) run?

1. 1930s

2. 1940s

3. *Duck Hunt*

4. Boy Scouts of America

5. Lleyton Hewitt

6. 1940s

1. What South American country has won the World Cup five times?

2. What was soccer star David Beckham's wife Victoria's career name before she married?

3. What four-letter word describes an arena for public roller-skating?

4. Which state minted Continental Dollars for the fledgling U.S. government in 1776?

5. What sport is featured in the movie *Raging Bull*?

6. Where did snowmobile innovator Joseph-Armand Bombardier establish his factory?

1. Brazil

2. Posh Spice

3. Rink

4. Pennsylvania

5. Boxing

6. Quebec, Canada

1. What horse, whose story has been told in several motion pictures, was the *Daily Racing Form's* Horse of the Year in 1938?

2. What decade saw the Grange Order of the Patrons of Husbandry established in Washington, D.C.?

3. What weapon completes the Olympic fencing trio along with the foil and épée?

4. What youth organization at different times claimed as members Laura Bush, Dionne Warwick, Sandra Day O'Connor, Katie Couric and Melissa Sue Anderson?

5. What basketball star for the Chicago Bulls and Washington Wizards had a Nike sneaker named for him?

6. What decade witnessed Pudge Heffelfinger become the first athlete paid to play American-style football by the Allegheny Athletic Association?

1. Seabiscuit

2. 1860s

3. Sabre

4. Girl Scouts of America

5. Michael "Air" Jordan

6. 1890s

1. What sport's 2004 Olympic tournament included set breaks in which a DJ played music for girls in orange bikinis to entertain the crowd?

2. What javelin thrower, high jumper, base runner and golfer did the Associated Press name as the Greatest Female Athlete of the first half of the 20th century?

3. What *Grey's Anatomy* actor has raced on the Indianapolis Speedway and drives professionally in *Grand American Cup* events?

4. What Scotsman in 1870 put his name to a fashion sewing pattern company, and later a long-running women's periodical?

5. Which has the least calories per pint— *Guinness*, skimmed milk or orange juice?

6. What martial art name means to strike with the feet?

1. Beach volleyball's

2. Babe Didrikson

3. Patrick Dempsey

4. James McCall

5. *Guinness*

6. Tae kwon do

1. How many teams take part in the World Cup finals?

2. What Japanese sport requires one participant to throw his or her opponent out of a "dohyo"?

3. What did his role in the 1968 movie *Winning* inspire actor Paul Newman to take up as a hobby?

4. What is the "inverted jenny"—a yoga position, an ailing donkey or a rare U.S. postage stamp?

5. What 1948 camera created by inventor Edwin Land revolutionized the speed with which photographs could be available to the shooter?

6. What European country did Shaquille O'Neal spend most of his adolescence in?

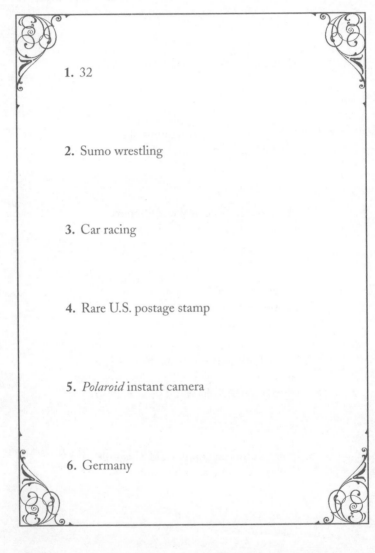

1. 32

2. Sumo wrestling

3. Car racing

4. Rare U.S. postage stamp

5. *Polaroid* instant camera

6. Germany

1. What actress did Olympic swimmer and movie *Tarzan* Johnny Weissmuller marry in 1933?

2. What D-word means bouncing a basketball as you move around the court?

3. What was Cy Young Award-winning baseball pitcher Jack McDowell's musical group, formed in 1992?

4. What decade did Ebenezer Butterick start a company, still in business, to make clothing patterns?

5. What is the link between Neve the snowball, Gliz the ice cube and the 2006 Turin Winter Olympics?

6. What year did baseball great "Joltin' Joe" DiMaggio marry actress Marilyn Monroe?

1. Lupe Velez

2. Dribbling

3. Stickfigure

4. 1860s

5. They were the mascots

6. 1954

1. What is the highest number on a standard roulette wheel?

2. What kind of card have you drawn in *Monopoly* if you win second prize in a beauty contest?

3. What drink would you expect to be served in Dublin if you asked for a "pint of the black stuff"?

4. What sport other than ice-skating was Tara Lipinski a national champ in?

5. Who was the first long jumper to leap over 27 feet?

6. What is *Major League Baseball's* oldest ballpark (built in 1912)?

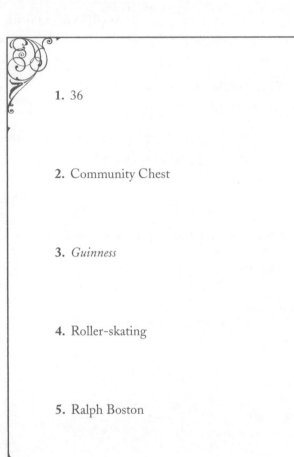

1. 36

2. Community Chest

3. *Guinness*

4. Roller-skating

5. Ralph Boston

6. Fenway Park in Boston

1. What name is given to the inedible plastic discs used instead of cash at most casino tables?

2. What is the only Olympic sport with a ruling against wearing more than the permitted amount of clothing?

3. How many tiles does each player pick at the start of a game of *Scrabble*?

4. Which Wimbledon court stages the main finals events?

5. What do the letters CPT stand for to someone who is new to bike riding?

6. What does a "miter gauge" on a home workshop table saw enable the sawyer to do?

1. Chips

2. Women's beach volleyball

3. Seven

4. Centre Court

5. Cycling proficiency test

6. Cut boards on an angle

1. What iron does a golfer most often use for high-angle shots, to place balls on the green?

2. What 6'2" tennis great has an equally talented, slightly shorter, sister?

3. What 1910s baseball player earned his nickname because his new spikes gave him blisters?

4. What name is given to the ground a skier would ski on and a fencer would fence on?

5. What game can you "squidge," "squop" and "pot out" in?

6. What is the heaviest of the three swords used in Olympic fencing?

1. Wedge

2. Venus Williams (sister of Serena Williams)

3. "Shoeless Joe" Jackson

4. Piste

5. Tiddlywinks

6. Épée

1. What part of Manhattan was the backdrop for many of the photos by James Van Der Zee?

2. What was designated the first National Scenic Trail in the U.S. in 1968?

3. What A-term is the alternative name for gymnastic uneven bars?

4. Whose ear did Mike Tyson bite in a 1997 fight dubbed "The Sound and the Fury"?

5. What Swiss player first became the world's top-ranked men's singles tennis player in February 2004?

6. Who was the only golfer to be named Associated Press Female Athlete of the Year during the 1980s?

1. Harlem

2. Appalachian Trail

3. Asymmetric bars

4. Evander Holyfield's

5. Roger Federer

6. Nancy Lopez

1. Who was the first Boy Scout to become a U.S. president?

2. What company marketed the first digital camera, the DCS-100, in 1991?

3. What two letters appear on the square where all players' tokens should be placed at the start of a game of *Monopoly*?

4. What sport is featured in the 1985 movie *Vision Quest*?

5. How many points are *E* and *O* each worth in a *Scrabble* game?

6. Who said to Lennox Lewis: "I want your heart, I wanna eat your children, praise be to Allah"?

1. John F. Kennedy

2. *Kodak*

3. *GO*

4. Wrestling

5. One

6. Mike Tyson

1. Which city's 1992 Olympic flame was lit by Paralympics archer Antonio Rebello?

2. What country has co-dominated international beach volleyball competitions along with the U.S. since the inception of the game?

3. What was the song the basketball team warmed up to in the 1951 motion picture *Harlem Globetrotter*?

4. What Pittsburgh Steelers quarterback held a national schoolboy record in the javelin?

5. How many days is the Olympic decathlon held over?

6. What team did basketball great Larry Bird play 13 seasons for?

1. Barcelona's

2. Brazil

3. *Sweet Georgia Brown*

4. Terry Bradshaw

5. Two

6. Boston Celtics

1. What Native American group has in its language the word "iditarod," meaning "a distant or far off place," but also the name of an annual Great Sled Race in Alaska?

2. What did a *Sony* advertisement claim is owned by one in three houses in the U.S.?

3. Which is longer—The Appalachian Trail or the Pacific Coast Trail?

4. What sport did Michael Weiss, Timothy Goebel, Michelle Kwan and Sarah Hughes perform in the 2000s?

5. What career did Arnold Schwarzenegger build for himself before acting and governing?

6. What distance is covered by the Olympic sprinter dubbed "the fastest man in the world"?

1. Athabaskan Indian

2. *PlayStation*

3. Pacific Coast Trail

4. Figure skating

5. Body-building

6. 100 meters

1. What decade first saw the America's Cup yacht race competition launched?

2. What British boxer had to stand and watch Cassius Clay given extra time between rounds after he'd knocked him to the canvas?

3. What team has won the baseball World Series the most times?

4. What country traditionally goes last in the Olympic opening parade?

5. When curling was reintroduced to the Olympics in 1998, what country won the women's gold medal?

6. Who played Babe Ruth in the 1992 bio film *The Babe*, a decades-later answer to William Bendix's depiction in the motion picture *The Babe Ruth Story* in 1948?

1. 1850s

2. Henry Cooper

3. New York Yankees (26 times)

4. The host country

5. Canada

6. John Goodman

1. What guessing game, named for an artist, revolves around famous people, initials and indirect questions?

2. What time period in U.S. history is photojournalist Dorothea Lange best known for documenting?

3. Who was the first modern athlete picked to play in pro football *and* baseball All-Star games?

4. What London venue stages the third tennis Grand Slam event played each year?

5. What two-letter abbreviation do weather watchers use when discussing a cumulonimbus cloud or thunderhead?

6. What was the name of the ape that Jumpman, or Mario, had to rescue the maiden from in an early arcade game?

1. Botticelli

2. Great Depression (1930s)

3. Bo Jackson

4. Wimbledon

5. Cb

6. Donkey Kong

1. What sport is mentioned in the full title of the Wimbledon Club along with that of lawn tennis?

2. What sport did the Kenosha Comets, Racine Bells and South Bend Blue Sox play in the 1940s?

3. What did colorful cousins Edwin Binney and C. Harold Smith invent in 1903?

4. Who signed 23 one-year contracts to manage the Dodgers?

5. What NFL team did Vince Lombardi end his coaching career with?

6. Who was Muhammad Ali's opponent when he regained the world title in what became known as the *Rumble in the Jungle*?

1. Croquet

2. Baseball

3. Crayons

4. Walter Alston

5. The Washington Redskins

6. George Foreman

1. What national anthem is traditionally played at the start of the Olympic closing ceremony?

2. How many pockets does a championship snooker table have?

3. What decade witnessed figure skater Ronnie Robertson complete the first triple Salchow jump?

4. What term for territorial and authoritarian surfers first appeared in the 1980s?

5. What city's 1980 Olympic games was the target of a U.S.-led boycott?

6. What did an ice cream man invent when he ran out of dishes, at the 1904 St. Louis World's Fair?

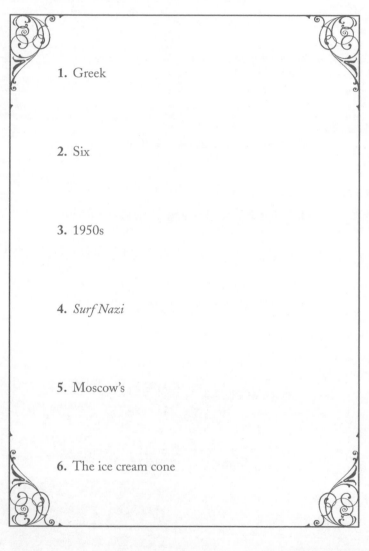

1. Greek

2. Six

3. 1950s

4. *Surf Nazi*

5. Moscow's

6. The ice cream cone

1. What odds are offered on *odd* in a game of roulette?

2. What tennis player was listed as the world's highest earning female athlete at the start of 2006?

3. How many degrees of black belt are there in karate, from student to Hanshi?

4. What grueling event in Barcelona saw Derartu Tulu of Ethiopia become the first black African Olympic champion?

5. What is the name of the home workshop machine used to "turn" wood?

6. What martial art was originated in 1882 by Japanese doctor Jigoro Kano?

1. Even

2. Maria Sharapova

3. 10

4. 10,000 meters

5. Lathe

6. Judo

1. How many colors were in the first boxes of *Crayola* crayons sold in 1903?

2. Who, in 1977, became the last British woman to win a Wimbledon singles title in the 20th century?

3. What actress was brilliant-haired basketball star Dennis Rodman married to for 10 days?

4. What decade brought women in as members of Kiwanis International?

5. What year did Jackie Robinson become the first African-American *Major League Baseball* player in the modern era, for the Brooklyn Dodgers?

6. Which type of bowling has the largest balls and pins—candlepin or duckpin?

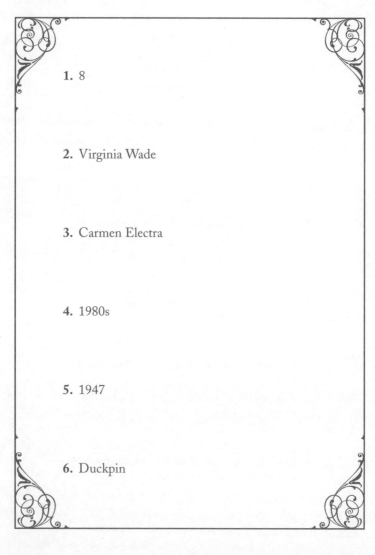

1. 8

2. Virginia Wade

3. Carmen Electra

4. 1980s

5. 1947

6. Duckpin

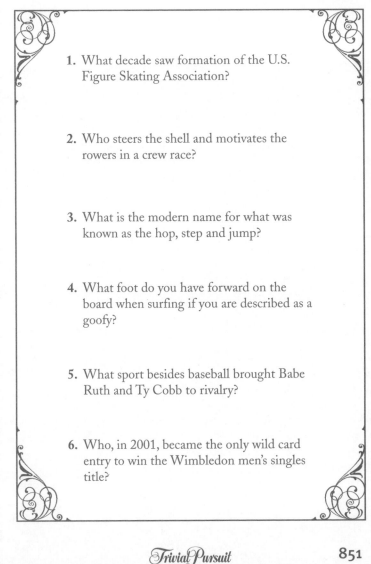

1. What decade saw formation of the U.S. Figure Skating Association?

2. Who steers the shell and motivates the rowers in a crew race?

3. What is the modern name for what was known as the hop, step and jump?

4. What foot do you have forward on the board when surfing if you are described as a goofy?

5. What sport besides baseball brought Babe Ruth and Ty Cobb to rivalry?

6. Who, in 2001, became the only wild card entry to win the Wimbledon men's singles title?

1. 1920s

2. Coxswain

3. Triple jump

4. Right

5. Golf

6. Goran Ivaniševic

1. How many points does a blank tile score if used as a *Q* in *Scrabble*?

2. What state provided the corn field that is backdrop to the "Shoeless Joe" Jackson film *Field of Dreams*?

3. What camera brand name did George Eastman launch in 1888?

4. What sport was played by the Mighty Pigs who were coached by Chief Wiggum on *The Simpsons*?

5. How many points is the outer white ring of an Olympic archery target worth?

6. What athletes chow down on protein-rich "chanko-nabe" to bulk up?

1. Zero

2. Iowa

3. *Kodak*

4. Ice hockey

5. One

6. Sumo wrestlers

1. What football defensive position is dubbed a "rover" or "monster"?

2. What Wimbledon championship offers the largest financial prize?

3. What color are the two stripes around the base of the World Cup?

4. What is the highest possible score in a 10-frame game in bowling?

5. How many pianists simultaneously plinked *Rhapsody in Blue* for the opening of the 1984 Summer Olympics?

6. What is the name of the competition in which Cub Scouts race handmade cars?

1. Safety

2. Men's Singles

3. Green

4. 300

5. Eighty-four

6. Pinewood Derby

1. What sport did the Baltimore Elite Giants, Kansas City Monarchs and New York Cubans play in the 1930s?

2. What brewer claims: "It takes 119.5 seconds to pour the perfect pint"?

3. Why do golf balls have up to 500 "dimples"?

4. What sport is the subject of the book *Sands of Time*?

5. What bowler won 26 Professional Bowlers Association titles, six PBA Senior titles and four National All-Star titles in five decades?

6. What medium does David Allen Sibley use in his *Guide to Birds* (2000) to illustrate his feathered subjects—painting, photos or line drawings?

1. Baseball

2. *Guinness*

3. To make them travel farther

4. Beach volleyball

5. Dick Weber

6. Paintings

1. What 6'11" hurler has risen an inch above 2001 World Series Arizona Diamondback ace Randy Johnson to be the tallest *Major League Baseball* pitcher ever?

2. Who was playing Phil Dent in the quarterfinals at Wimbledon in 1977, when he heard boos for the first time?

3. What nationality is Asafa Powell who broke the world 100 meters record three times in 2005 and 2006?

4. What Latin American nation became the first to host soccer's World Cup a second time, after cash-strapped Colombia was obliged to back out?

5. What color ball sits at the top of the triangle of reds at the start of a snooker match?

6. What is the more common name for an all-terrain bicycle?

1. Washington Nationals reliever Jon Rauch

2. John McEnroe

3. Jamaican

4. Mexico

5. Pink

6. Mountain bike

1. What Braves lefthander registered 363 career victories and 363 lifetime hits in the majors?

2. What decade claims the first patented golf tee?

3. What city was home to the historic *Major League Baseball* team called the Trolley Dodgers?

4. What game, invented by Canadian Dr. James Naismith in 1891, was played with a football until the late 1950s?

5. What *Law & Order: SVU* TV actress is daughter of a former Mr. Universe and Jayne Mansfield?

6. What year did the number of *Crayola* crayon colors increase from 48 to 64—1945, 1958 or 1967?

1. Warren Spahn

2. 1880s

3. Brooklyn

4. Basketball

5. Mariska Hargitay

6. 1958

1. Who pitched for the Brooklyn Robins in the 14-inning World Series game in which Babe Ruth was at the mound for the Boston Red Sox?

2. What is the most common form of chain and multiple sprocket gear system used on bicycles?

3. Whose 2006 demotion from top to 12th in the rankings meant that the U.S. had no representative in the women's tennis singles top ten for the first time since 1975?

4. What decade did the Georgia-to-Maine Appalachian Trail open in?

5. What team did legendary baseball player George Herman "Babe" Ruth move to after playing the 1918 season with the Boston Red Sox?

6. What U.S. president frequently played at the Augusta National Golf Club in Georgia and frequently hit the same loblolly pine with his ball?

1. Sherry Smith

2. Derailleur

3. Lindsay Davenport's

4. 1930s

5. New York Yankees

6. Dwight Eisenhower

DATE DE RETOUR
Veuillez rapporter ce volume avant ou
la dernière date ci-dessous indiquée.

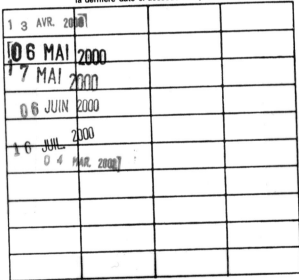

1 3 AVR. 2001			
06 MAI 2000			
1 7 MAI 2000			
06 JUIN 2000			
1 6 JUIL. 2000 04 MAR. 2002			

Galveston

Ace Books by Sean Stewart

PASSION PLAY
NOBODY'S SON
RESURRECTION MAN
CLOUDS END
THE NIGHT WATCH
MOCKINGBIRD
GALVESTON

Galveston

SEAN STEWART

ACE BOOKS, NEW YORK

GALVESTON

This is a work of fiction. Names, characters, places, and incidents are
either the product of the author's imagination or are used fictitiously, and
any resemblance to actual persons, living or dead, business
establishments, events or locales is entirely coincidental.

An Ace Book
Published by The Berkley Publishing Group,
a division of Penguin Putnam Inc.,
375 Hudson Street, New York, New York 10014.
The Penguin Putnam Inc. World Wide Web site address is
http://www.penguinputnam.com

First edition: March 2000

Library of Congress Cataloging-in-Publication Data

Stewart, Sean, 1965–
Galveston / Sean Stewart.
p.   cm.
ISBN 0-441-00686-8
I. Title.
PR9199.3.S794G35   2000
813'.54—dc21   99-35454
                                                  CIP

Printed in the United States of America

10   9   8   7   6   5   4   3   2   1

Galveston

Chapter One

LUCK

"POKER is a man's game," Josh's daddy used to say, "because it isn't fair."

He played every Saturday afternoon on the verandah behind the Ford mansion. Most Saturdays, when the sun began to fall into the Gulf of Mexico, Joshua Cane got the job of fetching his father home for supper. He liked going to the Ford place. Sometimes Sloane Gardner would be over, playing with the Ford twins. Mrs. Ford said Josh was sweet on Sloane, but really it was just that she was curious and gave him a chance to explain things. Everyone agreed Josh was a smart boy.

Even when Sloane and the Ford kids weren't there, Mrs. Ford always let him in and asked him how his mother was doing, and whether business at the pharmacy was good. When he had answered to her satisfaction, she sent him back to the cavernous kitchen, where Gloria the black cook would give him a treat. When his mother found out about the treats, she started sending along three red ibuprofen for Gloria's arthritis. Gloria said she didn't want to be paid, and Josh explained it was a gift. Gloria said his momma just didn't want to feel in debt. Josh figured she pretty much had the right of it.

April 12, 2015, was the hottest day of the spring yet. Josh waved to the Mexican gardener working in the flower bed beside the porch. He knocked on the door and a housemaid let him in. "Master Cane," she said, her curtsey lost under an armful of purple drapes. "I'm just taking these up to be mended. Your dad's on the back porch. Can you find your way?" Josh nodded and she headed upstairs. As Josh stepped into the cool air-conditioned hallway, sweat started up on his skin like water beading on a cold glass. A pair of housemaids sat at the dining room table polishing silver. They paused and bobbed their heads as he went by. No sign of any kids today. Back in the kitchen, Gloria had a pot of craw-dads boiling on the gas range. Clouds of mud-scented steam rose from it, blown apart by the slow chop of the ceiling fan overhead. Gloria was cutting garlic into a skil-let full of hissing butter, and there was a chess pie in the oven. Josh was almost too old to lick the beaters, but not quite.

Gloria frowned into the Fords' massive refrigerator. It had been eleven years since the Flood of 2004 had ended the industrial world, and with no spare parts available, refrigerators were becoming more precious—but of course the Fords had a giant two-door Frigidaire that would squirt out chilled water or ice cubes in two dif-ferent shapes, regular cubes or the little half-moons Joshua liked better. Their freezer was big enough to hold a dressed-out buck and enough doves to make pie for forty, which was what they served each September on the first weekend of whitetail season.

"Well, Joshua, try you one of those," Gloria said, pull-ing out a crockery dish in which a few dozen shrimps lay nestled in crushed ice.

"Thank you, ma'am." Josh took a shrimp, pulled off its legs, and split its shell with practiced fingernails. It was pleasantly cold and firm in his mouth. Munching happily, he stood peeking through the kitchen blind at

the back porch. He liked watching the menfolk play cards and lie to one another and laugh. It was as if there were two wholly different worlds, one for women like Mrs. Ford and Gloria and even his mom back at home in the pharmacy, and another one for men, who worried less and laughed more as they sat outside under the Gulf of Mexico sunset and drank rice beer from recycled Mexican beer bottles, Corona and Tecate and Dos Equis.

Except nobody was laughing tonight. Of all the men on the verandah only his father seemed really comfortable. It was his turn to deal. The sleeves of his cotton shirt were rolled up, and Josh could see the muscles in his forearms move as he shuffled and passed the cards back to be cut. Sam Cane was a notoriously lucky man. The others wouldn't have played with him if he didn't fold so often that there were still pots for the rest of them. Sam sipped from a glass of ice water. He never touched liquor when there was money on the table.

Sam's poker face was an easy smile. Josh's was a worried little scowl, and he still had a lot of tells. His hands shook when he was nervous on his bets, and his eyes tended to widen when he liked his cards. He knew the odds as well as his father did, now; he was smart and good at games and could beat his daddy at chess maybe one time in three. But when they dealt a pack of cards it was as if Josh were sitting there naked as a jaybird, while he never could see past his father's smile.

Around the table men picked up their hands. The game would be five-card draw, jacks or better. His father always said a man was a fool who didn't take advantage of being dealer by choosing a game where he got last choice to open. Directly across from his father sat Jim Ford. He had a big pile of chips at his place but looked nearly miserable. Josh couldn't figure it.

"You'd like to be out there playing, wouldn't you?" Gloria said, washing up a mixing bowl. Josh didn't an-

swer. "Well, go on anyway. Your momma's waiting on you."

"All right." Josh dropped the shrimp head in the slops bucket and pushed the back door open.

Outside the air was warm and sweet. Two hens were in the yard, each followed by a little peeping crowd of chicks, scuffling through the yard for seeds and doodle-bugs. Bumblebees drowsed and hummed among the rose beds and oleanders, which were all out in blossoms, pink and white. The sun was setting and the shadow of the Fords' big Victorian mansion lay deeply over the veran-dah and the yard beyond. Josh quickly closed the kitchen door behind him, mindful not to let the cool out. Six men turned to see him. They looked relieved.

"There you are, Josh," Jim Ford said, running his hand back through his hair. "I was about to figure you got eaten by wild dogs."

"Or carried off by hungry niggers," Carl Banks said. Carl was black. "Sam, your boy's here."

"Hey, Josh. —All right. I'll see that bet and raise you a hundred," Sam said, turning back to the table. Carl and Uwe Krupp folded immediately. That left Jim Ford, Vinny Tranh, Joshua's dad, and Travis Denton.

In all the years since Colonel Denton, a hero of the Confederate army, came to Galveston to make his living cheating cotton farmers, there had never been a civil Den-ton. Of the three great Galveston families, the Gardners were as gracious as could be, the Fords differed each from the next, but the Dentons always had that air of thinking a good thrashing was about what you deserved. Travis Denton was a mass of tells. His voice changed when he was under stress, and he sat leaning over the table with his shoulders high and tight. He even ordered his cards in his hand, right where everyone could watch him doing it. Josh despised a man who couldn't hold his cards.

Travis said, "If you want to bet it, Sam, put it on the table."

It was then Josh realized his dad was out of chips.

Sam Cane didn't say a word. Just looked at Travis, eyebrows up a mite, smiling. He had learned that trick from Josh's mom, that way of cutting out a joke in poor taste or a badly chosen phrase and putting a big fence of silence around it so that everyone had time to look it over. Men known to bluster and rage through any kind of argument ended up wriggling like perch on the hook of that silence.

Jim Ford took a swallow of rice beer from his Dos Equis bottle without meeting anybody's eyes. "Don't worry, Travis. He's good for it."

Josh's dad deliberately wrote out a chit on the back of a piece of paper and placed it in the pot. Looking around the table, Joshua saw there were scraps of paper in Carl's winnings, and Vinny's, and Travis Denton's. A feeling jumped in his stomach as if he were walking by a yard with a big dog unchained inside. His father always brought a bankroll of fifty times the minimum bet. "You can't win playing with scared money," he said. "Quit when you've lost forty-five times the minimum bet. Either you've got no luck, or the other players are way better than you, or the game is crooked. Any one of those is a good reason not to be there. So—in a five-dollar game, how much can you lose before you walk away?"

"Two hundred twenty-five dollars," Josh had said. He had always been good at math.

But something was wrong tonight. Either his father hadn't brought a big enough bankroll, or he hadn't quit when he was supposed to. The betting went around the table as Josh walked over to stand behind his father's chair. Sam Cane closed his hand.

"Won't even let the kid see your cards, Sam?" Carl Banks laughed. He had big white teeth and was vain about them. He had paid a tidy sum to Josh's mother to

set aside her store of Rembrandt Extra Whitening tooth-paste for him. They'd sold him the last tube a week ago. In another year they would have sold every tube of the real toothpaste from before the Flood. Josh's mother was already experimenting with making their own from in-structions in a book of herbal medicine. He had spent the morning chopping sage leaves fine and baking them to-gether with milled sea salt and then grinding the mixture into powder. Josh thought the new tooth powder tasted weird and salty, but his mother said they didn't have a choice.

Josh's father turned and reached up to tousle his hair. "He's a good boy."

"I don't want to see his cards. I still got tells," Josh explained to Carl. "I don't want to give away his hand."

"That's my boy. How many, Mr. Denton?"

Travis Denton took a card. Josh's dad only allowed one draw when he dealt. No sense letting chance run rampant, he said. Jim Ford took three cards, Vince took two. Josh's dad drew one card. It was possible he was drawing to a straight or flush, but without a lot more money in the pot to make it worth the gamble those were poor percentage draws. Josh put him on two pair, draw-ing for a chance at a full house. "Any fool can play his own cards," his father used to say. "The trick is putting the other fellow on a hand."

Sam Cane took a sip of his ice water. "Any bets?"

Vincent Tranh bet. He had a leathery, lined Vietnam-ese face and spoke in a soft South Texas drawl. He al-ways smelled of raw shrimp and chili paste. The KKK out of Beaumont had blown up his parents' shrimp boat in 1978, three years after they came to the States from Vietnam. Claimed they were setting illegal trot lines, which they probably were. They sold their house, bought another boat on the proceeds, and moved to Galveston while Vincent was still a boy.

Vince was the kind of player Josh's dad called a Rock;

usually he only stayed in with very good cards. If Vince was drawing two cards and betting, Josh put him on trips. If Vince didn't have three of a kind, he would at least be holding aces and a paint off. Nine times out of ten Sam would fold his hand if Vince was betting after the draw. He folded more hands by far than any of the other players.

This time he stayed in.

Travis Denton agonized; put his cards down; picked them up and stayed in. Jim Ford folded. Josh's dad called Vince's bet but did not raise. If he was bluffing he'd have raised, trying to drive Vinny out. Vinny was a conservative player. Then again, if he was dead sure of his cards, he would have raised moderately, trying to suck a little more juice into the pot. Josh judged the call to mean his father thought he could win, but wasn't sure. Two pair, most likely, hoping Vince hadn't been dealt trips. "Show 'em, Vince."

The shrimper laid down three queens. "They looked pretty good to me, Ace."

Travis Denton brought his own pre-Flood bourbon to the game and never shared. He knocked back a slug of it. "Fuck me."

Sam Cane smiled and laid his cards facedown on the table. "Vince, you always did have a way with women."

Vince hadn't so much as held a woman's hand since the Flood took his wife. She had been in the hospital delivering their first child when it hit. He had just gone home to sleep for the first time in thirty-six hours. When he woke up, the world had changed. Magic coalesced everywhere in the Flood, clotting around strong emotions, taking on flesh and will. Creatures born of survivors' joy and sufferers' pain, the relief of loved ones and presurgical dread, had warred throughout the University of Texas Medical Branch, leaving the hospital a shattered ruin. Vince had barely survived himself, joining the

Krewe of Thalassar parade while minotaurs stalked the Island's streets.

Vincent Tranh sorted his winnings. He stalled for a second over Sam's IOU before tucking it under a stack of blue chips.

Jim Ford stood back from the table, wiping the sweat from his forehead again and swiping at a mosquito. Sunset was fading to dusk in the rose garden out beyond the verandah. Darkening blue sky closed around the fronds of the tall palm trees behind Jim's mansion. A last burst of animal noise saluted the end of the day: roosters crowed, a pig squealed, cicadas boomed and buzzed. The blue-white lights in the swimming pool came on, making the water glow. The Gulf breeze rustled among the oleanders.

Jim Ford faked a smile for Josh. "You come to fetch your daddy home for dinner?"

"Yessir. I—"

"I ain't quite ready to quit," Sam Cane said. "Just one more hand."

Men studied the roses, or the sky. Carl Banks looked down at the table, not meeting Sam's eye. "I keep *my* wife waiting, there's hell to pay."

Josh knew this wasn't well calculated to get his father out of the game.

"I'm in," Travis Denton said, picking up the deck and shuffling. "Seven-card stud. Sit down if you want to play."

Vincent Tranh stood up. "I can't afford to stay in another hand. Sam's too lucky to keep losing. I don't want to be at the table when Ace finds his touch again."

"That's for damn sure," said Carl.

Little slips of paper were fluttering under chips all around the table. Josh counted seven of them. Something was terribly wrong. "Dad?"

"I'm right here," Sam said. "Jim? I'd hate to sit at your table without you having a piece of the action."

"Dad. Dad, Mom said—"

"Hush, Josh."

Jim fidgeted. "Hell, Sam. You're going to get the boy in trouble. Why not pack it up?"

"Because I feel lucky." Sam was still smiling his easy smile, but there was something else behind it, an edge. He did feel lucky, Josh was sure of it. So lucky, so confident that even those slips of paper weren't unnerving him. Sam turned around and fully met his boy's eyes. "Josh, I'm going to play another hand. I'd be happy for you to stay and be my good luck charm. But if you're worried about getting in trouble, you scoot along home to your mother. I'll be there directly."

Josh looked at his father, calm and easy sitting there, his pale blue eyes that trusted him, trusted his son. He had a frog in his throat that made it hard to speak. "I can wait out a hand," he said.

Travis Denton banged the cards on the table to square them and made a show of shuffling. "You in, Jim?"

Jim sighed. "Yeah, why not. Hell yes. Deal the damn cards."

Three of them in the hand, Travis and Jim and Josh's father. Vince and Carl and Uwe all made as if to leave, gathering up wallets and keys and caps, but as the two hole cards went down they stilled, standing around the table. The sky was darkening fast. It would have been hard to read the cards if not for the light that fell through the kitchen blinds to lie in bars across the table. One by one the city's roosters fell silent. The air seemed to sigh the day's last breath, rich with cicada song and the smell of magnolia. Night coming.

Josh couldn't help peeking when his father checked his hole cards. Four of clubs, ace of clubs. Travis dealt Third Street, the third card in the hand and the first one to be placed faceup in plain view. Four of hearts for Josh's dad. Josh's heart hammered in his chest. One pair by Third Street, with an ace for the side card. A playable

hand. Jack of diamonds to Jim Ford. Dealer showed a seven of hearts.

"Jack to bet."

"No bet."

"Sam?"

"Oh. I'll go in twenty, I reckon. Pass me that notebook of yours, would you, Carl?" He took the notebook from Carl and a pencil and wrote out an IOU.

"I'll see your twenty and raise you twenty more," Travis said. He bit another finger off the hand of bourbon in his shot glass.

"Shit," Jim Ford said, looking at Josh and his dad. He shovelled forty dollars in chips across the table.

Joshua's father wrote out another IOU.

It is a cold fact that after the Great Hurricane of 1900, the Galveston Relief Committee asked the Dentons to give temporary shelter to a group of orphans and the Dentons turned them down. They said they had no space or food or water to spare. A week later, when Will Denton, Jr., told the Colonel that business was bound to suffer from the exodus of survivors from the Island, the old man uttered one of the most famous comments in Island history. "Good," he said. "Remember, we both love to hunt and fish. The fewer people on the Island, the better the hunting and fishing will be." Two weeks after the hurricane, Will Denton, Jr., purchased a thirty-room mansion at 2618 Broadway for ten cents on the dollar.

The Colonel's great-great-great-grandson dealt out another round. "Nine of spades for Jim, no help there." He laid the five of diamonds in front of Josh's dad. "Possible straight. Dealer gets a king of hearts. And that'll cost you forty," he added, pushing four blue chips out into the middle of the table. Travis was trying to scare his dad's money. This was his way of putting the screws into Sam, trying to back him down or make him gamble everything not because he had the cards, but because he had to win.

"Forty?" Jim said. "With only four cards dealt?"

"What's it matter to you? Pay up or shut up, Jim. *You* aren't busted."

"I'll see your forty," Josh's father said. "And I'll raise you another."

Josh's mouth went dry. They always played a $5–$10 game, but somehow things had escalated and they were playing $20–$40. "Dad, what about putting borders on a game? You said—"

"Hush up, Josh."

Josh bit his lip until it hurt. He deserved it. What a horrible tell. He had just given away that his dad didn't have a monster hand.

"I'll see your raise and reraise again," Travis said. He pushed eight blue chips into the middle of the table. No more raises allowed on Fourth Street.

"Great blue Christ, Travis!"

"Jim, are you in or out? If you're in, put up your money. If you're out, shut the fuck up."

Jim Ford scooped up his cards. "I'm out, goddammit." He grabbed up his glass of beer and drank it down and set it back on the table, hard. "Sam, fold up for God's sake. You think you're having trouble with Mandy now? Christ, what the hell do you think is going to happen after this?"

Josh's dad looked up. "I'll ask you not to speak that way in front of the boy, Jim."

Jim Ford looked out into the rose garden that had filled up with darkness. "Sorry, Sam. I just . . ." A little green lizard about the length and heft of a man's finger slipped along the stone verandah and up the wall, watching for bugs drawn to the light that slivered through the kitchen blinds. Jim's eyes dropped down to the stone flags of his verandah. "I'll step in and see if supper's ready."

Josh's dad wrote out another IOU. Travis Denton said, "Feeling lucky, Sam?"

"The whole night, if you'll believe it."

Josh was staring at that lizard. It froze as a mosquito

bumped up against the kitchen shutters. Bump, bump, bump.

Travis laughed. "But you just keep losing."

Snap. The tongue shot out faster than Josh could ever hope to see. Sloane Gardner's mom, the Grand Duchess, still had a dandy computer from before the Flood and plenty of power to run it; they had a picture of a lizard's tongue snapping out to catch a fly on their CD-ROM encyclopedia. Curling out like a whiplash, no chance for the bug. You had to play it in slow motion, frame by frame, to see it at all.

Please, Josh said. Please, Dad. Don't do this. But the words wouldn't come out. He licked his lips, dry despite the sultry Texas night.

"Come on, Sam," Carl Banks muttered. "Come on, Ace."

Travis Denton dealt the Fifth Street card: a deuce of diamonds for Josh's father, a six of hearts for himself. "Still working on a possible straight over there. Dealer has three hearts showing."

Betting. More chips in the center of the table. More little slips of paper.

Josh's dad was sitting with a pair of fours, ace high. All he lacked for a straight was a three. Travis might be sitting on a pair, two pair, or possibly a flush. If he was holding pairs, a four in the draw would win it for Josh's dad with three of a kind. A three would give him a straight; still not good enough to beat Travis's flush if he did get two more hearts. Another ace or five for Sam would give him two pair. It was a good hand, a good situation, except there was too much money in the pot. There was way too much money in the pot. If Sam didn't get a favorable draw, he'd have a pair of fours ace high. You might win with that in seven-card stud, but you sure couldn't bet this high on it. Not as fast as Travis was laying down his bets.

Maybe he had nothing, maybe he was bluffing. "It's

easier to bluff a good player than a bad one," Sam always said. "A bad player only thinks about winning. A good player is willing to throw in and wait for a better hand. He doesn't get embarrassed about being bluffed. He doesn't let it get personal."

But this was personal. It's me, Josh thought. He doesn't want to be shown up in front of his boy.

Why hadn't he waited in the kitchen with Gloria just a few more minutes? Just enough to let his dad take a licking and then get out while there was still time. Dad and Mom would fight about it later, of course. Even Jim Ford knew that. There had been fights before. But now . . . Josh tried to imagine how much was written on all those little slips of paper, those little white flags fluttering under chips all around the table in the dark South Texas breeze.

Their Sixth Street card was a nine of clubs. Another rag, no use at all.

A mosquito settled on Sam Cane's neck. He ignored it. Josh watched it dip its head and begin to drink.

Travis bet. Josh's father called. "Let's get this done," he said. He never said things like that. He never showed himself anxious to see his last card.

A dove broke up from somewhere in the dim grounds, nothing but a sound of wings slapping until it got high enough to be silhouetted against the last blue ashes of light in the west. Josh prayed. Please, God, let my dad draw a three or a four. An ace or a deuce or a five would be okay, but a three or four would be better. I will be very, very, very good if you do this for me.

The last hole card came. Josh's father let it lie there what seemed like forever, then drew it smoothly into his hand, close to his chest, almost too fast for Josh to see— except he could tell it was paint. A face card.

Nothing.

Josh looked up and saw Travis staring at him. He couldn't put on his poker face. He just stood there, trans-

fixed, knowing every line of his body must scream that they had nothing in the hole, nothing nothing nothing.

"Like my boy, Travis?" Sam said easily. "You're looking at him awful hard. You weren't peeking, were you, Josh?"

"No, sir. I didn't see the last cards there, sir."

"Good boy."

"I promise. I couldn't see a thing."

Travis Denton raised his glass of bourbon to hide his face. His hand was shaking. "Looking right through him, Sam. Thinking hard. Seems like a fine boy, though."

Maybe he doesn't know, Josh thought. So what if I looked scared? I ought to look scared with this much money on the table.

"Betting, Sam?"

"I think so." Josh's father wrote something on a slip of paper and tore it neatly from the notebook. It looked too long to be a number. "I wonder if you'll oblige me and take my bet." He passed the piece of paper over.

Travis picked it up. He stared. "I . . . I don't know, Sam."

"That's my wager," Josh's father said, with just a hint of steel behind his smile. "You aren't a Banks or a Ford, are you, Travis? You're a Denton. You can take that bet."

Josh felt Travis's eyes return to him. He looked away, staring hard at the lizard clinging to the wall. Another dove went up and time seemed to open out forever, years and years of it between each slapping wing beat.

Travis took the piece of paper and laid it in the pot. "I call," he said.

Josh burst out crying. He hated himself for it; he grabbed a hand across his mouth and held it there, as if he could shove the sobs back down his own throat, but they tore out, sudden water blurring the stars above him. Tears spilled down his face as his father turned over his cards one by one.

"Pair of fours, you bastard!" Travis Denton whooped.

"By God you were bluffing after all, you son of a bitch! Three fat sevens over here, my friend. Read 'em and weep."

The air came out of the three men watching. Carl Banks leaned over and gave Joshua a hug. His arm was big, and he smelled of sage soap. Josh cried helplessly against his chest. It had been his tell that gave it away. His eyes that doomed his daddy's bluff.

"Sweet Jesus," said Vinny Tranh. He was holding Sam's last IOU.

Jim Ford was standing at the back door. "What's on it?"

For the first time Joshua's father wasn't smiling. His blue eyes were bewildered. "My address," he said.

Travis Denton gave Josh and his family two weeks to move out.

A thin ribbon of sand only thirty miles long and less than three miles from the Texas coast, Galveston Island had been baptized twice: twice thrust under and twice born again, gasping, into a new life.

The Island's first rough cleansing of the modern era came on the evening of September 7, 1900, when a hurricane that seemed destined for the Louisiana coast veered suddenly to the west and caught Galveston square. At that time the Island's highest point was eight feet above sea level. The storm surge crested at twenty. Sustained winds in excess of one hundred fifteen miles an hour ripped roofing slates off the houses and sent them screaming through the air like saw blades. The sea and the wind obliterated everything near the beach, gathered the debris and smashed it into the next line of buildings, over and over. The grinding thresher of rubble, twenty feet tall, scoured 1,500 acres bare, including nearly one third of the city. Where it had passed nothing remained standing: no house, no building, no dock, no tree, no shrub.

One out of every six Islanders died in the hurricane. Thirty-six hundred houses were destroyed. One man counted forty-three bodies left dangling among the trestles of an unfinished railroad bridge. Of the ninety-seven children in St. Mary's Orphanage, three survived. The bodies of nine, still roped with clothesline to a drowned nun, were found washed up miles down the beach. By sundown on September 8th, it had become clear that there were far, far too many dead to bury. Casualty estimates went from fifty, to three hundred, to a thousand, to six thousand killed. Bands of Negroes were rounded up at gunpoint to load the dead and the pieces of the dead onto barges. By the time they got to open water it was too dark to work, so the blacks were forced to spend the night with the stinking corpses. When morning came they tied stones to the bodies and heaved them into the sea.

The next day the dead came back, floating up all along the beach. The stones had not held them and they had slipped their ropes. After that the bodies were cremated on pyres that smoldered for weeks. The Island reeked with the smell of corpses burning.

The Island's second baptism came in 2004, during the week of Mardi Gras. This time Galveston drowned not under water, but magic. It had been rising since the end of the Second World War, a little more every year. When enough magic gathered at a certain time and place, it could be catalyzed by strong emotion. From that reaction a precipitate would fall, a minotaur: a secret lover for the lonely, or, for the bitter or the dispossessed, a nightmare made flesh.

In the spring of 2004 a cascade reaction began, magic kindling magic, the world awash in dreams. The bright rational day of the twentieth century was eclipsed, passing into a long night of spirits, where ghosts walked and a house or tree or road might wake to find its voice and will. In Texas, where people still knew their Bible, they called this cataclysm the Flood.

Over the seven days of Galveston's Mardi Gras, seventy percent of her population was lost. Hundreds died trying to flee when the sea threw down the causeway that linked the Island to the mainland. The mayor put out his own eyes to stop from seeing the ghost of his oldest son, killed years before in a car crash. The sound of screeching metal and shattering glass followed him into his blindness, stopping only when he blew out his brains with a Colt .45 he had grabbed from a policeman detailed to guard him. Hundreds of others followed his example, killing themselves with guns or pills or gas leaks, or running off the long jetties to drop, arms windmilling, into the warm waters of the Gulf of Mexico.

The citizens of Galveston were hunted by more than memories. Terror and madness birthed scores of minotaurs: scorpions the size of dogs, the Crying Clown and the Glass Eater and the Widow in her black dress, whose touch was death and who ate her victims.

However many died, more still fell into the Endless Carnival, where it was always Mardi Gras and always night, where revellers danced on with bloody feet and the singing never stopped. It was a wonderful, glorious riot of a party, thrown by cruel moon-headed Momus. Of the thousands who wandered into his dominion, only a handful ever came back to the real world again.

Each Mardi Gras Krewe sponsored a different event during Galveston's busiest tourist season, a dance or beer garden or concert. The Krewe of Harlequins were marching in their parade when the Flood hit. They were the first to see the magic jump from reveller to reveller, setting the drunks and drug users off like roman candles. When the carnival streets mazed up and the clowns went mad and the ghosts of Galveston's dead floated through the Strand on a chest-high tide, it was the Krewe of Harlequins, still marching in costume or gripping their floats, white-knuckled, who were of the magic enough to ride its wave, apart from it enough not to be rolled under and

drowned. Lucky Samuel Cane had been marching in that parade.

Just as minotaurs were forming out of fear and pain, the strongest Krewes brought their own gods into existence. The drowsing sea, on waking, crystallized around the Krewe of Thalassar. From the hopes and fears of sailors and fishermen she took her form and character, and she gave to the members of her Krewe some measure of protection. As people realized what was happening, they joined any Krewe they could, hoping that the demons of Mardi Gras would spare them. Some Krewes made it, others were broken. The Krewe of Brewe, for instance, was a gang of UT frat boys and party animals who thought of the Galveston Mardi Gras as a cut-rate Daytona Beach scene. If any god formed around their drunken fear, it had no use for them, and their Krewe shredded like wet newsprint in the Flood.

In the end, five major Krewes came through with their people intact: the Harlequins, the women of the Krewe of Venus, the socially active Krewe of Togetherness, the Krewe of Thalassar (originally the Texas A & M boat club), and the ancient and honorable Krewe of the Knights of Momus, which had been celebrating Mardi Gras in Galveston since the 1860s and was ably directed by their grand duchess, Jane Gardner.

Two women saved the Island, Jane Gardner and Odessa Gibbons. Cool, practical, and resourceful, Jane Gardner took advantage of her family name and position as the leader of the most powerful Krewe to direct her fellow citizens after the first tide of magic had receded. She formed work crews and volunteer fire brigades, set survivors to work tapping the natural gas lines that ran in from the Gulf of Mexico for power, and rationed water until the pumping stations could be repaired.

Odessa Gibbons was an angel, a person with a talent for feeling and using magic. She could move back and forth between the real Galveston and the endless party of

Momus's Carnival. Her job was to push all magical things into Mardi Gras: to stand in Galveston like the little Dutch boy with her fingers in the dike, holding the magic back. In the beginning the magic spilled everywhere, but in time Odessa wrestled her island back to some semblance of the world as it once had been. She was merciless in her duties. Islanders came to think of her as a witch; the Recluse, they called her, and their gratitude for her work in the Flood was gradually replaced with fear. Should a child begin to hear the speech of birds, or a woman gain a gift for healing beyond what medicine could explain, sooner or later the Recluse would hear of it. In a day or a week or a month thereafter, the person stained by magic would disappear. Taken into Mardi Gras, or "gone to Krewes," as the saying was.

Josh had often wondered if his lucky father would someday go that way.

Samuel Cane's wife Amanda had been one of only two pharmacists to come through the Flood unscathed and with her full stock undamaged. She was a respected member of the Krewe of Togetherness right up to the day Sam lost their house and their luck began to turn.

Galveston in those days was a bad place and a hard time to be unlucky. Josh's mom never for a moment tried to welch on her husband's bet. After the Flood, luck was omen, not chance, and you took it in deadly earnest. But you didn't risk your family's future on it, either, she said. The words Josh always remembered were, "Your father and I have decided it would be best if we stayed apart."

"Is that it?" Josh had said, turning on his dad, furious, tears in his eyes. "Aren't you even going to, to, to fight it?"

But Sam Cane said, "Sometimes you have to cut your losses."

Two weeks later, Travis Denton brought his wife and three children to inspect their new property. The kids

were playing in the attic when the conjunction of a gas leak and an electrical short blew the house to splinters. Travis and his wife died instantly. Two of the children perished in the fire; the third died a week later from his burns.

"You *see*, Mandy?" Sam Cane said, standing drunk and exultant in the doorway of the smelly little rental house where she and Josh were staying. "We *can* be together. God, it's a hell of a thing, it's a tragedy, but it was going to happen! That's why I had to keep playing. That's why I had to keep losing. If I don't lose the house, that's us down there, it's our teeth they're picking out of the street."

"No, Sam." Josh's mother sounded very tired. "I still love you. But no."

"Don't you understand, Mandy? I've still got it. I still have my luck!"

"I know," Joshua's mother said. "But you don't have us anymore."

Part One

Chapter Two

SLOANE

Josh is ten years old, still living the charmed life his father will lose in a game of cards the following winter. He is sitting next to Sloane Gardner in a deck chair beside Jim Ford's swimming pool and they are looking at the stars. It's one of Jim's magnificent parties; inside Open Gates, musicians have moved from playing "The Yellow Rose of Texas" to covering old Beatles tunes. The older members of the audience join in the chorus. Laughter and lamplight leak out between the shutters.

The kids have been banished to the backyard. Some of them sneak up to the marble verandah to peer in at the singers until a grown-up, strolling the balcony with a glass of palm whiskey, catches sight of the skinny silhouettes and waves them away. The rest of the kids are scattered around the pool, lounging in patio chairs or sitting on the side dangling their feet in the water. The underwater pool lights are on, making it glow a cool, wavering, unearthly blue. Bats whirl and veer, rags of darkness moving in and out of the night so quickly Josh feels more than sees them, tiny winds and shadows that feed on the mosquitoes.

One by one the kids fall asleep in the patio furniture

or are dragged away, bleary-eyed, by parents ready to go home. Josh, having maneuvered to sit beside Sloane, bites his lip to stay awake. He hopes she will talk to him and ask him questions, because she is the most curious of the kids and he is the smartest. She is quiet so long he is afraid she has fallen asleep, so he says, "You know, the stars at night really *are* big and bright, deep in the heart of Texas." She smiles, a very small, private smile, just between them. He explains how the stars twinkle because the column of air between the ground and space is bent and flawed, like bottle glass, so the stars look bigger some days than others, and ripple when you stare at them. His father hadn't told him that; he had read it in the encyclopedia on his mom's computer.

"So why do the stars disappear when you look at them?" Sloane asks.

"Do they?"

"Try it." She squints. "Pick a faint one in the corner of your eye and then stare right at it."

He tries it. "Oh."

"See? Why is that?"

"Well, probably it's . . ." And then Joshua stops, because he had been about to lie, which is unscientific. Instead he says, "I don't know," feeling that he has failed.

She gives him that sly look again, pleased. Her smile goes through him like a shiver on the surface of the glowing blue pool.

A long time later he's almost asleep in the patio lounger next to hers when he feels the dry brush of her fingers against his hand. He lies very still, not knowing what to do, afraid the smallest movement might scare the hand away. He can feel his heartbeat at the base of his thumb; it's like his whole being is concentrated in the skin of his left hand. Her hand creeps farther into his. Their fingers lace together. Laughter comes from the mansion behind them like wind moving through the leaves of the magnolia trees.

"Let's not tell the others," she whispers.

He squeezes her hand and nods, his heart tight in his chest, and stares up at the stars until the sound of her breathing slowly changes, and her warm fingers relax inside his own. He is half-asleep, blue and wavery, lit inside. Gone to water.

AFTER Amanda Cane lost her house and her husband—and her husband's luck—she and Josh moved into a series of smaller places. At first Josh was still invited to the better birthday parties, but time went on. Joshua's clothes grew shabby, his voice broke, Jenny Ford pretended not to see him during the Mardi Gras parade. Randall Denton made fun of him when they met on the street. But Sloane Gardner was the one Josh cared about. For years after they moved into the barrio he found excuses that would take him by Ashton Villa, where she lived with her mother the Grand Duchess. Or he would go to play chess downtown; he was a good player, he won a lot, and the games were played outside in the cobbled square across from the offices of the Ancient and Honorable Krewe of Momus, where Sloane was going more and more often to help her mother run the city.

Amanda Cane lost the lease on her pharmacy. Josh borrowed a wheelbarrow and moved his mom's stock into the front room of their little house on the wrong side of Broadway. Randall Denton, who was seventeen by this time, now ignored Josh entirely.

Then Amanda and Josh got busy with an outbreak of yellow fever. Josh spent more and more time in the library, researching herbal remedies for his mother's shop as the real medicines ran out one by one. Together they learned to make poultices from sage and plaintain to ease the pain of cuts and bruises, brewed up damiana tea for old people with constipation, made chili pepper paste to

ease arthritis, and experimented, cautiously, with morning glory extract for patients with asthma.

Josh developed a bad case of acne, and the pretty Mexican girls made fun of him. He tried to cure the acne by taking infusions of dandelion tea and steam facials made by pouring boiling water over dried yarrow. It didn't work. He kept waiting for a growth spurt that never came. Finally he had to admit that five foot three was as tall as he would ever be. Sloane, on the other hand, grew taller and more poised, and began wearing the smart, tailored clothes her mother favored. For more than three years Josh ducked into any convenient doorway if he saw her coming, and left his mother any errands that would have taken him past Ashton Villa.

He never did grow taller, but his face cleared up and his voice settled in its new register. His clothes were threadbare, but he kept them neat and clean. One day in 2023, just after his eighteenth birthday, he walked down to the Strand to buy some cheesecloth to replace a worn-out strainer. He was wearing a drab but clean shirt of grey Galveston cotton, a good pair of shorts, and a pair of rope sandals when Sloane happened to emerge from the Krewe of Momus building just as he was walking by. He tipped his head in a dignified salute. "Good morning, Sloane."

"It is, isn't it?" And she gave him the polite, impersonal smile that the daughter of the Grand Duchess must keep ready for her mother's citizens. She had not the faintest idea who he was. Josh was devastated.

So much for the fine, genteel life he was supposed to have lived.

Five years later, when the Grand Duchess fell ill, he found himself wondering whether Sloane might come into his shop one day, looking for remedies. A stupid fantasy. The Grand Duchess would have access to real doctors and whatever real medicine remained from before the Flood. He was irritated with himself. Sure, Sloane

Gardner would come to him for help—and what would he give her? Garlic cloves to rub on her mother's feet? Stinging nettle shampoo to put the shine back in her hair?

But as luck would have it, Sloane did come into his shop late that summer, barely conscious, with her dress ripped and blood running down her face.

ON the evening of August 23, 2028, Sloane Gardner sat in front of her vanity, trying to decide what she should wear for a difficult evening. She was booked for two very different occasions. The first was a party to which her mother had summoned Galveston's best society. The second was a secret meeting which would probably cost Sloane her life. She toyed with a case of brown eye shadow. It's the sort of night, she thought, that puts a lot of pressure on one's wardrobe.

A servant knocked on her bedroom door. "Do you need help, señorita?"

"No thanks, Consuela. You get yourself ready."

"Bueno. And your mother . . . ?"

"I'll dress Mother."

"Gracias." Obvious relief in Consuela's voice. None of the servants could stand seeing Jane Gardner reduced to her present pitiful state. Only a daughter was required to bear that.

It was now six o'clock in the evening. An hour and a half for Sloane to dress, then twenty minutes to throw an outfit on her mother, who would fume and complain about wasting even that much time on primping. Their guests would begin to arrive at eight. Allow at least two hours of mingling before Sloane could slip away. . . . It would be ten-thirty at the earliest, then, before she could walk to the haunted amusement park where the Lord of Mardi Gras dwelt and beg for her mother's life. The thought made her sick with fear. But everything else had failed. If she didn't try it, Jane Gardner would die.

Very likely she would die anyway.

Sloane's hands were shaking badly. It was going to be hard to get her makeup on. Damn. Her mother wouldn't be such a coward. As Momus's Consort, Jane Gardner had faced the Moon God every Mardi Gras since 2004. Sloane's godmother, Odessa, was a powerful witch, and Galveston's last surviving angel. For all Sloane knew, she might chat with Momus once a day and twice on Sundays. Sloane was not like those women. She needed the confidence of excellent mascara and well-made clothes. Once her eyes were done and she was wearing a tailored dress, it would be so much easier to be brave.

Sloane studied herself in the bureau mirror. She was tall and carried her weight on her legs: big feet, round calves, big hips and buttocks. I look like a pear, she thought dourly. That explains my psyche, too—easily bruised and squishy in the middle. Her waist and shoulders were slender. She had interesting breasts, she thought—large, but not the high round kind men seemed to admire. Hers hung down on her chest and then swelled at the bottom, with the nipples tilting up. More like squashes than melons. Sloane was what she called privately a Can-be. Her face was average, but well made-up and smiling, she could seem rather pretty. She wasn't smiling now; her skin was clammy and pale. Wincing at her own ugliness she reached for her eye shadow. Courage may come, and courage may go, my girl, but vanity will never fail you.

Most days Sloane tried to use the newer, cruder makeups they could manufacture here on Galveston Island, but tonight she applied the last of the precious pre-Flood stuff Odessa had given her on her sixteenth birthday. It was realistic to anticipate crying, either in fear or grief: non-streaking mascara was definitely called for.

"If you don't want to spend time fussing," Odessa once said, "be bold! The most exhausting use of makeup is to pretend you're not wearing any." This was depressingly

true. Sloane had watery hazel eyes, a pale complexion, and medium brown hair—more pear colors!—leaving her only two real choices. She could dye her hair black or red and then use black pencils and mascara, giving her eyes the contrast to blaze up greenly. This is what Odessa would do. Or she could spend ages in front of her mirror with soft brown eye shadow and pencils, smudging and blending.

Sloane smudged. After forty minutes she leaned back and looked at herself. It was dismaying to see just how subtle the effect was. Still, better to err on the side of sophistication.

She wondered if Momus would rape her. Surely not. Not his stepdaughter.

The air-conditioning droned on, fighting its long losing battle with the Texas summer. A ceiling fan turned overhead, making the mosquito netting around Sloane's bed shake and flutter. There had been no rain since the 4th of July; almost seven weeks now. Jane Gardner and her city were withering together.

Sloane stood and walked over to her window. The glass was hot to the touch. She looked into the backyard. Chickens scratched in the sun-baked courtyard behind the house. Santa Anna, the rooster, jumped onto the power shed where their two matched '02 Lexus engines whirred, powering Ashton Villa's computers and refrigerator and prodigious air-conditioning. The swimming pool was a bare concrete pit. Her mother had drained it by the end of July to encourage water rationing. "Unless you are running a police state, you have to have moral authority to lead," Jane said. She had been a lawyer, before the Flood.

First the face, now the dress. Sloane pulled open the doors of her enormous cypress wardrobe and picked through the ranks of clothes she had made herself, trying to find something she was willing to die in. The charcoal vest was attractive, in a quiet way, but it was diffident

and professional, designed with her role as her mother's executive assistant in mind. Not at all the thing to wear tonight. To walk under the moon's mad stare to the Carnival where cruel Momus dwelt would require more courage than you could reasonably ask of a business suit.

"My outfits are a kind of test," Sloane had told Odessa once. "Most people won't pay me a bit of mind, but the very smartest people will notice." She had been sixteen at the time, and very earnest.

"How will you know if you have succeeded?" her godmother asked.

Sloane considered. "Only half the women will notice me, and none of the men."

Odessa had laughed at that.

Sloane took out several gowns and matched them with shoes and shawls on the dressmaker's mannequin she kept beside her sewing machine. Sloane liked using the ancient Wheeler-Wright treadle model that had been in Ashton Villa since the turn of the twentieth century. It was a survivor, and she needed all the luck she could get.

She chose a full-length lichen-colored dress with brown trim, a scoop neck (not too low), and spaghetti straps that flattered her shoulders. She added a shawl of a different material, a lighter cotton with less body, colored a pale rose-tan with sassafras root dye. Then she added a filmy dark grey veil, dyed with pecan hulls. To the casual observer, having all three pieces of different cloths, unprinted and colored with local vegetable dyes, made the ensemble not much different than what a poor woman might throw together . . . except the pieces were exquisitely matched, and putting the darker cloth of the shawl and veil near her face served to subtly accentuate her eyes.

She would wear the veil back for the party, of course. But later, when she dared the fairgrounds where Momus dwelt, she might need something between her and the god's white stare.

She also wore her most powerful charm, the watch her mother had given her the year she began to menstruate. It was a steel-cased Rolex with gold accents and diamond chips at every hour. "Time is the first thing the magic takes away," her mother said. "Time doesn't pass in the Mardi Gras, not in the ways we understand. Time doesn't pass for savages, either. They live in a wheel that is always the same: winter, spring, summer, fall; winter, spring, summer, fall. To know the time of day, to know the day of the month, to know what year it is, and to have built something new and better since the last year on this day: that's civilization."

Sloane held the Rolex up to her ear and listened to it tick. Some days her mother's life, sliced up into ten-minute meetings and half-hour speech appearances, seemed horribly suffocating. On those days, the watch was the last charm she wanted to wear. But tonight its grave, reliable march seemed very reassuring. Tick, tick, tick. Something you could depend on. Sloane felt calmer now that she was dressed. She returned to the mirror and regarded herself. No beauty, but a young woman of hidden strengths. Not a politician, not a governor, not a leader. Not a Grand Duchess, she would never be able to live up to that. A facilitator, though. A woman who knew her duty.

A nicely turned-out sacrifice?

Sloane snapped her makeup case shut. Enough of that.

THEY had moved Sloane's mother to the parlor on the ground floor in June, when she got too weak to manage the stairs. She was sitting in her wheelchair looking out the front window at the flower beds that the sun by slow degrees had burned away. Jane had banished all the overstuffed Eastlake furniture from the parlor the day she moved in, replacing it with the spare rubbed-oak pieces from her room. "Nobody can think sensibly, surrounded

by this," she had said with a wave of her hand. She had more energy for hand-waving then.

Sloane put her makeup case on the austere Bailey-Scott end table by the bed. "Are you comfortable?"

Jane Gardner said, "It's like being buried alive, one shovel of dirt a day."

The Grand Duchess had started feeling poorly not long after Mardi Gras. By May they both knew it couldn't be arthritis, or the flu, or age. Sloane finally forced her to see her doctor. The diagnosis was devastating: Lou Gehrig's disease. While Jane's mind was as sharp as ever, a creeping paralysis had gripped her body. Her skin and limbs were going to die from the outside in, inch by agonizing inch. Eventually the paralysis would reach her heart, or her lungs, and she would die. The disease seemed to be progressing unusually fast; the doctor was worried there might be a thread of magic complicating its progress. Jane wasn't much taken with that idea. "Uneasy lies the head that wears the crown, eh? Good grief."

Sloane helped her mother reposition herself more comfortably in her wheelchair.

"I know you scheduled feeling sorry for myself from ten-thirty to ten-forty-five this morning," Jane said after a pause, "but my meeting with Randall Denton ran late and I just haven't had a chance until now." Her way of apologizing.

"If feeling sorry for yourself is too much bother, I can do it for you."

"Ha." Jane looked at her daughter and shook her head. "You look nice, dear. Not gaudy. Beats me what you do that takes so long, though. With the fine folk coming, do you suppose we better have Sarah polish up my chrome?" she said, glancing at her wheelchair. "That was a joke."

Sloane tried to smile. Her mother's speech had begun to slur, just the tiniest bit. Probably nobody else could notice it yet, the softness creeping into her consonants as it got harder and harder for her to make her tongue and

teeth do exactly what she wished them to. Sloane helped her mother take off her workday clothes. She could still manage most of it herself, but certain movements were pretty much beyond her now, particularly putting her arms behind her back to slip out of a sleeve or do up a zipper.

Down to her underwear, Jane grabbed a cane and shambled to the bathroom. When she emerged again, Sloane had a couple of outfits on the bed, waiting for her. "I figured the black gown might be good."

"A bit startling against this skin, don't you think?" Immured in the house for months by the disease, Jane Gardner's skin had grown pale and wrinkled, like an old mushroom.

"I brought some foundation—"

"No."

"For God sake's, Mother, you're going to look—"

"Like I'm dying?"

"You can't just give up!"

Her mother sank unsteadily onto the bed, took a breath, and rested her cane against the nightstand. Then she turned and studied Sloane for a long time. "It would be so much more comfortable for you if I pretended nothing was wrong. If I made like I would always be here to do the crap I do, and you would never have to."

Sloane said nothing, transfixed by the horrible feeling she had been caught out. Jane Gardner finally let her gaze drop. "I didn't do you any favors, letting you hide so much. You were such a scared little girl. But there are some things you can't run away from."

Sloane helped her mother into a charcoal pantsuit. Halfway through the effort Jane stopped wasting her breath complaining. Her face was drawn by the time she dropped back into her wheelchair. She sat resting with her eyes closed as Sloane slipped a pair of black pumps onto her feet.

At last she opened her eyes. "You remembered to invite everyone I told you to?"

"And the ones you forgot."

"Who did I forget?"

"Kyle Lanier." Ugly little bandy-legged man, Sloane thought. And then, You are so superficial.

Her mother tsked. "Quite right, Jeremiah's new deputy. He's a climber, isn't he?"

"His grandmother was a Rosenberg, but she married badly and they fell out of society. He's hungry to get back in."

Jane nodded. She respected Sloane's opinions on people. "It's the Fords and the Dentons who are key, still. Jim Ford's a good guy, but old and a bit of a softie." Sloane picked up the case of foundation. "Stop that," Jane said. Sloane put it down again. "You won't have any trouble with Jim, but his kids are a different story. He spoiled them rotten. You'll have to be careful how you handle them when Jim steps down. And Randall Denton is a snake with a spare set of fangs."

I'm not you, I'm not you, I'm not you. "At least some blush?" Sloane said.

"For Christ's sake, Sloane, I'm not going to my prom. I've spoken with Jim Ford and Jeremiah Denton. They understand the need for the Krewe to preserve a stable, united front after I die. Especially with this drought."

"Mom, I can't be you. Please listen to me."

"Honey, when I was your age I wasn't me either." Sloane's mother turned her head to look at her daughter. "One of the hardest lessons we all have to learn is how few choices life gives to a civilized woman with any conscience at all."

SLOANE wheeled her mother into the Gold Room where she would hold court, parking her beside the famous square piano on which the ghost of Bettie Brown still played a few nights every year. Since Jane Gardner had

moved into Ashton Villa after the Flood, the Gold Room, with its towering gilt-framed mirrors and French settees, had once again become the center of Galveston's social scene. Sloane was sure this must please Miss Bettie's ghost. Her mother thought this was being fanciful, which mostly proved that Jane Gardner, though a great leader, was still a woman of her time. Unlike Sloane, she had been born into a world almost without magic, whose assumptions she would never entirely shake.

Jim Ford was the first of their guests to arrive. Since the death of his first wife, Clara, there had been nobody to keep Jim from showing up for dinner parties at exactly the time written on the invitation. It was an open secret that he and his black housekeeper, Gloria, were now a couple, but he wasn't brave enough to bring her to this kind of soiree, despite the gentle encouragement of the Grand Duchess. A wise move, Sloane thought; his unpleasant children would never let him hear the end of it.

The Fords had controlled Galveston's wharf since the Civil War, and Jim carried his money with unthinking grace. Like a lot of men whose sense of style had been set before the Flood, he favored trousers with braces, comfortable boots, and light suit jackets. And a string tie! Sloane noted. Thank God Clara didn't live to see this.

Meow. Sloane reprimanded herself as she escorted him into the Gold Room. Bad girl. No mouse. "Rice wine?" she asked, walking to the giant cherrywood sideboard across from the piano.

"Thank you, Sloane." She poured him a drink and put in an ice cube, which she knew he liked but was embarrassed to ask for. He smiled when she returned with his drink. Glancing across the room to where her mother was consulting with Sarah, their housekeeper, he lowered his voice. "How is she?"

Dying. "In good spirits, as you can see."

"Your mother is an extraordinary woman."

"So she tells me." Sloane smiled. "Nobody believes it

more than me, either. You know, this morning we were worrying about whether there would be enough gunpowder to trade into Beaumont, but Mom told me not to worry. 'Jim will handle it,' she said."

He grinned, passing his hand over what had once been hair. Jim Ford was one of the three directors of the Krewe of Momus, along with her mother and Jeremiah Denton. Jim was so modest, and so happy to be well thought of, that flattering him was one of Sloane's most pleasant duties.

"Oh, don't you worry," Jim said. "Production is down a bit here, but the cannibals on Bolivar Peninsula are so bad this year that Beaumont's desperate for all the powder it can get. We'll up our price by a hundredweight of rice per fifty cartridges, say, and come out better than last year. As long as those cannibals don't start building boats, we're in good shape." He lowered his voice again. "Do you know . . . how much longer?"

Six months? Or weeks? Or days? "She hasn't said."

"It must be hard on you."

Not as hard as dying. Sloane shrugged.

Jim glanced around reflexively, making sure he was not standing next to a window or beneath a skylight where, unnoticed, a beam of moonshine might finger him. It was said Momus could see and hear anything lit by the moon. "Has *he* given you any sign?"

Ask me in six hours. Sloane shook her head. A tricky moment here, as Jim looked at her with such sympathy that it was hard not to break down, but she let the panic pass under her like a wave rolling in from the Gulf. "Would you excuse me, Jim? I need to consult with Sarah," she said, escaping under the cover of her practiced smile.

Guests trickled in and Sloane plied them with appetizers: oysters on the half shell, spicy tomato-pepper antipasto, rings of petite rice crackers, popcorn shrimp in silver bowls of crushed ice, and little sushi wraps made

by a Japanese woman the cook knew, seaweed around rice and stuffed with crawdad meat.

Sheriff Denton arrived, gracious as always, with Kyle Lanier at his side. Kyle was an ugly little schemer, with small brown eyes and a badly pocked face. When they had first met in their late teens, Kyle could never lift his gaze above Sloane's breasts, but she noted with some amusement that now that he had risen high enough for her political connections to matter, he did a very fair job of making eye contact. She ditched him as quickly and gracefully as she could.

Commodore Travis Perry of the Krewe of Thalassar was next to arrive, still smelling faintly of the sea, water-stains on the cuffs of his pants. Then came Horace Lemon, the chunky old black director of the Krewe of Togetherness. His curly hair was turning white at the ends, as if singed. Then Jane's doctor and her husband came, shortly followed by Ellen Geary, the current head of the Krewe of Venus.

The Krewe of Harlequins was last to be represented, Dietrich Bix arriving just before nine in a cap and bells. "Glad you could come," Sloane said as the elderly Bix kissed her knuckles. His was one of the invitations she had sent out on her own. The older Jane Gardner got, the more she avoided the Krewe of Harlequins. They were tiring and unpredictable, she said, which was true. "The Krewe of Momus wants to divide the pie by merit," Jane had once said. "Thalassar wants to divide it by risk. Togetherness wants everybody's share to be equal. Venus doesn't care what size the slices are, as long as a woman gets to serve it. But the Harlequins just want to pick the pie up and throw it in your face, and too bad if everyone goes hungry." More to the point, the Harlequins, alone of the five major Krewes, had always been dead set against Jane and Odessa's strategy of keeping the two Galvestons separate, with all the magic confined to the dark Carnival where Momus was king.

"You expecting the Recluse tonight?" Dietrich asked, bells jingling as he raised his lips from Sloane's hand. "I had a prank or two I meant to pull."

"I imagine Odessa will come."

"I reckoned as much. Thanks for the heads up," Bix said. "Don't want the witch to catch me doing a card trick and send me to Krewes for it." Sloane watched the Harlequin plunge into the crowd, wishing that daughters of the Ancient and Honorable Krewe of Momus could escape from Mardi Gras as easily as rumor said the Harlequins could.

She very badly wanted a drink.

Odessa made her entrance just after nine, preening like a peacock and pausing to frame herself dramatically in the doorway to the Gold Room. The crowd of guests went still. Dietrich Bix, who had been pulling a coin out of Commodore Perry's offended nose, palmed it and stood with his hands behind his back and his eyes downcast. There was no trace of sly defiance in his stance. Despite his joking earlier, he knew perfectly well that he was a marked man in Odessa's book, living in Galveston, like all notable members of his Krewe, on the witch's undependable sufferance.

Galveston's last angel had outdone herself: a plum-colored satin brocade sheath and sleeveless vest, over which she had draped yards and yards and yards of a fantastical sari of wafer-thin cotton, hand-painted with scores of miniature birds—a print that only a slender woman could possibly survive. On Sloane it would have looked like an explosion in an aviary. The draping was brooched into a graceful swirl at Odessa's hip, but as soon as she was inside she stopped, unpinned the brooch, and let the material fall, revealing a three-foot train that everyone else was going to have to spend the rest of the evening trying not to step on. Sloane winced.

Odessa caught Sloane's eye, smiled, and mimed throwing back a quick drink. The room emptied around her.

Jim Ford stopped to chat with her for several minutes; he had known her before the Flood. But everybody else feared her much too much to make casual conversation. The other Krewe leaders, exquisitely polite, paid their cautious respects and escaped as soon as decorum would allow.

As Commodore Perry excused himself from Odessa's company at a (prearranged) signal from one of his subordinates, Sloane approached and handed her godmother a tumbler with two fingers of palm whiskey inside. Odessa leaned back, studied Sloane's outfit, and cackled. "It's the poor little rich girl!" she cried, waving her drink. "You sly little mouse, you. And, doll! Your eyes! They're beautiful! They must have taken *hours*."

"Of course not." A hot prickle of embarrassment crept up Sloane's neck.

"The application of time and skill to frivolous things is the hallmark of civilized society," Odessa remarked. "Any savage can face down a lion or suckle a baby, but History begins with Cleopatra dyeing her hair, if you ask me. Another dreary day of toiling and spinning on Jane's behalf successfully concluded, I trust? How wonderful for you." Odessa presented her aging cheek for a kiss. "What do you think of my train? Too tasteful, yes?"

"It makes a very graceful loop when you brooch it."

"Brooched, you think? That seems like a waste." Odessa sipped her whiskey. "I expect you're right, but not all of us have your assets to work with, you voluptuous young thing."

Good grief.

"EVERYONE is always very keen to praise you Gardners for your public spirit," Randall Denton was saying to Sloane fifteen minutes later. "But the truth is, you're the least democratic gang on the Island."

She had just caught him staring at her breasts. She decided against making it obvious that she had caught

him, because she knew that it would be not Randall but herself, annoyingly, who would end up blushing and embarrassed. "Wine, Randall? Or will you not drink the liquor of tyrants?"

"Oh, we Dentons have never had any problems with tyrants," Randall remarked, accepting a glass of rice wine. He was a slender man in his late twenties, already balding. He had been one of the young men who set the current fashion for severe, tightly cut evening clothes: a narrow black fitted jacket over a collarless mandarin shirt, pants tailored skintight around the calves and ankles, and pointy black dress shoes so polished Sloane could see the chandelier reflected on their uppers. Sloane always thought the effect of the ensemble was to give Randall a predatory look, like a black-and-white wasp. The only splashes of color in his outfit came from the small gold and scarlet scorpions painted on the silk scarf draped around his shoulders in complete defiance of the sweltering Texas heat outside.

"For a hundred and fifty years you've managed to hoodwink this Island into calling 'civic leadership' what is actually the uncontrollable Gardner urge to run other people's lives," Randall continued. "As if the sun wouldn't recollect to rise without your benevolent reminders."

This so exactly articulated a thought Sloane had suppressed as disloyal dozens of times that all she could do was blink.

"What I. H. Gardner and the City Club did to this Island after the Hurricane of 1900 would have been called a 'bloodless coup' if it had happened in some swarthy banana republic," Randall added pleasantly. "Excellent mussels, these," he said, spearing one with a little two-tined oyster fork. "After 2004, your mother did the exact same thing. Did you think nobody noticed the parallel?"

"Then why didn't someone oppose her? Why didn't your father say something, or Jeremiah?"

"It seems to amuse Gardners to run things, and they do a tolerable job of it. We Dentons aren't keen on democracy either," Randall said with a smile. "We're just not hypocrites about it."

And so it went. Within an hour Sloane had spoken to everyone, been asked the same questions and given slightly different assurances, pleasant but impalpable in the manner of a good hostess. She waited until Sarah was in the Gold Room, passing through with a tray of pickled mussels, and then slipped back into the kitchen. From there she walked quickly along the covered walkway that led out to the stables.

Outside it was hot and breathless. She followed the walk around the front of the carriage house and then passed the public garden, its flowers wasted in the cracking earth. The centerpiece of the garden was a raised platform from which rose an open latticework dome. This was supposed to be wound about with flowers, but the vines had died and no petals obscured the motto old George Ford had ordered built into the iron tracery a century before: *One generation passeth away and another generation cometh: But the earth abideth forever.*

Apparently the author of Ecclesiastes had not shared her mother's vision of the march of civilization. But really, if you felt God, or gods, you couldn't believe in Jane Gardner's world, could you? That great order the older generation had grown up with, before the Flood, was based on the idea that the world was inanimate: a giant machine from which an intelligent person could assemble other machines, like cars and schools and child labor laws. But in a world alive, where that car might have a will and the gods would have their way . . . ? Jane Gardner would have said the twentieth century was founded on reason, but Sloane wondered if vanity might be closer to the truth.

Broadway, the boulevard that passed in front of Ashton Villa, had been the widest street in America when it was first built in the 1800s. Palm trees and live oaks grew by its sides and along the center median, creating a double tunnel of leaves. Tree roots had long since made the sidewalk a nearly impassable jumble of tilting concrete slabs. Sloane walked in the road itself, not far from the gutter, feet brushing through the thin covering of wilted salt grass, shepherd's purse, live-oak leaves, and brittle palm fronds that lay over the asphalt. There was no traffic. People preferred to stay indoors on nights when the moon was full. Only the Krewe of Momus would schedule business for such an evening.

Her shadow crept up, caught, and passed her as she walked by the hissing gas streetlamps in the better part of town. Her eyes hurt. Gardners weren't supposed to cry. At the far end of Broadway, where the Stewart Beach Amusement Park waited at the edge of the Gulf of Mexico, the moon was rising in a cream-colored haze. Sloane felt its gaze and dropped her head. Be small. Be silent. Two tears slipped over the edge of her aching eyes and crept down her cheeks. She wiped them off with the palm of her hand. Waste of water.

Every spring, the Mardi Gras parade followed the same route the Krewe of Harlequins had walked on that fateful night in 2004 when the world changed forever. They started at the old train station just west of downtown, long since turned into a railroad museum, then walked through the Strand, Galveston's tourist and business district, and finally stopped at the gates to the Stewart Beach Amusement Park, where Momus had established his court on the first night of the Flood.

Here, where Broadway ended at Seawall Boulevard, the gap between the real Galveston and the Galveston still locked in Carnival was only inches. Jane Gardner had ordered a tall fence erected in her first year in office, so those having business along the Seawall would be pro-

tected from seeing the unholy carnival seething below. Fairground noises drifted up over the fence to Sloane, the rhythmical barking of the hucksters at their stalls, the clink and clatter of baseballs hurled at milk jugs and BB guns fired at metal ducks. Faint strains of calliope music, inexpressibly sad.

Sloane hovered on the corner of Broadway and Sea-wall Boulevard. A single doorway had been left in the wooden fence; through it a set of concrete steps led down to the beach, and the world of magic. Next to the door stood a ramshackle ticket-taker's hut. Even by moonlight Sloane could see the gaily painted facade around the door, with clown faces and balloons, a Bearded Lady and a Wheel of Fortune. Silver letters on the door spelled out the motto of Momus's kingdom:

It Just Doesn't Get
Any Better Than This!

Sloane stood on the corner with her heart hammering in her chest. She lifted her left wrist up to her ear and listened to the patient *tick, tick, tick* of the Rolex, letting it steady her.

A snatch of mad calliope music greeted her as she headed for the ticket-taker's booth.

Chapter Three

MOMUS

THE night smelled of crabs and salt and wet sand. The dark air was murmurous with laughter and shouts and distant music, and under everything else the rhythmic roar and hush of the breaking sea. Sloane glanced back over her shoulder. The faint glow of the last gas lamp on Broadway seemed very far away. She forced herself to step onto the sidewalk and walk to the ticket-taker's booth.

"Evening, Sloane," said a voice from the shadows. "Feeling lucky, are you?" The voice sounded neither young nor old, male or female.

I will not faint. "I, I, I'm sorry," Sloane stammered. "You know my name."

"I know everybody's name."

"Oh. Ah, I didn't mean to trouble you. I n-need—" *For God's sake, woman, you're a Gardner. Stop sputtering like a ten-year-old.* "I need to see Momus."

"Hold out your hand," said the voice.

Goose bumps ran up Sloane's arm as she stretched out her arm toward the ticket-taker's booth. She flinched. "What are you going to do to me?"

"Give you a stamp. Hold out your hand."

"Is that all?"

"Admission is always free." The ticket-taker chuckled. "You'll do your paying inside. Hold out your hand."

Sloane squeezed her eyes shut. Pushing her hand under the ticket-taker's wicket and into the shadow beyond was like sticking it into a drawer full of spiders. Something stung her on the wrist, just below the steel band of her watch. She gasped and jerked her hand back. A silvery caricature of Momus glowed on her skin, a round head with two little horns and an evil grin. Even now, sick with dread, she remembered to say, "Thank you." You get more done with good manners than quick wits. Her mother hated it when Sloane said that.

She started down the concrete stairs to Stewart Beach. *Admission is always free. You'll do your paying inside.* I bet.

The noise of the Carnival grew louder with every downward step. Fairground smells eddied up the stairwell: barbecue and cigarettes, spilled beer and . . . popcorn! Sloane was amazed how easy it was to identify the aroma. She could have been no more than nine years old when the last bag of popcorn ran out.

When she got to the bottom of the stairs she did not plunge at once into the Carnival to look for Momus. Instead she hung back in the shadowy doorway, staring out at the scene before her. Aproned stall keepers hawked cold beer, nachos, sno-cones, pickled jalapeños and cotton candy, corn-on-the-cob and licorice and popcorn. Tongues of flame reached up from a dozen makeshift grills to lick barbecued ribs and chicken and brisket and shrimp, German sausage and hamburgers and ballpark franks, all bursting and blistering. The air was full of smoke, clouds of it, wafting up from barbecue pits, cigarettes, fire-swallowers' wands, and fat cigars.

There were hucksters' booths by the score, each with a different barker, adorned with bunting or blinking lights or bobbing balloons. People milled between them, trying

to knock over milk jugs with a baseball, to guess the weight of the Fat Lady, to ring the bell with one whack of a sledgehammer. They hurled pies at clowns and tossed rings at pegs and pulled mightily at a giant fortune wheel with gypsy letters that rattled and slowed and shuddered to a stop like an old heart giving out.

Even the weather was different in Mardi Gras than it had been outside, cooler and less humid. As her mother had warned her, it was always the same night in Mardi Gras: February 11, 2004. Sloane lifted her Rolex to her ear. To her enormous relief it was still ticking. It was said that clocks and watches ran badly in Carnival, or not at all, but the Rolex was a talisman as well as a machine, and some combination of superior workmanship and her mother's love seemed to be keeping it safe from harm. What charm could be proof against the spells of Momus's court, Sloane figured, if not a favor from his Duchess?

All the revellers in the crowd were wearing masks, it seemed. Sloane unpinned her veil and let it drop across her own face. No, wait—looking closer she realized that many in the crowd were not wholly human. A feathered woman stood on one leg like a heron, squinting hard as she tried to guess the Fat Lady's weight. A man munching on a D-cell battery as if it were a pickle passed not three feet from where Sloane was lurking. He had steel teeth and his fingers were ridged like pliers. Sloane cringed more deeply into the shadowed doorway. These must be people the magic had been working for years and years. Caught in the first days of the Flood perhaps.

Their clothes were extraordinary. They wore cotton, immaculately carded and woven impossibly tight—blue jeans and denim vests of a quality Sloane had only seen in photographs. Some of the women had taken advantage of the gorgeous weight and beautiful hang of rayon. Sloane saw rough silks and smooth jackets of cool linen, clinging jersey camisoles, and more lace than an army of grandmothers could knit in a year. All the clothes were

dyed in bright pre-Flood colors Nature only showed on flowers or fish—lemon yellow, glossy scarlet, copper and silver and ultramarine.

She soon found she could pick out the more recent arrivals by their clothes. Even the ones who had begun to lose their human form, growing whiskers or scales, were immediately recognizable by their rough cotton shirts, tire-rubber sandals, and the dingy, drab dyes Galvestonians made themselves from pecan hulls, live-oak bark, and broom.

With a shock Sloane realized something else: everyone seemed to be having fun. Men boasted, women smiled, children clapped and hopped, shrieking with excitement or chasing one another through the forest of adult legs. Somehow Sloane had always assumed that Carnival must be a kind of hell, full of tormented souls in a ghoulish parody of amusement. It had never occurred to her that it might really be a heck of a party. She blinked. *It just doesn't get any better than this.* She found herself smiling at her own obscure sense of disappointment. She must be more of her mother's daughter than she realized, a disapproving ant made surly by the sight of grasshoppers at play.

A cat-headed woman in a gold lamé sheath padded by Sloane's hiding spot.

Time to find Momus. Annoyingly enough, her legs wouldn't move. Come on now. Scared? she said to herself. You're the best-dressed woman in the place.

Sloane had spent a lot of time learning to be invisible; it had been part of her character from toddler days, the desire to sit quietly out of the way and observe others without being noticed herself. A useful skill for anyone acting as Jane Gardner's assistant, but a rotten trait in a grand duchess, as she had tried a hundred times—politely—to point out. But invisible was exactly what she wanted to be now.

Bodies pressed and jostled against her as she stepped

into the crowd. She hunched her shoulders, as any tall girl with large breasts learned to do, and kept her head down, careful not to risk eye contact. Now she wished she were wearing something less elegant than her lichen-colored evening dress. Nobody here is going to notice you, she told herself, but the old familiar dread that everyone was watching her spread like a flush across her skin.

"Peanuts! Hot roasted peanuts!" someone bellowed directly in her ear. "Cotton candy!"

"Everyone's a winner, ladies and gents!"

"—Virgen Sagrada has blessed me with oracular—"

"Beads! Beads!" cried a black woman entirely decked in necklaces of plastic beads. "Honey, you need some beads!"

"No, thank you," Sloane said, sidling toward a ringtoss as if she were extremely interested in the stuffed monkeys offered for prizes.

The black woman grinned. "You must be new, you think you don't need beads." She laughed. "Come see me when you know better, honey."

"Easy shot, miss. Easy shot for a monkey," said the ringtoss huckster, holding out a handful of plastic rings.

"Actually, I wanted to see Momus."

The huckster cupped his ear. "What was that? Speak up, honey. Two sets of rings?"

"Momus," Sloane yelled. "I need to see Momus."

The god's name dropped into the crowd like a stone falling into a pond. Silence washed out from her. Revellers glanced at one another and backed away. "Not so loud," the huckster hissed. "Want me to lose all my customers?"

"Sorry."

"Manager's tent," he growled. He pointedly turned his back and held out a handful of rings to a small boy wearing a snakeskin mask. "Take a few shots for free, sonny! Absolutely on the house, to show how easy it is to win

a prize. Someone has to win, ladies and gentlemen—why not you?"

Sloane backed away from the ringtoss, trying without success to see anything that might be the manager's office.

An emaciated young woman in a fancy dress yanked on her sleeve, bawling, "You always were a bit of a wet blanket, Sloane!"

"Omigod." Sloane stared. "Ladybird? Ladybird Trube?"

"The one and only."

"But how—"

Ladybird shrugged. "Either I'm crazy, I'm dead, or Odessa found out about the ghosts I kept seeing around our mansion and sent me to Krewes. To be perfectly honest, darling, I try not to dwell on it. I'm having a simply fabulous time, without Mother around to spoil it for once." She raised a plastic wineglass to her lips and sipped a pale drink from it. "You know she was blackballed by the Daughters of the Texas Revolution again? Those seven lean and hungry kine who guard the application process cast aspersions on our paperwork. Mother keeps using little bits of Scotch tape to fix things up. I say, Sloane, could you tell me the time?"

Sloane checked her watch. "Almost midnight."

Ladybird's breath stank of sweet liquor. She leaned heavily on Sloane's arm. "Thanks, doll. I don't know why I ask, really, since it never does get to dawn here, but one likes to know. There's a perfectly lovely party going on at your place, you know. Well, not quite your place, if you see what I mean. Miss Bettie will be playing that funny old square piano. Her taste in music is predictably antiquated, but she bangs away with great verve."

"I need to see—" Sloane tapped the caricature of Momus stamped on her wrist.

"Of course you do, dear." Ladybird gestured, drink in

hand. She was flamboyant as ever, her hair piled atop her head in grand Spanish señora style and held in place with three large tortoiseshell combs. "Right behind you, walk past the Bearded Lady and then along the side of the Genuine Human Maze. You can't miss it."

"Ladybird . . ." Sloane looked at the heiress to the Trube fortune. She would have made a wonderful eccentric old lady, Sloane thought. But these days it's not safe to be noticed; the most colorful flower is the first to get picked. "Shall I look for you on my way out?"

"I can't get out, Sloane." Ladybird smiled wearily. "When I walk out the door, up on Seawall Boulevard, you know, I'm not back home. I'm in this Galveston. Parties up and down the Strand. Grand drunks at your house. Cars that work. I've gone to Krewes, you see. It's the Mardi Gras. Wherever I am, there it is." She took another drink from her plastic wineglass and manufactured a smile. "I can't say I miss the old place much! You ought to stay."

"It does look sort of fun," Sloane said uncomfortably. "But I have things I have to . . . There's Mother and all."

Ladybird laid a finger next to her nose. "Say no more. Off you go!"

Sloane waved and headed for the Bearded Lady.

"Sloane?" Ladybird called. Sloane turned back. Ladybird was standing up on tiptoe, already obscured by the crowd milling between them. "What time did you say it was?" she shouted.

"Eleven fifty-two."

"Fabulous! Good night, and good luck with You Know Who!"

Sloane followed Ladybird's directions. In a few minutes she found herself standing outside a small hut with the word MANAGER painted over the door. The cries of the lost came faintly from the Genuine Human Maze behind her.

She found she wasn't knocking. Come on. You are the

daughter of the Grand Duchess. Still no knocking. If you don't do this, your mother will die. That almost did it. — And you will be doing her job, meeting by meeting, motion and motion seconded, for the rest of your life.

I am such a coward. She knocked.

"Come in!" The door popped open, and Momus stood before her, a hunchbacked moonfaced dwarf with two little horns atop his bald head. He wore a scarlet ringmaster's suit and tails and black boots darker than the space between the stars. "Stepdaughter! At last!"

Time stopped.

Sloane's mother always talked about magic as something impossible, something not real. The gods were wine or drugs that distorted your senses. Fever dreams and hallucinations. Nothing could be further from the truth. Standing before the hunchbacked god, Sloane knew that Momus alone was real. What she called life was a crayon drawing, crudely scribbled on a piece of paper, and Momus was the nail hammered through it to pin it to the universe.

As tall as she was, she found herself staring down at his bald old head. The god's white scalp, webbed with blue veins, showed the dips and ridges in the plates of his skull. His skin gathered, thickening and rougher, at the base of his horns. He had no eyebrows, though the bony ridges above his eyes showed clearly under his thin white skin. She felt a terrible urge to reach out and touch him, to feel the craggy bones, the skin like wax paper beneath her fingers. She saw herself, withered and old, sitting in front of her vanity mirror with a brush in her hand, her thin hair coming out in clumps. "Sorry," she whispered, seeing her old thighs, flabby and pale. Blue vessels broken into bruises all over them.

She gripped the steel Rolex.

Time jumped like a cricket caged in the god's hands. Momus grinned and set it free again. "Heard about your mother," he said. "Stiff, stiffer, stiffest, what a shame.

Should have had more fun, that's my philosophy. No sense being sober at last call." He took her arm. His touch was lonely drunks and suicides. Sloane imagined her teeth yellow, her pretty smile gone. No shoulders worth showing anymore. Big tits sagging inside a dowdy dressing gown. Empty house. Loneliness.

"Are you glad to see me, Stepdaughter?"

"Honored," Sloane meant to say—but the word turned in her mouth and "Horrified" came out instead. She yelped and covered mouth with her hand.

"You are not in your mother's house, Sloane. With me, you will speak only the truth." Momus patted her fondly. "That's the difference between a lawyer and a fool, my dear. A lawyer speaks to be heard, regardless of the truth. A fool must speak the truth, whether he will be heard or not."

Momus took her hand and began to walk. "Come, catch your breath." The noise of Carnival danced around her again, the laughter of drunks and the stall keepers' patter. Footsteps fled and faded within the Genuine Human Maze. They followed a small path down to the shoreline. Lines of silver surf crawled and whispered on the dark sand. Momus walked toward the beach with her arm clasped in his. The bright, noisy fairground dwindled behind them, as if washed away by the eternal thud and murmur of the surf. First came the crash of a wave smacking into the sand. Then, in the gap before the next wave fell, bubbles of foam expired with a faint lingering hiss, the same sound Sloane heard at Odessa's when the old witch poured her a glass of hoarded Dr Pepper.

"Are you going to kill me?" Sloane asked.

"No."

"Trap me here?" The god didn't answer. Whitecaps built and broke out from shore, ghostly in the moonlight. "Let me ask a favor," Sloane said. "Grant it or deny it as you wish, but let me ask and then let me go. Please."

"Ask away, Stepdaughter."

When you sup with the Devil, use a long spoon. Odessa used to say that. But it was too late to be wise now. "You must know that my mother is dying. Your consort," Sloane said. "It isn't right. It isn't time. Not yet."

The hunchbacked god stooped and picked up an empty shell from the beach. Its fragile walls had been broken at many points by the sea. He held it to the moonlight, then let it drop. "At the height of Rome, they say, there was a dwarf whose only job was to ride beside the Emperor in every procession and revue, and whisper one thing in the imperial ear: *'You will die, you will die, you, too, shall die.'* It comes to us all," Momus said. "Even to me, perhaps, although not for a long time yet." He waved back at the Carnival behind them. "Jane keeps one Galveston, I another, and the Recluse watches the door between the two."

Sloane knelt in the wet sand. "I beg you."

Momus pulled her up. "You'll ruin your dress." He sighed. "Tell me your wish, and I will see what I can do for the daughter of my consort."

"I just can't stand to see her die." Sloane couldn't stop herself from crying, tears spilling out of her and no way to stop them. "Will you help me?"

The sea broke and hushed, broke and hushed like the slow beating of the world's heart. "I will," Momus said.

Chapter Four

THE APOTHECARY

MOMUS showed Sloane back to the Carnival entrance on Seawall Boulevard. The very presence of the god was so overpowering it was all she could do not to faint, but she willed herself to look him in the eye, bit her lip until it ached, bobbed her head and even managed a curtsey when he bowed to take his leave. Then the door closed behind him and she fell against it, head spinning, her cheek pressed against the warm wood just under the silver letters of the slogan. *It Just Doesn't Get Any Better Than This!*

There were no lights, no sound of music playing. She was back in Galveston, her Galveston, where magic was not allowed. All the good and cautious folk were inside, with charms against the full moon hung on their doors and windows. Sloane stared at her city like a drunken hawk, dizzy and exultant. "Ha!" she yelled. The shout echoed back at her. A fierce grin spread across her face. She had done it. Sloane, dull dutiful Sloane—she had risked her sanity, she had braved the Carnival, she had saved her mother's life. Her mother would not die, and Sloane would not be entombed in the awful business of running Galveston. Elation rose through her, bubbles of

it popping and fizzing in her blood. So this is what it feels like to be brave! Like a champagne drunk—lovely, but not something you want to do very often.

Sloane staggered across Seawall Boulevard and hurried down the street. The first few blocks of Broadway were a desolate part of town, too close to the Carnival for decent people to live. Giant Victorian houses stood untenanted, their heads caved in by live-oak limbs. Many of them had been scavenged down to the skeleton, looted for firewood and metal fittings.

Sloane was having problems seeing, and her heartbeat was all wrong, as if the rhythm of the breaking sea had got inside her and messed it up. But she couldn't stop grinning and despite herself she started to run. She imagined herself sweeping into Ashton Villa. The last few guests would still be there, staring at Jane Gardner dumbfounded as she rose from her wheelchair. Jim Ford would be goggle-eyed and Randall Denton would begin a lazy round of applause as the Grand Duchess of Momus did the impossible and walked across the room. She would call for a servant and demand tea, then say, "To hell with tea!" and grip a flute of champagne with fingers that against all hope could feel again. Jane Gardner's rational mind would have no explanation for her recovery. It would be a miracle.

And then Sloane would stride into the Gold Room and everyone would look at her. Odessa would be the first to understand, and then everyone else, one by one, and last of all her mother would look across the room at Sloane and realize that her daughter had risked everything to save—

A shadow detached itself from a lamppost as Sloane ran by and stuck out its foot. She fell, smacking the pavement with her face. Her whole body froze for a split second, and then the pain hit like a shock wave, blinding her.

When she could think again there was a man crouching

over her. He smelled of shrimp and motor oil and beer. "Hey, sweet thing, why the hurry?" A hand lingered on her shoulder. Blood slipped down the side of her face, soaking into the parched roadway. Even though the sun had gone down hours before, the asphalt still held the day's heat. It burned against her cheek.

There was blood in her mouth. She blinked, trying to see. Another pair of hands grabbed her ankles and jerked her roughly to the side of the road, scraping her face again. "Get her in the house," said the man by her head. He hooked his hands under her arms and lifted her up. She screamed. The men dropped her, and her head smacked into the pavement again.

She groaned and someone slapped her hard on her bloody cheek. The first man was squatting on her chest, driving the breath out of her. He grabbed a handful of her hair and jerked her head up. She felt cold metal against her throat. "One more like that," he hissed, "and I'll cut you a new pussy. Got it?"

"Hey!" someone shouted suspiciously from down the block.

The man with the knife jumped up. "Mind your own fucking business," he yelled.

Heavy footsteps began to hurry toward them. Sloane struggled to lift her head, but the moon got in her eyes. She had a confused impression of a big man with a club lumbering toward them.

Sloane's attacker held his knife out in front of him. "I ain't joking, man. Keep moving."

The big man slowed to a walk, glancing down at Sloane where she lay in the road. From where Sloane was lying he looked gigantic, six and half feet if he was an inch, and square as the big refrigerator in Jim Ford's kitchen. Three hundred pounds easy. What she thought was a club turned out to be a homemade flounder gaff, a baseball bat with a giant nail sticking out of one end. He hefted the gaff, letting it smack into his enormous

hand with a meaty thunk. "You better be packing some serious firepower, son, and you better be able to get to it quick, 'cause I'm fixing to open a hole in you big enough to step through, you little jack shit."

The man holding Sloane's ankles dropped her and bolted.

"I'll give you a count of three. One, two, th—"

"Fuck you," said the man with the knife. Then he, too, turned and raced down the street.

The big man sighed gustily and squatted down in the road beside her. He smelled of seawater and sweat and beer. "You're all right," he said. "Can you move your head?" She shook it back and forth. He chuckled. "No? How 'bout your fingers and toes?" She wiggled them. "How many fingers?" he said, sticking his hand in front of her face.

Lots, she tried to say, but the words wouldn't come out right. His fingers were square and thick and smelled of fish. She gurgled a little. More blood seeped out of her mouth.

"Well, stunned or drunk, I reckon, but I don't think your neck's broke or anything. You fill out that dress all right, I'll give you that," he muttered. "They say more than a handful's a waste, but *damn*. And I got big hands." He eased one massive arm around her waist. "Okay, cupcake, up we go." He picked her up as easily as if she had been a cat and slung her over his back. His massive shoulder felt wider than her waist. "Ah, hell," he muttered. He headed back the way he had come, bent over, and retrieved a sack. "No point wasting a good night's work." A moment later Sloane found herself face-to-face with a bag full of stinking flounder. The bag jerked and twitched as the big man walked; Sloane would have sworn some of the fish inside weren't quite dead.

It occurred to Sloane that the big man hadn't asked her her name or where he should take her. He might be just another rapist, dragging her somewhere out of sight

to have his way with her. If so, she was in serious trouble. Nobody was going to rescue her from this giant. She tried to scream, but she had no breath, slung over his shoulder, and her "Help!" came out a whisper.

He chuckled. "Don't you worry, doll. Ol' Ham's got the cure for what ails you." He brought her and the sack of fish to a small house about two blocks away. He climbed up the front steps, pulled open the screen door, and banged on the wooden one behind it with a fist the size of a cantaloupe. "Josh!"

He had tilted her closer to upright in the act of knocking. As suddenly as she could, Sloane slashed at his face with her fingernails. She meant to gouge at his eyes but at the last instant she flinched and raked his cheek instead. "Hey! God*damn*," the big man roared. Sloane tried to twist away, but he jerked her off his back, grabbed her arms and pinned them to her sides, and forced her down, smacking her knees painfully against the porch. "Cut that out, you silly bitch!"

Stairs creaked. "Ham? What the hell?"

"Goddamn drunk skirt here just tried to poke out my eye! Shit. I'm bleeding."

"I have money," Sloane gasped. "I can pay you." Her cheek was stinging fiercely, and her head was pounding. "I know important people."

The other man, the one called Josh, opened his front door. "She probably thinks you're going to rape her," he said.

The big man froze. An instant later he jerked his hands off Sloane as if she were on fire. "Hey. You got the wrong idea, lady. Me and Josh are the good guys, swear to God."

Sloane knelt on the porch. Her head hurt, and she was dizzy and she felt like throwing up.

"You don't have to come in," said Josh, from the doorway of his house. "But I know a little first aid, and you look like you could use it."

"I'll . . ." Sloane struggled to her feet. "I'll be okay," she said, trying to find the porch stairs. Then she fell down.

Ham caught her. This time he picked her up as if carrying a fairy princess and crept inside, ducking his head to keep from bumping the ceiling, which was festooned with hanks of drying nettle and seaweed, and ropes of garlic and peppers. Josh's house was un-airconditioned and horribly hot. It stank of turpentine and sulfur, and the yeasty odor of fermenting rice beer.

A gas lamp came on, hissing softly. "Okay," Josh said. "Put her on the exam table." Sloane felt warm vinyl under her back. Someone put a cushion under her feet. The small man was standing over her. "I'm going to take a look at you. Don't be afraid."

"She can still move her fingers and toes. Two old boys was fixing to take advantage of her when I come back from Rachel's trailer with the rest of my catch."

"I don't smell any liquor. On her, that is."

Ham laughed.

The small man's fingers touched behind her ear and on the point of her chin as he turned her face. She blinked against the gaslight. His hands were hard and smelled of sulfur and chili peppers. He pulled her eyes wide open. "She's in shock. Pupils dilated. Grab a blanket from my room, would you?"

"You the boss, boss." The big man moved away, his absence suddenly emptying the front room.

Sloane's cheek and forehead were a lace of rough fire. She could taste gravel and blood in her mouth. Her eyes closed. When she forced them open she saw the one called Josh looking at her, like a man this time, not a doctor. His eyes flicked guiltily away from hers. The flame of the gas lamp flickered and trembled, making her dizzier and dizzier until she fell into it.

● ● ●

WHEN she came to there was a blanket snugged around her. She was lying on a doctor's examination table. The old vinyl surface creaked as she blinked and tried to look around. The house was cramped and cluttered; the front room only had space for a couple of chairs and the exam table on one side, a narrow corridor, and a long counter that ran the length of the other side. A stainless steel mixing bowl full of dried leaves and the head of a golf club sat on the counter. Behind it were rows and rows of shelves stocked with plastic Robitussin bottles and blue glass Vick's Vapo-Rub jars and Altoids Peppermint tins, plastic pop bottles with the labels scrubbed off, coarse cotton bags and beer bottles with wax plugs to seal them. Roots and leaves hung floating in jars of oil and alcohol, and animal parts, too; she was sure she saw chicken livers, fish, a plastic bottle full of rattlesnake rattles, and something that looked like a jar full of tongues.

"Ham, this is Sloane Gardner. You rescued the Grand Duchess's daughter."

"Are you shitting me, Josh?"

Sloane closed her eyes, fighting the urge to throw up. Her shoulder ached. She was beginning to warm up under the blankets. The house was warm and dim and full of strange thick smells. "Pharmacy," she murmured.

"Used to be," said the man named Josh. "Now it's just a witch doctor's hut."

"Frontier medicine," Ham said. "Apothecary shop."

"Apothecary shop." Josh squatted next to the head of the exam table, holding a mug. "Drink this, if you can. It's warm broth with something to help fight the shock."

He was young, with a bony face. Reserved. He wasn't really tiny except in comparison to his enormous friend, whom Sloane could hear lumbering about somewhere out of view. The reek of yeast was very strong, and it came to Sloane that the apothecary must ferment rice beer or palm whiskey here in his house. She struggled to sit up. The apothecary put an arm behind her back to support

her. She sipped at the broth. Something in it left a bitter, woody aftertaste. "Sorry to cause trouble," she said.

The small man took out a pocket watch and put his fingers lightly on her wrist. They settled; moved; settled. He took her pulse. "No trouble." His eyes met hers.

Sloane finished the broth and lay back on the exam table. Movement caught her eye. A tree roach the length of her thumb was crawling toward her feet. The apothecary didn't notice it. "How did you recognize me?" Sloane asked. "Have we met?"

"Everyone knows Jane Gardner's daughter." There was something odd and flat in his voice. "I'm Joshua Cane," he said.

She shrugged helplessly. "I'm sorry. Should I know you?"

The lines around his mouth and eyes tightened. He looked away.

He's angry about something. He's also attracted to me, Sloane realized, surprised. But why? . . . Well, a pear-shaped woman in a bloody dress—what's not to like? As Sloane stared at the apothecary a faint connection completed itself in the back of her mind. "But didn't I know you, once? When we were young?" She saw in his dour face that she was right. If you were a girl, she thought, you would have learned to smile when you were uncomfortable, instead of looking as if you had been weaned on a pickle. "Yes, I remember now. You knew things, back then."

"Josh knows a thing or two now," Ham rumbled. He was leaning against the pharmacy counter, patting his scratched cheek with a damp rag. "Lucky for you. No bedside manner at all, but Josh is smart and he'll do the right thing by you."

"You told Ladybird Trube once that all the seashells on the beach were fossils," Sloane said. She thought of Ladybird, flushed and drinking, lost somewhere in the fairgrounds. Or maybe by now she was somewhere in the

city, in that other Galveston where it was Mardi Gras forever, sipping champagne in the Bishop's Palace, or dancing in the Gold Room of another, slightly different Ashton Villa, where the ghost of Bettie Brown played ragtime tunes on her famous square piano.

"Did I?" Joshua's face grew less dour. "Yes, that's true. The island has rolled back toward the mainland over the last ten thousand years. The shells we find on the west beach today were actually laid down when that area was part of the Bay." He stopped. "I thought you didn't remember."

"I didn't at first." She looked again at the tiny, mildewing house, crowded with plants and stinking of fermenting rice beer. "What happened?"

"We lost our luck." He looked at her. "But I guess you folks have, too, haven't you? I'm sorry about your mother."

You don't have to be now, Sloane thought, with a brief return of her earlier elation. But it was never smart to anger the gods by being presumptuous, and she wasn't going to say, out loud, that her mother was well until she had seen the evidence with her own eyes.

The apothecary turned to his friend. "Ham, walk over to Ashton Villa, would you? Tell the Duchess her daughter is quite safe but could use a carriage to get home."

"Will do, Josh." Ham stooped to get through the doorway. Where he passed, drying bunches of sage and garlic swung lazily from the ceiling. The apothecary must use them to make his medicines, of course. Ham looked from Sloane to his buddy and back, and then gave what he probably thought was a sly wink. "You kids be good now!" he said, and then he tramped heavily down the squeaking porch stairs.

"I'm sorry about Ham," Josh said stiffly. "He's . . ."

"I'm not offended," Sloane said. Appalled, possibly. As if she were likely to roll around on the mildewed carpets, squashing a helpless roach and a doodlebug or two in the throes of lust for some down-on-his-luck phar-

macist. She suppressed the image with a shudder and wondered when she would stop noticing the awful smell of fermenting rice beer.

"I'm sorry I can't offer you better accommodations," Josh said, even more stiffly.

Oops. Apparently she wasn't censoring her expressions with her usual skill. "To tell you the truth, I was so busy being grateful I hadn't noticed the accommodations." Thank God the rest of the world was not like Momus's realm, where you could only speak the truth.

"I'm sure you must be looking forward to getting home," Josh said.

Sloane broke into a smile, sending a sharp twinge of pain through her bruised cheek. "Ouch. Yes, I am." Well, her triumphant return wouldn't be quite the entrance she had imagined, but in a way this might be better. A few cuts and bruises would make her look even more like a brave heroine who had endured great hardships to win back her mother's life. After the first round of champagne, she thought, I'll have one of the housemaids draw me a bath. Her mother had been implacable on the subject of frivolous baths, demanding that Ashton Villa conserve water irreproachably for the duration of the drought. But surely after a night like this, even she would agree that Sloane deserved to take as long and lingering a bath as she wanted.

Sloane got her elbows under her and gingerly sat up on the exam table. The nausea in her stomach was easing and she felt less drowsy, although her face still ached and her shoulder was beginning to throb where she had fallen on it. She winced.

"Head?"

"Shoulder. I think I fell on it badly." How stupid she had been, so caught up in her fantasies she hadn't seen the two thugs waiting for her.

"I've got some ointment that will help that." The apothecary ducked behind his counter.

"Why is there a golf club head sticking out of the mixing bowl?"

"It's not a golf club, it's a pestle. A Ping three wood pestle, to be exact. All the best witch doctors use them. Ah. Here we go." Josh reappeared holding a small tin that had once contained chewing tobacco. He popped it open. The red paste inside smelled so strongly of turpentine and hot peppers it made Sloane's eyes water. He moved behind her. "Right shoulder?"

"Y-yes."

His fingers touched the strap of her dress, hesitated, and then he began to slide it gently to one side.

Sloane pulled away from him. "I'll be fine," she said.

His hand left her shoulder. "Yes. Okay. That's fine. Take this home, Ms. Gardner. Have one of your servants rub it in gently and then cover it up with a nightshirt. No, on second thought, the stuff does *smell*," he said. "Better wear one of the servant's shirts. Don't want to ruin a good nightie."

That was a cheap shot. Hell hath no fury like an embarrassed man.

Joshua held out the tin and she took it. "The ointment will feel hot," he said. "Your maid should be careful not to touch her eyes, and she'll need to wash her hands afterwards."

"Thank you."

Joshua went behind his counter and began grinding with his mortar and pestle. They waited in awkward silence for the Gardner carriage. Damn, Sloane thought. If she were her usual self she would have handled the situation far more deftly. She would have been able to politely deflect his attentions in a way that left neither of them feeling embarrassed. As it was, the sound of the carriage wheels grinding to a stop outside was heartily welcome. "Goodbye," she said. "And thank you again."

Bill, the Gardners' stable hand, was waiting outside.

He helped her up into the carriage and then geed up his horses. The carriage rattled into motion, passing one ratty bungalow after another, some kept in decent shape, with little bits of garden, while others had gone completely to seed, with drought-stricken grass lying tangled around rusting car parts and salt-rotted tires. The ride home was agonizing for Sloane. Her heart was torn, one part desperate to celebrate her mother's recovery, the other hardly daring to hope, because the disappointment would be so unbearably bitter if somehow Momus had betrayed her.

"We never noticed you'd lit out," Bill said. He tugged his reins and turned his team onto Broadway.

"I try to be inconspicuous. Are there many guests left?"

"A couple." Sloane didn't like the sound of that. Surely a miraculous cure would have kept the whole gathering riveted. "Funny—" Bill paused as they clopped through a patch of moonlight. Then the canopy of live-oak limbs closed overhead. "Funny part of town for you to get to, Miss Gardner. Not so safe, I reckon."

"We should certainly get some of the streetlights fixed," Sloane agreed. "I'll suggest it to Mother."

Another silence. Bill pushed his team into a smart trot. Nobody was anxious to stay out under a full moon more than necessary. They passed the Bishop's Palace, the great mansion where Randall Denton now lived, and entered the familiar district of Galveston's great homes. All the streetlights worked here, of course. Sloane was pretty sure Joshua Cane would have remarked the difference.

"It don't take a genius to guess what you was up to," the driver said gently.

Sloane froze inside. "What?"

"With your mom so poorly, it ain't hard to figure what you might be doing at a doctor's house. But if you don't mind some advice, Josh Cane isn't going to help you. I got family that can't afford a real doctor, so when my cousin come down with pneumonia, she went to Josh.

He's a stiff-necked little cuss, but he's honest, I'll give him that. Told her what she really needed was to break into a real doctor's office and steal some penicillin. Probably good advice. She died two weeks later."

"I'm sorry."

"I guess what I'm saying is, Josh Cane does the best he can for the poor folk that can't do any better. But he ain't got any miracles to sell. You stick with a real doctor that went to school before the Flood and still has some of the old drugs left. That's my advice, and Josh will tell you the same if you ask him."

Sloane couldn't think of anything to say.

She did her best to sit calmly in the carriage, but when they arrived home she abandoned Bill to stable the horses by himself and hurried up the walk, ignoring the pain in her shoulder. She jerked the front door open, pushed past a startled housemaid carrying a tray of desserts, and burst into the Gold Room.

Her mother was by the square piano, still sitting in her wheelchair, pretending to listen to a conversation between Randall Denton and Kyle Lanier. Randall liked to give Kyle a few glasses of wine and then get him talking because his speech decayed into the white trash patois of his childhood in a way Randall found amusing. Sloane could tell her mother wasn't paying attention. She looked utterly drained, as if even the effort of conversation was a terrible exertion.

The room fell silent as the last few guests turned to look at Sloane, taking in her bruised face and cut cheek and the bloodstains on her beautiful lichen-colored dress. She felt her heart thudding dully in her chest. Her mother's eyes fluttered open. "Good God, Sloane," she murmured. "You look terrible."

Sloane walked across the room, cheeks burning. "How are you feeling?" she whispered.

"Better than you, by the looks of it. What were you doing out? You were supposed to be here," Jane Gardner

said. "I could have used a little more help, Sloane."

"I . . . I'm sorry. I didn't mean to be gone so long." Sloane took one of her mother's hands. It was lifeless, her bones like sticks stuffed into skin that didn't fit right anymore. It's too soon, she told herself. Of course it will take a while. It was childish to expect everything to be fixed in a flash. "It's nothing important. I fell down."

Her heart beat and beat against her ribs, hurting her.

Or maybe it just doesn't get any better than this.

Chapter Five

THE RECLUSE

LATE that night, as Sloane lay aching in her bed and stinking of Josh's bruise ointment, she decided she would have to beg off the next day's work—won't that make Mother even happier with me—and visit Odessa. Momus had lied to her. Or if he hadn't lied, he had tricked her. Either way, Sloane had made a bargain with a god and it wasn't working out. Odessa was the only person in Galveston you could go to with that kind of problem.

As a little girl Sloane had spent many a long, sultry day at Odessa's place, the old gambling joint called the Balinese Room that hung over the Gulf of Mexico at the bottom of 23rd Avenue. After lunch, Odessa always made her take a nap in the hammock by her workbench, and Sloane would lie with her eyes closed, the scratchy ropes making diamonds against the skin of her back and legs, determined not to go to sleep, trying to identify every sound: the stop-and-start whirr of Odessa's sewing machine, the heavy chop of the ceiling fan overhead, the maddening whine of a mosquito in her ear, shutters creaking and clacking, curtains fluttering.

" 'Dessa, why do they call you the Recluse?" she had asked one day when she was eleven.

"Do they?" Odessa said, not looking up from her sewing. This was a kind of fib Odessa often indulged in. What Odessa called "ladylike" was often not much different from what Sloane's mom called "lying." It wasn't hard to keep the rules straight, unless you were talking to both of them at once.

Odessa picked up the doll she was working on and studied it critically through her wire-rimmed bifocals. Her fingernails were very long and sharp, and they were always painted, bloodred or sea green or seashell white. Today they glimmered like mother-of-pearl. "If they do call me that, I suppose it's because I live alone and keep to myself. That's what a recluse is, honey. A hermit. Did you get anything from Vincent Tranh?"

"Uh-huh." Sloane dug Uncle Vince's handkerchief out of the pocket of her shorts. It was nothing special, made from rough Galveston cotton spun on the Island, but Odessa had asked for something he kept near him. "I told him I needed it to make a doll dress. He thinks all girls play with dolls."

"Aren't you a good little liar." Sloane squirmed. "Well, thank you, honey." Galveston's last angel considered the square of cloth for a moment, then cut out two matching tunic pieces and tacked them together.

"What are you making?"

"A shirt for my doll, doll."

Sloane turned on her side in the hammock so she could watch Odessa work. "Randall said it was from brown recluse, like the spider. Mom calls them fiddlebacks. He said his cousin got bit by one and her whole leg turned black and the meat fell right off it so you could see the bone and she died."

Odessa gave her a sharp look over the tops of her bifocals. "Randall Denton ought to learn to hush up." Sloane hushed up instead. Randall was three years older than her and a complete jerk, but she didn't want to get him in trouble with the witch.

Her godmother made a sleeveless shirt from Vincent Tranh's handkerchief, running it through the sewing machine. Then she slipped it over the head of the doll she had been working on since Sloane had arrived. It was a thin doll, with black hair and a sallow complexion.

"Hey," Sloane said. She squinted at the doll. "That's Uncle Vince." Odessa didn't answer. "Why are you making a doll of Uncle Vince?"

"Honey, this is 'Dessa's business."

"You made me bring you his handkerchief. You owe me an explanation."

"Ah, I hear your mother talking." Odessa put the doll down on her workbench and straightened, putting her hands on the small of her back and rubbing briefly. "All right, kiddo. The thing is, Uncle Vince has begun to see the Prawn Men."

"What?"

"He has begun to see the Prawn Men. He's getting so he can dip a finger in the ocean and tell the next day's weather. Find where the fish are hiding by smell. Yesterday he discovered he can drink salt water," Odessa said disapprovingly. "The magic is beginning to seep into him."

"How do you know that?"

"It is my job to know."

Sloane looked at her godmother, frightened. "But those things just make him a better sailor. He can bring home more fish and shrimp; there's more food for everybody. It's nothing bad."

Odessa looked at her sympathetically. "But it's magic, doll. And we don't let the magic in, here. That's how Galveston survives. I don't let it in." She turned back to studying the doll and gave its tummy a light poke with her long, shimmering fingernail. The doll flinched.

"But you have magic! You use it all the time!"

"That's different."

"Why!"

"That's my job," Odessa repeated. Sloane could see the doll struggling weakly in Odessa's hand. The witch stood up, ignoring it, and walked over to the shrines at the side of the room. Here, where the bandstand used to be in the swank Balinese Room restaurant, there were five votary cabinets, one for each of the Krewes: Momus, Togetherness, Thalassar, Venus, and Harlequin. She went to the Krewe of Thalassar's blue-painted votary, decked with sand dollars and starfish and bits of fishing rope. She opened one of the cabinet doors, kissed the Vincent Tranh doll lightly on the head, and popped it inside. "When someone springs a leak, you see, it can't easily be patched." Odessa latched the cabinet shut. "So we let the magic take them instead."

Faint bumping sounds came from inside the shrine.

"You're making Uncle Vince gone to Krewes!" Sloane cried in horror.

Odessa came back to the hammock and put her hand on the side of Sloane's face, ignoring the way the girl shrank from her. "Oh, kiddo, it's a hard old world we live in these days." Tears were glistening in the witch's eyes. Sloane hated her anyway. "I'm sorry you asked about the doll, but you had to understand sooner or later. Somebody will have to do this when I'm gone, you know."

"No!"

"No, not yet. For now the old Recluse will do it, and for a long time. Don't you worry." Her tone became more businesslike. "But now, I'm afraid I can't have you telling anyone about poor Uncle Vince. Stick out your tongue, doll."

Sloane shook her head, mute.

Odessa looked at her. Behind her bifocals, her eyes were green and unfathomable, like the sea. "Stick out your tongue, child."

Sloane wished afterward Odessa had used a spell. She should have held out, she should have forced her god-

mother to witch her. But the image of a little Sloane doll filled her mind, a little brown-haired figurine locked inside the Krewe of Momus shrine, bumping and scuffling in the darkness while the Momus puppet sat on top, dangling his legs and grinning like a wicked Humpty-Dumpty with horns.

She stuck out her tongue.

"There's a doll," Odessa said. And she touched the tip of Sloane's tongue with one long fingernail.

From that day on, Sloane could not say Uncle Vince's name or talk about him in any way. Not at the wake they held for him after he disappeared that spring, and not for many years afterward.

SLOANE thought of that day as she walked toward Odessa's house. It was hot and dry again. Drought-blasted vegetation creaked and whispered underfoot, withered grass and palm fronds and live-oak leaves dry and brittle as locust shells. At least the drought was keeping the horrible mosquitoes in check.

From Ashton Villa it was twelve blocks due south on 23rd Avenue to the Seawall and the Balinese Room pier, but it wasn't a very nice twelve blocks. Once she got on the seaward side of Broadway, the neighborhood rapidly deteriorated. Mangy dogs snarled at her as she went by. Roosters screamed from atop junked cars. A few blocks from Joshua Cane's apothecary shop she passed a front yard that had been fenced in with chicken wire. Five or six hens scratched in a dirt courtyard inside. Under a sign that said BEWARE OF GOD someone had nailed the carcass of a rat to a little wooden crucifix. Sloane kept her eyes downcast and hurried past.

She was grateful, as always, to leave the barrio behind and come out onto Seawall Boulevard. Salt grass had taken root in the cracked road, and sea purslane and camphor daisies that seemed to live off dew and sea spray, surviving even the drought. The pavement was littered

with the shells of crabs and oysters, dropped there by seagulls to smash and spill out their tender meat. The shells crunched and scraped beneath Sloane's feet as she crossed the road and stood for a moment, looking out at the ocean. A hazy salt light glittered over the Gulf, making her eyes smart. Rags of foam split and heaved on the sea's back. Waves broke twenty yards out from shore, their crests boiling brown and dirty white.

She thought of Vincent Tranh, gone to Krewes; lost at sea only days after Odessa had closed his doll inside the Krewe of Thalassar votary. The doll Sloane had helped to make. That would have been only a few months after Joshua Cane's father gambled away their house to . . . some Denton or other. She remembered Odessa tapping silence like a nail through her tongue. She tried to say Vince Tranh's name out loud. Her tongue lay dead in her mouth.

The Recluse was not a good woman to cross.

Sloane turned right and walked half a block to the Balinese Room pier. In the 1930s and '40s, the Balinese Room had been not only the swankiest nightclub in Texas, but the heart and soul of the Maceo mob empire. So completely had Sam and Rosie Maceo controlled the town that the Island was known as the Free State of Galveston, a pocket Atlantic City with palm trees, where every schoolchild ran odds sheets for Maceo bookies and the visiting sailor could find more prostitutes per capita than in Shanghai. By the time Sloane was a girl it had been sixty years since Guy Lombardo or Jimmy Dorsey had played the Balinese Room, but sometimes during her visits she could still hear their ghosts: glasses clinking, faint laughter, the rattle of a slot machine paying out. The smell of scotch and good Cuban cigars.

The nightclub had been built on a T-shaped pier, with a restaurant and kitchen in the stem of the T and a casino at the back, far over the ocean, where Odessa now slept. Sloane's shoes click-clacked across Odessa's weathered

boardwalk. The Gulf swell gathered and lapsed below, foaming around the barnacle-crusted pier posts. Sloane passed the guard's hut. Once upon a time, a sentry had been stationed there. If the cops or the Texas Rangers showed, his job was to push the buzzer that rang in the casino at the far end of the pier. There the blackjack tables and roulette wheels would fold up into the wall like ironing boards, and the wealthy mobsters and Houston high rollers would hastily sit down in front of pre-dealt hands of cribbage and old maid. No sentry stayed in the guard's hut anymore. Now it was home to the engine block of a '97 Lincoln Town Car with a carburetor reconfigured to run on propane. It hummed away, generating the power for Odessa's lights and refrigerator, her electric drill and soldering iron and sewing machine.

The front door of the Balinese Room was smoked glass. Sloane stood in front of her own dim reflection; today she wore charcoal slacks, a white cotton blouse, and a simple veil worn back to keep the sun off her neck. A green anole the size of her middle finger clung to the glass door, staring at her. He puffed his throat out into an angry bag as her reflection passed under him and disappeared inside.

Early on a hot morning the Balinese Room's red velour upholstery had the sad, dingy look that bars viewed in daylight always do. The Gulf breeze passed through Odessa's open shutters, making the fishing nets that decorated the walls sway and slap. Messy strands of spider-silk drifted, trembling, from chair backs and table legs. Sloane could see several more anoles, one frozen in the middle of a dinner plate as he made his way across a table, another clinging motionless to the back of a chair, eyeing her balefully.

Odessa looked up from her workbench. She was wearing sandals and a red kimono with mysterious golden birds patterned on it. "Hey, kiddo, I looked for you last night to say goodbye, but nobody seemed to know where

you were." She squinted, then rose, alarmed at the sight of Sloane's bruised face. She pulled Sloane into a warm hug. For the first time Sloane realized that the witch had grown old. She could feel the bumps of Odessa's spine beneath her fingers. The witch's thinning hair had turned wholly white, and her skin was brownish red, wind-chapped and leathery from too many years of salt and sun. Her back was beginning to bend over, and the breasts beneath her dressing gown hung flat. She smelled of sewing machine oil and ironed cloth, nail polish remover and Max Factor foundation.

The visions of Sloane's own ugly old age that had gripped her at Momus's touch flooded back over her.

Odessa drew back, holding Sloane by her shoulders. She reached up and felt her goddaughter's cheek, very gently, with the back of one hand. Her knuckles were swollen with arthritis. "Well, kiddo? Start talking."

Sloane told her the whole tale of her visit to Momus, her stupidity afterward in nearly getting herself raped, and her salvation in the arms of the giant named Ham and his friend the apothecary. When she came to the last part, about going home and finding her mother no better, it was difficult not to cry.

When she had finished, Odessa shook her head. "Some days you just can't win for losing. You try so hard to be a good little girl, don't you, Sloane? As if that was going to save you." Odessa's shoulders sagged and she ran one hand through her thinning hair. "And you've made a deal with Momus, too. It will take some work to keep you from Krewes now, child." She sighed. "I reckon this is a Dr Pepper problem," she said at last. "I've been saving a last few for emergencies and I think this qualifies. Want one, sugar?"

A few belts of whiskey might be better. "Yes, please."

Odessa passed through the heavy swinging doors at the back of the dining lounge and into the restaurant-sized kitchen. A moment later she returned with two glasses

full of ice. A refrigerator with a working ice-maker was one of the special luxuries Jane Gardner had always made sure to supply her. Odessa also brought an ancient two-liter bottle of Dr Pepper, the plastic coated with dust and webbed with cracks. She poured ceremoniously and they drank together. "I should have known something was up, the way you were dressed last night. I assumed you were putting on a good face for your mother's sake. It was a very brave thing to do, wonderfully brave, little mouse," Odessa said. "Very silly, too. Why didn't you tell me you were planning this?"

Because it was quite possible you had a little Jane Gardner doll in concrete somewhere, 'Dessa. "Sorry," Sloane said, eyes downcast. "I should have, I know. I was worried I would lose my nerve if I started talking about it." Which was also true.

"Ha. I can just see you." Odessa swirled her drink around, making the ice cubes clink. Water had already beaded up on the outside of her glass. "Can you remember the exact words you said to him?"

"Just that I couldn't bear for her to—" Sloane stopped. The color drained from her face. "No. That wasn't it either. I said, *'I just can't stand to see her die.'* " A range of horrible possibilities started to open up before her. "But he knew what I *meant*, 'Dessa!"

"Don't try that on me," Odessa said sharply. "Save it for someone you can fool. Nobody says anything to Momus that isn't the exact truth. That's just what you said and it's just what you meant."

"It wasn't the only thing I meant," Sloane whispered.

Her godmother shrugged. "If you want to sup with the Devil, you better bring a long spoon. Well, the damage is done now. 'I just can't stand to see her die.' It's not . . . it's not a happy choice of words, Sloane."

"I guess if I stay in Mother's room, watching her twenty-four hours a day, she'll live forever," Sloane said bitterly.

Odessa took a sip of her Dr Pepper. "Not to be hateful, doll, but there is at least one other way you wouldn't be able to see her die."

Sloane stared at her for a long moment. "Oh," she said. "You mean if I die first."

"It fits the letter of the bargain." The Recluse took a breath. "No, I think you will have to go back and renegotiate, dear. Only this time, I will help you and you will be less of a fool. Did you really think so little of me?" she asked with a flash of anger. She took off her bifocals and polished them up with a piece of cloth from her workbench. "Did you really think you were up to meeting Momus without my help?" She turned her back on the girl, gripping the top of her sewing machine. "Do you forget that there are people besides your mother who are counting on you?"

Sloane kept her eyes on the floor.

"Jane Gardner isn't the only person who needs a successor, Sloane. Who couldn't do her job? Anyone, any sufficiently dreary, practical-minded Krewe of Momus drudge can get a sewer line run or order a water main fixed when it begins to leak. What happens when the magic begins to leak, hey? What happens when nightmares start spilling into Jane's little empire and there's no Recluse there to shoo them off to Mardi Gras? I have taught you for a purpose, Sloane."

"Oh, good," Sloane said. "I was hoping there would be more to feel guilty about."

Somewhere at the back of the house a shutter banged, once, twice. Odessa laughed. She turned and tousled Sloane's short brown hair. "Quite right. What did you ever do to deserve two such terrible old ladies brooding over you? Still, the fact remains you have to try to renegotiate your deal. And for that we need quite another *you*, if you're going to be dealing with the old lunatic himself. We need someone a lot less *nice*."

She tapped her fingernails on her glass. "I'm going to

make you a mask," the witch said at last. Sloane's eyes widened. Odessa's masks were loaded with power. The Recluse drained the last of her Dr. Pepper. "There are some things you need a new face," she said, "to face."

A small collection of masks hung from the peg-board at the end of the bench. Sloane recognized some of them: *Hollow, Dry Salvage, Lizard, Burnt Hair.* "I'm almost done with this one," Odessa said, picking a polished copper domino off the bench. "Remember it?"

The cheekbones and eyebrows of the mask were marked out with 4 Meg SIMMs Sloane had salvaged for Odessa from an ancient PC clone she had found abandoned in the attic of Ashton Villa. "Sure. What are you going to call it?"

"*1999.*" The witch placed the cool metal gently against Sloane's face. It struck the breath from her like an electric shock, sweeping her up into a whining, buzzing, inhuman cascade of calculation, acquisition, construction, commerce. With shaking hands Sloane pulled it away and bent over Odessa's workbench, trying to breathe, waiting for the driving rhythms of that vanished industrial world to stop roaring through her blood. "Oh, gods. I knew it was different, but . . ."

"One thing to hear the stories, but it's another to feel it, isn't it, honey? That's what we lost," Odessa said. "So much, Sloane. We lost so much."

Sloane thought of Joshua Cane. His mother had dispensed real drugs in perfect little pills; now he was grinding up plants with a golf club head.

Odessa hung up the mask. "Let me just tidy up a bit." She cleared the workbench of all its bits of cloth, stuffing them into the cedar chest by the sewing machine that was already full to bursting with coarse modern Galveston cotton and treasures from before the Flood: lace and nylon stockings, bolts of flowered silk, polyester slacks and high-quality stonewashed denim with the Levi's buttons

still attached, crepe chenille and squares of grey jersey and meters of formal gaberdine. Odessa cleaned her work space, whisking a can of solvent under the bench, hanging her soldering iron and a T-square back on the pegboard. The loose stuff she put in two red fishing tackle boxes: screws and nails and loops of wire, wrenches and drill bits, files for metal and wood and glass.

When Odessa had the bench cleared to her satisfaction she made Sloane lie on it, facing the ceiling, with her head pillowed on a bolt of cloth. "This is going to take some time," she said, pressing one red fingernail against Sloane's lips. "Days, possibly. I'll send a message to Jane to let her know you're safe. You won't eat, you won't drink, you won't sleep. You will be the mask."

Odessa walked through the door to the kitchen and rummaged around. Sloane tried to call to her. Words gathered like heat in her mouth, but her lips would not open. They felt numb where Odessa's fingernail had touched. She tried harder, struggling desperately. A thin hiss of air leaked from her mouth. She gave up.

Odessa returned holding two striped straws. "Put these in your nose." Sloane's eyes widened. "You want to breathe, don't you? Don't worry, these are the wide ones, milk shake straws. Scavenged them from the Denny's down the street. I don't mind putting them in, but they'll tickle less if you do it."

Sloane took the straws and gingerly inserted them, one in each nostril. They smelled like old plastic. Odessa examined her, looking down through her bifocals, and then nodded. "Luverly," she drawled. "I b'lieve they add character."

The Recluse made several trips to the kitchen, returning with three large mixing bowls full of water, a can of plaster powder, a can marked "Danlo Dental Supply," and a jar of Vaseline. She wet a rag and gently wiped Sloane's face. The water was warm and smelled faintly of soap. "We were always different, your mother and I.

Jane is a creature of clay. Everything sticks to her so. No wonder she can't move, with all that weight bearing down. Me, I live in a world of water," the old witch said, touching the rag tenderly to Sloane's temples, to her lips. "Everything trickles away from me."

Odessa patted Sloane's face with a dry cloth, then opened up her jar of Vaseline and spread a thin layer over Sloane's face with her fingertips, paying special attention to her eyelashes and eyebrows. Next she fished an old nylon stocking out of the fabric chest. "We have to protect your hair, now, don't we, honey?" She pulled the stocking over Sloane's head and then wrapped a muslin bandana around the whole business.

Odessa picked up a pair of scissors and cut three pieces of cheesecloth into one foot by two foot rectangles. Then she sifted plaster powder into the biggest bowl of water. "Of course I didn't stick so well to Jane, these last few years. She dropped me easily enough. Can't say I blame her. Persnickety old lady, I am now. You'd never know I was pretty once, would you?"

She went back to the kitchen and returned with an electric mixer. "Noise," she warned, then she turned it on and began to beat the plaster. "No lumps. Like a good cake batter. Jane never did care to cook, either. Always wanted to eat out. Italian. Greek. Well, she came from those kind of people. Much richer than my momma. My momma taught me to cook. Chicken-fried steak, pound cake, corn bread. Black-eyed peas on New Year's Day." She lifted up a beater. Plaster dripped from it. "Good." She cleaned the beaters. "We had our different kinds of power, Jane and I."

She picked up the can marked Danlo Dental Supply. "Alginate. They make it from seaweed, actually, but I don't know how. I stole this from my dentist's office. Dr. Holub. He lost his mind the day after the Flood. Killed himself with a hatchet. Nasty business." She sifted the alginate into the second mixing bowl. "Used to make

dental impressions with this stuff." The electric mixer whirred again. When it stopped, Odessa's hand, blotched with liver spots, appeared suddenly over Sloane's face. "And now, dear, it's time to close your eyes." She touched Sloane's left eyelid with her long red fingernail, then her right. They slammed shut as if made of lead.

Sloane lay in the dark. Panic jumped like a cricket in her belly. Her heart was racing. She felt nearly as scared as she had standing before Momus. Sometimes, because she loved Odessa, she forgot how terrible Galveston's angel could be.

The alginate poured down around her eyes and ran over her face, wet cool billows of it, thick as cake batter, spreading over her cheeks and lips. It trailed off, then came again, a second wave starting at her forehead, seeping down into her eyeholes, a last slow spill across her nose. Odessa must be using a ladle. A third thick wave over her mouth and cheeks. Sloane found herself breathing hard, mouth closed, pulling air through the straws in her nose. She flinched, twisting away from the spill of alginate.

"None of that." A sharp tap on the top of her forehead and her face became inert. Odessa touched her left shoulder next. Numbness spread out from the touch, flesh going dead. Sloane whimpered. Now the other arm. Now her chest. Now her hips, her waist gone dead, her sex, the tops of her thighs. Odessa touched each leg. Sloane flexed her feet until her calves lost feeling, then her ankles, then her toes.

She was as good as dead. Her body no longer lived; she was wood and clay, sticks and stones. She was a blind dead thing, a stone underground, trapped in the dark with only the sound of her frightened breathing, unnaturally loud. Sloane had a sudden horrific thought: She wasn't a woman, she was one of Odessa's dolls, a thing with life but not volition, to be dropped in the sea or stuffed in a shoebox coffin and buried alive.

This is what it's like for Mother every day.

Another wave of cool syrup on her face. "I don't think either of us ever aged, until you were born," Odessa said. "I was there that morning. It was blustery outside, cold for here. Up to that moment, neither Jane nor I thought we would die. But when you see a baby, it turns your own hourglass over. Every time I saw you getting older, Sloane, I would feel myself getting older, too. Only you were climbing, and I was slipping. You grew breasts, I grew wrinkles. I lost track of my own birthdays when I started counting yours, and they came faster and faster. Some days it hurt so much to see you, Sloane. I loved you so much, maybe more than my own kiddos if I ever could have had some. Them I would have grown used to. But you flew through here like a singing bird, and then were gone again. Watching you play I could feel the seconds slipping away from me, one by one."

Sloane lay in the dark, paralyzed.

The alginate began to set immediately, stiffening to the consistency of hard cool gelatin. After three minutes Odessa tapped her on the scalp. "It should be set. Flex your face muscles for me now, sugar, to loosen the casting. I'm going to make a plaster mold. Remember those pieces of cheesecloth I cut? I'm dipping them in the plaster now. Good. Now I'm going to drape them over your face so we have some support for the alginate. That's it, baby. There's a pretty face under all that. I don't know why you hide it so. Veils and hoods and you always looking at the ground." The press of fingers around Sloane's scalp, her cheeks, her jaw and chin. Odessa's voice again, sounding tired. "Time will hide it for you soon enough."

Sloane's body felt heavy and lifeless on the witch's table, a parcel of meat, nothing more. The stiff milk shake straws stuck up her nose made her want to sneeze. The sound of her breath sucking through them seemed terribly loud, so she had to strain to hear Odessa's voice.

"I was as pretty as you once, if you can believe that. It was hard work to behave like a lady, those last few years before the Flood; the magic got into your blood like wine, if you were an angel. It would have been easy to take what I wanted." Odessa's old fingers were on the only exposed part of Sloane that could still feel, just at the nape of her neck, naked below the muslin wraps. Softly Odessa stroked her short hair. "The news was full of stories of angels and minotaurs, miracles and nightmares. All that winter I felt the magic rising under me, as if I were standing in the Gulf and the tide was coming in. You know how it is, the water up to your waist, your chest, and then each wave your feet lift off the bottom just a little and it's hard to stand firm. Then it's up to your neck, you turn your face up, a wave smacks you and there's salt in your mouth, you lose your footing, splash, find it again.

"I don't even know why I was spared, really. Most of us were lost in a heartbeat, I think. I had a girlfriend I saw dissolve the night the Flood came down. Seeped away like a sugar cube in a hot cup of coffee. And of course most that survived never got out of the Mardi Gras. For all I know, they're still there with your step-daddy."

The noise of Sloane's breathing was like a rhythmic wind. She wished she could feel her chest rising and falling with it. Wished she could feel a pulse beating at her numb wrists and ankles.

"People were going crazy," Odessa said. "The streets filled up with minotaurs. People kept expecting me to do something; I didn't know what to do. It was Jane who took everything in hand. She realized we had to get in the Krewes. She was the one who salvaged everything from the hospital before it went under. Somebody else thought of tapping the gas lines for fuel, but it was your momma that got it done. Seems like every time disaster strikes, the Island looks to a Gardner. Dentons were al-

ways in it for themselves alone, and Fords have one eye on the bottom line. People trust the Gardners.

"She was going all the time, she hardly slept. I would come into her place—this was before she moved to Ashton Villa—I would stagger in at maybe two or three in the morning, she would still be working. I had to stay in the room to make sure her nightmares wouldn't thicken, you know. That was the sort of thing that was happening those first six weeks and we wouldn't have made it if we'd lost her. She would fall asleep on the little couch with maybe her head in my lap, face all drawn from working, nearly too tired to dream, and I could never fall asleep myself. There was one dim light going, a Coleman lantern I think it was, I'd turn it down real low, just it hissing in the corner and me looking down at her face, all shadows."

Odessa's voice stopped, along with her fingers. "I admired her very much," she said. After a moment she took her hand off Sloane's neck. "But that was long ago. She doesn't come out to visit me anymore. Just sends the little messenger, hey, sugar? Just sends you."

Odessa's fingers returned, businesslike now, feeling around Sloane's face, gently wiggling the edge of the alginate mask with its plaster backing. In a moment it released from Sloane's forehead with a little tug, a whisper of air cool on her skin. Smoothly and steadily Odessa pulled the mask down. The straws slid out of Sloane's nose, the darkness against her eyelids lightened, gelatin pulled away from her mouth with a last kiss. Then Odessa tapped her once on each eyelid, and she could see.

ODESSA quickly greased the inside of the alginate mask with Vaseline, then filled it up with fresh plaster. Twenty minutes later the plaster had set. She worked off the alginate mold, and Sloane found herself looking down at a plaster impression of her own face.

Odessa drew a long breath and flexed her fingers. She glanced at Sloane through her wire-rimmed bifocals. "Now: let's see about finding a Sloane who's a match for old Momus, shall we?" From a can underneath her workbench she gathered a handful of clay.

Sloane struggled to speak.

"What's that?" Odessa said. "Oops. Sorry, doll," she said, tapping Sloane lightly on the lips.

Sloane's voice came back. "Thank God," she blurted, the words bubbling out from her like water from a kinked hose suddenly put straight. "Whew. Is there anything I can do to help?"

"Maybe later. For now . . . well, dear, your version of you is part of the problem, isn't it?" Odessa took a small ball of clay and stuck it to the end of Sloane's plaster nose. "The life mask should fit perfectly against your face, but now I'm going to change your contours a little. Some uptilt to that shy little nose of yours, for instance." She smoothed the clay onto the end of Sloane's nose, tilting it up, making it sharper and more like her own. "And the eyes . . . you have such downcast eyes, sugar. Always looking at the ground. Not the right spirit for Mardi Gras." Sloane watched as Odessa remade her face. Her eyes became thinner and more sly. Her muzzle thrust out; her cheeks grew higher and sharper. And where her own eyebrows were straight and unremarkable, the ones growing beneath Odessa's fingers swept up at the outside edges.

It was an hour of work, careful and meticulous. When it was done Odessa leaned back, pressing her hands against the small of her back. "There you go, my girl," she said, as Sloane leaned forward over her shoulder to examine the mask. "What do you think?"

A vixen looked up at her, a sly flirt with a dangerous smile. "That's not me," Sloane said.

"Not yet."

Odessa's fingers were grey and dirty, her glasses pow-

dered with plaster dust. "It's well into afternoon," she said. "What say we get a bite while we wait for that to set?" With a sigh she got up from the workbench and picked her way across the dining room, stiff from sitting so long. Sloane followed the witch as she pushed open the swinging door to the gigantic kitchen where the Maceos' staff of Chinese chefs had once cooked for two hundred people a night. It was immaculate. As messy as Odessa's workbench was, she always kept her kitchen spotless. She was a wonderful cook, with two different pecan pies to die for, one pale and light with a faint scent of vanilla, the other dark as Mississippi mud and dense as an anvil.

In the middle of the kitchen floor was a trapdoor that Odessa always left open. According to her, one of the Chinese potboys had been assigned to sit there with a line and catch fish for the dinner special during the Maceo days. Now the sound of the sea came welling up from the hole in the floor, along with a powerful briny smell of salt and wet wood. Odessa bustled in the kitchen, throwing together a lunch of fried redfish with red beans and rice.

After they had eaten, Odessa made a negative mask and then another positive one, this time in gypsum cement. She put a big pot of water on the stove to heat. Then she burrowed down to the bottom of her fabric trunk and pulled out a long hank of leather. Carefully she wrapped the leather over the cement face. Next she submerged the whole head in the hot water on the stove. She turned the gas off and let the leather steep for about ten minutes. Then she passed the bust to Sloane, telling her to knead and wring and twist it. "Your turn, sugar. This is a new life you hold in your hands. A chance to start all over. This is your new face. From now on you are the only one who will touch it."

Sloane stretched and pressed the leather, pushing it deeply into the mold's eye sockets with her thumbs and

pulling it taut across the vixen's high, sharp cheeks. When the leather was stretched tight and tacked down, Odessa handed her a curious tool she called a "sticketta," a wooden butter knife she had sanded down from a busted pool cue.

It was very hot. Sweat gathered thickly in Sloane's armpits and beaded on her forehead. She sat with the mask in her lap, rubbing and coaxing and pressing at the leather with the sticketta. Slowly she lost herself in her hands. She no longer heard the sea muttering around the pier posts below or the fan sweeping overhead; even her eyes seemed only another kind of touch, a confirmation of what her fingers already knew.

A face began to rise out of the leather, a laughing face, darker than her own and more knowing. It grinned at her and she felt uneasy, off-balance. She was intensely aware of the skin of her real face, tightening along the ridges above her eyes. Blood tingled in her cheeks.

It was a shock when Odessa broke the silence. "That's enough for now, sugar." Next she gave Sloane a hammer with a head made from steer's horn, sanded silky smooth. Sloane began pecking away with the pointed end, working on one feature at a time. The blows from the hammer compacted the leather, crushing it down, and forcing it ever more tightly onto the mold. It took her an hour to do her right eye and the plane of her right cheek. As soon as Sloane had covered one area with dimples, she would go over it again with the sticketta, rubbing the ridges down, smoothing away every tiny wrinkle and imperfection. Drawing it tight.

She felt her own skin pull taut between her cheekbones and her jaw. The corners of her eyes began to pull up, and even though her back was aching and she was desperate with thirst in the stifling heat, she felt herself start to smile.

Hours went by.

•　　•　　•

FOR a long time her mind was empty, still as a pool of brown water. Then, slowly, images and memories began to float to the surface. The tip of her hammer fell pattering over the mask, releasing little traces of leather smell and the memory of Momus standing next to her. She remembered how real he had felt, and the fish-belly whiteness of his skin. *Jane keeps one Galveston, I another, and the Recluse watches the door between the two.* The memory of that moment hung in her mind as she finished hammering along the plane of her left cheek. Then she picked up the sticketta and rubbed. And as she rubbed, she pressed the memory out, coaxing and stroking the surface of the mask until the memory began to fade, pressing and pushing until she had rubbed out the very last glimpse of his white skin, and all that remained was the smooth tight plane of leather under her fingers.

As an herb, crushed, gives forth a tiny burst of scent, so the blows of the hammer each brought forth packets of memory; breaths of desire, despair, hope, grief. Visions of pain, moments when for all her skill and effort she had not been invisible enough.

She rubbed them out.

It was amazing, that you could do this. It was incredible to her that she could take even an encounter with a god and erase it, drain it, smooth it away. But the longer she worked, the easier it became. She saw her mother, lying in bed and staring at Sloane, afraid to die and more afraid her daughter wouldn't live up to her responsibilities. The doubt in her eyes was humiliating, and Sloane was very glad to rub it out, pushing it away with tiny patient strokes of the sticketta.

Certain angles and ridges she left untouched: the twin arcs of her eyebrows and the cheekbones below them. In time these ridges came to stand out even more sharply, making hard shadows under the glare of the workbench light.

Jane and Sloane up late at night in her mother's office,

she shouldn't have been bored but she was, and she was ashamed of being bored. All she wanted to do was go to bed, go for a walk, work on a blouse that lay half-finished on her sewing table, trade gossip with Ladybird Trube, anything. Lazy. Frivolous. Weak, said a voice in her head. It was a bossy, resentful voice and it was always saying things like that. If you really cared about anything besides yourself you'd—

She rubbed it out.

I didn't do you any favors, letting you hide so much. You were such a scared little girl.

She rubbed that out, too.

Bent under her mother's wasting arms, helping her awkwardly to the downstairs bathroom and afterward watching her struggle to pull up her underwear again. She rubbed that out furiously, trembling with anger.

The drought. The look in the faces of the poor as they passed Ashton Villa. The poor themselves, big-bellied with rice, faces lined with thirst, yellow with jaundice, poxed or sunburnt or clammy with yellow fever: she made them all go away, rubbed them smooth and shiny and voiceless.

Resentful, clever Joshua Cane who desired her: gone.

Further back, Sloane sitting motionless before her vanity mirror, her mother behind her, carefully braiding her hair. Her own serious expression, her mother's sure touch, the great Jane Gardner terribly vulnerable, helpless with love for her daughter. "You are my sunshine," she had sung in a whisper, and she had kissed Sloane on the top of her head, and they had been safe together.

That memory made Sloane angrier still and she rubbed it out, rubbed and rubbed and rubbed.

The two of them playing together in the surf, Sloane a small child now, rare laughter in her mother's eyes and salt water beaded in her hair, Sloane like a bag of giggles that had burst open, laughing and whooping as her mother jumped her over each incoming wave—

Everything, every thought and feeling and memory that came up, she rubbed it out. She was so angry her whole body shook with it. Only after hours did the fury begin to fade, after hours and hours and hours, finally getting almost smooth enough, the soft brown surface of the mask like oil beneath her fingers.

Then she was rubbing out the last wrinkles one by one, feeling more cheerful all the time, flat and sharp and grinning. If it hadn't been for the fierce, stretched, tingling pain in Sloane's face, and a curious tightness in her chest, she would have said it was the best she'd felt in ages.

Chapter Six

THE MASK

As Sloane finished her work the high, blank feeling continued to sing through her. Humming to herself, she applied seven coats of lacquer to the inside of the mask, then smoothed it to a silky gloss with a strip of 400-grit extra-fine sandpaper. She dyed the leather a russet red, working the color in with a shaving brush, adding more some places than others, so the whole face took on the brindled look of an animal's pelt. With a pinch of cleanser from an ancient canister of Comet she rubbed some of the dye off, leaving pale highlights along the raised ridges of the mask so the sharp brows and cheeks stood out more dramatically. Then she cut face straps and attached them with rivets.

The only moment of discomfort came when she had to cut out the eyeholes. Odessa had her set the mask on a rounded piece of driftwood and handed her a gouge, a chisel with a slightly cupped blade. It was strange to see the mask staring up at her, something so like her own face and yet so very different. It made Sloane uneasy and she whacked the gouge harder than she had meant to. She felt a stabbing pain in her left eye, and it went dark on that side as soon as the mask's leather pupil had fallen

away. "Odessa—" The Recluse shook her head and moved the gouge over the mask's right eye. This time the pain was even worse, and when Sloane had finished she was blind.

The darkness she found herself in was full of noise. For an age there had been no sound but that of her own breathing, Odessa's fan, the restless sea below them both. Now, however, she could hear gusts of laughter, snatches of conversation, and the clinking of plates and cutlery. A piano tinkled in the background. Sloane lifted the mask toward her face. The sounds grew louder, as if she were approaching a crowded room. They faded again as she lowered it back to her lap.

She put on the mask. She could see perfectly well. Every table in the Balinese Room was crowded. Conversation roared around her. Candlelight glittered on silver and crystal. A woman in a black evening gown with pearls around her neck threw her head back and laughed, so close Sloane could have touched her. "Hey!" someone said, pointing at Sloane. Every head at the table turned to stare at her.

She tore the mask from her face and found herself back in quiet darkness. "Not yet," Odessa said. "And I'd choose a less public place to make my entrance, if I were you."

"I can't see."

"That will pass. Can I get you something to drink, doll?"

"Yes, please," Sloane whispered. For the first time she realized she'd had neither food nor water since Odessa had removed the mask from her face, hours and hours before. Her throat was hard and dry and stung with the fumes of lacquer and paint thinner and dye. She tried to speak up as Odessa left the room to get her a drink, but her voice was a croak. "What time is it?"

"Almost dawn," Odessa said over her shoulder. "It's nearly tomorrow."

• • •

THE sun came up as Sloane walked home. After so long inside it was strange to see broad light in the sky, to feel the horizon so far away. She carried the mask in her purse like a terrible secret. It was already hot outside, but it would get hotter still. Dry pots and pails sat under the gutters of every inhabited house. Roosters flapped and crowed as she passed, necks extended, screaming from fence posts and toolsheds and porch roofs. Chickens scratched in the barren dust. The high, tense energy that had filled her as she built her mask seemed to disappear with the sunrise, leaving her dizzy and exhausted.

She ran the last block to Ashton Villa, her stomach in a knot. Maybe her mother would have died while she wasn't around to see it. Or—and the hope was almost as terrible as the fear—maybe she would come home to find Momus hadn't betrayed her after all. Maybe there would be some sign that her mother was getting well. Just the full use of her arms would be a miracle. Anything to show that the disease had finally halted its inexorable advance.

She slipped into her house, crept across the foyer, and cracked open the parlor door. Though it was barely dawn Jane Gardner was awake and seated in her wheelchair. Her arms lay dead in her lap, the skin blotched with liver spots. The knot in Sloane's stomach pulled tight. "I'm back," she said.

"I see that."

"You're not—" Sloane bit her lip. "Can I get you anything?"

"I'm sure you're very tired," Jane Gardner said. She was looking at Bettie Brown's stuffed Bird of Paradise in its cage of glass. "When Odessa sent a message to say she was keeping you overnight I hired a nurse. She's bringing my tea."

"I—"

"I've said for weeks you shouldn't be spending so

much time on me. A nurse is more practical."

Sloane's face was burning. "I'm sorry."

"What are you apologizing for? I hate it when you apologize all the time," Jane said. Her p's when she said "apologize" were definitely losing their shape, becoming slurred and breathy, almost like f's. "Make good d'cisions and let that be the end of it." She turned her head away, facing the wine-colored portieres that separated the parlor from the dining room. In the distance, footsteps were approaching. Sloane could hear spoons rattling on a tea tray.

Numbly she turned and left the room.

ONE week later, just past dawn, Sloane found herself hovering on the sidewalk outside Joshua Cane's house. Her mother hadn't died yet. Sloane was just back from Mardi Gras. Beside her, drought-withered ivy hung from a faded metal signpost left over from the days before the Flood:

San Jacinto Neighborhood Association
CRIME WATCH
We report all suspicious activities
to our police department.

I'm the sort of thing these good people should report, Sloane thought wryly. Her head was pounding, her feet ached, and every now and then a little more blood oozed out of a shallow cut above her left knee. The stain had rubbed onto the inside of her right thigh as well. She was wearing a short tight cotton dress and silk stockings, not like her at all but they matched the mask—they matched the person she became when she put it on. What a tramp she must look, her dress splotched and smelling of booze, the beautiful silk stockings Odessa had given her on her twenty-first birthday slashed, laddered, and bloodstained after a night in Momus's kingdom.

For her mother to see her in this state was unthinkable. Nor could she show up at Randall Denton's mansion looking like this, or Jim Ford's, or the Trube Castle. She had to get changed, or at least cleaned up. Despite the awkwardness of her last visit to Joshua Cane's house, he was the only person she knew unimportant enough that she could risk being seen in her present state.

Besides, you rather like the idea of showing up on your admirer's doorstep in a short dress, don't you . . . ?

That was the last of the evening's wine talking. Hush, she told it.

By daylight the apothecary's house looked small and shabby, but its ten-year-old coat of paint left it better off than its neighbors. A worn suit in a closet full of overalls. Sloane tiptoed up to the front porch. The third step groaned, sounding unnaturally loud this early in the morning. Sloane winced, glancing around to see if any of his neighbors were watching her.

Joshua must have heard her on the steps, for a curtain twitched at the front window and his face appeared. A moment later he stood in the doorway. An early riser, apparently: he was already washed and dressed. "Am I in trouble?"

"Not that I know."

"In that case, come in."

The first time she had met Josh here, she had been in shock and it had been night. Her memory of him was a confused impression of hissing gas lamps, overpowering pharmacy smells, and hard fingers touching the strap of her dress. Today she saw him more clearly. He was roughly her own age, a small man in his early twenties with the fleshless face and wrists of someone who finds cooking and eating an annoyance. He had dark eyes under surprisingly heavy black brows, a bony face, and curly black hair cut very short. It was a neat job, but with no real understanding of hair. Does it himself, I bet.

Joshua Cane, she thought, exemplified the kind of pov-

erty that knows better—an excellent silk shirt, custom-tailored, with several tight, careful mends and two replaced buttons which didn't match the originals but were intended to. His shorts were newer, made out of the rough modern denim they spun here in Galveston from Amarillo cotton. Below the shorts his knees and ankles were bony. The soles of his sandals were made from tire rubber; the nylon straps had been cut from abandoned car seat belts.

He stepped aside and waved her in, looking at the nasty bloodstain on her leg. "Is that serious?"

"It looks worse than it was. Stupid accident with a broken bottle." Sloane dabbed at the stain, then stopped as her fingers came up red and sticky. "Oh, yuck." She looked up. "Do you have . . . ? I mean, could I—"

"There's a bathroom through that door, to your left."

"Thanks."

The bathroom was tiny and mildewed. Like most people too poor to have running water, Josh had a big water barrel next to his bathtub. An old plastic milk bottle with the top cut off served as a dipper. Sloane's stockings were stuck to her legs with dried blood. She took off her dress and stood in the tub, sloshing tepid water over her thighs. It seeped into her cut and began to sting furiously. Yikes! Salt water! Of course, a common man wouldn't be using freshwater to bathe in after four weeks of rationing. Joshua Cane didn't enjoy the privileges of living at Ashton Villa. Sloane felt like a spoiled rich girl.

There's a reason for that, Miss Gardner.

To her relief his towels were clean and didn't smell much. She dried off quickly and put her dress back on. There was a tiny bloodstain on the hem. That she could scrub out later, or cover in trim, but the stockings were a dead loss. When she returned to the front room, Joshua was behind the counter of his pharmacy, grinding away with his mixing bowl mortar and golf club pestle. "What are you making?" Sloane asked.

"Chili paste arthritis liniment. You remember Ham? His dad's hands hurt him pretty bad these days. Wanted to get this done before my morning rush," Josh said sardonically.

"You're doing this for free?"

"The Mathers are good as kin. I owe them more than the occasional jar of liniment," Joshua said. "What can I do for you, Ms. Gardner?"

Sloane grinned. "Raised by your mother, were you?"

"What?"

"Only sons brought up by women of my mother's generation call anyone 'Ms.' "

"I can stop."

"No, don't. It's quaint." Sloane laughed. "Lovely old-fashioned manners. Really." She held up the damp remains of her stockings. "I wasn't sure what to do with these." Besides walking through the streets with them bloody and ripped in my hands, that is. Maybe I should just leave them gaily flung over the back of the armchair in the parlor for Mom to find. Sloane shuddered. "They're ruined, but I didn't know where—"

"If you're throwing them out, I could use them." Sloane cocked one eyebrow and gave him an arch look. It was a new expression for her, one that had come with the mask. "Not to wear," Joshua added hastily. "To strain my tinctures through. Something finer than cheesecloth would be very useful from time to time." Sloane plopped the damp pile of wet silk on his counter. "So how was your night at the Mardi Gras, Ms. Gardner?" Josh said.

Sloane froze.

"You smell of cigarette smoke," Josh explained. "We haven't had tobacco on the Island in ten years. That was the last good money we made. Even my mom didn't mind charging an arm and two legs for that poison. Only time we ever got a Denton in our store. Sheriff Jeremiah's first wife came in desperate a few times before cancer got her."

"You're very smart, Mr. Cane."

"Hasn't made me rich, Ms. Gardner."

"Call me Sloane. Please." She stuck her hand over the counter. He smiled, put down his pestle, wiped his hand on his denim shorts and shook. His fingertips were hard, as she had remembered. All that grinding.

"Were you up all night?" Josh asked.

"I've been a bad girl, I'm afraid. As if there isn't work to be done." As if Mom doesn't need me now more than ever.

She had meant to see Momus and clarify their agreement, that's why she had put on the mask in the first place. But it was so strange in Mardi Gras, there was so much music and dancing, it had taken her a while to get her bearings. She had been caught up, somehow, in a wonderful party at the Bishop's Palace—only it wasn't the real Palace, where Randall Denton now lived, but a different, magical one where it was still February 2004 and there were cars in the streets and all the air-conditioning you could desire and marvelous exotic foods she hadn't tasted in her whole life. And water! All the water you could drink, and Coke, and wine, and beer that wasn't made from rice—anything you could imagine. They had lived like kings, before the Flood. They were still living like kings in Mardi Gras. The last night of the old world, playing on forever.

Sloane blinked. She had almost drifted off to sleep on her feet.

Josh turned and ran his fingers along one of the shelves behind his head, then pulled down a mason jar full of dried leaves. "Damiana. A mild stimulant and antidepressant, one of the few useful plants that grows wild here. The Mexicans use it all the time, call it *hierba de la pastora*. Not that anyone cares. This is what passes for medicine these days. They used to think it was an aphrodisiac." He glanced up. With the tingle of the Mardi Gras still in her blood, she gave him a sly smile. Odessa

would have been proud of that look, she thought. You naughty flirt.

He grinned, unscrewing the jar's lid. "You look like a good sneeze would knock you over. Can I give you a little something to pick you up? I'm thinking your days aren't a lot of fun right now."

"Not too much fun, no."

"I lost my mother a few years back," Josh said. "Diabetes." He took out a small handful of damiana leaves and closed up the jar. "I hope I die of a heart attack," he said. "It's bad when you can see it coming from so far away."

It was quite unbearable to listen to him try, in his awkward way, to comfort her, when instead of trying to save her mother all she had done last night was drink and dance. Sloane smiled her practiced smile. "We're just trying to take it one day at a time."

Joshua nodded, as if this meant something, as if it wasn't just mechanical bullshit of the kind she dished out all day, every day. "Did you happen to drink much last night? No, forget I asked. What I mean is, you're probably a little dehydrated. Let me make you a sip of tea."

He showed her into his kitchen and she followed, knowing she shouldn't, knowing he probably didn't have the money or the water to be wasting on her, knowing she should get back to Ashton Villa before she was missed. Instead she sank into a chair at Josh's kitchen table while he boiled precious water to make her a cup of damiana tea. The guilt she felt at having abandoned her mother to go dancing in the Mardi Gras all night didn't make it any easier to face returning to that dim parlor with the closed drapes and the wasted figure on the bed. The tea tasted strange, minty and a little bitter, but she was grateful for its warmth. After a few sips she crossed her arms on the table in front of her and put her head down to rest. Joshua Cane reminded her of Deputy Kyle Lanier, she decided, drowsing. Physically they were

both small, but more importantly each carried the sense of poverty like a grudge. The difference was that Kyle had been poor as a child, Josh well-to-do. Kyle was always running away from his past, where Josh Cane couldn't let go of his.

She realized she must have fallen asleep when a clatter woke her. Josh was putting a bowl and spoon in front of her. It felt as if hours had passed, but it must have only been minutes. A moment later he returned with a pot full of rice porridge and began ladling out a portion for her. "Brown sugar or molasses?"

"Sugar," she said, and then worried she had picked the more expensive alternative, and wondered what he would think of her if he knew she didn't know. Spoiled rich kid. Sloane watched a lump of brown sugar turn liquid, a dark stain spreading into the porridge. Her whole body recoiled from the thought of food, but she didn't want to seem rude or shame him so she blessed the porridge and forced herself to eat everything in her bowl, washing it down with sips of bitter damiana tea.

A rooster shrieked and strutted in the backyard. Joshua sat across from her, stirring molasses into his porridge. Damn. Bet the molasses was cheaper. When Ham had brought her here the first time, the apothecary had smelled of the pepper and yeast and sulfur he worked with. Today his clean shirt and pants both smelled faintly but pleasantly of early morning ironing.

"Thanks for this," Sloane said, holding up her cup of tea.

"Witch-doctoring," Josh said briefly. "Which reminds me, don't go picking your own damiana and drinking it by the quart. It's also a mild laxative."

Sloane laughed. "Thanks for the warning. Do you get a lot of customers?"

"No. I'm . . . my mother and I had a reputation for being unlucky," Josh said.

After an awkward pause Sloane said, "Thank you for

the tea, and your help." Careful of his pride here. "I'd like to pay you."

"I wasn't trying to get your sympathy."

Sure you were. "Of course not," Sloane said. "But I can afford to pay. You are allowed to be as proud as a Gardner, but not prouder. You can look offended while getting paid, but I won't let you avoid payment entirely. Deal?"

He eyed her sardonically. "Deal. . . . No, on second thought, I want something more. I want to know what it's like in the Mardi Gras."

It was Sloane's turn to flinch. She sipped her tea. "I'm not sure I can tell you. I've never really been there." He started to say something, but she shook her head. "I mean, it's not really me, it's someone else. Sly goes to parties, Sly plays dice, Sly drinks and dances. Sloane . . . Sloane is a good girl. She has to get up in the morning. Organize appointments. Take Mother to the bathroom."

"Sly?"

"That's what I call her. I mean, myself. When I'm over there. I don't use my real name, not in Momus's kingdom."

"Why Sly?"

If you saw the mask, you would know. Sloane shrugged.

Joshua finished his rice porridge and cleared the table, putting the dishes in his small sink. "How much time have you been spending over there?"

"Not much," Sloane said quickly. "I've only been there twice. Well, three times."

"Mm," Josh said, looking at her.

Sloane couldn't meet his eyes. "Joshua? Please . . . please don't tell."

"I wouldn't."

"I would be so ashamed."

He said, "I know what that feels like."

Then Sloane did something she never could have done

before she had put on the mask. She joined him at the sink, holding his eyes with her own, and took his hand, and sealed their bargain with a touch. The trace of a smile flickered over Joshua's face. "Let's not tell the others," he murmured. She looked quizzically at him, but he shook his head. "Your secret is safe with me, Ms. Gardner."

"Sloane? Please?"

"Sloane."

She squeezed his hand and then released it and finished her tea. "Thanks. I needed that." On aching feet she allowed him to see her to the front door. One more time, she thought. I'll go back just one more time to see Momus. After that, never again.

SHE walked home through the poor sections of town on the south side of Broadway, praying under her breath that she would not meet anyone she knew. Even though the day was hot she felt much too exposed in her short cotton dress, especially with her legs bare. What possessed me to wear a mid-thigh hem! There's only one explanation, she thought morosely. My mind is being controlled by a god who likes fat legs.

Her luck almost held. She came cautiously up 23rd Avenue and hung back behind a fat palm on the west side of Broadway, waiting for a moment the street was nearly empty. Then she hurried across, eyes downcast, and slipped through the front door of Ashton Villa.

"Up late again," said Sarah, the senior housemaid, materializing from the gloomy foyer. "And a night like your poor mother had," she added disapprovingly.

Oh, God. "Is she worse?"

Sarah shrugged. "Ask the nurse," she said pointedly.

"Sarah, you don't have to . . ."

"Don't *tell* on you, is that what you mean? I have my own work to do," Sarah said, and without waiting for an answer she headed back to the kitchen.

• • •

Two hours later Sloane sat beside her mother's wheelchair, awake by virtue of willpower and damiana tea. Her eyes felt like scoured glass. The damiana hadn't actually made her feel wakeful, just jumpy and nervous. She desperately longed for sleep.

They were sitting at the smaller table in the dining room, the circular one carved from Italian oak. Polished cabinets and tallboys around the room held Miss Bettie's silver, fifty place settings for a seven-course meal. Twenty matched chairs in the Elizabethan style, with blue velvet backs and cushions, sat around the formal cherrywood table that occupied the center of the room. Sloane found herself wondering how much of Joshua's house she could buy with the money it had taken to commission just one of the carved walnut cornices that hung over every window in the room. Similar thoughts wandered through her mind as she pretended to listen to her mother discuss Krewe business with Jim Ford and Jeremiah Denton.

Sheriff Denton was a quiet, intelligent Southern gentleman with the neat grey mustache and beard Sloane had seen in photographs of Robert E. Lee. He had Lee's weary grey eyes, too, that had looked, unflinching but at great cost, at too many years of grief and toil. Jeremiah was the one Denton of his generation viewed with universal respect. Jane Gardner had coaxed him into accepting the nomination for sheriff when Sloane was still a girl. Now he was serving his third term.

Sloane quietly shifted Jane's wheelchair so her mother could see both men without strain. "Well, Sheriff, the bad news is that the drought's hit Beaumont. Jim tells me they're going to have trouble bringing in the summer rice crop."

"Even if they do, the price is going to go up, up, up," Jim said. He brought out the Sony laptop he had carried to work every day for as long as Sloane could remember

and put it on the table. Flipping up the screen he said, "Let me show you some numbers."

Over the next hour the heads of the Krewe of Momus pored over their options. They discussed alternative foods, considered how best to increase pumping from the artesian wells across the bay that supplied the Island's water, and argued the value of rationing. Everybody stopped frequently to wish for rain.

It was a crucial conversation, desperately important to the Island's immediate future. Sloane followed hardly any of it. It was boring and she was exhausted. Each time she grimly set out to follow an argument or idea, her concentration slipped away like a minnow between her fingers. Instead she found herself staring at the way the lamplight gleamed on Jim Ford's bald spot, or her mother's fingers, so pitifully wasted and thin. She remembered those fingers resting over her own as her mother patiently taught her to type at the Compaq desktop in her playroom. Cut into that memory were others from her recent nights in the Mardi Gras: snatches of song, the sight of a laughing mouth, bubbles winking in a champagne flute.

How fearless they are, she thought, as the sober debate murmured on around her. Desperate they might be; but like all the members of her mother's generation, they didn't feel the malice of the drought. It was impersonal to them, an annoying accident of weather. They should be making sacrifices to it, or begging for help from the Sea. Instead they continued to act as if mankind alone of all creation had volition and purpose. As if the rest of the world was nothing but a clockwork, a blind machine, badly made and crotchety, which they were supposed to regulate and repair. They can't help it, she reminded herself. It's how they were raised. But how any thinking person could hold so naive a view in a world where Vincent Tranh could be gone to Krewes, where Momus ruled his kingdom from an amusement park two miles away—

that seemed like something worse than naiveté to Sloane. That felt like dangerous pride and pure blind folly.

"Sloane? Sloane?" She blinked. Jeremiah Denton was talking to her. "Is something wrong with your momma?"

Jane Gardner's eyes were wide, her lips grey. She was struggling to speak. "She can't breathe!" Sloane said. "Get a doctor!"

LATE that night in Sloane's bedroom, the little blue Dresden clock that had belonged to Miss Bettie's shy sister, Matilda, struck two. Sloane lay on her back staring at the pale white blur of mosquito netting around her bed. Her purse lay on top of her hand-painted French satinwood dresser. The mask was in her purse. From downstairs came the faint sound of a piano. Miss Bettie's ghost. Sloane had heard her play every night since bringing home the mask.

Her mother lay in the parlor downstairs, taking oxygen through a rubber mask. It had been very close that morning, very close. Sloane had tried to give her mother mouth-to-mouth, but in her panic she had done it wrong, forgetting to pinch her mother's nose shut, and the air had all escaped. By the time she realized what was happening the nurse had come and pushed her briskly aside.

The taste of her mother's mouth still sat horribly on her lips.

Sloane sat up, pulled aside her canopy of mosquito netting, and walked softly to the French doors that opened onto her balcony. In her stepfather's Galveston the party would be in full swing. But here in the real world the Island lay like a dead animal in the hot night. Gaslight lanterns burned in the better neighborhoods; the rest were dark. Far away, a few yellow lamps moved slowly over the Bay; night fishermen, out for squid or skate.

Her mother's mouth had tasted old, her lips soft under Sloane's lips. No lipstick, of course—Sloane hadn't been

there to put it on that morning. The nurse hadn't thought of it, and Jane Gardner wouldn't ask a stranger to do something that personal. Sloane couldn't think of a day in her mother's life she hadn't worn lipstick. It was part of her armor.

Even with her back to the mask, Sloane could feel it waiting for her.

She really had no business going back to the Mardi Gras. She needed to sleep. She needed to be well-rested and alert. She should never have forced her mother to hire a nurse. It was Sloane's responsibility to wheel her to the bathroom, wash her, dress her, read to her. However tired she was.

Whenever Sloane talked to her mother or Odessa about the first terrible year after the Flood, she would ask where they had found the strength to go on, with sickness in the streets and madness spreading by contagion, and worst of all the terrible weight of loss, of families drowned beneath the magic's tide. They both gave the same non-answer: "You do what you have to do."

When the choking weight of the Gardner name fell on her, presumably she would find the strength to bear it. If her mother's life wasn't the one Sloane wanted to lead— well, Jane Gardner hadn't asked for her burdens either, had she? Before the Flood she had been a successful young lawyer with a handsome husband and a condo on the beach. If Jane could lose her world and still persist, it was little enough to ask Sloane to give up her freedom.

One of the hardest lessons we all have to learn is how few choices life gives to a civilized woman with any conscience at all.

The Rolex ticked in exact accord with the blue Dresden clock on Sloane's dresser. She had taken to wearing the watch to bed and even in the shower. With Momus maybe watching her, she didn't feel safe taking off her most powerful charm anymore, although she had come to hate its maddening *tick, tick, tick* as she tossed and

turned, trying to sleep through the long, hot, Texas nights.

Perhaps, Sloane thought, the time she had spent in Mardi Gras over the past week had been a hidden blessing. Maybe it had been wrong of her to be gone so much, but the nurse was a brisk, efficient professional. Now that she was here, it was ridiculous for Sloane to feel guilty about letting her do her job. Sloane and Jane both felt the humiliation of Jane's weakness too keenly. Neither of them could smile or joke about Sloane pulling up her mother's underwear after a trip to the toilet.

Maybe Momus was cheating her, the bastard. Maybe he would keep Jane alive but never better than she was right now. A useless cripple. The moon god would probably find that cruelly diverting. Or maybe Odessa was right, maybe it was Sloane who would die first. That would take care of the question of which kingdom, exactly, she was supposed to inherit: Galveston, Mardi Gras, or Odessa's twilight territory in between.

Did any of them seriously expect her to succeed them? Sloane who could barely function as her mother's assistant? Sloane who didn't have the courage or strength of purpose to face Momus a second time and undo her previous mistake? *I just can't stand to see her die.* The stupidity of it made her want to scream. She who thought of herself as the cunning one, the one who had grown up with gods and witches and was supposed to understand them.

No, she had to go back. She had to confront Momus again. Not because she was brave. Because she was too much a coward to bear going through more days like this one. Too weak to bear the disappointment in her mother's eyes as Jane Gardner saw, more clearly every day, that her daughter would not be able to maintain what she had built.

The funniest thing, she thought, is that Mom would like Sly better than me. Sly didn't sit in the corner of the

room and pretend to be interested in the potted plants;
she joked, she wheedled, she bullied and coaxed. She was
more rakish, perhaps, than the Gardners allowed themselves to be, but Sly would enjoy Jane's job—at least the
parties and the politics of it. In a way, it wasn't a bad
thing she had spent so much of the last week being Sly.
Sloane had a lot to learn from her. Really, she would
make a better heir for her mother once she had mastered
the skills Sly had to teach her.

And black is white and chickens are pigs. I sure am
using a lot of energy to get in bed with myself, she
thought sourly. She groaned and rubbed her face with her
hands. She felt wide awake but fragile. It was hot and
humid and she was never going to get back to sleep.

Clocks ticked. Downstairs the piano tinkled a ragtime
tune.

Sloane closed her shutters and turned up the gas lamp
over the vanity. She went to her closet and picked out an
ensemble calculated to make her mother's eyes roll, fea-
turing a short-sleeved cotton dress, fitted snug around her
breasts and hips. She chose a pair of diamond studs to
match her Rolex. She finished the outfit with her best
shoes, the brown cloth ones with the copper buckles, and
a silk scarf looped around her throat, a present from
Odessa. Sly never wore a veil. She hurried over to the
night table to get the mask. This really will be the absolutely last time, she thought. The sound of the piano
came to her more clearly as she touched the leather, and
she felt her mouth tightening into a smile. Yeah, right.

Chapter Seven

THIRD STREET

THE moment Sloane put on her mask she felt much, much better.

Downstairs the piano tinkled and juked. Glasses clinked amid a dull roar of conversation. Gusts of laughter floated in from the garden outside. Sloane opened the French doors and stepped out on her balcony. This Galveston was ablaze with lights: tall streetlamps, lit windows in houses and office buildings, headlights from moving cars, and over everything the white stare of a full moon. There was a crowd milling around the grounds of Ashton Villa. Someone let off a Roman candle, sending pulses of golden fire into the night sky. Down on the ground a man in a gangster suit and a domino mask caught sight of her and whistled. She waved back.

She felt good. She knew, in a detached way, that she was a bad person for feeling happy, but the guilt that pressed on her all the time had suddenly receded. In the real Galveston it was a constant, pushing pain. Here—an annoyance. A mosquito bite.

SLOANE gasped and pulled the mask down her face so her eyes peeked over the top. Mardi Gras vanished, re-

placed by the dreary, drought-stricken city she would face again in the morning. Her hands were shaking like a junkie's, and she found she was listening for the faintest sound, as if she had woken from a nightmare. *You are not making this trip to have fun. You are going to see Momus. You are going to do your duty.*

She stared down at her trembling hands. Her panic contracted into fury. "The hell with it," she whispered, and she pushed the mask back on.

DOWNSTAIRS the Gold Room was packed. Uniformed staff passed through Ashton Villa bearing an incredible variety of food. And the drinks! Exotic juices made from fruits that only existed for Sloane in stories: apples and cranberries and lemons. There was alcohol of every description, and cream-topped pastries made from something far nicer than dry, flaky rice flour. A tray of crackers went by. She didn't even recognize half the toppings, like the purple vegetable embedded in an exotic cheese sauce, or the odd relish that smelled of basil and roasted garlic.

She could only imagine what Josh Cane would think of this breathtaking display of casual waste. *You'd think the little runt would have bigger shoulders, with all the chips he carries around on them,* she thought.

Moralizing bored Sly.

As she wandered out of the Gold Room, Sloane caught sight of a familiar figure. Ladybird Trube was down on all fours in front of the grandfather clock in the hallway. She had the case open and was groping around inside it, interfering with the pendulum. "Ladybird?"

The Trube heiress jumped and looked back over her shoulder. She had lost her tortoiseshell combs and her hair hung raggedly before her eyes. The hem of her evening dress was dirty and raveling. She attempted a smile. "Oh, hello," she said. "Do you happen to know the time?"

"What are you doing down there?"

"Clock's stopped. I thought I'd wind the old boy up, but I can't seem to . . ." She turned back, searching more desperately inside the mechanism. "Can't seem to find the goddamn *key!*"

"Ladybird? Do you know me?" Sloane said from behind her mask. She realized she wanted very badly for Ladybird not to recognize her. She wanted to be Sly here, not Sloane. She would be so ashamed to be seen.

"Don't believe we've had the pleasure." Ladybird stared into the clock case. Her shoulders slumped. Suddenly she slammed her head against the wooden frame of the clock, sickeningly hard. If the glass front had been closed she would have shattered it. "I just want . . ." SLAM "to know . . ." SLAM "the *time*." She slammed her head again and dropped to the carpet, sobbing.

Sloane crossed the foyer. "Now, honey," she remarked in Sly's careless voice. "You'll get bloodstains on that dress."

Ladybird was too busy sobbing to notice her. Thank God. There would have been a scene of the sort that doughy, dutiful old Sloane would have felt compelled to wallow in. Bound to dampen one's evening of fun. All in all, a narrow escape.

There was a card game running at the round table in the dining room. "Ante up, ladies and gentlemen!" the dealer said. He was sitting in the very spot where, sixteen hours before, Jane Gardner had nearly died. Only that had happened back in the boring, dowdy Galveston. In this much more pleasant city, Jane wasn't even in danger.

A little hit of guilt passed through Sloane, like a wave of nausea. Not that she wasn't going to find Momus. She was.

There were five players in the game. The dealer was a thin, balding, Asian man wearing a pair of round spectacles and sporting an enormously long mustache. On second glance Sloane saw that the mustache wasn't made

from hair at all, but long red tendrils like shrimp's feelers that drooped down below the edge of the table.

Sloane recognized the player next to him instantly: it was Miss Bettie herself, and in her prime, looking just as she did in the portrait that still hung in the Gold Room. She was a strong-featured woman just Sloane's age who had traveled by camel across the Sahara with thirteen giant cedar trunks in tow. She wore a purple evening gown and a feather boa that made a joke of its own extravagance. She was one of the few people Sloane had seen who wasn't wearing a mask. Of course, Miss Bettie had been a part of Galveston's magic long before the Flood rolled over the Island.

Next to Miss Bettie, a tall, angular woman dug her ante out of a silk clutch purse and tossed it into the middle of the table. Her fingers were dark and hard like talons. She was wearing a white evening gown and a very good bird mask on which perched a pair of opera glasses. No, on second thought it wasn't a mask. She had the head of an egret: white face, long straight bill, small yellow eyes, and a ragged fringe of white feathers where her hairline ought to be.

A gigantic man sat across from the dealer. He had a narrow waist but enormous, rounded shoulders, broader than Ham's. He smelled like a wild animal and radiated a barely contained ferocity. In one hairy fist he clutched a stick on which was pasted a papier-mâché half-mask of a meek, middle-aged man. Below the inoffensive mask, black hairs as thick as wire sprang up from a jutting muzzle, and two boar's fangs curled up from a wide-lipped mouth.

The last player was a cat-headed woman in gypsy skirts.

The shrimp-whiskered man looked up at Sloane and smiled. "Care to play? We lost our sixth."

The dealer is Vincent Tranh! She was sure of it. Of course he would be in Mardi Gras. Moping gutless

Sloane had sent him there. Guilt, embarrassment, more guilt: yawn.

She tried to say his name but the words died in her mouth, killed by Odessa's enchantment. "Call me Sly," she said. "I'd love to play, but I'm afraid I don't know how."

Shrimp-whiskered Vincent Tranh, gone to Krewes so long ago, pulled out a chair for her. "A pretty woman can always find help." Vince spotted a thin man leaning in the shadows by the portieres that led into the parlor. "Ace? Ace! Come over here and advise the young lady, would you?" He winked at Sloane. "Best damn card player I ever knew. Take his advice and you'll do fine."

The lean man came slowly to the table. He must have been handsome once, but now he was emaciated to the point of starvation, revealing too much of the skull beneath his skin. His left ear had been cut off, leaving only little nubs of scar tissue around the ear hole. If Sloane hadn't been wearing her mask, she would have been shocked and stammering.

The bland human mask in front of the beast-man's face trembled, threatening to slip. "I don't want his luck at the table," he snarled.

Vincent waved him off. "We won't be dealing Ace any cards, Rake. Just let him give her some pointers."

Sloane curled up one corner of her mouth in a lazy smile that felt very comfortable to Sly. "Don't worry. I hardly ever take good advice."

The player called Rake flexed his hairy fingers around the stick of his mask, making it tremble again. He spat on the floor. "First sign of cheating, he's a dead man."

Sloane smiled and held out her hand for Ace to kiss. He bent and brushed the back of her knuckles with his lips. "Charmed," he said, and he took up position behind her chair.

"Have you got the stakes?" asked the heron-headed

woman. "We're playing fifty-one hundred, with a ten-dollar ante."

Ah. A problem. Of course stupid Sloane hadn't thought to bring money with her. "How about this?" she said, taking the Rolex off her wrist. "The diamonds are real."

"That's a fine piece you have there," said Miss Bettie. She gave Sloane a long look. "Are you quite sure you want to part with it?"

She recognizes me, Sloane thought, dismayed. Miss Bettie wasn't fooled by the mask. She knew poor dutiful Sloane was hiding behind Sly's hard smile. Well, it shouldn't be that much of a surprise. After all, they had lived in the same house for twenty-three years now.

Really, what she should do was keep the watch, leave the table, go find Momus, go be brave. Or just take off the mask. Go back to the real Galveston, the one that mattered, the one where her mother was dying. The one she was supposed to inherit.

But the whole point of the mask was to create a tougher Sloane, a smarter, harder, more cunning woman to meet Momus. Someone who stood a chance. The last thing she could afford was to let the old, weak, mewling Sloane muddy the waters. It was Sly she had to count on, wasn't it? She had spent twenty-three years being Sloane, and look what it had made of her: a prisoner of everybody else's expectations. One who never lived up to them, at that.

Sloane found herself reaching across the table. Sly had taken off the watch and was holding it up for sale. "Will anyone give me three thousand?"

"I'll give you two," said the heron-headed woman.

"Done—"

"Make it twenty-five hundred," Miss Bettie said. "It will go so nicely with the diamond pendant Emperor Franz Josef gave to me. What a lovely man—and could he waltz!" As Miss Bettie pulled a wad of bills out of a sequined clutch purse, Sly tossed the Rolex across the

table. She felt wonderfully lighter without it.

Vincent dealt out the first three cards of a round of stud. Sloane got a six and a three in the hole, with another six showing: a pair already. "Low card must open the ante, that's dealer with a deuce showing," Vincent said, putting in another ten dollars. "Any other bets on Third Street? Fifty dollars to play."

Sloane pulled out three twenty-dollar bills. "I'll see your ten and raise fif—" She felt a slight pressure as Ace pushed ever so slightly on her shoulder. She glanced back at him, surprised.

"Throw 'em."

"By Momus's moon-sized balls, why would I do that?"

"Advice," the Rake growled. "No explanations." His lips pulled back, showing yellow fangs bedded in bloody pink gums.

Ace stood still and silent.

Sloane tossed her sixty dollars in the pot and smiled at the Rake. "I promised you I wouldn't do as I was told."

Miss Bettie folded. The Rake reraised with a queen showing, and the Heron called, with a ten of diamonds. The cat-faced woman, whose name was Lianna, folded, along with Vincent.

"My odds are improving," Sloane said, but knowing Ace disapproved of her play she didn't raise on her next three cards, just called the Rake, who raised at every card. The Heron seemed to be building a diamond flush, but her fifth and sixth cards were both spades and when the Rake raised again she folded, too. Sloane had been tempted to do the same, seeing the fury with which the Rake bet, but her sixth card was another three, giving her two pair. She decided to stay for the showdown. Every bet on the fourth, fifth, and sixth cards had been for a hundred dollars, leaving thirteen hundred and twenty dollars in the middle of the table when she called the Rake's last bet. "Show me what you've got."

"Queens and fours," he snarled.

Sloane winced and started to lay down her two smaller pair, but Ace swiftly took her hand and placed her cards facedown on the table. "Shh." He looked at the Rake. "You win."

Sloane counted her money. She had lost five hundred and sixty dollars, more than a fifth of her stake, in one hand. She glanced at Ace. "Guess I should have folded."

"Yep."

On his advice she immediately folded the next three hands, won a small pot on the fourth, and folded again on the fifth card of the next, just before the raising started in earnest. The hand after, it was Miss Bettie who had the low card and the first bet. The Rake and the cat-faced woman folded. The Heron and Vincent called. Sloane had a ten and ace down with a king showing and no chance of a flush. She started to close up her hand when she felt Ace's bony fingers on her shoulder again. "Raise," he said.

"Just what I was thinking," she said, and she threw sixty more dollars into the middle of the table. Ten minutes later she won a sixteen-hundred-dollar pot with three tens.

The Rake growled, a low, savage rumbling in the back of his throat. "I told you we shouldn't play with him." He threw back a long shot of bourbon. "I didn't sit down to be cheated."

"Nobody's cheating, nobody's cheating!" Vincent said, shaking his head quickly so the long fronds of his feelers swished against the table's edge.

"Beginner's luck," Sloane added brightly. She glanced back at her advisor.

"Get your money and leave the table," Ace said. "That's the best advice I've got."

THE Gold Room was a roar of clinking glasses and drunken song. Ace followed Sloane in, leaned close to her ear and murmured, "Knowing the Rake, he might just

wait out front to beat his money out of you." After the next song Sloane slipped down the hallway to the kitchen and the back door. A moment later Ace followed.

As they stepped out of the cool, dry, air-conditioned interior and onto the back lawn, the Galveston night closed over them like a warm bath. A pavilion tent strewn with bunting sat gaily where the piggery should be. Throngs of people chatted and set off firecrackers and mingled beside the swimming pool. Sloane looked longingly at the pool.

There was no henhouse against the back fence, and the generator shed was still a detached garage. The two Lexus engines that in Sloane's world provided power for the house, here were still inside functioning automobiles. There were no washing lines strung up from tree to tree, no stench of slops, no dusty buckets and pails waiting below the gutters for any precious rain. What a clever girl I am to come to *this* Galveston.

She followed Ace out the back gate of Ashton Villa and found herself standing on a level sidewalk next to Ford Street. The road was in good repair, with cars parked along it. The Rosenberg Library loomed across the street. In Sloane's Galveston it had become the headquarters for the Krewe of Togetherness. Here it housed only books. Well, check that. After twenty-four years of Carnival, it probably held things considerably stranger than books.

Ace began to amble south along the sidewalk. Sloane fell into step beside him. "Thank you for your advice. You even managed to make up for my mistake."

"Reckon the advice was worth a cut?" He didn't meet her eyes.

"That, sir, was not part of the deal," Sloane said. "It was all for chivalry, I thought."

After a long silence he said, "I'm starving."

"That's better." She found that Sly had an arch, bantering tone when she spoke. "Don't try to bargain with

me. Just appeal to my abundant generosity." She held out a few bills, but pulled them lightly away as Ace tried to take them. "No, no. What's the magic word?"

"Thank you, ma'am."

Sloane laughed. "Much better." She took his hand and closed his fingers around the money. "Pride heals," she said.

AN hour later she was sitting with Ace on the edge of the Seawall, each with a plate of barbecue bought from a stall in the busy Stewart Beach fairground. On the sand below them carnies and hucksters worked the crowd. A plume of flame flared briefly and then disappeared down a fire-eater's gullet. Revellers milled and joked through the fairgrounds, buying food and beer from the makeshift stalls, trying their luck at skittles or ringtoss or the shooting gallery, staring at the peep shows, singing, or just wading in the warm Gulf water. Light from the fierce moon glinted off the swell, making brief planes of shifting pewter in the night. Ghosts of foam glimmered and guttered on the sea's back, or ran hissing onto the sand.

"You need to know which hands to fold and which ones to play," Ace said between mouthfuls of charred brisket. "And you need to know it before your first bet. I hope you don't mind if I talk a bit. If I eat too fast I'll get sick."

Sloane sucked on the end of a rib, idly swinging her feet so her heels kicked against the Seawall. "Why did you want me to fold with a pair one hand and raise with nothing the next?"

"Nothing ace high, with a paint scare card showing," he corrected her. "Position. On the first hand, you had to bet before everyone else. You're telling them you have sixes right off the bat. With a small pair and not much of an off card—it was a three, wasn't it?—you're going to be chasing all the way on a hand like that. An animal

like the Rake will raise and raise and raise, punishing you for staying in with bad cards. Nearly any pair out there is going to beat you, not to mention any drawing hand." He licked his fingers. "Straights or flushes, I mean. Trips are your only hope, really, and with a bad off card it's just not worth the gamble."

Sloane grinned. "And my ace high nothing?"

"There you got to bet last. Everyone else called or folded, so we knew nobody had a premium pair. Plus the Rake was out of the game. You had a scare card showing and pretty tight players left, so I figured we'd be able to limp into Fifth or Sixth Street with a lot of possibilities. They didn't want to raise and get reraised, so we got two free cards—free card is when you get to draw without having to bet to pay for the privilege. We got free cards on Fourth and Sixth streets by being aggressive on Third and Fifth. You drew out your tens—" He shrugged and cut another piece of brisket with his plastic utensils. "Hey, presto."

Sloane found herself smiling. "You care about your cards, I see."

"Not anymore." The gaunt man beside her licked his fingers. "But I still know the game."

"So why are you starving? Can't you make a living playing cards?"

"Nobody will play with me. There are always games in Mardi Gras, dozens of them; but there's only one left that I am welcome to join." He glanced over at the manager's hut at the back of the amusement park and fingered his mutilated ear. "But the stakes are high."

"It doesn't seem . . . *manly* to bar someone from a game just because he's good."

"Lucky. Not just good. Lucky."

"Sounds like a nice trait to have."

"You'd think so, wouldn't you?" Ace finished his barbecue. He held the plate between his hands for a long time.

She laughed. "Go ahead. Lick it. I can tell you want to." He regarded her. Sly didn't give a damn. "Pride heals," she said.

THEY walked out onto one of the long stone jetties that stuck into the ocean. Built as a storm-protection measure at the same time as the Seawall, the jetties were made from giant blocks of granite. When they reached the end, with the warm water of the Gulf boiling away below them, Ace said, "You don't live here."

"Pardon?"

"You don't live in the Mardi Gras. Most people here can't get out, but you can."

"What makes you think so?"

"You have the tells. In the Mardi Gras it's always night, but your skin is tanned. You could be a new arrival, but I don't see any changes on your body. Your mask is just a mask. There's no magic been spilled on you, nothing funny about your hands or feet or hair. You walk in the street by habit, instead of on the sidewalk, and you walk like a tourist, staring. I can see you comparing this Galveston to the real one."

Sloane whistled. "Good eyes."

Water crashed and hissed dully around them. The moon hung directly over the fairground, like a giant white spotlight. Ace said, "When I was a young man, before the Flood, I spent a year in Peru teaching English. I met a bunch of Americans there. Eight or nine. And the would-be travelers passing through, the Around-the-World-on-a-Shoestring types." Ace studied the sea. "You don't pack up and hightail it to the ass end of nowhere on a whim. Every one of them was running from something. Maybe a bad marriage. Maybe they didn't like themselves and were hoping to change. I met one guy who'd had a brain tumor removed. You could see Fear standing behind that old boy with a whip. Him thinking maybe he could just outrun that cancer. . . ." A wave broke just be-

low them, forcing spray out of the cracks in the rocks.

"And you? What were you running from?"

"Never did figure it out," Ace said. "The Flood hit just after I got home."

A cloud drifted in front of the moon, and for a moment the world around Sloane grew darker. "You think I'm on the run, too, is that it?"

"That's none of my business. But you had better know."

A dim suggestion of movement caught Sloane's eye and she looked around. There was a man sitting on the side of the jetty with his feet in the water, perhaps ten paces away. No. Not a man, exactly. A tall figure with a sad face and long undersea whiskers that drooped to his waist. Bulging eyes and armored skin. The veil of cloud slid across the moon and the white light returned. The creature clambered down among the rocks and slipped into the sea. A moment later a faint reek like the smell from a bucket of shrimp came to her on the steady Gulf breeze. Sea boiled and ran over the place where he had disappeared.

A Prawn Man. She had heard Odessa talk about them.

"I've got nothing against running," Ace said. "Weak players hold on to hands that better ones throw away."

Sloane couldn't tell if he had seen the Prawn Man. There had been something very quiet in the creature's face. And sad. Or rather, something akin to sadness: the feeling Sloane got staring across the salt-grass flats at the end of the day. The loneliness of all things. No one knows anyone, not really. Each of us is locked inside our own skin, a creature marooned in the secret salt sea of the body.

The wind from the sea felt cold and she shivered. She knew she should shake off the vision. It was such a Sloane thing to feel; nothing about Carnival at all. She would feel better when she forgot it. And yet . . . these moments of apprehension, where she saw things, frag-

ments of disappointment or doubt that her mother never seemed to feel; these moments seemed to Sloane more real, more true of her, than her whole busy public life as a Gardner. As if acts and words were only things, like clothes, that might reflect but never define her.

This is stupid. She turned her back on the place where the Prawn Man had been.

Ace said, "I have a proposition for you. I need to eat and you have quick eyes. If you reckon on staying here, in Mardi Gras, I can teach you to play cards and win. I wouldn't want all your take, or even half. Just a cut."

Sloane felt her lips curl into Sly's smile. "I might be willing. But only so long as it amuses me."

"There's a nice little five-ten game going at the Railroad Museum if you want to get your feet wet."

No! said the dreary dutiful voice inside her. What about Mother?

Sloane smiled whitely. "I'd love to," she said.

AFTER the railroad station had closed down and been converted into a museum, someone had decided to populate it with statues. In the real Galveston, there were seven or eight of them, mostly dressed in the fashions of the 1940s and '50s, sprinkled about the wooden pews in the lobby as if waiting for their trains to be called. Sloane recognized one of them the moment she and Ace walked into the station, an old black man wearing a slouch hat and reading a newspaper, who seemed so real she had to knock his arm to be sure it was stone. "He sure looks bored," she said.

Ace shrugged. "He's been waiting a long time."

Sloane laughed.

"They're playing in a Pullman car out back," Ace said. "There's no percentage in going into the finer points of poker until you have a better feel for the game. For now, I'll just give you two good rules. First is, fold nearly

every hand. If you *can* fold a hand, if the cards let you, do. Then watch how the other folks play."

"And rule two?"

"If you're in, bet. Raise, don't call. Drive out all the weak hands early so they can't limp along for free and then draw out a straight or a flush at the end." He took a breath. "Well, those fellas won't let me near the table, so you best go on. I'll be waiting in the diner," he said, jerking a thumb back to the station cafeteria.

She walked out the back door of the Railroad Museum and followed the sound of laughter and the smell of cigar smoke to a luxuriously appointed Pullman car that had once been used by the infamous Will Denton, Jr. The air was thick with the smells of liquor and Havanas. Sloane played for a long time, losing only a little more than she won. At last she took a break to stretch her legs, walked back to the station, and found Ace at the counter in the diner, as he had promised. The statue of the old black man sat on the stool beside him, poring over a menu. Sloane reached out and tapped it on the hand. Cold stone and still as death. "I'll be damned," she said.

She talked over a few plays with Ace, the two of them walking around the marble lobby while crowds of revellers flowed around them, laughing and joking and peering at the museum exhibits. Then Sloane went back to play some more.

She did her best, and her best wasn't bad. Finally, after a pleasant win which brought her back near even, Sloane's thin bubble of exuberance popped. She felt as if she hadn't slept for days. When she found herself drowsing between bets she knew it was time to stop. She excused herself, stepped down from the smoky Pullman car, and walked back across the crunching gravel to the station entrance, yawning her head off. The dreary nagging sense of guilt that haunted Sloane in the real world seemed to be getting stronger as tiredness wore down the fine, high, blank hum that was being Sly.

Momus! Damn. I was supposed to see Momus. She had forgotten again. Another yawn gripped her. Well, she was far too tired to do anything about the Lord of Carnival now. That confrontation would have to wait for one more night.

Ace was nursing a cup of coffee in the railway station diner. "Leaving Mardi Gras?"

"Duty calls, I'm afraid." She yawned again. "Bed, too."

"When you come back, look for me here. If I'm not around, I'm playing with Momus, but that's a game you aren't nearly ready for."

She kissed him, something Sloane would never do. Then she took off the mask.

THE hum and buzz of Mardi Gras stopped as if chopped off with a knife. She was alone in sudden silence, standing in the empty foyer of the Railroad Museum. Grey light was just beginning to creep through the plate glass doors. Beside her, back in his accustomed pew, the weary old black man read his newspaper in the gloom.

She had failed again.

The knowledge twisted like a snake in her belly. She hadn't faced down Momus. She hadn't used the mask as she was meant to. Instead of helping her mother, instead of making Odessa proud, she had frittered away another precious night playing cards. All she had to look forward to was another morning of sneaking into her house like a disgraced teenager. Her mouth was dry and her throat raspy with cigar smoke. Her knees were weak with exhaustion. "Oh, God," she whispered. "What am I *doing*?"

All right. All right. She had screwed up again, she hated herself, fine. There would be plenty of time to hate herself in proper detail later. Right now she had to get right, she had to be able to do her work, to help her mother. She had to be able to get through the day. Another dose of that damiana tea, I think. She started for

the museum doors. The sound of her shuffling steps echoed in the empty station.

She walked up from the Railroad Museum to Joshua's house, trudging past the sign that read, "We report all suspicious activities to our police department," and wincing as she saw a neighbor or two staring at her from behind lifted curtains or venetian blinds. Lord only knows what his big friend Ham would say about me showing up like this. She imagined lewd stories circulating along the docks, and finally making their way up to her mother's ears—all gossip did, sooner or later. Ugh. Sloane kept her eyes on the ground, trying to ignore the stares as she climbed Joshua's front steps and knocked on his door.

Movement rumored from inside. "Visiting hours start at—Christ," Joshua said. "It's you."

"I'm happy to see you, too. Can I come in?"

The apothecary stepped aside.

Sloane was so tired her ears were buzzing with white noise and her eyelids felt as if Odessa had spelled them to stillness. "I'm hoping you have a bit more of that tea," she said, fumbling in her purse for the last of the money she had gotten for her Rolex.

"Where have you been?" His eyes narrowed. "At the Mardi Gras, of course." She could read the contempt in every line of his body. "You don't even know, do you?"

Dread bloomed inside her. "Don't know what?"

"Do you realize you've been gone four days?"

Sloane gasped. She actually fell against the wall. "It gets better," Joshua said coolly. "While you were off partying, your mother died. They buried her yesterday."

A whiteness like the stare of the moon filled Sloane's head. Her blood ran backward. Everything was wrong, impossible, perverse. "No," she whispered.

"I hope it was a hell of a party," Josh said.

Part Two

Chapter Eight

INSULIN

JOSH grabbed a canister of damiana tea from a shelf in his tiny front room. When he turned to show Sloane Gardner into his kitchen, she was gone. He stepped out onto his front porch, thinking to see her running for Ashton Villa, but the streets were empty. Sloane had vanished without a sound. He clattered down the porch steps, looking in the parched herb beds and even around the corners of his little house, in case she had passed out from shock or booze, but there was no trace of her. If it weren't for the smell of cigarettes and alcohol that lingered in his doorway, she might have been a mirage.

Josh came back inside and dithered, wondering what to make of it. Finally he hung the CLOSED sign from his front doorknob and walked down to the docks, hoping to catch Ham before he left for his day's work. He found his big friend at Pier 21. Ham was fussing with his company boat, an aluminum runabout with the Gas Authority's blue flame talisman painted on the bow. Ham's thick fingers probed delicately at the innards of the runabout's little Mercury 9.5 hp outboard motor.

In the early days after the Flood, it had quickly become clear that Galveston's best option for powering the city

was to run hot taps off the natural gas pipelines that
snaked in from the Gulf of Mexico to the crackers and
refineries in Texas City, and the vast Dow Chemical plant
north of La Marque. Most of the surviving houses in
Galveston had the gas laid on anyway. Using the ma-
chinery in the local auto-body shops, Ham's father and
dozens of mechanically minded survivors like him had
patiently retooled automobile carburetors to run on methane. Throw the car up on blocks in your backyard, and
every house could have its own small generator. Joshua's
childhood home had been powered by a trusty Toyota
4Runner engine, but in recent years he hadn't had the
money to buy the more reliable imports. He was currently
running a Ford Taurus that had been reconditioned twice
already and would probably crap out within the year.
Ham, who cared more, ran a 2001 model Delta 88. Like
most white guys, Ham was a Lincoln/Olds fan. Galveston's blacks preferred Caddy engines, when available, or
Buicks otherwise, particularly the Regal, whose turn-of-
the-century models had been unusually reliable. The Hispanics all swore by Chevies. "They're shitty cars for a
white man," Ham said one time, "but they run like velvet
for the damn Mexicans."

The Vietnamese pretty much all lived on boats, making
it a Mercury/Evinrude question, though they were said to
have a fine talent for reworking motorcycle engines for
their additional power.

This morning Ham had an oil-stained Houston Astros
baseball cap turned backward to keep the sun off the nape
of his neck as he bent over the delinquent outboard motor. He wiggled one of its electrical leads gently between
two enormous fingers. Sunlight turned the little hairs on
his neck into wires of gold against his brick-red skin. A
shirt of cheap grey Galveston cotton was cinched tight
over his gigantic chest and even more enormous gut,
bolted down by a bronze Smith & Wesson belt buckle
the size of a bread plate. Ham's daddy had been wearing

that buckle the night the Flood washed over Galveston,
making it the luckiest walkaway in the family. It had
come to Ham when his older brother, Shem, died from
alcohol poisoning after a palm whiskey binge at his bach-
elor party.

Josh was glad to catch Ham on the docks, rather than
out in the scrub somewhere checking for leaks in a gas
line, which was usually how he spent his days. "Sloane
Gardner showed up at my door this morning, if you'll
believe it, tricked up like a Mardi Gras whore."

Ham looked at him with interest. "All *right*! What happened?"

"Nothing," Josh said.

Ham slapped himself in the forehead with one beefy
hand. "I just thank the good Lord that I can look myself
in the mirror and say, Ham, you did your part. You did
not merely introduce the woman unto Joshua, you *carried
her into the house*! And lo! He did minister to her there,
but as a brother only, for his rain was puny and fell not
upon her parched hills." He shook his head, disgusted.
"When the day comes that your dick falls off from disuse,
at least I won't be stung by the bitter lash of self-
recrimination."

Alice Mather, Ham's mother, was a lifelong Sunday
school teacher, and her second boy had a biblical turn of
phrase. His Erotic Journeys of Paul were legendary. Ham
spat into the Gulf. "What the hell do you mean, nothing?"

"I mean literally nothing. She vanished." Josh wiped a
sheen of sweat off his forehead. The day was going to
be another cooker. "She wanted some damiana tea. I
turned to get it off the shelf. When I looked back, she
was gone. Disappeared."

Ham whistled. "No shit?"

"She must have gone back to the Mardi Gras. That's
all I can figure." Josh brought back the image of Sloane
Gardner standing on his front porch, swaying slightly
with exhaustion and booze, the smell of cigarettes still

on her. She had seemed prettier this time. Light in her eyes. The faint smile as she started to ask for tea, that pretty woman's smile, that asks forgiveness with no thought of being denied. Her dress had been ripped and stained and must have cost more than every stitch Joshua's mother owned for the last three years of her life.

Should I know you? What's your name?

Ham looked back over his shoulder at Josh, making the little motorboat rock. "Well, are you going to tell the sheriff? You know they've been looking for her."

"Not yet. I promised I wouldn't tell about her sneaking into Carnival."

Ham rolled his eyes. "Has this woman even greased your monkey wrench, Josh?"

"Ham—"

"I'm just saying you don't know her well enough to let your little head tell your big head what to do."

"Sometimes you are such a shit." Josh squatted down on the wooden dock.

"I'm serious, Josh." Ham abandoned his motor and sat with his fat arms resting on the weathered dock. "When we were little, you were the only kid I knew who had the guts to leave the magic alone. No praying, no walk-aways, no charms and bullshit. Remember when Mrs. MacReady's dryer broke and she started putting out charms to make it get better? You got me in there to help take it apart, you figured out the solenoid was busted, you and me faked up a new one."

"Which lasted about six months as I recall."

"The point is, you never gave in," Ham said. " 'Ham,' you used to say, 'I know the Mardi Gras is there, but once you let it get into your head, you'll never be a free man again.' Well, now I'm warning you: Mardi Gras and a rich skirt like Sloane Gardner, that spells trouble with a capital T."

Josh laughed. "God, I was a bossy little bastard."

"And I'm a better man for it," Ham said. "I always

told folks you were the smartest cookie in the neighborhood. Don't go making a fool out of me over this Gardner
girl, okay?"

"I'll try," Josh said, smiling. Ham turned back to his
motor, making the boat slosh and dip and jounce against
the floats that kept her aluminum hull from banging into
the side of the dock. Every now and then Josh caught
himself wondering why in hell the affable Ham put up
with his moodiness. Apparently Ham knew, even if he
didn't. "Where are you going today?" he asked.

"Pelican Island, to walk a line." Ham reconnected a
cable and eased the cowling back over the Mercury's
engine. "Guys in the plant saw a pressure drop on number
three line this week. I went out into the Gulf yesterday
to check the Christmas tree, but the pressure at the well-
head hadn't gone down. Then I pigged the line and
pushed out some crud, but the pressure at the plant didn't
much recover. So today I get the pleasure of walking the
line and cleaning the traps. If I can't find the leak on
land, then it's your boy Hammy in a wet suit on the ocean
floor checking for bubbles."

Josh smirked. "I guess I'll put you down for a flush
tonight, then?"

Ham scowled. Before any serious diving he had to put
mineral oil drops in his ears for a day and then sit with
a towel around his neck, complaining bitterly, while Josh
flushed the wax out of his ears with a turkey baster and
warm water. "You just love to see me squirm, you peck-
erhead."

Josh sat on the pier and let his feet dangle in the warm
Gulf water. The tire-rubber soles of his sandals turned
black and shiny. "My daddy had ostrich skin boots," he
said. "And loafers, Italian loafers. Ferragamo, I remember
the brand. He used to . . . I remember one Mardi Gras, at
the Krewe of Momus Grand Ball, he was the first one
out on the floor. He tried to get my mother to dance, but
she wouldn't, not with everybody watching, so he asked

some old lady, one of the Fords I think. He was a fine dancer. All night long women kept telling Mother how lucky she was. The only time she ever danced with him was in our kitchen."

The bells of St. Patrick's clanged out the half hour, rings of sound spreading sluggishly from the cathedral, muffled by the damp heat of the morning like ripples in molasses. The floating dock beneath Joshua rocked and creaked as a line of swell went by. The Mosquito Fleet, the band of shrimpers that headed out into the Gulf every morning, was already at the mouth of Galveston Harbor. A haze of gulls hung screaming and wheeling around the little flotilla.

Josh thought about Sloane Gardner.

A hideous mongrel, one ear eaten away by disease, limped onto the dock. The torment of fleas and mange had left the beast half-naked, its fur scoured off against concrete sidewalks or brick buildings. The dog snarled at Josh, then hobbled away.

"Ham, I think I'm going to join a Krewe."

"You?" Ham spat, this time to connote surprise. "After, what, six years of you telling me you don't need Krewes, can't afford 'em, don't believe in them? You want to join? What for? The back dues will kill you." A line of sweat went inching down his cheek. He rubbed at it with a finger the size and shape of a hearty breakfast sausage. "Now I wonder if this might have something to do with the pussycat I drug out of the moonlight last week."

"You know we held hands once? She didn't even remember me," Josh said. "As for joining a Krewe, it's just time, that's all."

Ham looked at him slantwise. "Uh-huh." He yanked the motor cord and his Mercury coughed into life in a small cloud of black smoke. Josh uncleated his bow rope. Ham headed out, his bulk pressing the nose of his boat down flat to the chop, aluminum hull glinting in the early

sun. A long V of wash broke and widened slowly behind him.

JOSH went home. The CLOSED sign still hung across his front door. He left it there. He kicked around the house a few minutes, then took Sloane's stockings down from the towel rack in the bathroom where they had been hanging. He meant to store them back with his seining equipment but instead he took them upstairs to his room. To his own contempt he found himself masturbating, thinking of Sloane. Not the Sloane he had seen that morning, the party girl giddy with wine and exhaustion, but the other, demure one. The Grand Duchess's daughter, who lived in Ashton Villa surrounded by servants. The one he should have been lusting after at fourteen. Instead he had been here, in this hovel, learning how to take corns off the feet of longshoremen and being sneered at by the pretty Mexican girls. Too unlucky to be a date even for the trailer park queens, though later they would come to him for their abortions, too broke to afford a real doctor.

When he got up from his bed he drank a small glass of water to hold off a dehydration headache he felt coming on. Then he checked on his chickens and took a look at his most recent batch of rice wine to make sure it was fermenting properly.

Today he would apply to join the Krewe of Momus. Couldn't put it off anymore. Sorry, Mom, he thought. She never wanted to be beholden to anybody, least of all the Krewes that had abandoned them after their luck left with his daddy.

He opened the top drawer of his desk and pulled out an old lab book. From between its unused pages he took the note he had found on the kitchen table the day his mother disappeared.

Dearest Josh—
  I am going away now.

We knew this day would come, and here it is. The choices are something quick and reasonably comfortable now, far away from the house—or ketoacidosis in two or three or five weeks, thirst and hyperpnea and coma. Not a hard decision. I think they call it the Lesser of Two Evils.

I don't want to go, don't ever think that. I worry, sometimes, that you believe I'm sadder than I am. You don't have to rescue me, Josh. You never did. There's nothing to rescue me from, it's just life, and I have been glad to live, and blessed with the best son I could have hoped for.

Then a line starting with *I wish*. The rest heavily crossed out.

Cry for me, if you need to, but laugh for me, too. I will always be
                    Your loving Mom

P.S. I wouldn't think of wasting the potassium chloride or the lanoxin for something like this, so don't bother checking. I haven't touched the stock. And remember to get those tinted bottles from the brewery next week!
P.P.S. I love you, kiddo. God bless.

As always he found it very difficult to read the letter. To grasp it. The words fled from his understanding as he read, like Sloane's faint stars, hidden when you looked at them.

AN hour later Joshua emerged from his house wearing his silk shirt and his nicest pair of pants, cheap Galveston cotton but carefully dyed to a pleasant yellow-tan. He had done the dyeing himself, cotton flowers with an alum-tannin-alum mordant, and then had the pants expertly cut and sewn by a seamstress down the street in

exchange for a quart jar of bruise, cut, and sting ointment and twenty genuine pre-Flood aspirins. He hadn't had many occasions to wear the pants; he had bought them to wear at Ham's brother's wedding.

Shoes were more problematic. Clearly his everyday sandals were not good enough for making an application to join a Krewe. His alternatives were the pair of battered boots he wore in winter or when hiking through the brush collecting plants for his shop, or a pair of black dress shoes of his father's that had been lying undisturbed in his closet for twelve years. His mother had tried to toss them, but Josh had snuck out to the garbage and brought them back in. If she noticed them, later, tucked away in the closet, she hadn't mentioned it.

He decided on the dress shoes. He pulled them carefully out of the closet, took them to the bathroom, and turned them upside down over the toilet. After a few brisk smacks, a brown recluse tumbled out of the left shoe into the toilet bowl. Josh took a dipper of salt water from the water barrel and flushed the spider away. Then he reamed the shoes out with a bottle-brush to make sure he'd gotten all the spiders. He scrubbed off the blotches of mold and rubbed them with powdered sage to take off the musty closet smell. The shoes were too large for him, but he found he could walk in them if he wore two pairs of socks and packed the heels and toes with cotton batting.

Amanda Cane had died four years ago, when the last of her stock of pre-Flood insulin gave out.

Here's an equation: status is power. Power is insulin. Insulin is life. Q.E.D. Status is life.

His mother had been willing to suffer. His mother had chosen to eat her bad luck when it came, as if somehow this would punish Joshua's father for failing them. As if her suffering was the best weapon she had to reach him. Joshua had never seen much sign that this worked. Sam Cane had visited them twice, maybe three times, and then

not again. There was a big service for Amanda, attended by all the people who had abandoned her in life. If you didn't do everything to lay the spirits of suicides, the Recluse said, they tended not to stay completely dead. But Sam didn't show. In the first few weeks after Amanda died, Joshua had been surprised—and angry—to find himself waiting for his father to appear, instead of keeping his mind on his mother and her sacrifices as he should have done. "Sumbitch should have showed," Ham had said at the time.

To which Josh had replied, "My daddy always knew to fold a losing hand."

Well. Time for Sam Cane's boy to play with enough of a bankroll to win. Josh sprinkled his armpits and the soles of his shoes with sage powder. He even washed out his mouth with a capful of ancient Listerine, though the taste was so foul he wondered if it could have gone bad. The plastic bottle was webbed with fine white cracks like the crow's-feet around old people's eyes.

Of Galveston's five Krewes, Joshua was the wrong sex to join the Krewe of Venus, and there wasn't much social advantage to be gained by joining the annoying Krewe of Harlequins. That left three: the old and powerful Knights of Momus, the seafaring Krewe of Thalassar, and the Krewe of Togetherness. It was the Krewe of Togetherness his mother had once belonged to. She had resigned when Josh was fourteen, unwilling to take Krewe charity when she could no longer afford the dues. Nor could she bear crossing into the civilized part of Galveston, to be stared at and pitied while she put in her mandatory hours of community service. Against his mother's will, Joshua had gone to them when he realized their supply of insulin was running out. The Krewe duty officer was politely sympathetic and put Amanda on a waiting list they both understood was too long to save her. Togetherness was not Joshua's first choice of Krewe.

You don't have to rescue me, Josh. You never did.

Which was quite true. He hadn't.

It was past nine in the morning when Joshua left his house to head downtown. The sun ran like hot syrup over his neighborhood. Chickens clucked and roosters crowed; reconditioned car engines hummed counterpoint to the cicadas that drowsed and buzzed in the trees. Crossing Broadway was heaven. You couldn't miss how much nicer it felt in the districts where the real people lived, under the shadowed canopy of live-oak limbs. Bluejays and mockingbirds flickered through the branches. The street was dappled with coins of early morning light. Horses and carriages rumbled down the middle of the road, while Josh and the other pedestrians walked in the dry gutter. The sidewalks here had been destroyed by live-oak roots long ago. Now jumbled slabs of concrete tipped and buckled at all angles beneath a ragged archway of oleanders, blooming white and pink. He wondered how many of the people living in these fine homes knew that the oleanders' elegant spear-shaped leaves were deadly poison.

Once on the Strand, Josh was constantly having to stand aside to let carriages by, supply carts mostly, packed with cotton or cloth or barrels of vinegar or beer or salt, pulled by patient-looking horses with big bags rigged behind to catch their droppings. Josh wiped the sweat from his forehead and then nearly dried his hand on his pants leg. He should have brought a handkerchief. Damn. He kept walking, his hand wet, until he came to the Cotton Exchange Building. He leaned against it as if merely pausing to catch his breath, leaving a damp palm print on the warm brick.

In five more minutes he had reached the Old Galveston Square Building, where the offices of the Ancient and Honorable Krewe of Momus were housed. Two tall doors confronted him, polished mahogany, tinted glass, brass handles. He pulled one briskly open, as if he had legitimate business here, and stepped inside.

The heels of his father's shoes tapped on the lobby floor of black and white marble tiles. His feet were sweating heavily inside the two pairs of socks. He took a moment to compose himself. Voices eddied from the central atrium, and laughter, and the low throb of air-conditioning. It was cool inside, sinfully cool and dry. Josh felt himself break out sweating, as if all the moisture in the air was condensing on him, the one hot damp thing in this cool, dry, perfect building. He wiped his hands on his pants, swore, and checked for stains. He couldn't see any, although he could feel the sweat in his armpits making his silk shirt damp.

The building was a hollow cube, three stories tall, each story with towering fifteen-foot ceilings. Light welled through the central atrium from a giant, frosted glass skylight. In front of Joshua was an old-fashioned elevator, a fancy wrought-iron cage faced with glass. Light winked and gleamed off its brass fittings. Across from it stood a machine that would press a penny into a decorative memento of the Strand, left over from Galveston's renaissance as a tourist attraction at the turn of the millenium.

Sculpted from papier-mâché, the gigantic head of Momus hung suspended from a single wire in the atrium well. His sinister smile floated at the level of the second-story floor, so his eyes seemed to be peering just over the railing. His two little horns curved up almost to the third story. The whole head slowly turned and twisted in the currents of cold air that fell from the A/C ducts high overhead. There was something disturbing in the quality of the god's amusement. Josh congratulated the Krewe on their honesty. Even they hadn't made the mistake of believing their patron was benevolent. Joshua entered the elevator and pressed the button for the third floor. Through the glass walls of the elevator, grinning Momus watched him ascend.

Two men and a woman were waiting for the elevator when the doors opened. "—worrying about her drove

Jane to her death," the woman was saying. Her eyes flicked briefly over Joshua Cane, resting for a moment on his face, as if he had missed a spot shaving.

"Excuse me," he said, stepping past.

"If she were alive, she would have been—" The elevator doors closed on their conversation.

Of course, Sloane Gardner must be a common figure here, passing through on the Grand Duchess's business nearly every day. Everyone in the building must be buzzing over her disappearance. It occurred to him that all his dressing up might well be wasted. The odds seemed pretty good that the Krewe, suddenly leaderless and heirless to boot, would decide it couldn't be bothered to interview witch doctors with pretensions.

Joshua entered the Krewe offices, left his name with a secretary, and settled in for a long wait. To pass the time he studied the paraphernalia on the walls: framed handbills from the late 1800s, pictures of Prohibition-era society women with spit-curled hair robed as Mardi Gras queens in satin and ermine, and everywhere the moon-faced grinning Momus, smirking over a banquet menu or on a lapel pin or etched on earrings worn by the Ford girls during the Depression, when the Momus balls had been at their most outrageously lavish.

Finally Josh was shown into a large office lined with oak bookshelves. A brass-trimmed ceiling fan circled over an oak desk with a pretty glass ink pot on it. A tall woman rose from behind the desk. "Fiona Barret," she said easily. "Pleased to meet you, Mr. Cane." Her teeth were whiter and straighter than the teeth of anyone who lived on Joshua's side of Broadway. She gave the impression of being naturally clean, as if mud wouldn't stick to her. He felt the dampness in his armpits as he reached to shake her dry, smooth hand.

She sat back down, took a duck-feather quill from the desk organizer before her, and held it poised over a pad of cheap Galveston paper milled from rice hulls. "So—

you were thinking of applying to join our Krewe?" He said that he was. "And have you discussed this with the members of your current Krewe?"

He told her that he wasn't currently in a Krewe. She looked at him. He looked down at the hardwood floor and explained that his mother had retired from her Krewe when he was not yet an adult, but that now he felt it was time for him to take up his community responsibilities. He betrayed his mother in the same calm, unemotional voice he used when examining his patients. It would be socially easier for him and Ms. Barret to come to an accord if any tension between them could be blamed on Amanda Cane, of course. The living are always in a tacit compact against the dead.

"I see." Ms. Barret dipped her quill and wrote a comment on her pad. "Mr. Cane, without meaning to discourage you, I must be candid about the obstacles you may face in your application."

He looked up but missed the rest of what Ms. Barret had to say because his dead mother was standing behind her. Her face was sallow, her hair was wet and stringy. Water dripped down her cheeks. Josh smelled mud and cold seawater. She was wearing her long tan raincoat, tightly buttoned despite the heat of the day. She had sewn it shut around her: cables of strong black thread stitched the raincoat's sides together. Its deep pockets bulged and sagged with stones or bits of brick. They, too, had been sewn shut. She gazed at him, wordless but with great intensity. Her eyes, which had been brown in life, were now as green as the sea. She shook her head, holding his eyes. A warning.

Fiona Barret coughed. "Mr. Cane?"

"I . . . I beg your pardon," he managed. "Would you mind repeating that?"

"Ten thousand dollars," she said with a frank smile. She rose, extending her hand in a manner clearly meant to end the interview. Josh felt himself rising, too, pow-

erless to resist. "Any time you wish to return with the first year's dues, do come back," she said pleasantly. "We will process your application at that time."

She couldn't see his mother. Couldn't feel the chill in the air. Couldn't smell the cold wet seaweed.

He thanked her, and when she showed him out to the elevator he thanked her again, unable to hear what she was saying. Chill damp waves of shock spread and rippled over his skin, making it crawl at his wrists, then his neck, his back, then the inside of one leg; unpredictable goose bumps prickling and spreading all over his body. He saw his mother's reflection in the glass wall of the elevator. Then the bronze doors shut and the apparition vanished.

In the last year before his mother's insulin was due to run out, she had begun visiting butchers and the town's two veterinarians, asking to be notified at the death of any pig or cow. Many times he had woken in his bedroom in the dead of night to hear her rummaging about, throwing on her boots and apron. An hour later he would wake again when she came back to the house with the dead animal's pancreas. Usually the owner tried to give it to her for free, but she insisted on paying.

From the pancreas she would make a raw preparation and use it in place of their dwindling supply of synthesized insulin. The injections raised brutal welts the size of duck eggs and hurt like hell. They were also not nearly as effective as the man-made stuff; she had to watch her sugar intake far more carefully, and live with days of climbing thirst until she gave in and slipped a nearly painless syringe of insulin into her arm.

One day the older vet—Vikram Chandri, whom she had known in the early days of the Krewe of Togetherness immediately after the Flood—stopped by with word of a pig to be butchered. This time she failed to go. Joshua reminded her twice as the day went on. At dinner

he started to bring it up again. It took the longest time for him to notice the tears running silently down her face. She put down her fork, and left the table, still limping badly from her last injection.

For several more weeks the vets continued to drop by with word of other opportunities, but Amanda never went, and Josh did not mention it again.

JOSH exited out of Old Galveston Square into the mid-morning heat. A white blindness waited behind his eyes, as if seeing his mother's ghost had been like looking at the sun, and now he blinked, dazzled, waiting for his sight to heal. He kept to the inner edge of the sidewalk, running one hand along the brickwork of the building he had just left. He took out his battered pocket watch and took his own pulse. One hundred twenty beats a minute. He stepped off the curb to cross the Strand at the corner of 23rd and was nearly run down by a big brewer's wagon. "Ain't you got eyes, you stupid sumbitch?" the driver yelled, working hard to bring down his rearing quarter horse.

Josh apologized and hurried across the street. People did get run over by wagon wheels—he'd treated some crushed legs, and gone to the funerals of a couple of men hit in the chest or higher—but usually you had to get drunk and pass out in the street after dark to get hit. He forced himself to pay better attention. On the other side of the street was a little open plaza. Josh sat on a bench there, waiting to recover. His skin gradually stopped creeping and for once he was glad of the strong sunlight.

For the last four years he had tried very hard not to imagine how his mother had died, but now he knew. She had sewn herself into her raincoat, filled the pockets with stones and sewn them shut, too, and then walked into the sea. Probably she had gone to the end of one of the long stone jetties that stuck out from the Seawall.

He had no idea why her ghost had appeared to him.

Had something in his mood drawn her, the memories that had come seeping back to him since Sloane Gardner arrived on his doorstep? Had Sloane brought a breath of magic with her out of Mardi Gras, to seize on him as he read his mother's last letter? He couldn't believe Amanda Cane was so adamantly opposed to him joining a Krewe that it had woken her from the grave. She hadn't left the Krewe of Togetherness out of principle, just lack of money to pay the dues, and a sense of shame that made it hard for her to be with those people after her marriage had failed.

The ghost had not tipped over the ink pot on Fiona Barret's desk, or really seemed to notice her at all. Just stood there, urgently visible, shaking her head. She was warning him: that's what he had felt. But warning him of what?

Joshua's vision cleared and his heart rate began to come down. The plaza was a good-sized corner lot that had been nicely paved with tile, including an outdoor chessboard complete with pieces the size of three-year-old children. About half were plastic pre-Flood originals; the newer replacement pieces had been carved out of driftwood and painted. He suddenly remembered the summer he had come here two or three times a week, when his dad was teaching him to play. How bland the game seemed on a little board at home compared to the physicality of moving these giant pawns and queens. The plastic pieces were no longer slick to the touch, but strangely feltlike after years of being scoured by the sandy Galveston wind and the brutal Texas sun.

His father had played a teaching game, describing both their positions move by move, creating opportunities for Josh to examine his tactics. He never let Josh win, though. He said it would make it more meaningful if he knew he really deserved it. Josh had believed this, although some days it felt hard to come close every time, playing carefully, doing his best, but always somehow

failing, his father giving less and less advice as the game drew to a close, until Samuel Cane played his black pieces in silence. Then his features would set into his calm, friendly poker face and he would win and win and win, and of course every time he won Josh had to lose.

AFTER twenty minutes Josh was too hot to sit out in the sun any longer. Well, if the Krewe of Momus wouldn't have him, he would try the Krewe of Thalassar. As he headed for the docks he noticed that dogs and roosters fell suddenly silent when he passed. The effect was so pronounced he found himself turning his head to see if his mother's ghost was following him. He never saw her. Perhaps the dogs could smell her near him; a scent of cold seawater and decay too faint for humans to detect.

The Krewe of Thalassar headquarters was located on the wreckage of the *Selma,* a 421-foot concrete ship. While the *Selma* had floated perfectly well, she turned out to be brittle. When a big swell first lifted her high and then dropped her sharply against the bottom of the bay in 1920, the concrete ship cracked in half and had remained there ever since. The Krewe of Thalassar was notoriously superstitious, and Joshua had never understood why they would choose a shipwreck for their base of operations, but Ham had explained that, as nobody had been killed or even seriously hurt when the giant ship went down, the *Selma,* looked at one way, was the mightiest sailors' walkaway in a town that had suffered terribly at the hands of the sea.

At Pier 23, the Krewe of Thalassar dock, a young black man about Joshua's age, tall and leanly muscled, stood in a motorboat cleated near the Krewe's methane fuel pump. He unhooked his gas can and swung it up onto the dock, then climbed out after it. An older Krewe man, missing his left hand, unhooked the fuel hose from the pump and began to fill the can.

Josh nodded at the sailor. "I'm thinking of joining up.

What's the chance I could get a lift out to the *Selma*?"

The old gas monkey laughed, showing a sprinkling of dirty teeth.

"The Krewe is for sailors," the black man said. "If you need help to get there, you got no reason to go." He wore dirty grey shorts and a baseball cap. He might have had a white grandparent, or a Mexican one, Joshua guessed; his skin was the color of coffee with one shot of milk. "You don't choose the sea, Joshua Cane. She chooses you."

"How do you know my name?"

"We keep track of the unlucky," the old gas monkey said. He held up the stump of his arm. "Won't nobody take me in a boat now neither, if it makes you feel any better." He flipped down the pump handle to shut off the flow of methane.

The young sailor shrugged. "Nothing personal, man." He swung the gas can back into his boat and hooked it up to his fuel line, then paused, looking over the back transom into the water. He glanced up at Josh. "Come here for a second." Josh stepped over to the edge of the dock, wary in case some practical joke was being planned that would have him in the drink. The sailor pointed down into the water just behind his engine. "You carry some heavy shit with you, my man."

Joshua's mother stood on the sandy bottom, staring up at him with blind urgency, her face partly obscured by a tangle of drifting seaweed and twists of her floating hair as she shook her head and held out her hands, palms up.

Go back. Beware.

JOSHUA'S interview with the Krewe of Harlequins went much better. First off, there was the beer. He absolutely couldn't justify spending money on food, but to walk home for lunch and back in the heat of the day could only make him sweatier and smellier. Instead he holed up in the Mikonos Cafe, a favorite haunt of Ham's, ig-

noring the smell of pork souvlakis and sour cream, and nursed his way slowly through one shot of palm whiskey and one cold glass of rice beer.

By the time he left Mikonos's it was early afternoon, the sun so fierce that even his shadow crouched beneath him to get out of the heat. It was an intense relief to get out of the glare and into the Grand Opera House, where the Harlequins were headquartered. First built in 1894, the Grand had seen all the giants at the turn of the twentieth century: Lionel Barrymore, Pavlova, Sarah Bernhardt, the Marx brothers and George Burns, Tex Ritter and his horse White Flash.

Josh also discovered what he should have guessed: his father had been a member of the Krewe of Harlequins. It was something of an in. Their dues were moderate, and community service was confined mostly to Mardi Gras duties. As a small-time brewer of beer, Josh had a leg up there. His interviewer grew quite excited when Joshua mentioned that his workshop chemistry was good enough to make a variety of invisible inks and crude fireworks.

The main problem with his candidacy was that he was not odd enough. "You seem like a calm, sensible young man," the interviewer said worriedly. They were sitting in the projection booth at the back of the mezzanine, looking down at the stage. "Not really our type. Although of course the ghost helps," he added.

Turning, Joshua was hardly surprised to look down and see his mother staring up at him from center stage.

The interviewer was a small balding man and terrifically ugly, his round forehead and face marred by several giant moles with hairs springing from them, stiff as pig bristles. "Something might come of that ghost, certainly, but I'm afraid I have to recommend waiting for a while on your application." He wiped at his mouth with stubby fingers. "I sense a definite leaning in you, a sense of unbalance which, properly uncontrolled, might be just the

ticket. We'll keep an eye on you, is what we'll do. We shall watch what the moon says, eh?"

Joshua did not feel calm and sensible. He felt frightened and weightless and slightly drunk. How off balance had he been, ever since Ham spilled Sloane Gardner onto his examination table with her cargo of memories? He remembered the shock on her face, the light in her eyes crumbling as she understood that her mother had died while she had been partying in the Mardi Gras. He shouldn't have been so spiteful about that. There was an angry tightness in the pit of his stomach that jumped out sometimes if he didn't keep himself under control. He remembered his mother's letter, and her ghost, staring and staring. He shook his head. "What if I told you I was a lot less sensible than you think?"

The ugly little man smiled. "Prove it."

THE beer at Martini's Crab Shack was even worse than the stuff Josh made at home, but whiskey was whiskey and the same everywhere. The kind of whiskey he could afford, anyway.

HIS fourth interview, at the Krewe of Togetherness chambers, was a complete disaster. Afterward, Joshua stumbled back to the Gas Authority pier and waited for Ham to return. The day he was having must have shown on his face; when Ham finally arrived he took one look at Josh and said, "Let's go fishin'."

From the Gas Authority slip they walked over to Ham's personal boat, *Lucille*. *Lucille* was a clapped-out aluminum rowboat with a 15 hp outboard on the back. Ham kept two modular fishing rods and a shitload of lures in a heavy red toolbox plastered with DANGER: EX-PLOSIVES stickers. He was widely known to carry old and temperamental blasting caps in the box to discourage theft. Joshua had never seen any such caps, but he was the one who had spread the story along the waterfront

when they were both teenagers. Every now and then he added a new story to embellish Ham's legend. Once this had gotten him in trouble, when Ham charged over to his house one day, furious to find that he was now known as a fish dynamiter. Exactly what curious line of sportsmanship that crossed Josh didn't know, but Ham had been as mortified as a preacher caught naked in a whorehouse.

Ham anchored *Lucille* off the rocks at the far southeast tip of the Island, looking across the strait at the tip of the Bolivar Peninsula. Slanting evening sunlight diffused into the air from the west. He lifted up the tip of his fishing rod and flicked it like a buggy whip, a surprisingly deft motion from a forearm as wide as a coffee can. Line hissed and whined as his silvery lure arced far out into the Gulf. It hung in the air, winking, and then hit the water, plop. "So maybe it wasn't the brightest idea to make a call on the Krewe of Togetherness," Ham said. The spool clicked as he began to reel in his lure. "Between the ghost and the no lunch and the booze and all. Not a great idea."

"Nope," Josh said.

"Did you spill any of your brother's blood upon the ground?" Ham said, playing his line with a couple of sharp tugs.

"No. No punches." Joshua grimaced. "I might have shaken the bastard once or twice. Just by the shoulders."

"Hm." Ham looked over at him with one shaggy eyebrow arched.

(Once, when they were both thirteen, they had been out walking together when Josh said, "I don't know why we stay friends, but I sure am glad of it."

"We stay friends because you think you're better than me," Ham had said, "and I let you."

That had shut Josh up in a hurry.)

He *was* accustomed to thinking of himself as the smart one, the forceful one, the dominant personality. But on a

day like this, having been bounced by four Krewes and
nearly arrested for drunk and disorderly behavior, he suddenly felt that it was Ham, standing by him solid as a
rock and jiggling softly on his line, who really had his
shit together.

Ham spat meditatively into the Gulf. "Cast, Josh. I'm
looking to eat tonight, even if you aren't."

The setting sun was nearly at their backs. Beneath
bright air the sea was dark with the shadow of the land.
Their own shadows stretched out farther still, hard to
track against the swell, broken into pockets and flashes
of darkness against the green water. Joshua cocked his
rod back, feeling the weight of the little steel lure bouncing and trembling at the end of his line. He snapped the
rod forward and felt the lure go sailing up, line whining
as it paid out, not nearly so far as Ham's cast but still
far, a beautiful arc of line hanging over the dark water,
gold as angel's hair in the low sunlight. When the lure
finally hit he could feel it, a little tremor up his arm and
into his core.

He felt absurdly, painfully grateful for the big man's
company.

"I also made a rude suggestion about the Krewe director's mother," Josh said after a while. "And his sister."

"Oh, my."

"I seem to remember that 'togetherness' was a theme,"
Josh added reflectively. Ham snorted. Josh slurred his
voice. "I'm just as good as any of you dinks. I'm a dink,
too. You think you're so much better than me just because yer *lucky*? Well, nobody stays lucky forever, you
know. Maybe one day you wake up and it's you who's
so fucking unlucky, maybe something happens to your
house or your family, and then I'm looking at you in the
gutter where I live and you'll come crawling to me! And
will I help you then? Eh? EH?" He hiccuped with great
dignity. "*I don't know!* How d'ya like *that*?"

Ham was wincing and laughing at the same time, his

big torso shaking beneath its acres of shirting. It made
the whole boat rock beneath them.

Josh sighed. "I did manage to throw up on Carl Banks
as they were dragging me out of the Krewe offices." He
looked down at his silk shirt, splotched all over where he
had tried to rub out the stains with seawater.

"You showed those pussies."

"Hey. You should have seen the other guys. They
won't be wearing *those* clothes again in a hurry."

Ham's small eyes screwed up even tighter and
squeezed out a tear of laughter. When the fit had passed
he reeled his lure in and cast again. "So was your mom
there for that one, too?"

Josh pulled in his lure, cocked his rod and cast. The
barbed spoon sparkled in the air, then fell into shadow,
drifting down into the dark waters. "Yeah."

"Is she here now?" Josh shook his head. "Do you know
what she wants?"

"Nope."

Two brown pelicans passed before them, low above
the water, wings beating heavily. Farther off, the last
stragglers of the Mosquito Fleet were coming in, each
shrimp boat hazed in a cloud of gulls. Their calls came
across the water, made thin and lonely by distance. "I
didn't used to need Galveston. Not our barrio, I mean the
real Galveston," Josh said. "I didn't even know I was
hungry for it. And now suddenly I want it so bad, Ham.
I want everything. I want my house back. I want my life
back."

"How about the girl?"

"Yes, damn it, I want the girl. I wish I'd never seen
her. I wish you hadn't brought her to my house."

"She'd had the crap kicked out of her."

"I know." Josh reeled in and hooked his lure to one of
the fishing rod's eyelets and slumped on his thwart. "The
day I've been having, I'll probably put the lure in my
eyes if I keep casting."

"Some days you jus' cain't win for losin'," Ham drawled. "Give me three more chances to catch us some dinner. I've got some rice and eggs at home if I don't."

"Find your leak?"

"On Line Number Three? Nope."

"Come by my place after we eat and I'll do your ears."

"Hoo boy," Ham said sourly. "Now you're talking." He threw out his line. The little aluminum boat rocked on the swell. Water chuffed and gurgled against her. "Your problem is, you keep expecting life to be fair," Ham said. "You think it ought to be like checkers or something. And if you make all the right moves you win. But it ain't. It's like fishing." He played his line. "You load your lure, you pick your spot—and that's all you can do, pardner. Some days they bite, and some days they don't."

"Maybe you're right. Maybe life is like that. But it shouldn't be," Josh said. "It didn't used to be. Back in the old days, before the Flood, it wasn't just luck."

Ham spat again. "Well, maybe that was a fluke, is my philosophy. Not natural. And the world woke up and put a stop to it purty quick, too."

"My mother had diabetes. It was 'natural' for her to die," Josh said. Ham's hand stopped for a second on his reel, then continued drawing his line in, the steady click-click-click of the mechanism soft and soothing in the evening air. "Is an animal all you want to be?" Josh asked. "You think it's wrong to strive for a world where merit counts for more than luck? I won't ever agree to that."

"Josh, you have a point." Ham made a face. "Lord, but I hate saying that. Which is too bad, 'cause I have to say it so damn often."

Despite everything, Josh smiled.

HAM caught a redfish on his last cast and they took it to the Mathers' house, where he lived with his parents and

his little brother—well, younger brother—Japhet. Ham board-grilled the fish, and he and Josh ate it with a side of rice and pinto beans and a shot of pepper sauce. Ham had his with a beer, as he said God had intended such meals to be eaten. Josh stuck to water. Japhet was home, and Ham's sister Rachel stopped by to visit with her husband and three kids. It was warm and crowded and familylike in a way Josh found deeply comforting at first, but as time wore on, the noise and smell and booming laughter began to wear on him. Ham's family was big and their house was small; Josh couldn't escape the feeling he would be crushed to death the moment he got caught between a Mather and the refrigerator.

It was full dark by the time he and Ham headed out. Of course in this neighborhood nobody kept the streetlights in good order, or the streets either, for that matter. Ham brought an old Coleman lantern and held it up, hissing, so Josh could see to get his key into his front door lock. With their eyes blinded by the lamp, Ham and Josh were caught completely by surprise by the armed men waiting for them inside. "Freeze!" someone shouted, and Josh heard a bunch of gun slides go back.

Chapter Nine

SHERIFF DENTON

"WHAT the h—"

Josh shut up as someone shoved a gun barrel hard into his face. The smell of cold steel tied his belly in a knot. Well, he thought, now I know what Mom was trying to warn me about. He wondered if he was about to die.

"We ain't moving," Ham said. "Right, Josh? Two statues, that's us."

The Coleman lamp hissed, throwing out its circle of hard white light. Josh could see four men: two behind his counter, one behind his examination table, and the one whose gun was pressed into his face. That one must have been standing behind the door. Three of them had handguns; the one behind the examination table had a pump-action shotgun. He chambered a round, ratchet-*click*.

"If you want the beer, take it," Josh said. He spoke with his doctor's voice, chilly and clinical. He had used it to keep calm when faced with any number of traumas—tumors and disfigurements and death. The cool, rational doctor's face was the only one he trusted not to give away his tells. It was the one he wore when he

couldn't afford to play scared. "Liquor isn't worth dying for. It's not worth killing for either."

"Howdy, Mr. Cane," said the man with the gun pressed against Joshua's face. He moved to stand in front of the apothecary, jamming the gun hard against his teeth. Joshua imagined the gun going off, his teeth shattering like dropped china, the bullet blowing out the back of his neck in a spatter of meat and bone.

It was a bad sign that the gunman was willing to be seen in the circle of lamplight. He wasn't afraid of being identified later. Josh looked him over as calmly as he could, trying to put him on a hand. The gunman's face was pitted with old scars, adolescent acne or possibly childhood smallpox. He had broken his front teeth at some point; both the upper ones sported gold caps. Expensive but vulgar; Sloane Gardner or Jim Ford would have picked something less obvious. He was about Joshua's height and build, small and lean; but instead of wearing patched scraps and hand-me-down shoes, he was dressed in a crisp shirt and vest, polished black boots and grey pants—ah. Charcoal uniform pants with a black stripe. City militia.

Josh allowed himself to relax. This was one of Sheriff Denton's men. "I suppose this is about the Krewe of Togetherness," he said. "I can pay reasonable damages, but the fault was not all on one—"

"Where is she, you little fuck?"

"Where is who?"

The militiaman punched forward with his gun, hard, splitting Josh's lip and making him stumble back. Blood sprayed into his mouth, and his teeth rang. The panic in his muscles suddenly balled into something hard and furious, and he started a wild punch—only to find his hand wrapped in Ham's big fist. Ham could crack crab shells with his fingers and pitch cinder blocks like horseshoes. Joshua's fist wasn't going anywhere.

"I'm sorry, fellas," Ham said peaceably. "We seem to

be getting off on the wrong foot here. What was it y'all were looking for?"

"Deputy Lanier," said the man with the shotgun. "We've got them. Let's take them in."

The deputy tapped Joshua's face with the barrel of his gun. "If I knew she was dead already, if there was no hope you left her alive, so help me God I'd blow your brains out in a heartbeat."

Joshua's mouth was full of blood. He swallowed it. Ham seemed in no hurry to let go of his fist. The fury in his stomach switched back to terror again. He ignored it, disgusted with himself, his voice even cooler and more distant. "Well, Deputy, you may have to hit me again, because I have no idea what you are talking about."

"I'm guessing Sloane Gardner," Ham said. "Judging from the high-class nature of the posse. Two government-issue Colt .45 automatics, a Glock 17, and if I'm not mistaken the fella with the shotgun back there is Sheriff Denton himself."

"Sloane!" Josh said. He shook his head. "I should have guessed."

Deputy Lanier belted him in the stomach with the gun barrel. Josh buckled at the knees and retched helplessly, vomiting his dinner of redfish and pinto beans onto the floor of his consulting room. The deputy stood over him. "That's Miss Gardner to you."

"Kyle! Quit that," Sheriff Denton said.

Sloane's elusive stars blinked and faded in front of Joshua's eyes. He got his breath and tried to struggle to his feet, but buckled again, heaving.

"Last I heard we still had trial by jury on this Island," Ham said. He didn't sound quite so calm. "And innocent until proven guilty."

"Bring them," the sheriff said.

AN hour and a half later, after fingerprints and processing, Sheriff Denton, Deputy Kyle Lanier, and Josh were

in the interrogation chamber in the basement of the County Courthouse. (At night any confidential business was carried out in rooms either windowless or heavily shuttered, to make sure no stray slivers of moonlight could let Momus in on the conversation.) The room had a smooth concrete floor, ancient fake wood paneling, two chairs, and a small vinyl-topped card table. Josh sat in one chair with his hands cuffed behind him. Kyle Lanier sat across from him with a clipboard and a sheet of rice paper, taking notes with an exquisite Waterman fountain pen. The only light came from a hissing propane lantern on the table. It lit Kyle's face unflatteringly from below, exposing the pitted skin of his neck and cheeks while filling his eyes with shadows.

Jeremiah Denton paced in the murk beyond the circle of lamplight. Occasionally he would approach, emerging from the gloom to rest his hands against the table's edge, lamplight winking on his gold watch chain. Josh wondered if the sheriff chose not to sit because he suffered from back pain. The stiffness in his gait as he walked and the deliberate way he placed his fingers on the table before putting weight on them suggested a touch of arthritis. He also seemed to have a slight dry cough, which could mean anything from ex-smoker to convalescence from bronchial infection to incipient tuberculosis.

After getting Joshua's version of the day's events, Sheriff Denton paused in his questioning. The lamp hissed. Kyle's pen scratched to the end of a line and then stopped. He blotted it on a rag. A silence built.

"Ham voted for you," Josh told the sheriff.

"You preferred my opponent?"

"I didn't vote."

"That's a mistake," Sheriff Denton said. "You owe it to yourself to have a voice in the direction of your community, and you owe it to your neighbors, 'that government of the people, by the people, for the people shall not perish from the earth.' But you were inquiring about

joining a Krewe today, weren't you? That was a sudden burst of public spirit."

"I would have thought you'd welcome it."

The sheriff coughed into his closed fist. Then he reached into the watch pocket of his vest and drew out a gold-plated Waltham. His fingers were stiff, and it took him a few moments to get the case open. Definitely some arthritis. He glanced at the watch, started to shut the case, then paused and courteously showed Joshua the time. It was thirteen minutes past midnight. Josh reminded himself not to read too much into the sheriff's small acts of consideration; that might be merely Jeremiah Denton's impeccable breeding. Nothing personal. Joshua's father had been blessed with an easy manner and a smiling, amiable poker face, but he had always played to win.

Sheriff Denton tucked his watch away. "Did you tell your friend Ham you intended to make applications to these Krewes?"

They were corroborating his story with Ham's. Josh hoped Ham remembered the morning the same way. "I believe I mentioned wanting to join."

"And what did he say about that?"

"He was surprised."

On the whole, Josh thought he was doing a good job of hiding his tells. This was critical, because his body was terrified. His pulse was racing, his stomach was tense, and he felt a cramp lodged like a stone in his throat. It was infuriating that his body felt guilty. Ham lived inside his meat, at home in his own bone and muscle. Not Josh. In Joshua's experience his body made bad decisions. It felt things it shouldn't. It gave him away.

"We have two witnesses who saw Sloane Gardner enter your house this morning," Sheriff Denton said. "Neither saw her leave."

"It's never the wrong time for my neighbors to mind someone else's business," Josh said. "As it happens, I didn't see her leave either."

"Could she have gone out your back door?"

"Hm." An opening. Josh studied the sheriff. If Sloane went out the back, that would explain why Joshua's gossiping neighbors had never seen her leave. On the other hand, other neighbors might have been out back early in the morning, tending chickens or working on their generators. And there were always the winos who loitered around his backyard hoping to scavenge table scraps, or better yet cakes of used yeast and fermented rice from the beer he made—anything that might have traces of alcohol on it.

Josh figured the odds were two to one the sheriff was waiting to catch him in a lie, with witnesses willing to swear Sloane hadn't left out the back. He met the sheriff's gaze dispassionately. "No, she didn't go out the kitchen door. There's no way she could have walked by me while my back was turned. There wasn't enough time, and I would have heard something."

Kyle's pen scratched across his sheet of rice paper.

"You claim this was the second time Miss Gardner had come to your house voluntarily, after being brought there without her consent by Mr. Mather."

"She was barely conscious when Ham—"

"We can come back to that," Sheriff Denton said. "You also claim that on both these visits Miss Gardner purchased some tea. Dami—?"

"Damiana. It's a mild stimulant. She was very tired."

Sheriff Denton paced away into the darkness, his back to Josh. His boot heels clicked slowly on the concrete floor. *Click. Clack. Click. Clack.* "May I ask why she chose your shop?"

"I had done her a service. I should add that Ham and I have learned our lesson, and solemnly promise never to be good Samaritans again."

"Don't get smart," Kyle said.

Sheriff Denton held up his hand for quiet. "Mr. Cane, did you find Sloane Gardner attractive?"

Joshua's heart jumped, and the cramp in his throat pulled tight like a knotted string. He shrugged, expressionless. "Somewhat."

"What does that mean, Josh? Did you think her plain or pretty?"

"Physically? I suppose she was tolerable. I've seen better."

Kyle wrote, shaking his head. The sheriff nodded. "How about her personality? Did you like her?"

"Yes."

"Why?"

"She wasn't stupid."

The sheriff regarded him. "Did you expect her to be?"

"I have learned not to take intelligence for granted."

Kyle laughed. "Arrogant little bastard, aren't you?"

"Kyle—" Sheriff Denton laid a hand on his deputy's shoulder. He coughed. He coughed again and cleared his throat. Another cough. "Pardon me, Mr. Cane. I need a drink of water. I will be back presently."

"But of course," Josh said. "Pray, don't worry on my account."

Sheriff Denton frowned as he walked slowly from the room.

Josh felt the front of his mouth with his tongue. His lip was fat and his mouth still tasted of blood and vomit. His stomach also hurt badly, a sharp aching pain in the gut where Kyle had punched him with his gun.

The door closed behind Sheriff Denton. Josh looked up warily as the deputy put down his clipboard. Kyle Lanier stood, stretching, and then came around the table. "The old fella has such beautiful manners, don't he?" Kyle shook his head and smiled. The gold caps on his front teeth winked in the lamplight. Except for his ugliness he looked very much the elegant young man Josh should have been. His shoulder-length hair was gathered in a small dirty-blond ponytail. He wore a rough cotton vest over a smooth shirt, and expensive pointy-toed

boots. His grey uniform pants were cut tight around his calves and ankles.

He walked past Joshua and behind him. Josh strained his neck trying to watch him, but with his hands cuffed to the chair back he could only turn so far. There was a long moment of silence. The skin on Joshua's back began to crawl. "What are you doing?"

Kyle tipped Joshua's chair backward until only his hand kept it from crashing to the floor. "My manners aren't so fine," the deputy said. "I'm what you'd call a self-made man, Josh. You see, I started out poor. I mean dirt-poor. When I was a boy my daddy used to whup me with a belt if I didn't bring my own dinner home at night. A crawdad or a squirrel or some damn thing. He used the buckle end, too. I didn't care for it at the time, but I tell you what, it was instructive. Did wonders for my character. I learned to work hard for what I wanted, and I didn't much go hungry."

"Put me down," Josh said. He spread his legs as wide as he could, searching for the floor with his toes. Kyle stepped beside the chair and drove his fist into Joshua's stomach as hard as he could, twice. The breath went out of Josh in fireworks of pain. His lungs kicked and strained for air.

"Sheriff Denton don't understand about the buckle end," Kyle said. "He thinks everybody is as good and fine and noble as him. I don't. Most people are animals, if you want my opinion. In the old days that got covered up a little, but now that the screws are back on you see folks showing their true colors. If you want to get any-where, you need to put the spur to 'em." This time Kyle punched Josh in the balls. Then he dropped the chair. Joshua's head bounced off the concrete floor and he blacked out.

When his eyelids fluttered open a few seconds later Kyle was standing over him. "Sloane Gardner was a friend of mine."

Air flooded back into Joshua's body. "I didn't—"

Kyle kicked him in the side, just above the kidney. "I recommend a full and complete confession. You know we won't kill you and your fat friend, even if you are found guilty. The sheriff don't believe in making ghosts." Josh curled up on his back, drawing his legs up around the horrible pain in his testicles and stomach and side. "In case you were wondering," Kyle added, "you are already one found-guilty son of a bitch. That's a done deal. We talked to the judge before we ever went to your house. It's over. The only difference a confession makes"—he kicked Joshua in the side again with his shiny leather boots—"is how much personal satisfaction I get from kicking the crap out of you for what you've done to Sloane, you freak."

Kyle heaved the chair up with Josh still in it and arranged him in front of the table. It hurt Josh terribly to breathe.

The door creaked open and Sheriff Denton returned. "What's going on? I heard a crash."

"The prisoner leaned back in his chair and it tipped over," Kyle said easily. "We're all right now."

"He beat me," Josh said raggedly.

Sheriff Denton looked seriously at Kyle. "Deputy?"

"I didn't touch him."

"See that you don't."

"Make him swear it," Josh said. "Make him swear it by Momus."

Sheriff Denton looked at him. "Son, you are here on a very serious charge. My advice to you is to be more helpful and stand a little less on your pride." The sheriff sighed. "Not that I wasn't stiff-necked myself, at your age." He coughed into his fist. "Let's get back to work."

Joshua tried to decide if he should tell them about Sloane's trips to the Mardi Gras, about the smell of cigarettes and liquor on her dress, the ripped stockings and the out-of-character recklessness in her smile the morning

she had stayed with him for breakfast. She had held his hand and trusted him when he promised to keep that secret. But it was hard to ignore his whimpering body. It wanted to tell everything right away. Of course its motives were pretty clear, and Josh was afraid it was influencing his judgment. Still, the sheriff meant to try him for murder, that was obvious now. Besides which, Ham wouldn't think twice about spilling the beans. He had no reason to be exiled or marooned for the sake of Josh's confidences. It would go a lot easier on Josh if his story and Ham's matched.

Sometimes you have to fold your cards and wait for a better hand.

Josh betrayed Sloane's secret, disliking himself and resenting her for making him a traitor. But when he told about Sloane's visits to the Mardi Gras, the sheriff didn't want to hear it. "You are actually implying that the Grand Duchess's daughter was in Carnival, not once but many times, by her own choice, while her mother lay dying?"

"Yes, sir."

"That doesn't sound like the Sloane Gardner I know," Sheriff Denton said. "She has always been a quiet, dutiful girl. I have known her since she was a child."

"So have I," Josh said. "Though everyone forgets it."

"Hm. Yes." The sheriff's eyes rested on Josh. "Do you know the Ten Commandments, young man? The last one is, Thou shalt not covet thy neighbor's house, thou shalt not covet thy neighbor's wife, nor his manservant, nor his maidservant, nor his ox, nor his ass, nor any thing that is thy neighbor's." The sheriff coughed. "I imagine daughters fall under the general law."

"I've been just that hungry," Kyle said softly. "I've wanted it so bad it made me puke. But I earned it, Josh. I earned what you tried to steal, you gutless fuck."

"You're vulgar and you're not very smart," Josh said. "Nothing you get will ever change that."

Kyle looked at him a long time before a slight smile

parted his lips, letting a gleam of gold escape from his capped teeth. "Speaking of not too smart," he said.

Joshua continued to look at Kyle with contempt, but his stupid body was scared. His mouth hurt where Kyle had jabbed him with the gun, his head hurt where it had banged the floor. It had been hours since he'd had a chance to pee and he needed to go badly. The pain in his balls had faded, but the hurt in his sides and stomach was growing slowly worse. He wouldn't show a lot of bruises, of course. How convenient for Kyle. It hurt to breathe. He wondered if the deputy might have cracked one of his ribs, kicking him, or damaged one of his kidneys.

Sheriff Denton paced back into the gloom. *Click. Clack. Click. Clack.* "Our two families never seem to cross in the best way, do they, Josh?"

It took Josh a moment to make the connection. "You mean our house?"

"I told Travis he shouldn't have collected on that bet. He should never have put Sam's family on the street, even if your daddy was foolish enough to gamble your house away. But Travis was . . ." The sheriff gave a short laugh. "A Denton, I suppose." He coughed into his fist. Gold chain clinked as he pulled out the Waltham pocket watch again. "Almost one." He closed the gold case with a click and settled the heavy watch back into his waistcoat pocket.

("You can always tell a rich guy by his watch," Ham had said once. "The less real work one of those fuckers has to do, the more he thinks about the time.")

The sheriff resumed his pacing. *Click. Clack. Click. Clack.* "Do you know there are members of my family who believe that fire was not an accident?" the sheriff said. "Randall Denton, for one, believes your father sabotaged the gas line."

"That's a lie!" Josh started to his feet, but the yank of the chair's weight against his cuffed wrists made him stumble and sit again.

"Shut up," Kyle said.

Josh forced his body to be still. Forced himself to ignore the shaking in his breath, the iron knot in his stomach. "It was all a long time ago," he said. "No hard feelings. A bet's a bet. My father made the wager and I lost it for him. A bet's a bet."

"What do you mean, you lost it?"

"I saw my father's cards. I knew he was bluffing and I gave away the bluff. I didn't have much of a poker face then."

"It's getting better," the sheriff said. He coughed into his hand, hard. Then he sighed and turned for the door of the interrogation chamber. "Excuse me, gentlemen; I need another drink of water. I'll be back directly."

Kyle put his clipboard down on the table and smiled at Josh.

"Please," Josh said.

The sheriff turned, his hand still on the doorknob. "Yes?"

"Don't leave me alone with him."

"Son, I am an old man and I need a drink of water. I'll be back soon enough."

"Then I'd like to request another guard. Please."

"Josh, I can't do that." Sheriff Denton paused and looked at him, old eyes grey under white brows. "Unless you have something important to say . . . ?"

Josh felt his heart thud once, twice, three times. Ah. So that's the way it was. The sheriff knew Kyle had beaten him. He was waiting for Josh to confess. If he didn't, Denton would leave the room and Kyle would beat him again. It was very well played. Really, it should have worked. "But I didn't do it," Josh whispered. To his horror he felt two tears begin to slide down his face. "I didn't do it!"

Sheriff Denton regarded him. "I need to get me a drink of water," he said. "I'll be back in directly."

•　　•　　•

IT had been a long time since anyone had beaten Joshua. His first year in the barrio it had happened a lot, but then Ham became his friend and the beatings had abruptly stopped. Most of the time Joshua never gave his body a second thought, concentrating instead on which drugs to mix, which cards to play, how he was going to pay the next month's rent. But when he was sick or hurting, unstrung with nausea or ringing with pain, it was impossible to live beyond the edges of his skin. All thinking suddenly fell away, except for a single clear understanding: *The meat is the only thing that matters.*

Later he would get well and forget the lesson, until the next wave of sickness came to remind him that the body is the only truth. Pain is master. Everything else is fantasy.

AFTER twenty minutes of brutal punishment, Kyle called two guards. They had to carry Joshua away. His knees wouldn't hold him up, and his body kept folding around the terrible pain in his gut. He was shivering.

He had peed himself sometime during the second beating. Nobody offered to get him clean clothes. It shouldn't have mattered, but as the guards dragged him to his cell, waves of humiliation ran through Josh at the reek of urine coming from his best pants, the ones he had dyed for Shem's wedding. His silk shirt was wet with pee at the waist. As much as he hated the guards, he was more terrified of being left alone, because then he would have to check his stinking pants for traces of blood in his urine.

One of the militiamen carried a Coleman lamp. Their shadows jerked and swayed at every step as they dragged him down a long tiled corridor. The ceiling was set with burned out fluorescent bar lights. Long broken and no way to fix or replace them. That was Galveston all over. All the real, true, steady lights going out, one by one, to be replaced by gaslight, firelight, moonlight. For one bright century men had moved beyond Nature's fickle,

shifting illumination, but then the Flood had come and they had fallen from the shadowless, well-lit twentieth century, back to these dark hallways and burning lamps.

The corridor ended at a heavy glass door with steel bars and steel mesh embedded in it. Its old electronic touch pad still worked, apparently; the guard without the lantern punched in a code, a series of chimes sounded, and the lock opened with a click.

Through the door was a small antechamber, beyond which was a second door, this one solid steel except for a small window and a key lock. One guard unlocked the door and held it open. The other shoved Joshua inside. Without anyone to lean on he stumbled and fell to his knees. The door slammed shut behind him. Flashes of lamplight flickered through the observation window for a few seconds, then dwindled and died. The guards must have withdrawn behind the antechamber's outer door.

It was not quite pitch-black. There were two long narrow windows on the far side of Joshua's cell, set near the ceiling at what must be street level. Pale bars of moonlight fell through them. Josh curled up on the floor, shaking and shaking. His mind spilled back and forth from one fear to another. He saw Kyle standing over him in the interrogation room. Fiona Barret's condescending smile. Sloane Gardner eating rice porridge at his kitchen table in the grey dawn, smelling faintly of smoke and liquor. When she lay dozing on his table he had come up behind her carrying her bowl of porridge and seen a crescent of bare skin through the armhole of her sleeveless dress, a glimpse of the gently curving side of her left breast. That memory melted into his mother's ghost, staring up at him from the sea floor behind the motorboat on Pier 23, then to the glossy sheen of Kyle's handsome leather shoes just before he kicked Joshua in the side.

Only when daylight began to creep into the cell, making things finally safe and definite and certain, did Josh manage a fitful doze.

C h a p t e r   T e n

THE TRIAL

JOSH would have said he never slept at all, except that waking was so hard. He heard a jangle of keys and voices approaching. By the time the cell door swung inward he had managed to force his eyes open. They felt stiff and swollen, like the rest of his body.

Two guards stood in the doorway, one older white guy with two days of stubble on his face, one younger Hispanic fellow with handsome features scarred by smallpox. Both guards wore the dark grey uniforms of the Galveston militia. Dyed with pecan hulls and . . . ferrous sulfate? Joshua couldn't remember.

"Come on, Cane. Time to rise and shine," the older man said.

"I can't."

The guard's hand fell on the butt of his nightstick. "You need help?"

"No thanks." Josh crawled to the side of the room and stood up, using the wall for support. He kept leaning on it as he shuffled down the corridors. He found it impossible to stand straight. Instead he walked hunched over, as if his muscles had knotted into place at some moment when he was curled around Kyle's foot.

They took him to a locker room. "Get in the shower," the older man said. "Paco, get him some clean clothes."

"Appreciate it," Josh whispered, fumbling at the buttons of his stained silk shirt.

"No one's doing you any favors, you sick bastard," said the guard. "We just don't want the judge to feel sorry for you."

Though Jane Gardner had trained as a lawyer, she hadn't believed them necessary for a population as small as Galveston's after the Flood. Disputes were argued in the old County Courthouse, but the defendants, unless incompetent, argued their own cases before a judge, without much care for legal technicalities. Josh thought the courtroom looked a lot like a church. Row after row of pews were filled with spectators who hushed as he was led in through a side door. In front of the pews were two tables, one for the defendant and one for the prosecutor. The high judge's bench dominated the far end of the room, where a pulpit or altar might have been. The guards sat him on a chair at the table to the left of the bench. The crowd began to whisper again, more loudly, pointing and staring at him.

It was already hot in the courtroom. The air conditioner strained and ceiling fans turned overhead, but the combination of another scorching hot day and a room crammed with more than a hundred spectators was far too much to overcome. Women flapped cloth fans, and men mopped at their foreheads with cotton handkerchiefs. Flies drowsed against the glass windows, and every now and then someone slapped at a roving mosquito. Josh wished he had forced himself to drink more in the shower. Too late now.

A second door opened at the side of the room and the judge made his entrance, murmuring a word or two to the bailiff and climbing up to his bench.

For the first time that morning Josh felt a surge of hope. Judge James Bose was to run this trial. Deacon

Bose was tough but fair. He had even known Joshua's mother, back when she was still active in the Krewe of Togetherness. Jim Bose was a farm boy, not a Gardner or a Denton. He had lost his left thumb in a combine accident. Josh had heard him speak the eulogy at the funerals of several of his patients; he could still remember the way the deacon held his Bible with both hands, made awkward by his missing thumb, his face stern and strong as he spoke. A deacon at the Island Church of Christ, he was a smart, hard, principled man and nobody's fool. Josh had seen him more than once on the wrong side of Broadway, bringing food and clothing for the poor, and reminding parents that they could always drop their kids off at Sunday school even if they didn't attend services themselves. He was past seventy now, but what hair he had left was as black as the Bible on the bench beside him.

The crowd shifted and whispered in the pews. Half the town must have jammed into the courtroom—Krewe officers in Corpus Christi cottons, dyed in colors the barrios never saw, scarlet and peach and indigo. Rich Hispanics with dresses of crepe chenille and old-fashioned suits; the women strung with rosary beads and crucifixes, the men with tiny ceramic hands and hearts dangling on necklaces to invoke the aid of El Mano Mo Más Poderoso and the Corazón Sagrado. Members of Sheriff Denton's Galveston militia, all in smartly pressed grey uniforms. Serious-looking black men from the Krewe of Togetherness. Fiona Barret and her family. Jim Ford. The entire staff of Jennifer Ford's *Galveston Daily News.* Randall Denton, elegantly turned out in a wasp-waisted coat and vest, eyed Josh with interest from the front row. Randall Denton made a point of having the best seat at any entertainment.

Standing at the back of the room and spilling into the hallways behind were all those second among equals: Vietnamese shrimpers, John Trachsel the horse man, a

few of Ham's buddies from the gas lines, Jezebel MacReady, who had made Joshua's best pair of pants—the same pants that were now probably in a garbage can somewhere inside the courthouse building.

Another murmur rose from the pews as Ham was led in, towering over his militia escort. He was still wearing the dirty yellow shorts and short-sleeved shirt he'd had on yesterday. He had to turn sideways to fit through the little wooden wicket to get to the prisoner's table. He settled himself in the chair next to Josh, which squeaked and complained under his weight. "Hey, buddy," Ham murmured. "We are in a shitload of trouble."

"Then it's a good thing we're innocent, isn't it?"

"Quiet," said the bailiff.

Sheriff Denton and Deputy Lanier entered and sat down at the table across from Josh and Ham. Deacon Bose banged his gavel. In the sudden silence he stood to face the courtroom. "Ladies and gentlemen, let's get started. Please rise." The crowd stood. After a moment's hesitation, Josh and Ham stood, too, and bowed their heads. "Heavenly Father," Deacon Bose said, "we are met here today under your sight to inquire after one of your children, Sloane Gardner. We ask that you bless these proceedings and lead us quickly and surely to an understanding of what has befallen her. We pray that you will restore her to us if you can. But if that is not your will, we hope that you will look on her, wherever she may be, in this world or the next, with all your tender mercies. All this we ask in the name of your son, Jesus Christ. Amen."

"Amen," the crowd murmured. Josh said his amen with everybody else; and, he thought bitterly, more honestly than most.

Deacon Bose sat; the rest of the courtroom followed in a rustle of pants and dresses. "Sheriff Denton, please rise." Jeremiah Denton stood up. "Sheriff, what is your contention?"

In a clear, steady voice, Sheriff Denton said, "We believe that Mr. Cane, in collusion with Mr. Mather, abducted Sloane Gardner, raped her, and probably killed her afterward."

The silence was terrible. Joshua's body betrayed him again as a burning flush spread over his face.

"Mr. Cane? How do you plead?"

"Not guilty."

"Liar," said a voice from the back.

"The next person who interrupts can spend a night in a cell for contempt of court," Deacon Bose said sharply. The bailiff glowered at the back of the courthouse. "This is not a theater. Although we would all like to see justice done swiftly, and Sloane found as soon as possible, I hold no case made before it is proven. Let's keep it clear and to the point, with no interruptions, please." He turned the full weight of his attention on Josh. "Mr. Cane, please tell us in your own words what happened from the time Mr. Mather brought Sloane Gardner to your verandah to the time you were arrested."

Josh told his story. His throat was still raw from retching and his stomach ached every time he breathed. He meant to stick just to his encounters with Sloane, but decided he had better make a cursory mention of his visits to the various Krewe offices, including the debacle at the Krewe of Togetherness. Sheriff Denton would doubtless bring up such a humiliating episode, and Josh didn't want it to look as if he had been hiding anything. He left his mother's ghost out of it. Deacon Bose took notes. Then he asked Ham for his version of events. He continued writing for some time after Ham had finished, then blotted his quill absently and put it down. "All right. Sheriff Denton, you may begin."

THE sheriff called Raúl and Conchita Fuentes as his first witnesses. Josh was surprised. The young couple lived six or seven blocks away from him and weren't likely to

have seen any of Sloane's comings and goings. Raúl had dressed up for the day in court in a faded serge jacket that had probably belonged to his father. He had the bandy legs of a lot of barrio kids who had grown up without enough food. Conchita must be nineteen by now. Her belly looked flat. Either his lectures on birth control had gotten through, or they had found a midwife to do their abortions.

"Mr. Fuentes, have you met the defendant?"

"*Sí.* Yes."

"When?"

"When my daughter was born. Last spring."

"Sheriff, why are you calling this witness?" Deacon Bose asked.

"It speaks to character, Judge."

"Very well. Be quick."

Josh was baffled. The Fuenteses' child had been born dead, but he had done everything he could.

"Would you describe Mr. Cane as a caring man?" the sheriff asked.

"No," Raúl said emphatically. For the first time he looked at Josh, a defiant glare. He was like so many of the young Tex-Mex guys, a scrawny little fighting cock. "He was a col' son of a bitch. He could have saved our baby. He just didn't want to."

The judge looked at Josh. "Mr. Cane?"

Josh was almost grateful to Sheriff Denton for starting with a case that was so clearly not his fault. "Mrs. Fuentes went into labor two months before term. Her nutrition was inadequate, and she admitted she had been drinking during her pregnancy. The baby was not breathing when it was born. I tried to provoke respiration for some time after delivery, but it just wasn't strong enough to survive."

"Did you ever tell Mrs. Fuentes about the dangers of drinking while pregnant?" Sheriff Denton asked.

Conchita was staring hard at the floor. "Once during

pregnancy," Josh said, "and once after the delivery."

The sheriff nodded thoughtfully. He turned toward the pews. "Mr. Cane, is it your habit to blame a mother for the death of her child?"

"I didn't—"

"Yes, you did. Just now, Mr. Cane. You expressed no remorse and not the faintest hint of your own responsibility. Not only did you do it here, in public—you also did it in Mrs. Fuentes's house, with her child's body not yet cold."

A cold shock spread through Joshua's chest, as if someone had touched an ice cube to his heart. The people of Galveston stared at him. "I'm sorry if I caused Mrs. Fuentes any distress," he said. "Raúl, Conchita, is that all you remember? Don't you remember that it was after midnight when you came for me? That I stayed with you past ten the next morning? Do you remember that I only billed you one chicken for my night's work and you haven't paid it and I haven't bothered you for it?"

As soon as he said it, Josh realized that had been a mistake. Nobody in the audience was going to understand how he could have the audacity to bill for a night's work when a poor couple had lost a child.

"A chicken and a pot of jam," Conchita whispered. "I brought the jam. It's all we got right now." To Joshua's horror she produced a small glass jar and placed it on the table.

"Do you remember what you said?" Raúl went on belligerently. "After little Maria died? You said, 'It's just as well.' To my wife you said this, after she was in labor for a day. 'It's just as well.' "

"The child never breathed!" Josh said. "Even if I could have revived her, there would have been massive brain damage—" Josh stopped. He was only making himself look worse.

" 'It's your fault your baby died, but it's just as well,' " Sheriff Denton repeated thoughtfully. The audience in the

pews looked at Josh with loathing. The sheriff glanced back at Deacon Bose. "It speaks to character," he said. "Mr. Cane, is it true that a shot of adrenaline is often administered to children who die during labor to aid in their resuscitation?"

"Sometimes," Josh said grimly. It wasn't hard to see where this was going.

"And did you have any adrenaline the night you attended the Fuenteses' delivery?"

"Yes."

"But you elected not to use it."

"That is correct."

"Why did you make that decision, Mr. Cane?"

"The medical term is triage," Josh said flatly. There was no way to get out of this without looking like a monster. "To divide patients into three categories. Those who will survive without treatment, those who will probably die even if they get it, and those for whom treatment is likely to make the difference between living and dying. When you have limited time or resources, you can only treat the last group. I only have a very little adrenaline left. In cases of asthma or anaphylactic shock it is going to make the difference between life and death."

"So you chose not to use it," the sheriff said. "Even though you had it right there. Even with the baby in front of you."

"In my judgment, there wasn't enough of a chance the child would survive and grow up to be an intelligent adult," Josh said. Conchita was staring at him helplessly. Her face had crumpled. Tears were crawling down her cheeks. "The right choice is not always easy. Sometimes you have to play bad cards well. I felt that preserving the adrenaline—"

"Perhaps for a client with more money?"

"Sheriff," the judge said. Sheriff Denton raised one hand in apology.

Conchita was crying on the stand, hand in front of her

mouth, trying not to make noise. Tears wrung out of her. Raúl put his hand on her shoulder and glared at Josh with pure hatred. Josh closed his eyes to keep from seeing them. "It's not about fairness," he said. "It's about what's best for everybody."

NEXT up was Josh's neighbor from across the street, Letitia Daschle, a fat German-Texan widow with skin the color of bread dough. She was a big nosy hen of a woman, all clucks and bosoms. She liked to complain about her trick knee and her arthritis, her allergies and her lumbago at every possible opportunity, hoping Josh might let some bit of wisdom drop for free, but she had always refused to have an actual billable visit.

"Mrs. Daschle, you saw Sloane Gardner enter Mr. Cane's house, correct?"

"Yes, sir."

"But you didn't see her leave?"

"No, sir."

"How long were you watching his door?"

"I wasn't watching it," she said huffily. "I just happened to be sitting near the front window."

Josh gritted his teeth. The prison-issue shirt was sticking to his sweaty back, and there were big wet patches under his arms. The courtroom was full of the smell of hot people.

The sheriff nodded sympathetically at his witness. "I understand, Mrs. Daschle. How long?"

"Maybe two hours."

"Thank you, that's very helpful. Mrs. Daschle, how would you describe Mr. Cane?"

"Standoffish. Not neighborly at all. Always kep' to himself."

"A loner."

"Loner," she said with satisfaction. "That's the very word."

"Thank you."

•   •   •

THEN came the winos to testify that Sloane Gardner had not left out the back door either. Josh smiled coldly at the sheriff throughout that testimony. Then came a succession of sailors and workmen with the Gas Authority, testifying that Ham had been boasting along the waterfront about how his pal Josh was getting his biscuit buttered by the Grand Duchess's daughter.

Josh wiped his sweaty forehead with the cuff of his grey prison shirt. "With friends like you, who needs enemies?"

"Sorry, bud," Ham mumbled. The big man was brick red past the ears.

The next witness was Aaron Barker, the black sailor who had refused to carry Joshua across to the *Selma*. He was in Thalassar dress whites, shorts and a shirt, and a pair of white canvas shoes with rubber soles.

"Would you tell the judge what you saw in the water behind your boat?"

"A ghost." The crowd moved and murmured. "A woman, under the water. Staring up at him," he said, pointing at Josh.

"Did you say anything about this ghost to Mr. Cane?"

"Oh, yeah. He saw it."

Sheriff Denton let a long silence stretch out. "Mr. Cane, you did not mention this ghost in your earlier testimony."

"It wasn't relevant," Josh said.

"Not relevant?"

"No, sir."

"I think it is. I suspect everybody in this courtroom is very interested to hear there was a ghost following you yesterday, Mr. Cane. Did you recognize this ghost?"

"Yes," Joshua said.

Six oak-bladed fans hung from the ceiling, all spinning. Sunlight from the windows glinted from the lacquered wooden blades. Like stars, Joshua thought. One

of the six had some kind of problem, turning much more slowly, as if wounded or sick. He couldn't feel the breeze from the fans at all.

Deacon Bose had never been involved in the medical wing of the Krewe of Togetherness. It hadn't been his office Joshua had waited in, cramping his heartbeat down into something small enough to fit inside his chest, his mouth going dry as a Krewe bureaucrat explained how of course his mother couldn't expect to jump the line ahead of others whose need for insulin was just as great, but she would be put on the waiting list . . .

"Mr. Cane, we are waiting."

"It was my mother," Joshua said.

"Mr. Barker, could you see the woman clearly enough to make out her face?"

"Not really," said the young sailor. "There was sea-weed floating in front of her. I could tell she was white, with dark hair."

"Mr. Barker, from what you saw, could it have been the ghost of the defendant's mother?"

"Sure. I suppose."

"Could it have been the ghost of Sloane Gardner?"

A gasp went through the crowd.

The witness's eyes widened. "I . . . yeah, I suppose." He nodded, slowly at first, then more strongly as he met the sheriff's eyes. "Yeah."

"But it wasn't," Joshua said. "It was my mother."

Sheriff Denton called the man who had interviewed Joshua for the Krewe of Harlequins. He testified that he had also seen the ghost of a dark-haired woman. Once again, she had been too far away for him to recognize. "It was my mother," Joshua said.

The sick ceiling fan limped overhead. Josh could feel the sweat at the waistband of the plain cotton pants they had given him. "Why?" Sheriff Denton asked after another long silence. "Why would your mother appear to you? Was she in the habit of doing this?"

"No."

"Then why yesterday? Why that day of all days?"

"I don't know," Josh said. "Probably to warn me that a lynch mob was going to arrest and try me for a crime I didn't commit."

Sheriff Denton turned away, addressing the courtroom. "I submit to the judge that the appearance of a ghost is a mark of omen." He paused. "Personally, I don't think it was your mother's ghost, Mr. Cane. I think it was the ghost of Sloane Gardner. And I think she was pursuing her killer."

The crowd murmured and nodded, staring at Josh. Under the blank haze of humiliation it occurred to him that he had not heard Sheriff Denton cough since the trial began.

"Mr. Barker, you may step down."

Josh jumped to his feet. "Deacon Bose, may I call a witness to the stand?"

"You may, Mr. Cane."

"Then how about one of my other patients?" Josh rasped. He turned to the courtroom. "They're in the back, of course. They don't get front row seats like Mr. Denton here. How about Daisy Thornton? I set her leg when a horse kick broke it. Or you, Mrs. Phipps," he said, catching sight of the neighborhood washerwoman. "How many times have I crawled into your shack and examined the shit in one of your kids' diapers?" She flinched and looked down. Easy, Josh told himself. Don't let anger get the best of you. You can't play drunk, scared, or mad. "How about Jezebel MacReady?" he called, his voice hoarse and ragged. "Mrs. MacReady, haven't you got a good word to say for me? Haven't I given you pills and lotions and what all for your arthritis for years, and all for a few jars of jam? I don't even like mustang grape jam. I got a crate of it at home now, all I do is trade it to the neighbors."

The black woman stared back at him. "That was the price we said. I paid it."

"Easy, Josh," Ham rumbled.

"I've lived with y'all for years," Josh said. "Come on now. I've done my duty. I've put in my time. Won't anybody stand up for me?" The silence was deafening. Row after row of faces stared back at him or turned away. Nobody stood to speak. "It's not fair," Josh yelled.

Sheriff Denton stirred. "They don't like you, Mr. Cane."

Joshua's anger began to cave in, collapsing into a ruin of shame. He had known, of course, that he didn't fit in. That was no shock. But for the first time he understood that his patients in the barrio only came to him *because they had no other choice.* He had never managed to conceal from them, not for an instant, how much he resented being trapped among them.

Ham rubbed his eyes with his fat fingers. "Oh, Josh."

Ham must have spent hours and hours defending him. Josh's face burned as if he were just now overhearing a hundred conversations. Ham patiently making excuses for him to the longshoremen and the milkmaids, the shrimpers and the house servants he met in bars after Josh was in bed. For all Josh knew, maybe not even the other Mathers liked him. Maybe Ham's sister, Rachel, thought he was a stuck-up prig who tried to show off by using big words. Ham's mother had always been quick to defer to Josh. Maybe what he had assumed was respect was actually tact, Mrs. Mather trying not to offend his pathetic vanity. He was a charity project, is what he was, tolerated because he had a few useful skills, protected by the shield of Ham's goodwill.

He felt his friend's giant paw on his shoulder, gently pulling him back to his seat. "Sit down," Ham rumbled. "Give the sheriff time to recover, you silver-tongued devil."

"I'm sorry," Josh said.

Ham lumbered slowly to his feet. He scratched at his neck. "You know, one thing about us Texans, we sure are neighborly." He looked around the crowded court-room. "Hey, Tex!" he called. "You got that leak on number three fixed yet? And howdy, Miz MacReady!" He gave a big old wave. "Yep. We sure like to be polite. And us Mathers, we're good at it. My mom gets to feeling hurt if her guests don't have three helpings of everything. My mom, she's been teaching Sunday school from time out of mind. Her manners got manners. We're just good ol' salt-of-the-earth friendly howdy-do neighbors."

He paused. "Josh ain't like that. Truth is, he's a Yankee at heart. He doesn't have the greatest bedside manner in the world. He doesn't much care how all's your kin is doing. And between you and me, I don't know if Josh Cane has cracked a Bible in a very long time."

Deacon Bose stirred. "If you're going somewhere with this, Mr. Mather, best get on with it, son."

"To the best of my recollection," Ham said, "Jesus Christ is pretty quiet on the subject of manners. What he does say is, 'By their fruits ye shall know them.' " Ham paused and looked around the room. "Well, look at what Josh Cane has done. He has worked his ass off for the people on the wrong side of Broadway, getting paid so little he has to sell beer to make ends meet. Thank God," Ham added piously, pausing to pat his ample gut. A little ripple of laughter passed through the room. "Josh has done a deal of good. To deny that just because he doesn't smile and say howdy at the same time—now *that* would be a sin."

"Amen," said Alice Mather. Josh looked at Ham's mother gratefully, and she smiled back at him, ignoring the rows of heads that turned to stare at her. Bless you, Josh thought.

Ham sat down.

•   •   •

SHERIFF Denton was wearing hand-tooled calfskin boots. The Mexican who made them lived in a fine house on Post Office Street now. At the end of the twentieth century his little shoe repair shop had made just enough money for his young family to be slowly starving. He had joined the Krewe of Togetherness in the spring of 2004 to try to make contacts, looking for a new line of work. Then the world ended and suddenly there were no more department stores stocked with new Tony Lama and Nocono Boot Company products. He became a wealthy man, a living example of the fickleness of fate.

Josh figured he could have eaten for three weeks on the price of Jeremiah Denton's boots. They had good wooden heels on them. When he paced slowly across the courtroom, the heels struck firmly, with authority. *Crack. Crack. Crack.* "Mr. Cane, would you care to explain how we came to find a pair of Sloane Gardner's stockings in your house?"

Crack. Crack.

"She said they were ruined while she was in Mardi Gras. I asked if I could have them." The crowd murmured. Josh spoke over them. "I needed them, as a mesh for seining. Screening. When I'm mixing a drug or a medicine, I often need to grind up dried leaves or minerals into powder. The stockings struck me as a good mesh screen."

"I see." *Crack. Crack. Crack.* Sheriff Denton walked toward Josh. "Mr. Cane, would you care to explain how we came to find traces of Sloane Gardner's blood in the stockings?"

"She was cut. In the Mardi Gras."

"I see." Sheriff Denton turned his back to Josh, pacing even more slowly, measured steps in those fine boots. "Mr. Cane, would you care to explain why we found significant amounts of drying semen in Sloane Gardner's stockings?"

Josh's heart kicked him in the chest like a mule. The

crowd roared. Deacon Bose slammed his gavel. Josh stared overhead at the circling fans and said nothing. His cheeks were burning.

"Mr. Cane? We are waiting."

Josh didn't even try to speak.

Sheriff Denton turned and jabbed at Josh with a finger. "By God, boy, I want to hear what you have to say. What is your explanation? What do you have to tell the judge? What do you have to tell Sloane's family? Why were her stockings stained with your semen?"

Ham surged up from his chair. "Mighty pink Christ on a barbecue," he growled. "It's as plain as the ears on a jackass, Sheriff. Josh asks for the stockings just like he said. Later he gives in to a moment of temptation and whacks off with them."

"Ham!"

"For Christ's sake, Josh, it's embarrassing, but it ain't a capital crime to do the five-finger mambo."

"I was asking Mr. Cane the question," Sheriff Denton snapped. "You had best save your wits for your own excuses, Mr. Mather."

"Easy there, Sheriff," Ham said. "My boy Josh here is on the delicate side. He embarrasses easy. I'm sure you'd admit that Miss Gardner was a peach. Are you telling me you never once in your life spent a romantic interlude in and amongst your own fingers?"

You could have heard a straw snap in the ensuing silence. Sheriff Denton said, "The trouble with people like you, Mr. Mather, is that you can't imagine anything higher than yourself. You think base thoughts and you feel base feelings, but instead of repenting them, you assume that you must be normal, that other men and women—decent, respectable men and women—are just like you." He turned his back so that he faced the crowd. "Mr. Mather, we are not like you."

Ham stood flushed and glowering, his massive jaw and gut out-thrust. "I hold *these* truths to be self-evident, Mr.

Denton: that ALL men are created EQUAL; that they are endowed by their creator with certain unalienable rights; that among these are life, liberty, and the pursuit of happiness."

"Not Jefferson," Josh moaned. "Not now."

"That to SECURE these rights, governments are instituted among men," Ham thundered, "deriving their JUST POWERS from the CONSENT OF THE GOVERNED, YOU PUSSY!"

Someone at the back laughed.

Sheriff Denton consulted his watch. "Mr. Mather, would you care to explain how we came to find two of Sloane Gardner's hairs in your boat?"

The crowd buzzed and leaned forward. Ham's jaw dropped open, then snapped shut. Josh twisted around to stare at his friend, shocked.

Sheriff Denton strode to the Deacon's bench, boots cracking crisply on the floor. "We have the hairs in this plastic bag," he said, laying it down on the judge's bench. "Obviously Sloane—or her body—was in Mr. Mather's boat some time recently."

Even at the back of the room, where Ham's friends and supporters stood, faces looked pale and shocked.

"Your Honor," Sheriff Denton said, "Sloane Gardner entered Mr. Cane's home in a dubious part of town. She never returned. Mr. Cane claims she went to Mardi Gras, fleeing her responsibilities to her family and her Krewe. I find that hard to believe. Mr. Cane spent the day attempting to join any Krewe that would have him. I submit he was looking for protection. We know he was pursued by a ghost. I submit that is no good thing. He claims it was his mother's. I suggest that he is a liar and this is another lie. I very much fear that the ghost attending him was the ghost of the young woman he had tricked, compromised, and killed. We found Miss Gardner's stockings in the defendant's house, matted with blood and semen. We found strands of her hair in Mr.

Mather's boat. They have been studied under a microscope and compared to hairs left in a brush at home. They are hers."

Jeremiah Denton turned and stared at the defendants. "Joshua Cane likes to think of himself as a charitable man, doing work among the poor. What he has never accepted is that he *is* the poor. I suggest to you that from the day his father gambled away the family fortune, Joshua Cane has lived in bitterness, filled with contempt for the unfortunates he lives among, and consumed with hatred and envy for those who still have what he believes should rightfully be his. Did he admire Sloane Gardner? Possibly. Was he jealous of her house, her breeding, her clothes, her fortune? I would bet my life on it." Jeremiah Denton paused. "My family, you may remember, has taken something the Canes felt was theirs," he said, "and paid a terrible price for it."

"I object!" Josh said hoarsely over the murmur of the crowd.

The sheriff ignored him. "It is true we have no body, Your Honor. But against the testimony of Mr. Cane and Mr. Mather we have three eloquent pieces of evidence. The word of witnesses who saw Sloane Gardner enter his house but never leave it. The bloody stockings in Mr. Cane's possession. And the hairs found in Mr. Mather's boat. Surely the story they tell is compelling."

Deacon Bose scratched out another line of notes. Joshua held up his hand. The effort made his arm shake. He'd had next to no food and less sleep for more than a day. His gut and ribs still ached badly from the beating Kyle had given him.

Deacon Bose looked up. "You may speak, Mr. Cane."

Josh dropped his hand and hunched down a little, then slowly stood. "I plead guilty," he said. The crowd let out a protracted sigh, and Sheriff Denton nodded.

Josh held up his hand for silence. "Guilty of many things. To the charge that I found Miss Gardner attrac-

tive, which seems to be most of Mr. Denton's case, I plead guilty. To the charge that I live in the wrong part of town, I plead guilty. To the charge that my house smells and I am not friends with many in this room, I apparently have to plead guilty, too. To the charge that I don't look fit to entertain any thoughts about a woman above my station, I also plead guilty, like a good little criminal, with the extenuating circumstance that my best clothes were ruined as I was beaten repeatedly last night by the brave men of Sheriff Denton's militia while my hands were cuffed behind me."

"Liar!" shouted someone in militia colors. Several people hissed.

"I will be the first to stipulate that my friend Ham gets drunk and says stupid things in bars," Joshua added, glancing at Ham, who had the decency to wince. "I've told you what happened. The issue of the stockings has been—explained. How Miss Gardner's hairs came to be in Ham's boat I cannot imagine, but I swear to you that he, and I, did nothing wrong. We two *saved Ms. Gardner's life.* That much is known. The rest is merely what Mr. Denton believes and conjectures and submits and fears. It's his word against ours." Josh looked at the courtroom. "Are we two really so different from you, that you would destroy our lives on nothing better than the sheriff's word?"

"Yes, faggot," said someone from the back.

Deacon Bose banged his gavel for silence. "Have you any further arguments, Mr. Denton? Mr. Cane? No?"

He consulted his notes. "My experience of the law," the deacon said at last, "has been that motive, while fascinating, is largely irrelevant in criminal cases. The physical evidence rarely lies. In the absence of a body, I cannot in good conscience find the defendants guilty of murder beyond a shadow of a doubt. However, I think the evidence warrants a sentence of exile, and that is the penalty I mean to impose."

In the back of the courtroom, Ham's mother and his sister Rachel began to weep.

"The court finds that Joshua Cane and Ham Mather are to be exiled from Galveston," Deacon Bose said. "They are to be set down far from our shores with the supplies mandated in the penal code, and banished henceforth, never to return, on penalty of death."

Part Three

Chapter Eleven

ASYLUM

COLD lightning went through Sloane as Josh told her of her mother's death. The instant he turned to make her tea, she grabbed her mask with shaking fingers and put it on, desperate for the high, blank feeling it brought.

The leather settled over her face and she was back in Mardi Gras. It was dark, and the energy of Carnival hummed and snapped in her veins, holding her up like a kite in a strong breeze. She made her way to Broadway. The big boulevard was full of revellers: jugglers and clowns, sword-swallowers and men who breathed fire. Stiff-legged stilt-walkers strode overhead, cautious as cranes. A woman with the claws and haunches of a cat bounded by on all fours with a dead bird in her mouth. Fireworks burst in the darkness, Roman candles and sparklers and Catherine wheels. Snakes of firecrackers lashed across the ground, crackling like gunshots.

The full moon grinned down at her. She stared back. The moon was so bright it stung her eyes. You lied. You lied, you son of a bitch.

I am Sly, I am Sly, I am the grin and the narrow eyes. The little jingle went around and around in her head as she made her way through the throngs to the Stewart

Beach Amusement Park. The moon burned like a white candle overhead, making the legend over the entrance gleam:

It Just Doesn't Get
Any Better Than This!

A geek in the Wild Boy cage was eating a live frog as she pushed her way past. The frog's legs still hung from his mouth, twitching. She ignored the come-ons of the shrimp-grillers and the hawkers in front of the Pussy Show tent, working her way past the Unicorn Cage and the Genuine Human Maze. She strode up to the manager's office just as Momus stepped out of it. "You lied," she said.

The hunchbacked dwarf looked up. "I never lie." Light from his eyes crept over her like frost, making her skin go cold and stiff. "Your exact words were, *I just can't stand to see her die.* You didn't. Be happy."

"You knew what I meant."

"Yes," Momus said, "I did."

She felt shame catch her again like a blow to the chest, squeezing her heart. If I weren't wearing the mask right now, if I were just Sloane, I would kill myself.

A dog ran by, wild-eyed. Someone had tied a sparkler to its tail. It vanished into the labyrinth of stalls, trailing a spray of white fire and lurching shadows. Momus said, "I am a moralist, in my way. I despise illusion." He took her by the arm. "Walk with me, Stepdaughter. I want to show you something."

Momus steered her around the side of the geek cage to a little alleyway that ran behind one line of exhibits. Where they walked the crowd went quiet and split around them. The god stopped at a small shed. The padlock on the back door fell open at his touch and he waved her inside. A cold white light fell from his blue-veined hands

and his round head, illuminating the interior as if by moonlight. It was a storage room. Props and bits of carnival equipment were jumbled everywhere within: rings for the ringtoss, balls and BBs, bowling pins and tin ducks for the shooting games, wigs and false teeth, spirit gum and lengths of crepe hair the same shade as the Bearded Lady's beard. There were cards and coins and mountebank's cups, collapsible swords and a moth-eaten gorilla suit that stank like a monkey.

Momus gestured at a bowling pin, the kind Sloane had seen people trying to knock over with a baseball at one of the stalls on the fairground outside. "Pick that up."

She did, grunting in surprise. "Wow. These are heavy sons of bitches." Sly swore more than Sloane ever had.

"They ought to be," Momus said. "They're made of lead."

"Lead!"

"Painted white afterward, of course. They look just like regular pins, but they're also wider at the base. It takes a very fine shot indeed to knock over one of these." He ambled over to another shelf and hefted up a jar of marbles. A placard pasted on it read, *Guess How Many and Win Our Grand Prize!* Momus tilted the jar forward. Looking down, Sly saw that there was another smaller empty container inside. The marbles that seemed to fill up the big jar were actually only a thin layer around the outside.

"Another cheat." Sloane felt her face pulling into Sly's sharp grin. "And the unicorn?"

"A goat with a fake horn glued to its head."

"The Bearded Lady?"

"She's a man."

Sloane chuckled. "And the geek? The wild boy I saw eating the 'live' frog?"

"Oh, that's real," Momus said. "He's just hungry."

She laughed out loud. "I thought you said you despised illusion?"

"This is not illusion," Momus said. "I don't lie, not ever. The world is full of lies, if called by other names. Advertisements. Policy platforms. Love poetry. Believe me when I tell you, Stepdaughter, you will never in a long life find a more honest statement than the motto of my kingdom." He tapped the lead bowling pin with a fingernail. "It just doesn't get any better than this. *That* is the cold truth."

"But it's a swindle."

"It's a lecture," Momus countered. He shook the marble jar and listened to it rattle. "It's a monograph, an experiment, a public demonstration of a basic law. Why do you think the sober men of your Krewe and the lunatics in the Krewe of Harlequins both bow to me? You think my carnival is a cheat because it should be fair. But life is not fair. The universe is not fair. The game is rigged. You can win for a time—find love, hope, happiness. But in the long run the house always wins. It *always* wins. That's the truth." He glanced at her and winked. "If you don't believe me, ask your mother. Which reminds me, Stepdaughter—how are you taking dear Jane's death? Bearing up?"

Sloane shrugged. "I want to kill myself," she said.

"Hm. That wasn't what I meant to say at all. I suppose it must be true, though. Can you stop me from feeling that?"

"Of course." Momus padded across the storage room to where she stood, plunged his hand into her chest and pulled out her beating heart. Sloane jerked and dropped like a puppet with her strings cut, smacking the side of her face on the plank floor. Beads rattled and a few pieces of ancient confetti drifted up and settled along with the dust. She lay on the floor, shaking. Momus squatted beside her. They looked at her heart together for a moment, the bloody organ shaking in his palm.

He patted the pockets of his waistcoat. "Now where . . . ? Ah. Here we go." From the hip pocket of his ringmaster's

suit he pulled out a doll. Sloane recognized it immediately. It was herself as a girl, only prettier, wilder, more exotic than she had ever been. Its dress was made of blue velvet, trimmed—more fancifully than Jane Gardner would ever have allowed—with lace from a veil she had lost a year ago. The doll's features were sharper and more beautiful than hers had ever been, and where Sloane's hair was mouse-brown, the doll's was fiery red. Her eyes were made from glinting jade buttons.

Momus stuffed her heart into the doll. "There we go, all tucked away. Doesn't that feel better?"

And it did. For the first time since she had heard of her mother's death, something loosened inside her ribs. She felt lighter inside. Much lighter, as if Momus had pulled an anvil out of her chest. She laughed and pointed at the doll. "Where did you get that?"

"The Recluse made it for me."

"Of course." Odessa must have stolen her veil. "How long ago?"

"A year, at least. We've been watching you, you know."

I'll bet you have. Thoughtfully Sloane touched the mask that fit like a second skin over her face. With her heart gone, she found she could think more clearly. Looking back, Sloane doubted that Odessa had ever really intended for the mask to help her challenge Momus. Surely the witch's purpose had been to give Sloane the power to walk in both Galvestons. And maybe, make her a little more like the daughter Odessa had never had. What had she said? *Jane Gardner isn't the only one who needs a successor, Sloane.*

Momus stuffed the doll back in his pocket. "It's interesting, how different people die. Your mother, now: she froze up, like a stone. But the Recluse: she's wearing through, like a piece of cloth. I talk to her more and more often these days. Right after the Flood she would send folk to Krewes all manner of ways: push them down the

stairs at Stewart Beach, lose them in the Maze, turn them into dogs or fish or brambles. Lately though she just tends to drown 'em, one after another. Hard to stay creative as you age, they say."

"What will happen if Odessa ever dies?"

"When, not if." Momus tapped the rigged bowling pin. "The house always wins, remember?"

"After she dies, then."

"What happens *after*," Momus said. "That's really the only question that matters, isn't it?" He winked. "In this case, your godmother and I finally came to an agreement, though we never could persuade poor Jane. As to what will happen after the witch dies, why, that's partly up to you, my dear. But I will tell you one thing: If there is no angel to stop me, the Harlequins will get all the magic they think they want."

"Fine with me," Sloane said. "I'm not interested in playing witch. Odessa will have to join the long list of people disappointed in me. And you know what? I don't care." Sloane's grin broadened. "Ooh, that felt good. I'll say it again. I don't care. I don't care what happens to you, or her, or me, or the whole rotten little Island." She curtseyed and backed toward the door of the little storage shed. "Thanks. About the heart, I mean."

Momus waved. "A trifle. It's hard on humans, spending time with gods. Bad for the skin," he said, as she backed out into the noise of the fairgrounds. "You might consider that, before seeking me out so freely."

SHE was Sly, wholly Sly, laughing and stumbling through the Carnival. Sly loosed like a hawk on the night.

She wandered the streets of Mardi Gras, completely carefree for the first time in her life. A mad energy sent her dancing through the mansions she knew so well, spinning and careening with gleeful abandon in the Fords' ballroom at Open Gates and the sprung-wood floor at the Bishop's Palace. She found friends in the night, and

champagne in crystal flutes at the Gresham Mansion, and bourbon at the Commodore Bar. She found music and dancing and games of chance, though she did not find Ace again. She lost Sloane and she found Sly. She found men and they found her.

She lost her purse and she lost her shoes. She danced along Seawall Boulevard in her stocking feet until she came to the Balinese Room. Strange sacrifices had been laid at the bottom of Odessa's pier: a bottle of wine, a handful of withered violets, a wreath of snakeskins stretched over a bone frame. A saucer of what Sloane took to be ketchup until she poked her finger in and licked it and the salt taste of congealing blood brought a rush of spit into her mouth.

A tiny, ferret-faced man with pliers and snips and wrenches at his belt came and knelt beside her. His knees as he lowered himself made a sound like sheet metal bending. In front of himself he had placed two car batteries and a pair of jumper cables which he touched together in a jerky rhythm, making sparks arc and gap in the darkness. "What are you doing?" Sly asked.

"Offering for the Lady," he grated. "Got two kids back on the Other Side. Need looking after. Bring the Lady gifts to keep an eye on them for me."

Sly blinked. "I never knew Odessa to take particular care of any family after she sent someone to Krewes. Look at the—" Tranhs, she still couldn't say. Poor Vince, that Sloane had betrayed. The silly bitch.

Sparks arced and jumped in front of the kneeling reveller. Sparks popped and hissed around his tin-colored face. "Have to do something," he said.

"Try drinking," Sloane suggested, backing away from the witch's house. She didn't really need to see Odessa tonight. Or ever again, come to think of it.

She headed back into town to drink. She drank and she drank and she drank. When she'd drunk too much to dance she spent a long, drowsy time of walking up and

down Galveston's streets, exhausted yet buzzing, her limbs twitching, driven forward as if by a clockwork in her back that would never run down. She backed into a doorway and pulled up her skirt and squatted to pee, warm wetness on her stockings. She had lost—it was wonderful—she had lost her ability to be embarrassed, but she had lost her talent for invisibility, too. She had nowhere near enough strength to keep the man in the dog mask from raping her, and the one with the monocle, and the one on stilts, but they couldn't hurt her. Afterward she stumbled down to Stewart Beach and threw herself on the dry sand next to the Seawall, determined to sleep, only to find herself rhythmically rocking, humming, digging little trenches in the sand with her toes, thirsty, dizzy, nauseated, sleepless. Rocking and rocking. Rocking and rocking.

The more of Sloane she lost, the better she felt.

'HEY." Someone shook her shoulder. "Hey!"

She curled more tightly in on herself. She was hard and dark, an undersea thing without feeling, a crab hidden on a beach. The voice was far away and faint, coming from above the water; the shaking was the swell of surf overhead.

The shaking intensified. "Get up, Sly. I ain't about to carry you."

There was sand under her cheek. It smelled of vomit and urine. She curled up tighter.

Two hands hooked under her armpits and pulled her into a sitting position with her back against the Seawall. She slumped over. "G'way!" She turned her head and blinked at the blur in front of her. "Ace?" The cardplayer wavered in and out of focus. "Hey, you old son of a bitch!" She giggled and then retched. "What brings you here?"

He looked at her sourly. "Just lucky, I guess. Can you walk?" She started to laugh and then stopped as he hauled

her upright. Gold and white stars flashed and faded in front of her eyes. Her knees buckled and she sagged in his arms. Ace grunted and straightened her up again. Somewhere in the distance a ragtime band was playing. Fireworks twinkled over the harbor and laughter echoed from a balcony across Seawall Boulevard.

Bit by bit she took her own weight on her legs. She bent over, breathing hard, hands on her knees. Her feet stung and throbbed. "A little support," she said. Ace offered his arm and she clung to it. The reek of her clothes rose up to her, stinking of vomit and urine and wine. "Damn. Ruined another pretty dress."

"I know a place to get you cleaned—uh-oh." A gang of young men in masks pounded down the Seawall steps to the beach, whooping and yelling. "Can you run?" Ace asked quietly.

"Nope. Too tired." Sly turned and grinned at the knot of revellers. Sloane would have tried to run, or cowered in the sand, hoping to remain unseen. Sly's grin grew broader. "Hey, fellas!" she shouted. Her voice was raspy and hoarse. Whoops and cheers greeted her. She picked out one of the leaders, a thin, curly-haired teenager wearing a gold domino mask and a Texas A & M T-shirt. Lost in the Flood before Sloane had even been born. "Hey, handsome!" she said, lurching into him and rubbing her filthy dress against his shirt. She sighed gustily with her vomit-foul breath.

He recoiled. "Beat it, skank."

"Filthy slut."

"Jesus, even my old man would have more pride."

"I got nothing but cold sores down below," Sly promised, rubbing against his thigh. "I don't have nothin' bad. C'mon, baby." Her chosen boyfriend cuffed her and backed away. She fell to her knees on the sand next to Ace. "C'mon, fellas," she said. Somebody spat at her. The revellers backed away, jeering and pretending to puke.

"That was close," Ace said when they were gone.

Sly struggled to her feet. "There's more than one way to skin a cat, as my momma says.—Oops!" She giggled. "Used to say."

Ace led her up to Seawall Boulevard and then turned east. A block down Ship Mechanic Street she let herself get distracted watching the fireworks over the harbor and slashed her foot open on a broken bottle lying in the street. Strangely, although she developed a slight limp, the foot didn't bleed, and she could barely feel the hurt. No heart, she remembered. A great improvement.

Distant Creole music wound through the night. They fell in behind a barbershop quartet on stilts and passed into a neighborhood of dilapidated Victorian houses just west of Big Red, the haunted UT Hospital. The street-lights were smashed, but the glare of the full moon made it easy to see. At 13th Avenue Ace stopped in front of a run-down three story house. The front porch sagged and part of the roof had fallen in. "Why here?" Sly asked.

"Nostalgia." He helped her stagger up the porch steps. "This is where we were living, me and my wife, the night the Flood broke. It was a shared house, seven of us in all. We called it the Asylum. That was funnier before the Flood. Me and Amanda were the only ones who made it through that week. We had it all to ourselves for the next ten years. They say it was bad after the Flood, and it was, but for a while there, with most people dead or gone, those of us who were left had a lot of stuff to choose from."

Sly blinked. "You weren't taken in the Flood?"

"Nope. I'm one lucky son of a bitch, remember?" He pulled open the screen door and tested the wooden one behind. It was unlocked. A musty, moldy smell rushed out of the darkness inside.

"Did the Recluse get you?"

"Sort of. She couldn't if I didn't want her to. I was too lucky," Ace said. "I guess I ended up in Hell pretty

much of my own free will. Which I've come to believe is the way most folks do it." He stood in the doorway for a long moment. "Sly, we need some light. Wait here on the porch." She slid down the wall and sat facing the street. "That's it. I'll be back directly." The porch boards squeaked and shifted as he left.

A mosquito whined around Sly's head, suddenly loud in her ear. The whining stopped and mosquito legs tickled her cheek, but she was too stupefied with tiredness to slap at it. Joke's on you: I've got no heart and no blood to suck, you scheming little bitch. She slid into sleep, grinning at the thought.

HER chin was on her chest and she had a terrible crick in her neck when Ace shook her awake. "Come inside. I've made up a pallet." He helped her to her feet. On a stair just inside the doorway Ace had set a candle. Darkness lapped at the shifting light it threw into the foyer of the ruined house. Shadows clung in the corners as if stuck to the cobwebs there. Banisters ascended into the upper darkness. Across the dusty hallway, a few shapeless hanks of rotten cloth dangled from a coat-and-hat stand. The stink of mold was overwhelming at first but faded gradually as she got used to it. Ace said, "There's a bathroom at the end of the hallway. I put a bucket of water and a bar of soap in there." He handed her a lump of fabric. "Here's a dress to change into."

"Where'd you get this stuff?"

"Spent some more of the money you made me."

The bathroom was awful, a riot of mildew crawling with roaches. They squished and crunched under her feet. She stripped out of her old clothes and put on the ones Ace had brought her, a loose grey blouse, knee-length skirt, and a pair of plain rope sandals. Dreary stuff, but beggars couldn't be choosers. Standing at the sink she washed her face, working a lather out of a ball of rough, clean-smelling soap with flecks of sage in it. She was

careful never to dislodge her mask, running her fingers up under it as gently as possible, inhaling its leathery smell like perfume.

Ace was waiting for her when she came out of the bathroom. "Better," he said. "Reckon you should take the mask off, too?"

"Never again."

He shrugged and led her into the kitchen. A second candle sat on a small table. Boxy pale blurs sat around the edges of the room: refrigerator, no doubt, and a stove, and probably a dishwasher or a microwave oven. He lowered her onto a puffy blue rectangle of plastic beside the table. What? Oh—swimming pool furniture. An inflatable raft. "We had one of these when I was little," Sly said. "I used to float around on it for hours, until my mother had the pool drained."

"Didn't trust the stairs up to the bedrooms. Didn't trust the mattresses either. Too many spiders."

"Yuck." Sly made a face and lay down on the inflatable raft, worried that any sudden pressure might cause the old plastic to burst or leak air. Ace took off his dark jacket and hung it on a chair back, then sat down at the kitchen table and started softly shuffling a pack of cards. He looked frail in his cotton undershirt. His chest was thin, and his round shoulders were beginning to hunch. His face in the flickering candlelight was gaunt and sad with shadows.

"Mister," Sly said at last, "you've lost a lot more than an ear."

"Wait awhile," he said. "You will, too."

Sly turned on her side, facing away from him so the candlelight wouldn't fall in her eyes. The plastic bed felt strangely cool where it touched her jaw, below the line of her mask. It had a strange smell, too: a faint remnant of the clean, artificial odor she always associated with the time before the Flood, so different from the smells of her world. Her Galveston smelled of mildew and steam, hot

cloth and sand. A memory from Sloane's childhood came
to her: sneaking into her mom's dresser drawers and
touching the crinkly plastic packages of panty hose Jane
had started hoarding immediately after the Flood. Every
year at Christmas, Galveston's Grand Duchess would
give one to herself as a present, letting Sloane play with
the cellophane wrapper and touch the stockings themselves, impossibly sheer and fine, like caramel-colored
spiderweb. Sly could still remember the way the muscles
in her mother's calves had bunched as she flexed her feet,
pulling on her panty hose. Disease hadn't yet wasted her
legs to sticks back then.

"Did you ever have any kids?" Sly said lazily.

"One boy." Cards riffled and fell. Ace squared up his
pack and shuffled, squared and shuffled. "When I first
came to Mardi Gras, I thought I'd never go back to the
real Galveston. I had folded my hand there, just like
you."

"Kind of cold for the kid. You didn't even miss him?"

"I lost him to Mandy fair and square, you see? I didn't
deserve him. He was better off without me. Mandy believed that for damn sure, and I guess I did, too. I guess
maybe I still do. But even so . . ." The cards tickered
together in a long waterfall, a dry, rushing sound like the
beating of insect wings. "One day the Prawn Men told
me Amanda had died. My wife, that was."

"I didn't know they could talk."

Ace squared his pack, held it in the middle with a little-
finger break, cut it one-handed and squared it up again.
"You have to be pretty patient."

"I guess you must be."

"Patience is the scar left behind when certain kinds of
hope have burned away." Ace was thin and sharp at the
edges from hunger, and after so many years trapped in a
night that never ended, his skin was waxy white. Paint a
joker on him and stick him in the pack for a spare, Sly
thought, grinning to herself.

Ace cut and shuffled. "Be that as it may. The thought of that boy alone—it ate me up. I decided I ought to go see him. Just observe how he was doing." Ace squared up his pack. "I didn't know any way to get back. I asked Miss Odessa to let me through, but she said her door was never going to swing that way, not if she could help it. So I found the only card in the pack to trump her. I played Momus for passage home. In the end I won, although the betting was heavy and I took some losses." Ace fingered the nubby scars around his ear hole. He smiled with no great humor. "Imagine if I weren't so damn lucky?"

Bugs were coming out of the darkness, drawn by the candle on the kitchen table. Sly watched a moth flutter and whirl around the flame until one of his wings burned and he fell to the table. Love is blind, she thought. "I hope the boy was glad to see you."

"You know, I never did talk to him. Watched him for a while. Followed him," Ace said. He licked his lips. "The way I figured it, he didn't need any more interruptions in his life."

Sly guffawed. "You were chickenshit, you mean. But hell, that was probably the smart thing to do." Sly put on Jane Gardner's tight-lipped, disappointed voice. "Children these days, they're more trouble than they're worth. Always let you down in the end."

"I took a good piece of change over to the parents of a friend of his," Ace said. "Asked them to watch out for him. A good piece of change."

Sly propped herself up on her elbow for a moment to look at the old man. "I guess pride doesn't heal as fast as I thought. You didn't have the decency to speak to your own son face-to-face? Man to man?" Ace's hands had gone still. With a snort, Sly settled back on her pool raft. "Well, good for you. Good riddance."

"I always try to fold my weaker hands," Ace said. "I don't bet more than I can afford to lose. But sooner or

later life deals every man a loss too terrible to accept."
He slid a card under the crippled moth and flicked it off
the table. "Anyone can win, Sly. It's how we lose that
measures us."

Sly laughed. She thought of all the rubes and simple-
tons still milling around Stewart Beach, throwing baseballs at lead bowling pins and shooting at tin ducks with
defective BB guns. "Sell philosophy to some other
sucker, old man."

Ace held his pack. After a moment he began to deal,
six hands of Texas Hold 'Em. Cards clicked and slid
against the tabletop, steady as rain falling. "Go to sleep,"
he said.

WHEN she had rested up enough, Ace taught her to play
poker. She sat across the kitchen table from him, studying
the cards by candlelight.

"Stay aggressive, that's rule number one." He laid out
three cards, ace and seven in the hole, another ace showing. "Your amateur calls on this hand, hoping to lure as
many people into the game as he can to fatten the pot.
Trouble is, the more people you have in the game, the
weaker those aces are. Say you're sitting over there with
a four-five-six. I let you drift along without paying for
the privilege, then by the time we come to the River, you
draw out on me."

"The River?"

"The last card down." Ace dealt out one complete hand
for seven-card stud. "Two cards go in the hole. Then
Third Street. Fourth street, also called the Turn, because
after Fourth Street bets double. Fifth Street. Sixth Street."
He laid the last card facedown. "The River."

"Where did that come from?"

"Never stopped to think about it." Ace turned up the
down card. "Styx, maybe. Lethe. The rivers of Hell. You
wouldn't know any of this stuff, you never went to
school."

"It's very annoying to be constantly told how ignorant you are by a generation of people who can't ride a horse or live without air-conditioning."

Ace laughed. "You know I can remember saying the exact same thing to my mother once, only it was 'can't program a VCR.' " He went back to the hand he had put down first, ace-seven-ace. "So if you're holding that ace-seven-ace, the right play is . . . ?"

"Raise. Drive out the drawing hands."

"Good. And the same goes for you. When you see an ace door card raise, respect the aces and throw away your cards. Don't play from behind." He gathered the cards up and squared them on the tabletop. "Winners throw their bad cards away. Losers stay in on hope. Hope is a sin, and you must punish it severely."

"All right." Sly laughed. "You don't have to get so excited."

"It's important." Ace dealt out six new hands up to Third Street. "Dealer shows paint, next is a rag, another rag. You've got a suicide king,"—the king of Hearts: for the first time Sly noticed that he seemed to be sticking his sword through his own head—"rag to your left, ten for the door card at the last position."

Sly looked at the hole cards in front of her: a four of diamonds and a six of clubs. Useless. What Ace would call "rags." "How do you bet?" he said.

(A brief unpleasant bubble of Sloane's memory drifted up, the taste of her mother's mouth as she tried to give her artificial respiration. Jane Gardner's strong eyes terribly frightened. The arms that had held Sloane as a baby hung useless at her sides. Jane Gardner at the River.)

"Sly? How do you bet?"

"I fold," Sly said. Letting the high, blank energy of the mask fill her and lift her up again.

AFTER what seemed like weeks of practicing he sent her out to play in a $5–$10 game. She went in with a two-

hundred-dollar bankroll, made one hundred forty more on a run of good hands, then lost sixty of it back and cashed her chips.

"You should have quit sooner," Ace said, when she returned to Asylum. "Once you win thirty times the minimum bet, make a note to yourself to quit if you slip back to twenty times minimum. That's a money-management thing. We called it a 'stop-loss,' back when I was going to be a stockbroker. I should have told you that."

Sly rubbed her face through the thin leather of the mask. "Sorry."

"You were getting tired, probably. Don't stay at the table once that happens. I boiled some water if you're thirsty."

Sly picked the candle off the kitchen table and looked through the cabinets over the sink, picking out a dusty mug with *You might consider thanking your lucky stars you were born in TEXAS!* on the side. The water was in a pot on the stove. "Hey. You cleaned the burners. And the counter. And the sink."

"And the window over the sink," Ace said.

Sly cocked an eyebrow. "Nesting?"

"Bored," Ace said. But he didn't meet her eye.

"If this is for me—"

"No payout required," he said. He looked at her square. "Nor wanted."

Sly leaned back against the stove, letting her dress ride up a little on her leg. "You might hurt a girl's feelings."

Ace said, "Sly, that's one hand I folded a long time ago."

THE next day she went back to the $5–$10 game in the Pullman car behind the Railroad Museum. Ace made her take his revolver, in case the game got ugly or the players lecherous. She played for a short time and lost. Ace was sweeping the foyer of the Asylum when she returned. "The Rake's in the game," she said. "He raises every-

thing. I kept folding out; only made it to the River two times. The first time he had the cards. The second I was sure I was over him, but a third player drew out for a flush."

Ace nodded and resumed sweeping. "Bad luck. Your instincts were basically right." Clouds of dust billowed around him, making Sly cough and sneeze. "Anyone who fast-plays all the time we call the Animal. This is one time you don't have to control the table. Throw in your rags, and be ready to make big money on your monster hands. With him, you drift. Let the Animal build the pot for you. With him at the table you can easily disguise a monster hand without worrying about giving anyone else a free card to draw out on you. The Animal does the taxing for you."

"Okay. I got it."

Ace pushed the screen door open and swept a cloud of filth onto the porch, and then down the steps into the yard. Sly lounged in the doorway, watching him. "You can't see dirt in the dark, Ace."

He returned to the porch and stood a moment with his hands on the broom handle, regarding her. "I keep trying to put *you* on a hand, Sly. There's paint for sure, you've had money and you've had some good life. You walk into the manager's office and Momus lets you go again. You're holding some cards, all right, but damned if I can figure what they are."

Pair of queens in the hole, dear—Jane Gardner and Odessa Gibbons. "Do you like this smile?" she said, grinning. "That's my poker face."

"You're learning," Ace said.

She went back to the $5 and $10 game. This time she won and won steadily, finishing seven hundred and twenty-five dollars up. She was high and clear, laughing and calculating at the same time.

She learned a new way of being invisible that Sloane had never thought about. It involved using her smile and

her breasts and her laughter as a screen, her mind slipping out to do its work unnoticed while all eyes attended to her body. Dietrich Bix, the Harlequin, had shown her a couple of magic tricks once, pulling nickels from her ears or making shells disappear, and they had all operated on the same principle. It was never the hand making the big gesture that worked the magic; it was the sly one, unnoticed, that did the stealing.

She picked up a bottle of wine and returned to Asylum in high good humor, humming and swaggering with the weight of Ace's revolver on her hip. She sat the older man down at the kitchen table, regaled him with war stories, and fished two hundred fifty dollars out of her purse. "One half of five hundred dollars! Not bad for a morning dusting the lintels or whatever you did, eh?" She brandished her bottle of wine. "Have a drink!"

Ace folded up the money and put it in his pants pocket. "No thanks."

"Come on! I want to celebrate! Next time I can move up to a bigger game, don't you think?"

"Maybe. You decide." He pulled on his worn black preacher's jacket. "I have a game of my own to go to."

"Good God, you've cleaned the whole first floor. How bored can one man be? What do you mean you have a game to go to? I thought you had been banned from every game in town."

"Every game but one." Ace slipped a pack of cards into the breast pocket of his jacket.

Sly blinked. "Momus?"

"You were right about me being a coward that first time I went back. I should have faced up to him." Half to himself, Ace said, "It's how we lose that counts. Keep the gun," he added. "I won't need it."

"Ace!" She grabbed him by the arm, which she had never done before. He had always been very scrupulous to make sure they did not touch. "You want to go back

to Galveston? Why? You threw in those cards, remember? What are you trying to do?"

He lifted her fingers gently off his arm. "Making my best five-card hand."

SHE found a $15–$30 game Ace had told her about. As he had warned, the players were much more aggressive, raising and reraising at a pace that put tremendous pressure on her bankroll. Sly played very tight at first, folding anything less than a premium pair on Third Street, watching the other players carefully to study their tendencies and the flow of the game. Ace had told her that the more competitive the game, the worse the winning hands were likely to be, and he was right. Nobody was allowed to limp along in the hopes of drawing out on Sixth Street or the River. Instead she saw more than one showdown won by a pair of jacks over rags ace high.

In time she began to play more actively, stealing one pot on Third Street with an ace door card and a quick raise-reraise. She won another hand on pure luck, kings in the hole with a jack at the door that filled out to a full house by Sixth Street, where she checked for the first time, appearing to waver to her opponent's probable trip queens. She brought the hammer back at the River, taking the table for nearly fourteen hundred dollars. Then she stayed in one hand too long and lost most of it back.

She finished three hundred dollars ahead and went barhopping. She picked up a handsome fellow with snake scales all over his skin, had a great time flirting and then cooled him off with a game of dares. On her turn she straightened out a safety pin and pushed it through her palm until the tip broke out the back of her hand. There was no blood, of course, and it barely hurt. She grinned at Snake and passed the pin over, watching the bulge in his pants wilt. He begged off the dare, to the derision of his buddies. She laughed until there were tears in her eyes.

On a whim she left the bar and wandered by Ashton Villa. It was her mother's house, and yet it wasn't. No roosters strutted behind this mansion, no pigs either, and the party going on inside was far more lavish and deca- dent than anything Jane Gardner would have counte- nanced. Looking up to her bedroom window on the third floor, Sly saw a woman staring out at her. It was Miss Bettie. As she watched, the old ghost tapped her wrist where a watch might have been, like a woman asking to be told the time.

Sly turned and hurried away.

SHE found Ace in the kitchen when she got home. He was leaning over the sink, holding a damp towel to the left side of his face. "You're back!" she said. "Are you hurt?"

"Lost my eye," he said. Red stains flowered slowly on his towel.

"I told you it was stupid to play Momus."

"On the first hand I put him on two pair and took him to the River on trip tens, but he drew out a diamond flush." Ace looked at her. "You're Sloane Gardner," he said.

She froze.

"In case you wondered," Ace went on, "you've got a tell when you're trying to think up a lie. Your mouth comes open and the tip of your tongue just touches your top lip. I can read you well enough, Sly. Sloane, I should say."

If I had a heart, it would be racing, she thought. It was crazy, childish really, how strongly she didn't want him to know she had once been Sloane Gardner. Didn't want anybody to know. She licked her lips and smiled. "That was a long time ago. It doesn't matter now."

Ace turned to face her, the bloody towel still held up to his ruined left eye. "Yes, it does. The city is all upset, Sly. Jane Gardner's dead. And Sloane Gardner, that

lovely, gentle girl, Sloane's been murdered. That's what they think." He grimaced. "Goddamn, this hurts." He poured steaming water from a pot on the stove onto his towel, wrung it out, and then slapped the hot cloth back onto his eye socket. "It wouldn't matter to me, Sly, only it's my boy they think killed you." `

"Your son?" Sly said, blinking.

"They put him on a boat last night and set off to maroon him. Headed up Beaumont way." Ace shrugged. "Josh and Amanda never had an ounce of luck after she left me. There was a day I was glad of that, but not now. Not for a long time. I would have given them every break I ever got, ten cents on the dollar."

"Joshua?" Sly said. "Joshua Cane! The apothecary." She laughed shakily. "And you must be Samuel Cane, the one who lost his house to Travis Denton. And the friends you gave money to, to look after your boy—that would have been Ham's family."

"Jim and Alice Mather. Real dependable folk. But not Joshua's family," Ace said. "I'm the only real family he has left."

"Goddamn," Sly said. "What a fix."

Red dribbles from the towel were staining Ace's undershirt. "Of course it's too late for Amanda now. But my boy's going to die if you don't get back and straighten things out."

"I'm sorry, Ace, but no." For once Sly's smile was nervous. "I'd do anything for you, you know that. Well, not anything. Quite a lot. But not this. I'm not going back. I like it here. I belong here."

"He'll die."

"So will I if I go back." Sly took out her winnings. With her left hand she heaped them on the table. Her right hand crept toward the .32 holstered at her hip. "Take the money. I'll keep a hundred for a stake. Well, two hundred. The rest is yours."

"Take off the mask, Sly."

"No!"

She had just gotten her hand on the butt of the revolver when he tackled her around the waist and drove her back over the kitchen table. She twisted furiously underneath him, trying to get her gun hand free. He grabbed for her mask, and she screamed and turned sideways and pulled the trigger of the .32. It bucked and roared, blowing out the bottom of its holster. A burst of fire ripped along the length of her leg, and their bodies crashed off the table together—

Chapter Twelve

SCARLET

SUDDENLY Ace wasn't there anymore and Sloane was falling to the floor of a ruined house in Galveston, the real Galveston where she had left her mother to die.

She wasn't Sly anymore. The mask was gone. Ace had it, back in the Mardi Gras.

She hit the floor and lay there, gasping. This house was very different from its double in the Mardi Gras. In Mardi Gras it smelled of mildew and the walls sagged, gone blowsy in the humid years, but it was still a house. Here Samuel Cane's home had been blown apart by a gas line explosion two weeks after he lost it to Travis Denton in a game of cards. Grey daylight poured in through broken windows and a giant rip in the smoke-blackened ceiling. Splintered rafters poked at the sky like shattered ribs. Sprigs of withered tansy and sea purslane grew up through the broken floor. Where the kitchen counters should have been there was only charred wreckage: burned boards and chunks of drywall, bits of glass and plaster, flecks of metal paint, blackened pieces of crockery. A ceiling fan blade, split and charred.

Sloane lay on the floor, waiting to be torn apart by guilt. She had abandoned her mother, and her mother had

died. And yet, when the grief and guilt came she could feel them only faintly and far away, like bugs bumping against the glass windows of Ashton Villa.

There was a tang of gunpowder in the air. Sloane looked down. She still held the .32. The bullet had blown out the bottom of its holster and left a burn line along her leg. She could barely feel it. She had no heart. That was it. Momus had taken out her heart.

She crawled across the floor to a pile of rubble and found a broken drinking glass and slashed her wrists with it. The glass bit and ripped through her skin, exposing the pink meat underneath, but she had no heart and no blood would come. Sloane dropped the glass.

Okay. Next plan. Well, she supposed she ought to put things right for Joshua Cane. She owed that much to Ace. Lucky for him.

But then, he was the luckiest man in Galveston, wasn't he? So everybody had always said. But what, exactly, did that mean? How could the luckiest man in Galveston, one stroke of fortunate chance at a time, come to be wifeless, childless, wordless, alone? Was his luck so shortsighted? Or maybe there were things Sloane didn't know, aspects of his story hidden from her, or even Ace himself. Maybe all his alternatives were worse. Could Joshua's exile somehow be part of Ace's good fortune? And if so, had it really been chance that Sloane had met Josh in the first place? Maybe the two men who attacked her as she stumbled out of the Mardi Gras had been merely the agents of Ace's luck. Or Momus's cunning. Maybe the whole web of events in which she was trapped was part of a sinister pattern that she would never understand.

Or maybe life was the best poker player of all. Win or lose, Fate never shows her cards, Sloane thought. You can never bluff her, never put her on a hand. All you can do is pick up each new card and form your best hand and play, and play, and play, until Fate takes your last chip and sends you from the table.

• • •

IT was hard to move in the real Galveston, as if the press of gravity was much greater. It was hot, too. In the endless night of Mardi Gras she had forgotten how hot the day could be. Sloane stirred, picking through the rubble until she could find a moldering stick of charred two-by-four. She rubbed her fingers over it until they were black. Then she marked her face: one long line above each eyebrow, turning up; one merry tilt at the corner of each eye. One high line on each cheek, marking the edge of Sly's fine, sharp bones.

Her mother's ghost whirred somewhere in the room, a distant mosquito. Unable to get to her.

It was nigh on noon when she stumbled out of the ruins of Ace's house. The sun was painfully bright. She felt it pushing on her, a dull ache of heat that beat in waves against the Island. There were no clouds; the sun had burned them and smeared them into a high white ash in the blank sky. Withered palm fronds rasped against her ankles as she walked home. The asphalt road burned her feet, but she did not notice it. Galveston's streets were empty. Everyone hiding from the sun. Rich folks' windows were shut tight to keep the air-conditioning in. Poor folks had their windows wide open in hope of a breeze. We fear Momus because he has a face, Sloane thought, but this is Texas, and the sun will always be more deadly than the moon.

She wondered how long she had been idling in the Mardi Gras. Days? Weeks? *Wasting time.* She circled the words like a moth around a candle flame. Time wasting, as her mother's limbs had wasted—time ebbing and dwindling, losing hope, wearing out.

Lost time. Time wandering, rootless, abandoned. The memories of her stay in Mardi Gras disappeared, draining away from her like raindrops vanishing into parched earth. Time lost that could never be recovered. Days gone that could never be made good.

I should have kept that watch.

A young Mexican came hurrying up from a side street, saw her, and stopped. He kissed his trembling fingers, made the sign of the cross, and backed away from her, one slow step at a time, as if she were a rattlesnake hissing in the dust. Sloane stared dumbly after him. Finally she thought to look down at herself. She was wearing one of Sly's dresses, a gold lamé number that was ripped at the shoulder, splotched with soot and singed at the hip where she had fired Ace's gun. I'll be damned. That boy thinks I'm a reveller. Sloane nearly smiled. Which I suppose I am.

She forced herself up to Broadway. A little farther and she would come to Ashton Villa. No, not a good idea. She couldn't face her mother's house, not yet. The Ford place, perhaps? Jim would help. Jim would try to set things right. A brewer's cart came rumbling slowly down the road, drawn by a brace of weary quarter horses. Sweat sparkled on their necks. She watched the horses rumble by, iron-shod hooves flashing and falling, the big cart wheels creaking and crunching along the road behind. She caught herself timing a suicide jump in front of them.

Oh, no you don't, my girl. She grabbed on to a streetlight to keep herself close to the curb. Not yet. Not so easy as that.

She continued along Broadway until she turned up the walk to the Ford place and knocked on the big front door. Like the double doors at Ashton Villa, it was made of cured cypress, the only wood that wouldn't rot away under the subtropical sun. Gloria opened the door. Sloane noted automatically that she was wearing one of Clara Ford's dresses, tailored to fit and with print hemwork liberally added. Probably enough to keep Jim from recognizing it as something that had belonged to his dead first wife; he never was too observant about that kind of thing. "God almighty!" Gloria said. Her eyes narrowed and she crossed her arms in front of her chest. "Is you a ghost?"

"No, ma'am. It's me, Sloane."

Gloria reached out and pinched her on the arm, hard. "Ow," Sloane said, knowing it was expected.

"Hunh. Well, I suppose it is you." Gloria shook her head. "Leastwise what's left of you. Come on in, girl, and set down. You look like what the cat drug in."

Two hours later Sloane was sitting by Jim Ford in his large carriage, facing forward. Sheriff Denton sat across from them. Deputy Lanier was up on the box, driving. From time to time Sloane could hear him gee up the horses, swishing the traces across their shoulders with a light smack.

It was late afternoon and fiercely hot, even with the white canvas canopy up. They were driving along the Seawall road toward the Balinese Room, but for once no breeze came off the Gulf to cool them. The sea lay flat, a dull green mirror glinting back flashes of the Texas sun. Now there were clouds, though, tall banks of them far to the southeast, the same gunmetal green as the sea. Jim's horses clopped steadily along. The carriage creaked and swayed, jerking over cracks in the pavement, big wheels grinding through the litter of broken shells on Seawall Boulevard.

It had been six days since Jane Gardner had died, Jim Ford said. Four since they had buried her. Three since Josh had told her of her death. Here in the real world three days had passed while in the Mardi Gras, where time ran strangely, Sly had left Sloane for dead, only to have Sam Cane resurrect her. Damn him.

Sloane had told Jim about the mask, told him that she had been escaping into the Mardi Gras and that her disappearance had nothing to do with Joshua Cane. Now they were all going to see the Recluse. Sheriff Denton said he needed to know why she hadn't come forward to support Joshua's story.

"Did you ever know Sam Cane?" Jim asked the sheriff.

Sweat had beaded up like dew on his bald head. "Joshua Cane's daddy. Used to play cards with me every Saturday. The boy would bring Gloria a pill for her arthritis. Good kid, back then. Now he's got a chip on his shoulder the size of a brick. Something changed him."

Poverty, Jim? Disappointment? Bitterness? Death? Sloane didn't say anything.

"I knew Travis Denton," the sheriff said.

"Of course. Of course you did. Terrible tragedy."

Sloane looked around the carriage. The bench was upholstered in cream-colored velour. Years of wear had made the color uneven: palest in the two spots where Jim and his wife had sat most often, and in the middle where the most sun had fallen; darker close to the sides, where the doors provided steady shadow. When Sloane was only a very small child, three or four at the oldest, she had noticed that sometimes it was simpler to observe the world than it was to be part of it. Sometimes, when you couldn't leave a bad place, you could escape it by turning into a watcher, a lizard on the wall. Mute as a shell on the beach.

Jim Ford tried again. "Sloane says she went into the boy's shop to get something for a cut on her leg. Says she left her stockings there on purpose, on account of they were all torn up."

"Wish we'd heard that sooner," the sheriff said.

"Yep." Jim shook his head sympathetically. Out over the Gulf, a glint of heat lightning sparkled over the distant cloud bank. "Wonder if there might be a drop of rain over yonder."

"Hope so," said the sheriff. He pulled out his pocket watch and checked the time. Sun winked on the crystal face. He frowned and tucked it back in his vest pocket.

Jim said, "It's a funny thing about that hair of Sloane's you found in Ham Mather's boat. Sloane says she was never in a boat."

"That she remembers," the sheriff said. "You told me

yourself she couldn't remember much that happened while she was"—he glanced back toward Stewart Beach—"over there."

Sloane was looking at her shoes. They were grey canvas shoes with rubber soles cut down from a tire. Gloria had sent a maid over to Ashton Villa to get Sloane a change of clothes. For the first time in what seemed like forever she was dressed the way she ought to be: neat white blouse and white cotton jacket to hide the sweat stains under her armpits, plain grey skirt that came a hand's span below her knees, covering the powder burns on her right leg. She wore no panty hose or stockings. The sun was slanting in from the west side of the carriage, laying a strip of light across Sloane's leg. She looked at the fine, fine hairs, gold spider-silk threads lying on her tanned legs.

"There may be many things the young lady does not remember," Sheriff Denton said.

"Maybe." Jim nodded, watching the cloud bank for more signs of lightning. "It's not impossible," he said.

They came to the Balinese Room. Kyle tied the horses to a rust-eaten street sign. When Sloane had been a little girl the sign had read "No Parking 12:00 A.M.–5:00 A.M."—but salt spray and windblown sand had scoured the writing off. Sloane got out of the carriage, feeling light-headed from the heat.

Sheriff Denton and Deputy Lanier started across the pier. Jim Ford offered Sloane his arm and they followed. Wood planks bleached dull silver by the remorseless sun creaked under their feet. They passed the guard hut, Sheriff Denton solemn and frowning like the Law. Sloane felt one of Sly's grins cross her face as she imagined a Maceo sentry pushing the hidden buzzer: inside, the band striking up "The Eyes of Texas Are Upon You," Chinese cooks playing deadpan and clogging the restaurant, while back in the casino roulette wheels and blackjack tables folded up into the wall.

Sheriff Denton pulled the front door open for his deputy. Sloane watched the gloom swallow them both. She caught Jim Ford looking at her. "You appear to be cheering up," he remarked.

Her mouth quirked in a small smile. "Odessa likes *me*," she said.

GALVESTON'S witch was sitting at her workbench. "Hello, Sheriff," she said without looking up. "Deputy Lanier. And Jim—always a pleasure."

They picked their way through the dim dining room. What light there was came obliquely through the north windows, raising a few gleams from the dusty silverware and the brightly painted Krewe altars on the raised bandstand. Jim and Jeremiah gave the altars as wide a berth as possible, but Kyle Lanier seemed unconcerned, passing directly in front of the bandstand and stopping to slouch against the back of the Harlequins' black-and-white checked altar with the mad clown puppet on top.

Hanging over the workbench was the wreath of snakeskins Sloane had seen placed as a sacrifice outside Odessa's house in the other Galveston. By daylight she could see them better. Water moccasins, mostly, with maybe a copperhead mixed in, on a frame made of what Sloane hoped were deer bones, forelegs and a few ribs. She wondered if the witch had just liked the way the wreath looked, or if it was a sacrifice she had accepted. Maybe she had been doing good works all these years, too, warding some from sickness or bad luck, watching over the families she had broken when she sent some gifted child or magically susceptible father into the moonlit Mardi Gras.

The sheriff took off his straw hat and turned it between his hands. "We have some questions we need answered, Ms. Gibbons."

For the first time Odessa looked around at them. She was wearing a silk kimono with birds of paradise printed

on it. Her lips and nails were bright pre-Flood red, and her foundation was immaculate. Sloane could smell the Revlon AquaNet that kept her hair perfectly in place. In her hand she was holding a Sheriff Denton doll the length of her forearm. It was wearing a black suit and tiny straw hat. Its eyes were made from pale blue chips of shell, its cheeks and jaw covered by a neatly trimmed grey beard of real human hair. A silver star was pinned to its little stuffed chest. "Yes, Jeremiah?"

Kyle fumbled for the gun at his side. "You set that down right now."

Odessa said, "I wouldn't threaten me, little boy."

"The hell—"

"Get your hand off your gun," Jim Ford said.

Kyle looked at Jeremiah Denton. The sheriff nodded. "Settle down, Kyle. Jim and Ms. Gibbons and me, we go back a while."

Odessa rose and came over to give Sloane a hug. "Are you okay, sugar?" she said softly. Sloane nodded. Behind her back, still trapped in Odessa's hand, the Sheriff Denton doll tugged feebly at Sloane's cotton jacket. Odessa let Sloane go. "Jeremiah, Jim—can I get you boys something to drink? I have Coke and Dr Pepper, rice wine and a few other spirits. Ice, too, which I hear is getting scarce."

"Ms. Gibbons," Sheriff Denton said quietly, "what are you doing with that doll?"

The Recluse regarded him. "My duty," she said.

Jim Ford faked a cough. "Goddamn. I could use a scotch and water if you've got it, Odessa."

"Jeremiah?" The sheriff doll wriggled weakly in Odessa's hand. She ignored it.

Sloane could see hairs lifting on Sheriff Denton's wrists. He couldn't take his eyes off the doll. "I don't want any of your drink."

"Suit yourself. Jim, I believe I'll join you." Odessa

turned and headed for the kitchen. "Y'all just talk amongst yourselves for a spell."

"Much obliged," Jim said.

"She's gonna bolt," Kyle said. He shouldered through the swinging door into the kitchen. The rest of them followed. Odessa was standing in front of her refrigerator, getting ice from the dispenser in the freezer. The Sheriff Denton doll lay on the counter next to two shot glasses, each of which contained a fat finger of bourbon. A big pot simmered on the stove, sending up coils of fetid steam, as if she were boiling seawater with the kelp and crabs still in it. The trapdoor in the kitchen floor was open; through it Sloane could see the dull green water, beginning to show a little swell now. A white wing flashed by as a gull swooped underneath the pier.

Odessa finished gathering a handful of ice and closed the freezer. A puff of cold air washed over them all. Sheriff Denton cleared his throat. "Ms. Gibbons, there's two young men been exiled when we couldn't find Ms. Gardner here. You said you didn't know anything about her disappearance. If you'd told about the mask, those boys might still be on the Island."

Odessa put ice in each of her glasses and handed one to Jim Ford. "Sheriff, making that mask was something done in confidence between Sloane and myself. How was I to guess you would make a damn fool of yourself and convict two innocent men?"

"You have a lot of mouth on you for an old lady," Kyle said, drawing his gun.

"Put it back, for God's sake!" Jim Ford said. But this time Sheriff Denton did not speak, and his hand was on the grip of his .38.

Kyle kept his gun out. "Power corrupts, I hear tell. I think you've gotten used to slinking out here, doing whatever you want."

"This is Galveston's only angel, for pity's sake!"

Kyle's lips pulled back enough to show his two gold-

capped teeth. "Funny, ain't it, Mr. Ford? If anyone else shows a bit of magic, they don't last long, do they? Gone to Krewes. The Recluse gets 'em. Some of us youngsters, we can't figure why we don't make us a few more angels. If one's so great, why not let a few more of 'em live? But she never does. Do you, Miss Gibbons? I'm going to take that doll of Mr. Denton now." He stepped carefully around the trapdoor. "Nobody ever voted for you, old lady."

Odessa said, "Boy, someone needs to learn you some manners." She quickly moved to the center of the room and held the Sheriff Denton doll poised over the open trapdoor.

A gun crashed like a blast of thunder and a bullet tore out Odessa's throat. The air was suddenly red with her blood, and her head fell impossibly on one side. Her body dropped like a heap of rags, blood spurting in horrible jets from the stump of her neck. She still clutched the sheriff doll in her hand. It wiggled and strained, turning its face as streamers of blood slapped against its cotton cheeks.

Only then did Sloane realize it was Sheriff Denton who had fired the shot. "I'm sorry," he whispered. He dropped his .38. His hand was shaking. "I had no choice. You saw what she was going to do. She was going to drop me down the hole. You all saw it." He swallowed. "I had no choice."

The blood stopped coming. Odessa's body went still. Sloane looked at the old witch, lying in a bloody heap in her beautiful kitchen. No more than a doll herself now. A few bits of bone and twists of rag. A silk robe. Some costume jewelry.

House wins again.

Goodbye, 'Dessa.

"SLOANE?" Sloane heard Jim Ford's voice dimly, as if from a long way off. Ever since falling back from the

Mardi Gras, she had been numb. Now she felt deaf as well, as if the crash of Sheriff Denton's gun had blotted out other sounds. Deep inside her, Odessa's ghost joined the ghost of her mother, the two of them drawn to her as if sensing her heat, whining and whirring, finding no purchase. She was glass. She was untouchable.

"Sloane, we need a blanket to put over her."

Sloane rose shakily to her feet and headed for the door which led back to Odessa's bedroom.

"Reckon I'll tag along," Kyle said.

Sloane looked at him. "Haven't you done enough?"

Kyle held the door open and waved her through with a grin and a flourish. "Just my duty, Ms. Gardner. Just my duty."

It had been years since Sloane had been in Odessa's bedroom. It had changed. She remembered it as quilts and dolls and knickknacks, a vanity and a big box of makeup and bottles of hair spray. Now sea and wind and light had spilled through it, washing the human things away. Dried seaweed lay in strands across the floor and furniture. The shutters were open and the mosquito netting around Odessa's brass bed hung in ribbons, twisting and fluttering in the Gulf breeze. Instead of sheets, her mattress was covered with a layer of cracked white shells. Here and there Sloane could see a sand dollar or a dried anemone. Two pink jellyfish lay where the pillows should have been. It was as if all these years Odessa had been holding back not only magic, but the Gulf itself, and it had worn her down at last.

A fragment of memory bobbed up, a younger Odessa, confident and matter-of-fact as she stuffed Vinny Tranh's doll into the Krewe of Thalassar's shrine. *When someone springs a leak, you see, it can't easily be patched.*

Something rustled in Odessa's walk-in closet. Kyle pulled out his gun and walked warily toward it. He laid his hand lightly on the doorknob and then jerked it open and stood quivering in the entrance with his .38 at the

ready. Sloane held her breath. Nothing moved. Kyle edged forward into the dim closet. "Hm. Maybe it was just a rat. Wait a min—ow!"

A little girl with fiery red ringlets scrambled out into the room, raced around Odessa's bed, and ran smack into Sloane—and it *hurt.* Sloane had a jumbled impression of flying hair, patent-leather shoes, and a scrap of blue veil. It's the doll! she thought. The doll with her heart inside.

Then grief and the ground hit her at the same moment and she shattered with the pain.

SLOANE and her mother and 'Dessa are having a picnic on the beach. Sloane is in 'Dessa's lap while Jane struggles with the Gulf breeze, trying to spread a white linen tablecloth on the sand. She reaches into a picnic basket and carefully pulls out a platter with a birthday cake on it. She sets the cake flat on one corner of the tablecloth, holding down another corner with her hand. Odessa laughs at her, and Jane looks up with a mock growl.

"Why didn't Sarah come?" Sloane whines.

"This is a special treat just for us," Jane says. "Honey, can you sit here and hold down this cloth?" Her hair isn't white yet, it's still long and brown. The breeze makes it into ribbons.

Sloane clings to Odessa's lap. "Don't you like Sarah?"

"Of course I like Sarah, but she's a servant. Odessa, can you lean over and get the silver out of that basket?"

"I like Sarah. She doesn't work all the time. *She* was at my real birthday party," Sloane says sullenly. She is rewarded by seeing her mother flinch. Jane drops her eyes, and her shoulders sag.

Now, reliving the instant, Sloane would give anything to take back that little burst of spite. But of course she can't. Her mother and Odessa have both gone where she can't rescue them, across the River, where not even the

smallest of her little cruelties and betrayals can be re-
deemed.

And it just doesn't—it can't ever, ever, ever—get any
better than this.

SLOANE fell to her knees, grabbing the doll. It was as if
the little girl had somehow slammed into a bruise Sloane
didn't know she had, one carried in her core, deep inside
the circle of her ribs. She gasped at the shock of feeling
again.

I can't be here. This is too much. I can't stand it. I
can't be here.

"Let me go!" the doll hissed, struggling and kicking.
She jabbed at Sloane and just missed skewering her with
something—a long hairpin. Sloane could remember losing it a year ago.

"That little brat drew blood," Kyle said, hobbling out
of the closet and rubbing his knee.

The doll bucked and twisted like a mad cat in Sloane's
hands. "I want to see Aunt Odessa!"

"You're an hour late and a bullet short. Stop fussing."
The girl answered with a yell and a kick. Kyle slapped
the child hard across the back of the head. She grunted
and went still. "That's better," Kyle said.

The doll with Sloane's heart inside was white and
shaking, but instead of crying she turned and eyed Kyle
with white hate. "My grandfather is going to get you for
that."

"Tell him to take a number." Kyle grimaced, rubbing
at his knee again. "Where the hell did you come from?"

The doll acted and spoke like a child of eight or nine,
but she was no bigger than a four-year-old, with very fine
bones, wiry muscles, and the heft of a big cat. "My
grandfather left me to stay with Aunt Odessa this afternoon. He has a very busy day today."

"What granddaddy would that be?"

Sloane squeezed the little girl's arms and willed her to lie, but she didn't. "Momus," the doll said contemptuously.

As Jane fusses with the birthday picnic, Odessa is looking out to sea, watching the chuckleheaded pelicans flap low across the wave tops and then land in their comical way, sticking their long beaks suddenly into the surf and falling over them. She grins. "Fifty million years of evolution for that?"

Sloane is studying a piece of birthday cake. The Grand Duchess of the Krewe of Momus watches nervously as she takes a bite. It's a pecan pound cake, crumbly and dry, not nearly as nice as something Sarah or Odessa would make. Sloane reckons her mother has tried to substitute rice flour from an old recipe without knowing to use extra eggs or syrup to hold the cake together. "Do you like it, honey?" Jane says.

Odessa looks for all the world to be entirely fascinated by the pelicans—but as Sloane opens her mouth to speak, her godmother's fingernails gouge sharply into her back, completely hidden from Jane's view. Sloane suppresses a shriek. "Great!" she squeaks in a spray of crumbs.

Sloane can tell her mother wants to believe her but can't quite manage it. "Really?"

More gouging. "Really, really great." Sloane's imagination stalls. She wipes her mouth with the back of her hand and forces herself to swallow the mouthful of dessicated pecan cake. "Um. Can I have something to drink, please?"

As Jane reaches for the Thermos, Odessa tickles Sloane in the ribs. The girl shrieks and thrashes, mussing the tablecloth until there's sand everywhere, laughing and laughing. Her mother smiles awkwardly and looks on, not quite sure how to join in. Then, disaster—Odessa gasps. "Oh, Jane! Honey, I knocked over your beautiful cake!" She abandons Sloane and fusses over the fallen

cake, trying in vain to blow the sand off it. She looks ridiculous, with her bum waggling high in the air, blowing like she's trying to stoke a fire, and pretty soon the frown that had started to form on Jane's face breaks into a smile. It's a wonderful performance by Odessa, and Sloane, who knows exactly what is going on, admires it enormously.

Finally Odessa looks up, crestfallen, her woebegone eyes made sadder with mascara, her lips vivid as Indian paintbrush. Jane laughs out loud. "Oh, you," Odessa says, and she leans across Sloane and tickles Jane this time, hands squirming under the Grand Duchess's grey jacket, making her fall back on the sand until she's wheezing and begging for mercy and her shirt pulls out of the waistband of her pants, showing little glimpses of skin. Finally the witch stops her onslaught. Jane's eyes are teary with laughter; she doesn't see the way Odessa is looking at her. It's a strange, vulnerable look: Odessa's red mouth is smiling, but her eyes are full of loss and longing. Sloane sees the look, but only sixteen years later, as she picks up the doll and turns away from Odessa's bedroom, does she begin to understand it.

I can't be here.

The doll wrapped around Sloane like a limpet, all knees and elbows, as if she could hide from Kyle by burrowing into Sloane's body. "What's your name?" Sloane murmured.

"Scarlet. I want 'Dessa!"

Jim Ford and Sheriff Denton looked up as Sloane came back into the kitchen. Jim blinked. "Sloane, who is that child?"

"Reveler," Kyle said. "The Recluse made her. She claims Momus is her grandfather."

Sheriff Denton's eyes narrowed. "We've had enough magic," he said.

Sloane watched, terrified, as his hand settled on the butt of his .38. "She's a child!"

The older man licked his lips. "She's a monster," he said.

Scarlet went rigid in Sloane's arms. Her eyes grew wide and she pointed wordlessly at Odessa's body, lying next to the trapdoor in the kitchen floor. "I know," Sloane whispered.

I can't be here.

I can, said Sly.

"There, there," she said. Her voice was surprisingly light and careless. Definitely Sly's voice. "Hush-a-by, baby. The nasty man over there shot your aunt Odessa," she said, pointing instructively at Sheriff Denton.

Scarlet's mouth trembled. Her china-doll eyes went wide and filled with tears. Her breath shook. She had the most astonishingly expressive face. Thoughts and feelings chased across it pell-mell, clear as fish flicking in a bowl. Sloane felt one corner of her mouth turn up in a sardonic smile. The kid wouldn't make much of a card player with those tells. "Come along," she said, putting Scarlet down and taking her hand. "Time to say bye-bye to Aunt 'Dessa." Scarlet shook her head and buried her face in Sloane's grey cotton skirt. Sloane *tsked.* "Now, Scarlet," she said reprovingly, "we always say goodbye to someone when they leave. It's manners." She peeled the child off her leg and together they crouched beside the dead witch.

"Sloane, what are you—?"

"Be quiet, Jim."

Yes, even without wearing the mask she definitely had a touch of Sly back. The high blank hum helped steady her. (Christ, how much of that feeling was pure rage.) She bowed her head over her godmother's corpse. "Our Heavenly Father," she said, not really caring who heard her prayer, Momus or the Jesus Odessa had learned about in Sunday school. Anyone who would avenge her was good enough. "Take care of your daughter as she comes

to join you. Forgive the sins she committed, but not those committed against her. For thine is the kingdom and the power and the glory, forever and ever, amen."

Sloane opened her eyes to see the blood-spattered Sheriff Denton doll still clutched in Odessa's dead hand. Her grin broadened. Now that's what I call a sign. "And as for you," she said, turning to Jeremiah Denton, "somebody needs to learn you to *play nice.*"

In a single smooth movement she grabbed the Sheriff Denton doll by one warm leg, spun, and pitched it, thinly shrieking, through the trapdoor. It tumbled down into the water, hit with a flat smack, and disappeared. A desperate cry ripped out of Sheriff Denton's throat. He dropped to his knees beside the trapdoor, staring down in horror.

"Good Christ," Jim whispered. "Girl, what have you done?"

"Serves him right," Scarlet said.

They all watched as the doll bobbed up. Its tiny fingers clenched and opened. Its bloody head twisted and turned to stay above water. The faint swell had begun to strengthen. Sloane recognized the low mutter of distant thunder. The heat lightning must be coming closer. Sheriff Denton's face was grey as he watched a long green wave gather up the doll and roll it under, smooth and gentle as a mother's caress. A moment later it surfaced again, farther out to sea, little legs and arms thrashing. "Wind's coming up off the land," Kyle said. Another roller swallowed the figurine. It took much longer to come up this time. The undertow had pulled it even farther from the shore.

"Sloane," Sheriff Denton whispered, watching the doll drift. "Sloane, why?"

Sloane grabbed Odessa's hand between hers and gripped it fiercely. She found herself grinning. "I hope you die." The words clotted in her throat and she spat them out. "I hope you die, you genteel murdering son of a bitch."

A shutter banged in the rising wind. The stifling heat began to break apart. The long drought was buckling at last, as if Odessa's blood had been the first drops of an approaching squall. Thunder growled, louder and closer. The doll went under again.

"Storm coming," Kyle said.

Sheriff Denton began to retch. He dropped to his hands and knees, heaving and coughing. A terrible contraction shook his frame, then another, and finally a rush of green seawater spurted from his mouth. He stared at it, puddled on Odessa's kitchen floor. Then his eyes rolled back and he fainted dead away.

Chapter Thirteen

HURRICANE

DEPUTY Kyle put his ear on Sheriff Denton's chest. "Still breathing well enough. Reckon it's mostly the shock. Man, you sure fixed him," he said, glancing over at Sloane.

"He deserved it."

Kyle shrugged. "Tell it to the judge."

Sloane found herself staring at the seawater the sherrif had spit up. He was going to Krewes for sure now. But then, weren't they all? Jane Gardner was dead. Odessa was dead. What would stop Momus and his magic from drowning the city? Fear began to build in Sloane. It was one thing to chafe at her mother's dogmatic opposition to anything remotely magical or divine—but something else to think of Galveston returning to the nightmare of the Flood, when madness had burst over the city, sweeping minds and lives away like so much flotsam on the tide.

Storm coming.

Jim Ford tore his eyes off the trapdoor and knocked back the rest of his bourbon. "Christ. Let's get Odessa decent and then get the hell out of here."

They covered Galveston's great angel with strips and

bolts of fabric taken from her sewing trunk, Sloane lifting out each length, checking for spiders, and carefully wrapping Odessa's body. The first layers of cloth turned dark and wet with blood. Sloane carried on, tucking the fabric under Odessa's shoulders, wrapping her up as if making a body cast of cloth mâché. Jim Ford tried to talk Scarlet into leaving the room, but she refused, sticking close to Sloane, watching everything.

"We'll send someone to take care of the body later," Jim Ford said at last. "In God's name, let's get the sheriff out of this accursed place."

"You're lying," Scarlet said flatly. "You won't send anybody."

"Shh, honey," Sloane said, but she thought the same, and refused to be hurried. When she had finished, Jim and Kyle carried the sheriff out to the carriage and laid him across one seat, with Jim and Sloane facing him, and Scarlet in Sloane's lap. The sheriff wasn't fully conscious, but he had begun to moan and cough.

While they had been inside, a wall of black clouds had built in the sky, cutting off the sun. The afternoon turned grey and ominous. The wind was coming hard off the land, ruffling the coats of the uneasy horses, making their traces swing and slap. Little scudding whitecaps curled and hissed on the darkening waters of the Gulf.

Kyle Lanier hopped up to the carriage box and geed the horses with a smart smack of the reins. They jerked into motion, rumbling down Seawall Boulevard. Sheriff Denton's head shook with the rattle and sway of the carriage. Up on the driver's box, Kyle began to whistle.

"I'm afraid Odessa was up to something," Jim murmured, glancing at Scarlet and shaking his head. "The kid's your spitting image, Sloane, only smaller."

"And prettier, Jim. Don't forget that."

Sloane watched the sea through the carriage window. The waterline was up over the skirt of riprap at the bottom of the Seawall, the waves pounding at the wall itself.

Incredible that the water could be coming in this fast against a land wind this hard. Not a good sign. Sheet lightning played over the approaching cloud face. The murmur of thunder was getting louder.

Sheriff Denton opened his eyes and coughed. Jim Ford reached to help him as he struggled to sit up, but the sheriff pushed his hand away. Another fit of coughing seized him. Keeping his bearded lips tightly closed he took out his pocket handkerchief, embroidered with crescent moons at each corner, and spat into it.

Kyle turned the carriage onto Broadway. People were spilling out of the grand houses along the boulevard: servants in uniform, tradespeople with their deliveries, rich children in neat shorts and pressed shirts, old-timers who could still remember Alicia, the hurricane of 1980. The land wind gusted and dropped, gusted and dropped, catching at hair and skirts and then letting them fall. Some people laughed, others whispered. The long drought was finally coming to an end.

The wind died for good. A raindrop fell on the canvas roof of the carriage with a sharp tap. Then another. Kyle gave the horses another smack and they picked up speed, rolling on toward Ashton Villa. Dark circles the size of quarters began to appear on the dusty sidewalk. The streets grew loud with a sudden clamor of birds, jays and grackles and mockingbirds calling out to one another, rising and circling, billows of them swirling through the live-oak limbs. Trapped smells rose up from the ground, released by the first touch of rain: tar, dust, warm brick, horse dung. Then the line of black clouds overspread the city, and the rain poured down, drumming on the canvas carriage top, battering the brittle palm fronds and the withered oak leaves—a sweeping, rolling rush of rain that shook the air like a great wave that would never stop breaking.

When they reached Ashton Villa, Sloane picked up Scarlet and dashed from the carriage, hunching her back

to protect the child from the rain. She arrived on the porch drenched and gasping, her skin puckered with goose bumps. Waiting to meet them at the door was Sarah, the Gardner's sharp-faced cook and senior house-maid for as long as Sloane could remember. A row of candles peeked out of the pocket of her apron. "You *tramp*," she said, grabbing Sloane and hugging her fiercely. She had to yell to be heard over the din of rain that thundered through the live-oak canopy and rushed gurgling into the curbside drains. "We thought we'd lost you, you little snake. We thought them boys'd killed you."

"I'm so sorry, Sarah. I didn't mean to worry anyone."

Jim Ford and Sheriff Denton joined them on the porch, shaking the rain out of their hats. "Everybody ought to worry, if God gived 'em the sense of a doodlebug," Sarah shouted. "There's a hurricane coming, or leastwise a gale. The glass is dropping faster than a whore's britches, twenty-nine inches and falling. I've turned the gas off already, and I've been setting out candles." Sarah stepped back and studied the little girl in Sloane's arms. "The Recluse teach you a trick for making babies, Sloane?"

"She's not human," Sheriff Denton said. "She may look like a child, but she is a reveller."

Sarah studied the doll, lips pursed. "Beats the hell out of the way I did it. No diapers neither."

"Don't worry about the girl," Sloane shouted. "I'll be keeping her with me." The deafening rain rolled and roared, as if the ghosts of the six thousand Islanders killed in 1900 were stirring uneasily in their graves. Sloane raised her voice. "Sarah, get your family and bring them here. We're on the highest spot on the Island. If the storm gets bad they'll be safer with us."

Sarah nodded, undoing her apron. "Thank you, Miss Gardner. I've got all the windows shuttered already and the chickens cooped up. I'll be back as quick as I can."

Sheriff Denton grabbed his deputy by the arm and

leaned in to shout in his ear. "Kyle, when you're done with the horses take Ms. Gardner and the changeling to her room—and see they don't leave it!"

A gust of wind came up, howling off the sea at last, twisting creaks and groans out of the live oaks that lined the boulevard. "Are you arresting me?" Sloane yelled.

"Keeping you out of trouble!"

The rain was a solid silver curtain falling from the iron canopy over the porch. Kyle Lanier broke through it and loped toward the street to stable the horses. By the time he reached the curb, Sloane could see only a black blur, obscured by the driving rain. She turned back to the sheriff, remembering the sight of his little puppet floundering in the swell under the Balinese Room. She felt Sly's grin on her face as she raised her voice to be heard over the squall. "If I were you, Jeremiah, I'd make for higher ground."

AN hour later wind roared around the house, rain battered the roof, and thunder boiled constantly overhead. Sloane was sitting at her sewing machine. She had found a piece of forest-green broadcloth and cut a child's tunic pattern out of it. She lined up the seams by the fitful light of a small oil lamp she had moved to her sewing bench. Her sewing machine stuttered and stopped, stuttered and stopped to the familiar pressure of her foot.

She was sewing partly to make a dry change of clothes for Scarlet and partly to calm herself. The storm building outside was the worst she could remember, and ever since Scarlet had run out of Odessa's closet and into her arms, Sloane had lost the blessed numbness that had protected her for the first few hours of her return to Galveston. This morning she would have felt the timbers of Ashton Villa shaking without giving a damn, but now she was haunted by visions of Scarlet crushed under a falling wall, Scarlet torn from her by the tide and drowned like the children of St. Mary's Orphanage who had perished in 1900. They

said there were more than forty scalps dangling from the
railroad bridge the morning after the big blow, bodies
tangled there by their hair and then torn free by the brutal
strength of the waves.

Stop that.

This was more than just a storm. This was the end of
Galveston as they had known it. At least they had the
Seawall between them and the Gulf, but with Odessa
dead, nothing now remained to hold back the tide of
magic. Sloane could feel it running through Galveston's
streets, sense it in the way Sly dwelt in her even when
she wasn't wearing her mask. Out there in the darkness,
Momus moved across the face of the waters, pregnant
with miracles.

Outside the wind grabbed at the shingles and slammed
the shutters back and forth, trying to smash its way into
the house. Sloane's bedroom felt terribly small, a wooden
box she and Scarlet had hidden in, shaken and hammered
by the storm. A blast of lightning filled the room with
sudden shadows, and instantly thunder was detonating
around them, rattling the picture frames on every wall.
Sloane's foot froze on the treadle of her machine. She
willed herself to breathe calmly and eased her foot back
down. Steady, steady. She ran out the last seam on her
improvised dress and held it up. Lightning flashed, out-
lining it. "Come here, Scarlet. I've got something dry for
you to wear."

Scarlet didn't move. She was standing with her nose
pressed against the French doors that led out to Sloane's
verandah. The verandah faced inland and thus was protected from the storm by the whole bulk of the mansion.
Lightning flared again. Sloane had a momentary vision
of palm trees bent double in the wind, fronds boiling,
blurred by rain. She imagined the hurricane spinning off
a tornado, their roof yanked off with a tremendous rip
like a bolt of cloth tearing. Scarlet blown into the sky
like a red leaf.

Reluctantly the little girl backed away from the French doors and let Sloane pull off her damp dress. Her skin was white as shells. Sloane pulled the green tunic over her head, watching a cloud of fiery red hair emerge through the neck hole, then Scarlet's fierce green eyes, sharp nose, thin red lips. "You have to learn not to make the sheriff angry," Sloane said.

"He shot Aunt Odessa!"

"He'll do the same to us if we give him reason," Sloane said, smoothing the doll's hair.

Scarlet slapped her hand away. "He'll shoot me whether I'm nice to him or not. I'm not human."

Somewhere downstairs one of the windows exploded. They both whirled and listened. Servants ran through the house, shouting for planks and nails to cover the gap. "You can pass for human, if you try," Sloane said.

"I don't lie," Scarlet said contemptuously.

"You should," Sloane said. "I do." She rummaged in her oddments drawer and found a black hair ribbon for Scarlet to wear as a sash, cinching the tunic around her tiny waist. "If you were my daughter, that's the first thing I would teach you."

"I'm not."

"Call it 'tact' or 'diplomacy,' but it's lying just the same, and there are lots of times we need to do it."

"Grandfather never lies."

"He is big. He doesn't have to," Sloane said. "We are small. And when you are small, my dear, so much of the world is bigger than you. You can't always get what you want by fighting. Sometimes you have to be cunning, or devious, or, God help you, polite. The world likes that in a girl, trust me." She tied a cute little bow in Scarlet's improvised sash. "Don't you look sweet! Won't that nasty little jabbing hairpin of yours come as a shock!"

The doll looked at her. "You're tricky," she said at last.

You bet. Look how I fooled my mother, ho ho. Sloane

closed her eyes. It was good to have a bit of Sly's selfish daring buzzing in her blood, but she would have been even happier to have the blessed blankness back. Sly's grin was never quite this fragile. It was so much easier to be her when you didn't care.

Gently Sloane held Scarlet by her bony shoulders and said, "Listen!" Timbers groaned in the attic. The servants shouted and cursed downstairs. Rain battered on the roof and sluiced onto Sloane's verandah. A blast of lightning struck so close the flash seemed to burst through the house, fierce actinic light spraying between each board in the walls. Then thunder smashed over Ashton Villa like a breaking wave. Sloane felt Scarlet jump and quiver between her hands. "Hear that?" she said, locking the girl's eyes with her own. "There are things in this life you have to hide from."

Scarlet stared back at her, white-faced.

The peal of thunder died away, replaced by others farther off, and the roar of the wind. "Shh, honey, it's all right," Sloane murmured, picking the girl up and holding her in her lap. For once Scarlet offered no resistance. "I'll take care of you," Sloane said. Oh, yes. Like I took care of Jane and 'Dessa. "Believe me," she said. Her eyes ached, but she refused to cry.

FOUR hours later a sudden calm fell. Scarlet cracked open the French doors to the verandah. "Definitely a hurricane," Sloane said. "The eye must be passing over us. Hey, don't go out there. You'll get your feet w—" But Scarlet had already slipped outside. Before Sloane could react, the girl hopped onto the iron railing around the verandah and then, quick as a cat, jumped up out of sight. The scrabble of small hands and knees sounded faintly through the ceiling.

Sloane clapped a hand over her mouth. Screaming would alert the guard Kyle Lanier had stationed in the hallway outside her room. Biting her lip to keep herself

quiet, she ran out onto the balcony, turned, and looked up at the roof. Crouched on all fours, Scarlet looked back over her shoulder with a fierce grin. "Coming?" the girl crowed.

"Get back this instant!"

Scarlet scrambled up the shingles. Ashton Villa's roof had a very gentle pitch to it, no more than ten degrees. Beyond the roof ridge the sky was impossibly clear and filled with stars. The rainwater puddled on the balcony felt cold on Sloane's bare feet. Scarlet reached the ridge and looked back. "Hurry up!" she called, waving.

A wide ornamental gable jutted out over the balcony. Scarlet had jumped to it from the wrought-iron railing. No human child could have made that leap. Sloane clambered cautiously onto the rail. It pressed painfully into her feet as she crouched on it like an unhappy gargoyle, one hand pushing hard into the brick wall of the house for balance. She looked down and then wished she hadn't. Three stories below, a moving sheet of water lay where the lawn ought to be. Lamplight from what must have been the kitchen shimmered on the floodwater. Either the rain had come so fast it was standing in the yard, or the ocean itself had come up over the Seawall and overspread the Island.

Horses were screaming in the stables out back.

Sloane straightened out of her crouch, swaying, and grabbed the rain gutter with her right hand. Next, a quarter turn of her upper body, so she was facing the gable. She leaned forward, braced her elbows on the roof, and pulled upward as hard as she could. Her feet left the railing and she was dangling above the verandah. That's when she discovered she wasn't strong enough to pull herself up. Leaning forward she could get most of her chest on the roof, but she couldn't swing her left knee up over the edge. Wet asphalt shingle grated under her forearms as she hung in space, ungainly as a frog on a trapeze.

The calm was broken by a stray gust of wind. This faint omen of the hurricane's return sent a lightning bolt of panic through Sloane and she scrabbled desperately up. The next thing she knew she had her hips on the roof. Blind terror, she thought, gasping. The best medicine.

She crawled to the roof ridge on her hands and knees. Scarlet was waiting for her. "Isn't this great?" the girl cackled.

"Oh, fabulous." Sloane considered throttling the little brat, but her hands were still shaking. She lay on the roof, trembling. When she could force herself to look around, she saw her island in ruins. Even here along Broadway, Galveston's spine and highest point, water had crested over the sidewalk like a flooding river, drowning flower beds and lapping at the porch steps of the great Victorian mansions. The wind had hurled the head of a palm tree through the Jacksons' bay window and pulled up the giant live oak in front of John Browning's house to throw it through his roof, cracking it open like an egg. The stumps of palm trees, their heads ripped off by the gale, lined the boulevard like broken masts.

Farther away, where the houses were smaller and the water higher, the damage was far worse. The air began to fill with wails and cries. A house with water up past the first story was burning fiercely on the second, smoke and light pouring from the attic windows. Ruptured gas line, no doubt. Horses were screaming throughout the city. Stables smashed, cows and pigs squealing and drowning.

Sloane got her breath back and grabbed for Scarlet, who avoided her easily. "Get back inside! The eye could pass at any time. You'll die if you're caught out in this!"

Scarlet went scooting along the roof ridge, quick as a monkey. "I'm going to the Carnival." She dropped over the front gable to land with an audible thump on top of the two-story iron porch at the front of the house. Sloane crawled after her, swearing. When she reached the front

gable she peered over, gripping the edge of the roof so hard her knuckles stood out, white as dice in the dim light. She could just see the top of Scarlet's head as she swarmed down an iron pillar at the side of the porch.

It should have been easy for Sloane to lower herself over the gable and drop to the top of the porch, but that area had never been intended to be used as a deck, and there was no railing. Sloane was so worried she would fall backward over the edge that when she finally gathered the courage to ease herself over the gable and drop, she pitched forward as she was landing and smacked her head painfully into the brick wall of the house.

Now she was on top of the pink iron double-decker porch above the front door. She wiped her forehead on her sleeve and then lowered herself down the same pillar Scarlet had taken. The whole wrought-iron porch was festooned with ornamental grillwork that her mother had thought ridiculously fussy. Tonight Sloane blessed every curlicue and cornice for the hand- and toeholds they provided.

In three minutes she was lowering herself into the prickly rosebush growing at the base of the porch. Scarlet was already wading away from the house in floodwaters up to her waist. Sloane splashed out and grabbed the girl, jerking her roughly up into her arms. Scarlet kicked and writhed. Sloane caught the girl's hand just as she was reaching for the long hairpin she had used to stab Kyle Lanier. "Do it and I'll break your arm," she said. Her voice was low and shaking with anger. "This is not a game. You cannot run away from me. I will take you to the Carnival if I can. But you cannot run away from me again."

Sloane strode forward, jerking Scarlet along with her. "You don't have to hurt me," the girl said. Sloane grunted and shifted so the girl was on her hip, her arms wrapped tightly around Sloane's shoulder. "Was that a lie, when you said you would break my arm?"

"I hope so," Sloane said.

Another gust of wind came up. Twenty-three stumbling, splashing blocks lay between Ashton Villa and Stewart Beach at the end of Broadway. We'd better be fast, Sloane thought, wading forward with one arm around Scarlet. Splash soaked her clothes, and for the first time in months she felt chilled. More and more people were coming outside. Children clustered on porches, whispering and staring at the devastation left by the leading edge of the hurricane. Wives held propane lanterns or oil lamps while their husbands furiously nailed boards across east and south facing windows. Many of the Broadway mansions were crowded with servants and relatives and even strangers off the street; more of these were trickling in all the time. A steady stream of refugees was floundering up to Broadway from the drowned piers of the back bay, and the poor residential neighborhoods farther south, where the wind had hit first and hardest.

Refugees began to clamor at the doors of the fine Victorian manors along the boulevard. The Jacksons and Jim Ford had their doors open and all their lights on, beacons guiding the battered and homeless to shelter. Bless them, Sloane thought as she floundered on through water up past her knees. But some of the mansions were dark, and armed men stood at others, warning off looters and vagrants.

Everyone watched the sky.

At the mouth of 18th Avenue the body of a drowned horse shifted gently in the flooded street. Sloane hurried on, jostling amongst the draggled refugees, scrambling over or around the toppled palms and live oaks blocking the sidewalk. With a shock she realized that the streets were full of revellers. As she passed 16th Avenue she saw a stilt-walker a block away, staggering like a drunken crane through the flooded street. Someone ran into his leg as she watched. He tumbled slowly backward, arms windmilling, and disappeared in a splash of spray.

Momus had set Carnival loose. The magic Jane and Odessa had tried so hard to keep at bay was sweeping back into Galveston on the wings of the storm.

A cat-faced woman jerked on Sloane's arm. Sloane searched for the reveller's name. Lianna, that was it. The cat-headed woman was wearing a badly ripped evening gown of emerald silk, now marred by water stains that would never come out. What a waste. Her slip was splattered with mud and worse. "Hey! Sly! I'm a friend of Vinnie Tranh's. You played poker with us."

"There's blood on your muzzle." Sloane had to yell to be heard over the noise of the crowd splashing through the streets.

"Flying glass," Lianna shouted back.

Scarlet wriggled in Sloane's arms. "Keep going! We have to see Grandpa!"

Sloane started to splash forward. Lianna loped beside her, her feline face screwed up in distaste at having to bound through the water. She licked a trickle of blood off her muzzle with a long pink tongue. "Mind if I come, too? I got nowhere else to go."

Sloane grunted and tried to run faster, floundering through the water as the the wind gusted up again, shaking fat raindrops out of the live-oak leaves. The crowd milling in the street grew abruptly more desperate, climbing up on mansion porches or pounding on doors. A tree had crushed the dome of St. Patrick's, and a horde of refugees had obviously spilled out of it to surround Randall Denton's place, the opulent Bishop's Palace. A stick arced out of the mob to smash one of Randall's windows. A shotgun blasted back from the porch. Someone screamed. The mob fell back, knocking Sloane down. She scrabbled up, spitting out a mouthful of water, Scarlet clinging to her like a monkey. The rain started coming down harder.

We're not going to make it, Sloane realized. And oh,

my God, Stewart Beach is *below the Seawall*. Christ, what have I been thinking?

"Keep going!" Scarlet yelled.

"We're not going to make it!" Panic tightened in Sloane's stomach. The wind picked up again. She turned and floundered desperately for the lights blazing from Randall Denton's mansion.

Randall stood on his front porch, holding a mob of refugees at bay with his antique Purdey double-barreled shotgun. "Get the hell back!" he yelled, waving the gun in a jerky arc across the line of faces staring at him. "Private property, damn you!" Lightning branched down from the southern sky, then a terrible pause, then the shuddering rumble of thunder. The eye of the hurricane was passing. The back wall of the storm swept toward them, swallowing the stars as it came. Cold rain began to fly again.

"Here it comes," Sloane whispered.

The crowd surged forward. Randall blasted a shot into them and a woman fell kicking and struggling into the water. Sloane kept waiting for her to scream, but she didn't, just thrashed and thrashed. It was hard to tell if she was hit or just scared. A stink of gunpowder eddied through the air. The rising wind made Randall's bathrobe whip around his legs as he chambered another round. "Who's next!"

The crowd pulled back. Sloane took a breath and stepped forward. The wind gusted and she almost fell. "Randall! Randall! It's me, Sloane!"

"The hell it is!" Randall jerked the gun around and trained it on her chest.

"Listen to me!" Sloane still clutched Scarlet in her right arm. Her left she held up over her head. With her arm raised she knew her thin cotton shirt would be clinging to her breasts. Sly knew how to play this hand. "Randall, please! Let me in. You know me."

He squinted into the darkness. "Sloane?"

She stumbled forward. "Randall, thank God! I thought I was going to die out here, with *them*." She was now clearly in front of the rest of the crowd, inching away from them with every step.

"Bitch!" someone yelled. A rock or stick hit the back of her head, hard. She yelped and stumbled forward, almost dropping Scarlet. Randall let off another blast from his shotgun. Sloane couldn't tell if anyone behind her was hit. She didn't turn around. The rain was roaring down now, churning white spray from the sheet of water covering the lawn.

"Randall!"

He waved her up the steps with the gun. "Come on! The rest of you filth STAY BACK!"

Sloane broke into a stumbling, splashing run toward the house. She wished she still had Ace's useful .32. Another bolt of lightning exploded over the Gulf. In the blinding instant of illumination, Sloane saw a dark figure at the end of Randall's balcony. It was a Prawn Man, perched motionless on the porch rail, staring out to sea. Then the lightning faded, and the Prawn Man was gone. Thunder rolled in like a shock wave, rattling the shutters of the Bishop's Palace.

Randall pumped his casings and chambered another round. "Sloane! Jesus, it is you! Who's the kid?"

"My niece." Sloane put Scarlet down and limped up the steps. "Oh, Randall!" she said, and she threw herself into his arms. He grabbed her around the waist, still brandishing the shotgun in his right hand.

"Come on!" he said, backing toward the door.

"Oh, Randall, thank God!" And then, bending within the circle of his arms, Sloane bit him as hard as she could just above the right wrist. He screamed and dropped his gun. In a flash Scarlet grabbed it and shoved it over the edge of the porch into the water. The crowd swept forward. Sloane pushed Randall back toward his front door. "Come in! Everyone!" she yelled. The mob roared and

surged forward. "No fighting! There's room for everyone! Even you," she added, shoving Randall into his own foyer.

"Bitch!" He hit her in the face, hard. The next instant he screamed, grabbing at the back of his knee, and crumpled to the ground. Scarlet jumped back, grinning, brandishing her hairpin.

Sloane's head was ringing and there was blood in her mouth. She picked out a big young man in a ripped shirt who was lumbering up Randall's steps. "You! Get Mr. Denton out of the way. Everyone inside!" Sloane shouted, waving frantically. "Everyone inside!"

The wind was screaming now, and the flying rain was mixed with hail. Lightning exploded overhead. A tremendous grinding crash filled the air as the church across the street foundered farther under the renewed press of the gale. The drenched mob poured through the front door of the Bishop's Palace like water coming through a breached dike. Muddy, battered, draggled people threw themselves down on Randall Denton's velvet upholstered sofas or sprawled on his gorgeous Persian carpets. Sloane had her commandeered deputy keep Randall behind her and out of the way. "Shoes against the wall. Manners, everyone!" Sloane shouted. "Nobody's here to cut your throat, Randall," she said over her shoulder. "They're just trying to stay alive."

Randall slumped sullenly against the wall in his drenched velvet bathrobe, moodily rubbing his injured wrist. "It's not manners to *bite*, Sloane."

She swallowed blood, feeling her teeth with her tongue to see if he had broken any of them when he hit her. "Well, we're even now."

The noise of the storm came roaring through the broken windows; Randall's heavy drapes shook and bulged as if a knife fight were going on behind them. Another tremendous peal of thunder shook the house, making the china in the cabinets rattle and Colonel Denton's medals

bounce in their red velour display cases. A blast of wind slammed open Randall's oak front doors and a volley of rain drenched the Persian carpet in an eye blink.

Sloane jumped to the doors and tried to shove them closed. She wasn't strong enough. Wind tore into the house to smack Randall's crystal chandelier and set it jangling like a wind chime. Then her fat young deputy threw his shoulder into the door beside her, and an instant later Lianna joined them. Together they heaved the door closed. As Sloane turned the dead bolts she could feel the cypress wood shuddering under her hands, vibrating with the force of the gale outside.

Sloane drew a deep breath and held out her hand to the heavyset boy. "Thanks. What's your name?"

"Japhet," he said stolidly, taking her hand and shaking it. "Japhet Mather, ma'am."

Recognition clicked in. This must be Ham's little brother. That sort of explained the six-foot, two-hundred-pound body with the twelve-year-old's head on top. Hi! she didn't say. I'm the reason your brother is outside in *this*, marooned somewhere on the Bolivar Peninsula. She grinned brightly. When in trouble, smile. That was one thing Sloane and Sly agreed on.

Glancing around, she saw one of Randall's housemaids peeping out from behind the doorway that led into the library. No sign of any other servants. The rest would be cowering in the kitchen, probably. Sloane dredged up the girl's name. "Hey, Lindsey!" The maid's face disappeared. "Your master needs some warm water and a bandage. Lindsey, I know you're there. Be a good girl. None of these people are going to hurt you."

"What about the *things*?" the maid shouted.

Sloane looked around. Oh—the revellers. More than one had rushed into the shelter of the Bishop's Palace. She spotted the Heron she had met in her first poker game in Mardi Gras, standing motionless on one leg over by

the china cabinet. Lianna jumped lightly on top of Randall's baby grand piano and curled up, licking her bloody muzzle. A stilt-walker, hunched double to get through the front door, straightened too fast and smacked his head on Randall's chandelier, making it shake and sway so diamonds of light veered wildly through the foyer.

"Monsters," Randall remarked. "Well, that's just great."

The human refugees, eyes wide with fear, were backing into the parlor, leaving the foyer and the great central staircase to the revellers. Sloane saw a man pick up a heavy crystal ashtray. A thin teenage boy with a bloody face drew a knife from his hip and held it out, blade trembling in his shaking hand. Better take charge of this situation *now*, before anybody else has a chance to think. "You—you look hurt," Sloane said, making eye contact with the knife-wielding kid. "Go to the back of the parlor and we'll get some treatment for you." He didn't move. Sloane pretended not to notice. "Anyone else injured?"

The mother of a crying child raised her hand. "I think my son's arm might be broken."

"Go to the far end of the room, away from the windows." The mother picked up her boy and limped across the room. A moment later a young woman followed, holding her shoulder. Then an older man with a blood-soaked piece of shirt wrapped around his knee. "Thank you," Sloane said gratefully. A moment later the bloody-faced teenager followed the rest. "Thank you, folks. Lindsey, get a basin of hot water and some clean cloths." The housemaid came slowly around the corner from the library. "If you don't have bandages in the house, we can use clean rags or pillow slips. Is there a doctor here?" Silence. "Anything close?"

"I know a little first aid," Japhet Mather said.

"Bless you. I'll help." Sloane turned to look at Randall. "Are you going to make trouble?"

"Later," he said with one of his old sardonic smiles.

"And that's a promise." Outside the hurricane raged and roared. "Very happy to be of service," he said loudly. The mob stared at him with loathing. "Please—make yourselves comfortable! Set a spell, pardner," he said, slapping Japhet on the back. "If any of you are hungry or thirsty, my staff will be pleased to rustle y'all some grub," he drawled.

Sloane's mouth fell open. "Now, don't look so shocked," Randall said. "You think I have no conscience at all?"

"Well, frankly—"

"Besides which, you'll be paying for every red cent of it," Randall said. He switched his smile back on. "Every mouthful of rice, every bloodstain on my carpet, every bottle of wine. Sloane? You look a little pale," Randall said solicitously. "Don't you worry your pretty—well, your not wholly unattractive—little head about a thing. I will *personally* take care of all the pricing and billing."

Sloane stared at the crowd of refugees currently trailing blood and mud over Randall's stupefyingly expensive antique furniture. "Oh, well," she said faintly. "That's all right, then."

"Nice of you to show up at last," Randall continued. Scarlet hissed at him. His eyebrows rose. "Though you might have done it a tad earlier, Sloane, for the sake of those two fellas we had marooned for killing you." Another blast of lightning rattled the chandelier. Randall shook his head. "Tsk tsk. Poor bastards." His face filled with transparently insincere concern. "Imagine what it must be like to be caught outside in this!"

Part Four

Chapter Fourteen

VENOM

Josh and Ham began their exile within twenty-four hours
of being sentenced. In the dark before dawn, they were
turned out of their separate cells and marched down to
Pier 23 at gunpoint. There they were forced into the hold
of the *Fat Tuesday*, a shrimper whose captain was a second cousin of the Gardners.

It was pitch-black in the *Fat Tuesday's* hold, nothing
for Josh to look at but fragments of humiliating memory.
The condescending smile of the woman in the Krewe of
Momus offices. Scar-faced Kyle Lanier, grinning as he
kicked Josh in the side with his shiny polished shoes.
Sloane Gardner lying on his ancient exam table, his little
front parlor stinking with yeast and fermenting rice wine.
His shelves loaded with pathetic witch doctor's potions
in salvaged pop bottles and Noxzema jars. The strap of
her dress just off her left shoulder. Her puzzled eyes—
I'm sorry. Should I know you?

Bound at the ankles with lengths of rope, Josh and
Ham sat three inches deep in seawater that was slimy
with algae and smelled of rotting shrimp. Josh could feel
bits of shrimp bumping against him, whiskers and legs
torn off during loading or unloading, left to float in the

brine. He had retched and retched after they were lowered in here, gut muscles still screaming with the beating Kyle Lanier had given him two nights before. He kept retching long after his stomach was empty, as if there were some toxin in his gut he couldn't manage to spit out. As if shame were a poison.

"Some of these sumbitches are still alive down here," Ham said, slapping at the water. Spray splattered over Joshua's face. "We oughta catch one of the little bastards. You ever eat a raw shrimp? Texas sushi," the big man said.

Joshua's stomach heaved. "Bowel parasites," he said. His face was hot and he felt feverish, stomach churning and churning. He thought of Sloane's lips closing around a spoonful of rice porridge. Fancy dress dyed in bright pre-Flood colors, the Mardi Gras smell of cigarette smoke clinging to her hair and clothes.

"God, I'm thirsty," Ham said, shifting noisily.

"Don't drink this stuff."

"No shit."

Josh stared into the darkness. Somewhere underneath them a motor kicked into life. The floor rocked as they began to move away from the dock. "Ham?"

"Yeah?" The floor tilted and subsided again as the *Fat Tuesday* came around and the swell took her gently abeam. The boat gathered speed, churning steadily into the Gulf.

"How did Sloane's hair get into your boat?"

Ham's voice came out of the darkness. "You dumb shit, the hairs were in the boat because Sheriff Denton put them there."

"They just *lied*?"

"Josh, sometimes I despair of you." Ham sighed gustily. "It's not like they hadn't found their killers. They just needed to get a conviction. You keep thinking they wouldn't do something like that to one of their own. But

guess what, Sherlock? To them, you're just another one of us."

"I grew up with her. We went to the same parties."

Another explosive *smack* showered Josh with filthy bilgewater. "I think I got the fucker. Feel around in there, Josh, and see if you find a flat shrimp." Joshua's stomach twisted up and he retched again. Ham coughed. "And it probably didn't help that the stockings were, ah . . ."

"Soiled."

"Right," Ham said. "Now, once they unload us out of this shithole, we're going to have to find some water. Reckon they'll take us west down to Corpus, or east up by Beaumont, in and amongst the cannibals?"

"I don't care."

"Hey, now. That ain't my buddy. The Josh I know was a surly little fucker who never gave up in his life," Ham said. "The Josh I know is the guy who came back every day when that mad dog bit Matt Biggs."

"Matt died, Ham."

"Of course he died, Josh," Ham said patiently. "He had the fucking rabies, didn't he? The point is, you stayed in there fighting when everybody knew he was a goner— and you didn't even like that lying little bastard. You're no quitter, Joshua Cane."

Josh closed his eyes against the sickening memory of that moment in the courtroom when he finally understood how thoroughly Galveston despised him. How much he was suffered to exist on the strength of Ham's goodwill. "There's a word for a guy who plays hands he ought to fold," Josh said. "A sucker." He hunched in the stinking water. "Ham?"

"Yeah?"

"I'm sorry you got dragged into—"

"Oh, shut the fuck up already."

A few hours out from the dock, Ham began to snore. The little cell of darkness moved on, carrying Joshua along

like Jonah in the belly of the whale. Water slapped and gurgled around him. The suffocating hold of the *Fat Tuesday* grew hotter and hotter. Josh slid down until he was lying on his back, trying to suck in the coolest air, just above the filthy bilgewater. He stopped noticing the smell of shrimp. Sometimes his eyes were open, sometimes they were closed. His stomach hurt, and his ribs.

He didn't realize he had fallen asleep until he woke to a blast of light as someone threw open the overhead hatch. He squeezed his eyes shut against the glare. The head of the *Fat Tuesday*'s captain appeared in the square of daylight. "Get up, you dogs." A mate unrolled a rope ladder into the hold. Josh climbed it. His legs shook, weak from hunger and thirst.

Abovedecks a stiff breeze was blowing from the land. Josh gulped the clean air, then grimaced as pain stabbed through his side. Cracked rib, probably. On the landward side of the *Fat Tuesday,* four deckhands were lowering the ship's launch into the water. Four more crewmen with rifles flanked the captain. He nodded at the launch. "In you go, boys."

Josh and Ham were lashed back-to-back with yellow nylon rope and dumped on a rear thwart. Ham said nothing when the sailors jerked the ropes tight, but to his shame Josh cried out. The sailors looked at him contemptuously. The launch headed for shore.

"At least there's a breeze," Ham said. His voice was cracked from lack of water. "How far have we come? Fifty miles maybe?"

None of the sailors answered. "Talk all you like. It's allowed," the captain said. He was a small, bearded man with hard eyes. "But if I were you, I'd save my spit."

The launch stopped fifty yards shy of the beach. Two sailors came back to untie them. The others sat with rifles at the ready. It was clear that if either Josh or Ham struggled or tried to escape, they would be shot at once. "Over you go," the captain said. A sailor gave Josh a poke with

his clasp knife to encourage him. Josh and Ham crawled over the side and stood waist-deep in the warm Gulf water.

While one sailor coiled and stowed the rope that had been used to bind them, the master's mate brought a small chest to the captain. He opened it. "By the articles of the Krewe of Thalassar and the justice of the court, any exiled person or persons must be supplied and equipped with certain provisions adequate to permit survival," he recited. "These items are as follows: one canteen." He lifted out a battered tin canteen and passed it to the mate, who handed it to Josh, who gave it to Ham, who dunked it in the sea and then held it up before his eyes. After a moment a small drip appeared at the bottom. Drip, drip, drip.

"This leaks," Josh said.

The captain scratched his beard. "A supply of matches and a waterproof container," he said. The mate handed Josh a handful of cheap wooden matches of the sort Joshua made up himself. Several dropped into the sea.

Joshua tried to imagine how many matches would stay dry through the long wade they had left to make it to the shore. "What about the waterproof container?"

"You have a metal canteen."

"There's water in it."

The captain shrugged. "That was your choice, not my concern."

"But it leaks—"

"One knife," the captain continued. His mate produced a Buck folding pocketknife with a two and a half inch blade.

"This is mine," Josh said, recognizing the initials he had scratched into the wooden handle. "My father gave it to me on my ninth birthday. The matches are mine, too, aren't they? Stolen from my house."

"Lastly, a gun and ammunition." The mate handed over a small revolver.

Ham slung the canteen around his neck and reached for the gun. Sweat was running down his wide red forehead. "A .32 caliber Colt," he said. The mate passed over a dirty cotton bag. Ham peered inside. "And six .38 caliber bullets. Thank you so very goddamn much. You know, y'all can just kiss my ass until my hat pops off." The captain nodded to his men. The launch motor kicked over and the boat began to slide away, leaving Ham and Josh standing in the Gulf swell, marooned. "You pussies!" Ham yelled. "If I die you can expect to see my ghost, you sons of bitches! I'll see you in hell!"

The launch put-putted away from them. Josh turned and waded toward the beach, holding the matches and pocketknife high above his head to keep them from getting wet. It partly worked. The shore looked much the same as it did beyond the Seawall on Galveston: dark firm sand up to the waterline, pale powdery sand above it that stretched back twenty yards to a low dune, no higher than Josh's waist. Behind that, a wide salt grass meadow.

Josh waded out of the sea and walked up the beach. The drought had withered much of the vegetation that capped the dune, but his apothecary's eye could still pick out sea purslane and camphor daisy, bitter panicum and gulf croton and small powder-grey leaves of sage. The strong land breeze made the whole plain seethe and tremble. Shifting waves of blue-green salt grass stirred and whispered. Farther inland Josh could see occasional thickets of scrub: chinaberry and baccharis and woolly-bucket, Chinese tallow and sugar hackberry. Over to the west, he spotted a stand of tall grass or reeds, cattails or wild bamboo or cane; the first good fortune they'd had in a while. Stands of cane and cattails meant fresh water, a pond or swale or creek line. Even if the drought had dried up the surface water, a cane thicket was a good place to dig for more. With luck there would be a black willow or two nearby, and he would be able to use the

bark as poor man's aspirin for their aches and bruises.

Ham was at the waterline, looking back to sea, shading his eyes with one thick hand. "The boat's heading west. If they're heading home, we're on the Bolivar Peninsula."

Josh turned and squinted into the afternoon sun, watching the *Fat Tuesday* recede. "Then we're in cannibal country, right?"

"I ain't ripe yet." Ham pointed at a thin dark band on the horizon. "Hey. Clouds. If it rains, we'll need some way to keep the water." He held up their canteen. It dripped steadily into the sea. Ham swore and rubbed one fat hand over his forehead.

God Josh was thirsty. He'd never felt so thirsty in his life. His voice was cracked, and his tongue felt like a hank of hot felt. "I'm dizzy," he said. "You?"

"Yeah. And my head aches like that fucking deputy was still kicking it. And I feel like throwing up."

Dehydration. "We need water. I think I saw some cane over yonder."

Ham squinted inland. "Come on, then."

They started down the beach. Even with the stiff wind coming off the land, it was brutally hot. Ninety-five degrees, maybe. Josh's clothes dried in a hurry. He didn't think he was sweating enough. Bits of reading came back to him: *At five percent water loss, patient will experience thirst, irritability, weakness, headache, possibly nausea.* Josh wondered how much internal bleeding he had done after Kyle had beaten him. More fluid loss there. *A ten percent deficit will result in more severe headache and nausea, possible inability to walk*—not there yet—*possible tingling sensation in limbs.* His feet hurt. *At fifteen percent, numb feeling spreads over the skin; also swollen tongue, deafness, dim vision, painful urination.*

Ham stopped. "Shit, I'm being fried alive." He gave Josh the canteen, gun, and bullets, then took off his shirt. His vast chest and gut were pale compared to his face and hands. Sweaty curls of hair ran from his flabby nip-

ples into a dark seam that thickened as it approached the waistband of his prisoner's pants. He wound his shirt around his head like a turban. "Better sunburn than heatstroke."

"Good idea." Josh followed his example.

"Us Mathers know a thing or two about living off the land. I'm gonna make those pussies wish they'd put a bullet in us when they had the chance," Ham said grimly. "I'm gonna stick my arm down that captain's throat till I reach his asshole and pull him inside out."

They started forward again, walking along the hardpacked sand. Wavelets broke and hissed foaming around Joshua's feet and then pulled back, sucking sand out from under his arches. Bits of shell jutted from the sand, blue or bone white.

More than fifteen percent water loss will result in death.

The stand of cane Josh had seen turned out to be cattails. When they came even with it they stood together on the beach, studying the thick pelt of tangled salt grass behind the dune. Josh figured it was about a third of a mile inland to the tall grass. Ham scratched at his jowls. His lips were cracking even in the sultry air. "I'm thinking maybe one of us checks over there for open water, and one of us does some serious beachcombing. What would it take to make a still?"

Josh licked his lips. It didn't do much good. "Sheet of plastic and a digging tool."

"Okay. You scavenge. I'll head over yonder." Ham unslung the canteen from around his neck, held it up, and then banged on its side with the barrel of the useless .32. It made a good, loud, unnatural noise. "Get out of my way, rattlesnakes, I'm coming through." He paused and shook his head. "Consider the parable of Joshua Cane. Banished for life for a pussy unplumbed, the poor dumb bastard."

"Next time."

"Yeah, yeah." Ham stepped up over the dune in his bare feet, belly swaying, and went tramping heavily through the salt grass, banging away on his improvised drum.

Josh scanned the beach for anything that might be of use. Even before the Flood the Bolivar Peninsula had been sparsely populated. Just a handful of second-rate seaside communities, summer cottages for those too poor to buy on Galveston; the occasional rancher with a few dozen head of cattle and a gift store along Highway 87; handfuls of men working the oil claims up the peninsula, and the gas stations, bars, and diners that serviced them. But even though there hadn't been many folk here before the Flood, the world had been so wasteful there was still plenty of litter to salvage if you looked carefully enough. Almost at once Josh found a fat length of sun-rotted nylon rope, black and yellow and thick as his wrist, lost from a tanker or container ship. He found a whole tire, a Goodyear AquaTread, lying just over the top of the dune where some storm had stranded it. This he dragged back to the beach, thinking they might want to cut it up later to make shoes, or possibly burn it, using the thick smoke to drive away the mosquitoes that would surely appear the moment the wind dropped. He looked at the tire and shook his head. What an empire. Even their garbage lasted forever.

It was getting harder for Josh to stand straight. He couldn't tell if he was getting sicker or the wind was strengthening. His head ached and ached.

He found a plastic pop bottle with the bottom torn out but the cap still screwed on. He put it inside the tire where it wouldn't blow away, not sure what he would use it for. He found two Budweiser cans, a twelve ounce that would hold water, and a twenty that leaked. He found a flat metal disk the size of a dinner plate; maybe the top of a pail of paint. They could use it as a digging tool, if he could figure out a way to shape it.

It was terrifying to him how quickly they had dwindled, as a species. His grandparents had lived in such astonishing *permanence*: going to universities a hundred years old, to study books centuries older still—a cumulative line of thought and accomplishment, each generation building on the foundation left by the last. Compared to that, the people Joshua doctored with his potions and charms were not much better than animals, born into makeshift houses, carried off by every drought and disease, breeding and dying like a year's crop of mosquitoes.

In the last century, doctors had won. They had made people well. All he could do was cut his patients' losses, delay the inevitable, play each losing hand of cards as well as he could. But Galveston always had her aces to play: typhoid, smallpox, spider bites, malaria. Recently he had begun to see tuberculosis, too, and something that looked a lot like yellow fever.

The thin bang of the tin canteen was getting louder again. Ham must be coming back.

Josh noticed a small hole at the base of the dune. Some kind of animal burrow, probably. Sunlight flashed from just inside it, as if from plastic. He reached inside and felt around for whatever had made that flash.

A snake bit him just above the right wrist and he screamed, a high crazy shriek that tore from his raw thoat. He jerked his hand back out of the hole and stared at the double puncture marks at the end of his right forearm. Two drops of blood beaded up, half an inch apart. He could hear Ham lumbering through the salt grass, running back to the beach.

How could he have been so stupid?

The trouble with being unlucky, Josh thought, staring, is that you have no margin for error. Pain stabbed up his arm from his wrist. All his life he had been playing bad cards well. He was smart and he worked hard, he made good choices, he had guts. Putting all that together he

could just manage to hold even. Never win, of course. Not Sam Cane's boy. And when those moments came when he slipped up, when he was stupid enough to fall in love and hold on to Sloane Gardner's stockings, or when, after a day without food or water, he lost his concentration and stuck his hand into a small hole in the side of a sand dune—that's where the knife went in. His father used to say, "If you make a mistake, a good player will always punish you for it." And it was true; whichever god had been dealing him bad hand after bad hand all his life applied a merciless penalty for every mistake.

In Joshua's experience, about half the people struck by a rattlesnake suffered little or no ill effect.

The lucky half.

HAM thundered through the salt grass and jumped down off the dune. He followed Joshua's eyes to the puncture marks on his wrist, then swung around and spotted the hole in the dune. "Good *Christ*, you dumb ass!"

Ham reached into Joshua's pocket, grabbed the knife, and flicked it open. Josh struggled out of his stupor. "No! Cutting me will just open up the capillaries and get the venom into my bloodstream faster."

"You sure? Okay, then. Tell me what to do, Josh."

"Draw a syringe and inject the antivenin. Duh."

Ham grabbed him by the shoulders. "Josh, don't fucking joke about it. Tell me what to do. Should I suck it out?"

"No! God, no. Vessels under your tongue will take the poison to your heart in one straight shot." Joshua's heart was hammering and hammering, every beat forcing the poison into his system. It had always struck him as funny, in a grim way, that the one thing you absolutely had to do after being bitten by a deadly snake was *stay calm*. "Ham, this bite is not a good thing."

"Tell me what to do, damn it!"

Josh closed his eyes. They had no mechanical suction.

"Squeeze it out, I guess." The area around the puncture was beginning to sting. Ham pinched it. Two fat drops of blood rolled out. "Harder," Josh said. Ham squeezed harder. Blood bubbled up from the wound. It hurt a lot. Josh clenched his teeth and nodded. Ham relaxed his fingers for a moment and then pinched harder still. Josh had seen him crack crab shells open between his forefinger and thumb.

"Josh, what else, buddy?"

"Well, I should stay still if I can. Can't panic." His wrist hurt. "I'm going to hold my breath."

"What?"

"When the CO_2 builds up in my bloodstream it will depress my heart rate." Josh took a big breath and held it. He closed his eyes and saw himself putting a needle full of raw pancreas solution into his mother's leg and slowly pushing down the plunger, counting to ten. Her thighs black and yellow with bruises, an old welt the size of a seagull's egg on her other buttock.

More blood oozed out of his wrist.

Ham patted him clumsily on the shoulder. "Sorry I cussed you out. Could have happened to anybody."

"You wouldn't stick your hand in there in ten lifetimes."

Ham's fat face looked bad after a day without water, blotchy with fatigue and the beginnings of sunburn on his cheeks and nose. "Buddy, I am no-shit scared. Don't you fuck off and die on me here."

"Okay." Already Joshua's right wrist felt terrible, puffy and burning with pain, even though Ham was no longer squeezing it. Next up: cleaning the wound. Josh turned his back to Ham and undid the buttons on his pants, wincing. Squatting in the sand he fished out his limp penis and held it above his right wrist. Ham's eyes widened. "Urine is sterile," Josh said. It hurt to talk. It took a long time for him to piss. Finally a little urine trickled out, dark yellow and strong-smelling. He rubbed it over

the puncture wound as thoroughly as he could. There wasn't enough to wash his hands but he tried.

"Son of a bitch," Ham whispered.

It took Josh a long time to get his pants buttoned up. Afterward he lowered himself to the sand, lying with his head pointing to the surf and his feet pointing toward the dune, naturally elevated.

The pain in his wrist brought tears to his eyes. It felt as if a match-head had ignited under his skin. He had treated several patients for rattler bites, including a malnourished three-year-old boy who had died. The boy had stepped on the snake while playing in the dirt street behind his parents' shack. Josh remembered how cool and clinical he had been at the bedside while the kid screamed. After the child died, his father had offered Josh a portion of their meager dinner of rice, promising they would add some chicken fat for him. He had politely refused. The father couldn't stop shaking his hand. The mother sat rocking the little body in her arms. He should have stayed for dinner, Josh thought. At the time he told himself he was doing the parents a favor. But that was a lie. What they needed was for someone to help eat the grief. He should have stayed.

"Son of a bitch," Ham said.

Josh rolled onto his left side. Ham was staring at the beach. The tide had come in. Way in, Josh realized. Surf was hissing up to within a few yards of where he lay, high above the waterline.

"Against the wind," Ham said. "It's running way over high tide and it's doing it *against the wind*. Look at the sky."

The southern horizon was black. Flicks and sheets of lightning winked across it. A storm had formed over the Gulf. That was what was sucking the hard wind off the land. It must be a hell of a storm to be pushing that huge swell inland against such a blow. Josh forgot to hold his breath. "Hurricane!" he whispered.

Ham scrambled to his feet. "We can't stay here, buddy. This whole beach will be underwater in an hour."

A glint of movement caught Joshua's eye. A dark triangular snake's head slid out of the hole where he had been bitten. A moment later the rest of the snake followed. It was well over five feet long, light brown with darker brown diamond-shaped markings, heavily barred with black rings, its tail the color of fresh cream. It turned and poured smoothly up the face of the sand dune.

"Western diamondback," Ham said. "He knows the storm's coming." They watched the snake vanish into the parched salt grass and sea purslane. Ham held out his hand. Josh took it and Ham pulled him up. They stood for a minute, looking out over the grassland. The wind gusted and abruptly died. A white egret rose from the withered plain and flapped heavily north. Josh doubted the land rose three feet above sea level from where they stood to the horizon.

"What was the storm surge on the Big Blow?" Ham asked.

"Twenty feet."

Ham cussed.

The burning in Joshua's wrist was getting very bad. "Ham, cut the sleeve off my shirt and wrap it around my arm. Not a tourniquet, just snug." It took Ham less than a minute to slash off the shirtsleeve and cinch it around his arm. The fingers on Joshua's right hand were beginning to burn, too. He forced himself to hold his breath, letting the CO_2 build up in his blood. His heart banged and banged against his chest, refusing to slow down. The north wind snapped back.

"We gotta go, buddy."

"Okay," Josh gasped.

They headed over the top of the dune, Ham first, following the trail he had left in the withered salt grass. Thirty paces inland the ground came up in a little rise, hard beneath Joshua's feet. Looking down he could see

cracked tarmac peeking through a half-knit carpet of grass and weeds. "Highway 87," Ham said.

"Can we follow it?"

Ham lumbered down the gentle slope on the other side. "Hell no. It runs along the coast."

Josh lurched after him. Birds scattered up around their feet and went winging inland, black grackles, sparrows, white-barred mockingbirds, and once a blood-red cardinal. At first Josh was terrified of stepping on another rattlesnake, but soon it was hard to think about anything but the pain in his right arm. He was dizzy and couldn't use his arm to balance. He fell down. "Come on, buddy," Ham said. Josh struggled to his feet, ran, fell down again. This time Ham grabbed his left arm and hauled him up.

The wind died again. In the sudden hush they could hear the mutter of distant thunder.

They went more quickly, a heavy gasping shuffle through the dry grass. No chance of Josh holding his breath anymore, he was gasping and choking for air. Dehydration and snakebite ganged up to make terrible cramps in his stomach and sides. Loops of salt grass tangled around his feet and he fell again, landing heavily on his dangling arm. Pain starred out like fireworks from the snakebite, so intense it left the rest of his body shuddering. His mind went blank, waiting for the waves of agony to subside.

Ham slung him over his huge shoulder in a fireman's carry and ran on. Josh bounced against his broad back. His right arm hung at full stretch, rattling horribly with every jarring stride Ham took. The big man was blowing hard, grunting and wheezing as he lumbered through the grass. "Stop!" Josh gasped.

"Easy there."

"I can keep up, I can—"

Ham stumbled, going down on one knee. "For Christ's sake, shut up!" He got up again, weaving, then leaned forward into a heavy jog, carrying Josh over his shoulder

like a broken toy. "Sorry, Josh. Can't wait on you anymore."

About a mile inland he lifted Josh carefully over an ancient barbed-wire fence. While Ham pushed down a fence post and picked his way across, Josh looked back the way they had come. The little swell of Highway 87 was still plainly visible, taller than the land they were standing on now. Josh stood doubled over and panting. He retched again. The cramps in his stomach and sides were worse. He felt a charley horse coming on, his right hamstring beginning to spasm.

"Damn," Ham said. "We got to have some shelter." He pointed to a stand of scrub at least another mile away. "I'm going to make for that."

The storm line cut off the westering sun. A dead calm came with the sudden gloom; the day went hushed and hot in the unnatural darkness. The withered prairie held its breath, as if waiting for a sign. Then a volley of gulls streaked from the black storm clouds, whistled overhead, and in a heartbeat had passed far into the north, like white arrows shot into the waiting stillness.

A gale followed like the shock wave of their passing, and the whole prairie bowed before it.

Chapter Fifteen

MAGGOTS

THE gale was blowing not south to north, as Josh had expected, but pouring hard from the east-southeast. The wind felt as if it were coming from a long way away, carrying mass and momentum, a broad river that flattened the plain under its weight. A raindrop smacked against Josh's back, shockingly cold on his hot skin. Then another drop stung his shoulder. Daylight went out like a doused lamp and then the rain came in earnest, a crashing cascade that left Josh drenched between one ragged breath and the next. The gale tore at his makeshift turban, making it snap and whip around him. The world was suddenly much smaller, a moving pocket of storm. Lightning burst overhead and thunder exploded around him like a bomb. Ham grabbed his left hand and they stumbled off together.

The drought-hardened ground turned to mud, squelching under their bare feet. Josh gulped at the water streaming down his face. In the stuttering lightning glare, the plain boiled like an angry sea. The rain was flying sideways. Josh doubled over with cramp. Ham jerked him forward into a run, but he fell with his swollen wrist under his body and passed out from the pain.

Ham picked him up. Josh bobbed like wreckage in the storm, wavering in and out of consciousness. His eyes opened and closed. The storm was a bedlam. Ham was carrying him, then dragging him, then carrying him again. Every time Josh felt himself surface, lightning burned a single stark image on his eyes.

Grass writhing like anemone arms.

Giant purple clouds with sucking starfish mouths.

A ball of wind-driven Spanish moss smacking into Ham's head, witching it suddenly into something furred and monstrous.

A thrashing alligator tangled in a barbed-wire fence.

Then they were in a thicket of screaming wood, where hackberry branches and cane chattered madly together. Josh found himself on the ground with his back against a tree, its convulsing boughs above him, limbs and twigs branching like capillaries, a whole circulatory system ripped out of some giant animal and held writhing over him.

Tin glinted in front of his face and then Ham was shoving the canteen in his mouth. He choked and coughed as he tried to suck water from it. The metal tasted sour but the rainwater was sweet as life.

More ventricles and arteries, this time made of lightning and sketched in white fire against the sky.

Another hank of Spanish moss came tumbling through the air to thud against the trunk of a nearby tree. Lightning guttered and flared again, and Josh realized it wasn't Spanish moss at all, it was his mother's face, dead white and clotted with seaweed. "Did you remember to bring the matches?" she asked.

"Yes, ma'am." He started up from the kitchen table and gave her the matches. His father began putting their chess pieces away. "Can't we play again?" Josh said.

"Again!" His mother smiled and shook her head. She lit the little oil lamp under the fondue pot she used for her experiments. The air smelled of mint and honey-

suckle and hot wax. She must be making hand lotion or soap or some such. "You've been playing for hours, Josh."

"I can't go out in this weather," he said reasonably. Shutters banged and the house beams creaked in the high wind as if to make his point. "I like playing a lot of games in a row. You learn more when you get in a zone."

"Like father, like son."

"Somebody once asked a grand master why there were no truly great female chess players," Josh's dad remarked. His wife turned around from her little pot and looked at him sardonically. "He said, 'I expect women have better things to do with their time than play chess.' "

Joshua's mother laughed.

"Can't we play again? Please?"

Samuel Cane put the last of the chess pieces away and closed the lid of the box. "If you want to play more, it will have to be poker."

"I like chess better," Josh said sulkily.

"That's because you're still a boy." His father was smiling, but Josh felt as if he had failed some obscure test.

His mom snorted. "So poker is a real man's game, eh?"

"Josh likes chess because it's fair. Each player controls exactly what happens on the board, and the one who plays best wins. That's what makes it a boy's game." Sam took a pack of cards out of his jacket pocket and decanted them with thoughtless grace. "A man's game should be like life."

Rain creaked and pattered across the kitchen windows. Josh had a dim sense of things swaying outside, palm fronds and spears of oleander. His father shuffled the cards in long liquid waterfalls that sounded like the wind outside, like the rain. "The best player doesn't always win. In real life, you get rags sometimes instead of paint. Winning is easy, Josh. Anyone can win. Losing, now . . ." He dealt quickly, two hands of five-card draw. Josh

picked his up. He knew his mom and dad had been married to different people, before the Flood, and those other people had died. A lot of people had died, and the world they knew had died, too. "We get a whole lifetime to learn just one lesson," Samuel Cane said. "How to lose with dignity."

Wind and rain beat against the warm house. Darkness waited outside its windows. When he looked down, Josh saw that the kitchen floor was gone, replaced by muddy prairie. Somehow the rain had worked its way inside. Pools of dark water were spreading between clumps of salt grass and camphor daisies, joining up, the water rising. A tangle of sea purslane was twined around his feet. "I think I disbelieve that," Joshua's mom said with a funny smile. "But you know, Sam, some days you're almost the man I thought you could be."

Joshua's dad laughed. "Don't bet on it," he said.

ONCE, much later, Josh came out of his delirium quite suddenly and unexpectedly, as if stepping through the wrong door by mistake. He was sitting in water up to his lap, lashed to a slender tree with a piece of what had once been Ham's shirt. The pain from his wrist was pure and terrible, but very distant. The howl of the storm had vanished, leaving an unearthly calm. Water rocked gently against him, smelling of salt and mud. The sky was clear. Overhead, stars glimmered like foam thrown hissing across a black beach.

Ham was tied to the next tree over. The big man's eyes were open, gazing out in profound solitude at the land and sea that had become the same unquiet thing. Even looking at him seemed intrusive somehow, shameful and unworthy.

Low to the horizon, a crescent moon drifted on the sea like a lost cradle. Trembling streaks of its yellow light fused and split on the face of the drowned land. The water rocked at Josh and rocked at him. Overhead, stars

flickered like remote candles, going out when he looked at them, flickering back to life as his eyes moved on. Stars wavering like luminous droplets of blue water, surrounding and eluding him.

THE next time Josh woke it was morning.

The sky was clear and the day was pleasantly cool—lower seventies perhaps, although the sun was well up. A fly buzzed around his head. He was still sitting with his back against a tree and water up to his lap. The plain had become a marsh, pools and rills of glinting water broken by clumps of salt grass and stands of reeds. The normal Gulf breeze was back. It shook the salt grass and the water both, so the whole landscape seethed and trembled. Wondering if the water was fresh or salt, Josh started to reach out, then stopped, groaning, as a sick ballooning pain billowed up from his right wrist.

"Morning, Josh!" Ham splashed into view from around the copse. He was naked, the tip of his cock just visible, waggling under the loom of his belly. His gigantic flabby chest was scoured red everywhere it wasn't bruised. His face was thickly stubbled with the beginnings of a beard. Exhaustion had left his eyes ringed like a racoon's. He grinned. "Son, you look like ten pounds of shit in a five-pound bag."

"Don't feel so great," Josh whispered. His back was aching from being strapped to this tree. The muscles in his sides and legs ached, too, reminders of the fierce cramps the rattlesnake venom had induced. Ham splashed over to his side and clubbed a mosquito to death on Joshua's thin chest. "There will be more of these little fuckers in a day or two." He squatted beside Josh, ignoring another mosquito and two flies settling on his enormous shoulders.

"Where are your pants?"

Ham pointed into the branches over Joshua's head. "When the wind started to die down I hung 'em up there

to collect rainwater while it was still falling. Guess I better get 'em down before they dry out. Want a drink?"

"God, yes." A minute later Josh was stretching his head up like a baby bird's as Ham slowly wrung the cloth out into his mouth, careful not to waste a dribble. Only after the last drop was gone did Josh say, "Should we have saved that?"

"Don't worry. I drank my fill and more last night. The canteen leaks at the bottom, by the way. If you screw the top on and hold it upside down it'll hold, mostly. I got it stuck in a tree branch over here." Ham squeezed his prison pants once more, wringing out a couple more drips for himself, then climbed into them, hopping and splashing in the muddy water.

"Ham?"

"Yeah?"

"I'm still tied to this tree." Ham cussed and bent to untie him. "How's my wrist?" Josh asked. He tried to make a fist. It was agony and his fingers barely moved. "I can't stand to look at it. Just tell me, please."

Joshua's eyes teared with pain as Ham gently lifted up his right arm and inspected it. "It don't look so hot," Ham said slowly. "It don't smell so good neither. I reckon your hand and wrist are still swole up about double. Josh, the meat here's turned black. It's black and it's kind of . . . melted." There was no amusement in Ham's voice anymore. "I think some of it's dripped off already. And it stinks."

"It's infected, then. Going necrotic." Another fly buzzed around Josh. Drawn by the smell, no doubt. He swallowed and shifted, trying to ease his aching back, bringing his knees up in front of him. Using his left hand he picked up his right arm and laid it as gently as he could across his knees, hissing with pain. "Ham, are we going to die?"

"Hell, no. We made it through the hurricane, didn't we? Too ugly to kill and too mean to die."

"What about water?"

The big man waved him off with magnificent nonchalance. "*No hay problemo, compadre.* All we have to do is follow Highway 87 till we find some buildings. First house we come to we look for a tarp or a shower curtain, and bingo, there's your still fixin's. Plus rain barrels, cisterns, wells. Any windmill you see, that's probably got a well at the bottom of it. It ain't like nobody lived here before the Flood."

"Won't most of the good stuff have been scavenged by now?"

"I doubt anybody's going to scavenge a stock tank. Those will be right where the farmers left 'em, and full up after last night's rain. Specially if we find a road that cuts inland a piece."

"What about food?"

"If you starve to death on a beach, you deserve to die," Ham said. "You are in and amongst Nature's All-You-Can-Eat-Buffet, my friend. You got your clams and crabs and oysters. Plus all the fish that got blown in and stranded. I've seen five or six flopping around already. One redfish stuck in a tree just yonder, damnedest thing I ever saw. —Josh, there's a fly on your wrist."

"Don't worry about it."

"Plus this morning I seen a couple head of drowned cattle hung up on barbed wire. And a alligator. Damn fine eating, gator." He trailed off. "There's another fly on you. Git, you little fuckers," he said, reaching forward to shoo them off.

"Leave them."

"What?"

"Leave them," Josh said. "In about an hour they'll have laid a batch of eggs in the meat of my wrist. Then I'll bandage the wound." Ham's eyes bugged out. "Maggot therapy," Josh said. "They used it all the time in World War One. You let the maggots hatch. They eat up all the infected flesh and then you flush 'em out."

Ham stared at the flies crawling on Joshua's wrist. "You don't mind if I puke, I hope."

"Not here," Josh said. "I don't want competition."

"Josh—"

"Can't have all my flies crawling over to your vomit—"

"Josh!"

"—and wasting their maggots," Josh finished, grinning. If Ham had retched, he would have laughed out loud.

THEY passed what was left of Ham's shirt repeatedly through the leaves of the little copse of hackberry trees, soaking up as much of the leftover rainfall as possible and wringing it into their mouths. At the back of the copse stood a small hunchbacked black willow. Josh had Ham cut away a few long strips of bark with the pocketknife, then peel out the softer inner bark. He stuck most of it in his pants pocket and chewed on the rest, hoping the salicylates there would give him some relief from the pain in his forearm and bring down his temperature, which he estimated was around a hundred degrees. Josh didn't know whether the fever was an aftereffect of Kyle's beating, the bout of dehydration, rattlesnake venom, or his infected arm. According to Ham he was much cooler than he had been in the middle of the previous night, which fit with his delirious dreams and moments of glassy lucidity.

He had lost their matches, of course. Not that they would have been any use after that deluge. Ham had done better; he still had the gun and mismatched bullets, for a miracle, as well as the canteen and knife. "What next?" Josh said.

Ham was busy peeling off more chunks of bark. "I figure you should rest up today, best you can. I'll find us some food. Then I'll cut some sandals out of this bark, elsewise our feet are going to get flayed to ribbons when

we walk. Especially after staying this long in salt water."
Josh lifted his foot out of the water. It was puffy and
wrinkled like a steamed raisin. "We'll move at night and
find shade during the day," Ham continued. "This afternoon, once it starts cooling down, we'll get over to the
highway yonder."

"Why the highway? Shouldn't we stick closer to the
trees?"

Ham started to spit, thought better of it, and swallowed
instead. "I like the idea of higher ground, for one thing.
For another it will be a lot easier to travel on the road.
Plus you're more likely to find a house along it. And
last"—he glanced into the water—"I like to see what I'm
stepping on."

"Maybe not all the snakes drowned, you think?"

"I *know* not all the gators did."

Josh gulped. He had been hoping for a drowsy day of
rest in the shade, but instead he started to imagine the
marshland teeming with alligators, stranded jellyfish, and
snakes: rattlesnakes, copperheads, cottonmouths, and water moccasins. "Ham, why don't you cut me two small
switches for a splint. Once I get this wrist bandaged up,
I'll follow you up to the road and rest there."

It was nearly midday by the time they got on the move,
picking their way through the marsh. Both men were naked from the waist up. Josh had lost his shirt in the hurricane, and Ham had torn his into strips to bandage
Joshua's elbow and lash them to the hackberry stand. It
wasn't nearly as hot as it had been for the weeks before
the storm, but it was still over eighty and unbelievably
muggy. After drinking quarts of rainwater the previous
night Ham was sweating rivers. Bugs clouded the air
around him, flies and marsh midges and the first mosquitoes coming back into the open after the big blow.
The air was hot and dank and smelled like mud and rotten
shrimp. Pools lay like broken glass between clumps of
salt grass. Sunlight splintered off of them. Josh walked

with his eyes screwed nearly shut against the glare.

A ton of fish had been stranded behind the accidental dike of Highway 87 when the sea receded. Josh could see them flicking around their feet as they walked, redfish and flounder and a few sea bass. The herons and egrets were feasting, striding through the marsh picking off fingerlings, baby snakes, and the croaking frogs that had begun to congregate atop every projecting log or clump of grass. At any one time there were always three or four flights of buzzards overhead, each marking the body of a drowned cow or a possum impaled on a barbed-wire fence.

It took more than an hour to get back to 87, and despite Ham's cheerful conversation, largely made up of helpful tips on alligator wrestling, Josh was exhausted. The highway was coated in a thick layer of mud the consistency of axle grease, studded with gasping fish, drowned birds, and ropes of seaweed. Josh sat Indian style, slumping forward so his head nearly touched his knees, his damaged arm tucked against his stomach. He hoped the maggot eggs were festering in his wrist. He drowsed unpleasantly while Ham went off to forage.

The big man returned well pleased with himself. "The swell's still running high, but there's a bit of sand showing at the top of the beach now. Lots of wreckage piled against the dune, too. I think we can get in and amongst some shelter there." He led Josh down the shore to where a massive live-oak limb, freshly splintered at the base, had been thrown against the sandy dune. Most of the leaves had been stripped away, but by piling seaweed and purslane and clumps of reed onto the twiggy lattice at the end of the limb, Ham manufactured a little shade.

Josh burrowed gingerly into the nest of twigs. It wasn't very comfortable, and instead of sleeping he spent an unrewarding hour trying to break off inconvenient branchlets with his left hand. Ham collected bunches of purslane, sea lettuce, and plantain to eat. "Thought we'd save

the meat and fish for when we can make a fire," he said. Josh had no appetite, but he forced himself to nibble the salty plants.

The afternoon was clear and the breeze light, but the sea was still riled up. Eight- and ten-foot waves built and broke thirty yards out. White spray rushed up the beach to within a few feet of where Josh and Ham were sitting, crowded side by side under the haphazard roof of seaweed and bracken, trying to find shade. Ham shook his head, munching on a handful of sea lettuce. "Hell of a blow."

"You figure the *Fat Tuesday* got caught in that?" Josh asked hopefully. He tried a plantain leaf. There was lots of mucilage in plantain; it figured in most of his poultices and potions for bruises and cuts. He should probably try packing some into the wound on his wrist, come to think of it, but he couldn't bring himself to open the dressing.

Ham had stopped eating. "I hadn't even thought. That hurricane was blowing east to west, so we must have got hit by the right side of the storm. Meaning the eye must have passed even closer to home."

"Serves the bastards right," Josh said. His mouth was bitter from chewing willow bark all morning.

Ham looked at him. "Fuck Galveston, eh?"

"Not my problem," Josh said. The plantain leaves still tasted faintly of brine. He wondered how much salt they were eating. "We better find some more water tonight."

"Those sailors gave me a goddamn rope burn when they tied us up," Ham said. "And how about the people in that courthouse? Never mind the sheriff and Deacon Bose, what about all those Gardner cousins and maids and kids that came just for the show. That's a hell of a way to get your jollies, ain't it? Serves them right if that storm taught *them* a lesson. Yes, sir."

Josh stopped eating. "What's wrong with you?"

"Why stop there?" Ham said, scratching at the stubble growing through his sunburned cheeks. His eyes were

narrow, and his fat face was ugly with anger. "Why not just scrape the fucking Island clean? Sure, maybe a few of the big houses will still be left standing, but at least you've killed off the riffraff."

"Did I piss you off somehow?"

"At least you'd have a *sterile working environment* for once," Ham said. He stared out at the furious ocean that still roiled and crashed along the shore.

Josh remembered the screaming squalls that had ripped off the water through the night. If the *Fat Tuesday* hadn't put into shore she must surely have been lost. "I didn't mean that I wanted everyone to die."

"Course not," Ham said. "You're a doctor, right? You take care of people."

"What do you want from me?" Josh said. "They kicked us out, Ham. If we go back they'll kill us both. I have tried and tried to do the best I could, and they just didn't want me, okay? Well, all right, I got the message."

"You little fucker," Ham said. He wiped his big red face with his hand. "We wanted you, Josh. Me and Shem and Penny and the Grooks and the Stephensons. That Bowles kid you saved who was dying of asthma. We wanted you. But we're not rich, so we just don't fucking count." His face was full of frustration and disgust. "Have you even figured out yet why you had the hots for the Gardner bitch?"

"What?"

"It's her *house* you want to fuck, Josh." Rolls of sun-burned flesh spilled over the waistband of Ham's ragged prison pants he grabbed his crotch and pumped his big hips. "You want to crawl up under the official and sanctified Duchess of the Krewe of Momus floorboards and hump her fine china and feel up all the swanks who come to her parties." Ham shook his head and spat, jaw working. "You're just a two-bit snob, Joshua Cane, and fuck me for ever telling anybody otherwise."

"That's not true." Josh felt parched and weak. He

shook his head. Remembered what they had all said about him in the courthouse. Remembered how nobody had defended him. Nobody but Ham.

The big man gathered up a handful of food. "I think I'll rest out on the beach."

"Ham. Jesus. Stay in the goddamn shade! We don't have the luxury to be stupid. You need to stay in the shade. Conserve water."

Ham eased his way out of their little bower of live-oak twigs. "It's hard to eat in here, Josh. Your fucking wrist stinks, if you want to know the truth."

"Ham."

"There's a fair little breeze out here," Ham said. "I'm jes' a rough ol' redneck, Josh. I ain't comfortable in no big fancy house," he said with an exaggerated drawl. "You can have the run of the mansion."

"This is childish."

"Childish?" Ham turned, quick as a fox, and shoved Josh back against the trunk of the wrecked oak with one huge hand around his throat. His whole body was shaking. "You . . ." He licked his lips. "Maybe you forgot that my sister Rachel lives in a double-wide, Josh. What do you figure her trailer park looks like this morning? Hey? But hell, it serves her right, don't it? Serves them all right for not recognizing your fucking genius." Josh fought for air. His friend's huge hand was hard as a brick, shoving against his windpipe. "People used to say, 'That Cane boy, he's a mean one, ain't he?' and I would tell them they were wrong. If you get past the prickles, I'd say, Josh is all right. But you aren't, are you, Josh? You're just a spiteful little fuck and nothing is ever your own fault and the world has done you wrong." Ham's fat arm was trembling with fury. "And because of you—*you*—I wasn't there for my family when they needed me. I have friends and kin who mean the world to me, and I sold them out for you." He dropped Josh in disgust. "So which one of us is stupider, eh? How many times have I saved

your ass? Whereas I got dick from you. Less than nothing. Maybe while I was out here watching you feel sorry for yourself, and stick your hand into rattler holes like no child of five should do, maybe my folks or my sister was getting drowned. Maybe my niece Christy, maybe she was getting a pane of glass through her neck because they didn't have enough help to board their windows up in time."

Josh felt sick with shame. He had never seen his friend like this. "Ham—"

"I don't want to hear it, you contemptible little fuck," Ham said flatly. He backed out of their makeshift hut. "I'll be outside," he said.

Josh watched him walk down the beach, looking west, toward Galveston.

Josh closed his eyes. Ham would get over it, he told himself. He always did. He'd heard the big man bluster before. He wasn't the type to hold a grudge. And yet . . . that flatness in Ham's voice as he backed out of the lean-to—that was something Josh had never heard before.

The lean-to that Ham had made, that Josh was using. *How many times have I saved your ass? Whereas I got dick.*

Ham's sister Rachel had two kids. Christ, Josh thought. What a prick he was. Even if somehow they had survived, they had terrible sewage problems in her run-down neighborhood. They'd be starting to see dysentery in a day or two. Cholera, too. Josh rubbed his eyes with his left hand and pressed his palm against his aching forehead. Ham was right. He was a mean, petty, vindictive snob. Hell, he thought, I wouldn't let me join a Krewe either.

The sound of Ham's footsteps was soon swallowed by the angry breakers and the hiss of surf against the sand. Gulls cried. Josh heard the piping of a gang of little shore plovers. Back when they were little, Sloane used to call

the big ones sandpipers and the little ones sandpeepers. She probably didn't remember that. He did. He remembered chasing after them with Sloane and Randall Denton and Jenny Ford, a whole pack of kids. Birds fluffing into the air, offended, the kids stringing out, most of them faster than him. He had stopped to pick up a sand dollar one time, he remembered, then put it back in the surf so it wouldn't dry out. By the time he looked up, the other kids were gone. They had run down the beach, nobody had waited for him. He was alone.

Josh's wrist ached and his body felt heavy as mud in the mid-afternoon heat. Exhausted and feverish, he fell into a long series of anxious dreams in which his mother needed something but he had lost it through pure carelessness and time was running out. The thing he was supposed to bring to her kept changing—a sand dollar, a Bible, a watch, a pair of black silk stockings spattered with blood. The dream seemed to go on and on, and his first reaction on waking was relief.

It was a sound that had woken him, a heavy metallic thunk, dull yet slightly musical. An odd sound. Opening his eyes, he was surprised to find that it was full dark out. Ham must have fallen asleep, too. Peering out through the lattice of twigs, all Josh could see was the dull glimmer of starlight on the waves breaking offshore. Ghostly ribbons of surf washed along the beach.

His head ached and he was thirsty. His mouth felt as if it were made of hot cloth. His wrist throbbed sharply when he tried to move. He fumbled at his pocket for another hank of willow bark. What the hell could have made that odd noise? It had sounded like someone dropping a cowbell wrapped in a tea towel. Grimacing, he started to crawl from their makeshift hut. Each pulse felt like a double rap with a tack hammer, one spike of pain from his right wrist and another ache a moment later in his pounding head. He poked his head out of the shelter and felt the cool wind on his face.

Someone jabbed him in the neck with a knife. "Move and I cut you right here," said a woman's voice. "George? I've caught the little one. Should I cut his throat?"

Chapter Sixteen

CANNIBALS

JOSH could see another figure stooped over the shadowy bulk of Ham's body. "This side of beef ain't dead yet," said the man called George in a businesslike East Texas drawl. "Can the little one walk?"

The woman holding the knife against Joshua's throat coughed, a dry hacking cough. "Can you walk?" He figured from her accent that she was black.

"Here's a hint," George said. "If you cain't walk, we'll cut your throat and leave you on the beach."

"I can walk."

"Attaboy." With a grunt George heaved Ham's body over so he was lying facedown in the sand. "This'un's a big sumbitch, ain't he? Hardheaded, too. I gave him plenty of whack with my baseball bat. Would have been a waste to kill him, but better safe than sorry, that's my motto."

"Why are you doing this?" Josh said. He thought about jumping back under the screen of brush, but that would leave him trapped. He was too weak and dizzy to hope to outrun his captors in a scramble along the beach. "We've got nothing worth stealing, not even food."

"Not even food?" George said with a laugh. "Hell, son, you *are* food."

Joshua's heart battered against his ribs like a trapped bird.

Cannibals.

Still chuckling, George pulled Ham's arms behind his back and lashed his wrists together with practiced speed. "Here's the deal, little man: After I get done with this big side of beef, you're going to stay still while I tie you up. Then we're going for a walk. If you make a break for it I will beat your friend's head like an egg and then haul ass after you. Comprende?"

"Why should I go along? You're just going to kill me anyway."

"Well, now, the game ain't over till it's over, that's my philosophy. Heck, I might let you go!" George said expansively. "That was a joke, son. Why ain't you laughing? Seriously, though, I got plenty of food, specially after a blow like this. Good workers, now—those are hard to come by. You'll be alive and un-et just as long as you are useful." George got busy down by Ham's ankles. "Nothing personal, friend. But it's a tough old world, and everybody's got to look out for number one. Martha, help him out of that lean-to and make sure he can walk."

The knifepoint teased Josh out into the open. He willed himself to stand up, biting his lips against a surge of dizziness. The woman named Martha coughed again. "He looks a little shaky to me. Skinny, too."

"You're so damn lazy, Martha." George came up behind Josh and began binding his wrists with what felt like wire. Josh screamed and thrashed as the loop jerked tight around his snakebit forearm. George punched him hard in the back of the head, and he fell facedown into the sand. George sat on his back. "Now, what in the hell? Give me some light, Martha. Oh, I see. Well, that's all

right. We'll just tie you by your elbows then. —There. That's better, ain't it?"

Josh tried to stop sobbing as the pain in his wrist receded. His arms were pinned tightly behind his back with his elbows almost touching. George rolled Josh over so he was lying on his back in the sand, then squatted over him with a knee on each side of his chest and gripped his chin to hold his head still. "You might want to close your eyes," George said.

"I can walk! I can walk! Don't kill me, please!" Josh kept his eyes shut tight.

"If I was going to kill you, would I waste time tying you up?" Josh heard a click, followed a moment later by a faint odor of kerosene on the Gulf breeze. His eyes flew open as a searing pain on his forehead made him buck and shriek.

Josh had been branded. "Welcome to the Bar V!" George said. Martha was holding a slender stamp made out of coat-hanger wire, glowing dull red. Josh writhed in his bonds, smelling the stink of his own burnt skin. George chuckled, taking the brand from Martha. A moment later he was squatting over Ham, stamping his forehead. The big man groaned and jerked, his great body curling and uncurling on the sand as George stepped off of him.

Seeing Ham utterly vulnerable, his ankles hobbled and his hands tied behind his back, made something click over in Josh, all his fear and pain precipitating suddenly into a cold, bitter anger. "If you really want us to walk, turn him around," Josh said. "If you hit him in the head he may have a concussion. Elevate his feet and give him some water so he won't go into shock."

A slender flame jumped in George's cupped hand—a silver cigarette lighter. That must have been what he had used to heat the branding wire. Shielding the lighter's wavering flame with his body, George peered at Josh. Josh stared back at his captor. George had been born

white, but burned by sun and wind to a ruddy mahogany. The leathery skin of his face was grooved and deeply lined. He had the used-up look of a man that has lived too hard and suffered too much from hunger and thirst and sickness. It was a look Josh had seen before, in his poorest and most brutalized patients. At first glance you would figure George for a strong man nearing seventy, but Josh guessed he was closer to forty-five. His hair was thin and kinked from malnutrition. Each side of his gaunt face was seamed with a long, deep scar. The flesh along the scars was puckered and gnarled from cheekbone to jaw. Above them, on his forehead, he bore a third scar, a barred V like the one he had branded onto Josh and Ham, but this one had been cut rather than burned in.

"You a doctor?" George said.

"Pretty much."

Martha coughed.

Josh lay on the sand with his arms lashed behind him and his ankles hobbled together. He drew his cool, professional detachment around him like a lab coat. It was the only covering he had left. "If you need Ham to walk, you'd better elevate his feet. I'd do it myself, but . . ."

Tears of pain started in Josh's eyes as George tapped the blistering brand on his forehead. "I give the orders here," he said. "You hear me, son?" Josh didn't answer. George reached around and gave his swollen wrist a squeeze. "Hear me?"

Josh gasped. "Yes, sir."

"That's all right, then," George said. A moment later he swung Ham's body around so his feet were up the shore. Then he dribbled a few drops of water into Ham's mouth from his canteen.

Ham recovered full consciousness within ten minutes. Half an hour later he and Josh were staggering slowly down Highway 87 under the stars, with their arms tied behind them and their ankles hobbled. Their captors walked behind them, Martha taciturn and coughing,

George in robust good spirits. Though the cold rage did not leave Josh, his strength quickly began to flag. The third time he fell in the road, George called a halt.

A thin band of sky was beginning to lighten on the eastern horizon. George had Josh and Ham lie back to back on the road. Josh could feel Ham's muscles begin to tense as George bent down to lash them together. George paused and then kicked Ham savagely in the stomach. "Don't go getting no ideas," he said with a chuckle. In a few seconds he used another hank of cord to tie their bound arms together. "Martha, I'm going to scout for some water and some grub. If they show any signs of moving, stick the little one and stay clear. I doubt the big one will get too far with his friend's body on his back."

Martha coughed. "I'm hungry," she said, eyeing Ham.

George laughed. "Not for long." Then he left them, striking inland. They could hear him splashing through the salt-grass marsh long after his dim form passed out of sight.

Grey light filtered slowly into the humid air. Josh and Ham lay back to back, with Josh facing inland. The Gulf breeze had died in the middle of the night. Grass and reeds rose motionless from the grey water that still covered much of the waterlogged prairie. Large humped shapes dotted the plain. Some were still, but others were moving, giant beasts as massive as live-oak trees that dipped and raised their great heads as if drinking. Suddenly Josh realized they were oil wells, solitary grazers of the kind they called cricket pumps, or dipping birds. He tried to wet his cracked lips. "Now I know why we didn't see any houses or barns," he said. "This land must have been leased to an oil company. There's cricket pumps all over it."

Ham grunted.

"They're cannibals," Josh said. "George says we're to work as slaves, near as I can gather. He says he won't

eat us till we can't work. How's your vision?"

"Kind of blurry. Not too bad. Feels like my head got kicked by a horse."

"It was an aluminum baseball bat. I saw it as our pal George was leaving."

"Easton Howitzer," Martha said with a chuckle. "B'longed to my brother. Had it since the Flood."

Josh squinted at Martha, who sat cross-legged on the road behind them. She was a lanky black woman with unhealthy yellow eyes and the sour look of someone with low expectations who had still been disappointed. Her cheeks were scarred like George's, but she had a different mark on her forehead, a diamond with a line through it. She was younger than George, he judged—thirty-five going on fifty. She would have been nine or ten when the Flood fell, and grown up during the bloody anarchy that followed.

George had been lean and sinewy, but Martha was painfully skinny. Too skinny, really. Even in hard times, the sea ought to supply enough food to keep more weight on her than this, Josh thought. The knuckle of her left ring finger was swollen twice as large as the other fingers on her bony hands. Arthritis? Scurvy? Her breasts hung low and flat beneath a long-sleeved cotton shirt. She wore polyester pants that had been patched and repatched with bits of other clothing, and a pair of rubber flip-flops on her feet. Josh looked at them enviously; his feet were already salt- and wind-chapped, his toes badly blistered. She still had her knife in her hand, an eight-inch blade with a non-slip molded rubber handle. It had once been a fat-bladed hunting knife, judging by the steel near the hilt, but years of sharpening had worn the blade thin and taken off any serrations, so now it looked more like a filleting knife.

Martha coughed. "Don' be looking at me."

"Help us get rid of George and we'll make it worth your while," Ham said.

Martha laughed. "That didn't take long. 'Xactly how you going to make it worth my while, beef? George and me got a place. George and me know the land, and we know the folks around here. You got jack. You know jack. Minute I let you out those ropes, you try to cut my throat."

"We wouldn't," Ham said.

"Then you even dumber than you look," Martha said. Josh didn't like the sound of that.

"Josh?" Ham said flatly, a while later.

"Yes?"

"Thanks again for getting me into this."

Josh watched the cricket pump heads lift up and down among the rushes. "You're welcome," he said.

Silence returned as the daylight broadened. A mosquito whined in Josh's ear. Another one settled on his cheek. He shook his head, trying to dislodge it. It rose for a second and then alighted again. His arms were tied behind his back. He watched the mosquito, eyes straining to keep focus, as it dipped into his skin. *Anopheles.* He wondered if it was carrying malaria or yellow fever.

Martha coughed again. A bell went off in the back of Joshua's brain. He looked sharply again at the swollen joint on her left ring finger. "How long—" He stopped, calculating.

"What?"

"Nothing," he said.

He had an idea, but he would have to wait for George to get back.

THEIR captor returned in excellent spirits, with four good-sized redfish in a plastic shopping bag. He turned the fish over to Martha to gut while he washed the bag out with seawater. "You get 'em with a bat?" Ham asked when he returned. "I figured you'd make a gig."

"Didn't have to." George grinned, taking a handful of tinder from his pack. "There's fish everywhere trapped

in these little ponds. All you have to do is kick up the bottom. When it's good and muddy they come up to see. Then you whack 'em, just like we whacked you when you wandered out onto the beach." He cleared a space on the highway and stacked up old ferns, cattail heads, and dropped pine needles. On top of the tinder he placed twigs, followed by larger bits of deadfall and driftwood the storm had thrown up. "Don't be sore, though. I'll give you a taste of breakfast this morning. Do your hearts good."

"George," Martha said.

" 'Muzzle not the ox that treads out the corn,' " George intoned. "They got to be able to walk, don't they? At least for today." He bent over his fire and flicked the silver cigarette lighter. The tinder flinched and smoked, reluctant to catch. Either water had gotten at it during the storm, or the ever-present Gulf Coast humidity had kept it moist. Finally a fan of pine needles went up, and little buds of white fire broke open on some of the smaller twigs.

George dug a battered tin skillet out of his pack. He waved at the long sky, the morning sun glinting on the salt-grass marsh, the gentle roar of the rollers breaking offshore. "A day like this makes you glad to be alive, don't it?"

"You'll excuse us if me and Ham don't spit up any hallelujahs," Josh said. They still lay tied back to back on the pavement.

George stopped and looked around, eyes merry. "What did you say your big friend's name was? *Ham?* My Lord, I might have to eat you boys after all! Ham! That's what I call a Sign."

"The little one, he's kind of stringy," Martha said, grinning.

George considered. "Not much of a roast, I'll admit, but I'd say he's halfway to jerky already. Six hours in a smokehouse, I reckon I could slip him into my back

pocket with space left over for a tin of chaw." Martha laughed in spite of herself, and George chuckled until he had to wipe the tears of laughter from his eyes and tend to the fire, which was threatening to go out. "You get busy with those fish now, Martha. I always loved to fish, even before the Flood. You boys are too young to re-member the world back then, I suppose. Even Martha here can't recall it, not really."

"We had a color TV and watched cartoons on Saturday morning," Martha said. "I had to go to a funeral after the neighbors ate my brother. I had red shoes."

"Nobody ate your brother," George said sharply. "Anyway he died after the Flood. You got it all mixed up. She don't even know how old she is. What year is it, honey?" Martha didn't answer. "See? Might as well ask a rattlesnake." George stuck out the skillet. Martha put in two redfish fillets.

George squatted in the road, holding his pan over the smoky fire. "Now I was a grown man. I remember. We had it easy then, that's the gospel truth. And sure, it was nice to watch a game on TV and drink a beer. But that's a life for a steer, not a man." He gestured at the wide world with his skillet. "Out here, today, it's survival of the fittest. It's tough. It's harsh. Are you the hunter or the hunted? But it makes you strong. In the old days, the government took away half of what you earned, gave it to the weak and the lazy blacks and drug addicts and gangs. White punks, too, it wasn't only blacks," he added, with a glance at Martha. "Nowadays you get a truer picture of what a man is really worth."

"Fuck you, you piece of shit," Ham said. Josh didn't point out he'd heard Ham say pretty much the same thing. "You cunt-sucking sister-fucker."

George jiggled his skillet over the fire and grinned. "Well, ain't nothing good about a fox, to hear the chick-ens tell it."

Martha turned her head away from the fish she was gutting and coughed, another dry hack.

"How long have you had that?" Josh said.

"Had what?"

"That cough."

"Oh." She shrugged. "Couple of weeks, maybe. It ain't nothing."

"Couple of weeks!" George said. "Try two months. Keeps me up all night and makes her wiggle when we do the nasty. It's a flu."

"It's a flu," Martha said.

Josh said, "Ever get night sweats, Martha?"

She cut the head off a second redfish with an angry chop. "Why don't you mind—"

"She does, too." George looked sharply at Josh. "I noticed it myself."

Josh wanted to cheer. He had George hooked now. "Hm," he said. The smell of frying redfish reached his nostrils, and his appetite rushed back for the first time in three days. His salivary glands clenched, though he'd drunk so little water that only a trickle of spit wet his mouth.

"You think she's got something," George said.

Josh shrugged.

"It's the flu," Martha snapped. She stared Josh down. Her wrist bones stood out clearly as she pulled the guts out of the fish and threw them in the roadside ditch. In full daylight her face looked even more gaunt, her scarred cheeks hollow and the bones of her forehead clearly visible under her skin.

"Martha, you might as well let the man ask some questions. If you're sick we need to get you some help," George said soothingly.

"You don't want to be weak," Ham said sarcastically. "It's a tough world out here. Dog-eat-dog. Survival of the fittest."

Bless you, Josh thought. You couldn't have said any-

thing better if I'd rehearsed you for an hour. "Do you ever get fevers in the afternoon?" Josh asked. "Say mid-afternoon to sunset?"

"No," Martha said.

"Have you been losing weight over the last few months?"

"No."

Josh glanced at George. George looked down at his skillet.

"Swelling in your joints? Not all over—maybe just one or two?" Josh saw George's eyes dart to the bulging knuckle on the ring finger of Martha's left hand.

"I got rheumatics in the family," Martha said.

Josh fell quiet.

"Well?" George said.

Josh blinked. "What? Oh, probably it's the flu. There's no way I could make a sure diagnosis anyway, not without a TB test."

"TB?" George said. "Tuberculosis?"

"He's making this shit up," Martha said angrily.

"I just wondered, because of the cough," Josh said. Ham twisted his head around to try to see Joshua's face. Josh shrugged. "It's probably the flu."

Martha put down her fish and stood up. She walked over to where Josh was lying on the road and kicked him in the stomach so savagely he doubled up against Ham's back, retching. "I ain't weak," she said. She stared at George. "Don't you believe any of this bullshit."

"I ain't worried," he said, looking into the skillet. But his previous ebullience was gone, and when the fish was cooked Josh and Ham didn't get any of it after all.

Josh had hoped that after the breakfast stop they would make camp for the day, but George pushed on. "I want to get home tonight," he explained. "The rate you boys are going, that could take a while." Josh couldn't talk him into giving them any food, but he grudgingly agreed to let them have water. Martha took a long pull off the

canteen, then gave each of them a swig. "One hell of a storm that was," George said, looking out to sea as he took the water from Martha. Josh noticed that he wiped off the mouth of the canteen with his shirt before taking a drink. He thought Martha noticed it, too.

George untied Josh from Ham and they set off, each still hobbled at the ankles and elbows. George pushed them into a waddling jog, shoving and yelling at them constantly. As the sun climbed and the day got hotter they slowed down even more. "I'm about out of patience," George said, tight-lipped. Some time later, he caught sight of another live-oak limb that the storm had thrown up on the beach. Jogging down off the highway he used the aluminum baseball bat to snap off a long switch. "This oughta help," he said, jabbing the splintered end of the stick hard into Ham's back. Ham grunted in pain.

He drove them harder, whipping their calves or jabbing them in the shoulders or back when they slowed down. It was a hellish journey. The brief respite from summer that had followed the storm had evaporated. The day was hot, as hot as it had been before the hurricane. The air was unbearably muggy, and as the day wore on it stank worse and worse of hot mud and rot and the decomposing bodies of stranded fish and livestock killed by the storm. Josh's eyes stung with constant sweat. He worried about dehydration. He fell again and again, only to have George jerk him back to his feet. Ham wasn't so lucky; when he fell, George just beat him with the switch until he got up on his own. Josh wondered if George was actually showing him a kind of favoritism, as if he had plans for him later and not Ham. Or perhaps George was just smart enough not to get too close to the big man. Even bound, Ham towered over the rest of them, and huge as he was, he might be able to do a lot of damage with a shoulder rush or a head butt.

Then there were the mosquitoes, clouds and clouds of

them. By mid-morning George called a halt. "Little bastards are going to eat us alive. Martha, git on into the
grass there and get some mud. I'll keep an eye on the
boys. You watch out for gators."

She nodded and headed down into the marsh. Josh
noticed she took the knife with her. George turned. "You.
Sit," he said, jabbing Ham behind one knee with his
switch.

Ham collapsed to his knees. His huge shoulders heaved
as he gasped for air. "So help me Jesus, if I ever get my
hands on you—"

"You won't, beef, so save your breath." George took
Josh by the arm and turned him so they were facing out
to sea, with their backs to Martha in the marsh. "Now,
Josh," he said quietly, "I think you and me could come
to an understanding. A big body, that's always useful for
a while. But a doctor . . . I can't make any promises, not
without talking to Martha, but I don't think there's any
call to waste that education by making you a field hand.
In fact, I think I could go so far as to say you might not
have to wear hobbles. Just a little nick in the hamstring,
you know, to make sure you stick around. With that and
my brand on you, I doubt you'd get rustled. You and me,
we could have a very profitable relationship."

Josh forced himself to remain cool and concentrate,
ignoring the pain in his wrist and the clouds of mosquitoes that had already covered his bare chest with bites.
"How about Ham?"

"Well . . . I tell you," George said after a moment, "a
big body like that, he'd be pretty useful to have around.
Couldn't let him roam without a hobble, of course. But
with me getting on and all, we could use a strong back
around the spread."

Josh took this to mean the big man was obviously dangerous and would get his throat cut the minute he had
conveniently walked himself to George's smokehouse.
"I'm relieved to hear that," he said.

George sidled closer. "Now, remind me a little bit about TB. How contagious is that, exactly?"

"Not really bad. You probably had some of the vaccines and boosters when you were in school."

George passed a hand over his stubbled head. "Hm. What about poor Martha, hey? What's her chances?"

"It's probably the flu."

George grimaced and lowered his voice still further. "I ain't so sure. Let's just say I have reason to believe she may have fibbed on a couple of those questions you asked her."

"Oh," Josh said. "If that's true, I'm afraid TB is a real possibility." A certainty, in fact; Martha had the most dead obvious case of the disease he had seen in years. "If it is tuberculosis, her outlook isn't very good. Six months, maybe. A year at the most."

George glanced behind them. Martha was up to her calves in the marsh, plastering handfuls of mud over herself to keep off the mosquitoes. She had covered up the bare skin of her face, wrists, feet and ankles, and was now beginning to coat her clothing as well. George turned back to face the sea. "That's hard. We been together a lot of years now. I took her in and looked out for her from when she was just thirteen years old. Lot of time. We had us three kids."

"The kids are at home?"

"Not really," George said. He shook his head. "We made a pretty good team, Martha and me. It comes to all men, though, right? Nature red in tooth and claw—my daddy used to say that. Live well today, you might die tomorrow. That's my motto."

The two men stood together, watching the waves break tirelessly on the shore.

George stirred. "Just out of curiosity," he said. "If some . . . if a gator, say, or an old coyote was to find the body of somebody who died like that, would they get TB from eating off of it?"

"From eating the corpse?"

"Out of curiosity."

"I wouldn't think so," Josh said in his coolest, considering, professional voice. "Certainly not if you didn't eat the swollen joints or the lungs. And of course cooking would eliminate the problem."

"I see," George said. "Coyotes don't cook, mind you."

"I guess not," Josh said.

Martha splashed through the ditch at the side of the road and hiked back up to the highway. "Not a word," George murmured. "Let's not get the poor girl rattled." He turned to Martha with a big smile. "Your turn to guard the henhouse, my dear." Josh noticed he took the baseball bat with him.

Josh looked for Martha and found her staring at him. Quietly he said, "George was just asking—"

"One more word out of you," Martha said, "and I'll cut off your dick."

Then she coughed.

THE day got hotter and there was no more talking. The mud on George and Martha caked and hardened. Josh and Ham moved in a cloud of mosquitoes. From time to time Ham would suddenly roar and shake his head like an angry bear and drop to his knees, rolling over and over in the road as if somehow he could crush the tormenting insects under him. The first time it happened, Josh expected George to beat Ham mercilessly, but there must have been some spark of fellow feeling, a hatred of the mosquitoes that unified them all. After a moment Ham staggered to his feet, fighting his balance and the ropes binding him, and then lumbered forward again. George said nothing about it.

Just after noon Ham dropped in his tracks. "If you're going to kill me, kill me. I'm done."

"What if I kill your friend?"

"Fuck him," Ham said. "If I can't keep running to save my own ass, I sure won't do it for his."

George laughed. "Everybody's always looking out for number one, that's my motto."

Josh sank to his knees. Gasping, he sucked in a mosquito, choked, and tried to cough it out. The temperature must be back in the nineties. The Gulf breeze still had not returned.

"Anyone for a drink?" George said, putting down his switch and his aluminum bat and slipping the pack from his shoulders.

Martha coughed. "I'll take one," she said, walking over. The pace and the hot day were telling on her, Josh thought. Not to mention lack of sleep and the effects of the TB that was wasting her away. Ham had spilled onto his front and lay gasping on the weed-choked asphalt. Only George seemed unfazed by the bugs and the stink and the pounding heat. His yellow teeth and eyes flashed in a smile from the midst of his mud-covered face. Right now, under the merciless Texas sun, he seemed like a different being from the rest of them, the sinewy invincible predator he pictured himself to be.

"Two hours' rest to get your wind, boys," George said. "A good push should get us home by—" He paused to think, tilting his neck up as he lifted the canteen strap over his head.

His arm was passing in front of his eyes as Martha reached up with a sudden slash and jerked her hunting knife across his throat. Blood spurted from his neck. George's eyes widened. He reached down to grab for his bat. The blood came harder, gobbets of it spurting with every heartbeat. It splashed over Josh's face, hot and salty and tasting of meat. Martha dodged back. George tried to yell; a weird bubbling hiss came out of his severed throat. He staggered after Martha, blood spraying from his neck. She backed easily out of range. He fell to his knees. Blood pumped from his throat. There was so much

of it, so much more blood than you'd expect, spattering the road like red rain. George lost consciousness and slid forward onto his face.

Martha watched him leak blood onto the road for a long time. "Git them before they git you," she said sourly. "That's my motto."

Ham was staring at her in complete bewilderment.

She wiped the blade of the knife on her leg. "Can you fix this TB thing?"

"It's probably the flu," Josh said.

"I know it ain't the goddamn flu," Martha said. "Can you fix it?"

"Yes," Josh lied.

"I think you just saying that to keep me from sticking you."

"I think you don't have a choice," Josh said. "You're a dead woman in six months if someone doesn't get you well. You have a flagrant case of *Mycobacterium tuberculosis* and I'm your only hope of living."

Martha considered. "All right," she said. She stepped forward and pulled the baseball bat out of George's hand. "End of the line for you, beef. I can't watch bof' of you all the way back to the smokehouse."

Ham struggled to rise to his knees. "Just try it, baby."

"Wait!" Josh shouted. "I want him alive."

"Fuck that," Martha said. She stuffed the knife in her belt and gripped the aluminum bat in both hands.

"You want me happy," Joshua said quickly. "If I'm happy, I make you well. If I'm not happy, you have no way of knowing if I'm giving you medicine or poison."

Martha stood quivering in the road. "God*damn* it," she said. Suddenly she swung down hard. Ham flinched, but it was George's head she hit. The aluminum bat crunched into his skull, partly caving it in. George's body jerked and then stiffened. "You didn't have to *listen*," Martha yelled. She coughed, another dry hacking cough. A couple of tears crawled down her muddy cheeks. She kicked

George in the side, and then again. He didn't seem to mind.

"We don't have to be enemies," Josh said quietly.

"You shut up," Martha said. "Got to think. Got to think hard." She shut her eyes. A moment later she opened them and kicked George's body again with a scream. "You think you was gonna do me that way?" She stopped to gather her composure. "I should have jes' killed you on the beach. Soon as you said you was a doctor." She shook her head. "He couldn't stand to be sick. This is your fault," she said, glaring at Josh. "If it wasn't for you this don't happen. An' he was a good provider."

"Martha, he was going to eat you," Josh said. "He was going to kill you and eat you. He pretty much told me that."

Even in the noonday sun there were mosquitoes around them, whining and settling. Josh's wrist was throbbing. It had been too long since he had opened the bandage over it. He wondered if any maggots had hatched inside the wound. Bound to have. In the heat of the day the stink rising from the damp bandage was sickening. Ham still knelt in the road in front of him. His vast back was sunburned and bruised and scraped from the jabs of George's switch. Cobbled with mosquito welts.

"If you kill us," Josh said, "you die for sure. If you kill just Ham, you die probably but not for sure. If you let us live, there's a chance I can save you. Let us go, Martha."

She passed one bony hand slowly through her short curly hair. "Why would you fix me up? Why not just kill me?"

"Making people well is what I do," Josh said.

A cloud of terns skirled overhead, tumbling inland off the sea, darting and circling one another. "Get on your knees by the beef," Martha said. "Fuck with me one second and I kill you."

Joshua shuffled over to Ham and sank to his knees.

Martha had them turn to face the sea and walked behind them. She must have switched the bat to her left hand and drawn the knife, because a moment later Josh felt her cut the rope that had lashed his elbows behind him. A wave of agony flashed up through his poor shoulders as his arms were released. A moment later his numb muscles began to tingle as the blood started flowing through them again. Martha cut the rope binding Ham's hands and dodged back out of range.

She glowered at Josh. "Now we even."

He nodded. They couldn't hurt her, not hobbled while she had her feet free, but as big and strong as Ham was, it would now be hard for her to kill them without putting herself at grave risk.

She coughed. She was losing her teeth from malnutrition. If she was prone to afternoon fever it was probably coming on now, especially on a hot day after a lot of exertion. "Truf or dare," she said. "Do I have this thing?"

"TB. Yes, you do."

"Am I gonna die?"

"Yes."

There was something haughty, even scornful in her air, despite the sunken cheeks. A starved, bitter pride he had seen in his patients sometimes. He thought he would probably look the same way when the time came for him to die. "Can you fix me up?" she asked.

"No."

"I figured," she said. "I figured you for a cheat the minute I saw you. How long I got?"

"Maybe six months," Josh said. She coughed again and spat. He wondered if there was blood in her spit, and if there was, how long it had been there.

The wind picked up. The little Gulf breeze was back. Martha nodded. "I'm taking the big pack. I ain't axing, I'm telling you. You best not come after me, I'll cut you where you stand, you hear me? I know these parts. You just git on." She picked up George's pack where he had

let it fall in the road, then patted down his pockets, ignoring his blood-soaked clothes, until she found the silver
cigarette lighter and fetched it out. She watched them all
the time, and when she was done she stood up again.
"Adios, doctor. All my life I been a stupid girl. It always
gets me into trouble. I jes' couldn't figure out another
way." She wiped her muddy face with her muddy hand.
"Short and sweet, that's my motto."

She walked backward down the road. They waited until she was a hundred yards away before Josh started
working on the ropes around Ham's ankles. When he
finally got them off, Ham swore and stretched out his
vast legs, knotted with cramps and bruises from George's
beatings. A charley horse seized him and he rubbed it
out. Then he started on Joshua's bonds. "Well, Josh, how
does Galveston look?" the big man rumbled. "Now that
you've seen a little of the world beyond?"

"Looking better," Josh admitted.

Ham shook his head, staring west along 87. Martha
had disappeared from view. "She just couldn't imagine
we could keep our word. Couldn't fathom that we would
all be better off if we worked together to get out of this
hellhole. My mom used to say the funniest thing about
salvation was that Christ would give it away for free,
anytime, to anyone—but damn near everybody is too
proud to ask."

Ham worked the ropes off Joshua's ankles. "You're a
better man than I am," Josh said. "I would have killed
her the first time I got the chance."

Ham regarded him. Instead of the reproachful look
Josh was expecting, the big man's face was expressionless. "I suppose you would, too," he said. He looked
away. "Funny how I always thought you were better than
that. I guess I just wasn't paying attention."

Chapter Seventeen

MARTIAL LAW

"I'M going home," Ham said, once they had rubbed the feeling back into their arms and legs.

"Are you crazy?" Josh said. "We can't go back to Galveston. There's a death sentence on our heads, remember?"

"Josh, I really don't give a good goddamn what you do." Ham found a second cigarette lighter and Josh's pocketknife in the pack Martha had left behind. "After a blow like this, you think they'll turn down a field medic and a pipeline man?" Ham said. "Of course, Islanders are known to be stupid."

"For Christ's sake." Josh pushed himself to his feet, gritting his teeth against the pain in his legs and wrist. He squinted against the dazzle of sunlight on the slough around them. The big man started walking west on 87. He didn't look back. After a moment Josh followed him.

As they trudged under the brutal sun Josh imagined Sloane Gardner, sitting in some air-conditioned mansion in the Mardi Gras, sipping exotic iced drinks, totally unaware that there had even been a hurricane—while back in the real world, he and Ham slogged on through clouds of mosquitoes, three quarters naked and gasping in the

insufferable heat, their piss turning dark orange and their feet nothing but blisters. Some people had all the luck.

Of course, they hadn't been eaten yet. Thank you, Lord, for these your tender mercies.

THE next morning Joshua found pink meat and blood in the wound on his wrist. The maggot therapy had been successful—if you could call getting eaten alive success. The little white crawling bastards had chewed away his infected flesh. Josh stared at them a long time. Beyond the first retching disgust, the sight struck him as a bleak revelation. This was what happened to everyone after the last card was dealt: the body died and worms ate it. He was just seeing that last hand a little early.

It took Josh an hour to clean all the maggots out, washing the wound over and over with seawater that burned like salt fire. When he was finally done he wrapped the wrist up with fresh bandages cut from George's shirt.

They walked at night and rested during the day, drinking from stock tanks. They ate steamed clams or baked fish every day, and once some meat from an alligator they found mostly dead and tangled in a ball of barbed wire. Ham finished it off with the baseball bat. The big man swore by alligator meat, but in Joshua's opinion sawing chunks out of its tail with the pocketknife was more work than it was worth.

They kept as quiet as they could and made no smoke if they could help it. "Lay low, beef," Josh had said in his best George accent. "So's we don't get rustled."

Ham didn't laugh.

Their luck held, for a change, and they met no other cannibals. They did leave the highway once, though. The whole third night of the trip they could see a blaze of lights on the road ahead. Just before dawn they came to the edge of a little town. A well-lit sign at the side of 87 proclaimed:

Welcome to Sunshine City,
Resort Capital of the Third Coast!
*"Visit Us Once, and You'll Never Want to
Leave!"*

For the first time since Martha had gone, they saw
people—lots of people, even in the dark before dawn. A
fresh-scrubbed teenage boy in pre-Flood shorts and T-
shirt rode a gleaming bicycle through the streets, delivering a morning paper. A smiling milkman gave him a
wave while setting out two bottles on the deck of a stilt-
legged vacation condo. In the condo next door, a glam-
orous couple carrying cups of hot coffee stepped onto
their porch to watch the sun rise. A pickup truck ghosted
to a stop outside the brightly lit windows of a donut shop
and spilled out a load of ruggedly handsome cowpokes
and oil-field workers who joked and laughed as they
passed inside.

"No mud on the streets," Ham muttered. "No broken
glass."

"No boarded-up windows."

"No watermarks on the houses. No seaweed around
their pillars. No nothin'," Ham said. "They didn't get a
drop of rain. There is some very heavy-duty magical-type
shit going on in there."

"Damn," Josh agreed. "I guess that stuff will happen
when you don't have the Recluse around." He stepped
back from the sign, gulping. " 'It just doesn't get any
better than this.' "

"I'm going around," Ham said, slipping down the side
of the embankment. A moment later Josh heard him
swear. He was crouched at the bottom of the mysteriously
dry ditch, staring at a human skeleton, fingers out-
stretched and clawing at the ground. "Fingers just even
with the sign," Ham said. "Poor sumbitch died trying to
crawl out."

They spent the next few hours giving the Resort Cap-

ital of the Third Coast an extremely wide berth.

Five mornings after Martha had left them, Highway 87 ended amidst the wreckage of the Point Bolivar Ferry Terminal. From here they could see Galveston Island, just over two miles away across the Bolivar Roads channel. They took their midday break amid the rubble of the abandoned ferry terminal, grateful for the shade. In the late afternoon, when the sun had begun to lose its bite, Josh scavenged for food while Ham looked for a way to get them across the channel. A ferry still sat in the berth—not floating anymore, of course, but settled on the sandy bottom with water well up over the car deck. Ham spent several hours trying to free one of its lifeboats with a ship's ax, only to find when he finally got the boat into the water that its boards were sprung or rotten or both. It sank like a brick.

Perched on the pier posts that lined the ferry berth, a collection of black cormorants watched the proceedings with amusement while they held their wings up to dry. They were primitive birds, lacking oil glands to make their feathers waterproof, and they were always having to dry them out. Josh had read that in a book.

After the lifeboat disappointment, Ham broke open the ferry's lockers with his ax and found twenty-seven life preservers. He kept one each for Josh and himself, and tied the other twenty-five together by their straps to make a raft.

They waited until twilight before putting their fleet of orange life preservers into the water and setting out across the Bolivar Roads. Ham had used his ax to cut down the oars from the useless lifeboat into small, crude paddles, but Joshua's right arm was still too weak for him to do much with his. He tried paddling at first, pulling with his left arm, but he quickly flagged. Ham watched him, expressionless. "Don't even bother," he said at last. "Just lie at the back of the raft with your legs in the water. Kick if you want to pretend to help."

"That's enough," Josh snapped. "You've made your point, I'm a little shit, I get it. Tell me what I'm supposed to say to apologize and I'll say it."

The big man dug in with his oar: one stroke, two. "There's sincere remorse," he said. Stroke, stroke. "Josh, just shut up."

"I notice for all that I'm in the doghouse, you're still rescuing me."

"Island's gonna need doctors," Ham said. "Even ones like you."

Ham paddled. Josh didn't think his kicking was doing any good, but he kept at it a good while so as not to give Ham the satisfaction of hearing him quit. The pressure of leaning down on his upper body got to hurting his wrist worse and worse, though, and finally he gave up. And then, stroke by stroke, Ham was carrying him. Again.

A sudden fear seized Josh that his drowned mother was drifting underneath them, but when he stared through a gap in the raft he couldn't see her. If she knew of any trouble coming, she kept it to herself.

Half an hour out from Point Bolivar, Ham turned his head. "If you need to talk, lithp. Thound carrieth over the water. Git in a boat off Loverth Point, you can hear a bra come undone at two hundred yardth."

"But why lisp?"

"Thut up and do what I tell you, Joth." Ham paddled. Some time later he said, "Your 'eth' ith eathily the loudeth noith in a whithper."

It was a calm night, with no danger of being swept out to sea. At the front of their bobbing quilt of life preservers Ham paddled sturdily away. It took a long time to cross the channel. Josh should have been relaxing. He was neither weak from hunger nor tortured by thirst, not running from a storm or hiding from cannibals. Overhead the stars were warm and liquid in the Texas sky. But instead of resting, he found himself getting angrier and

angrier at Ham. Yes, he had been thoughtless, but for Christ's sake, it was a little hard to ask a man who had been beaten, exiled, and then struck by a poisonous snake to be on his best behavior.

To the right, far across the Bay, vast fires and smokes rose inexhaustibly from the refineries of Texas City. With its miles and miles of smokestacks and condensation towers, crackers and tanks and weird constant gouts of flame, it looked like an industrial version of hell. There were kids on the Island who said Texas City was where the souls of the evil dead were condemned to roam. There was much sturdy common sense behind the theory, Josh always thought. He would send Deputy Lanier there in a heartbeat.

He wondered again what had happened to Sloane.

They inched toward Galveston. In daylight, she had looked much as usual from Point Bolivar, but by night it was easier to tell there was something wrong. The town was too dark. Great black gaps blotted her grid of street-lamps, and where there was light, it was often the red unsteady gleam of fires burning where no fires should be.

They had been aiming for the closest land to Point Bolivar, the beach in front of Old Fort San Jacinto, but instead they ended up south and east a few hundred yards, in the rocky shallows around the Big Reef, an area Ham knew well. He had dragged Josh out here when they were thirteen years old. Josh had brought a magnifying glass and cotton specimen bag; Ham a propane lantern, a flounder gig—a stick with a nail sticking out the end of it—and a pair of pliers. He made Josh hold the lantern over the reef pools. When the goggling flounder came up, bewitched by the lantern light, Ham gigged them and flipped them into the bag, where they jerked and thrashed so unnervingly that Josh had dropped it. Then, to cover up his shame at being a sissy, he had yelled at Ham for ruining his specimen bag. Ham had meekly apologized, grabbed the next spiked flounder by the tail, slammed it

headfirst into a nearby rock until it stiffened and died, and then placed it gently in the sack.

Josh winced at the memory.

When Ham had gigged enough flounder for the night, Josh, bored with standing around, had made the mistake of asking what the pliers were for. Ham had shown him how to catch the rock crabs that lived in the reef, and how to tear the left claws off the living animals. "If you take both claws they die," he gravely explained, dropping the fresh claw into the bag while the rest of the crab lurched crazily away.

All in all it had been a fascinating, disgusting night—but good eating afterward. Joshua had eaten a lot of suppers over at Ham's place that year. Suddenly, lying on the makeshift raft of life preservers, he understood that this had been a tactful kind of charity from Ham's mom, paying for Amanda Cane's pharmaceuticals and expertise in a form she wasn't too proud to accept: child care and good food for her son. Odd that he hadn't realized that before.

Ham lay at the front of the raft, using his paddle like a pole to push them through the Big Reef to the jumbled blocks of granite riprap that made up the shoreline. A gentle swell surged between the riprap and drained back again. Water slapped and muttered. Ham was just starting to ease his enormous body into the water and pull the raft onshore when he froze. "Joth!" he hissed. "Git up here."

Life preservers sank and bobbed under Josh's weight as he wiggled forward. At least he wasn't cold: the Gulf water was always warm in September, and the night air was sultry. His wrist stung where salt water had seeped through his latest cloth dressing, but the pain was so much less terrible than it had been earlier in the week it hardly seemed worth noticing. "What's up? —Oopth. Thorry," Josh said, remembering to lisp.

Ham pointed with his paddle. "Body," he said.

With only starlight and an old moon to see by, it took Josh a moment to make out what Ham was pointing at. A man-sized shape was floating facedown in the water. The body was wedged between two rocks, almost lifting free with each swell, then settling back, stuck like a piece of driftwood. There was something terrible about the way it moved, no different from a log or length of rope. Just an object now, no longer a living thing. Josh felt a moment of intense horror and pity. The thought of his mother, reduced to this, was worse than seeing her ghost. At least that apparition had retained something of her. It had seen him and known him. But this . . .

"Got a hole in hith head," Ham murmured. Looking more closely, Josh saw a cavity where the back of the head should have been. A large part of the skull was missing. Ham touched the back of the corpse with his paddle. The wood clicked against something stiff. Ham slid the paddle forward and lifted the head, turning it to one side. Instead of a man's cheek, they saw a sad, red creature with long shrimp's whiskers. Its face was stiff, something halfway between skin and shell. "Prawn Man," Ham murmured. "I heard about 'em, but I never theen one before." There was a small round hole just above the creature's left eye, another near his jaw. "Thomeone thot him. More than onth."

"Let's get away from it," Josh said.

Ham nodded, pushing off the rocks with his paddle. Eager as he had been to get back to the Island, he spent an extra fifteen minutes working down the shore, putting distance between them and the strange, sad corpse. It was a grim omen for their arrival.

The beach here was tumbled rocks at the base of a short hill. They rested for a while on a big slab of granite, getting colder as the breeze got at their pants—if you could call their sodden rags "pants" anymore. Once Josh's skin was dry, though, the night was nearly perfect, warm and humid.

Obviously their first order of business was to find out what had happened to Ham's family. Then they would decide what to do next. Josh insisted that they leave the life preserver raft somewhere easy to find, in case they were still under the death penalty and had to hightail it off the Island. Ham didn't argue the point.

From where they were sitting, the raised dike that marked the eastern terminus of Seawall Boulevard was less than a hundred yards away. They could walk along the road proper, making good time across the uninhabited end of the Island, but they would be easily visible to anyone coming along the road. "We'll walk through the salt grath bethide the road, out of thight, and make nearly ath good time," Ham decided.

Josh froze. "Can't."

"Do what you're told," Ham said.

"Can't. Too afraid I'll step on a snake."

Ham looked at him a long time. At last he said, "We'll take the road. Thlip down into the grath if we thee any-one." He started up the embankment without looking back.

It turned out not to matter. They didn't see another soul for the whole two miles up to Stewart Beach. At first Josh was elated at their good fortune, but the com-plete silence came to seem uncanny. "Ought to be thomeone out for flounder," Ham muttered. "Or crabbing. Or *thomething*."

"Look," Josh whispered. They were several hundred yards shy of Lyncrest Drive, the easternmost north-south road on the Island. Streetlights here had never been a priority, but now there were none. Either the gas lines had ruptured, or gas was being rationed. Three blocks farther along, at the intersection of Seawall Boulevard and the Ferry Road, they could clearly see a large fire. Not a blazing bonfire, but a dark mound with flames flickering erratically over its surface, and cracks and fis-sures of embering red. A moment later a terrible smell

hit them, of charred meat and hide. Josh drew a breath. "They're burning bodies," he murmured. "Just like after the Big Blow."

They'd be burning the dead animals, too. As low as the water supply had dwindled before the storm hit, it would be very difficult to keep the streets sanitary, especially with the sewer systems cracked and choked in the aftermath of the hurricane. There were bound to be hundreds of wounds to clean out, from flying debris, broken glass, dropped tree branches. The lack of clean water would hurt there, too. It would be a miracle if Galveston escaped an outbreak of cholera. Josh found himself going over the supplies in his house, trying to guess what injuries and illnesses he would find waiting.

Ham shook Josh's shoulder. His eyes were frantic. "Let'th go, let'th go!"

Josh nodded, a sinking feeling in his chest. Ham's sister Rachel and her kids lived in a trailer park on Tuna Avenue, in the neighborhood called the Fishes. Before the Flood it had been a decent part of town, but in the first years after 2004 the deeply haunted U.T. Medical Branch had lain between the Fishes and the rest of Galveston. People with family or resources fled the neighborhood. Those too stubborn to leave saw the abandoned lots fill up with squatters, refugees, and trailer homes like the one Rachel's family lived in. Dread began building in Josh. There couldn't have been much between the Fishes and the hurricane except the raised dike of Seawall Boulevard.

They slipped down Lyncrest Drive. On their right the empty flatland showed little sign of the hurricane's passing, but to their left tin roofs and plywood walls lay scattered on the ground like giant playing cards. Josh began to notice crude crosses in the ground, one, three, five— dozens of them, nailed together from broken broomsticks or two-by-fours, or twisted out of coat hangers. One small house that looked nearly untouched had five small crosses

in front. Two doors down they passed a tin shed with the walls blown down and nothing left standing but a gas stove with one burner still hissing. There were no crosses in the yard. Whether that meant the occupants had survived, or simply had nobody left to mark their passing, Josh couldn't say.

Ham was running by the time he turned onto Tuna Avenue. Back from Lyncrest, the devastation was slightly less complete. A working streetlight still twinkled at the intersection of Tuna and Ferry Road. A ghost tumbled underneath it for an instant, struggling and thrashing in an invisible tide. A wave they could not see rolled over the specter, and it disappeared.

"Josh?" Ham whispered.

"I saw it." Joshua's heart beat in his chest, hard enough to hurt. They shouldn't have been able to see a ghost that easily. If word got out that he and Ham were seeing visions, the Recluse would have them gone to Krewes before a week was out.

With a couple of blocks between them and the full brunt of the storm, the little houses here looked better. There were lights in several windows, but still they had seen no living person out of doors. "Curfew?" Josh breathed in Ham's ear. The big man shrugged and started lumbering across the road, crossing himself as he passed the spot where they had seen the drowning ghost.

In this neighborhood the Mexican houses were bright with the flicker of candles. Candles burned in their windows, on their porches, and along their garden walks; candles surrounded by paper shades or candles burning in tall magic glasses painted with images of the Sacred Heart or the Bleeding Lamb, La Virgen Sagrada or El Mano Más Poderoso, the Most Powerful Hand. There were other charms, too, in front of the black and anglo houses. Crosses and walkaways had been nailed to doors, or offerings left out on the porch—a fish, a plate of cold rice, presents wrapped in wax paper and left for any spir-

its who might need placating. One person had obviously dragged a heavy Texaco sign from an abandoned gas station and planted it in his yard, facing across the Bay, as if begging for protection from whatever spirits still dwelt among the eternal fires of Texas City. When the things men made could no longer protect them, they turned back to their gods and ghosts for salvation, Josh thought. It won't be long before we're cowering in caves again, believing every sickness to be a witch's curse.

Ham started to run, jogging heavily along the pavement in his bare feet. Josh picked his way more slowly after, worried he would step on a piece of broken glass or a board with a rusty nail poking through. He had lost four patients to tetanus and another handful to gangrene since his mother died.

Ham stopped at the 4th Street intersection where Rachel's home had once been. A moment later Josh joined him, and together they looked out at a nightmare. Clearly the hurricane had spun off a tornado. Bits and pieces of trailers lay smashed across a field of desolation; furniture, clothes, and dishes lay strewn in eddies of rubble. The trailers had been cracked like eggs, their contents shaken out and scrambled, then the shells beaten in for good measure. "Oh, my God," Josh whispered. He thought of Ham's sister, Rachel, cowering in their trailer. They would have taken the mattress off Rachel's bed and hidden under it, and it wouldn't have mattered a damn. He imagined the children screaming as the walls tore apart.

"Christy caught her first fish not three weeks ago," Ham said. Christy was Rachel's imperious curly-haired four-year-old. "A little pound-and-a-half speck' trout. Back of my boat with a hook and bobber. Piece of shrimp for bait. I should have been here," he said.

Josh felt the dull thudding of his heart, ten times, twenty times, thirty. "They weren't here."

Ham shook his head and spat.

"They wouldn't have stayed here, with that front com-

ing in. You saw the clouds. No way Rachel would have stayed put. She'd have moved them all. Jesus Christ, Ham. They weren't here." He could see the trailer tumbling end over end, each crunching impact. Rain driving sideways like machine-gun fire. Window casements crushed in, glass exploding like shrapnel. "They would have gone to your mom's place," Josh said. He knew he was babbling, but he couldn't stop. "Ham. Ham, I didn't mean this. Say something." He grabbed Ham's arm, and the big man smashed him to the ground without even turning around.

Breath caught and rasped in Josh's chest. "They weren't here," he whispered.

Still Ham stood staring over the devastated lot. Across the street a row of houses stood virtually untouched. Pure chance, tornadoes. A small one might level one house to the foundation and leave the next one with the shutters still attached. All in the fall of the cards. Josh could hear the whirring, snapping sound of his father's crisp waterfall shuffle in his ears.

"I bet they went to Mom's place," Ham said.

"Yeah."

Ham turned away. A moment late Josh got up and limped after him.

They went to the house where Ham had lived with his mother and father and kid brother Japhet. It had been damaged but not flattened. Most of the windows were broken, the chicken coop out back was gone, and the little evaporative A/C unit that had been Mr. Mather's particular pride and joy had simply vanished from the front room window where it used to hang. Ham burst through the front door into the dark parlor and was about to yell when Josh got a hand over his mouth. "There's nobody here!" Josh hissed.

Ham slapped his hand away and stood stock-still in the darkness, shoulders heaving. His parents' bed in the front room was empty. Josh felt his way along the wall to the

kitchen. The wallpaper was wet up past his waist. In the kitchen the gas to the stove wasn't working and Japhet's cot was gone.

"If they're dead I'm gonna break your neck," Ham said.

"They're not dead."

"Do you swear it, Josh?" Ham's voice was empty and terrible. "Swear it on your mom's ghost."

"They're alive," Josh said. "I swear it."

Ham headed for the front door. "I saw a light next door at the Rossis'. I'm gonna ask."

"Ham! If we're caught, the sheriff will shoot us this time."

"The Rossis like me," Ham said. He brushed past Josh.

"At least give me the gun," Josh said. "In case anyone tries to turn you in."

"The gun ain't loaded, Josh."

"Nobody else knows that."

Ham passed over the useless .32 and stepped through the tiny patch of ground to the Rossis' while Josh hunkered down at the corner of the Mathers' house clutching the gun awkwardly in his left hand. Ham banged on the door with his massive fist. One of the Rossis' shutters opened a crack. "Git home to bed, you darn kids, before I whup your little hineys red!"

"It's Ham Mather, Mrs. Rossi."

"Ham!"

"Where's my folks?"

The shutter swung open. Mrs. Rossi squinted at him suspiciously. "You're a ghost."

"And I'll haunt you forever unless you tell me where my folks are."

"No, you aren't neither," Mrs. Rossi said. "I can smell you from here. God bless, you big pig! They're at Mr. Cane's, Ham."

Joshua thought his heart would stop.

Ham stared stupidly up at Mrs. Rossi. "Josh's house?"

"Your mom said, 'It's a good tight house on higher ground, and somebody ought to get the use of it with the storm coming.' Folks left that place alone; you can imagine what kind of ghost that Josh would make, proud as he was. But your mom said if Josh was dead then you would be, too, and you'd keep him in line. She said you'd be back, though. She's got a lot of faith in Jesus, your mother has."

"They're alive," Josh said. It was like a death sentence had lifted from him. Relief did not begin to describe it. His heart was dazzled.

Ham was already backing from the door and breaking into a trot toward Joshua's house. Josh stood up from the shadows and came after him. As he passed Mrs. Rossi's window he caught a glimpse of her startled face. "Boo!" he said, snickering like a schoolboy, and then loped after his friend.

A small house full of Mathers, Josh discovered, is very full indeed. Ham was so tall that even bent over to crush his mother in a bear hug his head rustled among the ropes of peppers and clumps of sage hanging from Joshua's ceiling to dry. Mr. Mather was nearly as broad as his son, if not so tall, and his belly, thickly thatched with greying hair, eclipsed the waistband of the shorts he had worn to bed.

It was actually the kids who had woken first. After some knocking Josh heard a modest thump that turned out to be the sound of four-year-old Christy getting down from the low examination table where she and her sister Samantha had been billeted. "Shh!" she hissed through the door. "Evewybody's *sweeping*," she said sternly. Josh thought it was the most beautiful sound he had ever heard.

"Christy!" Ham said.

"*Shh!*"

"Christy, it's Uncle Ham. Get your mom, honey!"

"She's *sweeping*!" Josh grinned like a lunatic in the darkness, knowing exactly the pouting thrust of the lower lip with which Christy would be making her point.

This argument might have gone on all night (Christy was intractable on points of order) but fortunately the noise had woken Samantha, who was six and sensible. She ran immediately to the kitchen to get her mother. A moment later Rachel opened the door and gave a little scream. She held a hand over her mouth and tears started in her eyes at the sight of her brother. Ham reached out and hugged her. A moment later her husband, Ben, hurried in from the kitchen. Samantha was dispatched to wake up the grandparents, and Rachel fussed to light the lamp over the exam table. Christy tried to make everyone go back to bed. Ben offered Josh some of his own rice wine, the grandparents emerged from the master bedroom, Josh found another oil lamp in the kitchen, lit it, and brought it to the front room, and finally even Japhet's untroubled slumber was broken when the resourceful Samantha pinched his nose shut until he struggled into wakefulness, coughing and blinking.

It was a joyous homecoming, marred slightly for Josh by the fear that he might be trampled in the general enthusiasm. All of the Mathers were huge: Ham, his father, and Japhet were enormous slabs of flesh and bone. Rachel's husband, Ben, was skinnier, but well over six feet tall, with long gangly limbs that looked as if they needed extra joints to fold down to some reasonable size. What the women lacked in girth they made up for in various ways, Rachel in the bigness of her styled hair, Samantha in energy, and Christy in volume and pure will. Mrs. Mather alone seemed scaled to a human dimension, and after the first flesh-slapping paroxysms had settled down, Josh found himself with an urge to chat quietly with her, preferably in a narrow corner where none of the Mather men could fit, reducing the chances he would be squashed flat by accident.

"Now that you're here, we'll shift back to the old place," Mrs. Mather said. "As low as the glass was going the day of the storm, we knew it was fixin' to get ugly. I didn't like to think of Rachel and the girls out at the trailer with any kind of a wind."

"You did exactly right," Josh said quickly, so Ham couldn't accuse him of being mean-spirited.

"Japhet got caught out over at the Bishop's Palace," Ham's mom said. "That Miss Gardner is back, you know. She's got a whole passel of poor folk staying with Randall Denton, if you believe it. Our Japhet helped her a bunch the first night, and I've been lending a hand since during the daytime, though we try to get out at night. There's only room for so many to sleep, and it's better to leave it for those who've got no beds to go to, I think." Alice Mather paused, and, charmingly, colored just a little. "Miss Gardner lets me do a little of the organizing."

I'll bet, Josh thought, remembering how Ham's mother had looked after every kid in the neighborhood. The Gardners always did have a fine eye for delegating. The idea of Sloane Gardner working shoulder to shoulder with Alice Mather tickled him greatly. Another wave of gratitude went through him, as he remembered that during their trial it had been Alice Mather who had backed him, unafraid of the staring crowd and her disapproving neighbors.

"I'm afraid a lot of your medicine is gone," Ham's mother said. "Two mornings after the storm that deputy came and cleaned the place out. He took everything left from before the Flood—for sharing, he said, but of course this neighborhood never had any use out of it, not with you gone, Josh. I should have taken it over to Miss Gardner, I reckon, but it seemed too much like stealing, somehow."

"Josh." Ham stuck his great head, shaggy with seven days' beard, through the doorway into the kitchen.

"We're off the hook. Dad says your girlfriend showed up the day the hurricane hit."

"There's a parable," Mrs. Mather said, patting Japhet on the head as her youngest son wandered blearily into the kitchen. Hunting for a midnight snack, no doubt; Ham said the kid had been on a serious growth spurt lately. Mrs. Mather shook her head. "Miss Gardner—she told me to call her Sloane, but I haven't gotten used to that yet—Miss Gardner came back all dressed up for Mardi Gras, just like you said, Josh. The sheriff 'bout liked to arrest her, though we don't know why. There's revelers in the Bishop's Palace, too. Give me quite a turn, the first time I wandered up to the second floor. But Miss Gardner's got everyone behaving themselves. Her mother's daughter, I guess."

"They got a feller there got stilts instead of legs," Japhet said. "And a woman with feathers on her face that wears dresses that show her"—he glanced at his mother—"knees."

"Them with houses to go back to headed out the next day," Mrs. Mather continued, "but there's plenty as had no place to go."

Ham squeezed into the kitchen, followed by his father. "The Recluse is dead. Shot by the sheriff, the story goes."

"Good thing, too," Jim Mather said. "Elsewise we'd have lost your mom by now."

Ham blinked. Alice Mather colored. "It's nothing," she said.

"Angeling!" Japhet said. He scratched his belly, nodded and grinned. "I seen her myself. Two days ago this Vietnamese comes off a houseboat, sicker than a dog. Mom starts talking, he talks back, they git along—only she's talking English, he's hearing Vietcong! He's jibbering away, Mom's hearing regular American."

"What you call your speaking in tongues," Ham's daddy explained.

Alice Mather shook her head, blushing furiously.

"Well, here we are gossiping, while you boys must be starved half to death. Let's get you some eats." She began to move busily about the kitchen, not meeting anybody's eyes.

"Good Lord almighty," Ham breathed.

Mr. Mather shook his head. He was still smiling at his boy's return, but Josh could see the worry returning to the deep seams and creases of his face. "We're in for some heavy weather, with Miss Odessa gone. What this town will look like in ten years, I don't care to guess."

"The Lord will provide," Alice said. And damned if there wasn't a kind of power in her simple voice. Josh could feel her certainty enter him and calm him, like oil poured on turbulent waters.

"Amen," Ham said, and then he added, "I could eat a good-sized buck down to the antlers. Josh owes us, Mom. What's he got in the way of grub?"

Joshua's pantry was as full as it had been when he left. Maybe fuller. "We tried to eat our own food, best we could," Mrs. Mather said. "Dad's been meaning to get our place fixed up so we could move back, but there's been so much work to do for those worse off. Days of going through the rubble to save the quick and burn the dead. But now you're back, we'll get home first thing tomorrow."

"No, please, stay as long as you like," Josh blurted. The Mathers looked at him in surprise. "It, this hasn't been the luckiest house," he stammered. "I'm so glad, after everything—it means so much to me that you could be here, safe, when the storm hit. It means the world to me."

"We were pretty tickled about it, too," Jim Mather said drily.

After a week of scrounging for seaweed and clams, the pantry was a dizzying Pandora's box of smells: molasses, vinegar, cheap rice wine for cooking, honey, hot sauce, canisters of chili powder and dried mint leaves and pe-

cans, and of course jams and jellies made from mustang grapes, blackberries, mint and dewberries and choke-cherries, and pickled peppers and chowchow and garlic spread. On the kitchen cabinets sat a line of large ceramic canisters: the biggest one full of rice, another for rice flour, then acorn flour (Josh had found he could get some use out of the ubiquitous live-oak acorns if he washed and leached the flour to take the bitterness out). Then came a big jar for prepared sugar and a smaller bowl always filled with fresh sticks of sugarcane. Spices on a rack next to the stove: salt and crushed dried chili, thyme and sage.

He had nothing compared to the Fords and the Den-tons, but for the first time Josh realized how much richer he was than most of his patients. Mortified, he remem-bered himself in court, ridiculing the jam Jezebel MacReady had brought him in payment. And he had been surprised when no one spoke up for him. He lost the thread of Mrs. Mather's talk in a hot blush of shame.

Over a hasty meal of rice and shrimp with hot sauce—heaven!—Josh and Ham slowly caught up with the Gal-veston news in a babble of Matherese. The hurricane hadn't done nearly the damage of the Big Blow; the Is-land had been raised ten feet since then, and the Seawall had held back the tide—almost. Still, there had been plenty killed outright; something between two hundred and a thousand, depending on who you believed. Most of the killing had been done by tornadoes spun off the storm: at least six twisters were known to have touched down on the Island. A few people had drowned, and sev-eral had been killed by wind-driven debris. Old Katie Heinrich, whose arthritis Josh had been treating for years with hot pepper rubs and willow bark aspirin, had climbed on top of her house to escape from drowning, only to be picked off by lightning.

Strangest of all had been the end of Mardi Gras, when Galveston woke up the morning after the storm to find

revellers drowned in doorways or huddled among the refugees in the big Broadway mansions. "Not for long, though," Jim Mather said. "Sheriff Denton, he started rounding them up. Wanted them off the Island and out of the way, by any means. A lot of folks have been shooting them on sight. I've been saving my bullets until one gives me trouble, myself. Most of 'em ran out of town, or else they're hiding up in the Bishop's Palace with Sloane Gardner and Randall Denton."

"Mrs. Mather mentioned that before," Josh said. "Do you mean to tell me Randall Denton has turned philanthropist?"

"More like a gentleman hostage," Alice said. "Miss Gardner's got him there, just in case the other Dentons decide to storm the house and gun down all her revellers. She's got a soft spot for them."

"There's a curfew every night," Rachel's husband Ben said. "Sundown to sunup. Good thing you weren't caught coming last night, or they'd have throwed you in jail all over again."

After that the news got worse. Now sickness was the problem. Diarrhea was bad and getting worse—dysentery if we're lucky, Josh thought, and cholera if we aren't. There wasn't enough clean water to go around. Many of the cisterns had been polluted by salt water, and too many buckets and barrels aboveground had been broken or blown away by the wind. Still, there had been enough rain that the first couple of days everyone had been able to find something to drink. Better yet, the thirty-six inch pipe under the Bay that brought the Island's water from the mainland had survived the storm intact. Unfortunately, the pumping station had not. Ham shook his head, shoveling down food. He was just the sort of man who could have helped a lot in this fix.

As for Josh, the Mathers said he had been sorely missed. "It's not that the other doctors won't help," Rachel said. "But they like to stick with the old stuff—"

"The real medicine," Josh said dourly.

"Yeah. And there's not much of it left. I know they want to use it for the worst off . . ."

Big Jim Mather shook his head. "A rich feller who's got water and good food and a place to sleep, he gets over a scrape or a cough. But folks out here, they just get worse and worse."

"We're taking the sick in at the Bishop's Palace," Mrs. Mather said. And speaking in tongues, apparently! Josh thought, taken all over again with the marvel of it. "But we could dearly use a doctor, Joshua."

"Here's your chance," Ham said between mouthfuls. "Those other doctors need you. I bet you could get into the Krewe of Togetherness now. They're that short staffed, and there's good money to be made looking after Dentons and Fords."

Josh felt a slow burn of shame spreading across his face. "That's not fair."

Alice frowned. "Is there something going on between you two?"

"Not anymore," Ham said.

He bent noisily to his food. The other Mathers looked first at Josh, and then away, embarrassed. A silence seemed to spread out from him, until nobody was talking. Only the clink and clatter of Ham's fork broke the quiet. Many times, looking at Sloane Gardner or seeing the fine folk of Galveston filing into Jim Ford's place, Josh had felt like a beggar, staring through a window at a party inside he could never join. Now he felt that way again, only this time it was the warmth and cheer of the Mather household that had been suddenly withdrawn.

Him caught with his face pressed up to the window, staring in.

"Ham?" Alice Mather said.

"Good eats, Mom. Goddamn, I needed this."

Stiffly, Joshua said, "Mrs. Mather, I'll go to the Bishop's Palace first thing tomorrow."

Alice Mather nodded, still glancing, troubled, between Josh and her son. "Sloane will be so pleased!" Her eyes widened and she clapped a hand over her mouth. "There. I called her Sloane. We're mingling in high society now, Jim," she said, with a merry glance at her husband.

Josh said, "Mrs. Mather, in my opinion, you are the highest society on this Island." He figured there was no way for her to know he had never been more serious in his life. Ham's mother called him a rascal and slapped him lightly on the arm. It was as if her touch came from a thousand miles away. He had lost the right to feel it.

Chapter Eighteen

BAPTISM

DESPITE all Joshua's polite protests, Rachel and Ben had given him back his bed, making up pallets for themselves on the kitchen floor. Somehow the moment Josh woke in his small dark room he knew that they and the rest of the Mathers were deeply, dreamlessly asleep. Someone was shaking his shoulder. The freezing touch stung his skin and raised goose bumps along his back.

He twisted away from the ice-cold hand and sat bolt upright. A rich woman in a white dress was standing beside his bed. "Are you s-sick?" Josh stammered.

She regarded him, amused. "No, Mr. Cane. I'm dead."

A ghost. The hairs on Joshua's wrist and neck prickled and rose. The ghost's voice had the masterful confidence that only money can bestow. Even in the darkness of his room her skin glowed the dead white of a cut mushroom. She had a strong, ugly face, with a wide, expressive mouth. "Who are you?" he said.

"You have to ask? *Ou sont les neiges d'antan* indeed. There was a time I would have been known in this town," the ghost said. She gave him an odd smile and curtseyed. Her dress was as white as her skin, a fantastically ornate and old-fashioned collection of ruffles and lace. She

might have been dead a hundred years. "Elizabeth Brown, at your service."

"Miss Bettie," Josh whispered. He started to hope he was still asleep, then gave it up. Miss Bettie was not a dream. She was real. More real than he was himself, somehow. Her cold presence was so certain it made his own life seem fragile and inconstant, a candle flame flickering in the wind.

Miss Bettie held out a businesslike hand. "So you see, there's nothing you can do for me, Mr. Cane. But there is someone *else* who needs your help. Come with me, and hop to it, sir!" She pulled him out of bed, her fingers like vines of frost around his forearm. There was not a creak from the rickety floorboards or a rustle in the curtains as she paced soundlessly from the room.

Josh rummaged in his closet for a pair of pants, stopping only to rub the coldness out of his forearm. Miss Bettie. The most famous ghost on the Island, the woman who had made Ashton Villa the center of Galveston society a century before the Flood. Died of—Lou Gehrig's disease, come to think of it, just like Jane Gardner. What were the odds of that? Josh pulled on his pants with a dour smile. Well, he had finally achieved one of his aspirations: He was moving in the highest possible circle of Galveston society, a personal acquaintance of its undisputed queen. Even dead, Miss Bettie was incontestably fashionable.

He shrugged on a shirt and hurried downstairs, yawning. Miss Bettie was waiting for him in the front room. Mathers lay about the house like beached manatees, whiffling and snoring. They slept as if enchanted, oblivious to Joshua's passage. He followed Miss Bettie outside into the warm Galveston night. As unbearable as the day's heat had been, at night the South Texas air was soft as the flesh of flowers. Galveston lay sleeping. It was curiously private outside: No souls moved through the streets still choked with rubble and debris. If any roosters sur-

vived, they had not yet begun to wake and announce the
dawn.

"Ma'am, where are we going?"

"Not far."

"Not your normal part of town," Josh said, gesturing
around at the dilapidated bungalows and run-down tract
houses of his neighborhood.

Miss Bettie gave him an admonitory look. "It is all my
town, Mr. Cane."

Josh kept from rolling his eyes. The rich were always
high-handed, apparently. Even the dead ones. He followed the shimmer of her white dress along the street.
Odd that Miss Bettie should be abroad, and so clearly
visible, even to him. He had never shown much aptitude
for magic. Thank God, or the Recluse would have packed
him off to Krewes for sure. But then, the Recluse was
dead, wasn't she? Now spirits and revellers walked the
street in broad daylight, at least if you believed the Mathers. He looked at the ghost ahead of him. So it began:
the last long slide from civilization into total barbarity,
into a world of dreams and ghosts no different from the
Middle Ages. By the end of his life they'd probably be
living in caves and hunting deer with clubs. Though Miss
Bettie was a ghost, a miracle, she had been born in the
great rational past. It was George and Martha who were
the future.

They walked through the streets that he had hated and
feared when he first came here to live, until Ham had
given the neighborhood to him, carelessly generous. Inside the storm-beaten little houses slept the Mathers'
friends and neighbors, that Josh had never deigned to
make his own. But now he had let Ham get away, somehow, and for the first time since moving here as a boy
of ten, he was among strangers again, and utterly alone.

Miss Bettie led him six blocks to Widow Tucker's
house. Billy Tucker's motorcycle lay on the front lawn.
Billy kept his mother's yard covered in car parts, usually,

but the hurricane had washed some away, and thrown the rotten skeleton of a Buick Regal on her porch. The storm had smashed in all her front windows; jags and nails of glass still hung loosely from the frames, glinting. Someone had a lamp lit inside. Josh could hear a child whining as he started up the steps. Exhausted as he was, it was hard for Josh to put on his calm, clinical air. He struggled into it as he followed Miss Bettie up the walk.

The ghost stepped aside and waved him to the door. He knocked. The kid inside the house yelped. Josh knocked again. "Mrs. Tucker?"

"Is that the doctor?"

"Billy! Quiet." A woman's voice, hissing. Gina, Billy's wife. Twenty-six or -seven now, big hips. Josh hadn't delivered her kids, but every few months they came down with head lice and he would sell her a packet of louse ointment he made from sage and creosote bush. Josh didn't have a lot of faith in the ointment, but it gave him an excuse to lend out one of his three steel-toothed lice combs.

Locks turned. The door opened an inch, still held by a brass chain. Billy looked out. "Josh Cane! Good Christ almighty," he whispered. "You're dead."

"Not yet."

Billy rubbed his face. His eyes were bloodshot and it didn't look as if he had shaved since the hurricane. "The ghost brung you, didn't she?"

"Lucky for you," Miss Bettie said tartly. She hopped up on the hood of the Buick beached on Mrs. Tucker's porch and sat there, swinging her feet, her gorgeous white evening gown faintly glowing in the darkness.

Josh stuck his left hand slowly through the crack of the door. "Feel me. Still warm," he said.

Billy touched Josh's fingers, lightly, then felt his palm. "All right." He opened the door. "Hope to God Ham made it back."

"He did."

"Well, that's something, then."

Billy Tucker was a short, stocky fireplug of a man who cut cars for a living, swapping pieces from one motor to another, trying to keep the dwindling supply of generators in the ghetto running. Josh always noticed his hands, how thick the stubby fingers were, permanently black around the nails and crisscrossed with bumpy white scars from hacksaw cuts and torn sheet metal and battery acid burns. He smelled bad, of oil and mud and sweat.

A querulous child was lying on the couch.

Billy headed into the dingy interior of his mother's house, walking with the bowlegged sway of a man who had gone hungry too often as a child. "It's Joe," he murmured.

"Your mother asleep?" Josh asked quietly, following.

"Mum's dead. Hurricane got her."

Why not just scrape the fucking Island clean? Sure, maybe a few of the big houses will still be left standing, but at least you've killed off the riffraff. Another slow burn of shame crept across Joshua's face. He kept his head down where the Tuckers couldn't see it so well, grateful for the dim light.

Billy's wife Gina was kneeling on the floor by the couch where her ten-year-old son lay, his head jerking restlessly back and forth. The couch stank of mildew and seawater. Billy squatted down and put his hand on the boy's arm. Joe flinched and cried, pulling away. "He can't stand any noise at all," Gina whispered. She sat with her hands on her knees, staring at her son, tight-lipped. A Coleman lantern with a repatched wick glowed dimly on an end table beside the couch. Shadows pooled and drained around Gina's eyes as she rocked back and forth, looking at her boy.

"Turn off the lamp," Joe whined. He had his mother's thin face. "Turn it off!"

"We're keeping the damn lamp on so the doctor can see, Joe Daniel."

"Gina," Billy said.

"You ain't been with him for the last six hours. You ain't listened while he—" She closed her mouth. Still rocking.

"I know it," Billy said. He didn't try to touch her.

Joe jerked his head away from the dull glow of the lantern. He whined again and his head came back, as if he couldn't bear the rasp of the upholstery against his cheek. "The boy's feeling everything," Billy said. Josh felt the flesh on his back grow cold and begin to creep as Miss Bettie walked up behind them. Billy jerked his thumb at the ghost. "He was the first to see her."

Hypersensitive. Josh forced himself to ignore the little shock of horror that ran down into his belly.

He tried gently to feel Joe's forehead. The boy jerked away from his touch. Gina grabbed Joe's face and held it still. He thrashed and screamed, high-pitched shrieks. For all his struggling he didn't have much strength. His parents had little difficulty holding him still. Josh tried to let the screams bounce off his imaginary doctor's coat and examined the boy. Not much fever, if any. Maybe a degree. He laid his fingers on Joe's neck and felt the pulse racing under a paper-thin layer of skin. He pulled Joe's eyelids open. His pupils were widely dilated. Josh sat back and signaled the parents to let go of the boy. Then he retreated to the hallway where he could talk to them without causing Joe so much distress.

He found two little girls in the hallway on their hands and knees, one about eight, the other four. "Git back in bed before I smack you," Gina hissed.

"But, Mom, what's wrong with J—"

Billy tucked one girl under each arm and tiptoed up the stairs with them.

The wallpaper was blotched and bubbled to three feet above the baseboards. Josh tried to imagine the whole

Island vanished, rolled underwater. *Serves them right if that storm taught them a lesson. Yes, sir.*

Enough. He had a patient to tend. No time to indulge in pointless guilt. "Do you have any drugs in the house?" Josh whispered to Gina. "Mushrooms? Jimson weed?"

"Billy's mom grew a little pot in the garden out back. That's all I know."

"Did Joe eat anything different from the rest of you?"

"I didn't keep track of every dead rat, Josh." Gina's upper body was still rocking. "We've been eating whatever shit we could find. Mother Tucker's lucky we didn't eat her." She was only a few years older than Josh, but it seemed like far more. She had three kids and a husband, and already there was grey showing in the wisps of hair that hung in front of her gaunt face. "Found her in the bedroom. Glass came out of the window and took her head half off at the neck. You know what I ate today? Half a can of peanuts. Billy gave me his share."

Billy came down the creaking stairs. "We're all right," he said. "Don't mind Gina, she's just upset."

"I'm upset," Gina said.

"Did Joe act like he might have eaten or drunk anything unusual?" Josh asked. "Complained about his stomach? Trouble walking or breathing?"

"Well, he's gimped on one side, but that's on account of a stob," Billy said.

"Told him to stay out of the big houses," Gina said. "Wouldn't listen to me. Like waiting dinner on a stray cat. Goddamn boys." She took a deep breath. "Not your fault," she said to Billy. "You done what you can, I know that. I'm just upset. He gets worse every hour, and it doesn't matter what I do."

Billy reached out for his wife. She rocked stiffly in the circle of his arm.

"A stob?" Josh said carefully. A sharp stick. The Mathers used that word sometimes.

"Went salvaging—"

"Stealing."

"—over on Seventeenth Avenue," Billy murmured. "The second story of one of the fancy houses gived out and he fell through. Got a real sharp old splinter dug way up the calf."

"I boiled some seawater and washed it out," Gina said. "Did that boy screech. Wrapped it up good as I could in one of Mother Tucker's old pillowcases. Figured she wouldn't need 'em anymore. I'm so sorry, Billy."

Josh's heartbeat sounded dully in his own ears. Joe's mother rocked in her hallway, regular but without purpose, like a clock keeping no time. She couldn't know the horror Josh's mind had just leapt to, but she was the boy's mother and she knew something was terribly, terribly wrong with her child. "I better take a look at that leg," Josh said. Walking back into the Tuckers' living room, he glanced back at Billy. "Is there a kitchen table in this place?"

"Yessir. Why?"

Josh didn't answer. He knelt at the foot of the couch where Joe tossed and squirmed, restless as a burn victim. "Hold him," Josh said. Billy gently pinned his son's arms to his chest. Gina held his feet. Josh took the lamp off the coffee table, set it on the floor near the boy's legs, and turned it up as bright as it would go. Joe squealed and bucked. Josh peeled back a dressing of damp cotton from the boy's leg. It was an ugly injury, a deep puncture going in at the back of the calf. The flesh around the wound was tight and dull red. Josh's mouth went dry. "When?"

"Three days ago. Three and a half now," Gina said. "I changed that twice."

Josh held the cotton dressing to the lamplight, looking for traces of thin red serum leaking from the wound. He found them.

Josh palpated the boy's calf. Joe screamed and screamed. "Take it easy," Billy murmured. Josh squeezed

and kneaded. Slight crunchiness nearly up to the back of the knee. Gas bubbles. Joe screamed and screamed and screamed. Gina was staring at Josh, her face like stone. Billy held the boy tighter and tighter, crushing his arms against his chest. Joe screamed and screamed. Josh squeezed his calf again. Crunch, crunch.

Josh stood up. Joe kept screaming. "Shut up," Billy hissed. The kid flopped like a fish inside his arms. "Shut up! Shut up!"

Josh picked up the lamp and dimmed it. He set it on the coffee table. He found Gina still looking at him. "Don't make me wait all night," she said. "And don't lie to me. I never did like you, but I know you don't lie. Tell me straight."

"Your son has gas gangrene. He's going to die." Josh felt his calm clinician's manner slipping away from him. "I am so, so sorry."

"You can't do nothing."

"If this were back before the Flood I could. If I had any penicillin I could. If it was too late for penicillin I could send him to a hospital with IVs and anesthetic and real trained doctors and they could take his leg off at the hip and maybe save him." Christ, there were tears on Josh's cheeks, how dare he cry in front of the boy's mother, in front of a woman who was going to lose her child. He wiped them off and shook his head. "No. I can't do anything for him."

Joe screamed and struggled. The muscles bunched in Billy's arms. He was breathing real fast and hard. He sat back on his haunches.

There was a creak on the staircase.

"Then take off his leg," Gina said.

"I'm not a doctor."

"Try it. He's gonna die anyway, right?"

Billy slammed his hand down on the coffee table. "Gina, dammit, the man says—"

"He's a gutless sack of shit," Gina said. "And I don't care. He's gonna save our boy."

"Gina—"

"He's gonna try."

The cold white figure of Bettie Brown came up beside Josh. "Noblesse oblige," she murmured.

"I can't," Josh whispered. Gina stared at the men implacably until Billy bowed his head. Josh shook his. "I can't," he said. "I don't have—"

The stairs creaked again. The motionless Billy suddenly exploded. "I told you girls to stay in bed!" he yelled. Joe screamed again. Josh made out the shape of the older daughter crouched on the stairs just as Billy picked her up and threw her against the stairwell so hard it made the walls shake. She grunted, falling heavily down several stairs and then her father picked her up and threw her up to the landing, a blur of pajamas and a white leg cracking against the banister at the stair head. Up in the shadows the four-year-old started to cry.

"Bill," Gina said.

The car-cutter stood halfway up the stairs, his shoulders shaking. "Don't say a goddamn word."

"See what Mr. Cane needs," Gina said.

Billy turned, breathing hard. The anguish in his eyes was so terrible it killed Joshua's hysteria. It erased his right to suffer. Josh turned away, unable to bear that look. "Have you got a hacksaw?" he said.

The silence stretched out. "Billy?" Gina said.

"In my toolbox."

"I'll need rope, too, as much as you've got. And nylon fishing line." Clamps, clamps. "And needle-nose pliers, as many as you can find. Or even plastic clothes-pegs," Josh said. His voice sounded high and clipped and fake to him. "Gina, if there's any marijuana left, see if you can get Joe to take it. If he won't smoke, make him eat it. If he won't eat a brownie or something, just burn it under his nose. Liquor, too, if he'll take it. Get any walk-

aways you can find, the best charms you got." The Recluse was gone and the magic was back. Even if the walkaways didn't help Joe survive Joshua's butchering, at the very least they had to try to keep any minotaurs at bay. The good Lord knew there was going to be some pain here tonight, some horror and some unbearable fear for the magic to wrap itself around. Josh wished he hadn't lost the habit of praying. "Clear off the kitchen table," he said. "I'll put some water on to boil."

HALF an hour later they strapped the boy to the kitchen table with hanks of ancient yellow nylon rope, so old it felt fuzzy to the touch and its plastic fibers were frayed. Despite his hypersensitivity, Joe showed no signs of delirium. Gina told him Josh was going to cut off his leg and that he would have to be brave. He peed himself and bit his lip to keep from yelling. "Be a man," Billy whispered. Joe broke down and started begging. Josh thought about gagging him, but decided against it. He had to be able to tell if Joe swallowed his tongue.

Josh set Gina to boiling the five pound nylon fishing line he meant to use for sutures. He went through Widow Tucker's knives and found the biggest one, then set Billy to sharpening it to the thinnest edge the discolored old steel would hold. While Billy worked, Josh took strips from the kitchen curtains and cinched them painfully tight around his right wrist, to give it more support. He didn't dare risk trying to operate left-handed.

Billy put down his whetstone and traced the blade of the filleting knife lightly across his thumbnail. Then he let the blade slide. It caught in the groove in his nail. He handed it to Josh. "How about the saw?" Josh asked.

"It's sharp."

Josh pulled down Joe's pants but left him in his urine-soaked underwear. He swabbed the boy's leg with palm whiskey. It stank. Joe spoke, his voice raw and shaking.

"Pa says I ain't old enough for the hard stuff." It was supposed to be a joke.

Josh set out his instruments on the kitchen counter beside him: carving knife, hacksaw, two pairs of needle-nose pliers with a third rusty one boiling in a pan of seawater on the stove. He had already threaded two needles with fishing line, and he had lots of cotton waiting, dingy grey balls of local stuff. He would cut as fast as possible through Joe's flesh with the carving knife, using the hacksaw only for the bone. The key thing was not to sever the femoral artery. He would need to dissect the tissue out around it and clamp it off. If he cut the femoral, the boy would die in seconds, without much pain.

It would be a very easy mistake to make.

Nobody could blame him. Nobody could prove he had done it on purpose. It wasn't as if he had ever performed an amputation before.

Josh found Miss Bettie looking at him. Quietly she said, "Galveston expects your best, Mr. Cane."

He tried to decide where to cut. The higher the better, to make sure he stopped the gangrene. He held the hacksaw upside down and laid it on Joe's leg, trying to see how high he could go and still have room to maneuver without hitting the boy's other thigh. Joe peed a little more into his underwear but kept from screaming.

"Sponges," Josh said. He'd forgotten sponges to sop up the blood from the little vessels. The pliers he needed to save for bigger arteries where he couldn't control the bleeding with pressure.

He had read somewhere that in the days of sailing ships navy surgeons could take off a man's leg in three minutes from the first cut to the last stitch. The faster the better, of course. Less blood loss, less trauma.

Josh started to faint. He forced himself to breathe until his eyes cleared and he no longer felt like throwing up.

Joe started banging his head against the table. "Quit that," Gina said.

"Don't want to be awake," the boy said raggedly.

"Be a man!" Billy said, grabbing his son's head. The car-cutter's face was white. "Be a man."

Josh picked up the knife. Joe tried to smack his head again, harder, but the ropes strapping him down didn't allow enough play. He screamed.

Say ten minutes for a first timer, Josh thought. I can do that.

IT took eighteen. Josh nicked the femoral artery but didn't sever it. Blood spattered out of the boy in pulses, hard as the sprinklers in front of city hall. Twice Josh got the hacksaw blade stuck in the thigh bone and had to jerk it out and start cutting again. The second time Billy walked out of the room. There was blood every- where. Josh had started his cut wrong and almost didn't have enough flesh to cover the bone. He spent an eternity grabbing Joe's skin and tugging on it like a man trying to wrap a present with not quite enough paper. Gina never moved. Joe screamed until his voice was a stump, but he never fainted. Josh lost all hope in a merciful God then. If there was a God in heaven who gave a damn, that boy would have fainted.

But he didn't die.

When Josh had pulled his last suture tight, he dropped the needle on the table and palpated the boy's stump. He couldn't feel any crepitance, but maybe the gas bubbles were still small or maybe he was in no state to feel any- thing. Maybe he wouldn't have felt a pound of road gravel under Joe Tucker's skin. The boy had long since stopped screaming, he could only moan now. Josh put his bloody hand on Joe's neck. His pulse was weak and spidery. No surprise there. He must have lost, what, two pints of blood? Three? Four? A mosquito settled on Joe's cheek. Josh brushed it away, leaving a splotch of blood on the boy's face. Josh felt a hand on his arm. It was

Gina. She had blood in her dirty blond hair. "Thanks," she said.

Thank you for maiming my boy, thank you for butchering him in the clumsiest way you could. Thank you for making him a cripple, something for other kids to laugh at. Thank you for ending the life he thought he had in front of him.

"You're welcome," Josh said.

"WILL he live?" Miss Bettie asked.

"I don't know." Josh had gone out into the backyard. He was sitting, completely drained, on the wreckage of what had once been Widow Tucker's henhouse. Wan grey light was seeping into the east, though overhead the stars still burned in a black sky. "I couldn't feel any bubbles in what's left of his leg. As long as the gas doesn't come back, he'll be fine. As long as the wound doesn't get infected. As long as he doesn't get blood fever or peritonitis or lockjaw. As long as he gets enough to eat and good clean water to drink, he'll be fine, sure, yeah, he'll be fine," Josh said. His throat was tight with rage. "Of course if he'd had the sense to be born thirty years ago, he'd be dandy. Three grams of penicillin. That's all he needed. Three grams of penicillin the day he got stuck."

"We didn't have penicillin when I was a girl either," Miss Bettie said. "Very few people ever have, Mr. Cane. You seem to find it so unfair." The great lady of Galveston society climbed gracefully on top of an overturned pig trough and settled next to Josh. He could feel the cold falling from her shoulder. She looked searchingly at him. "Civilization isn't what happens in the absence of barbarity, Mr. Cane. It's what we struggle to build in the midst of it."

Josh bent over with his face in his hands. He had never felt so tired, not even in the hurricane, not even when George was whipping him along Highway 87. He was

drained all the way down to the pit of his stomach. Unbelievable to think that the last time the sun had come up, he was still two miles shy of the Point Bolivar Ferry Terminal. He had been a different man then. He had left Galveston a criminal with one friend in the world; he returned a free man with none. The houses and the neighbors, they hadn't changed, exactly; it was what they meant that was different. He had come home, and found himself a stranger to his own life.

He wanted the Tucker boy to live so badly he dared not even think it to himself.

"Why did you have to come for me?" Josh asked Miss Bettie. "Why not get a real doctor? Hell, why even come here at all? These aren't your people. You belong over there," he said, gesturing toward Broadway and the Strand, the few enclaves where the streetlights had already been repaired.

" 'One of the serious obstacles to the improvement of our race is indiscriminate charity,' " Miss Bettie recited. "Andy Carnegie, the old humbug. I suppose I am an indiscriminate woman. Carnegie also said that surplus wealth was a sacred trust, which one was duty bound to give away in one's lifetime. I've done him one better, haven't I?" she said with a laugh. "You should clean up." She passed him a plain grey tea towel. Taken from one of Widow Tucker's kitchen cupboards, no doubt. Josh stared at it, stupid with weariness, then began to wipe himself off.

A small miracle happened. Wherever Joe Tucker's blood had lain, Josh found his skin had turned milk white, as if dipped in acid. His hands were like salt. Strangest of all, his right wrist was dented but smooth, as if some of the muscle lost when the maggots cleaned out his wound was still missing, but the skin had already healed seamlessly over the top of it. Streaks and drops of whiteness straggled up his arms, past his elbows. He looked at himself in wonder. "And your face, Mr. Cane," Miss

Bettie said. He wiped his cheeks and his forehead and saw another section of the towel come back red. "Washed in the blood of the lamb," Miss Bettie said softly.

He stared at her. "Did you do this?"

"No, sir, not I."

"Then . . . ?"

Miss Bettie's lace and ruffles fluttered in a shrug. "Our little sandbar has gone under the tide at last, Mr. Cane. Who is to say what miracles shall come to pass?"

They sat together and watched dawn spill across the sky. At last Josh stirred. He should see how Joe was doing, he should talk to Billy and Gina. Tell them to hang their charms and feed their boy dandelion tea, make sure his electrolyte balance didn't go to hell. Soon he should present himself at the Bishop's Palace, where, they said, Sloane Gardner would be waiting. He tried to imagine what he would say, but his mind kept slipping to less personal, more important things: cholera and malaria, clean water and bandages.

He noticed Miss Bettie was wearing a watch, a steel Rolex with diamond chips. "What time is it?" he asked.

Miss Bettie glanced at him and laughed. "You do seem to have difficulty remembering, don't you? Well, then, I shall tell you. It's *now*, Joshua Cane. Always and only now."

Part Five

Chapter Nineteen

GOING UNDER

ON the seventh morning after the hurricane, Sloane woke
to the smell of bait. She was lying on a chaise in Randall
Denton's library. She fought to open her eyes. Dawn
hadn't come, though the darkness felt lighter than it had
when she had finally settled down to sleep just after three
in the morning. Something long and wet and stringy
brushed her cheek and then withdrew. Sloane gasped,
eyes widening. A sad, whiskered face leaned out of the
gloom, bringing a powerful stink of wet shrimp and craw-
dads. She had never heard of a Prawn Man coming so
close to anyone before. She waited for him to move or
speak. He did neither. He only watched, regarding her
with a deep, gentle melancholy, his long stiff-shelled
face tilted to one side, his eyes black and glistening
like roe. Sloane's eyes struggled under the weight of
the night. They fell shut, opened, shut again, the smell
of mud and cut bait like a drug in the dark air, until at
last she slipped back into sleep. Dreams closed over her
head, strange and slowly moving like the currents of a
dark sea.

When she woke again it was grey dawn. The Prawn
Man was gone, though a faint fishy odor lingered in the

air. Somewhere beyond the library window a mocking-bird called. The notes of her song were beautiful and sad, each line lilting up to end with a question, like the voice of a woman wandering through the underworld and calling for her family.

Or perhaps it was Jane Gardner, enchanted, searching for the city she had lost. Galveston was going under: Sloane could feel the magic seeping over the Island, bringing miracles with it and minotaurs and the Prawn Men who seemed to live within its current.

The morning after the hurricane rumors of minotaurs had begun to circulate. With so much fear in the air, and no Recluse to keep the magic from hardening around it, it was inevitable that pockets of dread and panic would precipitate into flesh. Sloane had heard of a little scalped girl who haunted the Fishes. It was said she had drowned when a tornado picked up the trailer home she had been hiding in, tore it to pieces, and flung it into the sea. The skin had been flayed from her head, and she was said to be drawn to long dark hair. There were reports of other minotaurs, too, the Glass Man and the Fat Boy, with his handful of knives, and a creature without a name that was said to haunt Pier 21, strangling its victims with slimy green tendrils like ropes of kelp.

What happens when nightmares start spilling into Jane's little empire and there's no Recluse there to shoo them off to Mardi Gras? It's a hard old world we live in now, kiddo. Oh, 'Dessa, why did you let yourself get killed? We need you so much now.

Not every marvel was dark. The first bold sign of the new magic Sloane had witnessed herself was the unfolding of the angel in Alice Mather. From the time Japhet had returned to the Bishop's Palace the day after the storm with his mother in tow, Sloane had been setting Alice more and more tasks. Mrs. Mather was competent and well-liked, and Sloane had needed all the help she

could get. At first there was no missing the fact that Alice
Mather was terribly worried about her son, no matter how
many times she expressed her belief that God would take
care of him. Alice had wanted very badly to keep busy,
and not just with her family. Sloane had obliged her.
Having jobs to do around strangers had been something
to hold on to as the days went by with no sign of Ham,
or the boat that had taken him into exile.

And then, curiously enough, Alice had begun to *shine*.
Her step got lighter and lighter. Hope came into a room
with her like the smell of fresh ironing. And finally three
days ago, Lindsey the maid had run into the study where
Sloane was working to tell her that Alice Mather was
speaking in tongues.

Sloane had always thought her mother didn't understand how *alive* things were. It was more obvious every
day. For instance, she'd had the seriously ill quartered in
Randall's ballroom for five days; now the ballroom itself
seemed to be sickening. The wallpaper had begun to blis-
ter and sweat, as if feverish, and the air tasted unhealthy
even when they left the windows open.

I should be glad Mother never saw her city come to
this.

In an improbable game of musical chairs, she now occupied Randall Denton's house. Sheriff Denton, on the
other hand, had moved his staff permanently into Ashton
Villa. Sloane would have been happy to trade, but the
sheriff had made it clear that if he caught her trying any
such thing he would put her under arrest and "round up"
the revellers, whatever that meant. Nothing good, Sloane
assumed. If she wanted to get out of the Bishop's Palace,
which she did, she should do it now, while the rest of
the city was either sleeping or busy coping with its own
disasters.

Sloane forced her eyes open. She had slept in her
clothes again, which she hated, but there wasn't space to

waste on privacy. The teenage boy with the hunting knife was sleeping on a pallet next to her. He'd lost his family in the storm and had no house to go back to. Scarlet, the little doll-girl with Sloane's heart inside her, lay a few feet away, curled like a cat in the big leather armchair.

Awake, Scarlet was a bristling, sulky kid packed with so much energy she seemed to give off sparks as she darted through the Bishop's Palace. She spent hours playing dominoes, very badly, with anyone who would give her a game. She was a furious loser, and gloated when she won. She stayed up past midnight every day, and made a point of being Momus's granddaughter. She disdained the ordinary humans stranded at the Palace, taking great pains to spend her time among the revellers instead, who treated her like a princess.

But no matter where Sloane fell asleep, each morning when she woke Scarlet was curled up a few feet away. Twice now nightmares had driven the girl to her in the middle of the night. She had burrowed under Sloane's arm, her small body shuddering. Slowly the shakes would fade and her breathing would slow down. She would sleep while Sloane lay awake, waiting for the long night to pass, afraid to move for fear of disturbing her.

Asleep, Scarlet was the most beautiful, the most fragile creature Sloane had ever seen. Visions haunted her: Scarlet shot by Sheriff Denton, or racked with malaria, or falling into the swimming pool in Randall's backyard and drowned. Image after dreadful image haunted Sloane's waking eyes until she squeezed them shut and forced herself to think of something else.

Outside the mockingbird sang and sang.

This hour before dawn was the only quiet moment of the day. The revellers had abandoned the ground floor of the Bishop's Palace to the human refugees. Snatches of song came floating down the central staircase until three and four every morning, along with the rattle of dice and

the clicking of dominoes and painfully obvious drunken tiptoeing into the kitchen.

In another hour, by five-thirty, Randall's housemaids would be tending to his chickens, and Mrs. Sherbourne, the cook, would be in the kitchen to start breakfast and begin adding to Sloane's alarmingly huge bill. Randall, predictably, had written out a contract for her to sign while the storm was still blowing. She had guaranteed to cover his damages and expenses, from her own pocket if necessary. At the time she had hoped the Krewe of Momus would foot the bill, but after a cautious exchange of messengers, Sheriff Denton had declared her an outcast from the Krewe.

"What gives him the right!" she had demanded. But as Randall had pointed out, with Jane Gardner dead, all Jeremiah had to do was bring Jim Ford around. No great feat for anyone with sufficient force of personality, as Sloane knew all too well.

This had required her to switch to a second plan: winning the money back. Every evening after dinner Mrs. Sherbourne began toting up the day's expenses. Then Sloane turned the house over for the last couple of hours before bedtime to Alice Mather and invited Randall upstairs to play cards. At first he was dubious about sitting among the revellers, but there was a part of him that enjoyed the exoticism of it, especially after he discovered that few of them were very good players.

Sloane was, though.

She couldn't possibly win as much as she was spending—Randall would have stopped playing if he realized he was losing *that* much money—but she had at least slowed the bleeding a little. Oh, yes, very noble. And all for a good cause, too, she thought sarcastically. Because the truth was, she enjoyed the card games. If she hadn't had that couple of irresponsible hours a day, she would have gone crazy. Downstairs, on the first floor, people

were sick or dying or grieving for family lost to the storm, while up among the monsters Sloane Gardner was laughing and drinking and, let's face it, having fun. Not what her mother would have done.

It also made for a very short night if you were up at first light the next morning. Sloane groaned inside.

She had heard from a couple of the revellers that Ace had been seen since the storm. One fire-eater who had snuck into the Bishop's Palace on the third day after the hurricane claimed that Ace and a few other human-looking revellers were running an unofficial shelter at the old Railroad Museum. As relieved as she had been to hear he was alive—of course she hadn't managed to shoot him, he was too lucky for that—the idea of facing him filled her with shame. Still, she owed him that. The leather chaise longue creaked beneath her as she got up, carefully stepping over the pale white boy sleeping on the floor.

Refugees littered the library and the billiard room, stretched on pallets made from Randall Denton's quilts and comforters. Sloane tiptoed over more sleeping bodies, grey humps in the dim house, here an out-thrust arm, there a bruised unshaven face. Behind Randall's pool table Sloane stepped over a woman and her child who had come in yesterday, both clammy with fever sweat. She turned the latch on the French doors that led to the back patio as quietly as she could, but the little girl's eyes fluttered open at the click. She stared soundlessly at Sloane. She couldn't have been more than ten. The mother stayed sleeping.

As much time as Sloane spent worrying about Scarlet these days, how much more must your heart catch watching a real child, a child you had borne and cared for every day for years and years? How unimaginably defenseless you would be. It shocked Sloane to imagine Jane Gardner that vulnerable. It brought a strange, shaky feeling to her chest when she thought about it. Maybe her mother had

been fighting for more than just Galveston. Fighting for her, Sloane. Holding back not just magic, but the *future*, the relentless wheel of time itself. Trying with all her great energy and intelligence to keep life and all its changes from hurting her child.

A mother's real duty was to prepare her child to live on her own. That was the pious thing people said to one another. But looking at Scarlet, or at that feverish ten-year-old girl lying on the floor, Sloane didn't buy it. If she were a parent, she thought, she couldn't do that. She would try with every breath to protect her child from any hurt, however small. However necessary or inevitable. It was ridiculous and impossible, but that's what she would do. Let the world try to break her if it could.

Sloane stepped outside. Later in the afternoon the sun would set the coast simmering in another ninety-five-degree day, but now, in the grey predawn, the air was cooler than it had been since April. The humid sixty-degree morning would have been delicious if not for the smell of corpse fires. Sloane walked through Randall's wrecked grounds, past his generator shed and his swimming pool. The pool was filled up with brackish water, littered with palm fronds and bits of shingle, leaves, and the bodies of several grackles and a squirrel. Yesterday there'd been a possum, but something had dragged it out. Even in the early dawn, wheels of buzzards turned over every part of the city. Thin ropes of smoke rose from the burning dead.

At 14th Avenue she passed a grey mare tethered to a streetlamp. In the early morning light the horse was grazing on the body of a dead dog, worrying the carcass with big yellow teeth. For some reason this seemed to Sloane the most terrible abomination the magic had spawned, worse than the men she had seen in Carnival with snake scales for skin or gills under their jawbones. She found herself wishing that Sheriff Denton would come and shoot the horrible mare and throw its body off the Island.

A quick spasm of pure hatred for the people of Galveston curdled Sloane's blood. As long as she could remember, the Islanders had feared and despised her godmother, Odessa. Called her a witch, a murderess, a monster. Wished she were dead or vanished. Sloane watched the horse put one heavy hoof on the dog's body and rip up another chunk of flesh. Well, my fellow citizens got their wish, she thought savagely. I wonder how they're liking it.

THE Railroad Museum was busier than she remembered it, noisy with the murmur of conversation and footsteps, doors opening and closing, plates and saucers clinking and clattering in the diner. Somebody seemed to be keeping the place clean. Here and there she could see a tuft of seaweed caught under a bench, but the floors had been mopped, and while she could see a few smashed windows, somebody had nailed boards across them and swept up the broken glass. The gas was up and running, with plenty of lights burning in brackets along the walls. Ceiling fans turned high overhead.

There were more people here, and more statues, too. In the real Galveston, before Odessa died, all the sculptures had been of folks dressed in the fashions of the 1930s and '40s, but today instead of the handful of old familiar statues, there were dozens and dozens of new ones: Japanese tourists and young women of Odessa's generation, with white teeth and tight shorts, and two middle-aged Hispanic women, frozen in mid-stride outside the ladies' room, both wearing dresses of dreary Galveston cotton from after the Flood. There was even a Karankawa Indian, one of the crying cannibals who inhabited the Island when Cabeza de Vaca first arrived. He was in the act of pushing open a door from the side of the station that faced the tracks and the abandoned railway cars, as if he had just ridden into town on the old

Southern Pacific cotton run. Even the old black man was no longer sitting on his accustomed pew, thumbing through his paper. Now that the tide of magic was rising into Galveston proper, maybe he could turn his page at last, or put the paper down and walk out into the day.

There were live people at the station, too. The rumors Sloane had heard were true; most of them were revellers who had been stranded in the Mardi Gras until the two Galvestons fell back together. Some still wore tattered ball gowns or clutched their party masks. Quiet voices and bloodshot eyes were the norm. Hangover, Sloane thought, putting her finger on the subdued quality of the crowd. The morning after history's longest night before.

She passed through the station as unobtrusively as possible, all Sloane, shoulders hunched and head bowed, with nothing of Sly in the tilt of her lips or the set of her head. Several people gave her long looks, but if anybody was sure they saw Sly, even without the mask, they didn't accost her. Curious, in retrospect, that Lianna had recognized her at once the night of the hurricane. Sly must have been very much in her then.

She picked her way through the crowd to the diner. Waitresses threaded their way between the crowded tables, carrying food out or dirty dishes back, letting out a sizzling sound from the grill every time they kicked open the swinging kitchen doors. Volleys of shouted Spanish flew through the air like brightly colored birds. The place smelled of hot butter and lard and pancakes cooking.

Ace was sitting at a corner table, pushing some refried beans around his plate with a fork. After a moment he put the fork down. He took a small sip of coffee and then sat wearily with the cup clasped between his hands.

Sloane gathered up her scraps of courage and approached his table. Hi! You might not remember me, but last time we met I tried to kill you. She left her hands

out of her pockets so he could see she wasn't carrying a gun. "Hey. Ace," she said. She meant to sound spritely, but it came out a whisper.

He looked up. "Ma'am?"

"It's me," she said. "Sl—Sloane Gardner." She swallowed. "Sly."

He wore a patch over the left eye Momus had taken from him, but his right eye widened. "God*damn*."

"Probably," Sloane agreed.

Samuel Cane's face broke into a smile. "Good Lord, I had no idea. I've never seen you in pants before, and the one time you had your mask off I was a tad preoccupied." Ace laughed again and waved at the chair across the table. "Sit! *Maria, una más aqui!* Have you had breakfast yet? It's rice and beans, or else beans and rice, take your pick."

"I was hoping for the ranch eggs."

"They lost a lot of chickens, and the ones left aren't laying much. But then, I forgot you're a Gardner. I guess you can afford chorizo and eggs even at post-hurricane prices." Sloane smiled and decided not to tell him she was already buying breakfast, lunch, and dinner for thirty—at the prices, God help her, Randall Denton thought fair. "You look younger," Ace said.

And you look older, Sloane thought. Much older. Ace looked as if he had aged ten years since she had seen him last. The lines around his mouth were deeply grooved, and his hair, which she remembered as salt-and-pepper, was almost entirely white. She glanced down at his plate. "You've hardly touched your beans."

"Little under the weather today."

They sat in silence for a while. Sloane searched his face for traces of Joshua. They were there. Father and son shared the same narrow, bony face and wide, straight eyebrows, though the effect of the features was very different on the two men. Josh's face was sharp and full of intelligence. Life had used his father harder, and longer;

weariness and wisdom lived in the rubble where calculation had been.

"Sorry I shot you," Sloane said at last.

"Tried to, you mean." Ace smiled. "If you're going to pack a piece, you'd better learn to shoot a mite straighter."

"I won't pick so lucky a target, that's all."

The waitress brought her a glass of water and a menu. "Have you heard from your son?" Sloane asked. "I told everyone he was innocent."

Ace stirred his coffee with a splinter of sugarcane. "I haven't heard anything. Word is they meant to set him down somewhere up the Peninsula the afternoon the hurricane blew up. Ship never made it back. Lost in the storm, I expect." He sipped his coffee. "Ever see that girl with your heart inside?"

"She's staying with me now, over at Randall Denton's place. The Bishop's Palace."

"I heard you'd fixed up a sick house there for poor folks that needed it." Ace deliberately forked up a mouthful of refried beans and swallowed it down. "How has it been to have a kid around?"

"Awful. I worry about her all the time." Ace nodded and reached for a bottle of hot sauce, sprinkling it over his refried beans. "She's loud," Sloane said, "she's sulky, she complains all the time, she never does what I tell her without arguing. I was never like that. My mother never had to worry about me falling out a window or running away."

Ace took a sip of water. "You don't get to pick your kids."

"She's not my daughter."

"Okay."

"She's not my daughter," Sloane said. She closed her eyes. Opened them. "She's who I wanted to be when I was eleven. Damn it. She's that bold, noisy, dramatic girl Odessa wanted me to be. I used to . . . I used to design

these dresses, glorious scarlet dresses with flounced sleeves and trains, or royal blue brocade."

Ace smiled. "I think I got an idea about the dresses."

Sloane winced. "That was the thing about Mardi Gras I always loved, making the costumes. And when I was there myself, with you . . . but I could never wear those dresses now. That was Sly, that wasn't me."

"What's Sly but you and three fingers of whiskey? Speaking of which . . ." Ace reached into his black preacher's coat and pulled a crumpled ball of leather from the breast pocket. It was the mask. "I believe this belongs to you," he said, handing it over.

The leather was a tingle in her hand. A shiver of possibilities rippled through Sloane, and she realized how much she had missed being Sly. God help her, but it was fun to be that willful, playful, fox-faced woman.

"Anyt'ing for you, señorita?" asked Maria the waitress.

"No. I should be going." Sloane closed the menu. "I guess it's stupid to be jealous of a little girl."

"Yep."

"Good seeing you," Sloane said. The tiredness was back in Ace's eye, and though it wasn't hot in the diner, there were tiny beads of sweat along his brow. His breakfast still sat all but uneaten in front of him. "You're running a fever."

"Oh, it's nothing. Everybody's sick. Lots of flu going around."

"If you get sick, if you need a place to stay, you can always find me at the Bishop's Palace," Sloane said. "You or anybody."

"Thank 'ee kindly, Miz Gardner," he said with a drawl and a smile. He sipped his coffee. "Sorry about your mom."

"Me, too," Sloane said.

THREE hours later, Sloane and Scarlet were grabbing a quick breakfast of rice porridge and molasses on Randall

Denton's patio. Sloane had started to cross herself before eating; Scarlet would have nothing to do with such pathetic charms, of course. It was ridiculous, Scarlet said, for Momus's granddaughter to be afraid of magic. She poked at the porridge with her spoon; she rolled her eyes; she kicked her feet against her iron deck chair and made disgusted faces.

Sloane tried to ignore her, drowsy with the hum of bees in the Denton gardens. The Dentons sure knew how to take their pleasures, Sloane had to give them that. Randall's patio was edged with honeysuckle and tumbles of forsythia, and the wrought-iron table at which they sat was shaded by a magnificent magnolia tree. The vegetation was gorgeous, lush and green. Sloane frowned at Randall, who was sitting in a patio chair with an accounts ledger open on his lap. "You haven't been conserving water, have you?"

"No," he replied equably, "but I have been encouraging it by buying up the excess from more conservation-minded souls. You didn't think your mother's edicts are what spurred the rash of civic-minded water-saving, did you? It was every man for himself until my money began leading the yokels along the path of virtue."

To Sloane's surprise, she had found herself very glad of Randall Denton's company. He was the only thing left over from her old life; in a way, even his greed was reassuring.

Lianna bounded through the French doors from the parlor. "They shot another Prawn Man, Sly. I just heard," she said, whiskers trembling. She prowled around the wrought-iron breakfast table. "That's seven of us in the last three days."

"What a shame," Randall murmured. "All right, that's another three sets of sheets ripped up for bandages since yesterday, two sets of servants' uniforms given away, as well as a pair of my pants—damn good pants, too—one Chinese vase, knocked over by the fellow with the stilts,

and of course another day's food, as recorded by my cook." He slid a piece of paper across to Sloane. "No, wait." He scribbled *2x rice pudding & molasses @ $3* and changed the total line at the bottom. "Sign here."

"We need to get to Grandfather," Scarlet said from the other side of the table. "This is disgusting," she added, pushing her rice pudding away.

"What do we do next?" Lianna snarled. "Wait until the sheriff breaks in here and shoots us all?"

"Eat your breakfast," Sloane said. She pulled a handful of poker chips out of her pocket and handed them to Randall, writing "paid" down the items on Mrs. Sherbourne's food bill until she ran out of chips. They lasted almost through yesterday's breakfast. Well, it was something. Then Sloane took the pen from Randall and crossed out the dollar amount for the Chinese vase. "I'll find someone to get you another pot."

Randall was wearing the tightly tailored pants he had helped establish as a style, back when his calves were better, along with a collarless cotton shirt that made a point of being impossibly white. "That's an antique—"

"So is this molasses."

"Then why do I have to eat it?" Scarlet sulked.

"Just be quiet and eat your breakfast," Sloane snapped. She didn't want any more of her porridge either, but forced herself to set a good example for Scarlet. Left to her own devices the girl would eat nothing but sweet yogurt and sugarcane.

Lord, it was going to be another scorching day. September . . . fourteenth? Only another couple of weeks until the summer broke for good.

Sloane forced her mind back to the problems of the present. "Randall? Is your uncle going to storm this house?"

"If he does, I expect my guns to be returned to me undamaged, with payment in full for every bullet you fire

in your glorious defense." Randall sipped from a cup of mint tea he had brought with him. He'll probably bill me for that, too, Sloane thought. Consultant's fee. Business breakfast. "I don't know, Sloane. I wouldn't have thought so, but your reappearance has put Jeremiah under considerable strain, you know. It makes it look as if the evidence against the two men convicted of, ah, getting rid of you, was not entirely legitimate. And of course the last week has been hard on everyone. But even so, Uncle Jeremiah has been behaving oddly. He never liked the revellers much, but since the hurricane it's become something of a mania with him. And he has a terrible cough," Randall said. Sloane wondered if the old man was still spitting up seawater. "Worse than that, he seems to be hearing things. We were chatting in the Gold Room at your old place and three different times he shushed me and held up his hands. Claimed to hear crabs scuttling around inside the piano. Once he actually lifted the top off to look down inside. Didn't hear a thing myself."

Wait a minute. "You've seen him?" Sloane asked.

"Yesterday. At your house. He's moved the sheriff's offices there until they get the building downtown fully repaired."

Sloane looked at Lianna. "Nobody told me Randall had left."

"I can't watch him every minute," Lianna bristled. Sloane closed her eyes. There were twenty-five or thirty refugees from the Mardi Gras now squatting in the Bishop's Palace. Sloane had begun to discover that, while many of them were great fun, "devotion to duty," "dependability," and other such stolid daily virtues were not the revellers' strong suit.

Bees bumbled among the vines. Randall watched them, considering. "Am I a prisoner then, in my own house, Sloane? Are you making me a hostage?"

Well, yes. "I guess not," Sloane said. "It wouldn't look

good, I suppose."

Randall grinned and sipped his tea. "Thanks for caring."

"We should get Grandfather," Scarlet said. She was using one of Randall's sterling silver spoons to draw patterns in her uneaten porridge.

"He would look after his own," Lianna said. "He would take care of us if he knew."

"What makes you think he doesn't know?" Randall said, amused. "You think none of these murders happened in the moonlight?" He put his cup down, stretched, and breathed in the scent of honeysuckle with great satisfaction, before glancing back at the cat-faced reveller. "The Dentons have been members of the Krewe of Momus since 1873, my feline friend, and at the risk of sounding sacrilegious, an excessive care for his worshipers has never been part of the jesting god's character. Named after the Greek god of derision, you know. Thrown out of Olympus for ridiculing the other gods. None of your Jesus cult loving-kindness. For that matter, I never heard that Jesus did much for the blacks when they were slaves around these parts either, however fiercely they believed."

"So what do you believe in, Randall?" Sloane said, exasperated.

"Keeping your head down and a ten percent return. Call me a traditionalist." He slid the accounts over to her again and held out his pen. "Sign the invoice, Sloane. — Ah. Thank you."

Sloane didn't like to think how much money she already owed him. Even if she ever managed to get Ashton Villa back, she might have to sell her mother's house to pay her debts. "You're such a Denton."

"And you have turned into a Gardner, much to my surprise." Randall gathered his papers. "I never thought you had your mother's stomach for it. Rather be off in

your room sewing or writing poetry. But here you are, a
do-gooder and a busybody after all. In my house, incon-
veniently." He stood. "I shall leave you to it. I am going
to stay with Mother tonight, and for the duration of Uncle
Jeremiah's siege, I think. Unless you've decided to hold
me hostage after all?"

"Don't go," Sloane said. Scarlet gave her a dirty look.
"I mean, why?"

"Much as I enjoy seeing my house full of mutants and
homeless people," Randall remarked, glancing pointedly
at the cat-faced Lianna and Scarlet, "not to mention rude
children, I don't believe this place is safe. It was one
thing for you and Alice Mather to play at good Samaritans here for the first few days after the storm. That was
mostly bumps and cuts and a few broken bones. But the
people coming here now are sick, Sloane. They have fevers. They are probably contagious with typhoid or dysentery or cholera or yellow fever. As lovely as it has been
to unite our strengths for the good of the adoring if
smelly masses, I don't intend to stay here and catch the
plague with you, dear."

"How will you know how much of your stuff we've
used?" Sloane argued weakly.

"Mrs. Sherbourne will keep track of it."

"Oh, so you don't mind leaving *her* here to catch the
plague."

"I'm paying her extra," Randall said briefly. "Or rather,
you are." He took a handkerchief out of the breast pocket
of his shirt and dabbed at the sweat beginning to bead
on his brow. "Besides which, now that the dead are slow-
roasting in their pyres, Uncle Jeremiah is turning his attention more seriously to the problem of the revellers
hiding out in my house. He's quite rabid about having
monsters on the Island. He warned me he might have to
cut off the water here, or the gas. I like a shower in the
morning, and I like it hot." Randall tipped his head.

"Good day, Sloane. And goodbye."

"Don't let him go, Sly!" Lianna said. "We need a hostage." But Sloane shook her head.

"Grandfather will fix you," Scarlet said.

Randall seemed unperturbed. "Momus will fix all of us, sooner or later," he said. "Until Carnival comes, I advise you to look somewhere else for rescue."

SLOANE went upstairs to Randall's study. She had told everyone she was going where she could concentrate, and she had tried, making lists of small jobs that needed doing, while all the time unable to figure out how to stop Sheriff Denton from executing the revellers.

What would Mom do? she asked herself. Easy, she'd be running the city. She was the Law, not the Outlaw. As for Odessa, she had her magic. Momus—well, gods did as they wished. Sloane couldn't do what any of them would have done. They were greater people than she. She quirked a small smile. So what was the small, sneaky, quiet, polite way to get out of this mess?

Pray?

Actually, that was good advice, she decided. With the magic running high over Galveston, the Mexicans clutching their votive candles and chanting Mass probably had the right idea. A small offering or two wouldn't hurt at all. And who had better ancestors to invoke than Sloane Gardner? Oh, it would make Mother spin in her grave to have me burning incense for her, Sloane thought. She grinned. For that matter, just finding she *could* spin in her grave would make her spin in her grave.

Her smile died. Even after having spent quite a while as Sly, she had let her mother down too badly to make light of it. Maybe she could pray to Bettie Brown; they had shared the same house together for years, after all. Even played a hand or two of cards in the Mardi Gras. Or Odessa, better still. She hadn't managed to save her godmother, but at least she had tried to avenge her. She

supposed she should feel sorry for having thrown Jeremiah Denton's doll into the sea, but she didn't. It had been a mean, furious, impulsive act, and she was so much prouder of it than all her polite, reasonable, carefully considered decisions.

I wonder if the sheriff would be willing to play stud to decide the issue. Or Texas hold 'em. Or jackpots, Sloane thought, as she closed her eyes. Hell, I'd let him deal and play with wild cards if he wanted. . . .

THE next thing she knew, a maid was touching her gingerly on the shoulder. "Ma'am?"

Sloane started up. It was hot and airless in the little study. Her eyes felt puffy and her face numb where it had been lying on the mahogany desk. "What? What?"

"I'm sorry to disturb you," Lindsey said. "Mrs. Mather brung her son, and a gentleman. A doctor." There was something odd about Lindsey's voice. Sloane blinked. The maid had a rag tied to cover her nose and mouth. Soaked in vinegar, to judge by the smell. Worried about catching a fever.

Sloane nodded. "A doctor. Good. That's good."

"It's, it's *the* doctor, ma'am. The one we all thought . . ."

Oh. "The apothecary. Mr. Cane." The maid nodded. "And Mrs. Mather's son Ham, is he there, too?"

"Yes, ma'am. Burned to a crisp with a big mark on his head. Branded like a cow, they say, by cannibals!"

"Thank God!" Sloane took one moment to be heartily glad that Josh and Ham hadn't died because of her, and another to be relieved on Alice Mather's part. How nice.

Now here comes the guilt. It was so predictable Sloane felt mad at herself as the shame rose in her. But she had earned this self-disgust. If she hadn't been out playing in the Mardi Gras, Josh and Ham would never have been arrested and exiled. Sloane looked at the small clock on Randall's desk. Just past noon. She had been asleep for

more than an hour. "Thank you. I'll be right down." The clock was very old; each tick felt labored and a little late. Brittle, elderly ticks. Sloane lifted her wrist to check her Rolex for the right time, then remembered that the watch was gone. She had thrown it away, her mother's most powerful charm. Thrown it away and been glad to get rid of it.

The maid curtseyed and turned to go. "Lindsey," Sloane said.

"Ma'am?"

"Do you have any makeup?"

"Me?"

"Yes."

"In the house?"

"Yes."

"A little, ma'am."

Sloane looked down at the desk, where her hands were lying. Flecks of faded red polish speckled her nails like peeling paint nobody had cared enough to sand away. "Could I borrow it?"

"It's just eyeliner and a pencil," Lindsey said doubtfully. "And cheap. Not from before the Flood or anything." The clock ticked slowly in the stuffy room. "All right," the maid said.

"Thank you," Sloane said. "Just bring the makeup, and then tell Mr. Cane I will be down directly."

In five minutes the maid was back. As well as eyebrow pencil and eyeliner, she brought a small bowl of water and a round tin with dull red lipstick inside, the sort you had to pick up on your fingertip and spread like liniment. "From Mrs. Sherbourne in the kitchen," Lindsey said. "And I brought one of Mr. Denton's handkerchiefs to blot with." Sloane was pretty sure that if she tried to speak she would cry. She settled for smiling. Lindsey smiled back through her vinegar-soaked rag. "Do you have a thing for the doctor?" the maid asked.

"No." Dipping her fingers in the bowl, Sloane traced cool water on her face. Without exactly meaning to, she found she was drawing the lines of the Sly mask on her cheeks—invisible tracks of coolness.

There are some things, Odessa had told her once, you need a new face to face.

Chapter Twenty

TREATMENT

ONCE Mrs. Mather had led Josh and Ham over to the Bishop's Palace she tactfully withdrew, saying she had to help Randall's cook put lunch on the table. She left the boys standing in the foyer while the housemaid ran upstairs to announce their arrival. The maid was wearing a rag face mask dipped in vinegar. Josh had long ago decided not to argue with these contraptions, which a lot of Islanders were wearing to fend off disease. He figured he had no right to be condescending, not when a good placebo was more effective than many of his remedies.

Ham tugged absently on the brim of an old nylon base-ball cap as he looked Randall Denton's place over. George's brand still marred his forehead, although Josh's was gone. Sometime during Joe Tucker's amputation he must have wiped his forehead with his bloody hands; his brand had been erased by a streak of salt-white skin. Josh found himself flexing his bleached fingers. The white skin was soft as a baby's bottom, and unnervingly sensitive; he had already burned himself once this morning, grabbing a cup of chicory that normally wouldn't have hurt him to hold.

Back in the old Galveston, he would have been

snitched out to the Recluse and gone to Krewes in a matter of days, with this kind of omen written on his flesh. But now the Recluse was dead and the Krewes had come to Galveston instead. He wondered if the Harlequins were liking the new world as well as they had anticipated.

Ham took in the marble fireplace across the foyer with its carved traceries of vines and gargoyle heads erupting from the mantle. He studied the great crystal chandelier overhead, and the gorgeous Persian carpet, now filthy with muddy footprints. He observed the polished baby grand in the piano room, the brass spittoons and velvet curtain pulls. He nodded judiciously. "So *this* is how the po' folk live." He tugged his cap over his ears and bent to examine the cherrywood display case Randall kept in his front hall, full of the trophies of Dentons past. The seat of his pants hung loosely from his hips and his neck was still an angry red from sunburn and the mosquito bites he hadn't been able to keep from scratching.

Josh joined him in front of the display case. "Those are the old Colonel's Civil War medals." Josh remembered getting the tour once, as a boy of eight. Randall's father had pointed out each item in the case, his hands shaking from the Parkinson's that would eventually kill him. "That's a signed letter from his friend William Jennings Bryan, who ran for president." Josh pointed to a stuffed parrot. "When someone came to Will Denton to ask for a loan from his bank, he used to bend his head down to this parrot—it was already dead and stuffed at the time—and then look back with a little smile and say his partner had refused the loan. And these are the plane tickets Randall's daddy decided not to use on the day before the Flood." Continental Flt. 204; a yellowing Hertz rental car coupon still peeping out from the decaying paper covers. "If he had decided to go, he would have been in New York City and swallowed with everyone else when it woke up."

"Hoo boy," Ham said.

They stood side by side, looking at the Denton heir-looms. "I'm sorry," Josh said. He felt sick. His heart was pounding and the palms of his hands were clammy with sweat. "I'm not going to make excuses. You and your family, you've been good to me. And I haven't always— I should have done better. I'm sorry." Ham showed no sign of having heard him. The blush of shame that had burned Josh so often over the last few days came back, stinging fiercely on the blotched white skin where Joe Tucker's blood had bleached his face. "So I guess I'm asking for another chance."

"You've had a ton of chances."

"I know," Josh said.

For the first time in days, Ham turned and looked him in the eye. "Is that finally the sound of genuine remorse?" A tiny quiver of relief went through Josh, and he remembered to breathe. "Are you going to turn over a new leaf?" Ham said. "Are you going to be a new and better Joshua Cane, full of care for others and actually looking beyond your own asshole?" The big man scratched under his cap. A few flakes of peeling skin drifted down from his sunburned scalp. "I don't know," Ham said. "And frankly, I don't care."

Josh could hear the blood running in his own eardrums, feel it pulsing in his neck and at the ball of his thumb.

Ham turned and ambled off, hooking his thumbs in the waistband of his pants. "I guess I'm not so mad anymore. Not like I was. But to tell you the truth, Josh, I find it exhausting just to listen to you. It feels like there's years and years and years of bullshit between us, and all I want to do is forget about it. So go ahead, turn over a new leaf. I'm all for it. But don't tell me about it. Because somewhere out there on the Bolivar Peninsula I just stopped giving a damn."

Josh's heart felt tight and dry and leathery, as if it had been hung in the rafters of his house with the thyme and

sage and garlic. "Fair enough," he said. "Some hands you just have to fold."

"I reckon," Ham said.

The housemaid trotted downstairs, her face-rag fluttering. "Ms. Gardner will join you directly," she said. "Can I get you gentlemen something to eat or drink?"

"We just ate," Josh said. The idea of food made him sick.

Ham beamed. "Chicory if you've got it, and I'd take a little snack if you have one handy."

"Very good." The maid bobbed and slipped back toward the kitchen.

"Like I'm going to miss a chance at working the Dentons for a free lunch," Ham said. "But be proud if you like. That's just the way your momma was. Too proud for everybody. Lot of good it did her."

"Ham, is there anything I can do—" Josh stopped. He gave a little laugh that felt like a knife in his chest. "Never mind," he said. "I just remembered something." Ham didn't ask what it was, and Josh realized he was still acting as if Ham cared, pathetic as a schoolboy turned down for a date. "Okay," he said.

Josh turned back, staring blindly through his own reflection in the Colonel's display case. What he had remembered all of a sudden, like a bubble rising to the surface of a deep sea and popping, was the sight of his father standing on their step a lifetime ago, drunk and penitent and exultant all at once. *Don't you understand, Mandy? I've still got it. I still have my luck!*

Even then his mother had loved Sam Cane. Josh was sure of that. It just didn't matter anymore. His tired mother had held Josh back, blocking the doorway with her body, her voice flat. *I know. But you don't have us anymore.*

Josh watched Ham walk away. After a lifetime of standing in that doorway behind his mom, he thought, it

was surprising to discover himself out in the street, and the door closing in front of him.

FOOTSTEPS thumped quickly down the stairs, and a moment later a tiny red-haired girl dashed into the parlor. "There's someone new. I heard voices. Oh," she said, coming to a stop and looking them up and down. "Humans."

Ham laughed. "What were you expecting?" he said, squatting down to meet her face-to-face.

The girl was the size of a toddler, but lithe and athletic as a ten-year-old, with a face Josh instantly recognized as being just like Sloane's, only much more dramatic. Her hair was fiery red and her skin white but completely unfreckled, a thing never seen in nature, not under the Texas sun. He wondered if his own hands would splotch and stain where Joe Tucker's blood had bleached them, or if they would stay milk white for the rest of his life.

"I was hoping for something interesting," the girl said. "This place is so boring. Nothing to do but wait for the sheriff to come and shoot us to death." She mimed a yawn and a stretch. "Exciting when it finally happens," she said with heavy irony. "But not much fun until then. You're fat," she added.

"You smell funny," Ham said instantly.

"I do not!"

Ham wrinkled his nose and snuffled. "Pee-yew."

"I don't smell funny!" the girl shouted. Ham shrugged. The child's nose quivered.

"Made you sniff!" Ham crowed.

"I wasn't playing!"

"You were and you lost," Ham said with satisfaction. "You're Scarlet, I bet. My niece Christy was telling me all about you this morning. You put on a puppet play for her."

"Christy makes a fine audience," Scarlet allowed. "Sometimes I let her play the humans."

"Good of you," Ham said gravely, and he stuck out his enormous hand, thick as a brick and pretty nearly the same color, for the girl to shake.

Josh watched them becoming friends. Ham always said most men were fools and blockheads, but somehow that opinion did not touch him at any depth. He liked people, he liked being around them, and he went out of his way to befriend them. He was always willing to talk, to men and women, fishers and land folk, the popular and the outcast. Josh had often wondered if it was his enormous size that made it possible. Ham just didn't fear people; ridicule bounced off of him, and nobody was stupid enough to actually take a swing. (Well, not twice.) Ham liked any man, red, brown, white, or black, as long as he worked like a son of a bitch.

The things that made Ham able to squat in his baggy pants in the Bishop's Palace and make friends with a little reveller girl (for it was obvious that was what she was) were probably the ones that had made him willing, all those years ago, to spend time with a nervous, proud, prickly kid who thought himself too good for his neighbors. And Josh, who was much less likely to say that most men were idiots, was a great deal more willing to believe it. He didn't like people very much, and he hadn't respected them.

He did now, a day late and a dollar short. Watching Billy and Gina Tucker hold down their boy while Josh cut off his leg had left one indelible thought in his mind: Everybody suffers. Rich or poor, black or white, even the cheeriest person he had ever met had known pain. Many had known more pain than him. Maybe most. Joshua had never given Billy Tucker a second thought until last night. Now he would do anything not to feel the anguish he had seen in the car-cutter's eyes. Once Josh had thought it was intellect you admired in a man, his ability to hold his tells and play his cards. How stupid he had been not to recognize the one thing everyone had in com-

mon: Sooner or later, every man lost more than he could bear.

Suffering was something Josh could respect. Suffering and the courage to stay at the table in the face of it. He closed his eyes and tried to shut out the memory of Joe Tucker, terrified, whispering, "Pa says I ain't old enough for the hard stuff."

The maid brought them two cups of chicory, a selection of rice crackers, and a pot of mustang grape jelly to spread on them. Ham had eaten three crackers of his own, fed one to Scarlet (she had confessed her name at last), and was working on a third cup of chicory by the time Sloane Gardner finally bothered to come downstairs and greet them.

She was a disappointment. In his mind's eye Josh had been expecting the superbly dressed woman with downcast eyes he remembered from the night Ham had first dragged her over to his shop. Or if not her, then the laughing party girl who had stripped off her ripped silk stockings and left them in his house. Or the woman he had fed damiana tea to, who reached out and held his hand, vulnerable, and trusted him with her secrets.

This Sloane Gardner was wearing a man's shirt that didn't fit very well and a plain pair of wrinkled pants. Her face was too small, her eyes set too close together. She hadn't been sleeping enough. Her skin was pale and puffy, with dark bags under her colorless eyes. She was just a body, like everybody else: a plain human tacked to an animal that was going to need sleep and food, that was going to sicken and die.

"Good afternoon," she said in a polite, reserved voice.

Josh nodded. "Ms. Gardner."

Ham lifted Scarlet off his lap, where she had been sitting. "You!" he said.

"Mr. Mather. I'm so pleased—"

Ham jabbed at her with a finger the size of a big dill pickle. "Thanks to you, Josh and I nearly bought the farm

out on the Peninsula, did you know that? Thanks to you, he got bit by a rattlesnake and I was nearly eaten by cannibals, and both of us had the shit kicked out of us by that hurricane." He rose from his chair and stood glowering down at her. Tall as she was, her eyes faced the mass of infected welts on his neck from his scratched mosquito bites. "What have you got to say about that?"

Sloane bit her lips, composed herself. "I am so sorry," she said softly. "I am so very, very—"

Ham clapped her thunderously on the back. "Right, then. 'Nuff said."

Sloane blinked. "But—"

"Ah, hell, honey. I've tied one on a time or two myself. No harm, no foul," Ham said, turning back and grabbing another rice cracker.

"Ham is very generous," Josh said. Bile rose in his throat.

The big man slathered on a thick layer of jam and stuffed the whole thing in his mouth at once. He pointed at Scarlet with the jam knife and said, "Nice kid," before he had quite swallowed, sending a small spray of rice cracker crumbs everywhere.

"Glad you think so," Sloane said dubiously.

"I think we should put them in the Guest Bedroom, don't you?" Scarlet said, cackling.

"Mmumph?" Ham said, cocking his head as he chewed.

"There seems to be a room in the Palace left over from Mardi Gras," Sloane explained. "It's got air-conditioning and polyester pillows and a TV that still works. Every now and then someone wanders into it by accident, but you never find it on purpose. Randall says he can remember it being renovated when he was a boy."

"We call it the Guest Bedroom because it never stays for long," Scarlet said.

Ham shook his head. "Good Christ in duck blind."

"I heard there were people needing medical attention,"

Josh said. "Or did they all get better during the rather long time we've been waiting?"

Sloane regarded him. "They're upstairs. When you've done with your snack, I would be grateful if you could have a look."

"I'm done."

Ham shooed them off. "Go ahead," he said through a mouthful of jammy cracker. "I'll catch you up."

"Your friend is very amiable," Sloane said as she led Josh up the central staircase to the second floor of Randall Denton's mansion. "I don't expect you to be so forgiving."

"Good," Josh said.

SLOANE showed him into the small ballroom at the back of Randall's mansion, where she had quartered the sickest and most injured. "You may want to move these patients," she said. "I think the room is getting sick."

Josh remembered the story of Vincent Tranh's wife, trapped in the UT Hospital when the Flood of 2004 hit. When the magic grew thick enough to clot around suffering and fear, a room full of sick people was not a good place to be.

Joshua's tire-rubber sandals clopped across the floor. He remembered this place from long ago—the blond dancing floor with parquet patterns all around the baseboards, the eight matched ceiling fans and the heavy swaying crystal chandelier. There had been a great stained glass window dominating the east wall of the room: Jacob wrestling the angel, a whimsical counterpoint to the gentler dancing that went on below. But the hurricane had smashed part of that window in, and what was left seemed very wrong. The angel was gaunt, his thin face wasted and flushed with fever. Jacob looked worse: conjunctivitis in one eye, the kinked hair of slow starvation, his face inflamed with pox. The very air seemed weary. Instead of the sounds of dancing feet and

a swing band playing, Josh would have to listen to the labored breathing of the sick. Instead of the rich aromas of wax and leather and perfume, the ballroom smelled of sour sweat and urine.

Sloane said there should be eight patients. Two were out on the shaded verandah for a few minutes of air. Probably suffering chills and anxious to get in the sun, Josh thought. One fellow was on the toilet in the bathroom, shitting his guts out. The other five lay on pallets of bedding on the sprung wood dancing floor.

Josh's first patient didn't look good. Her face was clammy with sweat. Her dark hair was lank and unwashed, heavily streaked with grey. She was probably only in her early thirties, but she looked much older. Joshua knelt down and felt her forehead with the back of his hand. Fever beat against his sensitive skin. About a hundred degrees; he found he didn't need to consult a thermometer. A little touch of magic in him, too, then, where Joe Tucker's blood had fallen. "Is the fever constant?"

"Sometimes worse, sometimes better," she said. "But even when it's gone, I feel so damn tired. I've got so much to do, the house is a wreck, and there's nobody else to take care of my niece and nephew. . . ." The woman's mouth worked, and a couple of tears slid down her cheeks. "But I'm so tir—"

"Fatigue," Josh said impatiently. "What about vomiting?" The woman shook her head, tears still streaking her face. "Stick out your tongue, please." Basically normal. Good. "Diarrhea?"

"A little."

Softly he turned the woman's head, checking for stiffness in the neck, looking for signs of conjunctivitis in her bloodshot eyes. "Delirium?"

"Two days ago, when her fever was really bad," Sloane said.

"What did you do for it?"

"For the hottest patients we keep the ceiling fan on full and wrap them in wet sheets. There was a supply of willow-bark aspirin, but we've used it up."

"Just as well. It was the wrong thing to do," Josh said. "Not that you could know that. This woman probably has malaria, which is usually accompanied by anemia and possible internal bleeding. Aspirin is a blood-thinner. Not a good risk."

"I'm sorry," Sloane said. "We didn't know."

"Malaria?" the sick woman said. "Oh, my God. What can you do?"

"Not much. Unless Ms. Gardner would like to take a trip to the Andes to collect the bark of the cinchona tree so we can make quinine. I suspect her calendar is full, though." For some reason Josh couldn't get rid of the cool tone in his voice, but his hands contradicted it. Never had they been so gentle as they were now, not even when holding a baby. He picked up the sick woman's wrist and felt for her pulse. It was quick and weak. "Good. Yes, malaria."

He looked at her for a long time, taking in her wan, lined face, her exhaustion and the waxy sweat of fever. "I'm really sick," she said, embarrassed, as if he might think she was malingering.

"I know." He met her eyes until he was sure she believed him. He did it because she was sick and he had no way to make her better; he had no comfort to offer her except to acknowledge her suffering. Because he owed her that, like he owed the Tuckers. Like he owed Ham and the Mathers and was going to keep on owing, for years and years and years, even if they never invited him into their house again. Even if they never said another word to him. Like he had owed Raúl and Conchita. That's where he had failed them when their baby was born dead. If he had to do it over again, he would have made the same decisions, he would have saved his adren-

aline, he wouldn't have changed a thing—except he would have respected their grief.

When he was sure this patient knew he had heard her suffering, he said, "Now, Sally—it is Sally, isn't it? I saw you once before about—" He felt her body tighten under his fingers and stopped himself from saying "a case of gonorrhea" just in time. "About a year ago," he finished. The woman gave him a grateful look. Josh knelt beside her pallet, still holding her hand. He felt her pulse beating against the thin skin of his hand. "Sally, listen carefully. You are very sick with malaria. That was the good news. The bad news is you're going to be very sick for the rest of your life."

Her hand clenched. He wanted to pull his away but forced himself not to. "The illness will come and go. You will have bad spells, like you did a couple of days ago: high fever, delirium, possibly bleeding, possibly jaundice. You'll know you have jaundice if your urine gets very dark." He wanted to sound different, to sound comforting, but that seemed like too much of a lie and he couldn't force himself to do it. "After each of these spells, you will feel better, maybe even better than you do right now, for three weeks or five or maybe even eight. Then will come another bad spell. All you can do is ride it out. Keep yourself as cool as you can, eat plenty of good food between bouts, and make sure to drink as much good clean water as you can manage."

"I'm never going to get better?" Sally said. "Isn't there a chance?" She tried to smile. "You can lie, just to keep my spirits up."

"No, I can't. I'm sorry," Josh said. "But you won't get all the way better, no. Even between bad spells you may still feel tired and irritable. Try to rest."

"Oh, sure," she said with the tired smile of a player whose bluff has been called. Of course there would be no rest for her. She would have to work, harder than he ever would, providing for children that weren't even her

own, the orphans of some brother or sister she had lost to sickness or to the storm. Josh thought of Gina Tucker, grim-faced, bullying him to save her boy.

"Malaria is a parasite," Josh said. "It resides in your liver. Periodically it breaks out into your red blood cells. It's carried by mosquitoes. Sally, even when you are feeling better, you can still spread the disease if a mosquito bites you first and then bites anybody else. It's important for you to try to rest and eat well, but it's even more important for everyone else on the Island that you sleep under good, tight mosquito netting every single night. *Every single night.* Do you understand?"

Her mouth worked. "Dr. Cane, we've got nothing—"

"Not true: you have malaria. It isn't fair." He shrugged. "But rotten as they are, those are the cards you got dealt, and now you have to make your best hand. Even if you can't win, you can help the odds of those around you. If you want to keep your niece and nephew from catching the disease, you will have to watch for mosquitoes for the rest of your life. Do you understand?"

Josh approved of the way she worked not to cry. "I'll try," she said.

WHEN Josh had finished making his rounds he withdrew with Sloane and Ham to the foyer at the top of the staircase. "Worse than I had hoped, better than I feared," he said. "I'm not positive about the fellow in the bathroom, but I'm guessing salmonella. He's got a fifty-fifty chance of making it. I think you have three cases of malaria, and three more enteric complaints, one complicated by dysentery. The malaria patients must be put under mosquito netting as much as possible; you should treat any mosquito as more dangerous than a rattlesnake. Sooner or later a case of yellow fever will crop up. It can be innocuous, or it can be even worse than malaria. It is also mosquito-driven. Keep everyone cool when you can, and make sure they have plenty of clean water to drink. Boil

it first. If you run out of fresh water, Ham can show you how to make a salt-water still. Serve dandelion tea; it's rich in iron and potassium, both crucial for patients with anemia or diarrhea. Last, the teenager with the scarred face has tetanus. I found a bad puncture wound in his shoulder, probably from a rusty nail embedded in a piece of debris. He'll die within the next three days."

Sloane paled. "Oh. My God."

"Good golly, Josh," Ham said irritably. "Try not to get all choked up about it."

Josh flexed his white fingers. "If I felt everything, I'd never move again. I've got damiana and jimsonweed to treat these people. What do you want from me, Ham? Hope?"

"People need hope to get well."

"You two supply it," Josh said. "I'm afraid I only have medicine to offer. Are there any other patients?"

"In the master bedroom," Sloane said. She hesitated. "I should warn you, these aren't exactly people."

"I beg your pardon?"

"They're revellers."

"Ah. On our way over here, one of Sheriff Denton's men stopped us in the street. He made me swear an oath I wouldn't treat any 'monsters.' "

Sloane closed her small eyes. She was tired, too, Josh thought. Not as tired as he was—she hadn't mutilated any ten-year-old boys today—but tired nonetheless. "You won't see them?" she said.

"Don't be ridiculous," Josh said. "Lead on."

Sloane laughed. "Whatever happened to a gentleman's word being his bond?"

"I'm not a gentleman," Josh said. "As the sheriff went to some pains to point out at my trial."

AFTER Josh had seen the revellers—another case of malaria; two with the DTs; one with septicemia, a goner for sure; three more he couldn't diagnose—he gave instruc-

tions to Sloane on how the patients should be handled, stressing once more the need for clean, boiled drinking water, then went down to the kitchen to grab a bite to eat and instruct the cook. For those suffering from diarrhea he told Mrs. Sherbourne to alternate chicken broth and dandelion tea sweetened with sugarcane: a basic formula for electrolyte replenishment, disguised as food they could understand. Then he sat at the dining room table and let the cook bring him some food, a fillet of sea trout pan-fried in garlic butter, with red beans and rice on the side. Ham inspected the generator shed outside, prospecting for materials to build a still, and then rejoined him for lunch.

Ham cut out a portion of his trout. "Damn this is good. Wonder why old George would think to eat us when he could fix this instead? Principle of the thing, I guess. Survival of the fittest." He chewed, savoring. Josh still felt dry and used up inside and could not interest himself in food. "Josh, I got a hell of a lot of mosquito bites back on the Peninsula. So did you. What are the chances . . . ?"

"Depends on if any of them were carrying."

The cook handed Ham a glass of milk and he drank it gratefully. Josh noticed her making a little note on a ledger on the kitchen counter. Shopping list? "When will we know?" Ham said. He started to scratch his bumpy neck, then stopped himself. "About the malaria and all?"

"Soon. If another couple of days go by without serious signs, we're probably okay. For now. But don't get bitten anymore. Wear layers on layers, no matter how hot it is. Rub garlic on your skin if you think that helps. There's going to be a real epidemic."

"Damn." Ham said the word with two syllables, *da-yum*. He shook his head and tucked into his lunch. "Nice digs," he said. "The table's so polished up I can see my own reflection."

"A hardworking maid will do that for you."

Ham ate and ate. At last he pushed back his plate, belched, and said, "So here you are, Josh. Back in high society again. Bossing around Randall Denton's servants. Giving orders to the Grand Duchess's daughter. Is it everything you thought it would be?"

Josh tinkered with his fish, dissecting the white flesh methodically away from its spine, remembering how he had cut through the meat of Joe Tucker's leg, exposing the bone. "It all seems smaller," he said at last.

AN urgent knock on the front door sounded just as Mrs. Sherbourne was clearing their plates away. Ham pushed himself up from the table and padded out into the front foyer. Josh came more slowly behind. Lindsey the housemaid was already at the door. "Another patient," she said, seeing him.

The patient was a gaunt man with white hair. He wore a patch over his left eye and his left ear had been cut off. His face was lobster red and filmed with sweat. His eye was red, too. "Get him up—Oh, my God," Josh said. He pulled himself together. "Get him upstairs." He looked around for the maid. "Wet some sheets, please. We need to bring down his fever." Sloane Gardner appeared on the landing, with her little girl Scarlet beside her. Josh looked up at her. "I'm going to need a separate room for this patient. It doesn't have to be big, but a bed with mosquito netting would be ideal."

"There's the children's bedroom," she said. "I'll lead the way."

"Excellent." Josh found Ham staring narrowly at him. "It's my father," he said.

Ham picked up Samuel Cane, carried him gently upstairs, and laid him in the bed Randall Denton had slept in as a boy, a small four-poster with a canopy of mosquito netting. Josh and Sloane filed into the room behind him. "I saw him this morning," Sloane murmured. "He looked sick then, but not like this."

"I saw him, too," Scarlet said, worming in between the bigger bodies to get a spot at the bedside. "Grandpa took his eye before I ever met you. Flicked it out like a marble."

Josh laid the back of his hand on his father's forehead. Sam Cane's skin was fiercely hot and damp and red, as if he were being steamed alive. Josh could feel the exact temperature with his white fingers, the way sailors who got the magic were said to be able to predict the next day's weather by sticking one finger in the ocean. His father was running 103.2 degrees. A terrible temperature for a man in his fifties. "Let's get those wet sheets," Josh said. "Turn on the ceiling fan, would you, Ms. Gardner?"

The sick man twitched and stared glassily at him. "Josh?" he whispered.

Josh leaned forward. "I can smell vomit on his breath."

"He couldn't eat this morning," Sloane said.

"Josh? Is that you? I'm hearing your voice," his father said. "I keep hearing voices."

"Patient shows some signs of delirium." Josh reached for his father's wrist. Sam Cane's forearm was very different than he remembered it. Those arms had always been so smooth, so tanned; he could still see the precise play of the muscles under his father's skin as he took a deck and cut it with one hand, split it and poured it into a waterfall shuffle that sounded as smooth and regular as a fan turning in the next room.

Now where his father's skin wasn't red it was terribly pale, sallow and white, like something growing under the floorboards. Age spots had crept over it like fungus, and the skin was baggy and wrinkled, the bones too obvious, not enough meat surrounding them.

Ham shifted in the doorway. "Answer him, Josh."

"Quiet, please." Josh flipped open his borrowed pocket watch and found his father's pulse easily, a sluggish throb under that hot pale skin. He counted only ten pulses in the first fifteen seconds, which seemed impossible. Scar-

let bounced on the end of the bed until Sloane grabbed her and pulled her away. Josh frowned at the pocket watch and started over. His father's heartbeats fell far behind the sweep of the second hand. Thirty-eight beats in a minute.

High fever and slow pulse—*Faget's sign*. The phrase drifted into Joshua's mind from some medical book he had read long ago.

"Fetch your mother for me, Josh," Sam Cane said. His mutilated head rolled weakly on the pillow. "Mandy? My head hurts so bad."

"Neck pain?"

"Josh?" Sam Cane's red eye rolled toward him again, holding on to his face unsteadily, like a drunk grabbing the edge of a bar.

Lindsey the maid appeared with a damp sheet, gave it to Josh, and quickly left the room, holding her facecloth tightly across her mouth and nose. Josh laid the damp sheet over his father. "Stick out your tongue," he said clearly. There was blood in Sam Cane's mouth: bleeding gums. His tongue was bright red around the edges, white and fuzzy in the middle.

"This man has yellow fever," Josh said.

"No." Sloane shook her head. "He's too lucky for that."

"Wasn't so lucky with Grandpa," Scarlet said. "I even felt sorry for him," she added.

"Josh?" Ace said. "Is that you?"

"He'll need clean water," Josh said. "If the fever comes down, we'll try to get some of Mrs. Sherbourne's dandelion tea into him. I'll need a clove of garlic, too, to rub on his skin. Anything to keep the mosquitoes off him. I may need to go back to my house to get a catheter tube."

Ham grabbed Josh by the shoulder. "For God's sake, answer him!'

"He's delirious," Josh said.

"He's your father!"

Josh removed Ham's hand. "Keep your bawling and hugging to yourself, Ham. You got your whole brood back, sows and piglets safe from the trailer park. Be happy."

Ham grabbed Josh's collar and slammed him against the wall so hard the ceiling fan rattled. Stars fizzed and popped in front of Josh's eyes like Mardi Gras sparklers, and the pain in his sunburned back made him gasp. "That's it," Josh hissed. He realized he was furious. "*Outsmart me.*"

"You little *fuck*," Ham said. His sunburned face was peeling everywhere, curls of skin flaking off the tops of his ears and the tip of his nose. Even after a week of privation he barely noticed Joshua's weight as he held him pinned against the wall a foot off the ground.

Sloane Gardner put one hand on Ham's big bicep. "I'm running out of bedrolls for the wounded."

Ham took a big, shaking breath. Then he let Josh drop, turned his back, and walked heavily out of the room.

Josh sat on the floor with his back against the wall, trying to catch his breath. Sloane Gardner turned to follow Ham. Lindsey the housemaid had already left, leaving Josh looking into the eyes of Scarlet, the little reveller girl. "Well," she said contemptuously. "I guess you showed him."

Two hours later Josh was still in Randall Denton's boyhood room. The ceiling fan was turned to its fastest setting, humming and whirring overhead. The room was full of collections: seashells and pocketknives and pebbles. Regiments of toy soldiers, whittled from driftwood or cast in lead, lined the window ledge, led by three prized specimens, GI Joes made from genuine pre-Flood plastic. An old corkboard with beetles and butterflies pinned to it was propped on top of the desk. The butterfly wings had moldered away in the humid Texas years, browning and crumbling off like scraps of newsprint, but the hard-

shelled insects were more or less intact: a grasshopper
and a June bug, a tiny purple doodlebug, an empty cicada
husk, and a big old tree roach the length of Joshua's
thumb. There was a dragonfly, too; its wings had turned
a blotchy caramel color with age. The wind from the
ceiling fan made the dragonfly and the cicada husk rustle
and scratch against the corkboard.

The mosquito netting over the four-poster bed fluttered, too. On the days when Josh had been sick as a boy,
he had watched the same thing, grey mosquito netting
rustling hour after hour. There was a smaller electric fan
with blue plastic blades on top of the writing desk. They
had turned that one on, too, letting its head swing slowly
back and forth.

"Joshua?" Sam whispered.

"Yes," Josh said.

"So that is you. I thought it was." They had stripped
off Samuel Cane's clothes, leaving him on the bed with
only a damp sheet around him. Through the shaking curtain Josh could see his dead white chest sticking out of
the sheet. "I don't feel very good, but I'm not so lost as
I was."

"Fever's down."

"I figured." Brass rails and steel springs creaked as his
father shifted in the bed. After a time Ace said, "Did I
imagine some big fellow hitting you, or did that really
happen?"

"That happened. Ham thought I wasn't being nice
enough to you."

Joshua's father gave a short, painful bark of laughter.
"Didn't know your momma, did he? Never got less sympathy from a woman in my life. 'Lie down and stop complaining. You just have the flu. I see *sick* people every
day.' "

Josh remembered lying in bed, coughing and coughing,
the stink of Vick's Vapo-Rub on his chest, the sound of
children playing in the street outside. He found a tight

smile starting on his face. " 'Mrs. Robinson, *she's* sick. Lost her whole left leg to a fiddleback bite since yesterday morning. *That's* sick.' "

" 'Chuck Yang, he's got a tumor the size of a grapefruit in his neck. *That's* sick.' "

Josh shook his head. "It was like it made her mad, when I got sick. Like it was a personal insult."

"Mandy always secretly believed you chose the cards you got dealt. Like bad luck was a person's fault."

"I suppose," Joshua said. He remembered the sounds of his mother getting out of bed in the middle of the night to collect raw pancreas. The fist-sized welts on her leg. "Guess what, Sam. You're sick now." He walked to the window, which looked over the back grounds of the Palace. Wet wash flapped lazily on clotheslines in the Gulf breeze. The swimming pool was littered with debris, palm fronds and live-oak leaves and fragments of shingle, bits of paper and cloth. Three ragged children with sticks were lying on their stomachs at the edge of the pool and slapping down. Trying to smack water-skaters, probably, or maybe frogs. He could see no sign of anybody watching out for them.

"It's yellow fever," Josh said.

"Remind me what that means."

"How long have you been sick?"

"Three days of fever, maybe."

"Today's a big day, then." Josh wished some grown-up would come out and tell those kids to get away from the edge of the swimming pool. "Either you go into 're-mission' or 'malignant phase.' You seem to be lucid, but maybe that's just the fever coming down for a spell."

"If it's remission, am I home free?"

"No. Just puts the malignant phase off."

"Oh. So sooner or later you have to draw the whole hand."

"Unless you fold," Josh said.

Josh remembered the swimming pool he had been sit-

ting at the night Sloane Gardner showed him how the stars went away when you looked at them. It still bothered him that she didn't remember that. *Let's not tell the others*, she had said. It was supposed to be a secret between them.

The desk fan reached one edge of its arc, blowing air across his face. He felt it most on his forehead, where Joe Tucker's blood had wiped away George's brand. "You want to know what's coming?"

"Not particularly," his father said. "I'll play them as they fall."

A blue jay flashed by the window in a cobalt streak. "Okay," Josh said. (Hemorrhages, anuria, delirium. Then jaundice, blistering fever, slow pulse, vomiting of black blood. More delirium and agitation, possibly leading to coma and death.)

" 'Less you need to tell me," his father said.

"No."

"Could I have a drink of water?"

Josh fetched him one. He drew back the curtain of mosquito netting and held the glass to his father's lips. Sam's tongue was still bright red, and when he finished sipping there were smears of blood on the edge of the glass. Josh let the mosquito netting fall. "Thought I'd see you at Mom's funeral."

"I came afterward. I meant to visit, but . . ." The fan swept, whirring, to the edge of its arc of motion, stopped, stuttered, and headed back the other direction. "Do you think I should have come more often?" Ace asked. "Your mother had strong feelings. She was doing the work of raising you up and I respected her decisions. But now I wonder if I should have come anyway."

"I guess that was your choice," Josh said.

"I guess so." His father coughed. "Josh, did the Mathers take some care of you?"

"Better than I ever deserved," Josh said.

"I gave them a fair sum, after the funeral. But of course

Jim and Alice aren't the sort who'd have stole it. Damn. My nose is bleeding." Ace laughed breathlessly.

Josh wiped his father's face. The rag came back bloody. "You paid the Mathers to take care of me," he said.

"I guess I knew you were tough enough to look out for yourself, but I figured a good home-cooked meal wouldn't hurt once in a while. Damn, it's hot in here."

"That's why they had me over for dinner all those times."

"I think I'll have another sip of water," Sam said.

Joshua remembered how loud the meals had been at Ham's house, thick arms reaching across the table, the dull clatter of silverware on wooden plates and bowls, or, if it was Sunday dinner, what was left of Alice Mather's china. The mismatched napkin rings Ham had lathed for his mom, Jim telling his kids to mind their mother, the taste of black-eyed peas with a little bacon fat cut in. And Joshua had always helped do the dishes. Even when Ham and his brothers were slumped out in the front room talking with their dad, Josh stayed behind with Rachel or Mrs. Mather because it was important to do his part. Because his mother had taught him not to be beholden to anyone.

"Pass me that towel, would you?" Samuel Cane's face was turning red again, the fever spiking up. Josh gave him the rag, but his hand was shaking too badly to use it. Josh wiped the blood off his father's lip himself. Samuel Cane's eye was red and he was blinking all the time, as if the light were hurting him. "Some days," he rasped, "you have to look pretty hard to see the luckiest man alive."

Chapter Twenty-one

OFFERINGS

WHILE Joshua Cane was nursing his father upstairs, Sloane was washing sheets and blankets. She had forced Scarlet to help, for once. The girl sulked and scowled and let the wet linen drag on the ground as she carried it outside to where Sloane stood with a bag of clothes-pins, hanging up laundry. "I'm bored," Scarlet said.

"Me, too," Sloane said, pinning up a pillowcase that had been used as a bandage. The bloodstain hadn't come out. Randall would call it ruined and charge her to re-place it, of course. Just because he was funny about it didn't mean he wasn't a cold-blooded son of a bitch who would screw her every way he could. "Mardi Gras is over, kid. You're living in the real world now. Everybody works. Everyone has work to do, even you. Get used to it."

"I don't see why you're so mad at me." Scarlet dumped an armful of wet laundry into Sloane's basket. "You ran away from all that work, too, from what I heard. I heard you went down to the beach even when your mom was dying."

Washline passed through the creaking pulleys as Sloane pushed the pillow slip away and clipped up a

badly stained towel. Ace had started vomiting black blood late in the afternoon, and even after washing the slip in the Denton's excellent pre-Flood washing machine, the marks still lingered. More internal bleeding to come, Josh had warned. "At least I knew I was doing something wrong."

"But you did it anyway," Scarlet said.

THERE were fourteen revellers in the house—fifteen if you counted Scarlet, which Sloane didn't. Kyle Lanier, the sheriff's deputy, called just before supper time to say, as politely as possible, that if the revellers weren't surrendered by the next day at noon, the sheriff would cut off all gas and water to the Bishop's Palace.

"People will die!" Sloane had said.

"That's up to you," Kyle had said, and tipped his hat. "Ma'am." He'd left two militiamen behind to watch the place.

It was official: They were under siege.

Supper time came. Alice Mather organized the few remaining human refugees in the house to take food around to their sick fellows. Sloane brought dinner up to the revellers herself. It was short commons now: rice pudding and molasses again, chicken broth for the sick, and dandelion tea. Mrs. Sherbourne couldn't kill any more chickens; they needed the rest for eggs. Sloane wanted to send a couple of her refugees down to the market to pick up more supplies, but she had no money to give them. In the end she had taken a few small items of Randall's she never saw him use, like his silver cigarette case. She wrote them down on Mrs. Sherbourne's account sheet and then told her agents to sell them and get extra food with the proceeds. They did it but didn't like it. "They thought we'd stole the stuff," one said.

Mrs. Sherbourne and Lindsey headed home to their families as soon as the dinner dishes were done. An hour later, Alice Mather gathered up Japhet and Christy and

got ready to leave the Bishop's Palace, too. "What if they won't let us back in tomorrow?" she asked, with a glance at the militia picket loitering at the front gate.

"Don't try," Sloane said. "This situation is getting ridiculous. I'll straighten things out with the sheriff tomorrow."

"What are you going to do?"

"Wait and see," Sloane had said, with her mother's calm, competent smile. She kept smiling until Alice was gone. Her mother always said both panic and levelheadedness were contagious, and that a leader's job was to spread the latter. Jane Gardner had lived through worse, far worse than this, and handled it magnificently. That's what everyone always told Sloane. She wondered if her mother had ever used that calm smile to hide so much hopelessness and confusion. She hoped so. She remembered her mother saying, *When I was your age, I wasn't me either.*

Not to mention, *You do what you have to do.*

Well, if Sloane was ever going to discover a cool, collected general inside herself, it had better happen in the next twelve hours. Come on, caterpillar, she thought bitterly. Grow wings and fly, damn you, fly!

Some time after nine o'clock she realized she hadn't eaten since her breakfast on the patio with Randall Denton. She slipped down to the darkened kitchen, caught one of the refugee kids crouched over a pot of molasses in the pantry and sent him back to his family. Twine baskets hung overhead, swaying lazily. A week ago they had been laden with garlic and onions and peppers—bell peppers, poblanos, anaheims, and habañeros. Now they were empty.

If Sheriff Denton cut the gas off they would run out of fuel for the motors in the generator shed. No electricity. No refrigerator. No washing machine; the laundry would have to be done by hand. No air-conditioning. No

fans. No lights except oil lamps, until the oil ran out. Then no lights at all.

People could live that way. Odessa's grandparents hadn't had any of those things. They had survived. Not if they had malaria, they didn't, Sloane answered herself. Not if they had yellow fever and there was no water to drink and no food to eat either.

Sloane went to grab a rice cracker, but they had all been eaten, so she settled for a spoonful of molasses instead. After a moment's pause she opened one of Randall's cupboards and took down a small saucer. What do gods eat? She started with a dollop of molasses and a clove of garlic. Then she grabbed a paring knife and cut three strands of her hair and put them on the saucer, too. It still didn't feel like quite enough, so she poked the end of her finger until a drop of blood welled out. She added that to her offering, and then carried the saucer out to Randall's patio and left it on the iron table underneath the magnolia tree. With luck, a god or ghost would get to it before the tree roaches did.

Good Lord, what Mother would say if she caught me doing this. *You make your own luck, Sloane!* Not anymore, Mom. Not always.

She stopped herself from imagining which dress they would have buried her mother in when she felt tears beginning to leak from her eyes. She couldn't afford to fall apart now, however badly she had acted. Even Jane Gardner would say so. She had to remain tough and focused and together.

Ha.

It was warmer outside than in the air-conditioned house, but the heat was less oppressive in the open, somehow. The humid night was clear, the stars bright but unsteady, flickering and blurred at the edges, as if seen through a heat ripple like the ones that came off the road on a hot summer day.

A glimmer of light from the back caught Sloane's eye.

Someone was out in the generator shed. Sloane stepped down the patio steps and followed the path to the backyard. A mosquito whined by her ear, faded and then returned. She slapped at her neck, panic washing through her. Couldn't afford to think of mosquitoes as just pests anymore. They were black widows now, scorpions and rattlesnakes with the deadly venoms of malaria and yellow fever in their stings.

When she cracked the door of the generator shed—"shed" was really the wrong word, it was bigger than a big garage and stocked with more tools than their place at Ashton Villa—she found Ham inside, squatting next to Randall's gargantuan gas-powered barbecue grill, surrounded by a jumble of large glass bottles, copper tubing, rubber seals, and hand tools. He glanced at her as she came in. "Hey, Miss Gardner."

"Call me Sloane. What are you doing?"

Ham stood and hefted a huge glass bottle filled with water onto the grill rack of the barbecue. "I heard they were thinking of cutting off your water supply, so I rolled over to Josh's place and fetched his still."

"Where did you get the water?"

"Swimming pool. I poured it through the pool skimmer to get out the leaves, but I wouldn't care to drink it just yet." He began attaching a short length of rubber hose to a curving beak at the top of the bottle. "How's Josh's dad?"

"Not great. Vomiting blood. Can I help?"

"Damn," Ham said. "Nah, I don't think so." He looked over and grinned. "Although if you don't mind sticking around awhile, just to piss Josh off, I'd be obliged."

Sloane laughed and hopped up on the seat of the Denton's old John Deere riding mower. Of course there hadn't been a lawn here for twenty years; it had long since been converted into a hen run and a piggery and a vegetable garden. Randall's dad had taken the blades out of the riding mower, and the Krewe of Momus used it

every year to pull floats in the Mardi Gras parade.

Ham got his length of pipe attached. He hooked his thumbs in the belt loops of his enormous pants and hitched them up his belly an inch or two. "If I had spent as much time sweet-talking girls as I did trying to make up with that ornery little son of a bitch, I'd have the three happiest wives in Galveston by now."

"Why did you bother?"

"Damned if I know." Ham squatted and fooled around with pipes and fittings and seals, attaching his copper tube so it ran into what Sloane guessed was a collection jar for the distilled liquid. There was a frown of concentration on his big face. His sausage fingers were quick and precise. "I think I felt sorry for him, at first. He didn't fit in so good, and there were a couple of kids who beat him up just on general principle. I thought of myself as the neighborhood cop, you know, so I stuck up for him. Little spiky kid. He owed me one, but you sure couldn't tell it. He made me feel bad all the time when we were kids. Made me feel stupid."

"Have you gotten to the part about why you were friends?" Sloane asked. "If you did, I missed it."

"Well, you see, I *was* stupid." Ham looked over at her. "Josh . . . he didn't see things like other kids did. You could tell he was going to make something of himself. The guys that beat him up, I knew them. I knew their brothers and their dads. I knew they were going to end up working, oh, warehouse jobs if they was lucky, getting pissed every night and hitting their girlfriends. My uncle Mordecai was like that. Josh wasn't. He made you want to understand things. My dad would teach me how to tune the engine on our boat, say. But Josh's mom had this encyclopedia on a computer that would show you how the engine *worked*, and why. And Josh was always interested in that stuff. He got me to take things apart and try to make new ones. He made me smarter." Ham stood up. "I'm a troubleshooter, first-class, with the Gas

Authority." He gave a comic scowl and flexed his arms. Biceps pushed up like fat tree roots from his upper arms. "If you've got a body like this, people always see you as a strong back first. If it hadn't been for Josh, I'd have been a stevedore, I reckon. Blown my back out at thirty or thirty-five, drunk myself to death at forty like my uncle Mordecai. If I didn't get drowned first, or axed, or shot in another man's bed." Ham shrugged and scratched at the mosquito bites on his fat neck.

To her surprise, Sloane realized she wanted to have sex with him. She looked at Ham incredulously. It was absurd. When Sloane fantasized about sex, her imaginary lovers were dashing and elegant and fabulously well-dressed. Dangerous, even. And yet, right now she could feel a little tingle inside her, Sly waking up and stretching. She found herself thinking about Ham's big meaty fingers unhooking hooks, undoing clasps with the same unexpected precision with which he could disassemble a motor. She imagined those fingers working the buttons on her shirt, a man's shirt she had filched from Randall's closet. Pushing a seashell button through, a building tension of resistance, the button tight between cotton lips, then slipping free. The whisper of cloth falling open.

Sloane blinked, looking up—*way* up—at Ham's broad face. Well, she wouldn't feel so damn tall anymore. Next to Ham she would be practically petite. "I think you're a wonderful friend to him."

Ham grimaced. "Not anymore." She looked at him curiously. Ham shrugged. "He just . . . he wore me out. I had a friend once, decided to kill himself over a girl. I listened to him talk about it every damn day, hours and hours for months and months. He even tried it, kinda— ate some foxgloves or something but didn't die from it. Anyway, finally he got better, but for the next year I was sick of the sight of him. And here's Josh. All those years I kept saying he was misunderstood, he had a tough life, blah, blah. But how long can you make excuses? Hurri-

cane comes, I'm saving his ass out on the Peninsula because he's hot for some skirt—begging your pardon—
while folks are *dying* here. And all he can think about is
me, me, me." Ham shook his head and spat.

Sloane said, "That's a lot of years to lose, even so. My
mother used to say, the thing about old friends is you
can't make any new ones."

Ham rubbed at his sunburned nose. "I'll live," he said.
"Hell, I don't even like myself when I'm around him
anymore. Like this afternoon. Since when do I need to
throw a guy into a wall? Josh's dad shows up for the first
time in ten years, only he's about to die and Josh can't
do squat for him. Time was I would have cut him some
slack. But right now everything about the little bastard
just pisses me off. Everything he says and does."

A few more peels of skin drifted off Ham's nose as he
rubbed it. Am I just slumming? Sloane thought. She tried
to imagine him in a nice shirt and jacket, subtle colors,
brown or maybe olive green. First thing she'd do, she'd
get rid of that belt and put him in suspenders. Would she
still like him, dressed up like one of her own?

Oh, yes.

"I just didn't catch up to him fast enough when his
dad showed up. My family, everyone's pretty simple.
Give us a present, we smile. Shout, we shout back. Give
us a beer, we get drunk. Josh is a ways twistier. I'm just
sick of trying to guess where he's at." Ham paused. "You
used to know the Recluse pretty well. I reckon you know
a thing or two about magic. Did you see Josh's hands?"

"I was going to ask about that."

"He took the leg off Billy Tucker's boy this morning
while I was still sawing logs," Ham said. "He's been real
funny ever since. Out of balance. I guess it's a hell of a
thing, cut off a kid's leg." The big man shuddered, making his chest and gut wobble under acres of shirting.

"How old was the boy?" Sloane asked.

Ham squeezed his brows together in thought. "Ten? Maybe eleven?"

"Hm." Sloane remembered the way Josh had looked at her when she first came into his house. That bitter, hungry look he shared with Kyle Lanier. Slowly she said, "I think I could name another boy who lost the life he knew at about that age."

"Oh," Ham said. His eyebrows rose. "You mean Josh his own self? I hadn't thought of that." He hooked his thumbs in his belt loops and hitched up his pants, giving her an admiring look. "I guess you can see around a few corners. Is that a Gardner thing?"

Sloane felt a little smile at the corner of her mouth. "No. Mother never had to be that . . . sly."

Ham ambled back over to the Dentons' giant gas grill, checked the propane tank, and turned it on. "I figure we oughta set this up outside the house proper. No sense pumping all this extra heat for the air-conditioning to fight with. Talking of your mom reminds me of a question I've been meaning to ask since we got back." Ham squinted up at the night sky. Only stars were out. "What's the deal with Momus?" he asked, more quietly.

"He was seen a time or two right after the storm. Drove one of Jenny Ford's servants crazy, I heard. It's counting down to the old moon. Maybe he's getting out less as the moon wanes."

Ham nodded. "But you figure when it comes full in another three weeks . . . ?"

"Look out."

Ham scratched under his chin. "So are you the one to deal with him, then? Seeing as how you've been in the Carnival and you were the Grand Duchess's daughter and all."

"I sure hope not," Sloane said. She remembered the white stare of the god, like frost falling on your heart. The visions she had had of her own old age, her legs blotched with veins. Under the circumstances, I suppose

I should be grateful for a chance to get old, but . . ."I'm still working on a way to get out of that."

He was courteous enough not to point out that she'd done pretty well at skipping out of her responsibilities so far.

Between the warm Texas night and Randall's Mercedes' motors running, the shed was already hot and humid. Sweat was beaded up on Ham's broad face. His cheap cotton undershirt stuck to his protruding belly and the flat mounds where his man's breasts pooched out. *Definitely need to get him some better clothes. Would I still like him in a muumuu?* Sloane wondered. She pictured him in something naughty, gathered under the breasts, a flimsy pink negligee with a feather boa trim swishing immodestly at the tops of his barrel-sized thighs. She snorted as a giggle got caught in her nose.

"What's up?" Ham asked with a grin.

Your hemline, big boy. "Nothing," Sloane said. "I'm just giddy with the heat." She felt sweaty herself, damp in her armpits and behind her knees and between her thighs. She uncrossed her legs, wishing she was wearing one of her skirts, maybe the one sewn together from handkerchiefs that fluttered and whispered as she walked. *Something easy to hike up a little, you mean? Good Lord, girl, you've got bigger things to think about.* She glanced at Ham. *Well, more important things.*

Ham fiddled with a few knobs on the barbecue. "Ma'am? Do you mind if I ask you a kind of personal question?"

"Don't know until I hear it," Sloane said with a little lazy smile that felt like one of Sly's. "You spins the wheel and you takes your chance."

He grinned. "Well." He pulled his shirttail up for a moment to wipe his forehead. "You strike me as a pretty smart girl, so I guess you know Josh is sweet on you."

" 'Sweet' isn't exactly the word I would have used. But I guess I had noticed that." *And used it,* she added

to herself. Made him a partner in crime when I was deserting my duty at home. Only I had a hell of a time, while he got beaten for it and exiled to the Bolivar Peninsula.

"So does he have a chance?"

The gas grill roared quietly to itself. Bubbles were forming at the bottom of the glass jar full of swimming pool water. "No," Sloane said at last. And then she did something she wouldn't have done before her time in Carnival. She raised her eyes and met Ham's for a long moment. "Not Josh," she said.

"Damn. Well, some days you git the bear, some days . . ." He trailed off, becoming aware that she was still looking at him.

"The bear gets *you*," she finished.

He squinted, puzzled.

Moron! Sloane looked away, embarrassed, feeling like she'd answered the door in her underwear and found her preacher on the step.

A shot exploded in the night, followed by a scream and another blast. Sloane and Ham stared at one another, electrified. "Shit!" Ham swore.

Sloane jumped down from the riding mower and ran outside. "That came from out back!" People were gathering at the lit windows of the mansion behind her, but she ran past the piggery and the piles of hurricane debris, stumbling in the gloom, looking for the door in the high stone wall at the back of the Bishop's Palace grounds.

There were voices on the other side of the wall. "Get her?" said one.

"I reckon. There was two of 'em, though. The other was real small, like a midget or a monkey."

Sloane found the wrought-iron gate and jerked it open. Outside, two men in militia uniforms swung around and trained their guns on her. A body lay sprawled across the sidewalk, under the streetlight on the corner. Sloane ran forward. "What have you done!"

"What I'm going to do to you if you don't stand still and shut up," said the older of the militiamen.

Sloane dropped to her knees next to the corpse. It was Lianna. The cat-faced woman lay utterly still. Sloane grabbed her arm and felt for a pulse, but she couldn't find one. "That's Sloane Gardner," one of the militiamen said.

Sloane put her ear against Lianna's chest. No sound of breathing. No heartbeat.

She remembered how adamant Lianna and Scarlet had been that morning about going to see Momus. And Sloane hadn't paid them any mind, because . . . ? Because she was a Gardner. That's what Randall would say. Because she had become her mother; she was running other people's lives for their own good, without listening to what they wanted. She remembered Lianna tugging on her arm the night of the storm. The first person to call her Sly when she didn't have her mask on.

"She's dead," Sloane said. "You killed her."

"Yep," said the burlier of the two guards with satisfaction. "Got her in one. Missed the little one, though. You're under arrest, by the way. Orders of the sheriff."

Sloane's blood froze. "What little one? Did she have— did you notice anything about her?"

"Sorry about this, Miss Gardner." The burly guard stuck his gun in his holster and fished out a pair of handcuffs. He pulled Sloane's wrists behind her back and cuffed her while his partner kept them covered. "As for the little monster, all I saw was a lot of red hair."

Sloane thought of Scarlet, eyes baggy with sleepiness, fighting to stay awake through one more hand of dominoes. Scarlet burrowing under her arm in the middle of the night, all defiance gone, begging for comfort from the only person left in the world she could claim it from. "She might have been a monster once," Sloane said. "Now she's just a little girl."

"For my part, I'm sorry she run off," the other guard said, holstering his gun. "Deputy Lanier put a hundred-dollar bounty on her."

Chapter Twenty-two

KREWE OF RAGS

JOSHUA was back in Randall's boyhood room, sitting inside the veils of mosquito netting with his father cradled in his arms, trying to get him to drink from a cup of cold dandelion tea. "Have a sip," he whispered. "There it is, just a little, that's good." The only light in the room came from an oil lamp on the writing desk.

Another drop of magic had gathered like dew on a shiny black beetle pinned to Randall Denton's corkboard and brought it back to life. Josh had first seen it twitch an hour ago. Now its little legs curled and stretched continuously as it tried to get free. Quite hopeless, of course; the pin through its back held it fast. Sometimes Josh thought he should free the bug, and sometimes he thought he should kill it. For now he just fed his father sips of tea and watched the beetle's thin black legs whisper and scrabble. Struggling and struggling.

Samuel Cane's face was a dull waxy red, no longer shiny with sweat. He was running out of sweat, running out of water. The last of his pee had dripped out with a bowel movement earlier. His shit and vomit were both black with digested blood. His liver wasn't making clotting factors anymore, that's what got yellow fever victims

in the end—internal hemorrhaging, hypovolemic shock, critical electrolyte imbalance, heart fibrillation.

"It's only yellow fever. Five percent mortality," Josh whispered. "That's all. Come on, lucky man."

There was a sharp knock on the door. Joshua's father jerked violently in his arms. Tea spilled onto his flushed naked chest.

"Josh? It's me, Ham." The big man opened the door.

"Goddamn it, I'm with a patient—"

"Shut up," Ham said. He was breathing heavily. "We're in a world of hurt. Did you hear the shots?"

"Maybe." Josh wiped the spilled tea off his father's chest with a sheet corner. "Someone injured?"

"No. Well, yeah, one of the revellers is dead. But they got Sloane," Ham said. "I was talking to her out in the generator shed, setting up a still, when we heard the shots. Before I could get my fat ass to the wall she was already out the gate and arguing with the militia. I didn't have my gun, so I sat tight while they cuffed her and hustled her off to Ashton Villa to see the sheriff." He paused. "Do you think I should have gone after them?"

"Of course. It would have been stupid but really brave."

"Pecker."

"Anything else?" Josh said.

"What are we gonna do now?"

"Why do you want my advice? I thought you were sick of the sight of me."

"I am. Doesn't make me a better card player, though. You're the smart one, remember? So tell me what the sheriff is going to do next, and how we're going to get Sloane back. Think of something."

"I'm flattered," Josh said.

Ham folded his big arms and waited. No brilliant ideas came to Josh. He wished one would so he could impress Ham, or spite him. He couldn't tell which he wanted more. Even knowing there was a good part of Ham that

despised him these days, it was pathetic how much he still wanted the big man to think he was smart. That's what he was supposed to be, right? That's all he had ever offered in return for Ham's friendship.

So Sam Cane had paid the Mathers to look out for him. Should have guessed.

Ham shifted impatiently. "I wouldn't say this in front of Sloane, but I won't kick much if the revellers, uh, go away. Especially if the alternative is having real human beings blown full of holes in a shoot-out."

Samuel Cane moaned and turned on the bed. Joshua felt for his father's pulse again. "Is Scarlet human?"

"That's different," Ham said. "She ain't . . . she's just a little girl."

"Mm," Josh said.

Sam Cane's pulse was down to thirty-four beats a minute. He gagged. Swiftly Josh reached to support his head, placing the empty teacup under his lips. The older man convulsed, bending forward and retching. His ribs heaved and the muscles in his flanks knotted in long, cramping waves until finally a dribble of black blood splattered into the cup. The retching passed. "Sixth Street," Josh said. "Don't fold now."

"Is he going to make it?" Ham whispered.

"I don't know."

There was a part of Josh, locked away, that hadn't stopped crying since the moment Gina Tucker told him he would have to cut off her son's leg. He thought of all the things Joe Tucker would miss, the games he would never play again. A cripple, for other kids to taunt and laugh at. He could never hope to be the handsome prince of any girl's dreams now. He'd have to live on charity and count himself lucky to get it.

Play those cards, kid.

Back on the corkboard, the little black beetle kicked and struggled. Ham hadn't noticed it yet. "Is my father human?" Josh said. His voice was contemptuous, but his

hand was gentle as he touched Sam Cane's cheek. "Look at him. He's an animal, a sick animal. Less human than Scarlet. Less human than the Prawn Men. We're just meat that dreams, Ham." Joshua brushed the sweat-slick hair away from his father's one good eye, then lowered him back onto his pillows. "You want to see monsters, think of George and Martha."

Ham touched the brand on his forehead, then let his hand fall. "I need a play, pardner."

It was so damn hard to be smart when all Josh wanted was to fall into a soft bed in a dark room and never be seen again. He tried to rub the tiredness out of his face. "I'm fresh out of cards," he said.

An hour later the bedroom door swung open. "Didn't I tell you to knock—"

"Howdy, Mr. Cane," said Kyle Lanier, looking very dapper in his militia greys. He appeared not to notice Ham glowering behind him.

Joshua remembered the interrogation room in the County Courthouse. The way Kyle Lanier had tipped his chair back and back and then let it drop, Josh's head slamming on the concrete floor. The gleam of lamplight on Kyle's shiny boots as he kicked Josh in the side and stomach. "What the hell do you want?"

"Sheriff Denton has called an emergency meeting of all the Krewes. It starts in half an hour at the Rosenberg Library, in the Krewe of Togetherness conference room. You and your pudgy friend are invited."

"We're not even in a Krewe."

"The meeting's about how to take care of the mob. I mean, the poorer citizens," Kyle said. "We need someone who can speak for them, and you're the lucky winners."

"What the hell have y'all done with Sloane?" Ham demanded.

"Miss Gardner is resting comfortably at home," the deputy said. "Where she should have stayed all along."

"I'm with a patient," Josh said. He was still holding the teacup black with his father's blood.

"I'll give you five minutes to finish up here," Kyle said. He winked at Ham. "I can see myself down."

"Just hop over the banister there. It's quicker," Ham growled.

Josh stood up as the deputy left. "This doesn't feel right at all." He began to pace in the little room. "Why would Sheriff Denton want to see either of us? If I was the sheriff, I wouldn't be inviting me to any meetings. I'd take my militia and storm this place. There's no paint over here worth worrying about, just rags. Anybody killed in the cross fire, well, that's too bad, but their kin won't have the clout to cause real trouble."

"If you're trying to cheer me up," Ham said, "it ain't working."

"In fact, if I can shoot the apothecary and his friend, that's a bonus," Josh said. "They're an embarrassment. They show I ran a crooked trial. Hell, they're more of a threat to my position than Sloane Gardner. Damn lucky for me they're sitting there where all the shooting is fixing to be."

"Josh, quit that."

"I've got to put him on a hand." Joshua shook his head. "No, if he wants to talk to us, he must be feeling pressure from the other Krewes about our trial. I mean, think about it, Ham. The militia's nearly running things in this town since the hurricane hit. With Jane Gardner dead, who is to be the new boss? Why, Sheriff Denton, I reckon. Only the other Krewes aren't going to want to give him power automatically, especially if maybe we're going to cause a lot of trouble for him with the poor folk."

"And don't forget the Recluse," Ham said. "If he really shot her, they'll want to know why." The big man absentmindedly pulled a curl of sunburned skin off his peeling nose. "So you think he wants to make nice with us?"

"Well, he hasn't shot us yet," Josh said. "For sure he

wants to get a sense of how the cards lie."

"I guess we've got to go to this meeting, huh? Seems like it's that or sit around here and wait for an 'accidental' bullet."

"I guess." Josh looked down at his father. "I'll be back directly. Try not to die in the meantime." He turned the lamp on the writing desk to a dull glow and slipped out of the room, carrying the teacup full of blood. Ham followed behind him. "Let's not give the sheriff the temptation of both of us disappearing," Josh said. "I'd like you to stay outside the Library while I'm inside talking, just in case this is an ambush. And I want a crowd around you. Enough people so you can't be disappeared without anyone noticing."

"How am I supposed to get a mob of people over to the Rosenberg Library after ten at night, Josh?"

"Use your native charm," Josh said with a tight smile. He walked briskly to the bathroom at the end of the hallway. He splashed his head in the barrel of salt water by the sink. The water felt shockingly cold on the blotches of white skin where Joe Tucker's blood had stained his hands and forehead. "Tell them we're having a parade. Galveston likes parades." His smile faded. "No, on second thought, don't. Tell them there's medicine," Josh said slowly. He turned to look directly at Ham. "Tell them there's medicine and fresh water and good food. Tell them the rich folks have been hoarding it. Tell them we're going to get our share."

"Is that true?"

"Who knows?" Josh dried his face on his shirt and then studied himself in the mirror. His face was a mess, red sunburned skin blotched with white. Lines of weariness were carved around his eyes and mouth.

"That's going to make a lot of people mad," Ham said, shaking his head. "Even if you outsmart Sheriff Denton, that's a promise you're going to have to keep somehow."

Joshua shrugged. "We can worry about that later," he

said. "Let's let those bastards play with some scared money for once."

Ham headed downstairs to where Kyle Lanier was waiting. Josh stopped for a last look at his father. Speckles of Sam Cane's blood were beginning to smear the pillowcase. Bloody nose or bleeding gums, it was hard to tell which. If full-scale delirium was coming, followed by coma and death, it couldn't be too long. Within the next day and a half, Josh guessed. Limp in, Ace. Just limp in to the River.

"Mr. Cane?" the deputy called.

"Coming," Josh shouted. He stepped quickly to the corkboard and pulled the pin out of the beetle struggling there. It tumbled to the ground, quivered, and then limped under the bed.

It was a comical bunch that headed out from the Bishop's Palace just before eleven that night. Josh and Kyle Lanier went first, then Ham, talking loudly with six or seven refugees that trailed alongside. Two more militiamen brought up the rear. Josh took a detour through the barrio, pretending he needed to drop off some of his doctoring kit at home. Ham picked up a fair throng once they got into the neighborhoods where there were car parts scattered over half the yards. "Water! Fresh water, and medicine for your sick!" Ham bellowed cheerfully.

"Nobody promised anything!" Kyle Lanier snapped.

"Shoot." Ham scratched in and amongst the folds of his fat neck. "Must have misunderstood. Hang on," he said loudly to the crowd gathering around them. "Deputy says I got that wrong. Maybe the sheriff isn't going to let you have any medicine after all."

"Big fucking surprise," said a voice from the darkness.

"That better?" Ham asked innocently.

"Why don't you just keep your fat mouth shut?" the deputy said.

The chatter in the crowd died away. Silence gathered

around them as they walked along the dark street. The militiamen both had their hands on the butts of their pistols. "Now, then," Ham said mildly. "There's no call to be rude."

It was the deputy who stopped talking. A good move. Josh bet he probably still had enemies on this side of Broadway; Ham Mather had nothing but friends. Black boys who used to go floundering with Ham joined in the procession, alongside Mexicans carrying magic candles and crucifixes. Dockworkers spilled out of the bars where they had been unwinding to see what the hell Ham was up to. Not far from the Krewe of Togetherness offices in the Rosenberg Library, a handful of his coworkers fell in, still wearing their Gas Authority overalls. By the time they reached the Library, Ham's crowd had swollen to more than a hundred people. More than came to our trial, Josh thought, although that other crowd had been considerably better dressed.

Josh stopped in front of the Library's main doors. "Deputy, Ham's going to stay out here, if you don't mind. I'll go in and talk to the sheriff."

"Expecting an ambush? Joshua Cane, you got to learn to trust a little bit," the deputy said.

"Maybe tomorrow."

Kyle shrugged and turned to Ham. "Sure you want to stay out here? There's deals to be made. From what I seen, I'm not sure I would trust Mr. Cane here to look out for my best interest, if I was you."

"Thanks for your concern. I like it just fine right here. Josh?" Ham said airily. "A quick word before you go inside?" Josh looked at Kyle, who nodded. Ham's arm settled like a tractor tire around his shoulders as they walked a few paces to the side. "Sell us out and I'll use your nuts for axle grease," the big man murmured. "Don't get in there and let all those Fords and Dentons go to your head now."

Josh stared down at the Library's marble steps. "Did you really think you had to say that?"

Josh allowed himself to believe he saw a flicker of embarrassment on Ham's face. "Just go play your cards. But do it quick, if you can. I know a bunch of these old boys, but not everyone. And I noticed there's more than one or two folks packing, if you know what I mean. As crazy and sick and hungry as everyone is, you don't want to keep a crowd like this standing around with nothing to do but play with their guns."

"Play with their constitutionally protected tools, you mean?"

"Piss off," Ham said.

Josh rejoined Kyle Lanier and together they walked up to the Library doors. Behind them, Ham raised his voice to the crowd. "Josh is going to go talk with the sheriff now about getting some good water and medicines and the like. Let's all be real calm and friendly. The Krewes know what's fair. I'm sure we can all trust the Dentons to do their duty," he said.

Josh smiled inside. "I'm sure we can trust the Dentons" was a sentence every Islander should understand pretty well.

"Ah, Mr. Cane," the sheriff said as Kyle led Josh into the Krewe of Togetherness conference room. "Everyone is here but Randall. We're almost ready to begin." Though it was hours past sunset, Sheriff Denton was wearing darkly tinted glasses. Must be on some medication that made him photosensitive, Josh thought.

Delegates were seated around a long cherrywood table the shape of a Tylenol tablet. The hurricane had smashed in the window at the end of the room, and it was warmer than it should have been, despite the ceiling fan that rattled overhead. Gas lamps hissed around the periphery of the room, leaving every other chair in shadow. The sheriff stood—none too easily, his arthritis must be bothering him—and introduced Josh to the assembled representa-

tives of the various Krewes: Horace Lemon, here for the Krewe of Togetherness, his black face deeply lined and weary. Commodore Travis Perry, Thalassar, a sun- and windburned man in his forties. "With Ellen Geary sick, Maria Gomez will speak for the Krewe of Venus," the sheriff said. He paused to cough. The cough was deeper and wetter than it had been the last time Josh had seen him.

"Is Ms. Geary running a fever?" Josh asked Ms. Gomez.

"Yes."

"Diarrhea or vomiting?"

Ms. Gomez looked at him. He suddenly remembered seeing her at the trial, sitting on the aisle in the third row. "Ms. Geary has a doctor," she said coolly.

Misplay. "Of course. Forgive me. I've been seeing patients all day long myself. The questions become automatic."

"Are you a doctor, then? I seem to remember you saying you were only an apothecary."

Josh said, "I'm what the poor people have."

"If you want to call them people," Randall Denton said, sauntering in. "The rabble outside seems scabby but vigorous. Travis, Horace," he said, nodding. Even at eleven o'clock at night he was immaculate in wasp-legged pants, a sand-colored shirt, and a scarf printed with colorful fish. Josh had actually thought about borrowing one of Randall's shirts to wear to this meeting; he was thankful now that he had decided against it. They were tailored too perfectly to hang right on him, and he would have looked like a servant caught pilfering from his master's closet. His own plain cotton shirt, speckled with drops of blood he had been unable to dab out, at least had a certain moral gravity.

Randall took the hand of the representative of the Krewe of Venus and kissed it with scrupulous insincerity. "Ms. Gomez. Always a pleasure."

She retrieved her hand and briefly wiped it off on her dress. Josh smiled inwardly. An instructive tell, there. Any distaste for a Denton might be played to his advantage.

"By the way," Randall Denton said, "I don't think Jim Ford will be coming. He's been a bit under the weather, and what with the lateness of the hour, he agreed that it might be best if he stayed home."

Meaning that with Sloane Gardner in custody, only the Dentons were here to speak for the Krewe of Momus. With every second it was looking more and more like Josh had put the Dentons on the right hand: the sheriff was trying to step into the power vacuum left by Jane Gardner's death.

"Shall we wait for a Harlequin?" Randall asked.

"I didn't invite any Harlequins," Jeremiah said. He lowered himself painfully back to his chair. "We know what they want. They bear some responsibility for what has become of us."

The sheriff's arthritis seemed markedly worse, his joints stiff and painful. Thinking about those dark glasses again, Joshua wondered if the sheriff was taking yarrow. He often prescribed it for colds and flus, as it helped break fevers and contained a mild anti-inflammatory, but occasionally a patient would report that it made his eyes painfully sensitive to light. The sheriff's cough was very bad, hoarse, wet and prolonged. To judge by the spots of color high on his cheeks he was running a fever, too.

He has pneumonia.

Josh blinked at the realization. He wondered what use he could make of this unexpected card. A gust of laughter came from the street below. So far Ham's crowd was still in a good humor.

"Kyle, take the minutes," Jeremiah Denton said. His deputy nodded. Horace Lemon slid a pad of paper across the table, along with an ink pot and a quill pen. Sheriff Denton coughed briefly into his fist, then took a long

rattling breath. Pneumonia, without a doubt. "Ladies and gentlemen, thank you for coming. I called this meeting so y'all can fire me."

Delegates blinked. "What?" Maria Gomez said.

The sheriff shrugged. "I am not a popular man right now. With Jane Gardner gone, somebody has to see about putting the Island back together. I've tried, but I'm not making many friends, especially on the other side of Broadway. The poor always suffer the most in any disaster, and the friends of Mr. Cane and Mr. Mather are particularly likely to distrust me."

I feel that way myself, Josh thought, but he kept his mouth shut like his Daddy always taught him and tried not to give away any tells.

"Then there is the question of the minotaurs and revellers," the sheriff said. "I want them off this Island. It's my firm belief that if we lack the strength of will to cleanse them from Galveston, in a year or two there will be nothing left that we could recognize by that name." The sheriff shrugged. He looked very old. "But to those too young to remember 2004, what I'm doing looks inhumane. I am not only encouraging the revellers to leave. My men have orders to shoot them in self-defense. That's an ugly policy. I need the power to enforce it. That's what I am asking for tonight." He leaned forward and put his hands on the table, so the cloth of his coat rustled on its surface. "We can wait for the minotaurs to pick us off one by one, or more horrible still, wait until we become monsters ourselves. It's a choice." The sheriff looked around the table. "And if this council decides that we are best off as a brother to dragons and a companion of owls, then so be it. I will retire. Perhaps I will leave the Island. But if you decide that humanity is a thing worth fighting for, then let me have your backing."

Josh stirred. "Exactly why am I here, Sheriff? I understand why you would need the authority of these other worthy folks, but . . . ?"

Sheriff Denton coughed. "To be frank, Josh, we need everyone to work together in these dark days. I need someone to talk to the poor folk, to the refugees, to the folks that have come to the Bishop's Palace because Sloane invited them in. I don't want a civil war here. I want those people included."

"Why me?" Josh said.

"You're their doctor. Mr. Mather is their friend. And you two, let's be candid, have a good reason to hold a grudge against my office. If you were willing to support the militia, I believe the people would see it was the right thing to do."

"And after all," Josh said, "the Krewe of Momus has always been in charge. And with Jim Ford not here, and Jane Gardner dead, and Sloane Gardner arrested, why, the Dentons are the Krewe of Momus, aren't they? Which reminds me to ask, why was it, again, that you arrested Ms. Gardner?"

"My men took her home," Jeremiah said. "Ashton Villa is where she lives, Mr. Cane. There's no call for her to be at Randall's house."

"No call to be inviting every mongrel off the streets to roll around in my sheets either," Randall added.

"How thoughtful of you," Josh said.

Kyle Lanier looked up from his notes. "Don't get smart, Cane."

"But while we're being candid," Josh said slowly, "I do have sort of a grudge with your office, Sheriff. Something about getting the crap kicked out of me and then being convicted of a crime I didn't commit, with the help of some faked-up evidence."

The sheriff shrugged. "Mistakes were made. It grieves me, but it has to be admitted."

"What if I said that wasn't good enough?" Josh asked. "What if I decided I wanted to test Galveston's justice? What if I said that I would be willing to support the militia, but only if the son of a bitch who faked the ev-

idence against me and Ham was caught and sent to jail?"

A long silence built. Josh wished he could see behind the sheriff's dark glasses. "Why, then," the sheriff said evenly, "we would launch an investigation into your charges of battery and false evidence." He paused. "We would make every effort to determine the guilty, and the guilty would be punished," he said.

Kyle Lanier's quill stopped moving across the sheet of rice paper. The deputy looked up, eyes narrow in his ugly face.

"I am a great lover of justice," Josh said.

Randall Denton laughed.

"Would you be able to sponsor me to join the Krewe of Momus?" Josh asked. "I have to warn you, I don't have the back fees, not just at the moment."

"Merit means more than money in times like these," the sheriff said.

Wrong. Merit won't buy you insulin, Sheriff. Josh frowned. "What if I said, no? What if I said, Sheriff Denton here shot the Recluse, that very Odessa Gibbons whose legacy he is claiming to defend? What if I said, Sheriff Denton was responsible for having me framed?" Josh gave Kyle Lanier a long look. Then he turned to Randall Denton. "What if I said, this man is out of control, he has involved the Krewe of Momus in bearing false witness, in single-handedly declaring martial law, in murder? He is injuring the Denton name!"

"If such a thing is possible," Maria Gomez muttered.

Sheriff Denton started from his chair. "Do you think you can come here in your dirty shirt and get yourself off by offering Randall my money and Kyle my job?" He caught ahold of himself. "Son, you have reached the limits of impertinence. I brought you here with an honest offer for your own good. Everyone around this table knows it. But don't think you can play hardball with me. You don't have the cards. Innocent or guilty, you were sentenced to exile from this Island, and I can have you

arrested between one breath and the next just for having set foot on Galveston again."

"You wouldn't dare," Josh said.

The sheriff regarded him. "Try me."

Maria Gomez cleared her throat. "Do you really think the magic is going to go away?" she said unexpectedly. "Now that the Recluse is gone, it's bound to be working in folks. I've—" She stopped, looking at the sheriff. "I've heard that, anyway."

Ha, Josh thought. I wonder what the representative of the Krewe of Venus has seen? He glanced down at his hands, still burned miraculous white where Joe Tucker's blood had spattered them.

Maria Gomez collected her thoughts. "Once the magic does start working on a person, there's nobody left to send her to Krewes, with Miss Odessa gone."

Travis Perry stirred. "A boat'll work as well as the Recluse's magic to get someone off the Island."

"But speaking of Miss Odessa," Horace Lemon said, "the Krewe of Togetherness for one would like to understand a little better the details of her death, Mr. Denton."

"Miss Gibbons was a great lady," Sheriff Denton said. "Of late she had begun to seriously abuse her power, but we must never forget what she did to save this Island. In 2004 it was Jane Gardner and Odessa Gibbons who showed us that to live free we must fight the magic to our last breaths—" Sheriff Denton stopped, coughed, pulled a handkerchief deliberately from the breast pocket of his coat and coughed into it, harder, a train of long wracking spasms. When he could finally draw breath, he folded the handkerchief carefully and tucked it back into his pocket. "This is not about the revellers' humanity," he said. "It is about ours.

"Once you say a thing with the shell of a crab or the face of a snake is human, you can't stop there. Why not marry them? Why not have their babies?" the sheriff de-

manded. His face behind those dark glasses was contorted with rage. "Will you let the human race vanish from the earth? Maybe Darwin is right, and we're nothing more than a fancy kind of monkey. Is that what you want? Do you want us to abdicate our position of sovereignty over the earth, a position entrusted to us by the almighty God? 'Duty is the sublimest word in our language. Do your duty in all things. You cannot do more. You should never want to do less.'—Robert E. Lee said that." Sheriff Denton looked around the table from behind his dark glasses. "I submit we have a duty to do."

"Yes, you're right to quote General Lee," Josh said slowly. "We have a civil war in Galveston. Again. And just like last time, the pure and unsullied South must protect itself from the foul, the subhuman, the manifestly inferior"—here Josh looked over into Horace Lemon's worn black face—"monsters."

Bodies shifted around the table. Lemon met Josh's eyes for a long moment, then turned to stare at the sheriff.

"The revellers aren't just a different color," Sheriff Denton said. "They are not human. The magic is not mindless, like sunspots or radiation. It twists people's characters, as well as their bodies."

"So does beer," Josh said. "So does whiskey. So does bigotry. Vincent Tranh is lying on the second floor of Mr. Denton's house tonight." Josh looked over at Travis Perry, the second—or was it third?—Captain of Thalassar since Vince had gone to Krewes. "He is sick with malaria, a genuine human parasite. It seems to be doing all right in his liver. He has a long mustache like a shrimp and his skin has changed color. You could say he is eccentric, if not actually crazy, from having spent the last thirteen years trapped in the Mardi Gras. But does he seem less human to me than a patient with advanced Alzheimer's? No, he retains more of himself than that. I could argue that physically he is no more changed than the late Grand Duchess was in the weeks before her

death." No more changed than Sam Cane, one-eyed and delirious, burning now in Randall Denton's childhood bed. Half-digested blood spilling from his mouth, staining Randall's expensive sheets. There was the sham of civilization for you, Josh thought, all laid bare in an instant.

For a moment he felt his face begin to dissolve into panic and exhaustion and despair. He schooled his features. No tells. Not now.

"You can't ask us to believe the Prawn Men are as human as you or I," Travis Perry said.

"The Devil can quote Scripture for his purpose," Sheriff Denton said. "But tell me, boy, are you really so soft on the revellers? Are you really that eager to have the magic come? If you think it will avenge you, you are mistaken. I've seen it before, my boy. I am old enough to remember the Flood, and believe me when I tell you that the poor and the sick will go first and worst."

Josh laughed. "Me, eager for the magic? Sheriff, you don't know me very well." Josh pushed back his chair and stood up. He walked to the window and pulled back the curtain. There was quite a crowd around the Rosenberg Library now, made up of the curious and the idle, the homeless and the sick, his patients and Ham's friends. If the revellers dared to show themselves, they would be part of that Krewe of outcasts. His father would be, too, if he survived. Someone in the crowd below caught sight of his silhouette, and a roar went through the throng. Heads turned and hands pointed up.

"Hear that, Sheriff?" Josh turned to face the old powers of Galveston. "Outside this window are the outcasts, the exiles, the nobodies nobody wants," he said. "Least of all me. You were right about that, Sheriff. To my shame." Josh remembered again the sick moment when he realized that Galveston thought no more of him than he had of it. " 'You have to play the cards you're dealt,' my daddy told me. I don't know how many times I must

have quoted that, without once seeing what it truly meant." He pointed out the window. "Well, ladies and gentlemen, *there are my cards.*"

The delegates stared at him, not understanding.

"It's a new day in Galveston," Josh said. "New rules. New powers. And one new Krewe. The Krewe of Rags. The Krewe of Rags," Josh said. "Of course I'm not really a member. They gave me a lot of chances to join over the last thirteen years or so. I turned them all down. Because I just couldn't bear to accept the cards I was dealt."

"Is there a point to all this?" Randall Denton asked.

"Sheriff, no man on this Island hates the magic more than I do." Josh turned away from the window. "I hate the new diseases. I hate that I have charms and weeds to give out instead of antibiotics and vaccinations. If this were 2004, I'd be in the streets with you, shooting any reveller you told me to. But it's not 2004," Josh said. He held up his hands, spattered white with the miracle of Joe Tucker's blood. "The magic is coming and coming and coming, and there's no holding it back anymore." Josh leaned over the table by Sheriff Denton. "*Those are our cards,* Sheriff. That's what life has dealt us this time around. And all we can do is play them as well as we can."

Jeremiah Denton no longer smelled of talcum powder and freshly ironed cloth as he had in the interrogation room. Now he smelled damp and salty. Not enough sleep, no time to change before the conference. "Would I love to join the Krewe of Momus?" Josh asked. "You know I would. Would I like to see you sacrifice Deputy Lanier there and send him to rot in jail? Oh, boy, would I like that. Two weeks ago I would have jumped at your offer, sir. But not now. Not because I'm soft on the revellers," Josh said. "Not because I'm half in love with the magic. Sloane is, you're right about that. I'm not. But the magic is rolling over everything now. Those are the cards. Letting you run around for a few months trying to hold it

back with bullets, Jeremiah Denton deciding who is human and who is not—that way truly does lie madness." Josh shook his head. "It hurts me to turn down your lovely bribe, but the Krewe of Rags votes no, sir. We vote to fire you. And I hope any other Krewe with a parcel of common sense will do the same."

The sheriff coughed. "There is no Krewe of Rags, Josh Cane. You are nothing. Your whole family has been nothing since you crossed the Dentons thirteen years ago." He coughed again, harder. "I'll have you arrested. Kyle, arrest—" Another spasm of coughing shook him, then another, then another. He bucked forward with the force of it and his tinted glasses fell to the table. The other delegates gasped.

Sheriff Denton's eyes were smooth blind pools of Gulf water, dark sea green, with neither whites nor pupils.

"*Madre de Dios,*" whispered Maria Gomez. "He's gone to Krewes!"

It was as if the sheriff had filled up with seawater, Josh thought, horrified. No wonder he was coughing all the time. He was drowning from the inside.

"Where are your principles?" Jeremiah Denton roared. Another cough racked him, and a faint briny odor eddied through the room. "Randall, where is your sense of family?"

Randall met his uncle's terrible seawater eyes, and then gave Kyle Lanier the slightest of nods. Kyle made his way around the table. At the last moment the sheriff saw him coming and scrabbled for the gun at his hip. Kyle grabbed his wrist. "Place your hands on the tabletop in front of you," the deputy said.

The sheriff stared at Kyle's hand as if it were a rattlesnake. "Judas!"

Kyle twisted the sheriff's arm up behind his back, smashed him with an elbow to the back of the head, and then drove the old man's face down into the conference table. "Think you were going to sell me out?" he hissed.

"I'll show you the buckle end, you backstabbing old fuck." He wrenched the armlock tighter. A strangled scream bubbled out of Sheriff Denton's throat, followed by a stream of salt spit.

"Ah, Deputy? A little decorum?" Randall Denton said.

Sheriff Denton coughed another weak string of salt phlegm onto the table. Kyle took a deep breath. "Yes, sir," he said in a calm, official voice. "I'll take it from here," he said.

"Deputy, what are you arresting him for?" Horace Lemon said wonderingly.

Kyle stared at him blankly.

"Murder," Josh said. "The murder of Odessa Gibbons."

"Forcible confinement of Sloane Gardner," Kyle added.

Joshua found he was sweating violently. So much for his poker face. "Tampering with evidence," he said. "At our trial? The hair he claimed to find in Ham's boat?" He licked his lips. "There's no point trying to protect him now, is there, Deputy?"

"That was wrong," Kyle Lanier said. "I told him that was wrong, but he wouldn't listen."

Maria Gomez swore softly and continuously in Spanish.

Josh watched Kyle Lanier handcuff his boss. In the stories Josh's mom had told him at bedtime, long ago, justice was always done; the bad guys died and the men in the white hats triumphed. But poker was a man's game, his father had said, because it wasn't fair. In real life there wouldn't be any justice. Ten days ago, Kyle Lanier had kicked Josh halfway senseless as he lay handcuffed to a chair and unable to defend himself. Josh glanced down. The deputy was wearing the same shiny pair of boots. Now, for all Josh knew, he might have to spend the next thirty years dealing with Kyle Lanier, prominent citizen. Kyle Lanier, keeper of the peace. Josh smiled sourly. It just doesn't get any better than this.

The sheriff was coughing and coughing. Maria Gomez kept staring from the puddled seawater on the conference table to Jeremiah Denton's blank green eyes. "But why?" she whispered. "If he was gone to Krewes already, how could he say all those things about cleansing the Island?"

Outside, Josh knew, Ham and his crowd of roughnecks would be getting impatient, telling vulgar jokes to pass the time, or lying about how much they could drink. Doing all the things Josh had always despised. "Sometimes," he said slowly, "I think the thing you hate the most is the one you fear you will become."

Chapter Twenty-three

THE RIVER

As soon as Kyle Lanier returned to Ashton Villa to free Sloane from her house arrest, she raced down to Stewart Beach, looking for Scarlet. When she got there she found that the wooden wall between the city and the amusement park was gone, torn away by the storm. The ticket-taker's booth was gone, too. Down below the Seawall, where Momus had held court among the hawkers and carnies, there was barely even debris left behind. The hurricane had scoured the beach clean, leaving nothing but sand and the low hiss of surf. The Genuine Human Maze was gone, and the stalls had blown away. Every huckster's booth and winking light, every board and stick of greasepaint had been lifted up and dispersed throughout the Island, or swallowed by the sea.

Sloane climbed back up from the beach and stood on Seawall Boulevard under an aging moon, the night warm around her like a shawl. Sweat made her bangs slick. She was literally sick with fear. Her thoughts began to fall apart into panic, but she bit her lip until the pain cleared her head. You're a Gardner. Act like it.

It had been so much easier to be Sly. It hurt so much to give a damn.

She pushed her sweaty hair back from her face. Well, then, she would have to search the streets, alley by avenue, just another desolate woman looking for a loved one lost in the storm. At least after three days in the same dress I look the part, she thought. Flotsam scavenging for jetsam.

For the next three hours she walked the streets of Galveston, calling Scarlet's name, but the girl didn't answer, and no one had seen her. At last she turned back to the Seawall, and walked to the 23rd Avenue intersection, where the Balinese Room should have been. The restaurant was gone, and all traces of Odessa with it. Even the pier had been ripped away and scattered by the sea. Only two barnacle-crusted posts remained behind, slanted and lonely as the last teeth in a witch's mouth. The sea swirled darkly around them. The Gulf had claimed Odessa's body as surely as it had taken Sheriff Denton's doll; there was nothing left of her godmother for Sloane to hold. She tried to close her eyes against the memory of Odessa with her throat shot out, blood spattering all over the kitchen. She was always so particular to keep that kitchen neat. Blood everywhere and no time to clean it up.

When someone springs a leak, you see, it can't easily be patched.

Sloane stood on the Seawall and cried.

Eventually the tears dried up. She remembered lying in Odessa's hammock, the sound of her sewing machine stopping and starting, shutters creaking and clattering in the Gulf breeze. Oh, well, another person I failed. I should be getting used to it by now. She half-smiled, remembering her godmother shaking her head over the top of a glass of Dr Pepper. *You try so hard to be a good little girl, don't you, Sloane? As if that was going to save you.*

Sloane drew a breath, turned her back on all that was left of the Balinese Room, and started for home. Either

Scarlet was dead, or in hiding, or maybe, just maybe, waiting for her somewhere. Sloane meant to go back to the Bishop's Palace, where she was supposed to be taking care of her refugees. She stopped dead, standing barefoot in the middle of Broadway in that black hour long after midnight but far from dawn. The thought of staggering into the Bishop's Palace for three hours of sleep, then to be woken before cock's crow to deal with complaints about the revellers upstairs, to help with breakfast, to give directions to Mrs. Sherbourne and Alice Mather—it was too much to bear. She had failed her mother, and Odessa, and now Scarlet, too. She couldn't face any more failures. Like a coward she slunk by the Palace, despising her own weakness, and headed for Ashton Villa. She would hide in the teak and porcelain luxury of her own room while whole families had lost their homes; tomorrow morning she would choose an outfit from her antique wardrobe, while Galveston's children were lucky to wear rags. As a reward for failing everyone, she would sleep tonight in her very own rich girl's bed. How proud her mother would have been.

She turned up the walk at Ashton Villa. Through a blur of tears Sloane saw a light flickering in one front window. She broke into a run. Pounding up the porch stairs she caught the faint strains of piano music. She yanked open the front door and ran through the foyer and into the Gold Room. There she stopped, panting and sobbing, her face wet with tears.

Miss Bettie, dead for eighty years but looking not much the worse for it, was sitting at the piano bench, playing Chopin with more feeling than skill. The great Texas belle was resplendent in an ecru evening gown and enough pearls to strangle an elephant. Her skin was dead white and luminous, reflecting a chilly glow as if lit by moonlight.

The only light in the Gold Room came from the small electric chandelier over the square piano. In the big arm-

chair next to it sat a statue where no statue should have been. Scarlet was sitting in the statue's lap, twisting a strand of her crinkly red hair around her finger and yawning prodigiously, like a cat. As Sloane froze at the other end of the room, Scarlet's impossibly green eyes widened and her mouth snapped shut in the middle of her yawn. She threw herself out of the statue's lap, pelted across the room, and leapt into Sloane's arms. There she clung like a limpet, her elbows and knees and sharp wrists digging into Sloane's flesh. "Where were you?" she demanded. "We were worried!"

Sloane held her and held her, rocking back and forth with her eyes closed.

Scarlet pointed at Miss Bettie, who had stopped playing. "I went down to the beach to find Grandpa, but he was gone and I met her instead. She brought me here."

"Of course I did," said the ghost, looking over the top of a pair of gold-rimmed spectacles. "It's my house. Where else would I go?"

"They shot Lianna," Scarlet said. Sloane put her down. "They would have shot me, but I was too fast. I was really scared. Did she die?"

"Yes," Sloane said.

The little girl wrapped her arms around Sloane's leg. "There, there," Scarlet murmured. Sloane recognized her own tone of voice. "It will be all right," the girl said gravely.

Sloane walked slowly toward Miss Bettie's end of the room. At first she had eyes only for the ghost, but then she found herself staring more and more intently at the statue sitting in the armchair. Light fell in glints and splinters from the chandelier, making highlights in the marble hands crossed in the stone woman's lap. She wore a smartly tailored suit with a charcoal skirt, grey jacket, and a white blouse. She was reading a paperback book, holding it just far enough away you could tell she needed reading glasses but thought herself too young for them.

"Oh," Sloane said—a tiny, heartbroken gasp. It was her mother, Jane Gardner herself, as perfect in every detail as the statues in the Railroad Museum had been.

But this wasn't the withered, sick woman Sloane had lifted from her wheelchair to bathe or sit on the toilet. This was Jane Gardner in her prime. The stone was so alive to every wrinkle in her cotton blouse, Sloane felt that at any moment her mother would hear a noise and look up. She would smile in her brief, busy way, and pull Sloane over to give her a brisk kiss and a chore to do. But the statue did not look up, the page did not turn, the white blouse did not rustle with any breath.

Sloane stared at Miss Bettie. "Did you do this?"

"I'm getting that question a lot these days," Miss Bettie said with some asperity. When she shook her head, it made her pearls rattle. "No, of course not, child. I have my talents, but sculpting is not one of them."

Sloane thought again of the old black man in the railroad museum, first reading on his pew, then hunched over a menu at the diner, and finally gone. If he had walked out into the light of Galveston's new day . . . ? "Is she—will she come back?" Sloane asked. A knife-thrust of dread went through her at the thought, and hope, too. Both hurt terribly, but she would have given her last breath to see her mother alive. Her heart was lost in such confusion.

"Will she live again? I don't know." Miss Bettie played a soft minor chord. "But Galveston has gone under the magic at last, you know. The line between our city and the Mardi Gras isn't the only one getting blurry." She played another little phrase on her piano, then pulled out the keyboard cover and closed it lovingly over the keys. "Come here, would you, dear?"

Still tightly holding Scarlet's hand, Sloane approached the piano bench where Miss Bettie sat, splendidly upright. For a woman who had been dead the better part of a century, she certainly had wonderful posture.

"Finishing school," Miss Bettie said, as if Sloane had spoken the thought out loud. "They polished us up like Mother's good silver when I was a girl. Could I put square corners on a sheet! You'd cut your shins on them when you fell out of bed in the morning. Always liked to make my own bed. You can't expect a hotel maid to care about a good square corner. Had to overtip at the Hyde Park hotel, the poor girl was so mortified I wouldn't let her do it. But that's neither here nor there." Miss Bettie patted the piano bench beside her. "Come here, Sloane."

Sitting next to her was like opening a freezer door. She took Sloane's fingers and gave them a squeeze. Her hand was cold as dirt. "Did you know I died of the very same disease as your mother? We both turned to stone," Miss Bettie said, looking at the statue of Jane Gardner with great tenderness and pity. Scarlet had crawled back into its stone lap. "I don't know if that's chance or fate. Or maybe something in the insulation," Miss Bettie added, frowning. "I'd get it checked, if I were you. But perhaps we were both compressed under the burden that comes with this house, with our position in society."

"What burden?" Sloane asked. "I always heard you spent your time waltzing around Europe and riding camels through the Sahara."

"That was in my youth," Miss Bettie said with a smile. "By heaven, I cut a figure then! Even if a girl isn't born with looks, a little personality and a large personal fortune can still carry her a good way." Sloane laughed. "A youth is not a bad thing to have," Miss Bettie continued. "You probably should have enjoyed yours more while you had the chance."

"It can't be too late—"

Miss Bettie interrupted, flapping a cold hand at Scarlet, who was perched on Jane Gardner's stone hair, idly swinging her feet. "Girl, get off your grandmother's head." With a pout Scarlet slid back into the statue's lap.

"Momus is gone and Momus is everywhere," Miss Bettie continued. "There are a lot of changes, Sloane. A lot of work for you to do. I came back from one of those jaunts to Africa to find my worthless older brother had squandered Daddy's money and left us two steps from the poorhouse. What a job we had keeping up appearances after that! I spent the last twenty years of my life in this town. Ran a hostel for sick women. Of course in my day ladies weren't encouraged to enter politics. A pity. I like to think I could have kept the Maceos from taking over our Island and turning it into a sort of cut-rate Atlantic City," Miss Bettie sniffed.

"Can we go to bed?" Scarlet said, yawning.

"Civic duty. That's what I'm talking about," Miss Bettie said. She held up her wrist. She was wearing the steel Rolex Sloane's mother had given her. Frost had crept over the crystal, so Sloane could just barely make out the time: 3:27 in the morning. "I've been saving this for you," Miss Bettie said, and she made as if to take it off.

"No!" Sloane cried. The ghost looked at her disapprovingly. "I mean, no, thank you." Sloane had the most terrible feeling that her mother was watching her, that at any moment the statue would turn its marble head and look at her with stony eyes that would see right through her and find her wanting. "I can't," Sloane said. Her breath caught in her chest. "I can't. I can't do it."

"Don't cry, girl," Miss Bettie said sharply. "Remember who you are."

"I'm not anybody," Sloane shouted, and she slammed her hand down on the piano, tears streaming down her face. "I've never been anybody, not in my whole life. All I've ever been is Not Jane Gardner. Not Odessa Gibbons." Her breath jerked and caught, her shoulders shook with it. She must look terrible, she thought. Lindsey's rotten mascara wouldn't be up to this. "Please," Sloane begged, too ashamed to meet Miss Bettie's frosty eyes. "Find someone else. I'm not cut out to save this Island.

I'm not cut out to be a princess. I'll only let you down."

"When the time comes, you'll do what you have to do."

"I didn't!" Sloane yelled. "I ran. Not Jane Gardner is all I know."

"There's more to you than that," Miss Bettie said. She reached under Sloane's chin and tipped her face up. The touch of her fingers was like ice against Sloane's throat.

"I'm an executive assistant," Sloane said. "Oh, I suppose Mother will always be a part of me. But . . ." But Odessa was part of her, too, with her witch's cackle and love of clothes. She was Scarlet, for that matter, or could be: dramatic and impetuous. And of course she was Sly. Even when she was being dutiful, deferent Sloane, she had never been Jane Gardner. She had been her executive assistant. Her job was to handle people: to flatter and coax, to wheedle and compromise and delegate, as she had with Randall Denton and Ace and Alice Mather.

"Oh," Sloane said.

Miss Bettie looked at her sharply.

Sloane met the old ghost's eyes. "I'll help any way I can," she said softly. "But unless we're very careful, what with Jeremiah gone, either Randall Denton or I will end up running the Krewe of Momus." She saw Miss Bettie begin to nod. "Which would be fine, if there wasn't a much better candidate available."

The ghost frowned. "There isn't anyone more suitable than you, Miss Gardner."

"Ah, but there is," Sloane said. "There's you."

"Her?" Scarlet said from over in the armchair.

"Me?" said Miss Bettie. Her hand dropped out from under Sloane's chin.

"But she's dead," Scarlet objected.

"It doesn't seem to have slowed her down." Sloane forced herself to take Miss Bettie's cold white hand. "Who has more creditability than Bettie Brown? Why, you are still acknowledged as the greatest society woman

in the Island's history, even after being, ah, indisposed for eighty years. And think what you could bring to the position. The Krewe of Momus has always been a stuffy lot. Do you really think it can adapt to this miraculous new world? With Jim and Randall and me bickering all the time? But you! You know more about magic than any of us," Sloane said reasonably. "For that matter, you also lived when there was no magic at all."

Miss Bettie gave Sloane a long, amused look. "Don't think I don't see why you're doing this."

"Just because I'm a coward doesn't make you less perfect for the job," Sloane said evenly. She wiped the tear tracks off her face and saw smears of cheap mascara on the side of her hand. "You even live at Ashton Villa. How convenient. I would be happy to lend a hand. If you needed an executive secretary, for example. Someone the other members of the Krewe know a little better. Someone, ah,—"

"Breathing," Miss Bettie prompted.

"That, too. I'd be happy to assist you." The corner of Sloane's mouth began to turn up in the smile she had once thought of as Sly's, but now had become simply her own.

"Rascal." Miss Bettie fingered her pearls, eyeing Sloane with grudging amusement. "There is a certain sort of impudence," the ghost said, "which I find it hard to disapprove of as much as I ought." Miss Bettie tapped her fingers on the frosted crystal of the Rolex. "Well," she said. "Hm." She frowned. "There are certainly things I would like to see done."

"Repairs to be made."

"Your mother was an excellent woman," Miss Bettie remarked, "but a little more elegance would not be amiss."

"I might suggest—"

"Don't," the ghost said. She put one chalk-white finger in front of her lips. "You have tempted me, Sloane Gard-

ner. That is enough for tonight. You go sleep on it. I will do some musing on my own."

"You really are the only person for the job," Sloane said. She rose and picked Scarlet out of Jane Gardner's unfeeling lap. Her smile faded. She was still waiting for her mother to turn the page of her book, to rise from her chair with a little sigh and go about her work. Sloane thought that if she were only not so tired, her heart would break: for Jane, and Odessa, and Ace, and Josh. Everyone on Galveston Island, really, living their little lives upon this sandbar until Time's inevitable wave came to carry them off. "We all have to serve," Sloane said. "We all have to help. Otherwise who could stand it?"

From Miss Bettie, a small, sad smile. "It just doesn't get any better than this," she said. And then, after a time, she moved her cold hand to cover Sloane's. "Or any worse either. This one life is all we are given, dear, with all its imperfections." She looked around the Gold Room, at the square piano and the chandelier, the twelve-foot mirrors and the gold wallpaper and the portrait of her arm in arm with the Emperor of Austria. "Oh, how I loved to live!" Miss Bettie said. "I loved it so well that I came back to it, despite all the suffering, when I could have chosen to sleep instead." The ghost looked at Sloane with eyes that had seen the chandeliers of Vienna and the dunes of the Sahara. The most famous Texan belle of her day, as gay as Sly and as dutiful as Sloane. "Even a civilized woman does have choices," Miss Bettie said. "She just has to choose well."

A few days later, Josh was thinking about Miss Bettie Brown as he walked toward Ashton Villa at dusk. Sloane Gardner had invited him to play cards. Josh suspected Sloane of trying to finesse a reconciliation between him and his father. It was the kind of meddling she liked to do. Ace had come through his fever. He was still very weak, but as soon as Josh had given the okay for him to

be moved, Sloane had sent a carriage to bring him to
Ashton Villa. It added insult to injury that she and his
father were now fast friends. There was a funny side to
that, but Josh had found it easy not to laugh.

At first he had said he couldn't make it, he was too
busy to play cards. Somehow she had coaxed him into
coming. A Gardner talent, that. Josh wondered if Miss
Bettie would be there. He hoped not. He had nothing
against the old lady personally, but she could only remind
him of the horror of taking off Joe Tucker's leg. And
besides, the last thing he needed was another sign of
magic. Piece by piece the last fragments of the twentieth
century were foundering under the tide of miracles creeping steadily over the Island. He had already begun to see
things which looked like diseases but weren't. One of
Ham's pals from the Gas Authority was watching his skin
thicken day by day into something hard and woody as
bark. Yesterday Josh had seen a woman with lesions
springing up all over her body, caused, he suspected, by
nothing but the guilt of having survived the storm that
had taken her son.

But then, Josh thought, even back when medicine
worked, doctoring was never a very good gamble. Sooner
or later, the house always wins.

The houses got larger and nicer as Josh walked out of
the barrio and turned onto Broadway. At Seventeenth Avenue a lamplighter was lifting his wick to the wrought-
iron streetlight on the corner. The flame caught, flickered,
and steadied within its white glass globe, hanging like a
small moon over the intersection. Josh glanced at the sky.
No sign of the real moon yet. Momus had been sighted
a handful of times in the last few days, looking older and
more withered each night, but so far he had never been
seen in the town before moonrise.

Josh wondered if Sloane was doomed to be Momus's
Consort. He hoped not, his mind fleeing uneasily from
what that might entail. Bettie Brown had announced her

intention to stand for the position of Grand Duchess, to
the bewilderment of almost everyone. The members of
the Krewe of Momus were supposed to vote on it later
in the week. Everybody agreed they ought to have the
matter settled before the next moon came full. And here
Josh had thought the Krewe of Rags would get the revellers and the monsters. Still not good enough for the
likes of Bettie Brown, apparently. Talk about being buried with a silver spoon in your mouth.

Slowly Josh walked on. Weariness sat in his joints like
rheumatism. Not that he could complain. If he had
worked hard since returning to Galveston, plenty had
worked harder. Two days ago he had found himself stopping by the Mather place, but Rachel was the only one
home, watching the kids. Without meeting his eye she
had told him that Ham was very busy. First there were
the natural gas lines to get back up and running. After
hours, half the folk on the Island had wheedled Ham into
helping rebuild their houses and toolsheds and piggeries.
He had towed away their garbage, replanted their gardens, patched boats and put shoes on a horse or two.
"Always ready to help anybody—you know how he is,"
Rachel had said. Yeah, Josh had said, that was Ham all
right.

Naturally the Krewe of Rags had chosen Ham to be
its leader. Not that people hadn't thanked Josh for his
part in overthrowing Sheriff Denton. But when push
came to shove, folk pretty much left Josh alone, except
when they were sick. Score one for me, he thought. How
clever I must be, to manage that.

It was possible he could join the Krewe of Rags if he
asked. He hadn't asked.

He found himself slowing down as he neared Ashton
Villa and it irritated him. It wasn't that he hadn't been
back to this neighborhood before. He had, plenty of
times, but always in daylight, when every specific detail—clothes on the line, kids playing, chickens cluck-

ing—said this was just another place, not steeped in his lost childhood. But in the deepening dusk, details melted away. The tall Victorian houses were reduced to the same silhouettes he remembered, and the smells leaking into the evening air, of poblano soup and shrimp étouffée, were the same as they had been dozens of evenings as he ambled home with his dad after an afternoon of cards at Jim Ford's house.

What had Ham said? It wasn't Sloane he was in love with, it was her house. Her wealth and position and fine friends. Probably true. But then, hadn't Ham been guilty of the same thing, really, when he decided to be Josh's friend? He might have stuck up for Josh out of general principles, at first. But he had stayed friends with him, year after year, exactly because Josh *wasn't* really part of the barrio. Because he represented something different from the rest of Ham's world.

So there, I win the argument, Josh thought dourly. And only a week late. But it had been ten years since he learned the schoolboy lesson that once you've been dumped, you can't just demonstrate the logical flaws in your girlfriend's reasoning and expect her to take you back. Life is like poker, not chess, and logic is only a tiny part of the game.

He couldn't see himself sending Ham flowers.

The shutters were open at Ashton Villa and the windows glowed with pale yellow gaslight. Josh found himself hesitating at the top of Sloane's walk. The ghosts of his childhood crowded around a little thicker, buzzing like mosquitoes. At least this place didn't smell like his mother's house. She wouldn't be waiting for him inside, melting wax in her little fondue pot or distilling thymol or boiling plantains for their mucilage.

Sloane met him at the door. "I was beginning to worry," she said. "Come on in. I've given the servants the night off. We have a card table set up in the back

room." She paused. "You know your father's here, don't you?"

"I guessed."

When he followed Sloane into the kitchen it wasn't the sight of Ace that threw him, sitting in a wheelchair by the kitchen table. Nor was he surprised to see Scarlet, the little reveller girl, in his father's lap. It was Ham he hadn't expected. The big man was bent over in front of the Gardners' fine refrigerator. "Are you out of beer, Sloane?" he said, rummaging. His butt crack showed. "Damn, but I'm thirsty."

Josh looked sharply at Sloane. "I see you've invited all sorts of people."

Ham stiffened at the sound of Josh's voice. "Oh, man." He straightened and turned. "Hey, Josh," he said uncomfortably.

This was so unlike the flat tone the big man had been using with him since they escaped from George and Martha that it made Josh instantly suspicious. "Or maybe you didn't invite Ham," he said slowly. "Maybe he's just here because . . . he stayed over last night?"

Ham wiped his forehead with the back of his hand. Sunburned skin was still peeling from his face like confetti. "Well, hell, what are we waiting for?" he blustered, dragging a couple of bottles of beer out of the fridge and setting them loudly on the table. "Let's play some cards!"

So Josh was right. Ham was here because he was staying here. Ham was sleeping with Sloane Gardner.

You had to appreciate the irony of it.

A smile so tight it made his face hurt settled on Josh. "Hell yes, let's play cards." He glanced at Sam Cane. "Are you in the game?" He had no doubt that his father was still so skilled, and so lucky, that he would easily overmatch anyone else at the table.

"Thought I'd just give Scarlet a few pointers," Ace said.

"A little bit of dinner first?" Sloane said brightly.

"Sarah made chili rellenos before she left." The smell of them woke Josh's appetite. He dug in while Ham fussed at the stove. The big man had brought a bucket of shrimp, and set about preparing a braise for them by dicing two fat cloves of garlic into a skillet of butter. Josh hadn't thought to bring anything himself. Of course. As if the fact that Sloane was rich excused him from making the simplest act of courtesy. Josh tried to wash the thought away with a quick bottle of beer.

The rellenos were stuffed poblano peppers, hotter than usual, with minced fatty pork and cilantro and other succulent things Josh could not identify. Within three bites his whole mouth was gently simmering, and he washed the relleno down with another beer. He noticed that he was the only person at the table not to cross himself like a Mexican before he started to eat. The habit had spread all over the Island now, as people tried to protect themselves with any charm or ritual or stupid chant.

After dinner Sloane broke out the cards. She told them she was staying up late almost every night playing for real money at the Bishop's Palace, slowly whittling away at her debt to Randall Denton. "Not that I still don't owe him the earth, but every little bit helps. Tonight, for once, I'd like to play just for fun."

A weak knock sounded at the back door. Sloane stood up to answer it. "Probably one of the servants forgot something. I was thinking we could bet with rice grains and pecans," she said over her shoulder. "I've got a collection of sand dollars upstairs we could use, too."

Josh heard the screen door squeak open. A gust of wind swept into the kitchen, surprisingly cold. "Oh," Sloane gasped, out of sight. The screen door banged shut. Sloane returned, white as Miss Bettie's fancy dress.

Behind her, paler than she, came an ancient man, thin and dry and brittle, as if twisted out of wicker. Josh knew instantly it was Momus. The god's skin was as white as a cue ball. Moonlight fell from it. "Heard there was going

to be a game," Momus wheezed. "Thought I'd sit in, just for one hand." His breath was short and his steps were crabbed, and he spoke in the thin voice of the very old. He smelled faintly of talcum powder and ice. Age and imminent death fell from him like the pale light from his skin. Josh felt himself shrivel up with fear.

"Grandpa?" Scarlet said, but she didn't leave Sam Cane's lap.

Joshua's father showed no tells. "Evening," Ace said. He tipped his head. Ham, who had been working near the stove, backed against Sloane's kitchen counter and stared wide-eyed at the god. Blood drained from his beefy face.

Momus rubbed his hands together with a sound like dry twigs scraping, and lowered himself into the empty chair between Josh and his father. "Well? Let's play, shall we? Who's up for a game? Sly, you'll play, won't you, doll? And Ace, of course. How about the little girl?"

"No!" Sloane cried. She seemed to catch hold of herself. Slowly one corner of her mouth turned up in a small, cold, reckless smile. "I'm in," she said.

Momus chuckled. His white stare fixed on Josh like a searchlight pinning down a fleeing fugitive. "And you must be Sam's boy. Ace taught you a thing or two, I bet."

"How to lose," Josh said, surprising himself. He hadn't meant to speak. He felt a little spark of fury answer the god's cold gaze. "I'm in."

Momus turned to look at Ham with eyes as old and barren as the last ice age. "How about you?"

"I can't," Ham whispered. He shook his head. "Too scared," he said. Shame filled his eyes at his own confession.

"Leave him alone," Josh said. Momus looked back at him with cold amusement. It felt as if the air had frozen in Joshua's lungs, but he forced himself to speak. "He

can't play worth a damn anyway," he said. "Four's enough."

Momus shrugged. "Just one hand. I was on my way out of town for a day or two. But I'll be back soon, I promise you, and much refreshed."

"I'll deal," Ace said, reaching for the pack.

The god laid his withered fingers on Ace's hand. "You're too lucky. It wouldn't be sporting." Not to mention that the god would have had to make the first bet, Josh thought, knowing his father's tactics well.

"I'll deal," Sloane said. A look passed between her and Sam Cane. He passed the cards to Josh, who cut and handed them back across the table to Sloane.

"Now, we're not going to play for rice and pecans," Momus said. "Poker means nothing if there's nothing at stake." He pulled a wallet from his breast pocket, counted off ten one-hundred-dollar bills, and laid them on the table. He peered around like an aging uncle who has made a joke. "Ante up, kids."

Ace studied the cash. "I believe I'll have to write you an IOU."

"Of course, of course. All bets made will be covered," Momus said. "I guarantee it," he added with a small white smile.

Sloane got a pen and some paper. She and Josh and Ace wrote out thousand-dollar IOUs and put them on the table. Then Sloane picked up the pack of cards. "Five cards, no draws," she said. "No wild cards."

"Deuces wild," Momus said.

"Dealer calls the game," Sloane said sharply. "No wild cards."

"Oh, all right."

It was an interesting choice of game, Josh thought, watching Sloane send card after card spinning across the flat tabletop. With Momus at the table it would have been insane to play any game with a lot of chances to bet,

such as Texas Hold 'Em or seven-card stud. Just looking
at the scarred and puckered flesh where Sam Cane's left
ear and eye used to be told you what kind of bettor the
god was. But if all Sloane had wanted was for Momus
to lose, she might have reasonably called as many wild
cards as possible, to give Ace's luck the most room to
maneuver. It wasn't just that she wants Momus to lose,
Josh thought. She wants to win herself.

He picked up his hand. Pair of eights with a king on
the side. With no draws it was an excellent hand.

"You to bet, Ace," Sloane said.

"No bet."

Everyone in the room looked at Momus. He studied
his cards, then laid them flat on the table. He rooted for
a moment in the pockets of his white linen pants and
produced a small pocketknife. "I've seen worse cards,"
he said. He opened the knife, laid his left hand on the
table, and cut off his middle finger just above the first
knuckle. A little blood oozed from the stump and quickly
congealed, paled over as if by frost. Momus folded the
pocketknife up and put it back in his pocket, then picked
up the finger and threw it in the center of the table, where
it lay amid the IOUs and hundred-dollar bills.

Ham turned and retched into Sloane's sink. The sound
seemed to go on and on, like the heaves of one of
Joshua's dysentery patients.

"Mr. Cane?" Momus said. "Your bet, sir."

"I fold," Josh said. There was no such thing as a playable hand against those stakes.

"Four thousand dollars!" Momus said, shaking his
head. "That's a lot of money to leave on the table, especially for you."

"Not enough to buy a new finger," Josh said. "Not
even before the Flood." He started to reach for his bottle
of beer, but his hand was shaking too much. "It wasn't
a fair bet. In three or four days the moon will be new
and you'll be whole again."

"Fair doesn't interest me," Momus said. "Sly, what do you say?"

"I'll see your bet with this, if you'll take it," Sloane said, and from her purse she pulled a leather mask and threw it on the table. It was russet and brown and brindled, sharp-featured like a fox.

Momus chuckled. "Very well. I accept that as a calling bet. Ace, back to you. Are you in or out?"

With a start Josh realized that his father was wearing his old poker face. There had been no trace of that calm, easy smile in the man who had lain in Randall Denton's bed, half-dead from yellow fever. Even when he was stronger, something had changed in him, as if the long years in Mardi Gras had burned the old Sam Cane away. But in this moment he was back as if resurrected, his voice light and his hands light on his cards, the very calm and grace and easiness of him, as if the last thirteen years had never happened. "I'll see that bet and I will raise it," he said. His eyebrows lifted just a fraction. "I'll bet my luck, sir. Will you care to see that wager?"

The god looked at him for a long, long time.

"Well, Momus? Are you in or out?"

And then, like a miracle, the god folded his cards. "Too rich for my blood," he said.

Josh's breath went out of him in a long sigh. Sam Cane had turned the tables on Momus. When the god had cut off his finger, he had been trying to scare the humans out of the game with a price too dear to pay. But in the new Galveston, with magic spilling everywhere—and perhaps new gods birthing even as they played—*luck* was a thing Momus could not dare to lose. "Jesus," Josh breathed. "Then it's over. You said you would only play for one hand."

"But the hand isn't finished," Momus observed. "Sly, will you see that bet or fold?"

Jane Gardner's daughter studied her hand. "Boy, I hate to lose on good cards, but I don't know what—" She

stopped, and her hard smile faded. "No, Sly doesn't have a bet. But I think Sloane does." She licked her lips. Her fingers started to tremble, making her cards quiver. "It's a funny thing to bet. Your luck."

"It's been my whole life," Ace said calmly. "For better and worse. Plenty worse."

Sloane nodded. "I'm thinking, then . . ." Sloane gathered her breath. It was strange how much less confident she looked than she had only moments earlier. "I bet *this*." And she looked around, taking in the kitchen and the hallway and the rooms beyond. "I bet Ashton Villa," she said. "I bet my house. My mother's house. My home."

Joshua's father looked at her. "That's a big bet."

Sloane took a moment to compose herself. Josh could see tears standing in her eyes. "You of all people should know."

"I accept that as a call," Sam Cane said. "I know what it is to lose that bet."

Josh remembered desolation sitting like ashes in his mouth as he trudged back from Jim Ford's house behind his father, his face wet with tears, his chest sore from the effort of swallowing his sobs, their house lost and it had all been his fault for giving away his father's hand. He couldn't know that the loss would be even more terrible than he had imagined.

Momus tapped Joshua's father on the wrist. "You're called," he said.

Ace turned over his cards. Nothing, king high. He had bluffed Momus out of the game. Sloane gasped and laid her hand on the table, showing a pair of queens.

"Miss Gardner wins," Ace said. He actually laughed. "Lady luck favors her own."

"How can you win someone's luck?" Scarlet asked, after her grandfather had gone. The cold air Momus left behind had begun to melt away into the Texas night.

"I bet it. I lost it. Momus will take care of the rest," Ace said.

The girl twisted in his lap to look up at him. "I better not take any advice from you, then."

Sloane pushed her chair back from the table and stood with a long, shaky intake of breath. She touched her hands to her face and rubbed her cheeks, as if feeling a tightness there. She walked slowly to the sink, where Ham still stood with his back bowed, resting his weight on his forearms with his head down. "You okay?" Sloane said. The big man shook his head. "It's all right to be afraid. Gods are like that."

"You stood up to him," Ham said hoarsely.

"I'm family. Besides, we've all seen him before."

"Not Josh," Ham said.

Sloane turned the taps and rinsed out the sink.

"If you're dizzy, keep your head down and remember to breathe," Josh said.

"Feels like when George dinged me with that baseball bat."

"Easton Howitzer," Josh said. He remembered Martha flailing furiously at George's head, crunching his skull in, leaving him in a puddle of blood on Highway 87. What had Momus said? *Fair doesn't interest me.* "Maybe get him a glass of water," Josh said.

Ten minutes later the color had come back to Ham's face, Scarlet was getting bored, and Sloane had written Josh an IOU for a thousand dollars. "For your expert medical advice," she said. "Plus I think I owe you for several cups of tea."

"I'm not sure it's that easy," Josh said gloomily. "I wouldn't be surprised if Momus finds some way to get that thousand dollars out of me yet. What are you going to do with that?" he added, glancing at the withered finger lying on the table.

"Throw it out," Ham said. "Good Lord."

"Are you kidding?" Sloane got a hot pad from above

the stove and wrapped it gingerly around the finger. "I gave away my best charm a few days before my mother died. Can you imagine a better walkaway to replace it?"

"Oh, *neat*," Scarlet said.

Sloane carried the finger out of the kitchen and returned a few minutes later. "As for your thousand dollars, I can always give it back, Josh. Or," she added, picking up the pack of cards, "you could win it from me."

"Jesus Christ on a unicycle!" Ham said. "You aren't seriously thinking of playing more poker!"

Sloane broke the deck one-handed, squared it, and shuffled, a long whispering waterfall. "I don't see why not. Momus said he was only going to sit in for one hand. And after all, who will have the guts to play again, now that we know *he* might sit in on any game?"

"Not me," Josh said.

"You got that right," Ham added, shuddering. For the moment he seemed to have forgotten that he currently despised Josh. Presumably he would remember soon enough.

Sloane cut the deck one-handed, fanned it, squared it with a sharp rap on the table and cut it again. Ace chuckled, watching her. "You just want to play because you're feeling lucky. I know you."

"No, you don't," Sloane answered. "You know Sly. Sloane, now, you've only just met."

Ace touched the brim of an imaginary cowboy hat. "I sit corrected."

"Where would you have gone to live if you had lost that hand?" Josh asked. He tried to imagine her shacked up with Rachel and her brood. Waiting under the covers of the bed he and Ham used to set toy soldiers on.

Sloane shrugged. Her short dark hair swayed a little by the side of her face, and Josh felt another rush of futile desire for her. "I don't know. Maybe I'd build a little shack down where the Balinese Room used to be," Sloane said softly.

"Are we going to play cards or not?" Scarlet said sulkily.

And in the end they did play, though this time they bet strictly with grains of rice, pecans, and sand dollars. At first Ham had the good cards, but he absentmindedly ate the better part of his early winnings and had to stay out of the big pots afterward. He had always been partial to pecans.

Ham was a decent home player, a veteran of many bar games who knew the basic odds, but he tried to limp in with a lot of drawing hands. Josh himself was a tight player and a conservative bettor, but he could afford to be as long as Sloane was at the table. As demure as she usually was, she played like a merry sadist. She gave away almost no tells, and seemed to enjoy winning a good deal more than a well-bred lady probably should.

Josh was content to take the hands he had the cards to win, and everyone conspired to make sure Scarlet won a pot every now and then. She was not a bad player, for a kid, but she still loved romantic hands, like flushes and straights. She also had a personal liking for jacks that made her stubborn about staying in with pairs of them beyond what the cards warranted. For the most part Ace restricted himself to analyzing each hand with her after it was over, but occasionally, unable to contain himself, he would lean and whisper something in her ear during play. "No advice," he promised. "I'm just pointing out tells." This happened twice while Josh was deciding to bet. He didn't like the feeling that his father could still see through him.

It occurred to him that the bluff his father had made to force Momus out of the game was nearly the same as the one that had failed against Travis Denton. Of course Momus was a better player, with more to lose, and thus was easier to scare. And unlike Josh, Scarlet had kept her poker face. Mind you, Sam Cane's bluff hadn't entirely

worked, had it? He'd lost the pot to Sloane Gardner. Once again Galveston's rich got richer, at the expense of the Canes. Maybe some things just weren't meant to change.

As the evening wore on and the electric fear that had come with Momus dissipated, weariness crept back into Josh to replace it. Or perhaps it was the beer. His attention wavered until he was following the cards no better than Ham, (although at least he wasn't eating his bankroll). Bleakly Josh tried to imagine what it would mean to live in a world where a dead woman might run the city's most powerful Krewe and a god could sit in on any hand of cards. In this dreaming world, Chance would always be king. Joshua's father would probably say it had been like that in the twentieth century, too. He'd say that tragedy had never been more than a car crash away, even before the Flood. Luck had just been disguised more then. Hidden a little. Well, Josh liked it hidden. The Galveston they were part of now was too unpredictable. Luck ran everywhere, unbalanced and uncatchable, like mercury from a smashed thermometer. Disaster lay coiled as close as a rattlesnake in the next dim crevice.

Ham was coughing tonight, a short, hacking cough Josh didn't like at all. The first time he heard it, his stomach knotted up tight as a ball of twine, and he realized he had been listening for that sound ever since the long day they had spent with Martha and George.

It was probably just a cold.

The night breeze grew cooler, coming through the screen door at the back of the kitchen. Sloane turned down the unnecessary lights, until it was just them in the kitchen, warm next to the stove and playing by the light of a single gas lamp, while around them the dim house creaked and settled. Outside, in the rest of the city, darkness would be lapping at the last lights, dousing them one by one. Joe Tucker would be dropping his crutches

to say his prayers, and then climbing awkwardly into bed. Somewhere in the night a child would wake sweaty and screaming with an ear infection. Prawn Men would sit on the stone jetties that stretched into the warm ocean, waiting for the moon to set.

Beyond the little line of houses, the Island would stretch, miles of empty salt-grass meadows and hackberry scrub. Across Galveston Bay, the infernal fires of Texas City would roar on. Desperate men and cannibals would look for shelter, ears straining for sounds of their own kind, ready to rob or butcher them. North of them, the whole vast continent lay, tormented by uneasy dreams, sleeping through the long night that had begun in '04. Who could say when day would ever come again?

Out the other way, from Galveston's southern shore, the Gulf of Mexico stretched like a desert of water, a darkness without end.

Josh folded his hand. Mrs. Mather would have a round of patients for him to visit tomorrow, and he had promised to drop in on Joe Tucker as well. He needed to make up more head lice powder and something for a rash of pinkeye going around. And aside from doctoring, there was always more beer to ferment to pay the bills.

Across the table, Sloane was fast-playing Ham again, laughing as he blustered and frowned and counted his bankroll. She was less mysterious, somehow, than she had been once, and livelier. All very well for her to be the champion of the revellers now, but Josh wondered how she would feel if she should wake up one day and find fox fur creeping across her cheeks. One thing to say, "Change is inevitable!"—another to deal with it when it's your goddamn life slipping like seawater between your fingers.

She's going to be a different sort of Gardner, he thought, watching Sloane. A good assistant to Miss Bettie ... most of the time. But every now and then, Josh suspected, there would come a day or three when Sloane

would disappear; only to turn up later, hungover, refusing
to say where she had been. Promising not to do it again.
Ham had warned him once about falling for Jane Gardner's daughter. The big man might should take his own
advice, Josh thought. Watching her play cards, fine and
fierce and laughing, Josh thought it would probably be
wonderful to be Sloane's lover—but very hard, too. As
hard as being married to Sam Cane, perhaps.

Josh glanced around at the circle of faces: Sloane
merry, Ham flushed with hot peppers and beer, little
Scarlet frowning and chewing on her lip. His father, old
now, and smaller than Josh remembered, wasted with
sickness. Ace had been stripped of his luck at last, the
fine luck that had cost him his wife, and his son, and his
friends, and his life in the world of men. Maybe it was
impossible for a human being to know what luck really
meant, Josh thought. Maybe only a god could bear it.

How fine Sam Cane had looked the night he lost their
house! Josh could still remember the smooth play of muscles in his father's forearm as he shuffled and dealt. And
here he was, so reduced, missing an ear and an eye, a
wife and a son, but still studying cards. A whole life
wasted on a game. A *game*.

It wasn't just the knowledge that loss was inevitable
that hurt Josh so profoundly. Part of the bitter wisdom
he had won on the Bolivar Peninsula was that life, even
human life, was more vulnerable than it was precious.
People were fragile, badly made machines, bound to
break down sooner or later. Men were born, they lived,
and they passed away. To the real powers of the world,
the sea and the sun and even the bright petty gods, they
mattered no more than the mosquitoes bumping against
Sloane's windows. It wasn't just that Josh was afraid of
losing: now, tonight, he couldn't see any point in playing
the game.

The table talk fell away from him, voices broken into
faint fragments. The light from the gas lamp went dim,

as if he had grown old between one breath and the next, his corneas stiff and yellowing. Choking dread descended on him, and suddenly he knew there was something terrible by the kitchen stove; something so frightening that if he were to look up, his heart would stop and he would die of fear.

He stared at his cards, splayed facedown in front of him. Their backs were blue, worked in a pattern of ivy. Terrible silence closed around him. The room grew icy cold. Goose bumps ran up his arms and down his back. He tried to speak, but he had no breath. His fingernails were blue. If he had been able to move, he would have thrown himself on the floor and crawled under the table and cowered with his head beneath his arms.

There was a horrible cold smell of rocks and seawater. Something touched his face: a hand. He struggled with every ounce of his strength to stare at the table, but the hand was stronger. It tilted up his chin, leaving him sickeningly exposed, as if someone had taken a scalpel and laid him open from his throat to his groin. He tried to close his eyes but he couldn't, he tried to scream but he couldn't. All he could do was die inside and meet his mother's eyes.

She was standing between his chair and Ham's. She wasn't old and she wasn't drowned. She was just as he had remembered her in his delirium during the hurricane: Amanda Cane at thirty or thirty-one, wearing a pair of cotton pants and a home-dyed cotton shirt. Her sleeves were rolled up to her elbows and her fingers were dusty with ground sage. She had looked this way before they lost the house, before the long years of bitter bad luck. Before the insulin ran out. She was smiling, and her eyes were full of love.

The smell of seaweed and cold sand was everywhere.

He wanted to die. He wanted to throw himself into her arms. He wanted her to tuck him into bed and read him a story. He wanted her to make baked chicken with rice

wine like she did on his birthday. He wanted to get her a cup of mint tea which they would share on the porch, as they did every Sunday morning while his father slept. There was a wisp of hair curling at the side of her face, and he would never have dreamed of touching it.

She leaned forward, cotton rustling, her sleeves pulling up, and kissed him on the forehead, once, in the lingering way she had when she was checking for fever.

Time stopped.

"JACKS and nines!" Scarlet crowed, reaching greedily for the pot and dragging it toward herself.

Ham shook his head and scooped up his pair of kings in a busted flush. "Brung a knife to a gunfight again," he growled. Sloane laughed at him.

"Can you see where you could have got one more bet off the sucker over there?" Ace asked, stacking Scarlet's sand dollars for her.

"Fifth Street?"

"Exactly right."

"Lock up your sons and husbands," Sloane drawled. "Scarlet's come to town!"

The kid arranged her pecans in groups of five.

Ham looked down at his bankroll, which had dwindled to a few grains of rice. "Josh, these women are wearing me out, and I recollect you wanted to make an early night of it. You ready to head home, or would you like to hang in for another few hands?" Ham prodded him in the arm. "Josh? Hey, Josh! In or out, pardner?"

"I think I need another beer," Sloane said, rooting around in her refrigerator. "Anyone else want a beer?"

JOSHUA blinked. He felt liquefied in the middle, like a frozen thing that had thawed. Two tears slid from his eyes. He ducked to wipe them off. The room was warm again, blessedly warm, and rich with the smell of braised shrimp and rellenos and beer and Sloane's perfume. He

hadn't realized before that she was wearing perfume. It was exquisite, a fragrance like green wood after rain, very faint. The flickering gaslight drew gleams from her dark hair. Beside him Ham coughed, covering his mouth with one meaty paw.

Joshua's father was looking at him sharply. He could tell that something had happened. Josh never could hide his tells from his dad.

"God, yes," Josh said. "God, yes, I'd like a beer." Sloane brought him one. He fell in love with her.

Ham was giving him a funny look. "In or out, compadre?"

Josh drew a long breath and laughed unsteadily. The smell of sea and cold sand was gone. "Deal me in," he said.

ACKNOWLEDGMENTS

To Christine and Philip, as always, I owe too much.

To Christopher Bullock, my stepfather, I owe a good deal more than I usually let on. I am deeply grateful for the sympathetic hearing he has given this book, and its author, over the last few years. He and Susan Allison, my editor, both liked and understood this novel before I did.

For a wealth of information on what must be the most interesting city in America, I am greatly indebted to Gary Cartwright's excellent *Galveston: A History of the Island*, and to Mike Reynolds, the Islander who loaned it to me, richly embellished with his own invaluable stories. Sound information on guns, Texas, and Life in the Ruins of Industry I got from the estimable Bob Stahl. Sage Walker, bless her, fielded medical questions with her usual grace. And my deepest thanks go to Scott Baker, Sean Russell, Linda Nagata, Tom Phinney, and especially Maureen McHugh, who kept me honest when I was trying very hard to lie.

Lastly, without the love and support of my mother, Kay Stewart, I might never have finished this book. Nor, come to think of it, any of the others.